Lecture Notes in Computer Science 13742

Founding Editors

Gerhard Goos
Juris Hartmanis

The series Lecture Notes in Computer Science (LNCS), including its subseries Lecture Notes in Artificial Intelligence (LNAI) and Lecture Notes in Bioinformatics (LNBI), has established itself as a medium for the publication of new developments in computer science and information technology research, teaching, and education.

LNCS enjoys close cooperation with the computer science R & D community, the series counts many renowned academics among its volume editors and paper authors, and collaborates with prestigious societies. Its mission is to serve this international community by providing an invaluable service, mainly focused on the publication of conference and workshop proceedings and postproceedings. LNCS commenced publication in 1973.

Benjamin Smith · Huapeng Wu
Editors

Selected Areas in Cryptography

29th International Conference, SAC 2022
Windsor, ON, Canada, August 24–26, 2022
Revised Selected Papers

Editors
Benjamin Smith
Inria and École Polytechnique
Institut Polytechnique de Paris
Palaiseau, France

Huapeng Wu
Electrical and Computer Engineering
University of Windsor
Windsor, ON, Canada

ISSN 0302-9743   ISSN 1611-3349 (electronic)
Lecture Notes in Computer Science
ISBN 978-3-031-58410-7   ISBN 978-3-031-58411-4 (eBook)
https://doi.org/10.1007/978-3-031-58411-4

This Springer imprint is published by the registered company Springer Nature Switzerland AG
The registered company address is: Gewerbestrasse 11, 6330 Cham, Switzerland

Paper in this product is recyclable.

Preface

Selected Areas in Cryptography (SAC) is Canada's annual cryptography research conference, held since 1994. The 29th edition of SAC took place at the University of Windsor, in Ontario, from August 24 to 26, 2022. Due to the ongoing COVID-19 pandemic, SAC 2022 was a hybrid event, with talks and discussion streamed online. The conference was preceded by a two-day summer school on August 22 and 23, with tutorials on isogeny-based cryptography and real-world post-quantum cryptography from Javad Doliskani, Benjamin Smith, and Douglas Stebila.

Each SAC conference covers four areas of research in cryptography. Three of these areas are permanent:

- Design and analysis of symmetric key primitives and cryptosystems, including block and stream ciphers, hash functions, MAC algorithms, cryptographic permutations, and authenticated encryption schemes;
- Efficient implementations of symmetric, public key, and post-quantum cryptography;
- Mathematical and algorithmic aspects of applied cryptography, including post-quantum cryptology.

The fourth area is selected as a special topic for each edition of SAC. For SAC 2022, this area was

- Theory and practice of isogeny-based cryptography.

We received 53 submissions; these were reviewed in a double-blind peer review process coordinated by the Program Committee. Regular submissions received three reviews; submissions involving members of the Program Committee received five reviews. Overall, our 34 Program Committee members, and their 28 subreviewers, wrote 172 reviews. Twenty-one of the submissions were accepted for presentation at SAC 2022 and publication in these proceedings.

There were three invited talks at SAC 2022. Nadia Heninger gave the Stafford Tavares lecture virtually: "On the passive compromise of TLS keys and other cryptanalytic adventures". Benjamin Wesolowski gave the second invited talk in person, on "Hard problems for isogeny-based cryptography". Finally, Wouter Castryck gave the third invited talk on "Efficient key recovery attacks on SIDH".

We would like to thank all of our colleagues who helped to make SAC 2022 a success, especially given the continuing complications all around the world due to the COVID-19 pandemic. We thank the Program Committee members for excellent work under a tight schedule. We are also grateful to the many others who participated in the review process: Gora Adj, Foteini Baldimtsi, Christof Beierle, Francesco Berti, Kevin Carrier, Arcangelo Castiglione, James Clements, Patrick Derbez, Thomas Espitau, Anna Lisa Ferrara, Manuela Flores, Clemente Galdi, Gayathri Garimella, Lydia Garms, Hosein Hadipour, Ryoma Ito, Amandine Jambert, Mikhail Kudinov, Norman Lahr, Fukang Liu, Liam Medley, Matthias Meijers, Mridul Nandi, Patrick Neumann, Richard Petri, Robert

Primas, Krijn Reijnders, and Florian Weber. We also thank the invited speakers for their excellent presentations, the summer school lecturers for animating a dynamic in-person event, and the SAC steering committee for their helpful advice and guidance. We are also appreciative of the financial support provided by the University of Windsor and by the Communications Security Establishment of Canada.

Finally, special thanks are due to Jo Asuncion for providing administrative assistance and we appreciate the help in the local arrangements offered by Lisa Geloso, Andria Ballo, Raqib Asif, Chen Zhang, and Hamza Bin Zaheer.

December 2023   Benjamin Smith
                                                                                                         Huapeng Wu

Organization

Program Committee

Riham AlTawy	University of Victoria, Canada
Melissa Azouaoui	NXP Semiconductors, USA
Paulo Barreto	University of Washington Tacoma, USA
Jean-François Biasse	University of South Florida, USA
Olivier Blazy	École polytechnique, France
Claude Carlet	Université Paris 8, France and University of Bergen, Norway
Wouter Castryck	KU Leuven, Belgium
Carlos Cid	Simula UiB, Norway and Okinawa Institute of Science and Technology, Japan
Craig Costello	Microsoft Research, USA
Luca De Feo	IBM Research Europe, Switzerland
Maria Eichlseder	Graz University of Technology, Austria
Aurore Guillevic	Inria Nancy, France and Aarhus University, Denmark
Kathrin Hövelmanns	TU Eindhoven, the Netherlands
Michael J. Jacobson Jr.	University of Calgary, Canada
Yunwen Liu	Independent Researcher
Subhamoy Maitra	Indian Statistical Institute Kolkata, India
Kalikinkar Mandal	University of New Brunswick, Canada
Chloe Martindale	University of Bristol, UK
Barbara Masucci	University of Salerno, Italy
Ruben Niederhagen	Academia Sinica, Taiwan and University of Southern Denmark, Denmark
Abderrahmane Nitaj	University of Caen Normandy, France
Lorenz Panny	Academia Sinica, Taipei, Taiwan
Elizabeth A. Quaglia	Royal Holloway, University of London, UK
Francisco Rodríguez-Henríquez	CINVESTAV-IPN, México and CRC-TII, United Arab Emirates
Yann Rotella	Université de Versailles Saint-Quentin, France
Simona Samardjiska	RU Nijmegen, the Netherlands
Nicolas Sendrier	Inria, France
Leonie Simpson	Queensland University of Technology, Australia
Benjamin Smith	Inria and École polytechnique, Institut Polytechnique de Paris, France

Djiby Sow	Cheikh Anta Diop University, Senegal
Douglas Stebila	University of Waterloo, Canada
Katsuyuki Takashima	Waseda University, Japan
Yosuke Todo	NTT Secure Platform Laboratories, Japan
Yuntao Wang	Osaka University, Japan
Huapeng Wu	University of Windsor, Canada

Additional Reviewers

Gora Adj	Hosein Hadipour
Foteini Baldimtsi	Ryoma Ito
Christof Beierle	Amandine Jambert
Francesco Berti	Mikhail Kudinov
Kevin Carrier	Norman Lahr
Arcangelo Castiglione	Fukang Liu
James Clements	Liam Medley
Patrick Derbez	Matthias Meijers
Thomas Espitau	Mridul Nandi
Anna Lisa Ferrara	Patrick Neumann
Manuela Flores	Richard Petri
Clemente Galdi	Robert Primas
Gayathri Garimella	Krijn Reijnders
Lydia Garms	Florian Weber

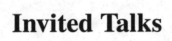

Invited Talks

On the Passive Compromise of TLS Keys and Other Cryptanalytic Adventures

Nadia Heninger

Computer Science and Engineering, University of California San Diego, 9500 Gilman Drive, La Jolla, CA, 92093-0021 USA
nadiah@cs.ucsd.edu

Abstract. It is well known in the cryptographic literature that the most common digital signature schemes used in practice can fail catastrophically in the presence of faults during computation. I will discuss recent joint work using passive and active network measurements to analyze organically-occuring faults in billions of digital signatures generated by tens of millions of hosts. We find that a persistent rate of apparent hardware faults in unprotected implementations has resulted in compromised certificate RSA private keys for years. Finally, we will put this work in the context of other cryptographic flaws that can be exploited in the wild.

Hard Problems for Isogeny-Based Cryptography

Benjamin Wesolowski

Institut de Mathématiques de Bordeaux, 351, Cours de la Libération, 33405 Talence,
France
benjamin.wesolowski@ens-lyon.fr

Abstract. Isogeny-based cryptography is one of the few branches of
public-key cryptography that promises to resist quantum attacks. The
security of these cryptosystems relates to the (presumed) hardness of
a variety of computational problems: finding paths in large "isogeny
graphs", computing endomorphisms of elliptic curves, or inverting group
actions. We present these problems, and analyse how they relate to each
other: which are equivalent, easier, or harder, and how they relate to
cryptosystems.

Efficient Key Recovery Attacks on SIDH

Wouter Castryck

Department of Electrical Engineering, KU Leuven, Oude Markt 13 - bus 5005, 3000
Leuven, Belgium
wouter.castryck@gmail.com

Abstract. It is well known in the cryptographic literature that the most common digital signature schemes used in practice can fail catastrophically in the presence of faults during computation. I will discuss recent joint work using passive and active network measurements to analyze organically-occuring faults in billions of digital signatures generated by tens of millions of hosts. We find that a persistent rate of apparent hardware faults in unprotected implementations has resulted in compromised certificate RSA private keys for years. Finally, we will put this work in the context of other cryptographic flaws that can be exploited in the wild.

Contents

Protocols and PRFs

Lattices and ECC

Profiling Side-Channel Attacks on Dilithium

A Small Bit-Fiddling Leak Breaks It All

Vincent Quentin Ulitzsch[1]([✉]), Soundes Marzougui[1], Mehdi Tibouchi[2],
and Jean-Pierre Seifert[1,3]

[1] Technical University Berlin, Berlin, Germany
`vincent@sect.tu-berlin.de`,
{`soundes.marzougui`,`jean-pierre.seifert`}`@tu-berlin.de`
[2] NTT Social Informatics Laboratories, Tokyo, Japan
`mehdi.tibouchi@ntt.com`
[3] Fraunhofer Institute for Secure Information Technology, Darmstadt, Germany

Abstract. We present an end-to-end (equivalent) key recovery attack on the Dilithium lattice-based signature scheme, one of the winners of the NIST postquantum cryptography competition. The attack is based on a small side-channel leakage we identified in a bit unpacking procedure inside Dilithium signature generation. We then combine machine-learning based profiling with various algorithmic techniques, including least squares regression and integer linear programming, in order to leverage this small leakage into essentially full key recovery: we manage to recover, from a moderate number of side-channel traces, enough information to sign arbitrary messages. We confirm the practicality of our technique using concrete experiments against the ARM Cortext-M4 implementation of Dilithium, and verify that our attack is robust to real-world conditions such as noisy power measurements. This attack appears difficult to protect against reliably without strong side-channel countermeasures such as masking of the entire signing algorithm, and underscores the necessity of implementing such countermeasures despite their known high cost.

Keywords: Dilithium · Lattice-based cryptography · Machine learning · Profiling attacks · Side-channel analysis · Integer linear programming

1 Introduction

The plausible advent of general-purpose quantum computers in the coming decades is a mounting threat to currently deployed public-key cryptography, and particularly digital signatures such as RSA signatures and ECDSA, since those

---

V. Q. Ulitzsch and S. Marzougui—Both authors contributed equally to this paper.

B. Smith and H. Wu (Eds.): SAC 2022, LNCS 13742, pp. 3–32, 2024.
https://doi.org/10.1007/978-3-031-58411-4_1

schemes are broken by Shor's algorithm [41]. It therefore appears increasingly important to design and implement quantum-resistant cryptographic schemes that are suitable for real-world deployment, whether in terms of security, performance or practicality of implementation. This is the aim of the ongoing NIST-led process to evaluate and standardize post-quantum primitives for public-key encryption, key encapsulation and signatures [36], which is now in its final stages, with four candidate algorithms already selected for standardization and an upcoming fourth round to analyze a few additional alternate constructions.

Post-quantum digital signatures can be based on a variety of cryptographic assumptions, ranging from collision-resistant hash functions to the hardness of solving large multivariate quadratic systems or finding isogenies between super-singular elliptic curves. Prominently among those are assumptions related to Euclidean lattices: two of the three digital signature schemes already selected for standardization by NIST, Dilithium and Falcon, are lattice-based schemes. Interestingly, those two schemes are instances of the two different design frameworks for lattice-based signatures: the hash-and-sign approach for Falcon and the Fiat–Shamir with aborts paradigm for Dilithium.

Hash-and-sign signatures based on lattices have a longer history, starting with GGH and NTRUSign [19,22], but the early constructions were quickly found to be insecure [34,35], as each released signature would leak a small amount of information of the signing trapdoor. The first successful construction dates back to a seminal paper of Gentry, Peikert and Vaikuntanathan (GPV) [18], who showed that a careful use of lattice Gaussian sampling could eliminate the statistical leaks that plagued earlier attempts. While the GPV scheme itself was not very practical, later developments improved the efficiency of lattice-based hash-and-sign signatures [11,14,15,32,38], and Falcon [38] is in particular quite fast and compact. However, like almost all schemes in this family, it retains the crucial reliance on lattice Gaussian sampling for its security. This makes it tricky to implement, validate, and protect against side-channels.

In contrast, the Fiat–Shamir with aborts paradigm, introduced by Lyubashevsky in [27], tends to give rise to simpler schemes, that have a structure similar to traditional Fiat–Shamir schemes like Schnorr signatures, but with a twist to deal with the fact that there is no uniform distribution on a lattice. Typically, those schemes only rely one one-dimensional discrete Gaussian sampling (as is the case for [13]; this is already considerably simpler than the lattice Gaussian sampling used in hash-and-sign signatures) or no Gaussian sampling at all (as is the case for [21]). Dilithium, in particular, belongs to the second category, and the submission document states that eliminating the reliance on Gaussian sampling is a deliberate design choice aiming at a greater ease of *secure implementation*, particularly against side-channel attacks [28]. Indeed, Gaussian sampling-based schemes have been the target of numerous devastating side-channel attacks [30].

Side-channel resilience has also been a point of focus of the NIST standardization process from the get-go. Indeed, the original call for proposals states that

Schemes that can be made resistant to side-channel attacks at minimal cost are more desirable than those whose performance is severely hampered by any attempt to resist side-channel attacks.

More recently, the PQC summary document for the second round (NISTIR 8309) notes that

NIST hopes to see more and better data for performance in the third round. This performance data will hopefully include implementations that protect against side-channel attacks, such as timing attacks, power monitoring attacks, fault attacks, etc.

The third round resulted in four candidate algorithm being selected for standardization, and the standardized algorithms can be expected to be deployed on large scale. It is thus of particular importance to understand to what extent and at what cost the selected schemes, including Dilithium, can be protected against side-channel attacks.

The reference implementation of Dilithium claims security against timing attacks, and as mentioned earlier, the scheme has been designed with particular consideration for side-channel resilience, but it does not necessarily offer protection against more powerful attacks like differential power analysis. In fact, some amount of side-channel leakage has been demonstrated in certain parts of the Dilithium signing algorithm. They have not been turned into a complete end-to-end attack so far, however, so implementers may be reluctant to embrace strong side-channel countermeasures like masking.

Indeed, while Migliore et al. [33] have described how Dilithium could be masked at any order, and hence protected against arbitrary-order power analysis attacks, this countermeasures comes at considerable cost. In fact, Migliore et al. restrict their practical evaluation to the masking of a simplified version of Dilithium, instantiated with a power-of-two modulus instead of the original prime modulus (which makes the countermeasure much less costly), and even so, they find that the first-order masked signature scheme is around five times slower than the unmasked scheme.

Contributions. In this work, we present a profiling-based power analysis attack on the Cortex-M4 reference implementation of Dilithium achieving essentially full key recovery. To the best of our knowledge, this constitutes the first end-to-end attack on a reference implementation of this signature scheme.

To describe our approach in a bit more details, we need to recall how Dilithium signature generation proceeds at a high level. It is roughly similar to Schnorr signatures in cyclic group $\mathbb{G} = \langle g \rangle$ of order p, which work by sampling some uniform random value y modulo p, hashing the message μ together with g^y to obtain $c = H(\mu, g^y)$, and returning the signature as (z, c) with $z = y + cs$ (where s is the private key and $a = g^s$ the public key). Verification is then carried out by checking whether $c = H(\mu, g^z/a^c)$. Accordingly, Dilithium proceeds as follows:

1. sample $\mathbf{y}$ as a random module element with uniform coefficients in some interval;
2. hash the message μ together with $\mathbf{Ay}$ ($\mathbf{A}$ a public matrix) to obtain $c = H(\mu, \mathbf{Ay})$, a ring element with sparse 0/1 coefficients;
3. let $\mathbf{z} = \mathbf{y} + c\mathbf{s}_1$ (where $\mathbf{s}_1$ is the first part of the secret key);
4. return the signature as $(\mathbf{z}, c)$ provided that a certain rejection condition is met (mostly stating that $\mathbf{z}$ has its coefficients in a small interval) and reject otherwise.

The starting point of our attack is identifying a power side-channel leakage in the first step: the generation of the random $\mathbf{y}$, which is carried out by constructing a certain random string, and expanding it into a module element (a vector of polynomials) using bit fiddling operations. Then, machine-learning assisted profiling lets us predict with relatively high accuracy whether a given polynomial coefficient in one of the components of $\mathbf{y}$ is zero or not. If we could do so with perfect accuracy, then the recovery of $\mathbf{s}_1$ would be a simple matter of linear algebra: indeed, for each zero coefficient $\mathbf{y}_i$ identified in this way, we get the relation $\mathbf{z}_i = 0 + (c\mathbf{s}_1)_i$, and since both $\mathbf{z}_i$ and c are known, this gives a linear relation on the coefficients of $\mathbf{s}_1$. Collecting sufficiently many of those reveals $\mathbf{s}_1$ in full.

However, the machine learning predictor is not perfectly accurate in practice, so two challenges naturally present themselves. On the one hand, we want to improve the accuracy of the predictor as much as possible, which is mainly a matter of improving the profiling phase of the attack (mainly by adjusting the hyperparameters of our ML model, and by carefully choosing the learning data). On the other hand, we need to solve a *noisy* linear system involving the secret key while minimizing the number of required traces. We consider several possible approaches to do so, and find that expressing the problem as an integer linear program offers the best results in practice for our particular setting.

We validate our attack by mounting it on the full reference implementation of Dilithium, executed on a Cortex-M4 implementation in a realistic attack setting, by capturing actual, noisy power traces and using them to train and apply our ML model, and then recover the full vector $\mathbf{s}_1$. Although $\mathbf{s}_1$ is not the entire secret key, it has been shown in previous work [20,39] that knowing $\mathbf{s}_1$ suffices to sign essentially arbitrary messages, so its recovery is essentially as good as full key recovery.

As an aside, we note that Dilithium has two variants that differ in the way the vector $\mathbf{y}$ is generated: one is deterministic (in the spirit of EdDSA) and the other is probabilistic (aiming at thwarting certain classes of implementation and fault attacks, in the spirit of signatures with hedged randomness [1]). However, our attack applies to both variants, since the bit-fiddling step we target is common to both of them. Moreover, our attack extracts information about the vector $\mathbf{y}$ per signature, from a single trace. Thus, while sampling a different vector $\mathbf{y}$ per execution does indeed thwart attacks that rely on aggregating traces, the randomization does not yield additional protection in our case.

All in all, this paper demonstrates a new power side-channel leakage in Dilithium, and leverages into an ML-assisted profiling attack that achieves essentially full key recovery. The attack relies on a novel, non trivial algorithmic decoding step based on integer linear programming, and is validated against the reference implementation of Dilithium.

Related Work. Side-channel attacks were introduced by Kocher et al. [25] and are considered one of the main threat against cryptographic algorithms deployed in embedded systems, and have also been demonstrated on larger devices like smartphones and desktop computers, as well as remotely over the internet. In a side-channel attack, an attacker does not exploit mathematical weaknesses or invalid behavior of an implementation but uses physical information to reveal secret data. The attacker measures physical information (for instance, power consumption, electromagnetic emanations, elapsed time, etc.) during the execution of cryptographic operations in order to gain information about sensitive internal data, including secret keys.

Although no end-to-end side-channel analysis of Dilithium has been presented so far, several earlier works did demonstrate potential side-channel leakage in various parts of the signing algorithm.

In [16], P. Fournaris et al. present a correlation-based differential side-channel analysis of the polynomial multiplication operation $c \cdot s_1$ during signature generation. The analysis considers various multiplication algorithms (schoolbook multiplication, NTT or sparse multiplier), and argues that mounting a correlation power analysis is *in principle* feasible with all of them. The authors also verify that the required leakage is detectable on power traces of Dilithium signature generation implemented on a commercial off-the-shelf embedded system board. However, they do not mount the full actual attack, evaluate the number of traces it would actually require in practice, nor quantify the sensitivity to measurement noise.

A more detailed theoretical analysis along the same lines is carried out by Ravi et al. [39], although only for schoolbook multiplication and sparse multiplication. The paper discusses the feasibility of key recovery in several idealized leakage models, and extends the evaluation of leakage noise effects. However, they again do not attempt to actually mount an attack on an actual implementation. Moreover, the NTT multiplication, which is used in the actual implementation of Dilithium, is not considered.

Aside from polynomial-multiplication-related vulnerabilities, several points of interest are identified by Migliore et al. [33] as leaking sensitive values, particularly in the rounding functions (low and high bits calculations), and the rejection sampling executed during signature generation. Using test vector leakage assessment on a Cortex-M3 implementation of Dilithium, they show that these functions do present detectable leakage, and can thus, again *in principle*, be exploited by differential power analysis. Again, however, they do not mount an actual attack (and only use those leakage points to evaluate the side-channel resistance of the *masked* implementation presented in the paper).

In a different direction, Groot Bruinderink and Pessl [20] present a fault injection attack on Dilithium which aims at creating a nonce-reuse scenario. They demonstrate that single random faults in the Dilithium signature can lead to nonce reuse. They perform their attack on an ARM Cortex-M4 microcontroller and prove that the success probability for all fault scenarios can reach 91%. An interesting feature of [39] and [20] is that they only consider the recovery of the main secret key element s_1, and therefore discuss how signing is possible using just that knowledge. The same techniques can be used in our setting as well.

Organization of the Paper. The remainder of this paper is organized in six sections. In Sect. 2, we give preliminaries on the Dilithium scheme and the use of machine-learning classifier in our side-channel attack. In Sect. 3, we give an overview on the attack and the attacker's model. Likewise, we analyze the weakness of Dilithium against machine-learning power side-channel analysis in Sect. 4. In Sect. 5, we present a detailed mathematical description of the attack strategy and its resistance against noisy measurements. Then, we describe our experimental setup for the profiling and the attack phases in Sect. 6 and present the results of our attack. We conclude the paper with Sect. 7, where we discuss possible countermeasures against our attack.

2   Background

2.1   Notation

For any integer q, the ring $\mathbb{Z}_q$ is represented by the set $[-q/2, q/2) \cap \mathbb{Z}$. We denote $\mathbb{Z}_q[X] = (\mathbb{Z}/q\mathbb{Z}[X])$ as the set of polynomials with integer coefficients modulo q. We define $R_q = \mathbb{Z}_q[X]/(X^n + 1)$, the ring of polynomials with integer coefficients modulo q, reduced by the cyclotomic polynomial $X^n + 1$. For any $\alpha < q$, R_α refers to the set of polynomials with coefficients in $\left[-\frac{\alpha}{2}, +\frac{\alpha}{2}\right]$. By default, we use the L^∞-norm: $\|\mathbf{v}\|_\infty = \max_i |v_i|$. We let S_η denote set $S_\eta = \{w \in R : \|w\|_\infty \leq \eta\}$.

By $vec(\cdot)$ we denote the function which maps a vector of polynomials in the ring R_q to the vector obtained by concatenating all coefficients of the respective polynomials.

In the following expressions, all polynomial operations are performed in R_q. Bold lowercase letters represent vectors with coefficients in R or R_q. Bold uppercase letters are matrices. Similarly, vector coefficients are represented by roman lowercase letters.

2.2   Dilithium Description

The Dilithium signature scheme is based on the Fiat-Shamir with aborts structure [27]. For a detailed overview we refer to Appendix C. Here, we only recall how a signature for a message μ is generated. The secret key vectors $s_1 \in R_q^\ell$ and $s_2 \in R_q^k$ are vectors of small polynomials, with each coefficients being chosen uniformly at random from a small range $\{-\eta, \ldots, \eta\}$. Signing a message μ

proceeds as follows: One first samples a commitment vector $\mathbf{y} \in R_q^\ell$ with uniformly random coefficients in the range $\{-(\gamma_1 - 1), \ldots, \gamma_1\}$. Next, one hashes the message μ together with $\mathbf{Ay}$, where $\mathbf{A}$ is public, to obtain $c = H(\mu, \mathbf{Ay})$, a ring element where τ coefficients are either -1 or 1 and the rest are 0. Finally, the output is the signature tuple $(\mathbf{z} = (c, \mathbf{s} + \mathbf{y}))$, provided that a certain rejection condition is met and repeat the signature generation otherwise.

The Dilithium specification comes with multiple sets of recommended values for the parameters q, n, k, l, η, d, γ_1, γ_2, β, w, and τ, depending on the desired security level [4]. Details about constraints and recommended values for these parameters are provided in the specifications [4] and Appendix C.

Our attack makes use of the fact that knowledge of only $\mathbf{s}_1$ is sufficient to achieve universal forgery, as shown in [20,39]. For the details of these forgery attacks we refer to Appendix D.

2.3 Machine-Learning Model for Profiling Side-Channel Analysis

Profiling side-channel attacks model an unknown distribution, which can only be approximated by an assumed statistical distribution of the leakage. The main idea behind a profiling attack is to learn this statistical distribution during a *profiling phase*, and then leverage the learned distribution during an *attack phase*. A famous way of executing profiling attacks is via so-called template attacks, which assume that the leakage follows a multi-variate Gaussian distribution [6].

Profiling attacks can also be executed by training a machine-learning model, e.g., artificial neural networks such as Multilayer Perceptron (MLP), Convolutional Neural Networks (CNN), among others [9,23,29,42]. Machine-learning models are capable of not only learning the parameters of an assumed (and thus fixed) leakage distribution, but also learning a model of the leakage distribution itself. Because of this flexible attack primitive, we employ MLPs in the present attack. For a more detailed exposition on machine-learning assisted profiling attacks, we refer to Appendix E.

3   Overview of the Attack

Attacker Model. The goal of this attack is to reconstruct the first part of the secret key of Dilithium. To this end, we conduct a profiling machine-learning-based side-channel attack and assume the following:

- In the profiling phase, the attacker has access to a clone device. The clone device is similar to the victim's device, but controlled by the attacker. Thus, the attacker can measure the power trace of the entire signing process while having knowledge of the secret key.
- In the attack phase, we assume that the attacker can trigger several signatures on the device under attack, where the same secret key is used for all signatures.
- There are no additional conditions on the secret key and on the messages used in the profiling and attack phases.
- Our attack can be mounted against both the deterministic and non-deterministic versions of Dilithium.

Main Idea. We present a profiling side-channel attack against the Dilithium reference implementation, targeting leakage in the signing procedure. In particular, we target the sampling of the commitment vector y. The vector y is generated by converting a (random) byte buffer into the vector's coefficients. The bit-unpacking function which handles this conversion leaks information about the coefficients.

We exploit this leakage as follows. During the profiling phase, we execute the signing process with random input messages on a device and collect the sub-traces corresponding to the power usage during the execution of the bit-unpacking function. We label the sub-traces with the sensitive internal data that will be leaked (in our case, whether the unpacked coefficients are zero or non-zero coefficients) and we train neural networks to infer the sensitive information from the power traces. Likewise, in the attack phase, by observing the power traces of the signature generation on a device of identical architecture, the trained classifier are used to recover the sensitive internal data generated during the signing algorithm. Together with known challenge vector elements (i.e., A, z, and c), we map the (potentially wrong) predictions obtained into a system of linear equations. We use the Least Squares Method (LSM) to get a solution candidate $\hat{s}_1$. Then, we uncover the secret key s_1 by solving an Integer Linear Program (ILP). Once we recovered s_1, the alternative signing procedures proposed in [20,39] allow us to generate valid signatures for arbitrary message, using only s_1.

4   Power Side-Channel Leakage in Dilithium

To assess the feasibility of power side-channel attacks against the Dilithium reference implementation, we proceed in two steps. First, we identified a leaking function in Dilithium's reference implementation [4]. We then trained and optimized Deep Neural networks (DNNs) to recover sensitive information from the leaking power traces. All experiments were conducted on an ARM Cortex M4 compiling the Dilithium reference implementation in NIST Security Level 2.

4.1   The Leaking `polyz_unpack` Function

We identified that the function used when generating the vector y (Algorithm 4 in the Appendix, Line 6) is a leaking. In the reference implementation of Dilithium [3], y is generated as follows. The initial randomness seed ρ' is extended through an Extensible Output Function (XOF) such as SHAKE-256 or AES-256. The resulting bit-string is then unpacked into ℓ polynomials, where each polynomial is unpacked separately. To unpack a bit-string into a polynomial, the bits are transformed into positive numbers from $\{0, \ldots, 2\gamma_1\}$. Then, the resulting numbers are subtracted from γ_1. Listing 1.1 in the Appendix lists the C code of the bit unpacking for one polynomial as found in the Dilithium reference implementation [3]. This bit-unpacking procedure leaks information about the polynomial coefficients through the power traces of its execution, which can be seen by leveraging Welch's t-test. To conduct the t-test, we collected power traces of executions of the `polyz_unpack` function, while unpacking either fixed (zero) or random coefficients. A t-test on the corresponding power traces clearly indicates a leak, as the t-test values suggest that there is a difference in the distributions of the power traces corresponding to the unpacking of a fixed vs. random coefficient. For details on the procedure and the results, we refer the reader to Appendix F.

4.2   Training Models to Learn Coefficients from Power Traces

We rely on DNNs to recover information about $\mathbf{y}$'s coefficients from the power traces. In an effort to maximize the DNN's performance, we use the profiling phase to not only search for weights that optimize classification performance, but also to optimize the DNN's architecture through hyper-parameter optimization. Note that during the i'th iteration of unpacking loop in the `polyz_unpack` function, different instructions are used to unpack the $(i)^{th}$ to $(i + 3)^{th}$ coefficients of the target polynomial. In order to optimize prediction performance, we train four different neural networks, one for each unpacked coefficient.

In detail, the training proceeds as follows. First, we collect a training set of power traces $X = \{x_1, \ldots, x_n\}$, $x_i \in \mathbb{R}^t$ on the cloning device, each trace corresponding to one iteration of the loop in `polyz_unpack`. We assign to each trace a binary label describing whether it corresponded to the unpacking of a 0-coefficient or not. A full-grid search over a variety of potential neural network architectures would be too extensive and suffer from combinatorial explosion. Instead, we use the Hyperband hyper-parameter optimization algorithm [26].

Concretely, we collected 64335 traces of executions of one loop iteration in the `polyz_unpack` function. We used those traced to assemble 4 data sets, one for each of the 4 neural networks. Each training data set contains 2176 traces corresponding to the unpacking of a 0 coefficient - the dataset is deliberately assembled to be unbalanced. For each of the 4 neural networks, we use Hyperband to determine the number of layers, the number of neurons in each respective layer, and the activation functions used. Table 1 depicts the resulting MLP architectures. An overview of the obtained accuracy, precision, recall, and specificity of each classifier, as evaluated on a validation set, is shown in Table 2.

5   Secret Key Retrieval

Equipped with the models trained in the *profiling phase*, as described in the previous section, an attacker can recover the secret key during the *attack phase*. In the attack phase, the attacker lets the victim device sign various (different) messages (these do not need to be known by the attacker), and collect the power trace snippets of the bit-unpacking function. We store the obtained traces along with all public information about the signature process (i.e., $\mathbf{A}$, $\mathbf{z}$, and c). With the recorded traces, the attacker is able to use the trained classifiers to obtain (noisy) information on whether the unpacked coefficients of the commitment vectors $\mathbf{y}$, were zero.

The rest of this section describes the algorithmic decoding method we use to elevate these (potentially wrong) classifications into a (equivalent) secret-key

Table 1. Architecture of the DNNs used to recover the $(i)^{th}$ to $(i+3)^{th}$ coefficient.

	Layer Type	(Input, output)	# Parameters		Layer Type	(Input, output)	# Parameters
Classifier 0	Dense	(548, 385)	211365	Classifier 1	Dense	(548, 385)	211365
	Dropout	(385, 385)	0		Dropout	(385, 385)	0
	Dense	(385, 17)	6562		Dense	(385, 17)	6562
	Dropout	(17, 17)	0		Dropout	(17, 17)	0
	Dense	(17, 97)	1746		Dense	(17, 97)	1746
	Dropout	(97, 97)	0		Dropout	(97, 97)	0
	Dense	(97, 1)	98		Dense	(97, 1)	98

	Layer Type	(Input, output)	# Parameters		Layer Type	(Input, output)	# Parameters
Classifier 2	Dense	(548, 465)	255285	Classifier 3	Dense	(548, 385)	211365
	Dropout	(465, 465)	0		Dropout	(385, 385)	0
	Dense	(465, 257)	119762		Dense	(385, 17)	6562
	Dropout	(257, 257)	0		Dropout	(17, 17)	0
	Dense	(257, 1)	258		Dense	(17, 97)	1746
					Dropout	(97, 97)	0
					Dense	(97, 1)	98

Table 2. Accuracy, Precision, Recall, and Specificity of the DNNs used to recover information about the $(i)^{th}$ to $(i+3)^{th}$ coefficient, respectively.

	Classifier 0	Classifier 1	Classifier 2	Classifier 3
Accuracy	0.999	0.999	0.999	0.999
Precision	0.999	0.997	0.999	0.998
Recall	1.0	0.999	0.999	0.996
Specificity	0.999	0.999	0.998	0.999

recovery. Throughout this section, we utilize the indices i, j to refer to the jth coefficient of the ith polynomial. For NIST 2-security level, $i \leq 256$ and $j \leq 4$. We assume that we collected power traces and the corresponding outputs for in total M signatures and denote by m to refer to the mth signature. The key retrieval proceeds in four steps. First, we define conditional equations in order to minimize the false-positive classifications. We then map the classifications into a system of linear equations. Finally, we recover the secret key from this system by leveraging the Least Squares Method and Integer Linear Programming. Algorithm 1 summarizes the key retrieval method, explained in detail in the following.

5.1 Step 1: Predicting Which Error Polynomial Coefficients Are Zero

Given that the probability of a coefficient $\mathbf{y}_{i,j}$ being equal to zero is very small, even tiny false-positive rates in our trained classifiers will be amplified to a high

---

Algorithm 1. Dilithium secret key retrieval

    Input A list of M signatures $(\mathbf{z}, \mathbf{c})$ and the respective power traces T
    Output The secret key $\mathbf{s}_1$

1: $L \leftarrow []$
2: **for** $(m, i, j) \in ((1 \ldots M) \times (1 \ldots k) \times (1 \ldots \ell))$ **do**
3:     **if** $|z_{i,j}| \leq \frac{(2 \cdot \eta + 1)^2 - 1}{12} \cdot \tau$ **then**
4:       $\hat{y}_{i,j}^m \leftarrow \text{classifier}(T_{y_{i,j}^m})$
5:       **if** classifier outputs $\hat{y}_{i,j}^m = 0$ **then**
6:          append (m, i, j) to L
7:       **end if**
8:     **end if**
9: **end for**
10: **for** $j = 1 \ldots \ell$ **do**
11:     for each prediction made on the jth polynomial, collect the respective challenge polynomials into matrix $\mathbf{C}$
12:     solve least squares $\mathbf{z} = \mathbf{C}\mathbf{s} + \mathbf{e}$ to obtain candidate solution $\hat{\mathbf{s}}$
13:     obtain correct secret key polynomial $\mathbf{s}$ by solving the integer linear program described in Sec. 5.4
14:     $(\mathbf{s}_1)_j = \mathbf{s}$
15: **end for**
16: **return** the secret key $\mathbf{s}_1$

---

amount of false-positives in the resulting equation system. To alleviate this problem and further reduce the amount of false-positives when deducing whether a certain coefficient $\mathbf{y}_{i,j}$ is zero, we define conditions on the corresponding coefficients $\mathbf{z}_{i,j}$ that allow us to filter out false-positive predictions. These conditions are be based on observations on the range and distribution of coefficients of the vector $(c\mathbf{s}_1)$ and $\mathbf{y}$.

The first observation is that $|(c\mathbf{s}_1)_{i,j}| \leq \beta$, where $\beta = \tau \cdot \eta$. Thus, assuming that $\mathbf{y}_{i,j} = 0$, it holds that $|\mathbf{z}_{i,j}| = |\mathbf{y}_{i,j} + (c\mathbf{s}_1)_{i,j}| \leq \beta$ as well. We can thus dismiss the possibility that a certain coefficient $\mathbf{y}_{i,j} = 0$ if the corresponding coefficient

$$|\mathbf{z}_{i,j}| > \beta \tag{1}$$

We further observe that each coefficient $(c\mathbf{s}_1)_{i,j}$ can be approximated by a normal distribution. Recall that c is a vector with coefficients in the set $\{-1, 0, 1\}$ and thus, each coefficient in the polynomial $c\mathbf{s}_1$ can be viewed as the sum of τ i.i.d. random variables uniformly distributed over the range $[-\eta, \ldots, \eta] \cap \mathbb{Z}$.

By a central limit theorem argument, this sum is close to a normal distribution with mean 0 and variance $\sigma^2 = \frac{(2 \cdot \eta)^2 - 1}{12} \cdot \tau$. It follows that if a given coefficient $\mathbf{y}_{i,j} = 0$, then

$$|\mathbf{z}_{i,j}| \leq 2 \cdot \sigma \tag{2}$$

with very high probability. Given the conditions in Eq. 1 and 2, we only invoke the machine-learning classifier to recover whether $\mathbf{y}_{i,j} = 0$ if $|\mathbf{z}_{i,j}| \leq 2 \cdot \sigma$. Otherwise, if $|\mathbf{z}_{i,j}|$ is larger than this threshold, we assume that $\mathbf{y}_{i,j} \neq 0$. These conditions allow a reduced number of false positives for a minor increase in false-negative.

5.2   Step 2: Mapping the Predictions into a Set of Linear Equations

In Step 2, we build a system of linear equations, which will be used to retrieve the secret key in Sect. 5.3 and Sect. 5.4. Assume that we traced M signatures in Sect. 5.1. We denote by $\mathbf{y}^m$, c^m, and $\mathbf{z}^m$ the commitment vector $\mathbf{y}$, the challenge polynomial, and the resulting signature value for the mth signature, respectively. From Sect. 5.1, we obtain a list L of triples (m, i, j), where each triple represents the assumption that $\mathbf{y}_{i,j}^m = 0$. Given a signature $\mathbf{z}^m$, we create a system of equations from this list in the following way. It holds that $\mathbf{z}_{i,j}^m = \mathbf{y}_{i,j}^m + (c\mathbf{s}_1)_{i,j}$. Thus, if $\mathbf{y}_{i,j}^m$ is indeed 0, we have: $\mathbf{z}_{i,j}^m = (c^m\mathbf{s}_1)_{i,j}$ Factoring in the erroneous classifications, we have a set of equations:

$$\mathbf{z}_{i,j}^m = (c^m\mathbf{s}_1)_{i,j} + e \tag{3}$$

where e is zero if the classifier's hypothesis that coefficient $\mathbf{y}_{i,j}^m = 0$ was correct, and $e \neq 0$ otherwise (then, $e = \mathbf{y}_{i,j}^m$). Thus, we want to obtain the secret key $\mathbf{s}_1$ from a system of linear equations: $\mathbf{z}^* = \mathbf{C}\mathbf{s}_1 + \mathbf{e}$, where $\mathbf{C} \in \mathbb{Z}^{|L| \times n}$ is derived from the challenge polynomials c, $\mathbf{z}^*$ contains the collected signature coefficients $\mathbf{z}_{i,j}^m$, and $\mathbf{e}$ is a vector of error coefficients. We make two observations about this equation system: First, assuming that the classifiers are mostly correct when asserting that a coefficient $\mathbf{y}_{i,j}^m = 0$, the error e is zero for the majority of the equations. Second, it holds that $||\mathbf{e}||_\infty \leq 2\sigma + \beta$. (Since if $|\mathbf{y}_{i,j}| > 2\sigma + \beta$, then $|\mathbf{z}_{i,j}| \geq 2\sigma$. But because of Eq. 2, we do not invoke classifiers for $\mathbf{y}_{i,j}^m$ where the corresponding coefficient $|\mathbf{z}_{i,j}| \geq 2\sigma$).

Before we turn our attention to retrieving the secret key $\mathbf{s}_1$ from this set of equations, let us first observe that we can split up the given problem into ℓ separate sets of equations, one for each polynomial in the vector $\mathbf{s}_1$.

Note that to obtain $c\mathbf{s}_1$ we multiply c with each polynomial in the vector $\mathbf{s}_1$ independently. For a given leak $\mathbf{y}_{i,j}^m$ at polynomial i, coefficient j, we observe that the equation $\mathbf{z}_{i,j}^m = \mathbf{y}_{i,j}^m + (c^m\mathbf{s}_1)$ is only influenced by the ith polynomial $(\mathbf{s}_1)_i$. As a result, we can create ℓ independent equation systems (one for each polynomial in $\mathbf{s}_1$) and solve for each polynomial of $\mathbf{s}_1$ separately. This will reduce the computational complexity in the following steps.

The rest of this section describes how to obtain each polynomial in $\mathbf{s}_1$ independently from the relevant set of equations, again collected into a vector $\mathbf{z}^* \in \mathbb{Z}^{|L|}$ and a matrix $\mathbf{C} \in \mathbb{Z}^{|L| \times n}$. For ease of notation, we will denote the polynomial we are currently solving for as $\mathbf{s} = (\mathbf{s}_1)_i$ for the remainder of this section.

5.3   Step 3: Obtaining a Solution Candidate from a Set of Linear Equations

Observe that since $||c\mathbf{s} + \mathbf{e}||_\infty < q$, there are no modular reductions involved in the given equation system. We can thus view the problem of obtaining a secret key polynomial $\hat{\mathbf{s}}$ from a system of linear equations $\mathbf{z}^* = \mathbf{C}\mathbf{s} + \mathbf{e}$ as an LWE without modular reduction problem. Using an approach described by [8], we obtain a solution candidate $\hat{s} \in \mathbb{R}^n$ by employing the least-squares method for each of the ℓ equation systems obtained in Step 2.

The least-squares method computes $\hat{s} \in \mathbb{R}^n$ as the vector minimizing the squared euclidean norm: $\|C\hat{s} - z\|_2^2$. We calculate $\hat{s}$ by employing the closed-form solution formula for least squares: $\hat{s} = (C^T C)^{-1} \cdot C \cdot z$. This solution candidate converges to a correct solution [8]. Given enough equations, it holds that $\lfloor \hat{s}_i \rceil = s_i$ for all $i \in \{1, \ldots, n\}$. Even with fewer equations, the solution $\lfloor \hat{s} \rceil$ is usually close to the correct solution s i.e., most of the coefficients are correct and some are wrong only by ± 1.

Thus, in practice, given enough equations, the following should hold for each coefficient in the least-squares solution $\hat{s}$:

1. Either rounding up or down should yield the correct solution, that is it should hold that $\lfloor \hat{s}_j \rfloor = (s)_j$ or $\lceil \hat{s}_j \rceil = (s)_j$ for all $j \in \{1, \ldots, n\}$.
2. If a coefficient $\hat{s}_j$ is close to an integer, the coefficient candidate should be correct. Formally, let $\text{dist\_nint}(x) = \min\left(x - \lfloor x \rfloor, 1 - (x - \lfloor x \rfloor)\right)$. Then, if $\text{dist\_nint}(\hat{s}_{1j}) \approx 0$, then $\lfloor \hat{s}_j \rfloor = (s)_j$.

The ILP introduced in the next step can leverage these observations about the candidate $\hat{s}$. Note that, since these conditions only hold when provided with enough equations, the least-squares step is optional. It can be left out to increase the attack's success chance at the expense of additional computation time.

5.4 Step 4: Solving an Integer Linear Program Leveraging the Solution Candidate

Recall that for most of the equations in our equation system it holds that $e = 0$, assuming that our classifier is correct in most instances. As a result, identifying the correct secret key polynomial s from the set of noisy equations amounts to identifying the secret key polynomial that maximizes the number of fulfilled equations.

We formulate the following Integer Linear Program (ILP) to identify a secret key polynomial s that maximizes the number of fulfilled equations in the list of equations L, where each equation is of the form $z_l^* = C_l s$.

To speed up the computation, the ILP allows to optionally factor in the solution candidate $\hat{s}$ obtained from the least-squares method.

$$\text{maximize} \sum_{l=1}^{|L|} x_l$$

subject to

$$\begin{aligned}
z_l - C_l s &\leq K \cdot (1 - x_l) && \forall l \in \{1, \ldots, |L|\} && (1)\\
z_l - C_l s &\geq -K \cdot (1 - x_l) && \forall l \in \{1, \ldots, |L|\} && (2)\\
(s)_i &\in \{\lfloor \hat{s}_i \rfloor, \lceil \hat{s}_i \rceil\} && \forall i \in \{1, \ldots, n\} && (3)\\
(s)_i &= \lfloor (s)_i \rceil && \forall i \in \{1, \ldots, N \mid \text{dist\_nint}(\hat{s}_i) \leq 0.01\} && (4)\\
x_l &\in \{0, 1\} && \forall l \in \{1, \ldots, |L|\} && (5)
\end{aligned}$$

Here, each binary variable x_l corresponds to whether the current solution candidate $\mathbf{s}$ fulfills the l'th equation. Constraints (1) and (2) ensure that if $x_l = 1$, then $\mathbf{z}_l^* - \mathbf{C}_l \mathbf{s} = 0$ (This is canonically known as the big-M method, we choose K as the maximum possible distance between $\mathbf{z}_l^*$ and $\mathbf{C}_l \mathbf{s}$). Constraint (3) and (4) factor in the information from our solution candidate $\hat{\mathbf{s}}$ obtained by least-squares. Note that constraints (3) and (4) are optional. Removing them guarantees a correct solution (assuming the majority of the equations are correct), but could incur additional runtime. We run two ILP-solvers in parallel (one with constraints (3) and (4), and one without) until we have solution $\mathbf{s}$ that satisfies at least $(1-\epsilon) \cdot |L|$ equations, where ϵ is our assumed false-positive rate (the percentage of equations that we assume to be wrong). In doing so, we ensure that the obtained solution should match the secret key polynomial of the secret key $\mathbf{s}$. While the Integer Linear Program is not guaranteed to be efficiently solvable, in practise, the ILP solver identified the secret key efficiently.

We perform step Sect. 5.3 and 5.4 ℓ times, for each polynomial equation independently. This yields a secret key candidate $\mathbf{s}_1$. We can then perform universal forgery as described in Appendix. D.

5.5   Alternative Attack Strategies

We also explored two alternative attack strategies: the *LWE with side information* technique by Dachman-Soled et al. [12], and *the ternary LWE attacks* by Kirshanova and May [24].

LWE with Side Information. The "LWE with side information" technique [12] provides a framework to integrate additional information about an LWE problem in the form of so-called hints. To this end, a given LWE instance is transformed into a Distorted Bounded Distance Decoding (DBDD) instance, which allows to keep track of a distribution of the secret vector. Hints can, for example, alter the secret distribution in a way that potentially makes the problem easier. After providing enough hints, it might be feasible to recover the LWE secret through lattice-reduction attacks. We explored the option of integrating the information obtained through the leaking implementation as hints until we can recover the secret through a lattice-reduction step.

Unfortunately, the entire framework essentially models the errors as normally distributed, whereas the errors in our setting have a high probability of being equal to zero, but can be fairly large with non-negligible probability as well. We can of course ignore the mismatch and pretend that the errors are Gaussian with variance equal to the real variance. However, probably due to this mismatch, we find that integrating even a large number of hints does not suffice to reduce the complexity of the underlying lattice problem to a feasible level. It would be interesting to consider to what extent the framework could be generalized to support such non-Gaussian errors.

Meeting Ternary LWE Keys. Recently, following up on results of May [31], Kirshanova and May [24] proposed a novel meet-in-the-middle (MITM) attack that can recover a ternary secret key $s \in \{0, \pm 1\}^n$ from an LWE instance $\mathbf{As} = \mathbf{b} + \mathbf{e}$ mod q, where the error $e \in \{0, \pm 1\}^m$ is also ternary, in asymptotic complexity $S^{0.25+o(1)}$ (where S is the size of the search space we need to consider for s, taking into account e.g. the sparsity of secrets). This is a large improvement upon the classical square-root complexity $S^{0.5}$ of straightforward MITM.

This attack setting is slightly different from our own, since our secrets and errors are somewhat larger, but contrary to May's earlier attack, whose complexity increases greatly for larger error bounds, the Kirshanova–May approach can in principle be adapted to larger errors at reasonable cost. As a result, one could consider applying this technique directly for key recovery. Unfortunately, a very coarse lower bound of the attack cost, obtained by assuming that secrets and errors are in fact ternary and computed using the estimator provided by the authors, shows that the approach is far from practical, and always much worse than the ILP.

One potential use of this MITM approach in our setting, however, could be as a postprocessing step after least-squares or ILP: it could help recover the exact secret once a sufficiently precise approximation has been obtained by other techniques, and only a few incorrect coefficients remain, so that the *difference* between the exact secret and the approximate one is a small, very sparse solution to a known LWE instance. A thorough analysis of this idea is left as future work. It would require working out and implementing the larger error variant of the Kirshanova–May approach on the one hand, and obtaining tight estimates for the Hamming weight of the difference between approximate and exact secret for varying number of samples in the attack on the other hand. Both of these problems are nontrivial research questions *per se* beyond the scope of the present work.

6   Experimental Setup and Results

We evaluate our attack in two settings. First, a practical evaluation that proves the efficacy of our attack through an end-to-end power side-channel attack carried out on a Cortex M4 with a ChipWhisperer Lite. We enrich this result with a theoretical evaluation of our secret key retrieval algorithm, simulating the noisy equations that would be given by the machine-learning classifiers. We provide all code as open source[1].

Practical Evaluation. To verify our findings, we tested our attack using two identical Cortex M4 CPUs equipped with two STM32F4 microcontrollers, where we used one device for training the classifiers, and the other device to mount the described attack. To conduct our experiments and collect power traces, we used the ChipWhisperer-Lite testing board [37]. As the ChipWhisperer Lite is limited to 24,400 samples per recorded trace and thus cannot be used to record the entire power trace of the Dilithium signature process, we collect only the relevant power snippets. For the details of our experimental setup, we refer

---

[1] https://github.com/fgsect/profiling-attack-dilithium.

the reader to Appendix G. In summary, we execute the profiling phase on a attacker-controlled device by collecting traces for attacker-known inputs to the bit-unpacking function. After training the model, we move to the attack phase. In the attack phase, the key pair generation was invoked once to generate the key under attack. Then a number of uniform, randomly chosen, messages were signed with this key on another cloning device, while tracing the power consumption.

We were able to recover the secret key s_1 by tracing the polyz_unpack() function for $756,589$ signatures. The trained machine-learning classifiers classified 2015 sub-traces as the sampling of a zero-coefficient, resulting in 2015 equations. Out of those, 24 equations were wrong, i.e. the machine-learning classifiers classified the sampled coefficients as zero when they were actually non-zero. After collecting all classifications, we ran the secret key recovery from Algorithm 1, where the ILP-Solver recovered the exact secret key after only a few minutes. We emphasize that the presented secret key retrieval method can also handle higher noise levels, as can be seen from the theoretical evaluation.

Theoretical Evaluation. Note that our key recovery algorithm will always identify the correct secret key, assuming that the majority of the inferred equations are correct. However, its run time complexity is not guaranteed to be polynomial. We find that a noisier equation system results in a higher, potentially even infeasible, run time of the ILP solver. To test the resistance of our secret-key retrieval method to noise, we conducted a theoretical evaluation of the secret-key retrieval algorithm, simulating noisy equations as returned by a machine-learning classifier. Algorithm 2 describes the theoretical evaluation framework.

To investigate the impact of the parameter choices, we evaluate in Table 3 whether the described attack was able to recover the key in under 30 minutes in at least 1 in 20 trials for different parameters. The results show that a lower true positive rate (=lower false negative) can be compensated for by collecting more signatures, while even a slightly higher false positive rate quickly becomes prohibitive. Attacking NIST security level 3 was only feasible with a very low false positive rate, while attacking NIST security Level 5 can be done via increasing the number of collected signatures.

7   Conclusion and Possible Countermeasures

In this paper, we presented a profiling power side-channel attack on the Dilithium signature scheme. Using a leak in a bit-unpacking function, we leverage machine-learning to recover noisy information about the vector $\mathbf{y}$. Together with the signature $\mathbf{z}$ and the message digest c, this small leak suffices to achieve the equivalent of key recovery with a moderate number of signatures.

Defending against our attack requires dedicated countermeasures against power side channel attacks. Masking Dilithium, as described by Migliore et. al. [33], constitutes such a countermeasure. The proposed masking scheme for Dilithium is based on Boolean and arithmetic masking. Each sensitive variable is split into $t + 1$ shares, where t is the so-called masking order. Every operation

Algorithm 2. Simulate noise in predictions from an assumed side-channel on $\mathbf{y}$

Input The number of signatures M to try, an assumed true and false positive rate, and a NIST security Level for Dilithium, defining the parameters k, ℓ, τ, η.

Output Whether $\mathbf{s}_1$ could be recovered in under 30 minutes computation time.

1: Generate M signatures
2: **for** $(m, i, j) \in ((1 \ldots M) \times (1 \ldots k) \times (1 \ldots \ell))$ **do**
3:    **if** $|z_{i,j}^m| \leq \frac{(2 \cdot \eta + 1)^2 - 1}{12} \cdot \tau$ **then**
4:       **if** $y_{i,j}^m = 0$ **then**
5:          Predict that $y_{i,j}^m = 0$ with probability true positive rate
6:       **else**
7:          Predict that $y_{i,j}^m = 0$ with probability false positive rate
8:       **end if**
9:    **end if**
10: **end for**
11: Use Alg. 1 to try to recover the secret key polynomial $\mathbf{s}_1$ from predictions

Table 3. Evaluation on the influence of different parameters on the success of the attack described in Algorithm 1, evaluated using the Algorithm 2

Security Level	False Positive Rate	True Positive Rate	Signatures	Total Equations	Wrong Equations	≥ 1 Success?
2	0.01	0.9	750000	3315	860	Yes
2	0.01	0.9	650000	2893	767	No
2	0.01	0.8	2000000	8451	2506	Yes
2	0.015	1	800000	4480	1484	Yes
2	0.019	0.981	800000	4393	1729	Yes
2	0.03	1	4000000	30811	12465	No
3	0.015	1	4000000	7750	3734	No
3	0.005	1	3500000	4792	1120	Yes
3	0.005	0.98	4000000	3491	701	Yes
5	0.015	1	800000	2233	889	No
5	0.015	1	3500000	9321	3631	Yes

that acts on the sensitive information is reformulated to act on each of the shares independently instead. Breaking a fully masked Dilithium implementation with the attack described in this paper would require to deduce the value of all shares of $\mathbf{y}$. Power consumption is inherently noisy, implying the potential for erroneous classifications on each share. As a result, the probability to correctly deduce the value of a coefficient $\mathbf{y}_{i,j}$ decreases exponentially with the number of shares.

However, the masking countermeasure described in [33] induces a performance overhead. Migliore et al. [33] measure that first-order masking already slows down signature creation by a factor of five. Arguably, the estimates given by [33] are a lower bound, as the authors replaced the real modulus by a modulus that is a power of two, which boosts performance of the countermeasure. The performance loss could impede the adoption of such countermeasure. On the other hand, considering that our attack only requires noisy information about the Hamming weight of the coefficients of $\mathbf{y}$, more efficient countermeasure are non-trivial to design[2].

We highlight that it was thus far unclear whether a dedicated countermeasure against power side-channels is needed for Dilithium at all: No end-to-end power side-channel attack against Dilithium had been demonstrated so far. Naturally, this could be taken as an indicator that Dilithium's countermeasures against side-channels attacks are sufficient for preventing power side-channel attacks also, especially when implementing the randomized version of Dilthium. This would allow implementations to skip masking in order to not suffer from its performance impact. Our results show that this is not the case. Consequently, our work calls attention to an urgent need of further defensive as well as offensive research: It is paramount for the implementation security of Dilithium to continue to explore possible countermeasures against power side-channel attacks in order to identify countermeasure that have only a minor impact on performance. In addition to that, offensive research is needed to uncover potential bypasses against existing countermeasures. This will ensure that protective measures taken to prevent power side-channel attacks are indeed sufficient.

Acknowledgments. The work described in this paper has been supported by the Einstein Research Unit "Perspectives of a quantum digital transformation: Near-term quantum computational devices and quantum processors" of the Berlin University Alliance. The authors acknowledge the financial support by the Federal Ministry of Education and Research of Germany in the program of "Souverän. Digital. Vernetzt." Joint project 6G-RIC, project identification number: 16KISK030 and the project Full Lifecycle Post-Quantum PKI - FLOQI (ID 16KIS1074).

A   Lattices

A lattice Λ is a discrete subgroup of $\mathbb{R}^n$ such that given $m \leq n$ are linearly independent vectors $\mathbf{b}_1, \ldots, \mathbf{b}_m \in \mathbb{R}^n$, the lattice $\Lambda = \Lambda(\mathbf{b}_1, \ldots, \mathbf{b}_m)$ is the set of all integer linear combinations of the $\mathbf{b}_i$'s, i.e.,

$$\Lambda(\mathbf{b_1}, ..., \mathbf{b_m}) = \left\{ \sum_{i=1}^{m} x_i \mathbf{b_i} \mid x_i \in \mathbb{Z} \right\},$$

where $\mathbf{b}_1, \ldots, \mathbf{b}_m$ is the basis of Λ and m is the rank. In this paper, we consider full-rank lattices, i.e., with $m = n$. An integer lattice is a lattice for which the basis vectors are in $\mathbb{Z}^n$. Usually, we consider elements modulo q, i.e., the basis vectors and coefficients, are taken from $\mathbb{Z}_q$.

---

[2] For example, restricting the masking to just $\mathbf{y}$ is not sufficient. As soon as $\mathbf{y}$ would be unmasked, an attacker could again retrieve all information necessary for the attack.

B   Learning With Errors

The Learning with Errors problem (LWE), a lattice counterpart to the classic Learning Parity with Noise problem (LPN), was introduced by Regev [40].

Definition 1. *Let n, q be positive integers, and χ be a distribution over $\mathbb{Z}$. For $\mathbf{s} \in \mathbb{Z}_q^n$, the LWE distribution $A_{s,\chi}$ is the distribution over $\mathbb{Z}_q^n \times \mathbb{Z}_q$ obtained by choosing $\mathbf{a} \in \mathbb{Z}_q^n$ uniformly at random and an integer error $e \in \mathbb{Z}$ from χ. The distribution outputs the pair $(\mathbf{a}, \langle \mathbf{a}, \mathbf{s}\rangle + e \mod q) \in \mathbb{Z}_q^n \times \mathbb{Z}q$.*

There are two important computational LWE problems: the *search problem* and the *decision problem*. The *search problem* is to recover the secret $\mathbf{s} \in \mathbb{Z}_q^n$ given a certain number of samples are drawn from the LWE distribution $A_{s,\chi}$. The *decision problem* is to distinguish a certain number of samples drawn from the LWE distribution from uniformly random samples.

C   Dilithium

The Dilithium signature scheme is based on the Fiat-Shamir with aborts structure [27]. It can also be seen as a variant of the Bai-Galbraith scheme (BG) [5]. The scheme has recently been selected as a one the four candidates for standardization by NIST, as a result of the NIST call for post-quantum cryptography algorithms.

Dilithium depends on parameters q, n, k, l, η, d, γ_1, γ_2, β, w, and τ. Details about constraints and recommended values for these parameters are provided in the specifications [4]. In this paper, we point the reader to the following set of recommended parameters: ($q = 8380417 = 2^{23} - 2^{13} + 1$, $n = 256$, $k = 4$, $l = 4$, $\eta = 2$, $d = 13$, $\gamma_1 = 2^{17}$, $\gamma_2 = q - 1/88$, $\beta = 78$, $w = 80$, $\tau = 39$). In addition, the scheme also uses:

- H: a collision-resistant hash function
- $ExpandMask$: A function used to deterministically generate the randomness of the signature scheme, maps a seed ρ' and a nonce κ to $S_{\gamma_1}^l$
- $ExpandA$: A function that maps a uniform seed $\{0,1\}^{256}$ to a matrix $\mathbf{A} \in R_q^{k \times l}$
- CRH: A collision resistant hash function

For complete details of these functions, we refer to [4]. The scheme is known to perform well in terms of its key size (i.e., Dilithium-II has a public key of 1,312 bytes and a signature of 2,420 bytes) and the signing process speed (i.e., its signing process takes 251,144 cycles and its signature verification takes 72,633 cycles on a Skylake CPU, AVX implementation) [4].

Dilithium employs various techniques to optimize performance. First, Dilithium is instantiated with Module-LWE. Module-LWE deals with matrix of "small" polynomials instead of a unique one as in Ring-LWE. Module-LWE addresses the limitation of R-LWE: the size of polynomials increases with security. For Module, only the number of rows and columns impacts security, not

---

Algorithm 3. *Key generation*

1: $\zeta \leftarrow \{0,1\}^{256}$
2: $(\rho, \varsigma, K) \in \{0,1\}^{256 \times 3} := \mathrm{H}(\varsigma)$
3: $(\mathbf{s}_1, \mathbf{s}_2) \in S_\eta^l \times S_\eta^k := \mathrm{H}(\varsigma)$
4: $\mathbf{A} \in R_q^{k \times l} := ExpandA(\rho)$
5: $\mathbf{t} = \mathbf{A}\mathbf{s}_1 + \mathbf{s}_2$
6: $(\mathbf{t}_1, \mathbf{t}_0) := Power2Round_q(\mathbf{t}, d)$
7: $tr \in \{0,1\}^{384} := CRH(\rho \parallel \mathbf{t}_1)$
8: **return** $(pk = (\rho, \mathbf{t}_1), sk = (\rho, K, tr, \mathbf{s}_1, \mathbf{s}_2, \mathbf{t}_0))$.

---

the size of polynomials-which can be set the same for all instantiations (256 coefficients for Dilithium).

Another optimization employed by Dilithium is the key compression mechanism to reduce public key size. The compression is done in two different ways. First, the sampling of $\mathbf{A}$ is done with an XOF function (Extendable Output Function), which generates a (deterministic) pseudo-random string from a small seed. Therefore, the public key contains the seed instead of the polynomial $\mathbf{A}$. Another compression is a per-coefficients truncation (or rounding) associated with a correcting code mechanism to guess truncated bits.

In the following section, we give a description of the key generation, signing, and verification processes of the Dilithium scheme.

Key Generation. The key generation algorithm is presented in Algorithm 3. The procedure starts off by generating a uniform seed ρ. Then, the function *ExpandA* maps a uniform seed to a matrix $\mathbf{A}$. Given that $\mathbf{s}_1$ and $\mathbf{s}_2$ are two secret random vectors, each coefficient of these vectors is an element of the polynomial ring R_q and is of small size at most η (See Tab. 1 in the Dilithium specification [4]). Next, the public key pk is computed as $\mathbf{t} = \mathbf{A}\mathbf{s}_1 + \mathbf{s}_2$ (Algorithm 3, Line 5). Note here that only the first d bits of $\mathbf{t}$ are public. This rounding technique yields to a public key size reduction.

Signing. The signing process is described in Algorithm 4. It starts with generating a vector of polynomials $\mathbf{y}$ with coefficients of absolute value less than a defined constant γ_1 [4] (Algorithm 4, Line 6). The signer retrieves the highest-order bits of $\mathbf{A}\mathbf{y}$ and computes $\mathbf{w}$. Precisely, each coefficient w_i of $\mathbf{A}\mathbf{y}$ is written in the form $w_i = w_{1,i} \cdot 2\gamma_2 + w_{0,i}$, where $|w_{0,i}| \leq \gamma_2$; $\mathbf{w_0}$, $\mathbf{w_1}$ are the vectors of coefficients $w_{0,i}$ and $w_{1,i}$ respectively. Then, a challenge c is generated as the hash of the message and $\mathbf{w_1}$ (Algorithm 4, Line 9). The potential signature is then calculated as $\mathbf{z} = \mathbf{y} + c\mathbf{s}_1$, where c is generated as a ring element having τ coefficients with values either -1 or 1, and the rest, 0. A rejection condition is applied to the signature $\mathbf{z}$ in order to avoid dependency of the signature on the secret key. The parameter β is set to be the maximum possible coefficient of $c\mathbf{s}_i$. Since c has a defined number of non-zero elements and the maximum coefficients in $\mathbf{s}_i$ is η, the absolute value of each coefficient in $c\mathbf{s}_i$ is less than or equal to $\beta = \tau \cdot \eta$. If any of the $\mathbf{z}$ coefficients is larger than $\gamma_1 - \beta$, then a rejection occurs

Algorithm 4. Signature generation

1:   $\mathbf{A} \in R_q^{k \times l} := ExpandA(\rho)$
2:   $\mu \in \{0,1\}^{384} := CRH(tr \parallel M)$
3:   $\kappa := 0, (\mathbf{z}, \mathbf{h}) := \perp$
4:   $\rho' \in \{0,1\}^{384} := CRH(K \parallel \mu)$ (or $\rho' \leftarrow \{0,1\}^{384}$ for randomized signing)
5:   **while** $(\mathbf{z}, \mathbf{h}) := \perp$ **do**
6:      $\mathbf{y} \in \widetilde{S}_{\gamma_1}^l := ExpandMask(\rho', \kappa)$
7:      $\mathbf{w} := \mathbf{Ay}$
8:      $\mathbf{w_1} := HighBits_q(\mathbf{w}, 2\gamma_2)$
9:      $c \in B_\tau := H(\mu \parallel \mathbf{w_1})$
10:     $\mathbf{z} := \mathbf{y} + c\mathbf{s_1}$
11:     $r_0 := LowBits_q(\mathbf{w} - c\mathbf{s_2}, 2\gamma_2)$
12:     **if** $\|\mathbf{z}\|_\infty \geq \gamma_1 - \beta$ and $\|\mathbf{r_0}\|_\infty \geq \gamma_2 - \beta$ **then**
13:        $(\mathbf{z}, \mathbf{h} := \perp)$
14:     **else**
15:        $\mathbf{h} := MakeHint_q(-c\mathbf{t_0}, \mathbf{w} - c\mathbf{s_2} + c\mathbf{t_0}, 2\gamma_2)$
16:        **if** $\|c\mathbf{t_0}\| \geq \gamma_2$ or the # of 1's in $\mathbf{h}$ is greater than $\mathbf{w}$ **then**
17:           $(\mathbf{z}, \mathbf{h}) := \perp$
18:        **end if**
19:     **end if**
20:     $\kappa := \kappa + l$
21:   **end while**
22:   **return** $\sigma = (\mathbf{z}, \mathbf{h}, c)$

---

and the signing process restarts (Algorithm 4, Line 6). In the same manner, the restart also occurs if the low-order coefficients of $\mathbf{Az} - ct$ is greater than $\gamma_2 - \beta$. The rejection probability as explained in [4] is low (between 4 and 7 per signature). The $MakeHint_q$ procedure (Algorithm 4, Line 15) produces hints to help guessing the shrunk bits of the public key.

The authors of Dilithium specify a deterministic and a probabilistic variant of the signature generation. In the deterministic version of Dilithium, a seed is added to the secret key and is used together with the message to produce the randomness $\mathbf{y}$ (Algorithm 4, Line 6) required for sampling $\mathbf{y}$. The non-deterministic version samples the randomness during signature generation. The non-deterministic version aims at prevent side-channel and fault attacks that exploit determinism [4].

Verification. The verification algorithm is described in Algorithm 5. The verifier computes the high-order bits of $\mathbf{Az} - ct$, and accepts if all the coefficients of $\mathbf{z}$ are less than $\gamma_1 - \beta$ provided that c is the hash of the message and $\mathbf{w_1'}$. A valid signature should satisfy:

$$HighBits_q(\mathbf{Ay}, 2\gamma_2) = HighBits_q(\mathbf{Ay} - c\mathbf{s_2}, 2\gamma_2).$$

To see why this is correct, observe that $\|LowBits_q(\mathbf{Ay} - c\mathbf{s_2})\|_\infty \leq \gamma_2 - \beta$ and $c\mathbf{s_2}$'s coefficients are smaller than β. Thus, adding $c\mathbf{s_2}$ will not cause carries.

Algorithm 5. Signature verification

1: $\mathbf{A} \in \mathbf{R}_q^{k \times l} := ExpandA(\rho)$
2: $\mu \in \{0,1\}^{384} := CRH(CRH(\rho \| \mathbf{t}_1) \| M)$
3: $\mathbf{w}_1' := UseHint_q(\mathbf{h}, \mathbf{Az} - c\mathbf{t}_1.2^d, 2\gamma_2)$
4: **if** $\|\mathbf{z}\|_\infty < \gamma_1 - \beta$ and $c = H(\mu \| \mathbf{w}_1')$ and # of 1's in $\mathbf{h}$ is$\leq \omega$ **then**
5:     **return** 1
6: **else**
7:     **return** 0
8: **end if**

D   Universal Forgery

In the following, we present two universal forgery attacks on Dilithium, which rely solely on the knowledge of $\mathbf{s}_1$, without knowing the vector $\mathbf{s}_2$. The first method was presented by Ravi et al. [39], the second method was presented by Groot Bruinderink and Pessl [20].

The method by Ravi et al. is based on the following observations. Assume an attacker has the knowledge of $\mathbf{s}_1$. Our goal is to generate a valid signature of a message. In the deterministic version of Dilithium, K is public and is used to deterministically generate randomness $\mathbf{y}$ (Algorithm 4, Line 6). The attacker proceeds from line 6 to 10 (Algorithm 4) by choosing $\mathbf{y}$, uniformly at random, from $S_{\gamma_1-1}^l$ in line 6 (Algorithm 4) and computing the signature $\mathbf{z}$ using the partial knowledge of $\mathbf{s}_1$ (Algorithm 4, Line 10). In the signature verification (Algorithm 5), the attacker requires the knowledge of $\mathbf{w}_1$. It is proven that $P[\mathbf{w}_1 = HighBits_q(\mathbf{w} - c\mathbf{s}_2)]$ is very close to 1 [4].

Note that $\mathbf{w} - c\mathbf{s}_2 = (-c\mathbf{t}_0) + (\mathbf{w} - c\mathbf{s}_2 + c\mathbf{t}_0)$. We write $\mathbf{u} = -c\mathbf{t}_0$ and $\mathbf{r} = \mathbf{w} - c\mathbf{s}_2 + c\mathbf{t}_0$. As we know that $P[\|\mathbf{u}\|_\infty \leq \gamma_2] \approx 1$, which means $\| - c\mathbf{t}_0\|_\infty \leq \|\mathbf{t}_0\|_\infty < 2^d < \gamma_2$. Hence, the attacker can compute $\mathbf{w}_1$ as: $UseHint_q(MakeHint_q(\mathbf{u}, \mathbf{r}, 2\gamma_2)) = HighBits_q(\mathbf{u} + \mathbf{r}, 2\gamma_2) = HighBits_q(\mathbf{w} - c\mathbf{s}_2, 2\gamma_2) = \mathbf{w}_1$.

The attacker needs to compute the hint matrix $\mathbf{h} = MakeHint_q(\mathbf{u}, \mathbf{r}, 2\gamma_2)$ without the knowledge of $\mathbf{t}_0$ ($\mathbf{u} = -c\mathbf{t}_0$). This was done by Ravi et al. in [39]. The authors of [39] showed that the function $UseHint_q(\mathbf{u}, \mathbf{r}, \alpha)$ can be inverted to produce the correct hint only if $\|\mathbf{u}\|_\infty \leq \alpha/2$. Therefore, in order to compute the hint $\mathbf{h}$, the attacker has access to $HighBits_q(\mathbf{u} + \mathbf{r}, 2\gamma_2) = HighBits_q(\mathbf{w} - c\mathbf{s}_2)$, where $\mathbf{r} = \mathbf{w} - c\mathbf{s}_2 + c\mathbf{t}_0$ and can easily be computed as $\mathbf{w} - c\mathbf{s}_2 + c\mathbf{t}_0 = \mathbf{Az} - c\mathbf{t}_1 \cdot 2^d$. Another condition to satisfy is: $\|LowBits_q(\mathbf{w} - c\mathbf{s}_2, 2\gamma_2)\|_\infty \leq \gamma_2 - \beta$ which the attacker cannot, as he is unknown to the value of $\mathbf{s}_2$. However, it has been proven in the Dilithium specification [4] that $P[\|LowBit_q(\mathbf{w} - c\mathbf{s}_2, 2\gamma_2)\|_\infty \leq \gamma_2 - \beta]$ is very close to 1.

Groot Bruinderink and Pessl [20] also present a method to achieve signature forgery after recovering the secret key $\mathbf{s}_1$. The method leverages the fact that $\mathbf{u} = \mathbf{t}_0 - \mathbf{s}_2$, which can be computed as $u = \mathbf{u} = \mathbf{As}_1 - \mathbf{t}_1 \cdot 2^d = \mathbf{t}_0 - \mathbf{s}_2$, approximately matches $\mathbf{t}_0$, given $\mathbf{s}_2$'s small coefficients. Thus, we can compute a hint $\mathbf{h}$ that will be accepted with probability using $\mathbf{u}$ only and instead of $\mathbf{t}_0$ and $\mathbf{s}_2$.

E   Machine-Learning Assisted Profiling Attacks

The main idea behind profiling techniques is that side-channel measurements follow an unknown distribution that can only be approximated by an assumed statistical distribution for the leakage. Among all, the template attack is the best-known method for profiling attacks, where an attacker assumes that the leakage follows a multi-variate Gaussian distribution [6].

The advent of machine learning techniques resulted into more profiling attacks later. These techniques allow the attacker to train a classifier to learn automatically from the profiling set of the statistics of the unknown leakage distribution. Thus, one advantage of machine learning over template attacks is that the profiling model is learned without any assumption about the statistical distribution of the leakage.

Profiling side-channel attacks are performed in two phases: profiling and attack. The profiling phase can be achieved by creating a template [2,10], or training a model e.g., artificial neural networks such as Multilayer Perceptron (MLP), Convolutional Neural Networks (CNN), among others [9,23,29,42]. When using an artificial neural network, the profiling phase requires network training to learn the target device leakage for all possible values of the sensitive variable. In this paper, we use MLP models as a methodology to achieve the profiling, which consist of: the input layer, at least one hidden layer, and the output layer.

The input layer directly receives the data, whereas the output layer creates the required output. The layers in between are known as hidden layers where the intermediate computation occurs. In the training phase, the hidden layers enhance the ability of MLP classifiers to learn a non-linear function $f : X \rightarrow Y$ by training on data sets X and Y. The set X represents the traces captured from the profiling device while Y is the label according to the selected leakage model such as the Hamming weight or value of the desired variable. MLP models are composed of multiple layers of perceptrons. The perceptron passes the input into a non-linear activation function and produces an output. Next, in the attack phase, the trained classifier is used to classify the captured traces from the victim's device and predict the sensitive information.

F   T-Test for Leakage Detection

To test whether the unpacking function as listed in Listing 1.1 leaks information about the coefficients of the generated polynomial through the power traces of its execution, we leverage Welch's t-test as follows.

```
void polyz_unpack(poly *r, const uint8_t *a) {
        unsigned int i;
        for(i = 0; i < N/4; ++i) {
                r->coeffs[4*i+0]  = a[9*i+0];
                r->coeffs[4*i+0] |= (uint32_t)a[9*i+1] << 8;
                r->coeffs[4*i+0] |= (uint32_t)a[9*i+2] << 16;
```

```
                   r−>coeffs [4∗ i +0]  &= 0x3FFFF;

                   r−>coeffs [4∗ i +1]  = a [9∗ i +2] >>  2;
                   r−>coeffs [4∗ i +1]  |= ( uint32_t ) a [9∗ i +3] <<  6;
                   r−>coeffs [4∗ i +1]  |= ( uint32_t ) a [9∗ i +4] << 14;
                   r−>coeffs [4∗ i +1]  &= 0x3FFFF;

                   r−>coeffs [4∗ i +2]  = a [9∗ i +4] >>  4;
                   r−>coeffs [4∗ i +2]  |= ( uint32_t ) a [9∗ i +5] <<  4;
                   r−>coeffs [4∗ i +2]  |= ( uint32_t ) a [9∗ i +6] << 12;
                   r−>coeffs [4∗ i +2]  &= 0x3FFFF;

                   r−>coeffs [4∗ i +3]  = a [9∗ i +6] >>  6;
                   r−>coeffs [4∗ i +3]  |= ( uint32_t ) a [9∗ i +7] <<  2;
                   r−>coeffs [4∗ i +3]  |= ( uint32_t ) a [9∗ i +8] << 10;
                   r−>coeffs [4∗ i +3]  &= 0x3FFFF;

                   r−>coeffs [4∗ i +0]  = GAMMA1 − r−>coeffs [4∗ i +0];
                   r−>coeffs [4∗ i +1]  = GAMMA1 − r−>coeffs [4∗ i +1];
                   r−>coeffs [4∗ i +2]  = GAMMA1 − r−>coeffs [4∗ i +2];
                   r−>coeffs [4∗ i +3]  = GAMMA1 − r−>coeffs [4∗ i +3];
            }
    }
```

Listing 1.1. C Implementation of the bit-unpacking function as in the Dilithium reference implementation [3], for NIST Security Level 2

We restrict our measurement setup to collect a power trace of one iteration of the loop executed in **polyz_unpack** function. This iteration i unpacks the $(i)^{th}$, $(i + 1)^{th}$, $(i + 2)^{th}$, and $(i + 3)^{th}$ coefficients. We now want to test which of the generated coefficients the power trace leaks information on: $(i)^{th}$, $(i + 1)^{th}$, $(i+2)^{th}$, or $(i+3)^{th}$. For each of the four coefficients, we follow a *fixed-vs-random* approach to identify if the power trace leaks:

1. We collect multiple power traces where the respective coefficient is unpacked to zero. We denote the set of traces so collected by L_A.
2. We collect multiple power traces where the respective coefficient is unpacked to non-zero and denote the set of traces by L_B.
3. For each sample in the collected traces, we then perform Welch's t-test to identify if the distribution from the traces in L_A in that sample is different from L_B.

The results of our t-test evaluations are depicted in Fig. 1. For each coefficient, we can see clear peaks in the t-test values that exceed the necessary value for a t-critical value for a confidence level of $p = 0.05$. This is a strong indicator that the power traces indeed leak information about whether a certain coefficient is zero or non-zero.

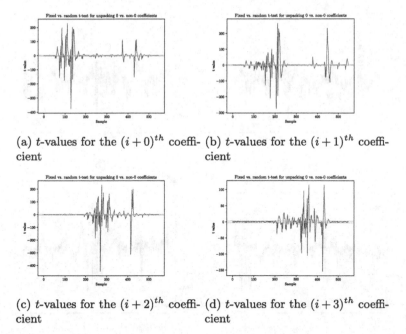

(a) t-values for the $(i+0)^{th}$ coefficient

(b) t-values for the $(i+1)^{th}$ coefficient

(c) t-values for the $(i+2)^{th}$ coefficient

(d) t-values for the $(i+3)^{th}$ coefficient

Fig. 1. t-values for a fixed vs. random t-test of the **unpack** function (using 21692 traces). The red line indicates the positive and negative t-critical value at a confidence value of $p = 0.05$. (Color figure online)

To visualize the difference, Fig. 2 illustrates traces of multiple executions of the unpacking routine to unpack the $(i)^{th}$, $(i + 1)^{th}$, $(i + 2)^{th}$, and $(i + 3)^{th}$ coefficients respectively. The blue lines correspond to the unpacking of the non-zero coefficients while the red lines to the unpacking of zero coefficients. In order to visualize the difference in the graph when the unpacking result is zero or non-zero, the power consumption traces are overlapped.

Although the difference is clear, an attacker cannot deduce the value of the unpacked coefficient from the power consumption trace with unaided eyes. Therefore, we train different machine-learning classifiers to predict the unpacked coefficient.

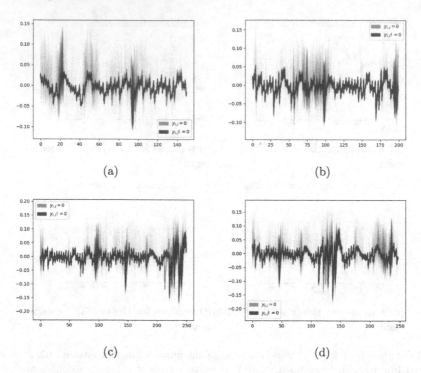

(a)	(b)

(c)	(d)

Fig. 2. Overlapped power consumption traces of the bit-unpacking of the polynomial **y**; the blue lines illustrate when the unpacked coefficient is zero and the red lines illustrate when the unpacked coefficient is non-zero; traces (a), (b), (c), and (d) corresponds to the unpacking of the the $(i)^{th}$, $(i+1)^{th}$, $(i+2)^{th}$, and $(i+3)^{th}$ coefficient, respectively. (Color figure online)

G Experimental Setup

Data Pre-processing. To facilitate our low-cost approach, we conduct the data collection for both profiling and attack in a phase we call *data pre-processing*. During this phase, we ran the Dilithium implementation [4] on an x86 Ubuntu 20.04 server machine. In the second stage, we used the profiling and attack devices to rerun sections of Dilithium code susceptible to leakage (i.e., the bit-unpacking function called multiple times during the signing process) and record power traces for the profiling and attack phases.

For the profiling phase, we signed a number of uniform and randomly chosen messages using random, individual keys. For the attack phase, the key pair generation was invoked to generate the key under attack and a number of uniform, randomly chosen, and attacker-known messages were signed. For both profiling and attack phase, we collected the internal inputs and outputs of the function susceptible to leakage of sensitive data (i.e., the unpacking function), and stored them along with all public information about the signature process. With this prepared data, we were able to rerun and analyze the parts of the code susceptible to leakage, individually.

Workbench. In our experiment, we considered two identical Cortex M4 CPUs equipped with two STM32F4 microcontrollers, named Device A and B. Device A will be used for profiling, while Device B is the device under attack. Our target is the bit-unpacking function polyz_unpack() which is called multiple times during the signing process.

As the ChipWhisperer Lite is limited to 24,400 samples per recorded trace and cannot be used to record the entire power trace of the Dilithium signature process, we used the data prepared in the pre-processing phase as explained above. During recording, the ChipWhisperer and the microcontroller both ran on the same 7,372,800 Hz clock. The sampling rate of the ADC was set to 4 samples/cycle with 10-bit resolution and a 45 dB low-noise gain filter. Collecting and storing all relevant traces was coordinated using a Python script.

Compilation. The Dilithium source code [3] was provided as a portable C implementation, which makes it suitable for compilation to different architectures.

The original benchmarking was done using the SUPERCOP benchmarking framework [7] on an Intel Core-i7 6600U (Skylake) CPU [4]. We compiled Dilithium using the gcc-arm cross-compiler *arm-none-eabi-gcc 9.2.1* on an Intel(R) Xeon(R) CPU E7-4870 running Ubuntu 20.04 and the default SUPERCOP [7] compiler options (*-O3 -fomit-frame-pointer -fwrapv*), with the necessary changes to cross-compile it for the two used devices. We used the SCIP Optimization suite [17] to solve the ILPs.

References

1. Aranha, D.F., Orlandi, C., Takahashi, A., Zaverucha, G.: Security of hedged fiat–Shamir signatures under fault attacks. In: Canteaut, A., Ishai, Y. (eds.) EUROCRYPT 2020. LNCS, vol. 12105, pp. 644–674. Springer, Cham (2020). https://doi.org/10.1007/978-3-030-45721-1_23
2. Archambeau, C., Peeters, E., Standaert, F.-X., Quisquater, J.-J.: Template attacks in principal subspaces. In: Goubin, L., Matsui, M. (eds.) CHES 2006. LNCS, vol. 4249, pp. 1–14. Springer, Heidelberg (2006). https://doi.org/10.1007/11894063_1
3. Bai, S., et al.: Dilithium reference implementation. https://github.com/pq-crystals/dilithium. Accessed 14 Apr 2020
4. Bai, S., et al.: Dilithium official website (2020). https://pq-crystals.org/dilithium/index.shtml. Accessed 20 Dec 2020
5. Bai, S., Galbraith, S.D.: An improved compression technique for signatures based on learning with errors. In: Benaloh, J. (ed.) CT-RSA 2014. LNCS, vol. 8366, pp. 28–47. Springer, Cham (2014). https://doi.org/10.1007/978-3-319-04852-9_2
6. Bartkewitz, T., Lemke-Rust, K.: Efficient template attacks based on probabilistic multi-class support vector machines. In: Mangard, S. (ed.) CARDIS 2012. LNCS, vol. 7771, pp. 263–276. Springer, Heidelberg (2013). https://doi.org/10.1007/978-3-642-37288-9_18
7. Bernstein, D.J., Lange, T.: eBACS: ECRYPT Benchmarking of Cryptographic Systems. https://bench.cr.yp.to/. Accessed 20 Dec 2020

8. Bootle, J., Delaplace, C., Espitau, T., Fouque, P.-A., Tibouchi, M.: LWE without modular reduction and improved side-channel attacks against BLISS. In: Peyrin, T., Galbraith, S. (eds.) ASIACRYPT 2018. LNCS, vol. 11272, pp. 494–524. Springer, Cham (2018). https://doi.org/10.1007/978-3-030-03326-2_17
9. Brisfors, M., Forsmark, S., Dubrova, E.: How deep learning helps compromising USIM. In: Liardet, P.-Y., Mentens, N. (eds.) CARDIS 2020. LNCS, vol. 12609, pp. 135–150. Springer, Cham (2021). https://doi.org/10.1007/978-3-030-68487-7_9
10. Camurati, G., Poeplau, S., Muench, M., Hayes, T., Francillon, A.: Screaming channels: when electromagnetic side channels meet radio transceivers. In: Lie, D., Mannan, M., Backes, M., Wang, X. (eds.) ACM CCS 2018, pp. 163–177. ACM Press, October 201. https://doi.org/10.1145/3243734.3243802
11. Chen, Y., Genise, N., Mukherjee, P.: Approximate trapdoors for lattices and smaller hash-and-sign signatures. In: Galbraith, S.D., Moriai, S. (eds.) ASIACRYPT 2019. LNCS, vol. 11923, pp. 3–32. Springer, Cham (2019). https://doi.org/10.1007/978-3-030-34618-8_1
12. Dachman-Soled, D., Ducas, L., Gong, H., Rossi, M.: LWE with side information: attacks and concrete security estimation. In: Micciancio, D., Ristenpart, T. (eds.) CRYPTO 2020. LNCS, vol. 12171, pp. 329–358. Springer, Cham (2020). https://doi.org/10.1007/978-3-030-56880-1_12
13. Ducas, L., Durmus, A., Lepoint, T., Lyubashevsky, V.: Lattice signatures and bimodal gaussians. In: Canetti, R., Garay, J.A. (eds.) CRYPTO 2013. LNCS, vol. 8042, pp. 40–56. Springer, Heidelberg (2013). https://doi.org/10.1007/978-3-642-40041-4_3
14. Ducas, L., Lyubashevsky, V., Prest, T.: Efficient identity-based encryption over NTRU lattices. In: Sarkar, P., Iwata, T. (eds.) ASIACRYPT 2014. LNCS, vol. 8874, pp. 22–41. Springer, Heidelberg (2014). https://doi.org/10.1007/978-3-662-45608-8_2
15. Espitau, T., et al.: Mitaka: a simpler, parallelizable, maskable variant of falcon. In: Dunkelman, O., Dziembowski, S. (eds.) Advances in Cryptology – EUROCRYPT 2022. EUROCRYPT 2022. LNCS, vol. 13277, pp. 222–253. Springer, Cham (2022). https://doi.org/10.1007/978-3-031-07082-2_9
16. Fournaris, A.P., Dimopoulos, C., Koufopavlou, O.: Profiling dilithium digital signature traces for correlation differential side channel attacks. In: Orailoglu, A., Jung, M., Reichenbach, M. (eds.) SAMOS 2020. LNCS, vol. 12471, pp. 281–294. Springer, Cham (2020). https://doi.org/10.1007/978-3-030-60939-9_19
17. Gamrath, G., et al.: The SCIP Optimization Suite 7.0. Technical report, Optimization Online, March 2020
18. Gentry, C., Peikert, C., Vaikuntanathan, V.: Trapdoors for hard lattices and new cryptographic constructions. In: Ladner, R.E., Dwork, C. (eds.) 40th ACM STOC, pp. 197–206. ACM Press, May 2008. https://doi.org/10.1145/1374376.1374407
19. Goldreich, O., Goldwasser, S., Halevi, S.: Public-key cryptosystems from lattice reduction problems. In: Kaliski, B.S. (ed.) CRYPTO 1997. LNCS, vol. 1294, pp. 112–131. Springer, Heidelberg (1997). https://doi.org/10.1007/BFb0052231
20. Groot Bruinderink, L., Pessl, P.: Differential fault attacks on deterministic lattice signatures. IACR TCHES 2018(3), 21–43 (2018). https://doi.org/10.13154/tches.v2018.i3.21-43
21. Güneysu, T., Lyubashevsky, V., Pöppelmann, T.: Practical lattice-based cryptography: a signature scheme for embedded systems. In: Prouff, E., Schaumont, P. (eds.) CHES 2012. LNCS, vol. 7428, pp. 530–547. Springer, Heidelberg (2012). https://doi.org/10.1007/978-3-642-33027-8_31

22. Hoffstein, J., Howgrave-Graham, N., Pipher, J., Silverman, J.H., Whyte, W.: NTRUSign: digital signatures using the NTRU lattice. In: Joye, M. (ed.) CT-RSA 2003. LNCS, vol. 2612, pp. 122–140. Springer, Heidelberg (2003). https://doi.org/10.1007/3-540-36563-X_9
23. Kim, J., Picek, S., Heuser, A., Bhasin, S., Hanjalic, A.: Make some noise: unleashing the power of convolutional neural networks for profiled side-channel analysis. IACR TCHES **2019**(3), 148–179 (2019). https://doi.org/10.13154/tches.v2019.i3.148-179
24. Kirshanova, E., May, A.: How to find ternary LWE keys using locality sensitive hashing. In: Paterson, M.B. (ed.) IMACC 2021. LNCS, vol. 13129, pp. 247–264. Springer, Cham (2021). https://doi.org/10.1007/978-3-030-92641-0_12
25. Kocher, P., Jaffe, J., Jun, B.: Differential power analysis. In: Wiener, M. (ed.) CRYPTO 1999. LNCS, vol. 1666, pp. 388–397. Springer, Heidelberg (1999). https://doi.org/10.1007/3-540-48405-1_25
26. Li, L., Jamieson, K., DeSalvo, G., Rostamizadeh, A., Talwalkar, A.: Hyperband: a novel bandit-based approach to hyperparameter optimization. J. Mach. Learn. Res. **18**(1), 6765–6816 (2017)
27. Lyubashevsky, V.: Fiat-Shamir with aborts: applications to lattice and factoring-based signatures. In: Matsui, M. (ed.) ASIACRYPT 2009. LNCS, vol. 5912, pp. 598–616. Springer, Heidelberg (2009). https://doi.org/10.1007/978-3-642-10366-7_35
28. Lyubashevsky, V., et al.: CRYSTALS-DILITHIUM. Technical report, National Institute of Standards and Technology (2020). https://csrc.nist.gov/projects/post-quantum-cryptography/round-3-submissions
29. Maghrebi, H., Portigliatti, T., Prouff, E.: Breaking cryptographic implementations using deep learning techniques. In: Carlet, C., Hasan, M.A., Saraswat, V. (eds.) SPACE 2016. LNCS, vol. 10076, pp. 3–26. Springer, Cham (2016). https://doi.org/10.1007/978-3-319-49445-6_1
30. Marzougui, S., Wisiol, N., Gersch, P., Krämer, J., Seifert, J.P.: Machine-learning side-channel attacks on the galactics constant-time implementation of bliss. arXiv preprint arXiv:2109.09461 (2021)
31. May, A.: How to meet ternary LWE keys. In: Malkin, T., Peikert, C. (eds.) CRYPTO 2021. LNCS, vol. 12826, pp. 701–731. Springer, Cham (2021). https://doi.org/10.1007/978-3-030-84245-1_24
32. Micciancio, D., Peikert, C.: Trapdoors for lattices: simpler, tighter, faster, smaller. In: Pointcheval, D., Johansson, T. (eds.) EUROCRYPT 2012. LNCS, vol. 7237, pp. 700–718. Springer, Heidelberg (2012). https://doi.org/10.1007/978-3-642-29011-4_41
33. Migliore, V., Gérard, B., Tibouchi, M., Fouque, P.-A.: Masking dilithium. In: Deng, R.H., Gauthier-Umaña, V., Ochoa, M., Yung, M. (eds.) ACNS 2019. LNCS, vol. 11464, pp. 344–362. Springer, Cham (2019). https://doi.org/10.1007/978-3-030-21568-2_17
34. Nguyen, P.: Cryptanalysis of the goldreich-goldwasser-halevi cryptosystem from crypto '97. In: Wiener, M. (ed.) CRYPTO 1999. LNCS, vol. 1666, pp. 288–304. Springer, Heidelberg (1999). https://doi.org/10.1007/3-540-48405-1_18
35. Nguyen, P.Q., Regev, O.: Learning a parallelepiped: cryptanalysis of GGH and NTRU signatures. In: Vaudenay, S. (ed.) EUROCRYPT 2006. LNCS, vol. 4004, pp. 271–288. Springer, Heidelberg (2006). https://doi.org/10.1007/11761679_17
36. NIST: Post-quantum cryptography standardization. https://csrc.nist.gov/projects/post-quantum-cryptography (2016–present)

37. O'Flynn, C., Chen, Z.D.: ChipWhisperer: an open-source platform for hardware embedded security research. In: Prouff, E. (ed.) COSADE 2014. LNCS, vol. 8622, pp. 243–260. Springer, Cham (2014). https://doi.org/10.1007/978-3-319-10175-0_17

38. Prest, T., et al.: FALCON. Technical report, National Institute of Standards and Technology (2020). https://csrc.nist.gov/projects/post-quantum-cryptography/round-3-submissions

39. Ravi, P., Jhanwar, M.P., Howe, J., Chattopadhyay, A., Bhasin, S.: Side-channel assisted existential forgery attack on Dilithium - A NIST PQC candidate. Cryptology ePrint Archive, Report 2018/821 (2018)

40. Regev, O.: On lattices, learning with errors, random linear codes, and cryptography. J. ACM **56**(6) (2009)

41. Shor, P.W.: Polynomial-time algorithms for prime factorization and discrete logarithms on a quantum computer. SIAM J. Comput. **26**(5) (1997)

42. Sim, B.Y., et al.: Single-trace attacks on message encoding in lattice-based kems. IEEE Access **8**, 183175–183191 (2020). https://doi.org/10.1109/ACCESS.2020.3029521

On the Weakness of Ring-LWE mod Prime Ideal q by Trace Map

Tomoka Takahashi[✉], Shinya Okumura, and Atsuko Miyaji

Graduate School of Engineering, Osaka University, Suita, Japan
u093809d@alumni.osaka-u.ac.jp, {okumura,miyaji}@comm.eng.osaka-u.ac.jp

Abstract. Lattice-based cryptography has attracted a great deal of attention due to the standardization of Post-Quantum Cryptography by the National Institute of Standards and Technology (NIST). The Ring-Learning with Error (Ring-LWE) problem is one of the mathematical problems that constitute such lattice cryptosystems, and it has many algebraic properties because it is considered in the ring of integers R of an algebraic number field K. This algebraic property makes it efficient, while it is also used for attacks. When the modulus q is unramified in K, it is known that the Ring-LWE problem, to determinate the secret information $s \in R/qR$, can be solved by determining $s \,(\mathrm{mod}\ \mathfrak{q})$ for all prime ideals $\mathfrak{q}$ lying over q. The χ^2–attack determines $s \,(\mathrm{mod}\ \mathfrak{q})$ by using a statistical test over $R/\mathfrak{q} \cong \mathbb{F}_{q^f}$. The χ^2–attack is improved in the special case where the residue degree f is two, called the two–residue–degree χ^2–attack. In this paper, we extend the two-residue-degree χ^2–attack to the prime–residue–degree and composite–number–residue–degree χ^2–attack. Thus, the χ^2–attack in not only two but also any residue-degree case can efficiently work. As a result, the previous attacks on $(q, f) = (67, 3)$ takes over 1.5 years but our attack takes only 129 s.

Keywords: Ring-LWE · Prime ideal · Trace map · attack

1 Introduction

With the ongoing standardization of post-quantum cryptography by the National Institute of Standards and Technology (NIST), lattice cryptography has received a great deal of attention. On July 5, 2022, four candidate algorithms have been selected for standardization [14], among which CRYSTALS-KYBER, CRYSTALS-Dilithium, and FALCON are lattice-based schemes. This is evidence that lattice-based schemes are attracting attention. The Learning with Errors (LWE) problem [13] is a problem that finds a solution to a linear system of equations with errors on a finite field, which is used to construct lattice-based cryptosystems. The Ring-Learning with Errors (Ring–LWE) problem [10], an LWE problem on the ring of integers of an algebraic number field, is known to be more efficient than the normal LWE problem. Many cryptographic schemes based on the Ring-LWE problem have been proposed [1,2]. Although

B. Smith and H. Wu (Eds.): SAC 2022, LNCS 13742, pp. 33–52, 2024.
https://doi.org/10.1007/978-3-031-58411-4_2

most cryptographic schemes including the NIST candidates based on the Ring-LWE problem use cyclotomic fields, a more efficient homomorphic encryption scheme based on a subring of a cyclotomic ring was proposed [3]. Therefore, it is important to analyze the difficulty of the Ring-LWE problem on any algebraic number field, which may give another advantage to a cryptographic scheme.

The Ring-LWE problem is defined over a ring of integers modulo q, R_q, which can be converted over a finite field $\mathbb{F}_{q^f}$ by using a prime ideal $\mathfrak{q}$ lying over q. The Ring–LWE problem on R_q is to determine the secret $s \in R_q$, whereas Ring–LWE problem on $\mathbb{F}_{q^f}$ is to determine the $s \pmod{\mathfrak{q}}$. In this paper, we refer to the Ring-LWE problem transformed on a finite field as the Ring-LWE (mod $\mathfrak{q}$). Especially when the modulus q is unramified in an algebraic number field K, determinate $s \pmod{\mathfrak{q}}$ is a very effective way to solve the Ring-LWE problem. The χ^2–attack was proposed in [5] as an attack for the Ring-LWE (mod $\mathfrak{q}$) problem. The χ^2–attack is not an efficient attack method because it is a brute force attack on a finite field and it requires a large number of samples. On the other hand, in [4], the χ^2–attack was improved in the case for $f = 2$, where f is the residue degree $R/\mathfrak{q} \cong \mathbb{F}_{q^f}$ which is called the two–residue–degree χ^2–attack. Then, the coset can reduce the number of statistical tests, and the Frobenius map can reduce the number of samples required for the attack.

In this paper, we extend the two-residue-degree χ^2–attack to the prime–residue–degree and composite–number–residue-degree χ^2–attack by using the trace map instead of the Frobenius map. Thus, the χ^2–attack in not only two but also any residue–degree case can efficiently work. Although both cases require some conditions as shown in Table 1, there exist exactly fields vulnerable to both attacks. We show that the number of operations in $\mathbb{F}_q$ of the trace map from $\mathbb{F}_{q^f}$ to $\mathbb{F}_q$ under the above conditions can reduce from $\mathcal{O}((n + C(n) + \log(q)M(n)) \cdot \log(n))$ to $\mathcal{O}(1)$. This will allow for more efficient attacks. In the χ^2–attack, it takes several years to solve the Ring-LWE (mod $\mathfrak{q}$) problem even with the small parameters used in the experiments. By using our attack, it is possible to solve the Ring-LWE (mod $\mathfrak{q}$) problem just in a few hours.

Our paper is constructed as follows. In Sect. 2, we describe the algebraic and lattice problems required in this paper, including the Ring-LWE (mod $\mathfrak{q}$) attack methods, the χ^2–attack, and the two-residue-degree χ^2–attack. Section 3 describes our proposed attack methods, the prime–residue–degree and composite–number–residue-degree χ^2–attack. We also show the existence of algebraic number fields that are vulnerable to our attacks. Section 4 shows an experimental comparison between the χ^2–attack and our proposed attacks, and Sect. 5 concludes our results.

2   Preliminary

In this section, we describe the mathematical facts required in this paper. We also explain attack methods on the Ring-LWE (mod $\mathfrak{q}$) problems [5,10], which is used as a reference for our research.

Table 1. The number of samples and statistical tests, and the conditions required for each Ring-LWE (mod q) attack.

Attacks	residue degree f	samples	statistical tests	conditions for the vulnerable field $R/\mathfrak{q} \cong \mathbb{F}_{q^f}$
χ^2–attack	$f =$ any	$\mathcal{O}(q^f)$	q^f	
Two–residue–degree	$f = 2$	$\mathcal{O}(q)$	q	
Prime–residue–degree	$f =$ any	$\mathcal{O}(q)$	q^{f-1}	• $\mathbb{F}_{q^f} \cong \mathbb{F}_q[x]/(x^f - c)$
Composite–residue–degree	$f = mn$	$\mathcal{O}(q)$	$q^{f-m} + q^{m-1}$	• $\mathbb{F}_{q^f} \cong \mathbb{F}_q[x]/(x^f - c)$ • $\mathbb{F}_{q^f} \cong \mathbb{F}_{q^m}[x]/(x^n - \sqrt[m]{c})$ • $\mathbb{F}_{q^m} \cong \mathbb{F}_q[x^n]/((x^n)^m - c)$

2.1 Algebra and Statistical Background

In this subsection, we describe the algebraic knowledge and Pearson's chi-square test used in our attacks.

Suppose that L is an extension field of a field K. Let $\mathrm{Aut}(L/K)$ be the group of all K-isomorphisms from L to L. When an algebraic extension L/K is normal and separable, L/K is called a Galois extension, and $\mathrm{Gal}(L/K) = \mathrm{Aut}(L/K)$ is called the Galois group of L/K. In particular, when $\mathrm{Gal}(L/K)$ is a cyclic group, the corresponding Galois extension L/K is called a cyclic extension. Suppose q is a prime power. Then $\mathbb{F}_{q^n}/\mathbb{F}_q$ is a cyclic extension of degree n and $\sigma \colon \mathbb{F}_{q^n} \to \mathbb{F}_{q^n}; \alpha \mapsto \alpha^q$ is the generator of $\mathrm{Gal}(\mathbb{F}_{q^n}/\mathbb{F}_q)$. There exists an irreducible polynomial $g(x) \in \mathbb{F}_q[x]$ of degree n such that $\mathbb{F}_{q^n} \cong \mathbb{F}_q[x]/(g(x))$. We use the symbol ξ to denote $x \pmod g \in \mathbb{F}_{q^n}$. Then arbitrary $\alpha \in \mathbb{F}_{q^n}$ can be represented as $\alpha = h(\xi) = \sum_{0 \le i < n} \alpha_i \xi^i (\alpha_i \in \mathbb{F}_q)$, where $h(x) \in \mathbb{F}_q[x]$ has degree less than n.

In this work, the computational complexity is evaluated in terms of the number of operations in $\mathbb{F}_q$ (sum, subtraction, multiplication, and division). Sum or subtraction of elements in $\mathbb{F}_{q^n}$ takes $\mathcal{O}(n)$ operations in $\mathbb{F}_q$, and multiplication is $\mathcal{O}(M(n))$ operations in $\mathbb{F}_q$. Division needs $\mathcal{O}(M(n) \log n)$ operations in $\mathbb{F}_q$. Here, $M(n)$ denotes the upper bound of operations in $\mathbb{F}_q$ on the product of 2 polynomials of degree n over $\mathbb{F}_q$, $M(n) = \mathcal{O}(n(\log n) \log \log n)$. $C(n)$ denotes the upper bound of operations modular polynomial composition, $C(n) = (O)(n^{1.67})$ [8].

Our attacks use the trace map to reduce the test space.

Definition 1 (Trace map). *Suppose L/K be a separable extension of degree n and $\bar{K}$ be the algebraic closure of K containing L. Let $\{\sigma_1, \sigma_2, \cdots, \sigma_n\}$ be the entire K-isomorphisms from L to $\bar{K}$. Then the trace map from L to K is defined as*

$$\mathrm{Tr}_{L/K}(\alpha) = \sigma_1(\alpha) + \sigma_2(\alpha) + \cdots + \sigma_n(\alpha).$$

The trace map has an additive homomorphism, $\mathrm{Tr}_{L/K}(\alpha + \beta) = \mathrm{Tr}_{L/K}(\alpha) + \mathrm{Tr}_{L/K}(\beta)$ for $\forall \alpha, \beta \in L$. For $\gamma \in K$, we have $\mathrm{Tr}_{L/K}(\gamma \cdot \alpha) = \gamma \cdot \mathrm{Tr}_{L/K}(\alpha)$. If $L \supset M \supset K$ is a finite separable extension, $\mathrm{Tr}_{L/K}(\alpha) = \mathrm{Tr}_{M/K}(\mathrm{Tr}_{L/M}(\alpha))$.

Suppose $q = p^k$ for prime number p, $f(x)$ is a degree n polynomial in $F_q[x]$, and d is a divisor of n. [8] proposed a trace like map algorithm to determine $\mathrm{Tr}_{\mathbb{F}_{q^d}/\mathbb{F}_p}(\alpha) = \alpha + \alpha^p + \alpha^{p^2} + \cdots + \alpha^{p^{kd-1}}$, where α is a random element in $\mathbb{F}_q[x]/(f(x))$. It requires $\mathcal{O}((nC(k) + C(n)M(k) + \log(p)M(n)M(k)) \log(kd))$ operations in $\mathbb{F}_p$. In particular, when $k = 1, d = n$ and $f(x)$ is monic irreducible polynomial, the trace like map is equivalent to the trace map from $\mathbb{F}_{p^n}$ to $\mathbb{F}_p$, which can be computed by $\mathcal{O}((n + C(n) + \log(p)M(n)) \log(n))$ operations in $\mathbb{F}_p$.

Pearson's Chi-Square Test [6,9]

Pearson's chi-square test is a hypothesis testing in which a hypothesis is tested from given samples. Suppose that a finite set S is divided into subsets of $S_1, S_2, \cdots S_r$. Let p_i be the probability that a random variable sampled with the assumed distribution is included in S_i. In this case, the expected value c_i of the number of samples included in each S_i for n samples is $c_i := np_i$. If the actual number of samples in the subset S_i is f_i, then we define

$$\chi^2 = \sum_{i=1}^{r} \frac{(f_i - c_i)^2}{c_i}.$$

For the risk ratio α, set $\delta = F_{r-1}^{-1}(\alpha)$. Here, $F_{r-1}(x)$ is the cumulative distribution function of the χ^2 distribution with $r - 1$ degree of freedom. If $\chi^2 < \delta$, then the distribution of the sample is consistent with the hypothesis. If $\chi^2 \geq \delta$, we reject the hypothesis.

The chi-square test has an applicability criterion that the expected values $c_i < 5$ should not be more than 20% of the total. To satisfy this applicability criterion, the chi-square test requires a sufficient number of samples. Our proposed attacks use the chi-square test under the hypothesis that given samples in $\mathbb{F}_q$ (or $\mathbb{F}_{q^f}$) are uniformly distributed. Therefore, at least $5 \cdot q$ (or $5 \cdot q^f$) samples are required.

2.2 Ring-LWE Problem Problem

Before explaining the Ring-LWE problem, we describe the discrete Gaussian distribution.

Definition 2 (discrete Gaussian distribution). *Let* $\rho_r(x) = e^{-\|x\|^2/r^2}$ *for* $r > 0$. *For a lattice* $\Lambda \subset \mathbb{R}^n$, *the discrete Gaussian distribution on* Λ *with width* r *is*

$$D_{\Lambda,r}(x) = \frac{\rho_r(x)}{\sum_{y \in \Lambda} \rho_r(y)}, \ \forall x \in \Lambda.$$

Lemma 1 is known about the discrete Gaussian distribution, which is used to show that algebraic number fields are vulnerable to our proposed attack [11].

Lemma 1. *Suppose $\Lambda \subset \mathbb{R}^n$ is a lattice. Let $D_{\Lambda,r}$ denote the discrete Gaussian over Λ with width r. Suppose c is a positive constant such that $c \geq \frac{r}{\sqrt{2\pi}}$. Let v be a sample from $D_{\Lambda,r}$. Then*

$$Prob(\|v\|_2 > c\sqrt{n}) \leq C^n_{c/r},$$

where $C_s = s\sqrt{2\pi e} \cdot e^{-\pi s^2}$.

In the paper proposing the Ring-LWE problem, the error and secret are selected from the dual space of the ring of integers $R^\vee$ [10]. However, for simplicity of the problem, the error and secret are often selected from R. In [12], it is shown that the two problems of dual Ring-LWE and non-dual Ring-LWE are equivalent. This paper proposes attacks on the non-dual Ring-LWE problem, without considering the dual space.

Let K be an algebraic number field of degree n with the ring of integers R. Suppose $\sigma_1, \sigma_2, \cdots, \sigma_{r_1}, \sigma_{r_1+1}, \cdots, \sigma_n$ are the distinct embeddings of K, such that $\sigma_1, \sigma_2, \cdots, \sigma_{r_1}$ are the real embeddings and $\sigma_{r_1+r_2+j} = \overline{\sigma_{r_1+j}}$ for $1 \leq j \leq r_2$. We define canonical embedding $\tau \colon K \to \mathbb{R}^n$ by

$$\tau \colon K \to \mathbb{R}^n \colon x \mapsto \begin{bmatrix} \sigma_1(x) \\ \vdots \\ \sigma_{r_1}(x) \\ \sqrt{2}\mathrm{Re}(\sigma_{r_1+1}(x)) \\ \sqrt{2}\mathrm{Im}(\sigma_{r_1+1}(x)) \\ \vdots \\ \sqrt{2}\mathrm{Re}(\sigma_{r_1+r_2}(x)) \\ \sqrt{2}\mathrm{Im}(\sigma_{r_1+r_2}(x)) \end{bmatrix}$$

Here $\tau(R)$ is a lattice in $\mathbb{R}^n$, with a basis $(\tau(w_1), \tau(w_2), \cdots, \tau(w_n))$, where $\{w_1, w_2, \cdots, w_n\}$ is an integral basis of R. In the non-dual Ring-LWE problem, errors of Ring-LWE are sampled from $D_{\tau(R),r}$, called discrete error distribution.

Definition 3. *Suppose $K/\mathbb{Q}$ is an algebraic number field with the ring of integers R and quotient ring $R_q = R/qR$ for integer q. Let $r > 0$ be a positive real number and fix $s \in R_q$. Then $\mathcal{R} = (K, q, r, s)$ is called a Ring-LWE instance, q is called modulus, and s is called secret. When a is chosen to be uniformly distributed on R_q and e is chosen according to $D_{\tau(R),r}$, $(a, b = as + e) \in R_q \times R_q$ is called a Ring-LWE sample, e is called an error.*

When analyzing the non-dual Ring-LWE error distribution, one needs to take into account the sparsity of the lattice $\tau(R)$, measured by its covolume in $\mathbb{R}^n$ [7]. This covolume is equal to $|disc(K)|^{1/2n}$. For the width r of the discrete error distribution, we denote the scaled error width r_0 as

$$r_0 = r/|disc(K)|^{1/2n} = r/|det(\tau(R))|^{1/n}.$$

There are two types of Ring-LWE problems: the decision Ring-LWE and the search Ring-LWE.

Definition 4 (search non-dual Ring-LWE). *Let $\mathcal{R} = (K, q, r, s)$ be a Ring-LWE instance. Given polynomially many samples $(a, b) \in R_q \times R_q$, the search Ring-LWE problem is to determine the secret s from the samples.*

Definition 5 (decision non-dual Ring-LWE). *Let $\mathcal{R} = (K, q, r, s)$ be a Ring-LWE instance. Given polynomially many samples $(a, b) \in R_q \times R_q$, the decision Ring-LWE problem is to distinguish whether the samples are Ring-LWE samples by $\mathcal{R}$ or samples selected according to a uniform distribution on $R_q \times R_q$.*

Suppose $\mathfrak{q}$ is a prime ideal in K lying over q. Then $\phi \colon R_q \to R/\mathfrak{q}; \alpha \mapsto \alpha \,(\text{mod } \mathfrak{q})$ is ring homomorphism, and $R/\mathfrak{q} \cong \mathbb{F}_{q^f}$, where f is called the residue degree. With the ring homomorphism ϕ, we can embed the Ring-LWE sample $(a', b' = a's' + e') \in R_q \times R_q$ into $(a, b = as + e) \in \mathbb{F}_{q^f} \times \mathbb{F}_{q^f}$. That is, we can use ϕ to convert the Ring-LWE problem on R_q into a problem on the finite field $\mathbb{F}_{q^f}$.

Definition 6 (search Ring-LWE (mod $\mathfrak{q}$)). *Let $\mathcal{R} = (K, q, r, s)$ be a Ring-LWE instance, and let $\mathfrak{q}$ be a prime ideal of K lying above q. Given an arbitrary many samples $(a, b) \in R_q \times R_q$, the search Ring-LWE problem (mod $\mathfrak{q}$) is to determine $s \,(\text{mod } \mathfrak{q})$ from the samples.*

The following lemma is known for the Ring-LWE (mod $\mathfrak{q}$) problem [5]. This lemma asserts that if we can determine all $s \,(\text{mod } \mathfrak{q}_i)$, we can solve the Ring-LWE problem on R_q by using the Chinese Remainder Theorem.

Lemma 2. *Let $K/\mathbb{Q}$ be a finite Galois extension of degree n with the ring of integers R, and let q be a prime unramified in K. Then there exists a unique divisor r of n and a set of r distinct prime ideals $\mathfrak{q}_1, \cdots \mathfrak{q}_r$ of R such that*

1. *$qR = \mathfrak{q}_1 \cdots \mathfrak{q}_r$*
2. *$R/\mathfrak{q}_i \cong \mathbb{F}_{q^f}$ for all i, where $f = n/r$*
3. *$R_q \cong \mathbb{F}_{q^{f_1}} \times \cdots \times \mathbb{F}_{q^{f_r}}$.*

2.3 Attacks for Ring-LWE (mod $\mathfrak{q}$)

The χ^2–Attack. Chen, Lauter, and Stange proposed the χ^2–attack to find the secret $s \,(\text{mod } \mathfrak{q})$ on the finite field by brute force [5]. The basic idea of this attack relies on the assumption that the distribution $D_{\tau(R), r} \,(\text{mod } \mathfrak{q})$ is distinguishable from the uniform distribution on the finite field $\mathbb{F}_{q^f}$.

In this attack, the following conditions are assumed.

- The modulus q is a prime of residue degree f in the algebraic number field K.
- Suppose $e' \in R_q$ are sampled from $D_{\tau(R), r}$. The distribution of $\phi(e')$ is distinguishable from the uniform distribution on $\mathbb{F}_{q^f}$.

The procedure of the attack is shown in Algorithm 1.

Algorithm 1. The χ^2–attack

Input: S: collection of Ring-LWE samples
Output: $s \pmod{\mathfrak{q}}$
1: Apply ϕ to samples $(a', b') \in R_q \times R_q$ to obtain samples $(a, b) = (\phi(a'), \phi(b')) \in \mathbb{F}_{q^f} \times \mathbb{F}_{q^f}$.
2: Guess the value of $\phi(s)$ from the elements of $\mathbb{F}_{q^f}$, calling the guess g.
3: Compute the distribution of $e' = b - ag \in \mathbb{F}_{q^f}$ for all samples.
4: If e' is not uniformly distributed on $\mathbb{F}_{q^f}$ for a particular g, output $s \pmod{\mathfrak{q}} = g$.

In the χ^2–attack, the statistical test is performed in $\mathbb{F}_{q^f}$, therefore $\mathcal{O}(q^f)$ samples are required for this attack. Furthermore, since the χ^2 test is performed for each guess g, the number of statistical tests is $\mathcal{O}(q^f)$.

The Two–Residue–Degree χ^2–Attack. In the χ^2–attack, both the number of samples and the number of tests depend on the order of the finite field $\mathbb{F}_{q^f}$. Therefore, it is difficult to attack when the residue degree is large. Chen, Lauter, and Stange showed that when the residue degree is two, the computational complexity of the attack can be reduced by using cosets and a Frobenius map [4].

In this attack, the following conditions are assumed.

- The modulus q is a prime of residue degree two in the algebraic number field K.
- Suppose $e' \in R_q$ are sampled from $D_{\tau(R),r}$. The probability that $\phi(e')$ lies in the prime subfield $\mathbb{F}_q$ of $\mathbb{F}_{q^2}$ is computationally distinguishable from $1/q$.

Suppose $\{t_1, \cdots, t_q\}$ is a fixed coset representatives for $\mathbb{F}_{q^2}/\mathbb{F}_q$. There exists a unique index i and $s_0 \in \mathbb{F}_q$ such that $\phi(s') = s = s_0 + t_i$. The number of statistical tests is reduced by finding s_0 and t_i, respectively. The Frobenius map, denoted as $\bar{a} := a^q$ ($\forall a \in \mathbb{F}_{q^2}$), allows the statistical test to be performed in a small sample space, thus reducing the number of samples required for the attack. The procedure of the attack is shown in Algorithm 2.

Algorithm 2. The two–residue–degree χ^2–attack

Input: S: collection of Ring-LWE samples
Output: $s \pmod{\mathfrak{q}}$
1: Apply ϕ to samples $(a', b') \in R_q \times R_q$ to obtain samples $(a, b) = (\phi(a'), \phi(b')) \in \mathbb{F}_{q^2} \times \mathbb{F}_{q^2}$.
2: For each j ($1 \le j \le q$), compute the distribution of

$$m_j(a, b) := \frac{\bar{b} - b - \overline{at_j} + at_j}{\bar{a} - a} \in \mathbb{F}_q.$$

3: If $m_j(a, b)$ is not uniformly distributed on $\mathbb{F}_q$ for a particular j, let s_0 the most frequent value and output $s \pmod{\mathfrak{q}} = s_0 + t_j$.

In the two–residue–degree χ^2–attack, the statistical test is performed in $\mathbb{F}_q$, and then $\mathcal{O}(q)$ samples are required for this attack. Furthermore, since the statistical test is performed for $t_1, \cdots, t_q$, the number of statistical tests is $\mathcal{O}(q)$.

3   Attacks on Ring-LWE (mod q) by Trace Map

In this section, we propose two attacks that reduce the number of samples by performing the statistical test on $\mathbb{F}_q$, and also reduce the number of statistical tests by using cosets $\mathbb{F}_{q^f}/\mathbb{F}_q$ or $\mathbb{F}_{q^f}/\mathbb{F}_{q^m}$. Although both cases require some conditions of $(\mathbb{F}_{q^f} \cong \mathbb{F}_q[x]/(x^f - c) \ (c \in \mathbb{F}_q))$ or $(\mathbb{F}_{q^f} \cong \mathbb{F}_q[x]/(x^f - c) \cong \mathbb{F}_{q^m}[x]/(x^n - c_1)$ and $\mathbb{F}_{q^m} \cong \mathbb{F}_q[x^n]/((x^n)^m - c) \ (c \in \mathbb{F}_q, \ c_1 = \sqrt[m]{c} \in \mathbb{F}_{q^m}))$.

In Sect. 3.1, we propose an attack using cosets $\mathbb{F}_{q^f}/\mathbb{F}_q$. Since $\mathbb{F}_q$ is a subfield of any extension field $\mathbb{F}_{q^f}$, it is an effective attack method for any residue degree.

If the residue degree f is composite, then $\mathbb{F}_{q^m}$ is a subfield of $\mathbb{F}_{q^f}$ for any divisor m of f. In the Sect. 3.2, we propose an attack on the algebraic number field whose residue degree is a composite number, using the cosets $\mathbb{F}_{q^m}$. If the algebraic number field has the composite residue degree, the attack using $\mathbb{F}_{q^m}$ is more efficient than the attack using $\mathbb{F}_q$. Therefore, an attack using $\mathbb{F}_q$ is an attack to a residue degree of prime numbers, while an attack using $\mathbb{F}_{q^m}$ is an attack to a residue degree of composite numbers. In this paper, we call the former attack the prime–residue–degree χ^2–attack, and the latter attack the composite–number–residue–degree χ^2–attack. Note that, the composite–number–residue–degree χ^2–attack needs to be added to the sample restriction.

In our proposed attacks, we use a trace map on a finite field to perform the statistical test on $\mathbb{F}_q$. [8] shows that the trace map over the finite field $\mathbb{F}_{q^n}$ can be derive by $\mathcal{O}((n + C(n) + \log(q)M(n)) \cdot \log(n))$ operations in $\mathbb{F}_q$ by considering the finite field elements as polynomials. However, by using Theorem 1 shown below, if $\mathbb{F}_{q^n} \cong \mathbb{F}_q[x]/(x^n - c)$, it can be derived by $\mathcal{O}(1)$ operations in $\mathbb{F}_q$, independent of the extension degree n.

Theorem 1. *Suppose* $\alpha = \sum_{0 \le l < n} \alpha_l \xi^l \ (\alpha_k \in \mathbb{F}_q)$ *is an element in* $\mathbb{F}_{q^n}$. *If* $\mathbb{F}_{q^n} \cong \mathbb{F}_q[x]/(x^n - c) \ (c \in \mathbb{F}_q)$, *the trace map on the finite field* $\mathrm{Tr}: \mathbb{F}_{q^n} \to \mathbb{F}_q$ *is*

$$\mathrm{Tr}(\alpha) = n \cdot \alpha_0.$$

Proof. The roots of $x^n - c$ are $c^{\frac{1}{n}} \cdot \zeta_n^j \ (j = 0, 1, \cdots, n-1)$, and so chose $\xi = c^{\frac{1}{n}} \cdot \zeta_n$, and any $\alpha \in \mathbb{F}_{a^n}$ can denote as $\alpha = \sum_{0 \le i \le n-1} a_i \xi^i = \sum_{0 \le i \le n-1} a_i (c^{\frac{1}{n}} \cdot \zeta_n)^i \ (a_i \in \mathbb{F}_q)$. The distinct roots $c^{\frac{1}{n}} \zeta_n^j$, $c^{\frac{1}{n}} \zeta_n^{j'}$ are conjugate, and so there exists $\sigma \in \mathrm{Gal}(\mathbb{F}_{q^f}/\mathbb{F}_q)$ such that $\sigma(c^{\frac{1}{n}} \zeta_n^j) = c^{\frac{1}{n}} \zeta_n^{j'}$. Moreover $\sigma(c^{\frac{1}{n}} \zeta_n) \ne \sigma'(c^{\frac{1}{n}} \zeta_n)$ for distinct σ, $\sigma' \in \mathrm{Gal}(\mathbb{F}_{q^f}/\mathbb{F}_q)$, and so $\sum_{\sigma \in \mathrm{Gal}(\mathbb{F}_{q^f}/\mathbb{F}_q)} \sigma(c^{\frac{1}{n}} \cdot \zeta_n) = \sum_{0 \le j \le n-1} c^{\frac{1}{n}} \cdot \zeta_n^j$. Therefore,

$$\mathrm{Tr}(\alpha) = \sum_{\sigma \in \mathrm{Gal}(\mathbb{F}_{q^f}/\mathbb{F}_q)} \sigma(\alpha)$$

$$= \sum_{\sigma \in \mathrm{Gal}(\mathbb{F}_{q^n}/\mathbb{F}_q)} \sigma \left(\sum_{0 \le i \le n-1} a_i \cdot \xi^i \right)$$

$$= \sum_{\sigma \in \mathrm{Gal}(\mathbb{F}_{q^n}/\mathbb{F}_q)} \sum_{0 \le i \le n-1} a_i \cdot \sigma(\xi)^i$$

$$= \sum_{0 \le i \le n-1} a_i \sum_{\sigma \in \mathrm{Gal}(\mathbb{F}_{q^f}/\mathbb{F}_q)} \sigma(c^{\frac{1}{n}} \cdot \zeta_n)^i$$

$$= \sum_{0 \le i \le n-1} a_i \sum_{0 \le j \le n-1} (c^{\frac{1}{n}} \zeta_n^j)^i = \sum_{0 \le i \le n-1} a_i c^{\frac{i}{n}} \sum_{0 \le j \le n-1} \zeta_n^{ij}.$$

$\sum_{0 \le j \le n-1} \zeta_n^{ij}$ is n and 0 for $i = 0$ and $i \ne 0$, respectively, and so $\mathrm{Tr}(\alpha) = n \cdot a_0$.

In both of Subsect. 3.1 and 3.2, we propose the basic approach and the improved approach. The basic and improved approach derive the trace value by $\mathrm{Tr}(\alpha) = \sum_{0 \le l < n} \alpha^{q^l}$ and $\mathrm{Tr}(\alpha) = n \cdot \alpha_0$, respectively.

3.1   The Prime–Residue–Degree χ^2–Attack

Basic Approach of the Prime–Residue–Degree χ^2–Attack

In the prime–residue–degree χ^2–attack, we assume the following conditions.

– The modulus q is a prime of residue degree f in the algebraic number field K. Moreover, there exists a irreducible polynomial $g(x) = x^f - c \in \mathbb{F}_q[x]$ $(c \in \mathbb{F}_q)$ such that $\mathbb{F}_{q^f} \cong \mathbb{F}_q[x]/(g(x))$.
– Suppose $c' \in R_q$ are sampled from $D_{\tau(R),r_0}$ and $e = \phi(c') = \sum e_l \xi^l$. The distribution of e_k is distinguishable from the uniform distribution on $\mathbb{F}_q$ for some index k $(0 \le k < f)$. Furthermore, the probability that $e_k = 0 \,(\mathrm{mod}\, q)$ is highest.

Suppose $\{t_1, \cdots, t_{q^f-1}\} = \{\sum_{1 \le l < f} \alpha_l \zeta^l \mid \alpha_l \in \mathbb{F}_q\}$ is the coset representatives for $\mathbb{F}_{q^f}/\mathbb{F}_q$. There is a unique index i and $s_0 \in \mathbb{F}_q$ such that $\phi(s') = s = s_0 + t_i$. The trace map $\mathrm{Tr}_{\mathbb{F}_{q^f}/\mathbb{F}_q} : \mathbb{F}_{q^f} \to \mathbb{F}_q$ is defined as follows.

$$\mathrm{Tr}_{\mathbb{F}_{q^f}/\mathbb{F}_q}(\alpha) := \alpha + \alpha^q + \alpha^{q^2} + \cdots + \alpha^{q^{f-1}}, \ \forall \alpha \in \mathbb{F}_{q^f}.$$

Let $\theta = \xi^{f-k}$. For each j $(1 \le j \le q^{f-1})$, $\forall a \in \mathbb{F}_{q^f}$ such that $\mathrm{Tr}_{\mathbb{F}_{q^f}/\mathbb{F}_q}(a\theta) \ne 0$, we define m_j as follows.

$$m_j(a, b) := \frac{\mathrm{Tr}_{\mathbb{F}_{q^f}/\mathbb{F}_q}(b\theta) - \mathrm{Tr}_{\mathbb{F}_{q^f}/\mathbb{F}_q}(at_j\theta)}{\mathrm{Tr}_{\mathbb{F}_{q^f}/\mathbb{F}_q}(a\theta)} \in \mathbb{F}_q.$$

We determinate $s \,(\mathrm{mod}\, \mathfrak{q})$ from the distribution of m_j. The following theorem holds for this m_j.

Theorem 2. *Let $a\theta$ be obtained uniformly at random from $\mathbb{F}_{q^f} \backslash \mathrm{Ker}(\mathrm{Tr}_{\mathbb{F}_{q^f}/\mathbb{F}_q})$ and $e = \phi(e')$, where e' is sampled from $D_{\tau(R),r}$. For each $1 \le j \le q^{f-1}$,*

1. If $j \neq i$, $m_j(a, b)$ is uniformly distributed in $\mathbb{F}_q$.
2. If $j = i$, $m_j(a, b) = s_0 + \dfrac{\mathrm{Tr}_{\mathbb{F}_{q^f}/\mathbb{F}_q}(e\theta)}{\mathrm{Tr}_{\mathbb{F}_{q^f}/\mathbb{F}_q}(a\theta)}$.

This theorem says m_j is not uniformly distributed if and only if t_i for the secret and the guessed value t_j match. From the assumption, the most frequent value of m_j is s_0 since $\mathrm{Tr}_{\mathbb{F}_{q^f}/\mathbb{F}_q}(e\theta) = \mathrm{Tr}_{\mathbb{F}_{q^f}/\mathbb{F}_q}(\sum e_l \xi^{f-k+l}) = f \cdot (e_k c)$. Then, the secret on the ideals can be obtained from $s = s_0 + t_j$.

Proof. Since $b = as + e$ and $s = s_0 + t_i$,

$$
\begin{aligned}
m_j(a, b) &= \frac{\mathrm{Tr}_{\mathbb{F}_{q^f}/\mathbb{F}_q}(b\theta) - \mathrm{Tr}_{\mathbb{F}_{q^f}/\mathbb{F}_q}(at_j\theta)}{\mathrm{Tr}_{\mathbb{F}_{q^f}/\mathbb{F}_q}(a\theta)} \\[2mm]
&= \frac{\mathrm{Tr}_{\mathbb{F}_{q^f}/\mathbb{F}_q}((as + e)\theta) - \mathrm{Tr}_{\mathbb{F}_{q^f}/\mathbb{F}_q}(at_j\theta)}{\mathrm{Tr}_{\mathbb{F}_{q^f}/\mathbb{F}_q}(a\theta)} \\[2mm]
&= \frac{\mathrm{Tr}_{\mathbb{F}_{q^f}/\mathbb{F}_q}(as_0\theta + at_i\theta + e\theta) - \mathrm{Tr}_{\mathbb{F}_{q^f}/\mathbb{F}_q}(at_j\theta)}{\mathrm{Tr}_{\mathbb{F}_{q^f}/\mathbb{F}_q}(a\theta)} \\[2mm]
&= \frac{\mathrm{Tr}_{\mathbb{F}_{q^f}/\mathrm{Tr}_q}(a(t_i - t_j)\theta) + s_0\mathrm{Tr}_{\mathbb{F}_{q^f}/\mathbb{F}_q}(a\theta) + \mathrm{Tr}_{\mathbb{F}_{q^f}/\mathbb{F}_q}(e\theta)}{\mathrm{Tr}_{\mathbb{F}_{q^f}/\mathbb{F}_q}(a\theta)} \\[2mm]
&= \frac{\mathrm{Tr}_{\mathbb{F}_{q^f}/\mathbb{F}_q}(a(t_i - t_j)\theta)}{\mathrm{Tr}_{\mathbb{F}_{q^f}/\mathbb{F}_q}(a\theta)} + s_0 + \frac{\mathrm{Tr}_{\mathbb{F}_{q^f}/\mathbb{F}_q}(e\theta)}{\mathrm{Tr}_{\mathbb{F}_{q^f}/\mathbb{F}_q}(a\theta)}.
\end{aligned}
$$

In the case of $j \neq i$, let $\delta = t_i - t_j \in \{\sum_{1 \leq l \leq f} \alpha_l \xi^l \mid \alpha_l \in \mathbb{F}_q\}$, then $m_j(a, b) = \dfrac{\mathrm{Tr}_{\mathbb{F}_{q^f}/\mathbb{F}_q}(a\theta\delta)}{\mathrm{Tr}_{\mathbb{F}_{q^f}/\mathbb{F}_q}(a\theta)} + s_0 + \dfrac{\mathrm{Tr}_{\mathbb{F}_{q^f}/\mathbb{F}_q}(e\theta)}{\mathrm{Tr}_{\mathbb{F}_{q^f}/\mathbb{F}_q}(a\theta)}$. Since $a\theta = \sum a_l \cdot \xi^{f-k+l}$ is uniformly random, a_i, a_j $(0 \leq i < j < f)$ can be assumed to be independent. Furthermore, from Theorem 1, $\mathrm{Tr}_{\mathbb{F}_{q^f}/\mathbb{F}_q}(a\theta)$ and $\mathrm{Tr}_{\mathbb{F}_{q^f}/\mathbb{F}_q}(a\theta\delta)$ also can be assumed to be independent. Since $\mathrm{Tr}_{\mathbb{F}_{q^f}/\mathbb{F}_q}(a\theta) \neq 0$, $Pr(\mathrm{Tr}_{\mathbb{F}_{q^f}/\mathbb{F}_q}(a\theta) = c, \ \mathrm{Tr}_{\mathbb{F}_{q^f}/\mathbb{F}_q}(a\theta\delta) = d) = \frac{1}{q(q-1)}$ for $\forall c, d \in \mathbb{F}_q$ $(c \neq 0)$. For $\forall z' \in \mathbb{F}_q$, let $z = z' - s_0$. From the following equality, we can derive that m_j is uniformly distributed when $j \neq i$.

$$
\begin{aligned}
Pr(m_j(a, b) = z') &= Pr\left(\frac{\mathrm{Tr}_{\mathbb{F}_{q^f}/\mathbb{F}_q}(a\theta\delta)}{\mathrm{Tr}_{\mathbb{F}_{q^f}/\mathbb{F}_q}(a\theta)} + \frac{\mathrm{Tr}_{\mathbb{F}_{q^f}/\mathbb{F}_q}(e\theta)}{\mathrm{Tr}_{\mathbb{F}_{q^f}/\mathbb{F}_q}(a\theta)} = z\right) \\[2mm]
&= \sum_{x+y=z} Pr\left(\frac{\mathrm{Tr}_{\mathbb{F}_{q^f}/\mathbb{F}_q}(a\theta\delta)}{\mathrm{Tr}_{\mathbb{F}_{q^f}/\mathbb{F}_q}(a\theta)} = x, \ \frac{\mathrm{Tr}_{\mathbb{F}_{q^f}/\mathbb{F}_q}(e\theta)}{\mathrm{Tr}_{\mathbb{F}_{q^f}/\mathbb{F}_q}(a\theta)} = y\right) \\[2mm]
&= \sum_{x+y=z} \sum_{c \in \mathbb{F}_q \setminus \{0\}} Pr(\mathrm{Tr}_{\mathbb{F}_{q^f}/\mathbb{F}_q}(a\theta\delta) = cx, \ \mathrm{Tr}_{\mathbb{F}_{q^f}/\mathbb{F}_q}(e\theta) = cy, \ \mathrm{Tr}_{\mathbb{F}_{q^f}/\mathbb{F}_q}(a\theta) = c) \\[2mm]
&= \sum_{x+y=z} \sum_{c \in \mathbb{F}_q \setminus \{0\}} Pr(\mathrm{Tr}_{\mathbb{F}_{q^f}/\mathbb{F}_q}(a\theta\delta) = cx, \mathrm{Tr}(a\theta) = c) \cdot Pr(\mathrm{Tr}_{\mathbb{F}_{q^f}/\mathbb{F}_q}(e\theta) = cy) \\[2mm]
&= \frac{1}{q(q-1)} \sum_{y \in \mathbb{F}_q} \sum_{c \in \mathbb{F}_q \setminus \{0\}} Pr(\mathrm{Tr}_{\mathbb{F}_{q^f}/\mathbb{F}_q}(e\theta) = cy) \\[2mm]
&= \frac{1}{q(q-1)}(q-1) \sum_{y \in \mathbb{F}_q} Pr(\mathrm{Tr}_{\mathbb{F}_{q^f}/\mathbb{F}_q}(e\theta) = y) = \frac{1}{q}.
\end{aligned}
$$

On the other hand when $j = i$, $m_i(a, b) = s_0 + \dfrac{\mathrm{Tr}_{\mathbb{F}_{q^f}/\mathbb{F}_q}(e\theta)}{\mathrm{Tr}_{\mathbb{F}_{q^f}/\mathbb{F}_q}(a\theta)}$.

Since the statistical test is performed on $\mathbb{F}_q$, we need $\mathcal{O}(q)$ samples. Furthermore, since the test needs to be performed on all the representatives, the number of statistical tests is q^{f-1}. $\mathcal{O}((n + C(n) + log(q)M(n)) \cdot log(n))$ operations in $\mathbb{F}_q$ are required for $\mathrm{Tr}_{\mathbb{F}_{q^f}/\mathbb{F}_q}(b\theta)$ and $Tr_{q^f/\mathbb{F}_q}(a\theta)$, and $\mathcal{O}(M(f) + (n + C(n) + log(q)M(n)) \cdot log(n))$ operations for $\mathrm{Tr}_{\mathbb{F}_{q^f}/\mathbb{F}_q}(at_j\theta)$. At a total, $m_j(a, b)$ need $\mathcal{O}((n + C(n) + log(q)M(n)) \cdot log(n))$ operations in $\mathbb{F}_q$. Thus, in the case of the basic approach, $\mathcal{O}((n + C(n) + log(q)M(n)) \cdot q^f log(n))$ operations in $\mathbb{F}_q$ are required. The algorithm for the prime–residue–degree χ^2–attack is shown in Algorithm 3.

Improved Approach of the Prime–Residue–Degree χ^2–Attack

From Theorem 1,

$$\mathrm{Tr}_{\mathbb{F}_{q^f}/\mathbb{F}_q}(\alpha\theta) = \mathrm{Tr}_{\mathbb{F}_{q^f}/\mathbb{F}_q}\left(\sum \alpha_l \xi^{f-k+l}\right) = \mathrm{Tr}_{\mathbb{F}_{q^f}/\mathbb{F}_q}(\alpha_k \cdot \xi^f) = f \cdot (\alpha_k \cdot c). \quad (1)$$

Algorithm 3. The prime–residue–degree χ^2–attack

Input: $\mathcal{S}$: collection of Ring-LWE samples
Output: $s \,(\mathrm{mod}\ \mathfrak{q})$, **NOT-RLWE** or **INSUFFICIENT-SAMPLES**
  for a, b in $\mathcal{S}$ **do**
    $a,\ b \leftarrow a\,(\mathrm{mod}\ \mathfrak{q}),\ b\,(\mathrm{mod}\ \mathfrak{q})$
  end for
  $\mathcal{G}_s \leftarrow \emptyset$
  for j in $1, \cdots, q^{f-1}$ **do**
    $\mathcal{E}_j \leftarrow \emptyset$
    for a, b in $\mathcal{S}$ **do**
      $m_j \leftarrow \dfrac{\mathrm{Tr}_{\mathbb{F}_{q^f}/\mathbb{F}_q}(b\theta) - \mathrm{Tr}_{\mathbb{F}_{q^f}/\mathbb{F}_q}(at_j\theta)}{\mathrm{Tr}_{\mathbb{F}_{q^f}/\mathbb{F}_q}(a\theta)}$
      add m_j to $\mathcal{E}_j$
    end for
    if $\mathcal{E}_j$ is not uniform **then**
      $s_0 :=$ the element(s) in $\mathcal{E}_j$ with highest frequency.
      add $s = s_0 + t_j$ to $\mathcal{G}_s$
    end if
  end for
  if $\mathcal{G}_s = \emptyset$ **then**
    return **NOT-RLWE**
  else if $\mathcal{G}_s = \{s\}$ **then**
    return s
  else
    return **INSUFFICIENT-SAMPLES**
  end if

Here, denote $at_j = \sum (at_j)_l \xi^l$, then

$$m_j(a, b) = \frac{\mathrm{Tr}_{\mathbb{F}_{q^f}/\mathbb{F}_q}(b\theta) - \mathrm{Tr}_{\mathbb{F}_{q^f}/\mathbb{F}_q}(at_j\theta)}{\mathrm{Tr}_{\mathbb{F}_{q^f}/\mathbb{F}_q}(a\theta)}$$

$$= \frac{f \cdot (b_k \cdot c) - f \cdot ((at_j)_k \cdot c)}{f \cdot (a_k \cdot c)}$$

$$= \frac{b_k - (at_j)_k}{a_k}.$$

The number of operations in $\mathbb{F}_q$ of $Tr_{\mathbb{F}_{q^f}/\mathbb{F}_q}$ can be reduced from $\mathcal{O}((n + C(n) + \log(q)M(n)) \cdot \log(n))$ to $\mathcal{O}(1)$ by (1). In the 4 section, we observed a significant reduction in attack time.

3.2   The Composite–Number–Residue–Degree χ^2–Attack

Basic Approach of the Composite–Number–Residue–Degree χ^2–Attack

In the composite–number–residue–degree χ^2–attack, we assume the following conditions.

- The modulus q is a prime of residue degree $f = mn$ in the algebraic number field K. Moreover, there exists irreducible polynomials $g(x) = x^f - c \in \mathbb{F}_q[x]$, $g_1(x) = x^n - c_1 \in \mathbb{F}_{q^m}[x]$, $g_2(x^n) = (x^n)^m - c \in \mathbb{F}_q[x^n]$ ($c \in \mathbb{F}_q, c_1 = \sqrt[m]{c} \in \mathbb{F}_{q^m}$) such that $\mathbb{F}_{q^f} \cong \mathbb{F}_q[x]/(g(x)) \cong \mathbb{F}_{q^m}[x]/(g_1(x))$ and $\mathbb{F}_{q^m} \cong \mathbb{F}_q[x^n]/(g_2(x^n))$.
- Suppose $e' \in R_q$ are sampled from $D_{\tau(R), r_0}$ and $e = \phi(e') = \sum e_l \xi^l$. The distribution of e_k is distinguishable from the uniform distribution on $\mathbb{F}_q$ for some index k ($0 \le k < f$). Furthermore, the probability that $e_k = 0 \,(\mathrm{mod}\, q)$ is highest.

Since $\mathbb{F}_{q^m} = \{\sum_{0 \le l < f, \, n|l} \alpha_l \xi^l \mid \alpha_l \in \mathbb{F}_q\}$, the coset representatives for $\mathbb{F}_{q^f}/\mathbb{F}_{q^m}$ is $\{u_1, \cdots, u_{q^{f-m}}\} = \{\sum_{0 \le l < f, \, n \nmid l} \alpha_l \xi^l \mid \alpha_l \in \mathbb{F}_q\}$. There is a unique index i and $s_0 = \sum_{0 \le l < f, n|l} (s_0)_l \xi^l \in \mathbb{F}_{q^m}$ such that $\phi(s') = s = s_0 + u_i$. The two trace map $\mathrm{Tr}_{\mathbb{F}_{q^f}/\mathbb{F}_{q^m}} : \mathbb{F}_{q^f} \to \mathbb{F}_{q^m}, \mathrm{Tr}_{\mathbb{F}_{q^m}/\mathbb{F}_q} : \mathbb{F}_{q^m} \to \mathbb{F}_q$ is defined as follows.

$$\mathrm{Tr}_{\mathbb{F}_{q^f}/\mathbb{F}_{q^m}}(\alpha) := \alpha + \alpha^{q^m} + \alpha^{q^{2m}} + \cdots + \alpha^{q^{(n-1)m}},$$

$$\mathrm{Tr}_{\mathbb{F}_{q^m}/\mathbb{F}_q}(\alpha) := \alpha + \alpha^q + \alpha^{q^2} + \cdots + \alpha^{q^{m-1}}.$$

Since $\mathbb{F}_q \subset \mathbb{F}_{q^m} \subset \mathbb{F}_{q^f}$ is a finite separable extension, $\mathrm{Tr}_{\mathbb{F}_{q^m}/\mathbb{F}_q}(\mathrm{Tr}_{\mathbb{F}_{q^f}/\mathbb{F}_{q^m}}(\alpha)) = \mathrm{Tr}_{\mathbb{F}_{q^f}/\mathbb{F}_q}(\alpha)$.

Let $\theta = \xi^{f-k}$. For $1 \le \forall j \le q^{f-m}$, $\forall a \in \mathbb{F}_{q^f}$ such that $\mathrm{Tr}_{\mathbb{F}_{q^f}/\mathbb{F}_{q^m}}(a\theta) \in \mathbb{F}_{q^m} \backslash \{0\}$, we set m_j as follows.

$$m_j(a, b) := \frac{\mathrm{Tr}_{\mathbb{F}_{q^f}/\mathbb{F}_{q^m}}(b\theta) - \mathrm{Tr}_{\mathbb{F}_{q^f}/\mathbb{F}_{q^m}}(au_j\theta)}{\mathrm{Tr}_{\mathbb{F}_{q^f}/\mathbb{F}_{q^m}}(a\theta)} \in \mathbb{F}_{q^m}.$$

Theorem 3. *Let a be obtained uniformly at random from $\mathbb{F}_{q^f} \setminus \mathrm{Ker}(\mathrm{Tr}_{\mathbb{F}_{q^f}/\mathbb{F}_{q^m}})$ and $e = \phi(e')$, where e' is sampled from $D_{\tau(R),r}$. For each $1 \le j \le q^{f-m}$,*

1. If $j \ne i$, $\mathrm{Tr}_{\mathbb{F}_{q^m}/\mathbb{F}_q}(m_j(a,b))$ is uniformly distributed in $\mathbb{F}_q$.

2. If $j = i$, then $\mathrm{Tr}_{\mathbb{F}_{q^m}/\mathbb{F}_q}(m_j(a,b)) = \mathrm{Tr}_{\mathbb{F}_{q^m}/\mathbb{F}_q}(s_0) + \mathrm{Tr}_{\mathbb{F}_{q^m}/\mathbb{F}_q}\left(\dfrac{\mathrm{Tr}_{\mathbb{F}_{q^f}/\mathbb{F}_{q^m}}(e\theta)}{\mathrm{Tr}_{\mathbb{F}_{q^f}/\mathbb{F}_{q^m}}(a\theta)}\right).$

Proof. If $i \ne j$, m_j is uniformly distributed on $\mathbb{F}_{q^m}$, and if $i = j$, $m_j = s_0 + \dfrac{\mathrm{Tr}_{\mathbb{F}_{q^f}/\mathbb{F}_{q^m}}(e\theta)}{\mathrm{Tr}_{\mathbb{F}_{q^f}/\mathbb{F}_{q^m}}(a\theta)}$. It can be shown as well as the Theorem 2. If $i \ne j$, $\mathrm{Tr}_{\mathbb{F}_{q^m}/\mathbb{F}_q}(m_j(a,b))$ is uniformly distributed on $\mathbb{F}_q$, since $\mathrm{Tr}_{\mathbb{F}_{q^m}/\mathbb{F}_q}$ is an additive homomorphism and surjective. If $i = j$, it is clear from the additive homomorphism of the trace map.

If $a = \phi(a') \in \mathbb{F}_{q^f}$ is chosen uniformly at random, then $\dfrac{\mathrm{Tr}_{\mathbb{F}_{q^f}/\mathbb{F}_{q^m}}(e\theta)}{\mathrm{Tr}_{\mathbb{F}_{q^f}/\mathbb{F}_{q^m}}(a\theta)}$ will be uniformly random on $\mathbb{F}_{q^m}$. In this case, it is impossible to distinguish between the distribution by $\mathrm{Tr}_{\mathbb{F}_{q^m}/\mathbb{F}_q}(s_0) + \mathrm{Tr}_{\mathbb{F}_{q^m}/\mathbb{F}_q}\left(\dfrac{\mathrm{Tr}_{\mathbb{F}_{q^f}/\mathbb{F}_{q^m}}(e\theta)}{\mathrm{Tr}_{\mathbb{F}_{q^f}/\mathbb{F}_{q^m}}(a\theta)}\right)$ and the uniform distribution on $\mathbb{F}_q$. Therefore, we restrict the sample a used in the attack to $\mathrm{Tr}_{\mathbb{F}_{q^f}/\mathbb{F}_{q^m}}(a\theta) \in \mathbb{F}_q \setminus \{0\}$.

If $\mathrm{Tr}_{\mathbb{F}_{q^f}/\mathbb{F}_{q^m}}(a\theta) \in \mathbb{F}_q$, then $\mathrm{Tr}_{\mathbb{F}_{q^f}/\mathbb{F}_{q^m}}(a\theta)^{-1} \in \mathbb{F}_q$, and so

$$\mathrm{Tr}_{\mathbb{F}_{q^m}/\mathbb{F}_q}\left(\dfrac{\mathrm{Tr}_{\mathbb{F}_{q^f}/\mathbb{F}_{q^m}}(e\theta)}{\mathrm{Tr}_{\mathbb{F}_{q^f}/\mathbb{F}_{q^m}}(a\theta)}\right) = \mathrm{Tr}_{\mathbb{F}_{q^f}/\mathbb{F}_{q^m}}(a\theta)^{-1} \cdot \mathrm{Tr}_{\mathbb{F}_{q^m}/\mathbb{F}_q}(\mathrm{Tr}_{\mathbb{F}_{q^f}/\mathbb{F}_{q^m}}(e\theta))$$

$$= \mathrm{Tr}_{\mathbb{F}_{q^f}/\mathbb{F}_{q^m}}(a\theta)^{-1} \cdot \mathrm{Tr}_{\mathbb{F}_{q^f}/\mathbb{F}_q}(e\theta).$$

From the assumption, the distribution of $\mathrm{Tr}_{\mathbb{F}_{q^f}/\mathbb{F}_q}(e\theta) = f \cdot (e_k c)$ can be distinguished from the uniform distribution on $\mathbb{F}_q$. By restricting the samples, m_j is not uniformly distributed if and only if the index $j = i$, so we can determine the value of u_j. $\mathrm{Tr}_{\mathbb{F}_{q^m}/\mathbb{F}_q}(s_0) = m \cdot (s_0)_0$ can be obtained from the most frequent value of $\mathrm{Tr}_{\mathbb{F}_{q^m}/\mathbb{F}_q}(m_j)$.

By applying the χ^2–attack, we derive $s_0 = \sum_{0 \le l < f} n_{|l}(s_0)_l \xi^l$. From $(s_0)_0$, guess the value of s_0 by brute force, and let g be that value. For $e' := b - a(u_i + g)$, determine s_0 by calculating the distribution of

$$\mathrm{Tr}_{\mathbb{F}_{q^f}/\mathbb{F}_q}(e'\theta) = \mathrm{Tr}_{\mathbb{F}_{q^f}/\mathbb{F}_q}((b - a(u_i + g))\theta).$$

In the case of $g \ne s_0$, since e' is uniformly random on $\mathbb{F}_{q^f}$ and $\mathrm{Tr}_{\mathbb{F}_{q^f}/\mathbb{F}_q}$ is an additive homomorphism and surjective, $\mathrm{Tr}_{\mathbb{F}_{q^f}/\mathbb{F}_q}(e'\theta)$ is uniformly random on $\mathbb{F}_q$. In the case of $g = s_0$, from $b = as + e$ and $s = s_0 + u_i$,

$$\mathrm{Tr}_{\mathbb{F}_{q^f}/\mathbb{F}_q}(e'\theta) = \mathrm{Tr}_{\mathbb{F}_{q^f}/\mathbb{F}_q}(b\theta - a(u_i + g)\theta)$$

$$= \mathrm{Tr}_{\mathbb{F}_{q^f}/\mathbb{F}_q}(a(s - (g + u_i))\theta + e\theta) = \mathrm{Tr}_{\mathbb{F}_{q^f}/\mathbb{F}_q}(e\theta) = f \cdot (e_k c)$$

Since the distribution of e_k can be distinguished from the uniform distribution on $\mathbb{F}_q$, s_0 can be obtained. Note that the calculation of the distribution of $\mathrm{Tr}_{\mathbb{F}_{q^f}/\mathbb{F}_q}(e'\theta)$ requires the use of a uniform random sample a, unlike the calculation of the distribution of m_j. The algorithm for the attack is shown in Algorithm 4.

Algorithm 4. The composite–number–residue–degree χ^2–attack

Input: $\mathcal{S}$: collection of Ring-LWE samples
Output: $s\,(\mathrm{mod}\ \mathsf{q})$, **NOT-RLWE**, or **INSUFFICIENT-SAMPLES**
  for a, b in $\mathcal{S}$ **do**
    $a,\ b \leftarrow a\,(\mathrm{mod}\ \mathsf{q}),\ b\,(\mathrm{mod}\ \mathsf{q})$
  end for
  $\mathcal{G}_s \leftarrow \emptyset$
  for j in $1, \cdots, q^{f-m}$ **do**
    $\mathcal{E}_j \leftarrow \emptyset$
    for a, b in $\mathcal{S}$ **do**
      if $\mathrm{Tr}_{\mathbb{F}_{q^f}/\mathbb{F}_{q^m}}(a\theta) \in \mathbb{F}_q \setminus \{0\}$ **then**
        continue
      end if
      $m_j(a,b) \leftarrow \dfrac{\mathrm{Tr}_{\mathbb{F}_{q^f}/\mathbb{F}_{q^m}}(b\theta) - \mathrm{Tr}_{\mathbb{F}_{q^f}/\mathbb{F}_{q^m}}(au_j\theta)}{\mathrm{Tr}_{\mathbb{F}_{q^f}/\mathbb{F}_{q^m}}(a\theta)}$
      add $\mathrm{Tr}_{\mathbb{F}_{q^m}/\mathbb{F}_q}(m_j(a,b))$ to $\mathcal{E}_j$
    end for
    if $\mathcal{E}_j$ is not uniform **then**
      $(s_0)_0 :=$ the element(s) in $\mathcal{E}_j$ with highest frequency.
      for g in $\mathcal{G}_{s_0} = \{c \in \mathbb{F}_{q^m} \mid \mathrm{Tr}_{\mathbb{F}_{q^m}/\mathbb{F}_q}(c) = \mathrm{Tr}_{\mathbb{F}_{q^m}/\mathbb{F}_q}(s_0)\}$ **do**
        $\mathcal{E}_g \leftarrow \emptyset$
        for a, b in $\mathcal{S}$ **do**
          $e' \leftarrow b - a(g + u_j)$
          add $\mathrm{Tr}_{\mathbb{F}_{q^f}/\mathbb{F}_q}(e'\theta)$ to $\mathcal{E}_g$
        end for
        if $\mathcal{E}_g$ is not uniform **then**
          add $s = g + u_j$ to $\mathcal{G}_s$
        end if
      end for
    end if
  end for
  if $\mathcal{G}_s = \emptyset$ **then**
    return NOT-RLWE
  else if $\mathcal{G}_s = \{s\}$ **then**
    return s
  else
    return INSUFFICIENT-SAMPLES
  end if

Improved Approach of the Composite–Number–Residue–Degree χ^2–Attack

For any $\mathbb{F}_{q^m}$ element $\beta = \sum_{0 \leq l < f,\ n|l} \gamma_l \xi^l$ ($\gamma_l \in \mathbb{F}_q$) and $\mathbb{F}_q$ element $\alpha = \sum_{0 \leq l < n} \beta_l \xi^l = \sum_{0 \leq l < f} \gamma_l \xi^l$ ($\gamma_l \in \mathbb{F}_q$, $\beta_l \in \mathbb{F}_{q^m}$), we have following equality from Theorem 1.

$$\mathrm{Tr}_{\mathbb{F}_{q^f}/\mathbb{F}_{q^m}}(\alpha) = \mathrm{Tr}_{\mathbb{F}_{q^f}/\mathbb{F}_{q^m}}\left(\sum_{0 \leq l < n} \beta_l \xi^l\right) = n \cdot \beta_0 = n \sum_{0 \leq l < f,\ n|l} \gamma_l \xi^l, \quad (2)$$

$$\mathrm{Tr}_{\mathbb{F}_{q^m}/\mathbb{F}_q}(\beta) = \mathrm{Tr}_{\mathbb{F}_{q^m}/\mathbb{F}_q}\left(\sum_{0 \leq l < f, n|l} \gamma_l \xi^l\right) = m \cdot \gamma_0. \quad (3)$$

Since we are restricting the samples used in the calculation m_j to $\mathrm{Tr}_{\mathbb{F}_{q^f}/\mathbb{F}_{q^m}}(a\theta) \in \mathbb{F}_q \backslash \{0\}$, we have $\mathrm{Tr}_{\mathbb{F}_{q^f}/\mathbb{F}_{q^m}}(a\theta) = \mathrm{Tr}_{\mathbb{F}_{q^f}/\mathbb{F}_{q^m}}(\sum a_l \xi^{l+f-k}) = n \cdot \sum_{0 \leq l < f, n|l} a_l \xi^{l+f-k} = n \cdot a_k \xi^f$. We denote $au_j = \sum (au_j)_l \xi^l$, then

$$m_j(a,b) = \frac{\mathrm{Tr}_{\mathbb{F}_{q^f}/\mathbb{F}_{q^m}}(b\theta) - \mathrm{Tr}_{\mathbb{F}_{q^f}/\mathbb{F}_{q^m}}(au_j\theta)}{\mathrm{Tr}_{\mathbb{F}_{q^f}/\mathbb{F}_{q^m}}(a\theta)}$$

$$= \frac{n \cdot \sum_{0 \leq l < f,\ n|l}(b_l - (au_j)_l)\xi^{l+f-k}}{n \cdot a_k \xi^f}$$

$$= \frac{\sum_{0 \leq l < f,\ n|l}(b_l - (au_j)_l)\xi^{l+f-k}}{a_k \xi^f}.$$

We can write $\mathrm{Tr}_{\mathbb{F}_{q^m}/\mathbb{F}_q}(m_j(a,b))$ as

$$\mathrm{Tr}_{\mathbb{F}_{q^m}/\mathbb{F}_q}(m_j(a,b)) = m \cdot \frac{(b_k - (au_j)_k)\xi^f}{a_k \xi^f}$$

$$= m \cdot \frac{b_k - (au_j)_k}{a_k}.$$

From Theorem 3, when $j = i$, $\mathrm{Tr}_{\mathbb{F}_{q^m}/\mathbb{F}_q}(m_j(a,b)) = \mathrm{Tr}_{\mathbb{F}_{q^m}/\mathbb{F}_q}(s_0) + \frac{\mathrm{Tr}_{\mathbb{F}_{q^f}/\mathbb{F}_q}(e\theta)}{\mathrm{Tr}_{\mathbb{F}_{q^f}/\mathbb{F}_{q^m}}(a\theta)}$. So, we have

$$m \cdot \frac{b_k - (au_j)_k}{a_k} = m \cdot (s_0)_0 + \frac{f \cdot e_k \xi^f}{n \cdot a_k \xi^f},$$

$$\frac{b_k - (au_j)_k}{a_k} - (s_0)_0 + \frac{e_k}{a_k}.$$

From the assumptions, the most frequent value of $\frac{b_k - (au_j)_k}{a_k}$ is $(s_0)_0$ when $j = i$. From $(s_0)_0$, guess the value of s_0 by brute force and find the secret on the ideals. We denote $g' = a(u_i + g) = \sum_{0 \leq l < n} g'_l \xi^l$, and we have

$$\mathrm{Tr}_{\mathbb{F}_{q^f}/\mathbb{F}_q}(e'\theta) = \mathrm{Tr}_{\mathbb{F}_{q^f}/\mathbb{F}_q}((b - g')\theta) = f \cdot (b_k - g'_k) \cdot \xi^f.$$

In the improved approach, we calculate the distribution of $(b_k - g'_k)$, instead of $\mathrm{Tr}_{\mathbb{F}_{q^f}/\mathbb{F}_q}(e'\theta)$.

From (2) and (3), it is possible to replace $\mathrm{Tr}_{\mathbb{F}_{q^m}/\mathbb{F}_q}(m_j)$ with $\frac{b_k - (au_j)_k}{a_k}$ and $\mathrm{Tr}_{\mathbb{F}_{q^f}/\mathbb{F}_q}(e'\theta)$ with $b_k - g'_k$. $\mathcal{O}(M(f))$ operations in $\mathbb{F}_q$ is required for both of $\frac{b_k - (au_j)_k}{a_k}$ and $b_k - g'_k$. Both of $\mathrm{Tr}_{\mathbb{F}_{q^m}/\mathbb{F}_q}(m_j)$ and $\mathrm{Tr}_{\mathbb{F}_{q^f}/\mathbb{F}_q}(e'\theta)$ are $\mathbb{F}_q$ elements, so they are calculated $\mathcal{O}(q^{f-m+1})$ and $\mathcal{O}(q^m)$ times, respectively. From this, the total complexity of this attack is $\mathcal{O}((q^{f-m+1} + q^m)M(f))$.

Selection of the Subfield. The computational complexity of the attack varies greatly depending on which subfield $\mathbb{F}_{q^m}$ is used. From Theorem 1, the computational complexity of $\mathrm{Tr}_{\mathbb{F}_{q^m}/\mathbb{F}_q}(m_j)$ and $\mathrm{Tr}_{\mathbb{F}_{q^f}/\mathbb{F}_q}(e'\theta)$ is $\mathcal{O}(M(f))$. That is, when the number of statistical tests $q^{f-m} + q^{m-1}$ is the lowest, the computational complexity of the attack is also the lowest. Let $f(m) = q^{f-m} + q^{m-1} (2 \leq m \leq f/2)$, then

$$f'(m) = -q^{f-m}\log q + q^{m-1}\log q$$
$$= (-q^{f-m} + q^{m-1})\log q.$$

$f(m)$ has minimum value when $q^{f-m} = q^{m-1}$, i.e., $m = \frac{f+1}{2}$. When the residue degree f is a composite number, the attack is most efficient when using the cosets $\mathbb{F}_{q^f}/\mathbb{F}_{q^m}$ with the largest divisor m of f.

3.3   Vulnerable Field

In the attack proposed in Sect. 3.1 and 3.2, it was important that the distribution of the error coefficients e_k is distinguishable with the uniform distribution on $\mathbb{F}_q$. In the Ring-LWE problem on the composite field $\mathbb{Q}(\zeta_p, \sqrt{d})$, it was shown that there exists a bias in the distribution of errors on the finite field $\mathbb{F}_{q^2}$ in [5]. In this section, we show that our attacks are valid for similar composite fields.

For an odd prime p and residue degree f, let d be an integer that is coprime with p and no f-th root of d in $\mathbb{Z}$. We chose an odd prime q such that $q \equiv 1 \pmod{p}$ and no f-th roots of d in $\mathbb{F}_q$. We assume that the integral basis of the ring of integer of $\mathbb{Q}(\sqrt[f]{d})$ is $\{1, \sqrt[f]{d}, \sqrt[f]{d}^2, \cdots, \sqrt[f]{d}^{f-1}\}$ and $g(x) = x^f - d \in \mathbb{F}_q[x]$ is a f-th irreducible polynomial over $\mathbb{F}_q$.

For $M = \mathbb{Q}(\zeta_p)$, $L = \mathbb{Q}(\sqrt[f]{d})$, let K be the composite field $M \cdot L$, R its ring of integers and quotient ring $R_q = R/qR$. We assume that $K/\mathbb{Q}$ is an algebraic extension with extension degree $f(p-1)$. This algebraic number field K is not a Galois extension. However, modulus q has residue degree f in K, and $R/\mathfrak{q} \cong \mathbb{F}_{q^f} \cong \mathbb{F}_q[x]/(x^f - d)$ for all prime ideal $\mathfrak{q}$ lying over q since the prime number q splits completely in M and is inert in L.

Theorem 4. *For p, f, d, q, K, R defined above, let $c = d^{\frac{f-1}{f}}$. For $r_0 < \sqrt{2\pi} \cdot c$, we set*

$$\beta = min\left\{\left(\frac{c\sqrt{2\pi e}}{r_0} \cdot e^{-\frac{\pi c^2}{r_0^2}}\right)^{f(p-1)}, 1\right\}.$$

If $e = \phi(e') = \sum_{0 \le l < f} e_l \xi^l$ for e' sampled from the discrete error distribution $D_{\tau(R), r_0}$, the probability that $e_{f-1} = 0$ is at least $1 - \beta$.

Proof. The integral basis of R is

$$\{1, \zeta_p, \cdots, \zeta_p^{p-2}, \sqrt[f]{d}, \sqrt[f]{d}\zeta_p, \cdots, \sqrt[f]{d}\zeta_p^{p-2}, \cdots, \sqrt[f]{d}^{f-1}, \sqrt[f]{d}^{f-1}\zeta_p, \cdots, \sqrt[f]{d}^{f-1}\zeta_p^{p-2}\}.$$

Here, the operation by $\phi: R_q \to R/\mathfrak{q} \cong \mathbb{F}_{q^f}$ is expressed as $\zeta_p \mapsto \alpha$ using α, the root of the p-th cyclotomic polynomial (mod q). By the map ϕ, $p-1$ basis from the $(p-1)i+1$ to the $(p-1)(i+1)$ corresponds to the x^i part of $\mathbb{F}_{q^f}$. Let $\sigma_{i,j}(0 \le i \le f-1, 1 \le j \le p-1)$ be the distinct embeddings from K to $\mathbb{C}$, and τ be canonical embedding. We can say $\sigma_{i,j}(\sqrt[f]{d}^u \zeta_p^v) = \sqrt[f]{d}^u \zeta_f^{ui} \zeta_p^{vj}$, so for $0 \le u, u' \le f-1$ and $0 \le v, v' \le p-2$,

$$\langle \tau(\sqrt[f]{d}^u \zeta_p^v), \tau(\sqrt[f]{d}^{u'} \zeta_p^{v'}) \rangle = \sum_{i=0}^{f-1}\sum_{j=0}^{p-2} \sigma_{i,j}(\sqrt[f]{d}^u \zeta_p^v) \overline{\sigma_{i,j}(\sqrt[f]{d}^{u'} \zeta_p^{v'})}$$

$$= \sum_{i=0}^{f-1}\sum_{j=0}^{p-2} \sqrt[f]{d}^{u+u'} \zeta_f^{(u-u')i} \zeta_p^{(v-v')j}$$

$$= \sqrt[f]{d}^{u+u'} \sum_{j=0}^{p-2} \zeta_p^{(v-v')j} \sum_{i=0}^{f-1} \zeta_f^{(u-u')i}.$$

The norm of the integral basis is $\|\tau(\sqrt[f]{d}^u \zeta_p^v)\| = \sqrt[f]{d}^u \sqrt{f(p-1)}$. When $u \ne u'$, $\langle \tau(\sqrt[f]{d}^u \zeta_p^v), \tau(\sqrt[f]{d}^{u'} \zeta_p^{v'}) \rangle = 0$ since $\sum_{i=0}^{f-1} \zeta_f^{(u-u')i} = 0$. The set of $p-1$ bases, $(p-1)i+1$ to $(p-1)(i+1)$, are orthogonal for different $i(1 \le i \le f-1)$. Therefore, $e \in R$ can be expressed as $e = \sum_{i=0}^{f-1} e_i \sqrt[f]{d}^i$ and $\|e\|^2 := \|\tau(e)\|^2 = \sum_{i=0}^{f-1} \|e_i\|^2 \sqrt[f]{d}^{2i}$. Note that $e_i \in \mathbb{Z}[\zeta_p]$. In particular, if $e_{f-1} \ne 0$, then $\|e\| \ge \|e_{f-1}\| \cdot \sqrt[f]{d}^{f-1} = d^{\frac{f-1}{f}} \cdot \sqrt{f(p-1)}$. If $c = d^{\frac{f-1}{f}}$ for Lemma 1, then $\text{Prob}(\|e\| > c\sqrt{f(p-1)}) \le \left(\frac{c\sqrt{2\pi e}}{r} \cdot e^{-\frac{\pi c^2}{r^2}}\right)^{f(p-1)}$.

4 Comparison with the χ^2-Attack

In this section, we attack the Ring-LWE (mod $\mathfrak{q}$) on the composite field shown in Sect. 3.3. The distribution is calculated using the chi-square test. The number of samples is $10 \times q^f$ for the χ^2-attack and $10 \times q$ for our attacks, and the risk ratio for the chi-square test is $\alpha = \frac{1}{10 \times q^f}$ for both of them. The experimental environment is CPU: Intel(R) Core(TM) i5-7200U CPU @

2.500 GHz, RAM: 8.0 GB, OS: Windows10, and SageMath version 9.2 was used [15] (Tables 2, tb:compare4.1 and tb:compare4.3). All the relevant code is available and can be found at https://github.com/TakahashiTomoka/RingLWE.git.

Table 2. Algorithm 1: The χ^2–attack

p	d	q	f	r_0	No. Samples	Success	Run Time (sec.)
11	504	67	3	4.1	$67^3 \times 10$	-	5.4×10^7 (est.)
13	4872	157	3	9.1	$157^3 \times 10$	-	9.1×10^{12} (est.)
13	503	53	4	5.0	$53^4 \times 10$	-	3.2×10^{14} (est.)

Table 3. Algorithm 3: The prime–residue–degree χ^2–attack

						Basic approach		Improved approach	
p	d	q	f	r_0	No. Samples	Success	Run Time(sec.)	Success	Run Time (sec.)
11	504	67	3	4.1	670	10/10	1471	10/10	129
13	4872	157	3	9.1	1570	12/12	22808	12/12	1667
13	503	53	4	5.0	530	-	6.0×10^4(est.)	12/12	3553
11	507	67	6	7.0	670	-	1.6×10^9(est.)	-	4.3×10^7(est.)

Table 4. Algorithm 4 : The composite–number–residue–degree χ^2–attack

						Basic approach		Improved approach	
p	d	q	f	r_0	No. Samples	Success	Run Time(sec.)	Success	Run Time (sec.)
13	503	53	4	5.0	530	12/12	795	12/12	63
11	507	67	6	7.0	670	10/10	174267	10/10	9330

The computational complexity of both the χ^2–attack and the attack method proposed in this paper is determined by residue degree f and modulus parameter q. In the case of the χ^2–attack, even with the smallest parameter $(f, q) = (3, 67)$ used in this experiment, it took more than 1.5 years to solve Ring-LWE (mod $\mathfrak{q}$). By using the prime–residue–degree χ^2–attack, we succeeded in solving it in less than 30 minutes even with the basic approach. Comparing the basic approach with the improved approach, the attack time was reduced by more than 90% for all the algebraic number fields used in this experiment. In the improved approach, only one multiplication in $\mathbb{F}_q$ is required for the trace map, whereas its computational cost depends on the residue degree f and modulus parameter q in the basic approach. That is, a significant reduction in computation time can be expected when the residue degree and modulus parameters become large. It is also confirmed that $e_{f-1} \neq 0$ with higher probability than that shown in Theorem 4.

5 Conclusion

In this paper, we proposed two attacks, the prime–residue–degree and composite–number–residue–degree χ^2–attack, that focuses on the algebraic properties of the Ring-LWE problem. Our attacks again showed that the algebraic property of the Ring-LWE problem can be used for attacks as well as for efficiency. In our proposed attack methods, we introduced θ as an attack condition. This θ can be set very flexibly. Currently, the only algebraic number field that is vulnerable to our proposed attacks are those described in Sect. 3.3. However, it is necessary to discuss the existence of vulnerable algebraic number fields from the viewpoint of attack flexibility. In addition, we believe that the attack using prime ideals can be applied not only to the Ring-LWE problem but also to other LWE problems. The study of attacks on other LWE problems is also an issue for future research.

Acknowledgement. This work is partially supported by JSPS KAKENHI Grant Number JP21H03443, and Innovation Platform for Society 5.0 at MEXT. We would also appreciate anonymous reviewers for their insightful comments and suggestions.

References

1. Alkim, E., Ducas, L., Pöppelmann, T., Schwabe, P.: Post-quantum key exchange - a new hope. In: 25Th USENIX Security Symposium (USENIX Security 16), pp. 327–343. USENIX Association (2016)
2. Arita, S., Handa, S.: Subring homomorphic encryption. In: Kim, H., Kim, D.C. (eds.) ICISC 2017. LNCS, vol. 10779, pp. 112–136. Springer, Cham (2017). https://doi.org/10.1007/978-3-319-78556-1_7
3. Arita, S., Handa, S.: Fully homomorphic encryption scheme based on decomposition ring. IEICE Trans. Fundam. Electron. Commun. Comput. Sci. **103-A**(1), 195–211 (2020)
4. Chen, H., Lauter, K.E., Stange, K.E.: Security considerations for Galois non-dual RLWE families. In: Avanzi, R., Heys, H.M. (eds.) SAC 2016. LNCS, vol. 10532, pp. 443–462. Springer, Cham (2016). https://doi.org/10.1007/978-3-319-69453-5_24
5. Chen, H., Lauter, K.E., Stange, K.E.: Attacks on the search RLWE problem with small errors. SIAM J. Appl. Algebra Geom. **1**(1), 665–682 (2017)
6. Cochran, W.G.: Some methods for strengthening the common χ 2 tests. Biometrics **10**(4), 417–451 (1954)
7. Elias, Y., Lauter, K.E., Ozman, E., Stange, K.E.: Provably weak instances of ring-LWE. In: Gennaro R., Robshaw M., (eds.) Advances in Cryptology – CRYPTO 2015 - 35th Annual Cryptology Conference. Lecture Notes in Computer Science, vol. 9215, pp.63–92, Springer (2015). https://doi.org/10.1007/978-3-662-47989-6_4
8. Erich, K., Victor, S · Fast polynomial factorization over high algebraic extensions of finite fields. In: Proceedings of the 1997 International Symposium on Symbolic and Algebraic Computation, pp. 184–188. ACM (1997)
9. Kouichi Saka, Takahiro Mizuhara, C.U.: Reidaityuusin Kakuritsu Toukei Nyuumon (Introduction of statistics), vol. 14. Gakujyutsu Tosyo Syuppan (2016)
10. Lyubashevsky, V., Peikert, C., Regev, O.: On ideal lattices and learning with errors over rings. J. ACM (JACM) **60**(6), 1–35 (2013)

11. Micciancio, D., Regev, O.: Worst-case to average-case reductions based on Gaussian measures. SIAM J. Comput. **37**(1), 267–302 (2007)
12. Peikert, C.: How (not) to instantiate ring-LWE. In: Zikas, V., Prisco, R.D. (eds.) SCN 2016. LNCS, vol. 9841, pp. 411–430. Springer, Cham (2016). https://doi.org/10.1007/978-3-319-44618-9_22
13. Regev, O.: On lattices, learning with errors, random linear codes, and cryptography. J. ACM (JACM) **56**(6), 1–40 (2009)
14. The National Institute of Standards and Technology (NIST): Post-quantum cryptograph. https://csrc.nist.gov/Projects/post-quantum-cryptography/selected-algorithms-2022
15. The Sage Developers: SageMath, the Sage Mathematics Software System (Version 9.2) (2020). https://www.sagemath.org

2DT-GLS: Faster and Exception-Free Scalar Multiplication in the GLS254 Binary Curve

Marius A. Aardal and Diego F. Aranha[(✉)]

Department of Computer Science, Aarhus University, Aarhus, Denmark
{maardal,dfaranha}@cs.au.dk

Abstract. We revisit and improve performance of arithmetic in the binary GLS254 curve by introducing the 2DT-GLS scalar multiplication algorithm. The algorithm includes theoretical and practice-oriented contributions of potential independent interest: (i) for the first time, a proof that the GLS scalar multiplication algorithm does not incur exceptions, such that faster incomplete formulas can be used; (ii) faster dedicated atomic formulas that alleviate the cost of precomputation; (iii) a table compression technique that reduces the storage needed for precomputed points; (iv) a refined constant-time scalar decomposition algorithm that is more robust to rounding. We also present the first GLS254 implementation for Armv8. With our contributions, we set new speed records for constant-time scalar multiplication by 34.5% and 6% on 64-bit Arm and Intel platforms, respectively.

Keywords: Binary elliptic curves · Software implementation · GLS254

1 Introduction

Elliptic Curve Cryptography (ECC) has become the *de facto* standard for instantiating public key cryptography, with security based on the conjectured-as-exponential hardness of solving discrete logarithms over elliptic curve groups (ECDLP problem). Scalar multiplication, in particular for the unknown point scenario, is the most expensive operation in cryptographic protocols with security guarantees based on the ECDLP. Since its introduction in 1985, there was plenty of research in finding efficient and secure implementation strategies, and choosing optimal parameters to improve performance [3,6,22].

An early milestone in this research was the idea due to Gallant-Lambert-Vanstone (GLV) [14] of exploiting efficient endomorphisms to accelerate scalar multiplication. In the large characteristic case with the curve $E : y^2 = x^3 + b$ defined over $\mathbb{F}_p$ for prime p, it initially manifested as evaluating $\psi : (x,y) \rightarrow (\beta x, y)$ for β a non-trivial cube root of unity. The technique was later generalized to Galbraith–Lin–Scott (GLS) curves defined over $\mathbb{F}_{p^2}$, and to exploit two or more endomorphisms as in the FourQ curve [25] and the genus-2 case [5]. In the characteristic 2 case, Koblitz curves are the classical example of curves equipped with endomorphisms [29]; a class later extended to include binary GLS curves [17].

B. Smith and H. Wu (Eds.): SAC 2022, LNCS 13742, pp. 53–74, 2024.
https://doi.org/10.1007/978-3-031-58411-4_3

Beyond performance, implementation security is also relevant, especially on embedded targets where side-channel attacks are more feasible. The classical countermeasure against these attacks is to formulate the arithmetic in a *regular* way, such as constant-time implementation against timing attacks. This translates to removing secret-dependent branches and memory accesses, and employing *complete* point addition formulas without corner cases [30]. Additional care needs to be taken for a correct and secure implementation when exploiting endomorphisms, such as using the GLV-SAC recoding technique [11] or by explicitly proving correctness of the specific scalar multiplication algorithm [6,10].

In this paper, we revisit the implementation of scalar multiplication in binary GLS curves at the 128-bit security level by improving efficiency and correctness of implementations of the GLS254 curve. Our contributions are:

- A variant of the GLS scalar multiplication algorithm that changes the computation/storage trade-off to use a 2D table. The resulting 2DT algorithm spends more precomputation to reduce point additions in the main loop.
- The first proof of correctness for the GLS scalar multiplication algorithm with the λ-projective group law from [28]. We show that there are no corner cases in the main loop of the algorithm (with exception of possibly the last iteration), which enables the use of faster incomplete formulas.
- Faster dedicated formulas to reduce the cost of precomputation, and a table compression technique that exploits the endomorphism to reduce storage.
- A refined scalar decomposition algorithm that can be easily implemented in constant time. The algorithm has robust parity and length guarantees that fill some gaps in previous works [28].
- An efficient formulation of arithmetic in $\mathbb{F}_{2^{254}}$ targeting Arm processors. The field arithmetic uses the interleaved representation proposed in the CHES'16 Rump Session [27]. We take the opportunity to include this formulation in the formal research literature, initially presented informally. Furthermore, this also closes affirmatively a question posed in [21] about the efficiency of binary curves in Armv8 processors, deemed "unclear".

With these contributions, we obtain speed records in the 64-bit Armv8 and Intel platforms, improving on previous results by 34.5% and 6%, respectively. While the latter speedup may seem small, we remark that it comes after decades of successful research in improving performance of ECC, so diminishing returns are expected. Due to the upcoming move to post-quantum cryptography, these techniques could be of limited practicality, but we believe they are relevant for applications not necessarily needing long-term security and involving the computation of many scalar multiplications, such as private set intersection protocols [31]. The proof and table compression technique may find further application in accelerating GLV/GLS scalar multiplication in pairing-based cryptography.

The rest of the document is organized as follows. Section 1 discusses preliminaries on binary GLS curves and their efficient implementation. Section 3 introduces the 2DT-GLS algorithm and its correctness proof. Section 4 pushes these ideas further by presenting the scalar decomposition algorithm, followed by dedicated formulas in Sect. 5. Section 6 discusses the implementation of field arithmetic in Armv8, with experimental results in Sect. 7. The interested reader will also find a treatment of point compression for binary GLS curves in the Appendix of the full version [1], together with detailed formulas.

2   Preliminaries

An ordinary *binary elliptic curve* in Weierstrass form is defined as

$$E/\mathbb{F}_q : y^2 + xy = x^3 + ax^2 + b \tag{1}$$

with $q = 2^m$ and coefficients $a, b \in \mathbb{F}_q$, $b \neq 0$. For any extension field $\mathbb{F}_{q^k}$, the points $P = (x, y) \in \mathbb{F}_{q^k} \times \mathbb{F}_{q^k}$ that satisfy the equation form an abelian group $E_{a,b}(\mathbb{F}_{q^k})$ together with a point at infinity ∞, which acts as the identity. The group law is denoted with additive notation $P + Q$, such that the scalar multiplication operation is written as kP.

2.1   Binary GLS Curves

In the interest of defining notation for later use, we briefly summarize the theory of binary GLS curves from [17].

Let E be an ordinary binary curve as defined previously. From Hasse's theorem, $\#E(\mathbb{F}_q) = q + 1 - t$ for some trace t satisfying $|t| \leq 2\sqrt{q}$. Pick some $a' \in \mathbb{F}_{q^2}$ with $\mathrm{Tr}'(a') = 1$, where Tr' is the field trace from $\mathbb{F}_{q^2}$ to $\mathbb{F}_2$ defined as $\mathrm{Tr}'(c) = \sum_{i=0}^{2m-1} c^{2^i}$. It can be shown that $E' = E_{a',b}$ is the quadratic twist of E over $\mathbb{F}_{q^2}$ with $\#E'(\mathbb{F}_{q^2}) = (q-1)^2 + t^2$, and that E and E' are isomorphic over $\mathbb{F}_{q^4}$ under an involutive twisting isomorphism ϕ.

An endomorphism ψ over $\mathbb{F}_{q^2}$ can be constructed for E' by composing ϕ with the q-power Frobenius map π as $\psi = \phi\pi\phi^{-1}$. Evaluating ψ over points $P \in E'(\mathbb{F}_{q^2})$ only requires field additions [28].

The curve E' would in this scenario be referred to as a binary GLS curve. Assume $\#E'(\mathbb{F}_{q^2}) = hr$ where h is a small cofactor and r is prime. Let $\mathcal{G}$ be the unique order-r subgroup $E'(\mathbb{F}_{q^2})[r]$. Then ψ restricted to $\mathcal{G}$ has an eigenvalue $\mu \in \mathbb{Z}$ so that for $P \in \mathcal{G}$, $\psi(P) = \mu P$. The eigenvalue satisfies that $\mu^2 = -1 \bmod r$.

2.2 λ-Projective Coordinates for GLS Scalar Multiplication

In [28], Oliveira et al. introduced the λ-projective coordinate system. To date, it is empirically the most efficient point representation for binary elliptic curves. Given an affine point $P = (x, y)$ with $x \neq 0$, its λ-affine representation is (x, λ) with $\lambda = x + \frac{y}{x}$. In λ-projective coordinates, the affine point can be represented by any triple (X, Λ, Z) with $X = xZ$, $\Lambda = \lambda Z$ and $Z \neq 0$. The point at infinity can now be represented as $\infty = (1, 1, 0)$. The curve equation in (1) is correspondingly transformed to

$$(\Lambda^2 + \Lambda Z + aZ^2)X^2 = X^4 + bZ^4. \tag{2}$$

Algorithm 1: Constant-time scalar multiplication (Oliveira et al. [28])

Input: $P \in \mathcal{G}$ in λ-affine coordinates, $k \in [1, r - 1]$, window size w
Output: kP in λ-affine coordinates

1 Decompose k into subscalars k_1, k_2.
2 $c_j \leftarrow 1 - (k_j \bmod 2)$ for $j = 1, 2$.
3 $k_j \leftarrow k_j + c_j$
4 $\ell \leftarrow \lceil \frac{m}{w-1} \rceil$
5 Compute width-w length-ℓ odd signed regular recoding $\overline{k}_1, \overline{k}_2$ of k_1, k_2.
6 Compute $T[i] = (2i + 1)P$ for all odd $i \in \{0, \ldots, 2^{w-2} - 1\}$.
7 Convert T to λ-affine coordinates using a simultaneous inversion.
8 Perform a linear pass over T to recover $P_{j,\ell-1} = \overline{k}_{j,\ell-1}P$ for $j = 1, 2$.
9 $Q \leftarrow P_{1,\ell-1} + \psi(P_{2,\ell-1})$
10 **for** i **from** $\ell - 2$ **downto** 0 **do**
11 $\quad$ $Q \leftarrow 2^{w-2}Q$
12 $\quad$ Perform a linear pass over T to recover $P_{j,i} = \overline{k}_{j,i}P$ for $j = 1, 2$.
13 $\quad$ $Q \leftarrow 2Q + P_{1,i} + \psi(P_{2,j})$
14 $Q \leftarrow Q - c_1 P - c_2 \psi(P)$
15 Convert Q to λ-affine coordinates.
16 **return** Q;

The constant-time binary GLS scalar multiplication algorithm from [28] is included in Algorithm 1. It is a constant-time left-to-right double-and-add algorithm using λ-projective coordinates, combining the Joye-Tunstall regular recoding algorithm [20] with the GLV interleaving technique. For the GLV method, the scalar k is decomposed into two subscalars k_1, k_2 such that $k \equiv k_1 + k_2\mu$ (mod r) and the subscalars are of roughly half the length of k. The two smaller scalar multiplications can then be computed in an interleaved fashion to save half of the point doublings.

The Joye-Tunstall regular recoding algorithm ensures the regular form of the algorithm and allows for a width-w windowing strategy. Specifically, the subscalars are recoded into $\ell = \lceil m/(w-1) \rceil$ odd signed digits of $w - 1$ bits using Algorithm 6 from [10] (which is a constant-length modification of Algorithm 6 from [20]). By initially computing a table $T[i] = (2i + 1)P$ for all positive digits (in a phase known as the precomputation), the main loop can process the scalars one digit at a time, reducing the number of iterations by a factor $w - 1$. To be resistant against (cache-)timing attacks, each lookup requires a linear pass over the entire table, and there can be no branches dependent on c_j, k_j. An additional consideration is that the regular recoding algorithm requires the subscalars to be odd. To ensure this, the subscalars are modified to be odd in line 3, and at the end the result is corrected at the cost of two point additions.

However, both [28] and the subsequent [27] suffer from a lack of rigor. First and foremost, no proof has been presented for correctness of the scalar multiplication algorithm. The λ-projective group law formulas are incomplete, so it could potentially fail in corner cases. It also relies on *ad-hoc* tricks for constant-time scalar decomposition, with no proof of correctness or length guarantees.

2.3   GLS254 and the Choice of Parameters

Previous works have benchmarked their implementation of scalar multiplications over a GLS curve specially crafted for efficiency at the 128-bit security level. For the GLS254 curve, one chooses $m = 127$, such that the base field can be defined as $\mathbb{F}_q \equiv \mathbb{F}_2[z]/(z^{127}+z^{63}+1)$ and its quadratic extension as $\mathbb{F}_{q^2} \equiv \mathbb{F}_q[u]/(u^2+u+1)$. The curve coefficients should be chosen to have minimal Hamming weight such that multiplying by them is as efficient as possible. We performed a parameter search that reproduced the curve chosen at [27]. By fixing $a' = u$ and searching for the shortest $b = (z^i + 1)$ such that the curve has order $2r$ for prime r, we were able to confirm that $i = 27$ is the smallest choice, giving a 254-bit r. This means that a multiplication by b can be computed with a single shifted addition.

To protect against Weil descent and generalized Gaudry-Hess-Smart (gGHS) attacks [15,18], several precautions must be taken. We pick m to be prime, as is the case for GLS254. In addition, the choice of b must be verified to not allow the attack, which happens with negligibly small probability for random b [17]. We used the MAGMA implementation of [8] available at https://github.com/ JJChiDguez/gGHS-check to clear our particular choice. This particular check, together with the curve generation method geared towards efficiency, satisfies rigidity concerns [4]. We stress that the ECDLP in binary curves remains infeasible for the parameter range used in this work [12].

3   Scalar Multiplication in GLS Curves

In this section, we begin by presenting a new scalar multiplication variant for binary GLS curves. It combines the Shamir-Straus' trick [9] for multiple scalar multiplication with a new table compression technique using the GLS endomorphism. We refer to it as the 2DT variant because it builds a two-dimensional table $T[i,j] = iP + j\psi(P)$ instead of $T[i] = iP$. Then, in Subsect. 3.2, we prove that the GLS scalar multiplication algorithms are exception-free.

3.1   The 2DT Variant

As in some *fast* variants of the Shamir-Straus' trick [9] for multiple scalar multiplication, the idea is to precompute $T[i,j] = iP + j\psi(P)$ for odd i,j. In the scalar multiplication loop, we then save roughly one point addition per iteration of the main loop by computing $2Q + T[i,j]$ instead of $2Q + T[i] + \psi(T[j])$.

This method was previously deemed noncompetitive due to the blowup in the size of the table. Because the subscalar regular recoding uses signed digits, we need to efficiently retrieve $s_1 iP + s_2 j\psi(P)$ for any $i,j \in \{1, ..., 2^{w-1}-1\}$ and sign combination $s_1, s_2 \in \{\pm 1\}$. The standard approach would be to build a table of $iP \pm j\psi(P)$ and then use conditional negations to get the two other combinations. The 2D table would then store $2^{2(w-2)+1}$ points. Even with specialized formulas for the precomputation, the cost in terms of storage and field operations is too high compared to the conventional 1DT algorithm.

The crucial new observation is that the efficiently computable GLS endo-morphism ψ can also be used to compress the 2D table by a factor of 2. As $\psi^2(P) = -P$ for any $P \in \mathcal{G}$, we obtain the identity

$$-\psi(T[j,i]) = iP - j\psi(P).$$

It implies that we can generate all combinations from a table that only stores $iP + j\psi(P)$ for positive i, j. The rest of the combinations can be efficiently retrieved using conditional negations and conditional applications of ψ.

This compression trick not only halve the amount of precomputation needed, but also halves the time needed to do a linear pass through the table in the main loop. With new specialized group law formulas for the precomputation (see Sect. 5), the 2DT algorithm is able to compete for the constant-time scalar multiplication speed record (see Sect. 7). The 2DT variant is presented in Algo-rithm 2. For $w = 2$, the only difference is that a complete formula must be used for $2Q + P_1$ at $i = 1$ as well.

Algorithm 2: Constant-time 2DT scalar multiplication

Input: $P \in \mathcal{G}$ in λ-affine coordinates, $k \in [1, r - 1]$, window size $w > 2$
Output: kP in λ-affine coordinates
1 Decompose k into odd subscalars k_1, k_2 using Algorithm 3.
2 $\ell \leftarrow \lceil \frac{m+1}{w-1} \rceil$
3 Compute width-w length-ℓ odd signed regular recoding $\overline{k}_1, \overline{k}_2$ of k_1, k_2.
4 Compute $T[i,j] = (2i+1)P + (2j+1)\psi(P)$ for all odd $i, j \in \{0, \ldots, 2^{w-2} - 1\}$.
5 Convert T to λ-affine coordinates using a simultaneous inversion.
6 Perform a linear pass over T to recover $P_{\ell-1} = \overline{k}_{1,\ell-1}P + \overline{k}_{2,l-1}\psi(P)$
7 $Q \leftarrow P_{\ell-1}$
8 **for** i **from** $\ell - 2$ **downto** 1 **do**
9 $\quad$ $Q \leftarrow 2^{w-2}Q$
10 $\quad$ Perform a linear pass over T to recover $P_i = \overline{k}_{1,i}P + \overline{k}_{2,i}\psi(P)$
11 $\quad$ $Q \leftarrow 2Q + P_i$
12 Repeat the steps for $i = 0$, but use a complete formula for $2Q + P_0$.
13 Convert Q to λ-affine coordinates.
14 **return** Q;

3.2 Proof of Exception-Free Scalar Multiplication

We will now prove that the scalar multiplication algorithms presented here and in [28] (with a minor modification) is correct on all valid inputs. The core issue is that the underlying λ-projective group law formulas from [28] are not complete, meaning that they output the wrong result in some corner cases. Without these exceptions, correctness would be trivial.

One could explicitly handle these exceptions in constant time using com-plete formulas, but this would come at a high performance cost. Here, we prove that exceptional cases can only occur in the last iteration(s) of the main loop.

By using complete formulas at the very end, correctness is ensured at only a minor performance penalty.

For clarity, the proof will be tailored to the 2DT algorithm. However, it can be easily adapted to the 1DT algorithm. The proof can be seen as a two-dimensional extension of the argument from Proposition 1 in [6]. We will for now assume that the scalar decomposition produces subscalars of bit-length at most $m + 1$, and defer the discussion about how to achieve this to Sect. 4. The proof crucially relies on the structure of the lattice discussed in [13,14] that emerge in the GLV method for scalar decomposition;

$$\mathcal{L} = \{(x, y) \in \mathbb{Z}^2 : x + y\mu \equiv 0 \ (\text{mod } r)\}.$$

Here r is the large prime order of $\#E'(\mathbb{F}_{q^2}) = hr$ and μ the eigenvalue of ψ restricted to $\mathcal{G}$. For our purposes, it is very useful to think about $\mathcal{L}$ as the lattice of decompositions of zero (as done in [10]).

Our proof requires that the norm of the shortest non-zero vector in $\mathcal{L}$ is at least $(q - 1)/\sqrt{2}$. The structure of $\mathcal{L}$ is determined by the order of $E'(\mathbb{F}_{q^2})$. The bound required on the shortest norm might not be obtainable in general, so we focus on the subclass of GLS curves most relevant for cryptography. As the (affine) point $(0, 0)$ is always in $E'(\mathbb{F}_{q^2})$, $2|h$. To ensure that the discrete log problem in $\mathcal{G}$ is as hard as possible, the optimal choice is to pick a curve with $h = 2$, which is easy in practice. Restricting our proof to this subclass of GLS curves, we can give an explicit solution to the SVP in $\mathcal{L}$.

Lemma 1. *Let $q = 2^m$. Let E' be a binary GLS curve with $\#E'(\mathbb{F}_{q^2}) = 2r$ for an odd prime r. Let $E/\mathbb{F}_q$ be the curve such that E' over $\mathbb{F}_{q^2}$ is the quadratic twist of $E(\mathbb{F}_{q^2})$. Define*

$$v_1 = \left(\frac{(q-1)+t}{2}, \frac{(q-1)-t}{2}\right) \text{ and } v_2 = \left(\frac{(q-1)-t}{2}, \frac{-(q-1)-t}{2}\right),$$

where t is the trace of the q-th power Frobenius endomorphism on E. Then v_1, v_2 form an orthogonal basis for the lattice $\mathcal{L}$. $\|v_1\| = \|v_2\| = \sqrt{r} = \min_{v \in \mathcal{L}\setminus\{0\}} \|v\|$.

Proof. Smith gives in Sects. 6 and 4 of [32] the basis $v_1' = (q - 1, -t)$, v_2 for $\mathcal{L}$. However it is not orthogonal and $\|v_1'\| = \sqrt{2r}$. The latter follows from $\#E'(\mathbb{F}_{q^2}) = (q-1)^2 + t^2$ (see Theorem 2 in [13]). We make the small adjustment of replacing v_1' with $v_1 = v_1' - v_2$. It can easily be checked that the basis v_1, v_2 is orthogonal and that $\|v_1\| = \|v_2\| = \sqrt{r}$. □

For the sake of proving scalar multiplication exception-free, the importance of Lemma 1 is showing that the minimal norm in $\mathcal{L}$ is large. This is what enables the subsequent proof to succeed. Note that we also require m to be prime, which is needed for security reasons anyways.

Theorem 1. *Let the notation be as in Lemma 1. Let $m > 4$ be prime and $2 \leq w \leq m$. Then Algorithm 2 is exception-free.*

Proof. Let us start by identifying the exceptional cases of the λ-projective formulas. The formula for $P + Q$ breaks down whenever $P = \pm Q$, $P = \infty$ or $Q = \infty$. The point ∞ does not have a λ-affine representation, so these last two cases are only a concern when the points are λ-projective. The $2P$ formula has no exceptional cases. Finally, the atomic formula for $2Q + P$ breaks down when $P = \pm 2Q$ or $Q = \infty$.

We will argue that all the exceptions that can occur in Algorithm 1 encode an element of $\mathcal{L}$. By this, we mean that they define some $z_1, z_2 \in \mathbb{Z}$ such that $z_1 P + z_2 \psi(P) = \infty$. Then $(z_1, z_2) \in \mathcal{L}$.

If $(z_1, z_2) \neq (0,0)$, we can show that either $|z_1|$ or $|z_2|$ must be at least an m-bit integer. v_1, v_2 form an orthogonal basis of $\mathcal{L}$, and are both a solution to the SVP in $\mathcal{L}$ with norm $\sqrt{r}$. Using the Hasse bound we get that $\|v_1\|, \|v_2\| \geq (q - 1)/\sqrt{2}$. Now assume for contradiction that $|z_1|, |z_2| < q/2$. Then

$$\|(z_1, z_2)\| = \sqrt{z_1^2 + z_2^2} \leq \sqrt{2\left(\frac{q}{2} - 1\right)^2} = \frac{q - 2}{\sqrt{2}} < \|v_1\|, \|v_2\|.$$

This is a contradiction, since v_1, v_2 have minimal norm in $\mathcal{L} \setminus \{\mathbf{0}\}$. Thus, it must be the case that $|z_1| \geq q/2$ or $|z_2| \geq q/2$.

We now have all the tools needed to prove that no exceptions occur in Algorithm 2, and we will start with the precomputation stage. Assume that an exception did occur in the computation of $iP + j\psi(P)$ for some odd $i, j \in \{1, \ldots, 2^{w-1} - 1\}$. $P, \psi(P) \neq \infty$, so there can only be an exception if $iP = sj\psi(P)$ for some $s \in \{\pm 1\}$. Then $(i, -sj) \in \mathcal{L} \setminus \{\mathbf{0}\}$. However, this is a contradiction, as neither $|i| = i$ nor $|-sj| = j$ are m-bit integers.

Next is the main loop. Let $Q_i = z_{1,i}P + z_{2,i}\psi(P)$ denote the value of Q after iteration i. No exception occurred in the precomputation stage, meaning Q is correctly initialized to $Q_{\ell-1} = \overline{k}_{1,\ell-1}P + \overline{k}_{2,\ell-1}\psi(P)$. Then at iteration i,

$$Q_i = (2^{w-1}z_{1,i+1} + \overline{k}_{1,i})P + (2^{w-1}z_{2,i+1} + \overline{k}_{2,i})\psi(P).$$

Observe that as long as no exceptions occur, we have the invariant that

$$0 < |z_{j,i+1}| \leq |z_{j,i}| \leq 2^{(\ell-i)(w-1)} - 1 \text{ for } j = 1, 2.$$

Assume the first exception occurs at iteration i. The $w - 2$ doublings are exception-free, so the exception must have been caused by the computation of $2Q_{i+1} + P_i$. Q_{i+1} cannot have been ∞. This is because $2Q \neq \infty$ for any $Q \neq \infty$ and the incomplete $2Q + P$ formula does not output ∞ for any P, Q on the curve. Hence, the first exception must have occurred because $2^{w-1}Q_{i+1} = sP_i$ for an $s \in \{\pm 1\}$. This is equivalent to

$$(2^{w-1}z_{1,i+1} - s\overline{k}_{1,i})P + (2^{w-1}z_{2,i+1} - s\overline{k}_{2,i})\psi(P) = \infty$$

Define $z'_{j,i} = 2^{w-1}z_{j,i+1} - s\overline{k}_{j,i}$. Notice that $-s\overline{k}_{j,i}$ is a valid digit of the regular recoding. The invariants for $|z_{j,i}|$ also hold for $|z'_{j,i}|$. Hence, $(z'_{1,i}, z'_{2,i}) \in \mathcal{L} \setminus \{\mathbf{0}\}$.

Since m is prime, it holds for all $2 \leq w \leq m$ that

$$2^{(\lceil \frac{m}{w-1} \rceil - 1)(w-1)} - 1 \leq 2^{(\frac{m}{w-1} + \frac{w-2}{w-1} - 1)(w-1)} - 1 = 2^{m-1} - 1$$

This means that $|z'_{1,i}|$ and $|z'_{2,i}|$ are of at most $m-1$ bits while $i \geq \ell - \lceil \frac{m}{w-1} \rceil + 1$. The implication is that the first exception could not have occurred in these iterations, so we must have that $i \leq \ell - \lceil \frac{m}{w-1} \rceil$.

For $w = 2$, this means that $i \leq 1$. For all other w, this means that $i = 0$. But these are exactly the iterations that use a complete formula for the computation of $2Q_{i+1} + P_i$ for the respective values of w. Thus, it is impossible for the first exception to occur in these last iterations. The conclusion is that there can be no exception in the main loop.   □

4   Scalar Decomposition with Parity and Length Guarantees

The GLV method for scalar decomposition needs a bit of care when required to run in constant-time while preserving length guarantees. The GLV method uses a reduced basis $\{u_1, u_2\}$ of some sublattice $\mathcal{L}'$ of $\mathcal{L}$ (see Sect. 3.2) to solve the CVP problem for $(k, 0)$ in $\mathcal{L}'$ using Babai rounding [14]. For a given basis, there exist unique constants $N, \alpha_1, \alpha_2 \in \mathbb{Z}$ such that

$$(k, 0) = \beta_1 u_1 - \beta_2 u_2,$$

where $\beta_i = \frac{\alpha_i}{N} k$. The subscalars k_1, k_2 are then computed as

$$(k_1, k_2) = (k, 0) - b_1 u_1 - b_2 u_2,$$

where $b_i = \lceil \beta_i \rfloor$. The magnitude of the subscalars can then be bounded by some expression depending on the norm of the basis vectors.

The issue for constant-time implementations is the computation of the b_i's. Ideally we would compute them using divisions, but unfortunately divisions do not run in constant time in most processors[1].

The standard solution was first introduced in [5] and further analyzed in [10]. The idea is to approximate the computation of the b_i's using integer divisions by powers of 2, which can be implemented in constant-time using shifts. Choose some integer d such that $k < 2^d$, and precompute the constants $c_i = \lfloor \frac{\alpha_i}{N} 2^d \rceil$. Then at runtime compute b_i as $b'_i = \lfloor \frac{c_i}{2^d} k \rfloor$.

This approach introduces rounding errors. It was shown in Lemma 1 of [10] that b'_i will either be b_i or incorrectly rounded down to $b_i - 1$. This does not affect the correctness of the decomposition. However, it does negatively impact the bounds on $|k_1|, |k_2|$. If the bounds become too loose, we might need more iterations of the main loop of the scalar multiplication to ensure correctness.

We present Algorithm 3 for constant time scalar decomposition using the optimal basis from Lemma 1. In Lemma 2 we prove that it outputs subscalars of

---

[1] See https://www.bearssl.org/constanttime.html.

at most $m + 1$ bits. Without rounding errors it would be m, but the extra bit does not affect the number of iterations of the main loop (see Corollary 1).

In fact, not handling rounding errors leads to more efficient scalar multiplication. Using the fact that the rounding errors are one-sided, we introduce a new trick to ensure that the k_1, k_2 are always odd, without affecting the length guarantees. The two point additions needed to correct for even subscalars (see Subsect. 2.2) are no longer needed, leading to a simpler and faster algorithm. Note that this optimization applies to both 1DT and 2DT scalar multiplication.

Algorithm 3: Constant-time fixed-parity scalar decomposition for binary GLS curves with $h = 2$

Input: $k \in [1, r - 1]$
Consts.: $N = \#E'(\mathbb{F}_{q^2})$, $d = \lceil \frac{2m}{W} \rceil \cdot W$, for W the machine word size.
$\qquad c_i = \lfloor \frac{\alpha_i}{N} 2^d \rceil$ for $i = 1, 2$ and $\alpha_1 = q - 1 + t$, $\alpha_2 = q - 1 - t$.
Output: Odd k_1, k_2 such that $k_1 + k_2 \mu \equiv k \pmod{r}$

1 $b_i \leftarrow c_i k \gg d$ for $i = 1, 2$ and
2 $(k_1, k_2) \leftarrow (k, 0) - b_1 v_1 - b_2 v_2$
3 **if** $\alpha_1 \equiv 0 \pmod 4$ **then** $(u_1, u_2) \leftarrow (v_2, v_1)$
4 **else** $(u_1, u_2) \leftarrow (v_1, v_2)$
5 $p_i \leftarrow k_i + 1 \bmod 2$ for $i = 1, 2$
6 $(k_1, k_2) \leftarrow (k_1, k_2) - p_1 u_1 - p_2 u_2$
7 **return** k_1, k_2

Lemma 2. *Let the notation be as in Lemma 1 and assume that $h = 2$ and $m > 4$. Algorithm 3 on input $k \in [1, r - 1]$ outputs a valid decomposition k_1, k_2. The subscalars are odd and $|k_1|, |k_2| < 2q$.*

Proof. Let k_1, k_2 be the output of the GLV method on input k and let k_1', k_2' the output of Algorithm 3. We start with correctness. Per definition, $(k, 0) + \mathcal{L} \in \mathbb{Z}^2/\mathcal{L}$ is the set of valid decompositions of k. Algorithm 2 produces (k_1', k_2') by adding integer multiples of v_1 and v_2 to $(k, 0)$. Hence, $(k_1', k_2') \in (k, 0) + \mathcal{L}$.

Next, let's bound the magnitude of the subscalars. The basis vectors are orthogonal with norm $\sqrt{r}$. By the same argument as in Lemma 3 of [13] it follows that $\|(k_1, k_2)\| \leq \sqrt{r/2}$. To make the analysis independent of r, we can upperbound it as $r \leq (q + 1)^2/2$ using the Hasse bound. Then $\|v_1\|, \|v_2\| \leq (q + 1)/\sqrt{2}$ and $\|(k_1, k_1)\| \leq (q + 1)/2$.

It can be easily verified that α_1, α_2, N are specified such that $(k, 0) = \beta_1 v_1 + \beta_2 v_2$. Since $k < r \leq (q + 1)^2/2 \leq q^2 \leq 2^d$, it follows from Lemma 1 of [10] that b_i' is either b_i or incorrectly rounded down to $b_i - 1$.

Let r_i be the bit that is 1 if such a rounding error occurred when computing b_i'. Let s_i be the bit that is 1 if v_i was subtracted from (k_1, k_2) at line 8. Then using the triangle inequality, we can derive the bound on the subscalars.

$$|k_1'|, |k_2'| \leq \|(k_1', k_2')\|$$

$$= \left\| \sum_{i=1}^{2} (\beta_i - (b_i - r_i + s_i)) v_i \right\|$$

$$\leq \left\| \sum_{i=1}^{2}(\beta_i - b_i)v_i \right\| + \|v_1\| + \|v_2\|$$

$$\leq \left(\frac{q+1}{2}\right) + 2\left(\frac{q+1}{\sqrt{2}}\right)$$

$$< 2q \qquad\qquad\qquad\qquad (\text{Assuming } m > 4)$$

Finally, we will show that k_1', k_2' are odd. The proof of Lemma 1 establishes that t is odd. $\frac{(q-1)+t}{2} = \frac{(q-1)-t}{2} + t$, meaning exactly one of the coordinates of v_1 are odd. By symmetry, only the other coordinate of v_2 is odd. Because $\alpha_1 = 2\left(\frac{(q-1)+t}{2}\right)$, $\alpha_1 \equiv 0 \pmod 4$ exactly when the 1st coordinate of v_2 is odd. Then u_i is the basis vector with the odd i-th coordinate. Subtracting (k_1', k_2') by u_i flips the parity of k_i' but leaves the parity of the other subscalar unchanged. $p_i = 1$ exactly when k_i is even, meaning that the subscalars output are odd. $\square$

Corollary 1. *Let $m > 4$ be a prime number. For any window size $2 < w \leq m$, the number of digits needed to recode the subscalars output by Algorithm 3 is the same as one would need for the subscalars output by the GLV method with no rounding errors. For $w = 2$, one more digit is required.*

5   New Formulas for Faster Precomputation

The 2DT scalar multiplication variant represents a different strategy for utilizing precomputation. The table grows quadratically faster than its 1DT counterpart, so reducing the cost of its precomputation is crucial. For both the 1DT and 2DT variants, we present more efficient strategies for the precomputation stage. The 2DT precomputation (Algorithm 5) uses the 1DT precomputation (Algorithm 4) as a subroutine, which makes a case for the fairness of our optimization efforts.

The precomputation algorithms depend on several new atomic group law formulas. Compared to doing the operations using the existing formulas from [28], they provide a significant saving in the number of field multiplications and squarings needed. Because these formulas are derived by combining the original group law formulas, they do not introduce additional exceptions. The new formulas that are nontrivial to derive are included in the Appendix of the full version [1]. An overview of the cost of the specialized λ-projective group law formulas is given in Table 1.

It follows from the same argument as in Theorem 1 that the new precomputation algorithms are exception-free. At any step we compute $iP + j\psi(P)$ for small coefficients i, j, where at least one of them are nonzero. Then $(i, \pm j) \notin \mathcal{L}$, meaning that there cannot be any exceptions.

Algorithm 4: Precomputation-1D

Input: $P \in \mathcal{G}$ in λ-affine coordinates, window size $w > 2$.
Output: Table T of size 2^{w-2} with $T[i] = (2i+1)P$ in λ-affine coordinates.

1 $T[0] \leftarrow P$
2 $T[1] \leftarrow 3P$
3 **for** i **from** 0 **to** $2^{w-3} - 2$ **do**
4 $\quad \lfloor\ T[2i+3], T[2i+2] \leftarrow 2T[i+1] \pm P$

5 Convert T to λ-affine coordinates using simultaneous inversion.
6 **return** T

Algorithm 5: Precomputation-2D

Input: $P \in \mathcal{G}$ in λ-affine coordinates, window size $w > 2$.
Output: Table T of size $2^{w-2} \times 2^{w-2}$ with $T[i,j] = (2i+1)P + (2j+1)\psi(P)$ in
$\qquad\qquad$ λ-affine coordinates.

1 $R \leftarrow$ Precomputation-1D(P, w)
2 **for** i **from** 0 **to** $2^{w-2} - 1$ **do**
3 $\quad \lfloor\ T[i,i] \leftarrow R[i] + \psi(R[i])$

4 **for** j **from** 1 **to** $2^{w-2} - 1$ **do**
5 $\quad|\quad Q \leftarrow \psi(R[j])$
6 $\quad|\quad$ **for** i **from** 0 **to** $j-1$ **do**
7 $\quad|\quad\ \lfloor\ T[i,j], T[j,i] \leftarrow R[i] \pm Q$
8 $\quad \lfloor\quad\ \lfloor\ T[j,i] \leftarrow \psi(T[j,i])$

9 Convert T to λ-affine coordinates using simultaneous inversion.
10 **return** T

Table 1. Cost of the λ-projective group law formulas with respect to the number of multiplications, multiplications by curve coefficients a and b and squarings $(\tilde{m}, \tilde{m}_a, \tilde{m}_b, \tilde{s})$ over the extension field $\mathbb{F}_{q^2}$. For the mixed point representations, Q is λ-projective while P, P_1 and P_2 are λ-affine. The formulas that have not been derived or that provided insignificant speedups are marked with '-'.

Op.\Rep.	Projective	Mixed	Affine
$2P$	$4\tilde{m} + \tilde{m}_a + 4\tilde{s}/3\tilde{m} + 4\tilde{m}_a + \tilde{m}_b + 4\tilde{s}$	-	$\tilde{m} + 3\tilde{s}$
$3P$	-	-	$4\tilde{m} + \tilde{m}_a + 4\tilde{s}$
$P + Q$	$11\tilde{m} + 2\tilde{s}$	$8\tilde{m} + 2\tilde{s}$	$5\tilde{m} + 2\tilde{s}$
$P \pm Q$	-	$12\tilde{m} + 5\tilde{s}$	$6\tilde{m} + 4\tilde{s}$
2Q+P	-	$10\tilde{m} + \tilde{m}_a + 6\tilde{s}$	-
$2Q + P_1 + P_2$	-	$17\tilde{m} + \tilde{m}_a + 8\tilde{s}$	-
$P + \psi(P)$	-	-	$3.5\tilde{m} + 1.5\tilde{s}$

6   Binary Field Arithmetic for Arm

This section details our Arm implementation of the GLS254 curve. The focus will be on the field arithmetic. It was implemented specifically for the platform, relying heavily on 128-bit Arm Neon vector instructions to achieve high performance. The rest of the curve implementation is almost exclusively written in C, and therefore does not differ much from the Intel implementation from [28].

Specifically, our implementation targets Armv8 AArch64, which introduces some new useful instructions for cryptographic implementations. In particular, we take advantage of the new PMULL vector instruction for 64-bit binary polynomial multiplication, a direct analogue of PCLMULQDQ for Intel. For convenience of implementation, we use C intrinsics for the Arm Neon vector instructions.

This section first details the implementation of the base field $\mathbb{F}_q$ with $q = 2^m$ and $m = 127$, then how we implement the quadratic extension field $\mathbb{F}_{q^2}$ on top.

6.1   Arithmetic in the Base Field $\mathbb{F}_q$

Representation of Elements. One benefit of the choice of field, is that the bit vector representation of $a \in \mathbb{F}_q$ is 127 bits long, meaning that we can fit it in a single 128-bit Neon vector register. We denote $a[0], a[1]$ as respectively the least significant and most significant word of the 128-bit register that stores $a \in \mathbb{F}_{2^{127}}$. $a[0]$ stores the bit vector for the terms z^0 to z^{63}, $a[1]$ terms z^{64} to z^{126}. We will sometimes use the notation $a = \{a[0], a[1]\}$ to show the contents of the register.

An efficiency issue for Arm AArch64, compared to AArch32, is that it cannot reference the upper word $a[1]$ of a 128-bit register as a separate 64-bit register [16]. Instead, one needs to use the Arm Neon instruction EXT. It takes two registers a, b and outputs $\{a[1], b[0]\}$. The lower half of this output can then be referenced for further computation. Table 2 gives an overview of all the Neon instructions that we used for our implementation.

Table 2. Arm Neon 128-bit vector instructions used. The first 128-bit operand is denoted a, the second b. The output is also stored in a 128-bit register.

Symbol	Description	Neon Instruction
$\oplus, \wedge$	Bitwise XOR, AND	EOR, AND
$\ll_{128}, \gg_{128}$	Logical shift (no carry between words)	SHL, SHR
pmull_bot	Multiply binary polynomials $a[0], b[0]$	PMULL
pmull_top	Multiply binary polynomials $a[1], b[1]$	PMULL2
extract	Outputs $\{a[1], b[0]\}$	EXT

Polynomial Multiplication. The polynomial multiplication algorithm takes as input two binary polynomials $a, b \in \mathbb{F}_q$ and outputs their polynomial product c. The degree of c can be up to twice the degree of the operands. Hence it must be stored in two 128-bit vector registers c_0, c_1, where c_0 stores the lower half.

For polynomial multiplication we use the Arm Neon implementation from [16]. It efficiently performs 128-bit polynomial multiplication using the new PMULL instructions. While they managed to implement it using 3 multiplications with the Karatsuba algorithm on AArch32, the high number of EXTs this would require on AArch64 meant that they instead opted for an algorithm with an extra PMULL.

Polynomial Squaring and Field Multi-squaring. Polynomial squaring of an $a \in \mathbb{F}_q$ can be trivially implemented as $c_0 \leftarrow \text{pmull\_bot}(a, a)$, $c_1 \leftarrow \text{pmull\_top}(a, a)$.

For multi-squaring in settings where it does not need to be computed in constant time, we implemented the technique from [2,7]. It uses lookup tables that are precomputed offline to compute the reduced result of a^{2^k}. However, for smaller Arm processors like the Cortex-A55, this method only outperforms the naive loop implementation for $k > 12$. This is a lot higher than the threshold of $k > 5$ for Intel [28]. It is an example of the higher cost of memory access on smaller devices, which results in a lower yield for precomputation strategies.

Modular Reduction. To compute a field multiplication or squaring, the result of the polynomial algorithm must be reduced modulo $f(z)$. We here present novel algorithms for efficient modular reduction, using exclusively Arm Neon vector instructions. Like the polynomial multiplication algorithm from [16], they attempt to minimize the number of accesses to the top half of the 128-bit registers, each of which incurs the cost of an EXT.

For reducing the result of a polynomial multiplication, we use Algorithm 6. It implements the lazy reduction technique from [27]. Instead of reducing $f(z)$, we reduce by the redundant trinomial $z \cdot f(z) = z^{128} + z^{64} + z$. Reductions by $zf(z)$ are roughly 40% faster than proper reductions by $zf(z)$. The result can have degree up to 127 instead of 126, but as the result still fits in a 128-bit register, this makes no difference. As $(c \bmod zf(z)) \bmod f(z) = c \bmod f(z)$, one can easily recover the properly reduced result from the output of the lazy reduction. This is done by conditionally adding $z^{63} + 1$ to it when bit 127 is set.

Algorithm 6: Lazy reduction by $z \cdot f(z) = z^{128} + z^{64} + z$

Input: 254-bit polynomial stored in two 128-bit registers c_0, c_1.
Output: 128-bit register a storing $c(z) \bmod f(z)$.
Temps.: Uses 128-bit registers t_0, t_1, t_2.

1 $t_0[0] \leftarrow 0$
2 $t_1[0] \leftarrow c_1[0] \gg 63$
3 $t_0 \leftarrow \text{extract}(c_1, t_0)$
4 $t_2[0] \leftarrow c_1[0] \oplus t_0[0]$
5 $t_1[0] \leftarrow t_1[0] \oplus t_2[0]$
6 $t_0 \leftarrow \text{extract}(t_0, t_1)$
7 $a \leftarrow c_0 \oplus t_0$
8 $t_2 \leftarrow t_2 \ll_{128} 1$
9 $a \leftarrow a \oplus t_2$
10 **return** a

It is possible to reduce a squaring slightly faster, exploiting the fact that the result only has bits set at even positions. Thus, we can remove the logic from Algorithm 6 that handles the carry of bit 191 from the left shift by 1. Concretely, this means removing lines 2 and 5, and replacing t_2 by t_1.

Field Inversion. Field inversion is done in the same way as described in [28], using the Itoh-Tsujii algorithm [19]. We generated our addition chain for $m-1 = 126$ using McLoughlin's *addchain* library [26].

$$1 \to 2 \to 3 \to 6 \to 12 \to 24 \to 30 \to 48 \to 96 \to 126$$

The cost of a field inversion is therefore $m - 1$ squarings and 9 multiplications. The steps after 30 involve multi-squarings with $k > 12$. When the inversion does not have to be in constant time, these steps can then be sped up using the table-based multi-squaring approach.

6.2 Arithmetic in the Extension Field $\mathbb{F}_{q^2}$

The elements of $\mathbb{F}_{q^2}$ can be represented as polynomials $a_1 u + a_0$, with coefficients $a_0, a_1 \in \mathbb{F}_q$. Therefore, we need two 128-bit registers to represent them. The extension field arithmetic can be implemented from the base field arithmetic, using the identities presented in [28].

In [27], Oliveira et al. present an algorithm for simultaneously reducing both coefficients of an element in $\mathbb{F}_{q^2}$ at the cost of only a single base field reduction. We have included the Arm Neon implementation in Algorithm 7.

Algorithm 7: Lazy simultaneous reduction by $zf(z) = z^{128} + z^{64} + z$ for coordinate-wise reduction in $\mathbb{F}_{q^2}$ (Oliveira et al. [27])

Input: Unreduced polynomial stored in interleaved 128-bit registers
c_0, c_1, c_2, c_3.
Output: 128-bit register a storing $c(z) \bmod zf(z)$.
Temps.: Uses 128-bit register t.

1 $c_2 \leftarrow c_2 \oplus c_3$
2 $t \leftarrow c_3 \ll_{128} 1$
3 $c_1 \leftarrow c_1 \oplus t$
4 $c_1 \leftarrow c_1 \oplus c_2$
5 $t \leftarrow c_2 \gg_{128} 63$
6 $c_1 \leftarrow c_1 \oplus t$
7 $t \leftarrow t \ll_{128} c_2$
8 $c_0 \leftarrow c_0 \oplus t$
9 **return** c_0, c_1

However, the reduction algorithm requires the field elements to be kept in an interleaved representation. For an $a \in \mathbb{F}_{q^2}$, let a_0, a_1 be the 128-bit registers storing each of its coefficients. Then the interleaved representation of a is

$$a'_0 = \{a_0[0], a_1[0]\}, \ a'_1 = \{a_0[1], a_1[1]\}. \tag{3}$$

Note that a'_0, a'_1 store a_0 in the lower half and a_1 in the upper half. The larger input to the reduction algorithm must also be in an interleaved representation. Let c_0, c_1, c_2, c_3 be the non-interleaved 128-bit registers storing the result of a polynomial multiplication or squaring. Because this result is computed using the identities from [28], the result is already reduced as a polynomial in u, but has coefficients that need further reduction in $\mathbb{F}_q$. Then c_0, c_1 store the unreduced constant coefficient and c_2, c_3 the other. The interleaved representation c'_0, c'_1, c'_2, c'_3 of these unreduced coefficients continue the pattern from (3). c'_0, c'_1 are c_0, c_2 interleaved, and c'_2, c'_3 are c_1, c_3 interleaved.

In order to reap the benefits of the reduction algorithm, we had to implement the $\mathbb{F}_{q^2}$ arithmetic directly in the interleaved representation. To do this, we manually merged and interleaved the base field algorithms to compute the identities from [28]. The only exception is inversion, where a standard base field inversion is used as a subroutine, which again uses all the arithmetic operations discusses in the previous section. While the abstraction between base field and extension field is somewhat broken for the sake of performance, the base field implementation is still the crucial foundation.

7 Results and Discussion

Our implementations, together with SAGE scripts for verification and operation counts, can be found at https://github.com/dfaranha/gls254.

7.1 Operation Counts for Binary GLS Scalar Multiplication

Table 3. The cost of the scalar multiplications with respect to the number of inversions, multiplications and squarings ($\tilde{i}$, $\tilde{m}$, $\tilde{s}$) over $\mathbb{F}_{q^2}$. The total cost in field multiplications are estimated using $\tilde{i}_{\text{non-ct}} = 18\tilde{m}$, $\tilde{i}_{\text{ct}} = 27\tilde{m}$ and $\tilde{s} = 0.4\tilde{m}$ based on our benchmarks, and rounded to the nearest integer. "prev" denotes the cost for previous work.

Variant\ w	3	4	5	6
Precomp.				
1DT (prev)	$\tilde{i}+12\tilde{m}+6\tilde{s}$	$\tilde{i}+38\tilde{m}+14\tilde{s}$	$\tilde{i}+90\tilde{m}+30\tilde{s}$	$\tilde{i}+194\tilde{m}+62\tilde{s}$
1DT	$\tilde{i}+6\tilde{m}+4\tilde{s}$	$\tilde{i}+31\tilde{m}+13\tilde{s}$	$\tilde{i}+81\tilde{m}+31\tilde{s}$	$\tilde{i}+181\tilde{m}+67\tilde{s}$
2DT	$2\tilde{i}+36\tilde{m}+11\tilde{s}$	$2\tilde{i}+158\tilde{m}+43\tilde{s}$	$2\tilde{i}+594\tilde{m}+155\tilde{s}$	$2\tilde{i}+2234\tilde{m}+571\tilde{s}$
Main loop				
1DT (both)	$1273\tilde{m}+764\tilde{s}$	$979\tilde{m}+680\tilde{s}$	$819\tilde{m}+628\tilde{s}$	$738\tilde{m}+608\tilde{s}$
2DT	$823\tilde{m}+633\tilde{s}$	$676\tilde{m}+591\tilde{s}$	$593\tilde{m}+561\tilde{s}$	$554\tilde{m}+553\tilde{s}$
Total				
1DT (prev)	$2\tilde{i}+1309\tilde{m}+780\tilde{s}$	$2\tilde{i}+1041\tilde{m}+704\tilde{s}$	$2\tilde{i}+933\tilde{m}+668\tilde{s}$	$2\tilde{i}+956\tilde{m}+680\tilde{s}$
1DT	$2\tilde{i}+1281\tilde{m}+768\tilde{s}$	$2\tilde{i}+1012\tilde{m}+693\tilde{s}$	$2\tilde{i}+902\tilde{m}+659\tilde{s}$	$2\tilde{i}+921\tilde{m}+675\tilde{s}$
2DT	$3\tilde{i}+861\tilde{m}+644\tilde{s}$	$3\tilde{i}+839\tilde{m}+634\tilde{s}$	$3\tilde{i}+1189\tilde{m}+716\tilde{s}$	$3\tilde{i}+2790\tilde{m}+1124\tilde{s}$
Est. mult.				
1DT (prev)	$1666\tilde{m}$	$1368\tilde{m}$	$1245\tilde{m}$	$1273\tilde{m}$
1DT	$1633\tilde{m}$	$1334\tilde{m}$	$1211\tilde{m}$	$1236\tilde{m}$
2DT	$1182\tilde{m}$	$1155\tilde{m}$	$1538\tilde{m}$	$3303\tilde{m}$

Throughout our work, we have used field operation counts as a measure of the complexity of the scalar multiplication variants. With an understanding of the relative cost of the operations, the count gives a platform-independent estimate of the relative performance of the algorithms. In particular, it guided our choice of window size. However, it crucially does not capture the space-time trade-offs of a particular architecture. For the variants discussed in this paper, which are precisely different strategies for how to use space, this trade-off has a significant impact. This will be apparent in the next subsection.

Table 3 gives an overview the operation counts for the variants. Additions and multiplications by the curve coefficients are ignored due to their insignificant impact on performance. We include the costs of the 1DT algorithm without the new formulas and scalar decomposition to highlight the impact of our contributions. For the sake of fairness, it has been modified to be exception-free in the same way as the others.

As expected, the 2DT algorithm spends more time on precomputation and less in the main loop. We see that the model predicts $w = 5$ to be the sweet spot for 1DT and $w = 4$ for 2DT. Notably, 2DT $w = 3$ is predicted to be faster than 1DT $w = 5$ using only half the amount of space.

For a simpler comparison, we estimate the total cost in terms of field multiplications. The relative cost of each operation will of course differ from processor to processor, so we tried to go for the middle-ground based on our benchmarks. With this simplification, the model predicts that 1DT with $w = 5$ should be 2.7% faster from our contributions. The 2DT approach with $w = 4$ is predicted to be 7.2% faster than 1DT in previous work with $w = 5$, and 4.6% faster than 1DT with $w = 5$ from this work. Non-constant-time field inversion is used to convert points from projective to affine in the precomputation table only, since it does not depend on the (secret) scalar.

7.2 Implementation Timings

We start by describing our benchmarks for the Armv8 AArch64 implementation, written from scratch. We used the ODROID C4 single board computer, as we wanted a smaller device that could be representative for the majority of Arm devices. It comes with a Quad-Core Cortex-A55, which is considered a mid-range processor. We employ `clang` from LLVM 13 with optimization level `-O3`.

Table 4. Benchmarks (in clock cycles) of the field arithmetic on an Arm Cortex-A55 2.0 GHz. The cost of reduction is included in the cost of the multiplication and squaring. Base field reduction is mod $zf(z)$. Op/m_b, Op/$\widetilde{m}$ denotes the cost relative to respectively base/extension field multiplication.

Field op.	$\mathbb{F}_{2^{127}}$		$\mathbb{F}_{2^{254}}$	
	Cycles	Op/m_b	Cycles	Op/$\widetilde{m}$
Multiplication	35	1.00	68	1.00
Reduction	16	0.46	15	0.22
Squaring	18	0.51	26	0.38
Inversion (ct.)	1 716	49.03	1 815	26.69
(non-ct.)	1 165	33.29	1 228	18.06

The benchmarks for our field implementation are presented in Table 4. Notice that non-constant time inversions that use lookup tables are roughly 33% faster.

Table 5 presents our scalar multiplication timings in GLS254 and comparisons to related work. Compared to Intel, there are not a lot of efficient implementations specialized for Arm at the 128-bit security level. FourQ [10] is the closest competitor on Intel, and they also provide specialized implementations for Arm [25]. We benchmarked their Armv8 AArch64 implementation on our machine and included their Armv7 timings from [25] for the sake of fairness. A notable outlier is Lenngren's implementation for Curve2559, which is a much closer competitor on Arm than any Curve25519 implementation on Intel.

As the first GLS254 implementation for Armv8, we are able to claim the constant-time scalar multiplication speed record by 34.5% in comparison to the previous state of the art. Contrary to the operation counts in Table 3, it is the 2DT $w = 3$ algorithm that is the superior variant. We do not compare against [24] due to the radically different choices of target platform.

Table 5. Constant-time variable base scalar multiplication benchmarks that are mostly performed on an Arm Quad-Core Cortex-A55 2.0 GHz. Memory is measured in terms of the number of elliptic curve points stored in the online precomputed table.

Implementation	Algorithm	Memory	Cycles
Lenngren [23] (Cortex-A55)	Curve25519	0	157,182
Longa [25] (Cortex-A55)	FourQ	8	191,184
Longa [25] (Cortex-A15)	FourQ	8	132,000
This work (Cortex-A55)	GLS254 1DT $w = 5$	8	92,460
	GLS254 2DT $w = 3$	**4**	**86,525**
	GLS254 2DT $w = 4$	16	91,682

Table 6. Protected variable base scalar multiplication benchmarks for 64-bit Intel Core i7 4770 Haswell at 3.4 GHz, and Core i7 7700 Kaby Lake at 3.6 GHz, both with TurboBoost disabled. Memory is measured in terms of the number of elliptic curve points stored in the online precomputed table.

Implementation	Algorithm	Memory	Cycles
Longa et al. [10] (Haswell)	FourQ	8	56,000
Longa et al. [10] (Kaby Lake)	FourQ	8	47,052
Oliveira et al. [28] (Haswell)	GLS254 1DT $w = 5$	8	48,301
Oliveira et al. [27] (Skylake)	GLS254 1DT $w = 5$	8	38,044
This work (Haswell)	GLS254 1DT $w = 5$	8	45,966
	GLS254 2DT $w = 3$	**4**	**45,253**
	GLS254 2DT $w = 4$	16	47,184
This work (Kaby Lake)	GLS254 1DT $w = 5$	8	36,480
	GLS254 2DT $w = 3$	**4**	**35,739**
	GLS254 2DT $w = 4$	16	38,076

For our Intel implementation, we extended the AVX-accelerated code from [31] with the new formulas and 2DT variant. Due to space limitations, we report timings for field arithmetic in the Appendix of the full version [1]. The scalar multiplication benchmarks are presented in Table 6. We benchmarked our code on an older Core i7 4770 Haswell processor, and a Core i7 7700 Kaby Lake as the closest to the Skylake in [27]; both using `clang` from LLVM 13 and optimization level -O3. For 1DT $w = 5$, we achieve small speedups of 4.8% in Haswell and 4.1% for Skylake over the previous state of the art. The 2DT $w = 3$ variant achieves a further speedup of 2%. Surprisingly, 2DT $w = 4$ performs relatively poorly due to expensive conditional moves within the longer linear pass. The cumulative speedup over previous work is around 6% on both machines. In comparison to FourQ, our timings are 24% faster and set a new speed record for constant-time scalar multiplication in Intel processors.

Removing the linear pass for the sake of experimentation, 2DT $w = 4$ outperforms the other variants on all the platforms benchmarked, as predicted by the operation counts. The relative cost of the linear pass seems to be the determining factor for how much of a speedup the new approach yields in practice. In general, the linear pass incurs a relatively high cost, favoring solutions that minimize the size of the lookup table. Hence, we see that the 2DT $w = 3$ variant claims the speed record across the board, using only half as much space as the previous record holder 1DT $w = 5$.

Acknowledgements. We thank Aurore Guillevic for discussions about preliminary results of this work, and Jonas Tambjerg Morthorst for help on the early Arm implementation. This work was partially supported by the Danish Independent Research Council under the project 1026-00350B (RENAIS).

References

1. Aardal, M.A., Aranha, D.F.: 2DT-GLS: faster and exception-free scalar multiplication in the GLS254 binary curve. Cryptology ePrint Archive, Paper 2022/748 (2022). https://eprint.iacr.org/2022/748
2. Ahmadi, O., Hankerson, D., Rodríguez-Henríquez, F.: Parallel formulations of scalar multiplication on Koblitz curves. J. UCS **14**(3), 481–504 (2008)
3. Bernstein, D.J.: Curve25519: new Diffie-Hellman speed records. In: Yung, M., Dodis, Y., Kiayias, A., Malkin, T. (eds.) PKC 2006. LNCS, vol. 3958, pp. 207–228. Springer, Heidelberg (2006). https://doi.org/10.1007/11745853_14
4. Bernstein, D.J., Lange, T.: SafeCurves: choosing safe curves for elliptic-curve cryptography. https://safecurves.cr.yp.to/
5. Bos, J.W., Costello, C., Hisil, H., Lauter, K.: High-performance scalar multiplication using 8-dimensional GLV/GLS decomposition. In: Bertoni, G., Coron, J.-S. (eds.) CHES 2013. LNCS, vol. 8086, pp. 331–348. Springer, Heidelberg (2013). https://doi.org/10.1007/978-3-642-40349-1_19
6. Bos, J.W., Costello, C., Longa, P., Naehrig, M.: Selecting elliptic curves for cryptography: an efficiency and security analysis. J. Cryptogr. Eng. **6**(4), 259–286 (2016)
7. Bos, J.W., Kleinjung, T., Niederhagen, R., Schwabe, P.: ECC2K-130 on cell CPUs. In: Bernstein, D.J., Lange, T. (eds.) AFRICACRYPT 2010. LNCS, vol. 6055, pp. 225–242. Springer, Heidelberg (2010). https://doi.org/10.1007/978-3-642-12678-9_14
8. Chi, J.-J., Oliveira, T.: Attacking a binary GLS elliptic curve with Magma. In: Lauter, K., Rodríguez-Henríquez, F. (eds.) LATINCRYPT 2015. LNCS, vol. 9230, pp. 308–326. Springer, Cham (2015). https://doi.org/10.1007/978-3-319-22174-8_17
9. Ciet, M., Lange, T., Sica, F., Quisquater, J.-J.: Improved algorithms for efficient arithmetic on elliptic curves using fast endomorphisms. In: Biham, E. (ed.) EUROCRYPT 2003. LNCS, vol. 2656, pp. 388–400. Springer, Heidelberg (2003). https://doi.org/10.1007/3-540-39200-9_24
10. Costello, C., Longa, P.: Fourℚ: four-dimensional decompositions on a ℚ-curve over the Mersenne prime. IACR Cryptol. ePrint Arch. 565 (2015)
11. Faz-Hernández, A., Longa, P., Sánchez, A.H.: Efficient and secure algorithms for GLV-based scalar multiplication and their implementation on GLV-GLS curves (extended version). J. Cryptogr. Eng. **5**(1), 31–52 (2015)

12. Galbraith, S.D., Gaudry, P.: Recent progress on the elliptic curve discrete logarithm problem. Des. Codes Cryptogr. **78**(1), 51–72 (2016)
13. Galbraith, S.D., Lin, X., Scott, M.: Endomorphisms for faster elliptic curve cryptography on a large class of curves. In: Joux, A. (ed.) EUROCRYPT 2009. LNCS, vol. 5479, pp. 518–535. Springer, Heidelberg (2009). https://doi.org/10.1007/978-3-642-01001-9_30
14. Gallant, R.P., Lambert, R.J., Vanstone, S.A.: Faster point multiplication on elliptic curves with efficient endomorphisms. In: Kilian, J. (ed.) CRYPTO 2001. LNCS, vol. 2139, pp. 190–200. Springer, Heidelberg (2001). https://doi.org/10.1007/3-540-44647-8_11
15. Gaudry, P., Hess, F., Smart, N.P.: Constructive and destructive facets of Weil descent on elliptic curves. J. Cryptol. **15**(1), 19–46 (2002)
16. Gouvêa, C.P.L., López, J.: Implementing GCM on ARMv8. In: Nyberg, K. (ed.) CT-RSA 2015. LNCS, vol. 9048, pp. 167–180. Springer, Cham (2015). https://doi.org/10.1007/978-3-319-16715-2_9
17. Hankerson, D., Karabina, K., Menezes, A.: Analyzing the Galbraith-Lin-Scott point multiplication method for elliptic curves over binary fields. IEEE Trans. Comput. **58**(10), 1411–1420 (2009)
18. Hess, F.: Generalising the GHS attack on the elliptic curve discrete logarithm problem. LMS J. Comput. Math. **7**, 167–192 (2004)
19. Itoh, T., Tsujii, S.: A fast algorithm for computing multiplicative inverses in $GF(2^m)$ using normal bases. Inf. Comput. **78**(3), 171–177 (1988)
20. Joye, M., Tunstall, M.: Exponent recoding and regular exponentiation algorithms. In: Preneel, B. (ed.) AFRICACRYPT 2009. LNCS, vol. 5580, pp. 334–349. Springer, Heidelberg (2009). https://doi.org/10.1007/978-3-642-02384-2_21
21. Kales, D., Rechberger, C., Schneider, T., Senker, M., Weinert, C.: Mobile private contact discovery at scale. In: USENIX Security Symposium, pp. 1447–1464. USENIX Association (2019)
22. Koblitz, A.H., Koblitz, N., Menezes, A.: Elliptic curve cryptography: the serpentine course of a paradigm shift. J. Number Theory **131**(5), 781–814 (2011)
23. Lenngren, E.: AArch64 optimized implementation for X25519. https://github.com/Emill/X25519-AArch64
24. Liu, Z., Longa, P., Pereira, G.C.C.F., Reparaz, O., Seo, H.: FourQ on embedded devices with strong countermeasures against side-channel attacks. In: Fischer, W., Homma, N. (eds.) CHES 2017. LNCS, vol. 10529, pp. 665–686. Springer, Cham (2017). https://doi.org/10.1007/978-3-319-66787-4_32
25. Longa, P.: FourQNEON: faster elliptic curve scalar multiplications on ARM processors. In: Avanzi, R., Heys, H. (eds.) SAC 2016. LNCS, vol. 10532, pp. 501–519. Springer, Cham (2017). https://doi.org/10.1007/978-3-319-69453-5_27
26. McLoughlin, M.B.: addchain: Cryptographic Addition Chain Generation in Go, October 2021. Repository https://github.com/mmcloughlin/addchain
27. Oliveira, T., López-Hernández, J.C., Aranha, D.F., Rodríguez-Henríquez, F.: Improving the performance of the GLS254. Presentation at CHES 2016 Rump Session (2016)
28. Oliveira, T., López-Hernández, J.C., Aranha, D.F., Rodríguez-Henríquez, F.: Two is the fastest prime: lambda coordinates for binary elliptic curves. J. Cryptogr. Eng. **4**(1), 3–17 (2014)
29. Oliveira, T., López-Hernández, J.C., Cervantes-Vázquez, D., Rodríguez-Henríquez, F.: Koblitz curves over quadratic fields. J. Cryptol. **32**(3), 867–894 (2019)

30. Renes, J., Costello, C., Batina, L.: Complete addition formulas for prime order elliptic curves. In: Fischlin, M., Coron, J.-S. (eds.) EUROCRYPT 2016. LNCS, vol. 9665, pp. 403–428. Springer, Heidelberg (2016). https://doi.org/10.1007/978-3-662-49890-3_16
31. Resende, A.C.D., Aranha, D.F.: Faster Unbalanced Private Set Intersection. In: Financial Cryptography. LNCS, vol. 10957, pp. 203–221. Springer (2018)
32. Smith, B.: Easy scalar decompositions for efficient scalar multiplication on elliptic curves and genus 2 Jacobians. CoRR **abs/1310.5250** (2013)

Differential Cryptanalysis

Key-Recovery Attacks on CRAFT and WARP

Ling Sun[1,2,3,4], Wei Wang[1,3], and Meiqin Wang[1,3,4]($\boxtimes$)

[1] Key Laboratory of Cryptologic Technology and Information Security,
Ministry of Education, Shandong University, Jinan, China
{lingsun,weiwangsdu,mqwang}@sdu.edu.cn
[2] State Key Laboratory of Cryptology, P. O. Box 5159, Beijing 100878, China
[3] School of Cyber Science and Technology, Shandong University, Qingdao, China
[4] Quan Cheng Shandong Laboratory, Jinan, China

Abstract. This paper considers the security of CRAFT and WARP. We present a practical key-recovery attack on full-round CRAFT in the related-key setting with only one differential characteristic, and the theoretical time complexity of the attack is $2^{36.09}$ full-round encryptions. The attack is verified in practice. The test result indicates that the theoretical analysis is valid, and it takes about 15.69 h to retrieve the key. A full-round key-recovery attack on WARP in the related-key setting is proposed, and the time complexity is $2^{44.58}$ full-round encryptions. The theoretical attack is implemented on a round-reduced version of WARP, which guarantees validity. Besides, we give a 33-round multiple zero-correlation linear attack on WARP, which is the longest attack on the cipher in the single-key attack setting. We note that the attack results in this paper do not threaten the security of CRAFT and WARP as the designers do not claim security under the related-key attack setting.

Keywords: Differential attack · Zero-correlation linear attack · Related-key · CRAFT · WARP

1 Introduction

Differential cryptanalysis [4] is one of the most fundamental cryptanalytic methods regarding symmetric-key primitives. It investigates how an input difference propagates through the cipher. If a particular output difference appears in a non-random way, this observation can be used to construct a distinguisher or recover keys.

For now, security against differential cryptanalysis is a baseline for modern symmetric-key primitives. Consequently, the probability of the distinguisher utilised in the differential attack typically is close to 2^{-n}, where n is the block size. However, for ciphers without related-key security, we can find differential distinguishers with extremely high probabilities. If these ciphers are misused in malicious cases, efficiently retrieving the key is more meaningful than distinguishing attacks. Moreover, according to Kerchhoffs' principle [10], the security of the encryption scheme should rely solely on the secrecy of the key. Hence, the motivation is to accomplish efficient key-recovery attacks on CRAFT [3] and WARP [1], two ciphers without related-key security, in the related-key setting.

B. Smith and H. Wu (Eds.): SAC 2022, LNCS 13742, pp. 77–95, 2024.
https://doi.org/10.1007/978-3-031-58411-4_4

1.1 Our Contributions

This work centres on the security of CRAFT and WARP, and the results are summarised as follows.

Practical Related-Key Differential Attack on Full-Round CRAFT. The previous related-key attack [8] with only one differential characteristic on CRAFT [3] has unrealistic time complexity, and we manage to propose a practical one. According to the theoretical analysis, the data complexity of our attack on full-round CRAFT is $2^{35.17}$ chosen plaintexts; the time complexity is $2^{36.09}$ full-round encryptions; the memory complexity is negligible. Given that the complexity of the new attack is practical, we try to verify it in practice. The test result indicates that the theoretical analysis is valid, and it takes about 15.69 h to retrieve the key. A summary of cryptanalytic results on CRAFT in the related-key attack setting can be found in Table 1.

Related-Key Differential Attack on Full-Round WARP. Since WARP [1] applies the same S-box as CRAFT, we wonder about its differential property in the related-key attack setting. With the automatic searching method, we first identify 384 full-round related-key differential characteristics with probability 2^{-40}. One characteristic is employed to accomplish the key-recovery attack. Based on the theoretical analysis, the data complexity of our attack on full-round WARP is $2^{44.58}$ chosen plaintexts; the time complexity is $2^{44.58}$ encryptions; the memory complexity is negligible. Because the complexity of the full-round attack is impractical, we attempt to launch an attack on a round-reduced version of WARP. We consider a 27-round version of WARP and remark that the key enumeration procedures remain the same. The test results demonstrate the validity of the theoretical attack. Excluding the time to collect right pairs, the runtime of the round-reduced key-recovery attack is about 44.50 h. A summary of cryptanalytic results on WARP can be found in Table 1.

33-Round Multiple Zero-Correlation Linear Attack on WARP. When analysing the security of WARP, we notice that the designers expected that the longest attack on the cipher in the single-key attack setting does not exceed 32 rounds. We propose a 33-round multiple zero-correlation linear attack, and it is the longest attack on WARP in the single-key attack setting as far as we know. A sketch of the 33-round attack can be found in Table 1.

Outline. Section 2 reviews two target ciphers and presents the main idea of the differential attack in this paper. The practical key-recovery attack on CRAFT in the related-key attack setting is given in Sect. 3. In Sect. 4, we propose the full-round related-key differential attack on WARP. Section 5 investigates the security of WARP against the multiple zero-correlation linear attack. Section 6 concludes the paper. [17] is the full version of the paper.

Table 1. Summary of cryptanalytic results on CRAFT and WARP.

Cipher	Setting	Attack	Round	Time	Data	Memory	P_S	Ref.
CRAFT	RK	Differential	32	$2^{85.00}$	$2^{31.00}$	$2^{41.00}$	97.72%	[8]
				$2^{32.00⊛}$	$2^{35.17}$	2^{6}	–	[8]
				$2^{36.09}$	$2^{35.17}$	neg	100%⊗	Section 3
WARP	SK	Differential	21	$2^{113.00}$	$2^{113.00}$	$2^{72.00}$	–	[11]
		Differential	23	$2^{106.68}$	$2^{106.62}$	$2^{106.62}$	92.09%	[18]
		Rectangle	24	$2^{125.18}$	$2^{126.06}$	$2^{127.06}$	86.20%	[18]
		Rectangle	26	$2^{115.90}$	$2^{120.60}$	$2^{120.60}$	97.67%	[13]
		Integral	32	$2^{127.00}$	$2^{127.00}$	$2^{108.00}$	–	[9]
		Zero-correlation	**33**	$\mathbf{2^{127.01}}$	$\mathbf{2^{97.71}}$	$\mathbf{2^{100.00}}$	**50.00%**	Section 5
	RK	Differential	41*	$2^{37.00}$	$2^{37.00}$	$2^{9.59}$	–	[18]
		Differential	**41**	$\mathbf{2^{44.58}}$	$\mathbf{2^{44.58}}$	neg	100%⊗	Section 4

SK stands for the single-key attack setting. RK stands for the related-key attack setting.
⊛ The attack uses eight related-key characteristics with distinct key differences. *Eight pairs* of keys are required.
The time complexity of the attack *might be wrong* since it should not be less than the data complexity.
* The attack recovers 60 bits of the key and is *not a complete* key-recovery attack.
⊗ The success probability is estimated with practical tests.

2   Preliminaries

In this section, we first review the two ciphers studied in the paper. Note that some irrelevant details are omitted. See Beierle *et al.* [3] and Banik *et al.* [1] for more information about the ciphers. Following that, the main idea of the differential attack in this paper is introduced.

2.1   Specification of CRAFT

CRAFT [3] is a lightweight block cipher with 64-bit block, 128-bit key, and 64-bit tweak. In the encryption phase, the internal state is viewed as a 4×4 square array of nibbles, and the nibble located at the i-th row and the j-th column is denoted as $I_{i,j}$, where $0 \leqslant i, j \leqslant 3$. Also, the 4×4 square array can be seen as a vector by concatenating the rows, and I_ℓ stands for the ℓ-th nibble of the vector in this expression, where $0 \leqslant \ell \leqslant 15$. With these definitions, the equation $I_{i,j} = I_{4\cdot i+j}$ holds.

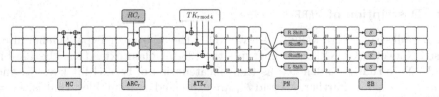

Fig. 1. Full round function $\mathcal{R}_r$ of CRAFT.

After initialising the state with the plaintext, the cipher iterates 31 full round functions ($\mathcal{R}_r$, $0 \leqslant r \leqslant 30$) and appends one linear round function ($\mathcal{R}'_{31}$) to yield the ciphertext. Each $\mathcal{R}_r$ applies the following five involutory operations, while $\mathcal{R}'_{31}$ only involves the first three operations. An illustration of $\mathcal{R}_r$ can be found in Fig. 1.

MixColumn(MC) Each column of the state is multiplied with the following involutory matrix

$$M = \begin{bmatrix} 0x1 & 0x0 & 0x1 & 0x1 \\ 0x0 & 0x1 & 0x0 & 0x1 \\ 0x0 & 0x0 & 0x1 & 0x0 \\ 0x0 & 0x0 & 0x0 & 0x1 \end{bmatrix}.$$

AddConstants$_r$(ARC$_r$) The round constants are generated with one 4-bit linear feedback shift register (LFSR) and one 3-bit LFSR, whose states are denoted by $a = (a_0, a_1, a_2, a_3)$ and $b = (b_0, b_1, b_2)$. In each round, $a_0\|a_1\|a_2\|a_3$ and $0\|b_0\|b_1\|b_2$ are firstly XORed with the state nibbles $I_{1,0}$ and $I_{1,1}$. After that, the two LFSRs get updated.

AddTweakey$_r$(ATK$_r$)] The 128-bit key K is split into two 64-bit keys K_0 and K_1. The formation of tweakeys involves the application of the permutation $\mathcal{Q} = (12, 10, 15, 5, \ 14, 8, 9, 2, \ 11, 3, 7, 4, \ 6, 0, 1, 13)$ on the sixteen nibbles of the 64-bit tweak T, and the i-th nibble of $\mathcal{Q}(T)$ equals the $\mathcal{Q}(i)$-th nibble of T, where $0 \leqslant i \leqslant 15$. Then, four 64-bit tweakeys TK_0, TK_1, TK_2, and TK_3 are derived as

$$TK_0 = K_0 \oplus T, \ TK_1 = K_1 \oplus T, \ TK_2 = K_0 \oplus \mathcal{Q}(T), \ TK_3 = K_1 \oplus \mathcal{Q}(T).$$

In the r-th round, the tweakey $TK_{r \bmod 4}$ is XORed with the cipher state.

PermuteNibbles(PN) The involutory permutation $\mathcal{P}$ is utilised to update the nibble positions of the state, i.e., $I_i \leftarrow I_{\mathcal{P}(i)}$ for all $0 \leqslant i \leqslant 15$, where $\mathcal{P} = (15, 12, 13, 14, \ 10, 9, 8, 11, \ 6, 5, 4, 7, \ 1, 2, 3, 0)$.

SubBox(SB) The S-box S in this operation is the same as the one exploited in Midori [2] and is applied to each nibble of the state. The table for S is given in the following.

x	0x0	0x1	0x2	0x3	0x4	0x5	0x6	0x7	0x8	0x9	0xa	0xb	0xc	0xd	0xe	0xf
$S(x)$	0xc	0xa	0xd	0x3	0xe	0xb	0xf	0x7	0x8	0x9	0x1	0x5	0x0	0x2	0x4	0x6

2.2 Description of WARP

The overall structure of WARP [1] is a variant of the 32-branch Type-2 Generalised Feistel Network (GFN) [19]. It encrypts the 128-bit plaintext $\mathcal{M}$ via the 128-bit key $\mathcal{K}$. Note that $\mathcal{K}$ is denoted as the concatenation of two 64-bit keys $\mathcal{K}_0$ and $\mathcal{K}_1$ as $\mathcal{K} = \mathcal{K}_0\|\mathcal{K}_1$. Further, $\mathcal{K}_0$ and $\mathcal{K}_1$ are expressed as 16 nibbles, that is, $\mathcal{K}_0 = \mathcal{K}_0[0]\|\mathcal{K}_0[1]\|\cdots\|\mathcal{K}_0[15]$ and $\mathcal{K}_1 = \mathcal{K}_1[0]\|\mathcal{K}_1[1]\|\cdots\|\mathcal{K}_1[15]$, where $\mathcal{K}_i[j] \in \mathbb{F}_2^4$, $i \in \{0, 1\}$, and $j \in \{0, 1, \ldots, 15\}$.

In the encryption phase, the plaintext $\mathcal{M}$ is loaded into a 128-bit internal state $\mathcal{X}_0$, which is represented in nibbles as $\mathcal{X}_0 = \mathcal{X}_0[0]\|\mathcal{X}_0[1]\|\cdots\|\mathcal{X}_0[31]$. The round function (cf. Figure 15 of the full version [17]) of WARP is composed of the following operations:

▷ 16 applications of the S-box S, which also is the same as the one in Midori, with outputs being $\mathcal{Z}_r[i] \triangleq S(\mathcal{X}_r[2 \cdot i])$, $0 \leqslant i \leqslant 15$;
▷ 16 XOR operations, with outputs being $\mathcal{W}_r[i] \triangleq \mathcal{Z}_r[i] \oplus \mathcal{K}_{r \bmod 2}[i]$, $0 \leqslant i \leqslant 15$;
▷ 16 XOR operations, with outputs being $\mathcal{Y}_r[2 \cdot i + 1] \triangleq \mathcal{W}_r[i] \oplus \mathcal{X}_r[2 \cdot i + 1]$, $0 \leqslant i \leqslant 15$;
▷ two XOR operations, with outputs being $\mathcal{Y}_r[2 \cdot i + 1] \leftarrow \mathcal{Y}_r[2 \cdot i + 1] \oplus RC_r[i]$, where $RC_r[i]$'s are constants and $i \in \{0, 1\}$;
▷ a permutation π, which is listed in the following, applied to 32 nibbles $\mathcal{Y}_r[0]$, $\mathcal{Y}_r[1]$, ..., $\mathcal{Y}_r[31]$, where $\mathcal{Y}_r[2 \cdot i] \triangleq \mathcal{X}_r[2 \cdot i]$ for all $0 \leqslant i \leqslant 15$, with outputs being $\mathcal{X}_{r+1}[\pi(j)] = \mathcal{Y}_r[j]$ for all $0 \leqslant j \leqslant 31$.

j	0	1	2	3	4	5	6	7	8	9	10	11	12	13	14	15
$\pi(j)$	31	6	29	14	1	12	21	8	27	2	3	0	25	4	23	10
j	16	17	18	19	20	21	22	23	24	25	26	27	28	29	30	31
$\pi(j)$	15	22	13	30	17	28	5	24	11	18	19	16	9	20	7	26

The round function is iterated 41 times from $r = 0$ to 40, and the nibble shuffle operation π is skipped in the last round.

2.3 Differential Attacks with High-Probability Characteristics

Differential cryptanalysis [4] studies how an input difference propagates through the cipher. For the iterated cipher, a *differential characteristic* describes not only the input and output differences but also the internal differences after every round function. The *right pair* for the given differential characteristic should fulfil all differences defined in the characteristic. The proportion of right pairs to all pairs validating the input difference is the *differential probability* of the characteristic. In contrast to differential characteristics, a *differential* only clarifies the input and output differences and should comprise all differential characteristics with input and output differences identical to those of the differential.

The first step in the differential attack is to find differential distinguishers with relatively high probabilities. In theory [12], the distinguisher should be differentials. However, searching for all characteristics and evaluating the differential probability of the differential are not manageable tasks in most cases. Hence, a standard measure is finding some dominating characteristics with significant differential probabilities and employing the sum of these probabilities to approximate the probability of the differential.

As in Fig. 2(a), after constructing a round-reduced differential distinguisher, the general key-recovery attack implements the following procedures.

1. Appending several rounds before and after the distinguisher.
2. Collecting multiple pairs of plaintexts with specific differences.
3. Enumerating subkeys involved in partial encryption and decryption phases.
4. Performing the statistical hypothesis testing to sieve subkey candidates.
5. Testing the surviving key candidates with plaintext-ciphertext pairs.

It can be noticed that the general method only exploits the input and output differences of the distinguisher. However, as illustrated in previous literature [5,7,16], given right pairs satisfying the known differential characteristic, more messages about the right pair can be inferred from the internal differences and can be employed to launch more efficient attacks. The differential attacks in this paper are based on this observation.

We start with the discussion on the S-box. Given a possible differential propagation $\delta_i \to \delta_o$ for the S-box S, we can calculate all right pairs validating this propagation. Denote $\mathbb{I}_S(\delta_i, \delta_o)$ (resp., $\mathbb{O}_S(\delta_i, \delta_o)$) the set of input (resp., output) values of right pairs. As an instance, for the S-box of CRAFT and WARP, we have $\mathbb{I}_S(\text{0x5}, \text{0x7}) = \{\text{0x0}, \text{0x5}, \text{0xa}, \text{0xf}\}$ and $\mathbb{O}_S(\text{0x5}, \text{0x7}) = \{\text{0x1}, \text{0x6}, \text{0xb}, \text{0xc}\}$. The right pairs for other possible propagations can be found in Appendix A of the full version [17].

The main idea of the differential attack in this work is shown in Fig. 2(b). Firstly, we search for a differential characteristic with a high probability p and confirm that the differential containing this characteristic does not have other significant characteristics with a probability greater than p. Then, $\mathcal{O}(p^{-1})$ random pairs are queried to find right pairs for the differential characteristic. Suppose that the characteristic activates an S-box with propagation $\delta_i \to \delta_o$ in a particular round; the values of the right pair at the input and output of the active S-box are known. Based on this message, we perform subkey enumeration inside the differential distinguisher and check whether the values of the right pair at the input of the active S-box fall into the set $\mathbb{I}_S(\delta_i, \delta_o)$. The key guess will be accepted if the condition is met by each right pair. Additionally, if more than one active S-box exists in the differential characteristic, this procedure can be done concerning other active S-boxes (cf. Fig. 2(c)).

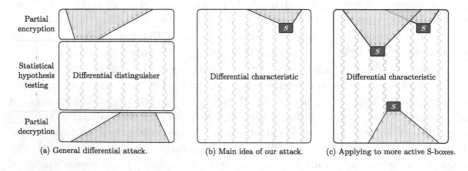

(a) General differential attack.   (b) Main idea of our attack.   (c) Applying to more active S-boxes.

Fig. 2. Methods to implementing differential attacks.

3   Practical Related-Key Differential Attack on CRAFT

In this section, we first check the differential properties of CRAFT in the related-key and related-tweakey settings. After that, a practical key-recovery attack on CRAFT is introduced.

3.1   Related-(Twea)Key Differential Properties of CRAFT

In [8], the authors created several iterative 2-round related-key differential characteristics for CRAFT. These 2-round characteristics were used to construct 28-round differential characteristics with probability 2^{-28}, which enable the authors to realise the full-round attack. However, if only one characteristic is utilised, the time complexity is 2^{85}, and the attack is unrealistic. Given the extremely high probability of the distinguisher, we wonder about the possibility of implementing a practical key-recovery attack on CRAFT.

Table 2. Upper bounds on differential probabilities of CRAFT in RK and RTK settings.

Round	1	2	3	4	5	6	7	8	9	10	11
$-\log_2(P_{RK}(r))$	0	0	2	4	4	6	6	8	8	10	10
$-\log_2(P_{RTK}(r))$	0	0	0	2	4	4	6	8	8	8	10
Round	12	13	14	15	16	17	18	19	20	21	22
$-\log_2(P_{RK}(r))$	12	12	14	14	16	16	18	18	20	20	22
$-\log_2(P_{RTK}(r))$	12	12	12	14	16	16	16	18	20	20	20
Round	23	24	25	26	27	28	29	30	31	32	-
$-\log_2(P_{RK}(r))$	22	24	24	26	26	28	28	30	30	30	-
$-\log_2(P_{RTK}(r))$	22	24	24	24	26	28	28	28	30	30	-

$P_{RK}(r)$ is the maximum differential probability for r-round characteristics in the RK setting.
$P_{RTK}(r)$ is the maximum differential probability for r-round characteristics in the RTK setting.

Motivated by this issue, we first search for the complete upper bounds on the differential probability of CRAFT in the related-key (RK) and related-tweakey (RTK) settings. The automatic searching method in [16] is applied, and the test results are listed in Table 2. Note that there are full-round differential characteristics with probability 2^{-30} in both settings. Then, we adopt the approach in [16] to find out all full-round differential characteristics in the two settings.

In the RK setting, 384 full-round differential characteristics are returned and can be divided into sixteen groups, denoted as $\mathbb{G}_0^{RK}$, $\mathbb{G}_1^{RK}$, ..., and $\mathbb{G}_{15}^{RK}$. Each group is composed of 24 characteristics, and all characteristics in the same group follow the same differential pattern. Note that all of the sixteen full-round differential patterns are iterative. The differential pattern in $\mathbb{G}_7^{RK}$ is illustrated in Fig. 3, where δ_i and δ_o are nonzero differences, and $\delta_i \to \delta_o$ should be a possible differential propagation for the S-box with probability 2^{-2}. The remaining

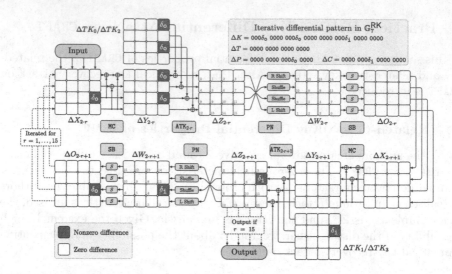

Fig. 3. Iterative differential pattern exploited in $\mathbb{G}_7^{\mathsf{RK}}$. We omit the $\mathtt{ARC}_r$ operation.

fifteen differential patterns can be found in the Supplementary Material[1]. These results are in accordance with the analysis in [8].

In the RTK setting, we obtain 7680 32-round differential characteristics. These characteristics can be partitioned into 28 groups, and we use $\mathbb{G}_0^{\mathsf{RTK}}$, $\mathbb{G}_1^{\mathsf{RTK}}$, ..., $\mathbb{G}_{27}^{\mathsf{RTK}}$ to represent them. All characteristics in the same group share the same differential pattern. Each of the first sixteen groups $\mathbb{G}_0^{\mathsf{RTK}}$, $\mathbb{G}_1^{\mathsf{RTK}}$, ..., $\mathbb{G}_{15}^{\mathsf{RTK}}$ is composed of 384 differential characteristics, and all of the 6144 differential characteristics are generated with 2-round iterative characteristics. As an illustration, the differential pattern in $\mathbb{G}_7^{\mathsf{RTK}}$ is provided in Figure 9 of the full version [17]. The remaining fifteen differential patterns can be found in the Supplementary Material. It can be noticed that for all $0 \leqslant i \leqslant 15$, the differential pattern in $\mathbb{G}_i^{\mathsf{RK}}$ corresponds to the special case of the differential pattern in $\mathbb{G}_i^{\mathsf{RTK}}$, where the tweak has no difference. In each of the remaining twelve groups $\mathbb{G}_{16}^{\mathsf{RTK}}$, $\mathbb{G}_{17}^{\mathsf{RTK}}$, ..., $\mathbb{G}_{27}^{\mathsf{RTK}}$, there are 128 characteristics. These differential characteristics also utilise iterative structures, while the number of iterative rounds is four. Figure 10 of the full version [17] exhibits the differential pattern in $\mathbb{G}_{16}^{\mathsf{RTK}}$. The differential patterns in $\mathbb{G}_{17}^{\mathsf{RTK}}$, $\mathbb{G}_{18}^{\mathsf{RTK}}$, ..., $\mathbb{G}_{27}^{\mathsf{RTK}}$ are given in Supplementary Material. As far as we know, we are the first to give the differential characteristic in the RTK setting.

3.2 Practical Key-Recovery Attack on CRAFT

Now, we aim at a practical key-recovery attack with one differential characteristic in the RK setting. The differential characteristics operated in the following

---

[1] https://github.com/SunLing134340/CRAFT-and-WARP.

discussion belongs to $\mathbb{G}_7^{\mathsf{RK}}$, and we fix $\delta_i = \mathtt{0x5}$ and $\delta_o = \mathtt{0x7}$. With the automatic method [16], we verify that there is no characteristic with a probability larger than 2^{-55} in the same differential apart from the optimal characteristic with probability 2^{-30}.

To facilitate the key-recovery attack, we first query N random pairs of plaintexts (P, P') validating $P \oplus P' = \Delta P = \mathtt{0x0000\ 0x0000\ 0x0007\ 0x0000}$. On average, $N_R = N \cdot 2^{-30}$ right pairs can be identified. So, the data requirement of the attack is $2 \cdot N$ chosen plaintexts. After obtaining right pairs, we execute the subsequent procedures to recover the values of the pair (K, K'). In the following, we use T to denote the tweak. The pair of tweakeys are represented with (TK_0, TK_1, TK_2, TK_3) and $(TK_0', TK_1', TK_2', TK_3')$. Note that the value of T is known in the attack. Once the j-th nibble of TK_i is recovered, the value of $K_{i \bmod 2}[j]$ can be computed with $TK_i[j]$ and T.

Step 1: recovering partial keys in the first two rounds. Note that the right pair must follow the differential characteristic in Fig. 3. Since the unique active S-box in the second round propagates the input difference δ_i to the output difference δ_o, the values of the right pair at $W_1[11]$ should fall into the set $\mathbb{I}_S(\delta_i, \delta_o)$. These known values enable us to recover the values of three nibbles of $TK_0 \| TK_1$.

An illustration of this step can be found in Fig. 4. To check the value at $W_1[11]$, we enumerate the value of the 12-bit tweakey $TK_0[0, 11] \| TK_1[7]$. With the known information on the related-tweakey, the values of $TK_0'[0] = TK_0[0]$, $TK_0'[11] = TK_0[11] \oplus \delta_o$, and $TK_1'[7] = TK_1[7] \oplus \delta_i$ are obtained. For each right pair (P, P'), partial encryption is performed, and we check whether $W_1[11]$ and $W_1'[11]$ belong to the set $\mathbb{I}_S(\delta_i, \delta_o)$. The guess for the tweakey will be accepted as a candidate if the verification is passed for all right pairs.

Observing the differential characteristic (cf. Fig. 3), we find that the two predictions $W_1[11] \in \mathbb{I}_S(\delta_i, \delta_o)$ and $W_1'[11] \in \mathbb{I}_S(\delta_i, \delta_o)$ should be true or false simultaneously. Since the propagation $\delta_i \to \delta_o$ holds with probability 2^{-2}, the set $\mathbb{I}_S(\delta_i, \delta_o)$ contains four elements. So, given the right pair, the probability that the random guess for the tweakey validates $W_1[11] \in \mathbb{I}_S(\delta_i, \delta_o)$ is 2^{-2}. Accordingly, on average, we can get the correct value for the tweakey with $N_1 = 6$ right pairs. With the value of T, we retrieve the value of the 12-bit key $K_0[0, 11] \| K_1[7]$.

Step 2: recovering partial keys in the last two rounds. After investigating the active S-box in the second round, we move to the active S-box in the 29-th round. From Fig. 3, the unique active S-box in the 29-th round follows the propagation $\delta_i \to \delta_o$. Therefore, the values of the right pair at $O_{29}[11] = X_{30}[11]$ should belong to the set $\mathbb{O}_S(\delta_i, \delta_o)$. Figure 5 of the full version [17] displays the key-recovery procedure in the last two rounds. Note that the value of $TK_2[0, 11] \| TK_3[7]$ can be derived from the result in the first step, and we only need to enumerate the value of the 4-bit tweakey $TK_3[15]$. For each right pair (P, P'), we check the validity of the condition $X_{30}[11]/X_{30}'[11] \in \mathbb{O}_S(\delta_i, \delta_o)$. The guess for the tweakey will be saved as a candidate if the verification is passed for all right pairs. The correct tweakey guess can be identified with $N_2 = 2$ right

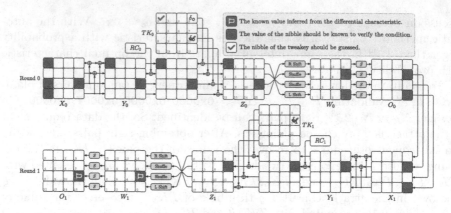

Fig. 4. The first step of the attack on CRAFT.

pairs based on a similar analysis as the first step, After that, the value of $K_1[15]$ can be computed with the known tweak T.

Step 3: recovering partial keys in the first four rounds. In this step, we go back to the head of the cipher and implement key-recovery regarding the first four rounds. The study centres on the known value of $W_3[11]$, and Figure 11 of the full version [17] shows the key-recovery procedure. With the previous analysis, the value of $TK_0[0, 11]\|TK_1[7, 15]\|TK_2[0, 11]\|TK_3[7, 15]$ is known. We enumerate the value of the 28-bit tweakey $TK_0[2, 3, 5, 8, 12]\|TK_1[1, 6]$ and check whether each right pair (P, P') fulfils the condition $W_3[11] \in \mathbb{I}_S(\delta_i, \delta_o)$. On average, with $N_3 = 14$ right pairs, we uncover the correct guess of the tweakey. Then, the value of $K_0[2, 3, 5, 8, 12]\|K_1[1, 6]$ can be recovered.

Step 4: recovering partial keys in the last four rounds. To control the time complexity of the attack, we focus on the tail of the cipher in this step. As shown in Figure 12 of the full version [17], the analysis is based on the known values of the right pair at $O_{27}[11] = X_{28}[11]$. The values of $TK_0[0, 2, 3, 5, 8, 11, 12]$, $TK_1[1, 6, 7, 15]$, $TK_2[0, 2, 3, 5, 8, 11, 12]$, and $TK_3[1, 6, 7, 15]$ are known, and we enumerate the value of the 12-bit tweakey $TK_3[9, 13, 14]$ and check the validity of the condition $X_{28}[11] \in \mathbb{O}_S(\delta_i, \delta_o)$ for each right pair. The correct guess of the tweakey can be found with approximately $N_4 = 6$ right pairs. Following that, we calculate the value of $K_1[9, 13, 14]$.

Step 5: recovering partial keys in the last six rounds. In this step, we still pay attention to the tail of the cipher and manipulate the known values of the right pair at $O_{25}[11] = X_{26}[11]$. To keep the key-recovery attack practical, we interchange the order of $\mathtt{ATK}_r$ operation and $\mathtt{ARC}_r \circ \mathtt{MC}$ operation for $r \geqslant 30$. Correspondingly, the tweakey involved in $\mathtt{ATK}_r$ operation is replaced from $TK_{r \bmod 4}$ to $ETK_{r \bmod 4} \triangleq M(TK_{r \bmod 4})$ so that the correctness of the encryption can be guaranteed.

The key-recovery procedure can be found in Figure 13 of the full version [17]. Note that the value of $TK_2[0,2,3,5,8,11,12]\|TK_3[1,6,7,9,13\text{-}15]$ is known. By the equation between $TK_{r\bmod 4}$ and $ETK_{r\bmod 4}$, we derive the value of $ETK_2[0,8,11,12]\|ETK_3[1,6,7,9,13\text{-}15]$

$$ETK_2[0] = TK_2[0] \oplus TK_2[8] \oplus TK_2[12],$$
$$ETK_2[j] = TK_2[j] \text{ for } j \in \{8,11,12\},$$
$$ETK_3[1] = TK_3[1] \oplus TK_3[9] \oplus TK_3[13],$$
$$ETK_3[j] = TK_3[j] \oplus TK_3[j+8] \text{ for } j \in \{6,7\},$$
$$ETK_3[j] = TK_3[j] \text{ for } j \in \{9,13,14,15\}.$$

In order to compute the value of $X_{26}[11]$, we should guess the value of the 28-bit tweakey $ETK_2[2,3,5]\|ETK_3[0,2\text{-}4]$. If the condition $X_{26}[11] \in \mathbb{O}_S(\delta_i,\delta_o)$ holds by each right pair, the guess for the tweakey will be accepted as a candidate. Therefore, with about $N_5 = 14$ right pairs, we recognise the correct guess. Based on the retrieved value of $ETK_2[3,5]$, the value of $TK_2[13] = TK_2[5] \oplus ETK_2[5]$ and $TK_2[15] = TK_2[3] \oplus TK_2[11] \oplus ETK_2[3]$ can be determined. Consequently, we recover the value of $K_0[13,15]$. Beyond that, with the value of $ETK_2[2]\|ETK_3[0,2\text{-}4]$, we develop the following 20-bit information about the unknown value of the tweakey

$$TK_2[10] \oplus TK_2[14] = TK_2[2] \oplus ETK_2[2],$$
$$TK_3[0] \oplus TK_3[8] \oplus TK_3[12] = ETK_3[0],$$
$$TK_3[2] \oplus TK_3[10] = TK_3[14] \oplus ETK_3[2],$$
$$TK_3[3] \oplus TK_3[11] = TK_3[15] \oplus ETK_3[3],$$
$$TK_3[4] \oplus TK_3[12] = ETK_3[4].$$

These messages allow us to guess fewer bits in the next step.

Step 6: recovering partial keys in the first six rounds. In this step, we go back to the head of the cipher and utilise the known values of the right pairs at $W_5[11]$. The key-recovery procedure is exhibited in Figure 14 of the full version. For now, we know the value of $K_0[0,2,3,5,8,11\text{-}13,15]\|K_1[1,6,7,9,13\text{-}15]$. To compute the value of $W_5[11]$, we enumerate the value of the 36-bit tweakey $TK_0[1,4,6,7,10]\|TK_1[0,2\text{-}4]$. As the value of $TK_2[10] \oplus TK_2[14]$ is uncovered in the fifth step, the value of $TK_0[14]$ is determined after guessing the value of $TK_0[10]$. Then, for each right pair, we inspect the validity of the condition $W_5[11] \in \mathbb{I}_S(\delta_i,\delta_o)$. On average, with $N_6 = 18$ right pairs, we can locate the correct guess of the tweakey. After that, we get the value of the 40-bit key $K_0[1,4,6,7,10,14]\|K_1[0,2\text{-}4]$.

Step 7: exhaustively searching for the remaining keys. After executing the preceding steps, the value of the 8-bit key $K_0[9]\|K_1[5]$ is unexplored. We exhaustively search for the value of $K_0[9]\|K_1[5]$ with $N_7 = 1$ right pair.

Theoretical Complexity Analysis. To ensure the success of each step, the number of right pairs for this attack should be no less than $N_R = \max\{N_i \mid 0 \leqslant i \leqslant 7\} = 18$. Accordingly, the data complexity of this attack is about $2 \cdot 18 \cdot 2^{30} \approx 2^{35.17}$ chosen plaintexts. The time complexity T_1 to collect plaintext-ciphertext pairs is about $2^{35.17}$ full-round encryptions. Apart from that, the time complexity T_2 of the sixth step dominates the key-recovery phase. Once the verification condition $W_5[11] \in \mathbb{I}_S(\delta_i, \delta_o)$ is not passed for at least one right pair, the tweakey guess is dropped. Therefore, T_2 is bounded by $2 \cdot \sum\limits_{i=0}^{17} 2^{36-2 \cdot i}$ 6-round encryptions. Approximately, we have $T_2 = 2^{35}$ full-round encryptions. Overall, the time complexity of this attack is $2^{36.09}$. The memory complexity of this attack is negligible.

Practical Runtime. Since the complexity of the attack is practical, we try to confirm the attack in practise. All tests are realised on one AMD EPYC 7302 16-Core Processor, and all programs use a single thread. To begin with, we fix $K\|T$ with the following randomly selected values

$$K = \text{0x6c6b 0xd022 0x4dc5 0x65e3 0x1d4d 0x5753 0xa30f 0xa6d8},$$
$$T = \text{0x08a2 0x3a1b 0x40f6 0x376f}.$$

With 2^{35} randomly generated pairs of chosen plaintexts, we collect 49 right pairs for the full-round differential characteristic in $\mathbb{G}_7^{\text{RK}}$ with $\delta_i = \text{0x5}$ and $\delta_o = \text{0x7}$. The runtime for this approach is about 9.2 h. Although we find more than $N_R = 18$ right pairs, only 18 right pairs are employed in the subsequent tests. The output and the runtime for the seven steps are listed in Table 3. It can be noticed that we cannot determine the unique correct candidate in some steps. We think the reason is that the tweakey is XORed before the S-box operation sometimes. In this case, if the input set $\mathbb{I}_S(\delta_i, \delta_o)$ is taken in the verification condition, more than one tweakey candidate can validate the condition. The good thing is that the auxiliary candidates are sieved in the following steps. At last, we catch the unique correct key. To sum up, the practical time complexity of the attack is about 15.69 h. All source codes can be found in the Supplementary Material.

Table 3. Test results about `CRAFT`.

Step	1	2	3	4	5	6	7	Total
Runtime	0.001 s	0.001 s	189.30 s	0.001 s	0.39 h	6.05 h	0.001 s	6.49 h
#{Candidates}	4	4	1	16	1	1	1	1

#{Candidates} is the number of tweakey candidates after conducting each step.

Remark 1. Although we specify $\delta_i = \text{0x5}$ and $\delta_o = \text{0x7}$ in the attack, each of the remaining 23 characteristics in $\mathbb{G}_7^{\text{RK}}$ can facilitate a practical key-recovery attack in RK setting.

Remark 2. We also try characteristics in $\mathbb{G}_i^{RK}$ with $i \neq 7$ and find that the time complexity might be impractical with characteristics in $\mathbb{G}_0^{RK}$, $\mathbb{G}_1^{RK}$, $\mathbb{G}_2^{RK}$, $\mathbb{G}_3^{RK}$, $\mathbb{G}_{12}^{RK}$, $\mathbb{G}_{13}^{RK}$, $\mathbb{G}_{14}^{RK}$, and $\mathbb{G}_{15}^{RK}$.

4   Related-Key Differential Attack on WARP

After realising the practical related-key differential attack on CRAFT, we are curious about the differential property of WARP in the related-key attack setting since it applies the same S-box as CRAFT.

4.1   Related-Key Differential Property of WARP

Table 4. Upper bounds on differential probabilities of WARP in the RK setting.

Round	1	2	3	4	5	6	7	8	9	10	11
$-\log_2(P_{RK}(r))$	0	0	0	2	4	6	6	8	8	10	10
Round	12	13	14	15	16	17	18	19	20	21	22
$-\log_2(P_{RK}(r))$	12	12	14	14	16	16	18	18	20	20	22
Round	23	24	25	26	27	28	29	30	31	32	33
$-\log_2(P_{RK}(r))$	22	24	24	26	26	28	28	30	30	32	32
Round	34	35	36	37	38	39	40	41	–	–	–
$-\log_2(P_{RK}(r))$	34	34	36	36	38	38	40	40	–	–	–

$P_{RK}(r)$ is the maximum differential probability for r-round characteristics in the RK setting.

We exploit the automatic searching method in [16] to explore the optimal related-key differential characteristics for WARP, and Table 4 presents the test result. Similarly to the case in CRAFT, there is a full-round related-key differential characteristic with a high probability, say 2^{-40}. With a further study, we discover 384 41-round differential characteristics with a probability of 2^{-40} in the RK setting. These characteristics can be divided into sixteen groups, which are denoted as $\mathbb{G}_0^{WARP}$, $\mathbb{G}_1^{WARP}$, ..., and $\mathbb{G}_{15}^{WARP}$. Each group consists of 24 characteristics, and all characteristics in the same group follow the same differential pattern. All of the sixteen full-round differential patterns are iterative. The differential pattern in $\mathbb{G}_6^{WARP}$ is demonstrated in Fig. 5, where δ_i and δ_o are nonzero differences, and $\delta_i \rightarrow \delta_o$ should be a possible differential propagation for the S-box with probability 2^{-2}. The remaining fifteen differential patterns can be found in the Supplementary Material.

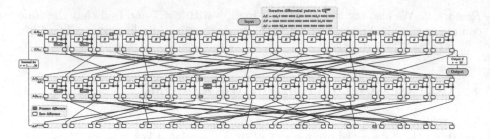

Fig. 5. Iterative differential pattern used in $\mathbb{G}_6^{\text{WARP}}$

4.2   Key-Recovery Attack on WARP

Now, we discuss the key-recovery attack on the full-round WARP with one characteristic in the RK setting. The differential characteristic belongs to $\mathbb{G}_6^{\text{WARP}}$, and we fix $\delta_i^{\text{WARP}} = \texttt{0xa}$ and $\delta_o^{\text{WARP}} = \texttt{0x5}$. With the automatic method, we confirm that there is no characteristic with a probability higher than 2^{-70} in the same differential apart from the optimal characteristic with probability 2^{-40}.

To implement the key-recovery attack, we first query N^{WARP} random pairs of plaintexts $(\mathcal{P}, \mathcal{P}')$ with

$$\mathcal{P} \oplus \mathcal{P}' = \texttt{0x0000 0x0000 0x0000 0x0000 0x0000 0x0000 0x0a00 0x0000}.$$

Approximately $N_R^{\text{WARP}} = N^{\text{WARP}} \cdot 2^{-40}$ right pairs can be obtained. Thus, the data complexity of the attack is $2 \cdot N^{\text{WARP}}$ chosen plaintexts. After collecting right pairs, we conduct the following steps to retrieve the values of the pair $(\mathcal{K}, \mathcal{K}')$.

Step 1: recovering partial keys in the first three rounds. The right pair must follow the differential characteristic in Fig. 5. As the unique active S-box in the fourth round propagates the input difference δ_i^{WARP} to the output difference δ_o^{WARP}, the values of the right pair at $\mathcal{X}_3[12]$ should fall into the set $\mathbb{I}_S(\delta_i^{\text{WARP}}, \delta_o^{\text{WARP}})$. These known values enable us to recover the values of three nibbles in $\mathcal{K} = \mathcal{K}_0 \| \mathcal{K}_1$. The key-recovery procedure of this step is illustrated in Fig. 6. To compute the value at $\mathcal{X}_3[12]$, we guess the value of the 12-bit key $\mathcal{K}_0[2,8] \| \mathcal{K}_1[6]$. For each right pair $(\mathcal{P}, \mathcal{P}')$, we check whether $\mathcal{X}_3[12]$ belongs to the set $\mathbb{I}_S(\delta_i^{\text{WARP}}, \delta_o^{\text{WARP}})$. The key guess will be accepted as a candidate if all right pairs pass the verification. On average, with $N_1^{\text{WARP}} = 6$ right pairs, we find the correct guess for the key.

Step 2: recovering partial keys in the last three rounds. This step concentrates on the tail of the cipher. From Fig. 5, the values of the right pair at $\mathcal{X}_{38}[25]$ should fall into the set $\mathbb{I}_S(\delta_i^{\text{WARP}}, \delta_o^{\text{WARP}})$. Based on this observation, the key-recovery procedure in the last three rounds is demonstrated in Figure 16 of the full version [17]. We enumerate the value of the 16-bit key $\mathcal{K}_0[1,6,12] \| \mathcal{K}_1[5]$ and check whether the condition $\mathcal{X}_{38}[25] \in \mathbb{I}_S(\delta_i^{\text{WARP}}, \delta_o^{\text{WARP}})$ is satisfied by all right pairs. The correct key guess can be identified with roughly $N_2^{\text{WARP}} = 8$ right pairs.

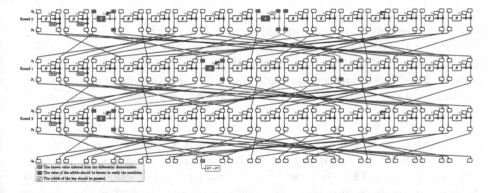

Fig. 6. The first step of the related-key attack on WARP.

Step 3: recovering partial keys in the first five rounds. After recovering partial keys in the last three rounds, we go back to the head of the cipher and implement key-recovery in the first five rounds. The enumeration is based on known values of the right pair at $\mathcal{X}_5[12]$, and the attack procedure is illustrated in Figure 17 of the full version [17]. We guess the value of the 20-bit key $\mathcal{K}_0[11, 14, 15]\|\mathcal{K}_1[12, 13]$ and check whether each right pair fulfils the condition $\mathcal{X}_5[12] \in \mathbb{I}_S(\delta_i^{\text{WARP}}, \delta_o^{\text{WARP}})$. With $N_3^{\text{WARP}} = 10$ right pairs, we uncover the correct guess for the key.

Step 4: recovering partial keys in the last five rounds. Again, we move to the tail of the cipher, and the analysis is centred on the known values of the right pair at $\mathcal{X}_{36}[25]$. Figure 18 of the full version [17] exhibits the key-recovery procedure. The value of the 24-bit key $\mathcal{K}_0[0, 3\text{-}5]\|\mathcal{K}_1[14, 15]$ is enumerated, and we inspect the validity of the condition $\mathcal{X}_{36}[25] \in \mathbb{I}_S(\delta_i^{\text{WARP}}, \delta_o^{\text{WARP}})$ for each right pair. The correct guess for the key can be identified with about $N_4^{\text{WARP}} = 12$ right pairs.

Step 5: recovering partial keys in the first seven rounds. In this step, we go back to the head of the cipher and exploit the known values of the right pair at $\mathcal{X}_7[12]$. The key-recovery procedure is shown in Figure 19 of the full version [17]. We guess the value of the 24-bit key $\mathcal{K}_0[13]\|\mathcal{K}_1[2, 3, 8\text{-}10]$ and check the validity of the condition $\mathcal{X}_7[12] \in \mathbb{I}_S(\delta_i^{\text{WARP}}, \delta_o^{\text{WARP}})$ for each right pair. The correct key guess can be identified with about $N_5^{\text{WARP}} = 12$ right pairs.

Step 6: recovering partial keys in the last seven rounds. This step focuses on the tail of the cipher. The analysis relies on known values of the right pair at $\mathcal{X}_{34}[25]$, and the key-recovery procedure is shown in Figure 20 of the full version [17]. We guess the value of the 16-bit key $\mathcal{K}_0[7, 9, 10]\|\mathcal{K}_1[1]$ and verify the condition $\mathcal{X}_{34}[25] \in \mathbb{I}_S(\delta_i^{\text{WARP}}, \delta_o^{\text{WARP}})$ for each right pair. The correct key guess can be obtained with about $N_6^{\text{WARP}} = 8$ right pairs.

Step 7: exhaustively searching for the remaining keys. After performing the previous six steps, the value of the 16-bit key $\mathcal{K}_1[0, 4, 7, 11]$ is unexplored. We exhaustively search for the value of $\mathcal{K}_1[0, 4, 7, 11]$ with $N_7^{\text{WARP}} = 1$ right pair.

Theoretical Complexity Analysis. To facilitate the analysis of each step, the number of right pairs for this attack should be no less than $N_R^{\text{WARP}} = \max\{N_i^{\text{WARP}} \mid 0 \leqslant i \leqslant 7\} = 12$. Hence, the data complexity of this attack is about $2 \cdot 12 \cdot 2^{40} \approx 2^{44.58}$ chosen plaintexts. The time complexity T_1^{WARP} to gather plaintext-ciphertext pairs is about $2^{44.58}$ full-round encryptions. Since T_1^{WARP} dominates the whole attack, the time complexity of the attack is $2^{44.58}$. The memory complexity of this attack is negligible.

Experimental Runtime for the Round-Reduced Attack. Since the complexity of the full-round attack is impractical, we try to launch an attack on a round-reduced version of WARP. We consider a 27-round version of WARP and note that the previous analyses also hold. The platform to run the test is the same as CRAFT. To begin with, we set $\mathcal{K}$ with the following randomly picked value

$$\mathcal{K} = \texttt{0x3b09 0xfaab 0x8d77 0xf7f1 0x0fa4 0xd8f6 0x91f7 0x6f1e}.$$

As the probability of the 27-round differential characteristic is 2^{-26}, we generate 2^{31} pairs of chosen plaintexts randomly and get 32 right pairs. The runtime for this approach is about 2.02 h. Due to the relatively weak diffusion of the Feistel structure, we find that using $N_R^{\text{WARP}} = 12$ right pairs will raise the number of surviving key candidates in the test. Thus, we use 17 right pairs to complete the test. The output and the runtime for the seven steps are listed in Table 5. Although the number of remaining candidates exceeds the expected value in several steps, the unique correct key can be recovered after performing the seven steps. All source codes can be found in the Supplementary Material.

Table 5. Test results about WARP.

Step	1	2	3	4	5	6	7	Total
Runtime	0.004 s	0.28 s	0.22 h	16.77 h	27.51 h	0.14 s	0.34 s	44.50 h
#{Candidates}	16	1024	4096	4096	4	4	1	1

#{Candidates} is the number of tweakey candidates after conducting each step.

Remark 3. A discussion on the performances of characteristics in other groups can be found in the full version [17].

5   Multiple Zero-Correlation Linear Attack on WARP

When analysing the security of WARP, we notice that the designers expected that the longest attack on the cipher in the single-key attack setting does not exceed 32 rounds. In this section, we propose a 33-round multiple zero-correlation linear attack, and it is the longest attack on WARP as far as we know. A brief review of multiple zero-correlation linear attack can be found in the full version [17].

5.1   21-Round Zero-Correlation Linear Approximations

The automatic method in [6,14,15] is utilised to search for zero-correlation linear approximations. We evaluate the search space such that both the input and output masks activate only one nibble. As a result, we find that the longest zero-correlation linear approximation covers 21 rounds. The thirty 21-round zero-correlation linear approximations returned by the solver can be partitioned into two groups. The first group is composed of 15 approximations

$$0x0000 \ 0x0000 \ 0x0000 \ 0x00\Gamma_i 0 \ 0x0000 \ 0x0000 \ 0x0000 \ 0x0000$$

$$\xrightarrow{21\text{-round}} 0x0000 \ 0x0000 \ 0x0000 \ 0x0000 \ 0x0000 \ 0x0000 \ 0x0000 \ 0x000\Gamma_o,$$

where Γ_i and Γ_o are nonzero nibbles meeting $\Gamma_i = \Gamma_o$. The approximations in the second group are

$$0x0000 \ 0x0000 \ 0x0000 \ 0x0000 \ 0x0000 \ 0x0000 \ 0x0000 \ 0x00\Gamma_i 0$$

$$\xrightarrow{21\text{-round}} 0x0000 \ 0x0000 \ 0x0000 \ 0x000\Gamma_o \ 0x0000 \ 0x0000 \ 0x0000 \ 0x0000.$$

We manually verify the contradiction in the approximations, and the illustration can be found in the Supplementary Material.

5.2   33-Round Multiple Zero-Correlation Linear Attack on WARP

In this section, we propose a multiple zero-correlation linear attack on 33-round WARP. This attack exploits the first group of 21-round zero-correlation approximations in Sect. 5.1 from round 6 to 26. The key-recovery attack is illustrated in Figure 8 of the full version [17]. To control the time complexity of the attack, we equivalently move the XOR operations with the key in the r-th round to the $(r+1)$-th round for $0 \leqslant r \leqslant 5$. The tail of the distinguisher applies a similar strategy. The XOR operations with the key in the r'-th round are moved to the $(r'-1)$-th round for $27 \leqslant r' \leqslant 32$. N_Z plaintext-ciphertext pairs are required, and the detailed attack procedure is given in Appendix D of the full version [17].

Complexity Analysis. We set the advantage as $a = 1.00$ and the success probability P_S as 50.00%. We obtain the data requirement of the attack is $N_Z = 2^{97.71}$. The time complexity of the attack is composed of the time complexity in the key enumeration phase as in **Step 0–Step 17** and the time to check the remaining 36-bit key exhaustively. Thus, the total time complexity of the attack is $2^{127.01}$. Since the counter $C_0[z_0]$ constitutes the most significant memory, the memory complexity is roughly 2^{100}. Given that the time complexity achieves $2^{127.01}$, we claim that the success probability of the attack is 50.00%, and it cannot be improved by repeating the entire work as the time complexity will go beyond 2^{128}.

6   Conclusion

This paper first focuses on the security of CRAFT and WARP in the related-key attack setting. For full-round CRAFT, we present a practical key-recovery attack with only one differential characteristic, and the theoretical time complexity is $2^{36.09}$ encryptions. The practical test is conducted and indicates that the theoretical analysis is valid. A full-round key-recovery attack on WARP is proposed, and the time complexity is $2^{44.58}$ encryptions. The theoretical attack is implemented on a round-reduced version of WARP, which guarantees validity. Moreover, we give a 33-round multiple zero-correlation linear attack on WARP, which is the longest attack on the cipher in the single-key attack setting as far as we know.

Acknowledgements. The authors would like to thank the anonymous reviewers for their valuable comments and suggestions to improve the quality of the paper. The research leading to these results has received funding from the National Natural Science Foundation of China (Grant No. 62272273, Grant No. 62002201, Grant No. 62032014), the National Key Research and Development Program of China (Grant No. 2018YFA0704702), and the Major Basic Research Project of Natural Science Foundation of Shandong Province, China (Grant No. ZR202010220025). Ling Sun gratefully acknowledges the support by the Program of TaiShan Scholars Special Fund for young scholars.

References

1. Banik, S., et al.: WARP: revisiting GFN for lightweight 128-bit block cipher. In: Dunkelman, O., Jacobson, Jr., M.J., O'Flynn, C. (eds.) SAC 2020. LNCS, vol. 12804, pp. 535–564. Springer, Cham (2021). https://doi.org/10.1007/978-3-030-81652-0_21
2. Banik, S., et al.: Midori: a block cipher for low energy. In: Iwata, T., Cheon, J.H. (eds.) ASIACRYPT 2015. LNCS, vol. 9453, pp. 411–436. Springer, Heidelberg (2015). https://doi.org/10.1007/978-3-662-48800-3_17
3. Beierle, C., Leander, G., Moradi, A., Rasoolzadeh, S.: CRAFT: lightweight tweakable block cipher with efficient protection against DFA attacks. IACR Trans. Symmetric Cryptol. **2019**(1), 5–45 (2019). https://doi.org/10.13154/tosc.v2019.i1.5-45
4. Biham, E., Shamir, A.: Differential cryptanalysis of DES-like cryptosystems. In: Menezes, A.J., Vanstone, S.A. (eds.) CRYPTO 1990. LNCS, vol. 537, pp. 2–21. Springer, Heidelberg (1991). https://doi.org/10.1007/3-540-38424-3_1
5. Canteaut, A., Lambooij, E., Neves, S., Rasoolzadeh, S., Sasaki, Y., Stevens, M.: Refined probability of differential characteristics including dependency between multiple rounds. IACR Trans. Symmetric Cryptol. **2017**(2), 203–227 (2017). https://doi.org/10.13154/tosc.v2017.i2.203-227
6. Cui, T., Chen, S., Fu, K., Wang, M., Jia, K.: New automatic tool for finding impossible differentials and zero-correlation linear approximations. Sci. China Inf. Sci. **64**(2) (2021). https://doi.org/10.1007/s11432-018-1506-4
7. Daemen, J., Rijmen, V.: Plateau characteristics. IET Inf. Secur. **1**(1), 11–17 (2007). https://doi.org/10.1049/iet-ifs:20060099

8. ElSheikh, M., Youssef, A.M.: Related-key differential cryptanalysis of full round CRAFT. In: Bhasin, S., Mendelson, A., Nandi, M. (eds.) SPACE 2019. LNCS, vol. 11947, pp. 50–66. Springer, Cham (2019). https://doi.org/10.1007/978-3-030-35869-3_6
9. Hadipour, H., Eichlseder, M.: Integral cryptanalysis of WARP based on monomial prediction. IACR Trans. Symmetric Cryptol. **2022**(2), 92–112 (2022). https://doi.org/10.46586/tosc.v2022.i2.92-112
10. Kerckhoffs, A.: La cryptographie militaire. Journal des Sciences Militaires 5–38
11. Kumar, M., Yadav, T.: MILP based differential attack on round reduced WARP. In: Batina, L., Picek, S., Mondal, M. (eds.) SPACE 2021. LNCS, vol. 13162, pp. 42–59. Springer, Cham (2022). https://doi.org/10.1007/978-3-030-95085-9_3
12. Lai, X., Massey, J.L., Murphy, S.: Markov ciphers and differential cryptanalysis. In: Davies, D.W. (ed.) EUROCRYPT 1991. LNCS, vol. 547, pp. 17–38. Springer, Heidelberg (1991). https://doi.org/10.1007/3-540-46416-6_2
13. Lallemand, V., Minier, M., Rouquette, L.: Automatic search of rectangle attacks on Feistel ciphers: application to WARP. IACR Trans. Symmetric Cryptol. **2022**(2), 113–140 (2022). https://doi.org/10.46586/tosc.v2022.i2.113-140
14. Sasaki, Y., Todo, Y.: New impossible differential search tool from design and cryptanalysis aspects. IACR Cryptology ePrint Archive, p. 1181 (2016). http://eprint.iacr.org/2016/1181
15. Sasaki, Yu., Todo, Y.: New impossible differential search tool from design and cryptanalysis aspects. In: Coron, J.-S., Nielsen, J.B. (eds.) EUROCRYPT 2017. LNCS, vol. 10212, pp. 185–215. Springer, Cham (2017). https://doi.org/10.1007/978-3-319-56617-7_7
16. Sun, L., Wang, W., Wang, M.: More accurate differential properties of LED64 and Midori64. IACR Trans. Symmetric Cryptol. **2018**(3), 93–123 (2018). https://doi.org/10.13154/tosc.v2018.i3.93-123
17. Sun, L., Wang, W., Wang, M.: Key-recovery attacks on CRAFT and WARP (full version). Cryptology ePrint Archive, Paper 2022/997 (2022). https://eprint.iacr.org/2022/997
18. Teh, J.S., Biryukov, A.: Differential cryptanalysis of WARP. IACR Cryptology ePrint Archive, p. 1641 (2021). https://eprint.iacr.org/2021/1641
19. Zheng, Y., Matsumoto, T., Imai, H.: On the construction of block ciphers provably secure and not relying on any unproved hypotheses. In: Brassard, G. (ed.) CRYPTO 1989. LNCS, vol. 435, pp. 461–480. Springer, New York (1990). https://doi.org/10.1007/0-387-34805-0_42

Differential Analysis of the Ternary Hash Function Troika

Christina Boura, Margot Funk$^{(\boxtimes)}$, and Yann Rotella

Université Paris-Saclay, UVSQ, CNRS, Laboratoire de mathématiques de Versailles,
78000 Versailles, France
{christina.boura,margot.funk,yann.rotella}@uvsq.fr

Abstract. Troika is a sponge-based hash function designed by Kölbl, Tischhauser, Bogdanov and Derbez in 2019. Its specificity is that it is defined over $\mathbb{F}_3$ in order to be used inside IOTA's distributed ledger but could also serve in all settings requiring the generation of ternary randomness. To be used in practice, Troika needs to be proven secure against state-of-the-art cryptanalysis. However, there are today almost no analysis tools for ternary designs. In this article we take a step in this direction by analyzing the propagation of differential trails of Troika and by providing bounds on the weight of its trails. For this, we adapt a well-known framework for trail search designed for KECCAK and provide new advanced techniques to handle the search on $\mathbb{F}_3$. Our work demonstrates that providing analysis tools for non-binary designs is a highly non-trivial research direction that needs to be enhanced in order to better understand the real security offered by such non-conventional primitives.

Keywords: Differential cryptanalysis · Troika · Ternary design

1 Introduction

Almost all symmetric-key cryptographic schemes known today are defined over the binary field $\mathbb{F}_2$. However, recent advances in cryptology imply that ternary symmetric constructions could fit better in some particular contexts. A first notable example is a cryptocurrency and distributed ledger technology called IOTA. This platform is based on a ternary architecture and its security relied, among others, on the security of a ternary hash function. For this purpose, a hash function called Curl-P was designed for IOTA, but was soon after found to have devastating security issues [8]. Curl-P was then replaced by Kerl, another ternary hash function that could be seen as an adaptation of SHA-3 to $\mathbb{F}_3$. This adaptation was however not natural and led to a particularly inefficient design. For this reason, Kölbl, Tischhauser, Bogdanov and Derbez proposed in 2019 Troika [9], a ternary hash function claimed to be secure and efficient at the same time.

Even if the advantage of a ternary construction is not completely clear in the IOTA paradigm, ternary symmetric designs could be very meaningful in other

B. Smith and H. Wu (Eds.): SAC 2022, LNCS 13742, pp. 96–115, 2024.
https://doi.org/10.1007/978-3-031-58411-4_5

settings. For example, in a completely different context, Debris-Alazard, Sendrier and Tillich designed in 2019 Wave, a ternary code-based signature scheme [7]. While this scheme is asymmetric, it needs the generation of good quality ternary randomness. Troika would then be a natural candidate for this purpose, as hash functions are regularly used as random number generators.

In the last 30 years, cryptanalysis of traditional binary schemes has been extremely developed. On the other hand, almost nothing is known about the security of ternary symmetric schemes, starting from their resistance against very basic attacks as the differential one. In this article we propose to take a step into this direction by providing an enhanced analysis of the hash function Troika against differential cryptanalysis. The goal of our work is two-fold. First, we aim to provide the first third-party differential analysis against this function by giving concrete upper bounds on the probability of its differential trails. Second, we develop non-trivial techniques for searching differential bounds for ternary designs. We believe that our work can serve as a starting point for the analysis against differential cryptanalysis of ternary designs to come.

Our Contributions. Troika is a sponge-based construction whose round function has a design very similar to KECCAK. Searching for good differential trails for KECCAK is a very complex task due mainly to its large state and its weakly aligned inner components. Dedicated algorithms for generating all trails for KECCAK below a given weight, leading to upper bounds on the probability of differential trails for a certain number of rounds were developed in [5,10]. These articles were the starting point of our work. We adapted and extended them for the ternary case and applied them to Troika. This adaptation was not straightforward and we needed to develop advanced techniques to be able to compute on trits (i.e. elements of $\mathbb{F}_3$) in a reasonable time. Most of our improvements concern the tree traversal used to generate out-kernel 2-round trail cores. This applies to the computation of the so-called *runs*, a way to organize the differential patterns of a state. More precisely, we defined an equivalence class notion on the runs that permitted us to treat less trail cores and we improved a specific order relation such that fewer collisions between runs occur, leading to more efficient tree pruning. This permitted us to scan all trail cores up to weight 41 and to prove that there do not exist 6-round trails with weight lower than 82. In comparison, the designers of Troika were only able to provide results on smaller versions of Troika by using a SMT-based approach. Their approach could not apply to the original version of the function because of its large state.

Eventually, we show that adapting the existing tool from KECCAK to Troika is a highly nontrivial problem, even if the design strategy of both primitives is similar. This is mainly due to the fact that, contrary to the binary case, active trits can take two values (1 or 2), leading to a huge number of trails to treat. Thus, providing interesting bounds for Troika is not possible without introducing new ideas to prune the search tree efficiently. More generally, our work highlights that adapting existing tools and methods from $\mathbb{F}_2$ to $\mathbb{F}_3$ is a challenging task and indicates that more research efforts are needed towards this direction.

The rest of the article is organized as follows. In Sect. 2 we recall classical notions regarding differential trail search on symmetric primitives. Section 3 presents the specifications of Troika while Sect. 4 describes the general strategy used to scan all trail cores of a certain weight. Our algorithms for generating 2-round trail cores for Troika are described in Sect. 5. These 2-round trail cores can then be extended to 6-round trail cores with the techniques described in Sect. 6. Section 6 also describes the direct search of 3-round trail cores of a particular profile, called *in-kernel* that can be generated relatively easily without the techniques of Sect. 5. Finally, Sect. 7 presents some statistics on the trails we managed to scan.

2   Differential Cryptanalysis

Differential cryptanalysis is a powerful attack against symmetric primitives that exploits input differences that propagate through the primitive to some output difference with high probability. We recall in this section basic definitions regarding differential properties.

Notation. Let $\mathbb{K}$ be a finite field. We want to study a substitution-permutation primitive f from $\mathbb{K}^n$ to $\mathbb{K}^n$. Typically for Troika, $\mathbb{K}$ is the field $\mathbb{F}_3$. We write $+$ for the usual coordinate-wise addition in $\mathbb{K}^n$ and use the operator $-$ in the usual way. We call *state* the value of the variable of $\mathbb{K}^n$ which is progressively updated through the substitution permutation network. We denote by $R_0, \ldots, R_{r-1}$ the r round functions that are iteratively applied to the state i.e. $f = R_{r-1} \circ \cdots \circ R_1 \circ R_0$. For $k \in [0, r-1]$, the round function R_k is the composition of a nonlinear map χ, a linear map λ and a round constant addition ι_k, that is to say $R_k = \iota_k \circ \lambda \circ \chi$. The state is divided for the nonlinear layer into disjoint parts of equal size, called *boxes*. A nonlinear map, called *S-box* and supposed here to be bijective, is applied to each box of the state.

Differentials. Let $f \colon \mathbb{K}^n \to \mathbb{K}^n$ be a permutation. A *differential* over f is a couple $(\Delta_{\text{in}}, \Delta_{\text{out}}) \in (\mathbb{K}^n)^2$. The difference Δ_{in} is said to be an *input difference* while the difference Δ_{out} is called an *output difference*. The *differential probability* of a differential $(\Delta_{\text{in}}, \Delta_{\text{out}})$ over f is defined as

$$\text{DP}_f(\Delta_{\text{in}}, \Delta_{\text{out}}) := \frac{\#\{x \in \mathbb{K}^n : f(x + \Delta_{\text{in}}) - f(x) = \Delta_{\text{out}}\}}{\#\mathbb{K}^n}.$$

If $\text{DP}_f(\Delta_{\text{in}}, \Delta_{\text{out}}) > 0$, we say that the input difference Δ_{in} is *compatible* with the output difference Δ_{out} through f and call $(\Delta_{\text{in}}, \Delta_{\text{out}})$ a *valid* differential over f. The *weight of a valid differential* $(\Delta_{\text{in}}, \Delta_{\text{out}})$ over f is

$$\text{w}_f(\Delta_{\text{in}}, \Delta_{\text{out}}) := -\log_{\#\mathbb{K}}(\text{DP}_f(\Delta_{\text{in}}, \Delta_{\text{out}})).$$

Differential Trails. When the dimension n of the domain of the iterated function f is large, it is in general not possible to compute the exact differential probability of a differential over f. Thus, we try to approximate this probability by studying sequences of differences, called differential trails. In the following, we denote by $f = R_{r-1} \circ \cdots \circ R_0$ an iterated function from $\mathbb{K}^n$ to $\mathbb{K}^n$. For $k \in [1, r]$, a k-round differential trail over f is a sequence $Q = (q^{(0)}, q^{(1)}, \ldots, q^{(k)}) \in (\mathbb{K}^n)^{k+1}$ where for $0 \leq i \leq k-1$, $(q^{(i)}, q^{(i+1)})$ is a valid differential over R_i. The *differential probability* of Q is defined as

$$\mathrm{DP}_f(Q) := \frac{\#\{x \in \mathbb{K}^n : \forall i \in [1, k], \ f[i](x) - f[i](x + q^{(0)}) = q^{(i)}\}}{\#\mathbb{K}^n},$$

where for $i \in [1, k]$, $f[i] = R_{i-1} \circ \ldots \circ R_0$. If we write $\mathrm{DT}_f(\Delta_{\mathrm{in}}, \Delta_{\mathrm{out}})$ for the set composed of all trails over f of the form $(\Delta_{\mathrm{in}}, q^{(1)}, \ldots, q^{(k-1)}, \Delta_{\mathrm{out}})$, then $\mathrm{DP}_f(\Delta_{\mathrm{in}}, \Delta_{\mathrm{out}}) = \sum_{Q \in \mathrm{DT}_f(\Delta_{\mathrm{in}}, \Delta_{\mathrm{out}})} \mathrm{DP}_f(Q)$.

Computing the exact probability of a differential trail is in general out of reach. Instead, we try to approximate it, looking locally at the differentials that form the trail. The *weight of a differential trail* $Q = (q^{(0)}, q^{(1)}, \ldots, q^{(k)})$ over f, defined as

$$\mathrm{w}_f(Q) := \sum_{i=0}^{k-1} \mathrm{w}_{R_i}(q^{(i)}, q^{(i+1)}),$$

is a value used to approximate the differential probability of the trail. We expect to have $\mathrm{DP}_f(Q) \simeq (\#\mathbb{K})^{-\mathrm{w}_f(Q)}$. The weight of the trail Q is easy to calculate as for all $i \in [0, k-1]$, $\mathrm{w}_{R_i}(q^{(i)}, q^{(i+1)}) = \mathrm{w}_\chi(q^{(i)}, \lambda^{-1}(q^{(i+1)}))$. This last quantity can be computed as the sum of the weights of the differentials given by the restriction of $(q^{(i)}, \lambda^{-1}(q^{(i+1)}))$ to the domain and co-domain of the S-boxes. To estimate the security of a primitive against differential attacks, it is essential to ensure that there do not exist differential trails with low weight.

Trail Cores [5]. A k-round differential trail over f will be represented as follows:

$$b_0 \xrightarrow{\chi} a_1 \xrightarrow{\lambda} b_1 \xrightarrow{\chi} a_2 \xrightarrow{\lambda} \cdots \xrightarrow{\lambda} b_{k-1} \xrightarrow{\chi} a_k \xrightarrow{\lambda} b_k,$$

where for $i \in [1, k]$, $b_i = \lambda(a_i)$ and $\mathrm{DP}_\chi(b_{i-1}, a_i) > 0$. Since the S-boxes are bijective, if a differential (b, a) is valid over χ, then the nonzero boxes of the difference a are located at the same positions as those of b. These boxes and their corresponding S-boxes are said to be *active*.

The choice of the difference b_0 and the choice of the difference a_k of the k-round trail do not affect the number of active S-boxes. For this reason it is convenient to specify only the central part of the trail, namely $(a_1, \ldots, b_{k-1})$. This defines a set of differential trails

$$\langle a_1, \ldots, b_{k-1} \rangle := \{Q = (b'_0, a_1, \ldots, b_{k-1}, a'_k, b'_k) : Q \text{ is a } k\text{-round trail over } f\}$$

called a *k-round trail core* of f. The *weight of a k-round trail core* $\langle a_1, \ldots, b_{k-1} \rangle$, written $\mathrm{w}\langle a_1, \ldots, b_{k-1} \rangle$, is the minimum of the weights of the trails that belong to the trail core. To make this explicit, the notions of minimum direct and reverse weight of a difference are introduced. The *minimum reverse weight* of a difference $\Delta \in \mathbb{K}^n$ is given by

$$\widetilde{w}^{\mathrm{rev}}(\Delta) = \min_b \{w_\chi(b, \Delta)\},$$

where the minimum is taken over the differences $b \in \mathbb{K}^n$ such that (b, Δ) is a valid differential over χ. The *minimum direct weight* of $\Delta \in \mathbb{K}^n$ is

$$\widetilde{w}^{\mathrm{dir}}(\Delta) = \min_a \{w_\chi(\Delta, a)\},$$

where the minimum is taken over the differences $a \in \mathbb{K}^n$ such that (Δ, a) is a valid differential over χ. The weight of a 2-round trail core $\langle a, b \rangle$ is then $w\langle a, b \rangle = \widetilde{w}^{\mathrm{rev}}(a) + \widetilde{w}^{\mathrm{dir}}(b)$. If $k \geq 2$, the weight of a k-round trail core $\langle a_1, \dots, b_{k-1} \rangle$ is

$$\widetilde{w}^{\mathrm{rev}}(a_1) + \sum_{i=1}^{k-2} w_\chi(b_i, a_{i+1}) + \widetilde{w}^{\mathrm{dir}}(b_{k-1}).$$

Following the same approach as in [10], we gradually generate differential trail cores, starting from short trail cores and extending them in the forward and backward direction.

3 Troika Description

We denote the finite field with 3 elements by $\mathbb{F}_3$. We call an element of $\mathbb{F}_3 = \{0, 1, 2\}$ a trit and an element of $\mathbb{F}_3^3$ a tryte.

The Troika Round Function. Troika is a hash function from $\mathbb{F}_3^*$ to $\mathbb{F}_3^{243}$. It follows the sponge construction [1] with a rate of 243 trits and a capacity of 486 trits. Therefore, the state is a vector of 729 trits. The permutation f used inside the sponge construction is composed of 24 rounds. Each round follows the KEC-CAK [2] philosophy and is composed of 5 step functions: a nonlinear layer Sub-Trytes, two shuffling layers ShiftRows and ShiftLanes, a parity-mixer AddColum-nParity and a round constant addition AddRoundConstant$_i$. Taking the same notations as in KECCAK-f, we abbreviate them here respectively by χ, ρ_r, ρ_ℓ, θ and ι_i. We also denote by ρ the composition $\rho = \rho_\ell \circ \rho_r$ and λ the whole linear layer. The round function R_i is then given by $R_i = \iota_i \circ \lambda \circ \chi$, where χ is the nonlinear layer and $\lambda = \theta \circ \rho$ is the linear layer.

Notations and Definitions. The round function operates on a state of 729 trits, organized as a three-dimensional array of size $9 \times 3 \times 27$ trits. In the following, x will always be an integer between 0 and 8, x_B an integer between 0 and 2, y an integer between 0 and 2 and z an integer between 0 and 26. Moreover, coordinates along the x, y and z axes will always be considered modulo 9, 3 and 27 respectively. We use the letter A to denote a state, that is either seen as an element of $\mathbb{F}_3^{729}$ or as a three-dimensional array. We write $A[x, y, z]$ for the trit of A of coordinates (x, y, z). The box of A of coordinates (x_B, y, z) is the tryte $(A[3x_B + i, y, z])_{i \in [0, 2]}$. We call a box-column a triplet of boxes that have the same x_B and z coordinates. The different parts of the state of Troika are illustrated in the full version of our paper [4].

We denote by $e_{(x,y,z)}$ the canonical state whose components are all zero, except the component of coordinates (x, y, z) that equals 1.

Definition 1. (trit-activity pattern) *The trit-activity pattern of a state A is the vector $\overline{A}$ of $\{0, 1\}^{729}$ that indicates the nonzero trits of A, called active trits. It is defined as $\overline{A}[x, y, z] = 0$ if $A[x, y, z] = 0$ and $\overline{A}[x, y, z] = 1$ otherwise.*

Definition 2. (box-activity pattern) *The box-activity pattern of a state A is the vector of $\{0, 1\}^{729}$ denoted by $\mathsf{box}(A)$ and given by $\mathsf{box}(A)[x, y, z] = 1$ if the box of A containing the trit of coordinates (x, y, z) is active and $\mathsf{box}(A)[x, y, z] = 0$ otherwise.*

Definition 3. (box weight) *The box weight [3] of a state A is the number of boxes of A that are active. It is denoted by $\mathrm{w}_{\mathrm{box}}(A)$.*

The Nonlinear Layer. The map SubTrytes, here denoted by χ, is the parallel application of 9×27 S-boxes of size 3 trits. The minimum reverse and direct weights of a state are easy to compute. Indeed, by computing the differential distribution table of the S-box, one can verify that for all differences $A \in \mathbb{F}_3^{729}$, $\widetilde{w}^{\mathrm{rev}}(A) = \widetilde{w}^{\mathrm{dir}}(A) = 2\,\mathrm{w}_{\mathrm{box}}(A)$.

The Shuffling Layers. The permutations ShiftRows and ShiftLanes move the trits of the state along the x and z axes, without modifying their value. For a complete description of these layers we refer to [9].

The Parity-Mixer. The map AddColumnParity, written here θ, is a column parity mixer [11]. The *parity plane* of a state A is the bi-dimensional array of size 9×27 that indicates the parity (0, 1 or 2) of each column of A. It is denoted by $P(A)$ and defined as

$$P(A)[x, z] := \sum_{y=0}^{2} A[x, y, z] \bmod 3.$$

It is said that the column of A of coordinates (x, z) has parity $P(A)[x, z] \in \mathbb{F}_3$. The θ-*effect plane* of A is the bi-dimensional array of size 9×27, denoted by $E(A)$ and defined as

$$E(A)[x, z] := P(A)[x - 1, z] + P(A)[x + 1, z + 1].$$

If $E(A)[x, z]$ is zero, the column of A of coordinates (x, z) is said to be *non affected* by θ. Otherwise, the column is said to be *affected* by $E(A)[x, z] \in \mathbb{F}_3$. The map θ is defined as

$$\theta(A)[x, y, z] := A[x, y, z] + E(A)[x, z].$$

The set $K := \{A \in \mathbb{F}_3^{729} : \theta(A) = A\}$ is called the *column-parity kernel* (or *kernel* for short). Moreover, the set $\mathbb{F}_3^{729} \setminus K$ is denoted by N. A state belongs to the kernel if and only if all its columns have parity 0. Given a k-round trail core $\langle a_1, b_1, \ldots, a_{k-1}, b_{k-1} \rangle$, its *parity profile* is written $|X_1| \ldots |X_{k-1}|$ where $X_i = K$ if $b_i \in K$ and $X_i = N$ otherwise. The column parity mixer θ does not change the parity of the state: $P(A) = P(\theta(A))$. Indeed, $P(\theta(A))[x,z] = \sum_{y=0}^{2} A[x,y,z] + 3E(A)[x,z] \bmod 3 = P(A)[x,z]$. Therefore, $E(A) = E(\theta(A))$ and the inverse function of θ is given by

$$\theta^{-1}(A)[x,y,z] = A[x,y,z] - E(A)[x,z].$$

Z-Equivalence Classes. The four step functions χ, ρ_r, ρ_ℓ and θ are invariant with respect to the translation along the z-axis i.e. they commute with functions that translate the state in the z direction. Differential trails are thus considered up to translation along the z-axis.

4   General Strategy for Differential Trail Search [10]

Our objective is to analyze the resistance of Troika against differential cryptanalysis by providing a lower bound on the weight of any trail over a given number of rounds. We explain in this section the general strategy we followed for doing so. As Troika's round function has a similar design to KECCAK-f, we naturally adopted the same strategy as the one used in [10]. This strategy permits to lower bound the weight of 6-round trail cores by extending trail cores on 3 rounds.

4.1   Overview of the Steps

All 6-round trail cores of weight less than a bound W can be generated by

1. collecting all 3-round trail cores of weight up to $W/2$,
2. extending these 3-round trail cores by 3 rounds in the forward direction and in the backward direction.

Remark 1. In [10], it is sufficient to collect all the 3-round trail cores up to weight $\lfloor W/2 \rfloor$ since the weight is necessarily an integer in $\mathbb{F}_2$.

To cover the space of 3-round trail cores $a_1 \xrightarrow{\lambda} b_1 \xrightarrow{\chi} a_2 \xrightarrow{\lambda} b_2$ up to some weight, the search space is split according to the parity profile of the trail cores. Trail cores of parity profile $|K|K|$ can be generated efficiently (see Sect. 6). For trail cores of parity profile $|K|N|$, $|N|K|$ and $|N|N|$ we use the same steps as in [10], recalled in the following lemma.

Lemma 1. [10] *Let T_3 be the weight up to which we want to collect the 3-round trail cores and T_1 be a parameter that can be adjusted.*

All $|K|N|$-trail cores up to weight T_3 can be generated by

1. *collecting all $|K|$-trail cores $\langle a, b \rangle$ with $\widetilde{w}^{rev}(a) \leq T_1$ and extending them forward outside the kernel,*
2. *collecting all $|N|$-trail cores $\langle a, b \rangle$ with $\widetilde{w}^{rev}(a) + \widetilde{w}^{dir}(b) < T_3 - T_1$ and extending them backward inside the kernel.*

All $|N|K|$-trail cores up to weight T_3 can be generated by

1. *collecting all $|K|$-trail cores $\langle a, b \rangle$ with $\widetilde{w}^{dir}(b) \leq T_1$ and extending them backward outside the kernel,*
2. *collecting all $|N|$-trail cores $\langle a, b \rangle$ with $\widetilde{w}^{rev}(a) + \widetilde{w}^{dir}(b) < T_3 - T_1$ and extending them forward inside the kernel.*

All $|N|N|$-trail cores up to weight T_3 can be generated by

1. *collecting all $|N|$-trail cores $\langle a, b \rangle$ with $2\,\widetilde{w}^{rev}(a) + \widetilde{w}^{dir}(b) < T_3$ and extending them forward outside the kernel,*
2. *collecting all $|N|$-trail cores $\langle a, b \rangle$ with $\widetilde{w}^{rev}(a) + 2\,\widetilde{w}^{dir}(b) \leq T_3$ and extending them backward inside the kernel.*

To exhaustively generate the 2-round trail cores that respect the constraints of the above lemma, we use a tree traversal, as defined by Mella et al. in [10]. We recall this technique in Sect. 4.2 and define the specific trees used for Troika in Sect. 5. The extension phase is explained in Sect. 6.

4.2 Generating 2-Round Trail Cores as a Tree Traversal

For simplicity, we explain the method presented in [10] to study 2-round trail cores of weakly aligned primitives in the case of primitives defined on $\mathbb{F}_2^n$. This technique exploits the specific features of the linear layer to take simultaneously into account the weights $\widetilde{w}^{rev}(a)$ and $\widetilde{w}^{dir}(b)$ of a 2-round trail core $\langle a, b \rangle$.

More precisely, given a bound W and two weightings α and β, a tree traversal is performed to find all trail cores $\langle a, b \rangle$ satisfying $\alpha\,\widetilde{w}^{rev}(a) + \beta\,\widetilde{w}^{dir}(b) \leq W$ and possibly some other restrictions. We denote by $c_{\alpha,\beta}$ the function that associates to a pair $(a, b) \in (\mathbb{F}_2^n)^2$ the quantity $\alpha\,\widetilde{w}^{rev}(a) + \beta\,\widetilde{w}^{dir}(b)$. In the following, after having fixed a pair (α, β), we will call the quantity $c_{\alpha,\beta}(a, b)$ the cost of the trail core $\langle a, b \rangle$.

The idea is to generate trail cores of the form $\langle a, b \rangle$ by adding progressively to a variable $(a, b) \in (\mathbb{F}_2^n)^2$ initialised to $(0, 0)$ some vectors of $(\mathbb{F}_2^n)^2$. These vectors are called units and must be defined according to the distinctive features of the round function. The cost of the trail core $\langle a, b \rangle$ is checked each time a unit is added. This process is stopped when all the trail cores that could be obtained by adding more units would have a cost higher than W.

The Tree Traversal. More formally, the algorithm is a tree traversal. A node of the tree is a list of units, called *unit-list*. A unit-list of the form $L = [u_1, \ldots, u_n]$ is associated to the vector $(a_L, b_L) := \sum_{i=1}^{n} u_i$ and to the cost $c_{\alpha,\beta}(a_L, b_L)$. A unit-list L is said to be complete if $b_L = \lambda(a_L)$, that is to say if it is associated to a 2-round trail core. It is not always the case (see the tree defined in Sect. 5.3). The root of the tree is the empty unit-list. A child of a unit-list L is a unit-list of the form $L \parallel [u]$, where u is some particular unit that does not belong to L. To avoid having two unit-lists with the same units in a different order, an order relation on the units is chosen and units are only added in ascending order. This order relation organizes the edges of the tree and must therefore be chosen to ensure good properties of the tree.

During the tree traversal a lower bound on the cost of all of the current node's descendants is calculated. The tree is pruned if this lower bound is higher than W. The goal is to define the units and the tree organization in order to be able to prune the tree efficiently. There should be no descendant of a node L that has a cost much lower than this L's cost. A node should have as few brothers as possible.

Finally, if there exists an equivalence relation on trail cores – like the z-invariance – then it is possible to visit only one representative per equivalence class. The order relation on the units induces an order relation on the unit-lists, given by the lexicographic order. A unit-list is said to be *canonical* if it is the smallest representative of its class. We are interested in the set formed by all canonical unit-lists of cost below W. As the Lemma 1 of [10, Section 3.2] shows that a unit-list that is not canonical cannot have a canonical descendant, the tree is also pruned if a non canonical unit-list is encountered.

Lower Bounding the Cost. To discuss how to give a lower bound on the costs of the descendants of a unit-list, we distinguish as in [6] between two types of active coordinates, the stable ones and the unstable ones. An active coordinate of (a_L, b_L) is said to be a *stable coordinate* of L if it is active for any pair $(a_{L'}, b_{L'})$ where L' is a descendant of L and *unstable* otherwise. By counting only the contribution of the stable coordinates of L we obtain a lower bound on the costs of the descendants of L.

This bound might be improved by studying the behavior of the unstable coordinates of L. For that, we search for some sets of passive or unstable coordinates that necessarily contribute to the cost of the descendants of L. We say that a subset I of the passive or unstable coordinates of (a_L, b_L) is an *activity invariant* of L if for every descendant L' of L there exists a coordinate $i \in I$ such that i is an active coordinate of $(a_{L'}, b_{L'})$. If all the coordinates of an activity invariant belong to boxes that have not already contributed to the bound, then this bound can be increased by adding a lower bound on the contribution of that activity invariant. This process is summarized in Algorithm 1 of Appendix A.

5   Generating 2-Round Trail Cores in Troika

We present in this section the trees used to exhaustively generate the 2-round Troika's trail cores of a given parity profile that also respect a cost constraint.

The cost of a 2-round trail core $\langle a, b \rangle$ depends only on the positions of the active trits, but in some cases we will also need to know the exact difference. For this reason we introduce the notion of *mixed states*.

Definition 4. (Mixed state) *A* mixed state *is a three-dimensional array of size* $9 \times 3 \times 27$ *whose cells can take either the value* 0, 1, 2 *or* $\boxtimes$, *where the value* $\boxtimes$ *stands for an active trit of unspecified value. It can also be seen as a vector of* $\{0, 1, 2, \boxtimes\}^{729}$.

We say that a difference $A \in \mathbb{F}_3^{729}$ is *compatible* with a parity plane p and a mixed state M if $P(A) = p$ and if for all coordinates (x, y, z), $A[x, y, z] = M[x, y, z]$ if $M[x, y, z] \in \{0, 1, 2\}$ and $A[x, y, z] \neq 0$ otherwise.

Addition of mixed states is defined as the component-wise addition. Only the commutative addition $0 + \boxtimes = \boxtimes$ and the usual addition modulo 3 can occur in our algorithms. The definitions of the trit shuffling ρ, the box weight and the cost functions $c_{\alpha,\beta}$ are extended to mixed states. We denote by $m_{(x,y,z)}$ the mixed state whose components are all zero, except the component of coordinates (x, y, z) that equals $\boxtimes$.

5.1   Generating $|K|$-Trail Cores

We define the tree used for the generation of trail cores $\langle \rho^{-1}(b), b \rangle$ with $b \in K$ and valid cost. As the difference b of such trail cores belongs to the kernel, its columns have either zero, two or three active coordinates. A node of the tree represents a couple of mixed states $(\rho^{-1}(M), M) \in \{0, \boxtimes\}^{729} \times \{0, \boxtimes\}^{729}$ where M has zero, two or three active coordinates per column. All nodes can be obtained by summing units of the form:

1. $\boxtimes_{x,z} := (\rho^{-1}(m), m)$, where $m = m_{(x,0,z)} + m_{(x,1,z)}$,

2. $\boxtimes_{x,z} := (\rho^{-1}(m), m)$, where $m = m_{(x,0,z)} + m_{(x,2,z)}$,

3. $\boxtimes_{x,z} := (\rho^{-1}(m), m)$, where $m = m_{(x,1,z)} + m_{(x,2,z)}$,

4. $\boxtimes_{x,z} := (\rho^{-1}(m_{(x,2,z)}), m_{(x,2,z)})$.

Units are characterized by their coordinates (x, z) and their patterns $\boxtimes$, $\boxtimes$, or $\boxtimes$. Their ordering is arbitrary. We just need to have $\boxtimes_{x,z} < \boxtimes_{x,z}$ for all x and z.

Units have to be added to the unit-list in ascending order while respecting two constraints. A unit of type 4 can only be added to a unit-list that already contains the unit of type 1 of same coordinates (x, z). A unit of types 1, 2 or 3 cannot be added if there is already in the unit-list another unit of same coordinates (x, z). Thereby, the mixed state M of a node $(\rho^{-1}(M), M)$ cannot have a column with only one active coordinate. Moreover, this ensures that all coordinates of a unit-list are stable and consequently that the cost function $c_{\alpha,\beta}$ is monotonic with respect to units addition.

To obtain the differences b of the desired trail cores $\langle \rho^{-1}(b), b \rangle$, it just remains to generate, for each node $(\rho^{-1}(M), M)$ reached during the tree traversal, the differences compatible with the zero parity plane and the mixed state M.

5.2   Reducing the Problem of Generating $|N|$-Trail Cores to that of Generating Parity-Bare States at the Input of θ

For the generation of trail cores of the form $\langle \rho^{-1}(c), \theta(c) \rangle$ with $c \in N$, our approach is the same as in [10]. Unlike the generation of $|K|$-trail cores, we were not able to define a tree whose nodes have only stable coordinates. The difficulty comes from the column parity mixer: activating trits at the input of θ can deactivate trits at the output of the function and vice versa. The rationale behind the tree's units and the order relation among them is to gradually choose the columns' values on either side of the map θ in an appropriate order that limits the number of unstable coordinates.

As in [10], we reduce the problem of that of finding a good tree containing all trail cores $\langle \rho^{-1}(c), \theta(c) \rangle$ such that c is a *parity-bare* state. That means that the unaffected columns of c have as few active trits as possible for their parity, namely zero for columns of parity zero and one for the other unaffected columns. Once the parity-bare states are generated, we no longer have to care about the θ-effect and can define trees as in Sect. 5.1 to recover from the parity-bare states all the wanted $|N|$-trail cores. Indeed, any out-kernel state can be obtained by summing a parity-bare state and an in-kernel state that only adds extra active coordinates to the unaffected columns of the initial parity-bare state. We refer to the full version of this paper [4] for a detailed description of the tree used to add extra active coordinates in the unaffected columns of a parity-bare state.

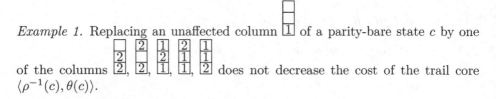

Example 1. Replacing an unaffected column $\boxed{1}$ of a parity-bare state c by one of the columns $\boxed{\substack{2 \\ 2}}, \boxed{\substack{2 \\ 2}}, \boxed{\substack{1 \\ 2}}, \boxed{\substack{2 \\ 1 \\ 1}}, \boxed{\substack{1 \\ 1 \\ 2}}$ does not decrease the cost of the trail core $\langle \rho^{-1}(c), \theta(c) \rangle$.

5.3   Generating Parity-Bare States at the Input of θ

We now present the tree used to organize the trail cores $\langle \rho^{-1}(c), \theta(c) \rangle$ such that c is a parity-bare state. The idea is to choose the columns of the difference c in an order that makes it possible to control the parity plane and the θ-effect plane of c.

To describe more easily the tree's units and the order relation among them, we introduce the notion of *diagonal coordinate d* of a column. The (x, z)-coordinates and (d, z)-coordinates of a column are related by the change of coordinates $(x, z) = (d + 2z \bmod 9, z)$. In the following, the letter d will always be an integer taken modulo 9 that refers to a diagonal coordinate. The coordinates of a column are implicitly given using the (d, z)-coordinates.

General Form of Units. A unit of the tree is an element of $\mathbb{F}_3^{729} \times \mathbb{F}_3^{729}$ whose values at the input and output of θ correspond to the values of a column, affected or not, before and after θ. More formally, a unit is a pair of the form

$$\begin{pmatrix} t_2 \\ t_1 \\ t_0 \end{pmatrix}_{x,z,t} := \left(\rho^{-1} \left(\sum_{i=0}^{2} t_i e_{(x,i,z)} \right), \sum_{i=0}^{2} (t_i + t) e_{(x,i,z)} \right).$$

It is characterized by its (x, z)-coordinates, by a triplet $(t_0, t_1, t_2) \in \mathbb{F}_3^3$ that is the column value at the input of θ and by a trit t that is the θ-effect applied to obtain the column value at the output of θ. To obtain a pair of the form $(\rho^{-1}(c), \theta(c))$ by summing units, the parity-plane and the θ-effect plane formed at the input of θ have to be consistent.

Runs and Loops. Similar to what is done for KECCAK [2] and XOODOO [6], to link the parity plane and the θ-effect of a state, we group all its columns of non-zero parity in sets called *runs* and *loops*. The following definitions are motivated by the fact that the θ-effect applied to a column of coordinates $(d_0 + 1, z_0)$ depends on the parity of the columns of coordinates (d_0, z_0) and $(d_0, z_0 + 1)$.

Definition 5. *Let A be a state. For an integer $\ell \in [1, 26]$ and some coordinates (d_0, z_0), we consider the set r formed by the columns of A of coordinates $(d_0, z_0), \ldots, (d_0, z_0 + \ell - 1)$. If all the columns of r have non-zero parity and if the two columns of coordinates $(d_0, z_0 - 1)$ and $(d_0, z_0 + \ell)$ have parity zero, we say that r is the* run *of A of coordinates (d_0, z_0) and of length ℓ.*

Definition 6. *If a state admits a set of columns of coordinates $(d_0, 0), \ldots, (d_0, 26)$ that all have non-zero parity, we say that this set is a* loop.

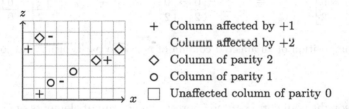

Fig. 1. Parity and θ-effect planes of a run of (d, z)-coordinates $(0, 1)$ and of length 5

The set formed by all the non-zero parity columns of a state can be partitioned into runs and loops. Each run or loop determines a part of the θ-effect plane. More precisely, if a state A admits a run of coordinates (d_0, z_0) and of length ℓ, then this run determines for all $i \in [-1, \ell - 1]$, the value of $E(A)[d_0 + 1, z_0 + i]$. The columns of coordinates $(d_0 + 1, z_0 - 1)$ and $(d_0 + 1, z_0 + \ell - 1)$ are always affected.

From Supra-Units to Units. Since a trail core $\langle \rho^{-1}(c), \theta(c) \rangle$ formed from a parity-bare state c that has a loop has a cost too high for our search, we restrict the nodes of the tree to trail cores formed from parity-bare states that have only runs. However, the existence of loops for Troika, is a consequence of the particular θ mapping used in Troika and this effect does not appear in KECCAK. The existence of these loops is due to the fact that all the diagonal coordinates form 9 disjoint sets. We use this property later to improve the lower bound on the cost of a trail.

Every parity-bare state with n runs can be decomposed into n parity-bare states with only one run. These latter have only unaffected null columns, unaffected columns with a single active trit and affected columns of parity zero. Such a decomposition is not unique. To make it unique, we adopt the same conventions as in [2] and [6]. The runs of the decomposition must not overlap. Moreover, if the initial state admits affected columns of non-zero parity, these columns have to be decomposed into an unaffected column with a single active trit at $y = 0$, whose value is the parity of the initial column, and an affected column chosen accordingly. We call this rule the non-zero-$y0$ convention. Under these conventions, the existence and the uniqueness of the decomposition can be proved as in [6, Section 7.3.2] by exhibiting a deterministic procedure that removes from a parity-bare state with n runs a parity-bare state with one run to get a parity-bare state with $n - 1$ runs. It removes the columns of a run as well as the columns affected by this run, using the non-zero-$y0$ convention to split the affected columns of non-zero parity and only remove the suitable part of such columns.

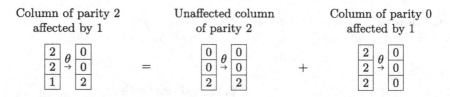

Fig. 2. Decomposition of an affected column of non-zero parity using the non-zero-$y0$ convention

All the sought trail cores can be expressed as a sum of elements of $\mathbb{F}_3^{729} \times \mathbb{F}_3^{729}$ of the form $\left(\rho^{-1}(A), \theta(A) \right)$ where A is a parity bare state with only one run. We call these elements *supra-units*. Since there are too many possible supra-units,

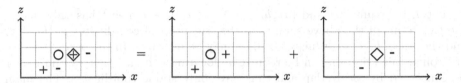

Fig. 3. Parity and θ-effect planes of a parity-bare state with 2 runs and its decomposition into parity-bare states with 1 run. The affected column of non-zero parity has to be split according to the non-zero-$y0$ convention. The symbols are explained in Fig. 1

they cannot directly be used as units. A finer subdivision is therefore used. It relies on the units introduced before, that enable to form the supra-units one by one. With this refinement, many supra-units have a common ancestor, which is important for the tree pruning.

We define a partial order relation on the supra-units. For that, we characterise a supra-unit $\left(\rho^{-1}(A), \theta(A)\right)$ with the coordinates (d, z) and the length ℓ of the run of A. The partial order is given by the lexicographic order on $[d, z, \ell]$ and supra-units are put in the unit-list in ascending order.

Two types of units are used. Those that are said to be affected correspond to affected columns of parity zero at the input of θ; those that are said to be unaffected correspond to unaffected columns with only one active trit at the input of θ. Each supra-unit of coordinates (d, z) and length ℓ is the sum of:

- ℓ unaffected units with (d, z)-coordinates $(d, z), \ldots, (d, z + \ell - 1)$,
- 2 affected units of coordinates $(d + 1, z - 1)$ and $(d + 1, z + \ell - 1)$,
- from 0 to $\ell - 1$ other affected units that could be in positions $(d + 1, z), \ldots, (d + 1, z + \ell - 2)$.

These units are indexed from 0 to 2ℓ and added to the unit-list in ascending order of indexes. The i-th unit has coordinates $(d + 1, z - 1 + \frac{i}{2})$ if i is even and $(d, z + \lfloor \frac{i}{2} \rfloor)$ if i is odd.

Importance of the Ordering of Supra-Units. The ordering of units resembles the one of [10], except that here, the partial order on supra-units allows us to detect more active coordinates that are stable for a unit-list. This results in an improvement of the bound computed with Algorithm 1 (given in Appendix A). We were able to increase the 3-round weight target from 33 to 41.

The only way for active coordinates of a unit-list to turn passive is when an unaffected unit is added to a unit-list that already contains an affected unit of same coordinates, or vice versa. By the non-zero-$y0$ convention, the only overlaps allowed are of the form:

$$\begin{pmatrix} t_2 \\ t_1 \\ t_0 \end{pmatrix}_{x,z,t} + \begin{pmatrix} 0 \\ 0 \\ t_0' \end{pmatrix}_{x,z,0} , \text{ where } t_0 + t_1 + t_2 = 0, \ t \in \{1, 2\} \text{ and } t_0' \in \{1, 2\}.$$

Let L be a unit-list and $(a_L, b_L) = \sum_{u \in L} u$. If a unit-list has only one of the two terms of the above sum, then the trit of a_L of coordinates $\rho^{-1}(x, 0, z)$ and the trit of b_L of coordinates $(x, 0, z)$ may be unstable. In the particular case of Troika, this criterion can be refined by locating columns that can no longer be concerned by an overlap and thus have only stable coordinates. The main remark is that overlaps only involve affected units of a supra-unit of diagonal coordinate d and unaffected units of a supra-unit of diagonal coordinate $d+1$. The ordering of supra-units implies that unaffected units that belong to a supra-unit of diagonal coordinate $d > 0$ are not concerned anymore by overlaps since supra-units of d-coordinate $d - 1$ can no longer be added to the unit-list. Similarly, if we write d_{last} for the d-coordinate of the supra-unit that is being formed or that just has been completed, then all the affected units belonging to a supra-unit of coordinate $d < d_{\text{last}} - 1$ cannot be involved in a new overlap.

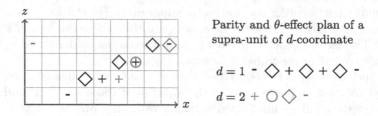

Parity and θ-effect plan of a supra-unit of d-coordinate

$d = 1$ $\cdot$ $\Diamond$ + $\Diamond$ + $\Diamond$ $\cdot$

$d = 2$ + $\bigcirc \Diamond$ $\cdot$

Fig. 4. Columns overlapping

Lower Bounding the Cost. We use Algorithm 1 to compute a lower bound on the costs of node's descendants. The criterion used to distinguish between stable and unstable coordinates of a unit-list L is explained above. It remains to describe the activity invariants of L. Suppose that the difference $\rho(a_L)$ has an affected column of coordinates (x, z). For every descendant L' of L, this column remains affected and thus $a_{L'}[\rho^{-1}(x, 0, z)] \neq b_{L'}[x, 0, z]$. In particular, at least one of these two trits is active. Suppose now that the difference $\rho(a_L)$ has an unaffected column with only one active trit of coordinates $(x, 0, z)$. Whether or not this column becomes affected for a descendant L' of L, there will always be an active trit among the set $\{a_{L'}[\rho^{-1}(x, 0, z)], \; b_{L'}[x, 0, z]\}$. Moreover, since the columns of coordinates (x, z) at the input and output of θ will always have a non-zero parity, the same is true for the sets $\{a_{L'}[\rho^{-1}(x, i, z)] : i \in [0, 2]\}$ and $\{b_{L'}[x, i, z] : i \in [0, 2]\}$.

An Improvement for the Tree Traversal. The fact that we are working over $\mathbb{F}_3$ does not facilitate the tree traversal. If we entirely specify the value of the differences for all the active trits, there will be too many possibilities to treat. But, if we do not specify the value, the behaviour of the column parity mixer θ is too complicated to understand. To deal with this situation we introduce an equivalence relation on parity-bare states used to reduce the search space during the tree traversal.

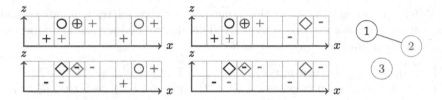

Fig. 5. Parity planes and θ-effect planes of four parity-bare states that are scalar-equivalent and their associated graph.

Definition 7. (Components of a parity-bare state) *Let A be a parity-bare state with n runs and $A = \sum_{i=1}^{n} A_i$ its decomposition into parity-bare states with one run defined in Sect. 5.3. We form a graph $\mathcal{G}_A$ whose vertices are numbered from 1 to n. The i-th and j-th vertices are connected by an edge if and only if the parity-bare state $A_i + A_j$ has an affected column of non-zero parity. If this graph admits k connected components $C_1, \ldots, C_k$, then we call the elements of the set $\{\sum_{j \in C_i} A_j : i \in [1, k]\}$ the* components *of A.*

Definition 8. (Scalar-equivalence) *Let A^1 and A^2 be two parity-bare states that have k components $C_1^1, \ldots, C_k^1$ and $C_1^2, \ldots, C_k^2$. The parity-bare states A^1 and A^2 are* scalar-equivalent *if there exists some scalars $\lambda_1, \ldots, \lambda_k \in \{1, 2\}$ and a permutation σ of the set $\{1, \ldots, k\}$ such that $C_i^1 = \lambda_i C_{\sigma(i)}^2$ for all $i \in [1, k]$.*

We say that two complete unit-lists L and L' are scalar-equivalent if the differences $\rho(a_L)$ and $\rho(a_{L'})$ are scalar-equivalent. Two complete scalar-equivalent unit-lists describe trail cores that have the same trit-activity pattern. We organize the tree to have only one representative per equivalence class. At the end of the tree traversal, we generate from each representative the elements of its class.

6 Dealing with $|K|K|$ Profile and Extensions

The space of 3-round trail cores with parity profile $|K|K|$ can be directly scanned up to some limit weight. Once all trail-cores of a certain length have been obtained, they must be extended. Extensions are treated differently depending on their direction (backward or forward) and their type (inside or outside the kernel). In the following two paragraphs, we give the idea behind these techniques. Details can be found in the full version of our paper [4].

Generating 3-Round Trail Cores of Parity Profile $|K|K|$. To search for trail cores of the form $\langle \rho^{-1}(b_1), b_1, a_2, \rho(a_2) \rangle$ with $b_1 \in K$ and $\rho(a_2) \in K$, the first step is to generate a subset $\overline{A_2} \subset \mathbb{F}_2^{729}$ that contains all trit activity patterns that are good candidates for $\overline{a_2}$. For that, we derive necessary conditions on $\overline{a_2}$ from the fact that the differences b_1 and $\rho(a_2)$ must be in the kernel. More precisely, if $\langle \rho^{-1}(b_1), b_1, a_2, \rho(a_2) \rangle$ is a trail core of parity profile $|K|K|$, then a column of $\rho(a_2)$ cannot have exactly one active trit. Moreover, as $b_1 \in K$, a box-column of b_1 cannot have exactly one active box. Due to the fact that the differences b_1 and a_2 have the same box activity pattern, a box-column of a_2 cannot have exactly one active box. Thereby, we deduce the two following necessary conditions on $\overline{\rho(a_2)}$ and on $\overline{a_2}$:

- If $\overline{\rho(a_2)}[x, y, z] = 1$, then $\overline{\rho(a_2)}[x, y + 1, z] = 1$ or $\overline{\rho(a_2)}[x, y + 2, z] = 1$;
- If $\overline{a_2}[x, y, z] = 1$, then it exists $i \in \{0, 1, 2\}$ and $j \in \{1, 2\}$ such that $\overline{a_2}[3x_B + i, y + j, z] = 1$, where $x_B = \lfloor \frac{x}{3} \rfloor$.

To take into account the weight constraint, we compute only from the trit activity pattern $\overline{a_2}$ of a difference a_2, a lower bound on the weight of trail cores of the form $\langle \rho^{-1}(b_1), b_1, a_2, \rho(a_2) \rangle$, denoted by $\widetilde{w}^{3\text{-round}}_{\min}(\overline{a_2})$. The set $\overline{A_2}$ is formed by all the trit activity patterns $\overline{a_2}$ that respect the necessary conditions and that lead to a bound $\widetilde{w}^{3\text{-round}}_{\min}(\overline{a_2})$ below the limit weight.

The second step is to generate all $(|K|K|, W)$-trail cores, by extending backward inside the kernel (if possible) the 2-round trail cores $\langle a_2, \rho(a_2) \rangle$ that satisfy $\overline{a_2} \in \overline{A_2}$ and $\rho(a_2) \in K$.

Extensions. For the forward extension, the authors of [10] exploited the fact that the KECCAK S-box is quadratic, a property that does not hold for Troika. To extend a trail core outside the kernel in the forward and backward direction or inside the kernel in the backward direction we use a step-by-step approach to control the extensions' weight. Our approach shares some similarities with the method of [10] but is necessarily different because the inner components of the two functions are not the same.

7   Results and Conclusion

We have covered the space of all 3-round trail cores up to weight 41 and showed that there exists no differential trail over six rounds with weight below 82. It results in a better bound than the one obtained with the SMT-based approach. Adapting the framework of [10] for the field $\mathbb{F}_3$ was harder than expected. Dealing with trits rather than bits complicates the analysis and we were not able to take a cost target for the search as high as for KECCAK.

Our experimental results have been obtained on a Intel Core i5 processor running at $2.4\,\text{Hz}$ and a single core was used for each experiment. Our code is publicly available[1]. We assume that we cannot do considerably better as the number of trails to scan would rapidly be a limiting factor. This is why we did not try to run the code longer even though it may be possible to get a slightly better bound.

For the generation of 3-round trail cores of parity profile $|K|K|$, we were able to cover the space up to weight 65. This search takes advantage of the small size of the S-boxes, which gives restrictive conditions on the box-activity pattern of an in-kernel difference. For the generation of 3-round trail cores with parity profile

---

[1] https://github.com/MargotFunk/troikaDifferentialCryptanalysis.

$|K|N|$, $|N|K|$ and $|N|N|$, increasing the target weight drastically increases the number of 2-round trail cores to investigate and extend into 3-round trail cores.

Figure 6 reports the number of 2-round trail cores that have to be collected in order to apply Lemma 1 with $T_3 = 41$ and $T_1 = 11$. It also represents the number of found $|K|K|$ trail cores per weight. The weight distribution of the 3-round trail cores up to weight $T_3 = 41$ depending on the parity profile of the trail cores can be found in the full version of our paper [4].

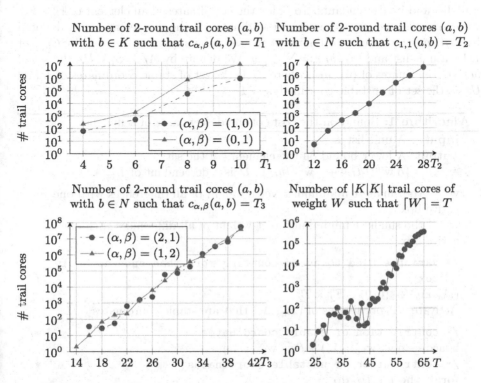

Fig. 6. Number of trail cores for different cost functions. Trail cores are considered in the four graphs up to z-invariance. In the second graph, trail cores are also considered up to scalar-equivalence.

The execution time for the generation of all 3-round trail cores for the four different parity profiles is given below.

Parity profile	Direction	Time	Parity profile	Direction	Time
$|K|K|$	backward	22 m 40 s	$|K|N|$	forward	5 m 7 s
				backward	5 h 19 m
$|N|N|$	forward	9 h 16 m	$|N|K|$	forward	6 h 32 m
	backward	17 h 7 m		backward	26 m 10 s

Acknowledgements. The authors are partially supported by the French Agence Nationale de la Recherche through the SWAP project under Contract ANR-21-CE39-0012.

A Appendix

We recall here the algorithm used in [6] to give a lower bound on the costs of a unit-list and its descendants. To index the coordinates of an element of $\mathbb{F}_2^n \times \mathbb{F}_2^n$, we distinguish between the set of coordinates of the first component, denoted by C_a, and the set of coordinates of the second component, denoted by C_b. Let L be a unit-list and $(a_L, b_L) := \sum_{u \in L} u$. We denote by $A_L = S_L \cup U_L$ the set of active coordinates of (a_L, b_L), where S_L is the set of stable coordinates of L and U_L is the set of unstable coordinates of L.

Algorithm 1: Bound on the costs of the descendants of a unit-list

input : A unit-list L

output: A lower bound on the elements of the set
$$\{\alpha\, \widetilde{w}^{\mathrm{rev}}(a_{L'}) + \beta\, \widetilde{w}^{\mathrm{dir}}(b_{L'}) : L' \text{ is a descendant of } L\}$$

$w_a \leftarrow$ the smallest minimum reverse weight of all differences with one active box

$w_b \leftarrow$ the smallest minimum direct weight of all differences with one active box

```
/* variable used to avoid counting more than once an active
   box                                                        */
```
$(\Delta_a, \Delta_b) \leftarrow (0,0) \in \mathbb{F}_2^n \times \mathbb{F}_2^n$
Activate all coordinates of (Δ_a, Δ_b) that are stable coordinates of L.

```
/* contribution of stable coordinates                         */
```
bound $\leftarrow \alpha\, w_a\, w_{\mathrm{box}}(\Delta_a) + \beta\, w_b\, w_{\mathrm{box}}(\Delta_b)$
```
/* contribution of unstable coordinates                       */
```
forall the $u \in U_L$ **do**

  if *there exists a small activity invariant* I_u *of* L *containing* u **then**

    forall the $i \in I_u$ **do** Note the contribution c_i of i
$$c_i \leftarrow \begin{cases} 0 & \text{if } i \in C_a \text{ and } i \text{ belongs to an active box of } \Delta_a \\ 0 & \text{if } i \in C_b \text{ and } i \text{ belongs to an active box of } \Delta_b \\ \alpha\, w_a & \text{if } i \in C_a \text{ and } i \text{ belongs to a passive box of } \Delta_a \\ \beta\, w_b & \text{if } i \in C_b \text{ and } i \text{ belongs to a passive box of } \Delta_b \end{cases}$$

    ```/* Take the minimum of the contributions   */```
    $c \leftarrow \min\{c_i : i \in I_u\}$
    if $c > 0$ **then**
      bound $\leftarrow$ bound $+ c$
      Activate all the coordinates of (Δ_a, Δ_b) that belong to I_u.

return bound

    ```

References

1. Bertoni, G., Daemen, J., Peeters, M., Van Assche, G.: On the indifferentiability of the sponge construction. In: Smart, N. (ed.) EUROCRYPT 2008. LNCS, vol. 4965, pp. 181–197. Springer, Heidelberg (2008). https://doi.org/10.1007/978-3-540-78967-3_11
2. Bertoni, G., Daemen, J., Peeters, M., Assche, G.V.: The Keccak SHA-3 submission, January 2011. http://sponge.noekeon.org/. Submission to NIST (Round 3)
3. Bordes, N., Daemen, J., Kuijsters, D., Van Assche, G.: Thinking outside the super-box. In: Malkin, T., Peikert, C. (eds.) CRYPTO 2021. LNCS, vol. 12827, pp. 337–367. Springer, Cham (2021). https://doi.org/10.1007/978-3-030-84252-9_12
4. Boura, C., Funk, M., Rotella, Y.: Differential analysis of the ternary hash function troika. Cryptology ePrint Archive, Paper 2023/036 (2023). https://eprint.iacr.org/2023/036
5. Daemen, J., Van Assche, G.: Differential propagation analysis of Keccak. In: Canteaut, A. (ed.) FSE 2012. LNCS, vol. 7549, pp. 422–441. Springer, Heidelberg (2012). https://doi.org/10.1007/978-3-642-34047-5_24
6. Daemen, J., Hoffert, S., Assche, G.V., Keer, R.V.: The design of Xoodoo and Xoofff. IACR Trans. Symmetric Cryptol. 2018(4), 1–38 (2018). https://doi.org/10.13154/tosc.v2018.i4.1-38
7. Debris-Alazard, T., Sendrier, N., Tillich, J.-P.: Wave: a new family of trapdoor one-way preimage sampleable functions based on codes. In: Galbraith, S.D., Moriai, S. (eds.) ASIACRYPT 2019. LNCS, vol. 11921, pp. 21–51. Springer, Cham (2019). https://doi.org/10.1007/978-3-030-34578-5_2
8. Heilman, E., et al.: Cryptanalysis of Curl-P and other attacks on the IOTA cryptocurrency. IACR Trans. Symmetric Cryptol. 2020(3), 367–391 (2020). https://doi.org/10.13154/tosc.v2020.i3.367-391
9. Kölbl, S., Tischhauser, E., Derbez, P., Bogdanov, A.: Troika: a ternary cryptographic hash function. Des. Codes Cryptogr. 88, 91–117 (2019). https://doi.org/10.1007/s10623-019-00673-2
10. Mella, S., Daemen, J., Assche, G.V.: New techniques for trail bounds and application to differential trails in Keccak. IACR Trans. Symmetric Cryptol. 2017(1), 329–357 (2017). https://doi.org/10.13154/tosc.v2017.i1.329-357
11. Stoffelen, K., Daemen, J.: Column parity mixers. IACR Trans. Symmetric Cryptol. 2018(1), 126–159 (2018). https://tosc.iacr.org/index.php/ToSC/article/view/847

Another Look at Differential-Linear Attacks

Orr Dunkelman[1] and Ariel Weizman[2(✉)]

[1] Computer Science Department, University of Haifa, Haifa, Israel
orrd@cs.haifa.ac.il
[2] Department of Mathematics, Bar-Ilan University, Ramat Gan, Israel
relweiz@gmail.com

Abstract. Differential-Linear (DL) cryptanalysis is a well known cryptanalytic technique that combines differential and linear cryptanalysis. Over the years, multiple techniques were proposed to increase its strength. Two recent ones are: The partitioning technique by Leurent and the use of neutral bits adapted by Beierle et al. to DL cryptanalysis.

In this paper we compare these techniques and discuss the possibility of using them together to achieve the best possible DL attacks. We study the combination of these two techniques and show that in many cases they are indeed compatible. We demonstrate the strength of the combination in two ways. First, we present the first DL attack on 4-round Xoodyak and an extension to 5-round in the related key model. We show that the attacks are possible only by using these two techniques simultaneously. In addition, using the combination of the two techniques we improve a DL attack on 9-round DES. We show that the partitioning technique mainly reduces the time complexity, and the use of neutral bits mainly reduces the data complexity, while the combination of them reduces both the time and data complexities.

Keywords: Differential-Linear Cryptanalysis · Partitioning · Neutral Bits · Xoodyak · DES

1 Introduction

1.1 Differential and Linear Cryptanalysis

The two main statistical cryptanalytic techniques are differential cryptanalysis [10] and linear cryptanalysis [27]. Differential cryptanalysis was introduced

The first author was supported in part by the Center for Cyber, Law, and Policy in conjunction with the Israel National Cyber Bureau in the Prime Minister's Office and by the Israeli Science Foundation through grants No. 880/18 and 3380/19.
The second author was supported by the European Research Council under the ERC starting grant agreement n. 757731 (LightCrypt), by the BIU Center for Research in Applied Cryptography and Cyber Security in conjunction with the Israel National Cyber Bureau in the Prime Minister's Office, and by the President Scholarship for Ph.D. students at the Bar-Ilan University.

© The Author(s), under exclusive license to Springer Nature Switzerland AG 2024
B. Smith and H. Wu (Eds.): SAC 2022, LNCS 13742, pp. 116–136, 2024.
https://doi.org/10.1007/978-3-031-58411-4_6

by Biham and Shamir [10]. It analyzes the development of differences of plaintext pairs through the encryption process. Let E be an n-bit block cipher consisting of r rounds, and denote the input of the i'th round by X_i. A differential with probability p of t rounds of E is a statistical property of the form $Pr[X_{i+t} \oplus X'_{i+t} = \Omega_O \mid X_i \oplus X'_i = \Omega_I] = p$, denoted by $\Omega_I \xrightarrow{p} \Omega_O$. Differential attacks exploit (high probability) differential characteristics for key recovering.

Linear cryptanalysis was published by Matsui [27]. It analyzes the development of parities of state bits of a single plaintext through the encryption process. A linear approximation with bias ϵ is a statistical property of the form $Pr[C \cdot \lambda_O = P \cdot \lambda_I] = \frac{1}{2} + \epsilon$, for two masks λ_I, λ_O, and $\cdot$ denoting the scalar product. The quality of such linear approximation is measured by the absolute value $|\epsilon|$. Linear attacks exploit (high bias) linear approximations for key recovering.

Given the strength of both differential and linear cryptanalysis, modern block ciphers are designed to withstand these attacks. A new block cipher should ensure that there are neither high-probability differential characteristics nor high-bias linear approximations for "many" rounds of the cipher [30], and some design methodologies have been developed to achieve that (e.g., the wide trail strategy [16]). The result is ciphers with a sufficient number of rounds such that there are no differential characteristics of probability $p \gg 2^{-n}$ and no linear approximations of bias $\mid \epsilon \mid \gg 2^{-\frac{n}{2}}$.

1.2 Differential-Linear Cryptanalysis

While it is possible to provide resistance against "long" differential characteristics and linear approximations, "short" characteristics (with high probability or bias) are inevitable. This fact led to the development of several cryptanalytic techniques which exploit two "short" characteristics instead of one "long" characteristic. Such techniques look on the cipher E as a decomposition[1] $E = E_1 \circ E_0$, and combine two "short" characteristics, one for E_0 and the other for E_1, as one "long" characteristic for E.

The first combined technique is the *Differential-Linear* (DL in short) cryptanalysis of Langford and Hellman [21]. DL cryptanalysis studies the relation between the parity of state bits of two ciphertexts generated from two plaintexts with a fixed difference. Given a difference Ω_I and state bits λ_O, DL cryptanalysis considers plaintexts pair $(P, P' = P \oplus \Omega_I)$, and checks whether the corresponding ciphertext pair (C, C') satisfies $C \cdot \lambda_O = C' \cdot \lambda_O$. Such a DL characteristic

---

[1] We note that some works divide the cipher into three sub-ciphers $E = E_1 \circ E_m \circ E_0$ (e.g., [3,11–13,25,26]). This is mostly done to better understand the transition between the two main sub-ciphers E_0, E_1 and most importantly the dependencies between the two sub-ciphers. The emphasis of this paper is the external rounds (rather than the internal rounds and the transition). Our results are independent of these works and thus we use the simpler description of DL attacks. We note that both partition and neutral bits may still result in subtle dependencies which may impact the transition, and hence we experimentally verified our results whenever possible.

$\Omega_I \to \lambda_O$ relies on a differential characteristic $\Omega_I \xrightarrow[E_0]{p} \Omega_M$ and a linear approximation $\lambda_M \xrightarrow[E_1]{\epsilon} \lambda_O$, and the probability of the DL characteristic is:

$$Pr[C \cdot \lambda_O = C' \cdot \lambda_O \mid P \oplus P' = \Omega_I] = \frac{1}{2} + 2p\epsilon^2.$$

Later, additional combined attacks were published, such as the boomerang attack [32], the amplified boomerang attack [19], and the rectangle attack [9].

Consider a DL attack based on a differential characteristic with a probability of p and a linear approximation with a bias of ϵ, the bias of the full distinguisher is $2p\epsilon^2$, and the data complexity of the corresponding DL attack is $\mathcal{O}\left(p^{-2}\epsilon^{-4}\right)$. Therefore, even a small improvement of the inner characteristics may have a large impact on the data complexity (and as a result also on the time complexity) of the attack.

Previous Works. Two previous works show how dependencies between plaintext pairs can improve DL attacks:[2] Leurent [22] extends the partitioning technique of [6] to DL characteristics on ARX ciphers. Using some properties of the modular addition operator, Leurent shows how to partition the data into disjoint subsets (the partition is done both in the differential part and the linear part), such that each subset satisfies the DL characteristic with a higher bias. As a result, in each subset, the bias is significantly higher, resulting in a gain stemming from the squaring of this bias.

Beierle et al. [4] suggest a different approach, which adapts the idea of *Neutral Bits* [7]. For the differential part, Beierle et al. suggest to look for a subspace $\mathcal{U} \subseteq \mathbb{F}_2^n$, such that given a plaintext pair (P, P') satisfying the differential part, then $\forall u \in \mathcal{U} : (P \oplus u, P' \oplus u)$ also satisfies the differential part (with high probability). Therefore, one right pair w.r.t. the differential characteristic produces a (possibly large) set of pairs all of which have the same parity at the entrance to the linear part.

1.3   Our Contributions

The main goal of this paper is to study the combination of these two techniques, partitioning and neutral bits, to minimize the attack's data and time complexities. We describe the techniques, compare them, and discuss the possibility of combining them in Sect. 3. Then, in Sect. 4, we present the first DL distinguisher on 5-round Xoodoo [14], and show that the use of these two techniques together allows a key-recovery RK attack on 5-round Xoodyak [15], which is impossible using each technique separately.[3] Finally, we show how the combination of the

---

[2] A similar idea is used in the chosen-plaintext linear attack of Knudsen and Mathiassen on DES [20].

[3] More precisely, we show that each subset in the partitioning (which is defined according to the key material) determines a good value for the non-neutral bits. Without the combination, the distinguisher cannot be used for a key recovery attack.

two techniques can improve two previous DL attacks: We achieve the best DL attack on 9-round DES [1], which improves the previous DL attack of [8] by a factor of about 2^8 (in Sect. 5), thus, showing that partitioning works also for S-box based constructions.

2   Notations

- e_i $(0 \leq i \leq n-1)$ denotes the n-bit word with zeros in all bits but the i'th bit, and $e_{i_1,\ldots,i_j} = e_{i_1} \oplus \cdots \oplus e_{i_j}$.
- The probabilities of differential characteristics are denoted by p, and the biases of linear approximations are denoted by ϵ.
- For a DL distinguisher, a cipher E is treated as a decomposition $E = E_1 \circ E_0$. A differential characteristic with a probability of p on E_0 is denoted by $\Omega_I \xrightarrow[E_0]{p} \Omega_M$, and a linear approximation with a bias of ϵ on E_1 is denoted by $\lambda_M \xrightarrow[E_1]{\epsilon} \lambda_O$.
- For a boolean function $f : \{0,1\}^m \to \{0,1\}^n$, the Difference Distribution Table (DDT in short) is the $2^m \times 2^n$ table, which is defined by:

$$\mathrm{DDT}^f[\Omega_I, \Omega_O] = |\{(X, X') \mid X \oplus X' = \Omega_I \wedge f(X) \oplus f(X') = \Omega_O\}|.$$

3   Partitioning, Neutral Bits, and Combination of Them

3.1   DL Cryptanalysis with Partitioning

The partitioning technique was first proposed to improve the cryptanalysis of ARX ciphers. In [6] Biham and Carmeli suggest the partitioning technique to improve linear cryptanalysis on FEAL-8X [28]. Leurent [22] extends this technique to DL cryptanalysis, and uses it to improve a DL attack on 7-round Chaskey [29]. We present here the technique in the DL settings.

The main idea of the partitioning technique is as follows: Let $\Omega_I \xrightarrow{\frac{1}{2} \pm 2p\epsilon^2} \lambda_O$ be a DL characteristic, based on $\Omega_I \xrightarrow[E_0]{p} \Omega_M, \lambda_M \xrightarrow[E_1]{\epsilon} \lambda_O$. As mentioned above, the data complexity of an attack based on such a characteristic is $\mathcal{O}(p^{-2}\epsilon^{-4})$. Assume that one can partition the data into s disjoint subsets of plaintexts $A_1, A_2, \ldots, A_s$, such that there is one right subset A_i in which the differential characteristic holds with significantly higher probability $p_i \gg p$, while for all other subsets the differential characteristic does not hold. Formally, denote the probability of the differential characteristic in a specific subset A_i by p_i, we assume that: $\exists 1 \leq i \leq s : p_i \gg p \wedge \forall j \neq i : p_j \approx 0$. One can now run the DL attack in each subset A_i independently, resulting in a data complexity of $\mathcal{O}(s \cdot p_i^{-2}\epsilon^{-4})$: Generating about $s \cdot p_i^{-2}\epsilon^{-4}$ plaintext pairs, and performing the original attack on each subset. Therefore, if $s \cdot p_i^{-2} < p^{-2}$ then the attack's complexity is reduced.[4]

---

[4] The partitioning can be applied to plaintexts, ciphertexts, or any other criteria. For example, in [22] the partitioning is performed also according to the values of the ciphertexts.

3.2 Neutral Bits

In [7] Biham and Chen presented the *neutral bits* technique to improve collision and near-collision attacks on SHA-0. This idea is used also in secret key cryptanalysis (e.g., in [18]). Here we adapt the definitions of Biham and Chen to differential characteristics on block ciphers.

Definition 1. *Let $\Omega_I \to \Omega_O$ be a differential characteristic, the i'th bit of the block, e_i, is called a neutral bit (w.r.t. $\Omega_I \to \Omega_O$) if for each input pair (P, P') that satisfies the characteristic, the pair $(P \oplus e_i, P' \oplus e_i)$ also satisfies the characteristic.*

Using such neutral bits, an adversary can create many right pairs given one right pair. In addition, Beierle et al. [4] use t neutral bits to create neutral linear subspace with 2^t neutral vectors: Given t neutral bits $i_1, \ldots, i_t$ they use all the vectors of the linear subspace $\mathcal{U} = span\{e_{i_1}, \ldots, e_{i_t}\}$ (i.e., vectors of the form $v = \sum_{j=1}^{t} \alpha_j \cdot e_{i_j}, \alpha_j \in \{0,1\}$) as neutral vectors.[5]

Reducing Attack's Complexity Using Neutral Bits. Let $\Omega_I \xrightarrow{\frac{1}{2}+2p\epsilon^2} \lambda_O$ be a DL characteristic that relies on a differential $\Omega_I \xrightarrow[E_0]{p} \Omega_M$ and a linear approximation $\lambda_M \xrightarrow[E_1]{\epsilon} \lambda_O$. The data complexity of an attack based on such a characteristic is $\mathcal{O}(p^{-2}\epsilon^{-4})$. As was done in [4], assume that we have a neutral subspace $\mathcal{U}$ (w.r.t. $\Omega_I \to \Omega_M$) with $|\mathcal{U}| \geq c \cdot \epsilon^{-4}$ for a small c, then it is possible to reduce the data complexity by a factor of p^{-1}: Generate p^{-1} plaintext pairs $(P_i, P'_i = P_i \oplus \Omega_I)$, and ask for sets of ϵ^{-4} plaintext pairs of the form $\{(P_i \oplus u, P'_i \oplus u) \mid u \in \mathcal{U}\}$. For the set where (P_i, P'_i) is a right pair w.r.t. the differential, then all the pairs $(P_i \oplus u, P'_i \oplus u)$ are right pairs w.r.t. the differential. Hence, once we have such a pair, then we have ϵ^{-4} plaintext pairs that satisfy the differential part, which is sufficient to detect a bias of ϵ^2 in the ciphertext pairs.

When the neutral subspace is not big enough,[6] it is possible to use a neutral subspace w.r.t. the beginning of the differential (and not the entire differential): Assume that $E_0 = E_{01} \circ E_{00}$, and the differential $\Omega_I \xrightarrow[E_0]{p} \Omega_M$ is composed from two shorter differentials $\Omega_I \xrightarrow[E_{00}]{p_0} \Omega_1, \Omega_1 \xrightarrow[E_{01}]{p_1} \Omega_M$ (for $p_0 \cdot p_1 = p$), and we have a neutral subspace $\mathcal{U}$ w.r.t. $\Omega_I \xrightarrow[E_{00}]{p_0} \Omega_1$ with $|\mathcal{U}| \geq p_1^{-2}\epsilon^{-4}$, then it is possible to reduce the data complexity by factor of p_0^{-1}.

In addition, Beierle et al. [4] show that it is possible to use probabilistic neutral bits (PNBs, in short) [2]: Given an input pair (P, P') that satisfies the

---

[5] It should be noted that not always all the vectors in the linear subspace are neutral (see [7] that discusses such examples). However, in all of the cases discussed here this is the scenario.

[6] Similar issue also affected chosen-plaintext linear cryptanalysis [20].

differential, the pair $(P \oplus e_i, P' \oplus e_i)$ also satisfies the characteristic with high probability[7] (see also [17]).

Beierle et al. [4] use these two observations to offer an improved DL attack on Chaskey [29], which achieves better results than achieved by [22] using the partitioning technique, and to perform an improved DL attack on Chacha [5].

3.3 A Comparison Between Partitioning and Neutral Bits

We note that these two previous techniques actually improve the data complexity in two different ways:

1. In the partitioning technique, the adversary identifies a subset of the data in which the probability of the differential (or the bias) is higher than for random data. This subset is identified according to an external condition on the data (and not on the pairs among themselves), and therefore cannot be chosen in advance.
2. In the neutral bits technique, the adversary generates subsets of data in advance (with an internal condition on the pairs among themselves), such that in each subset all the pairs satisfy the differential part together (or not).

In other words, the goal of the partitioning technique is to increase the bias by using a partial subset of the data in which the bias is higher. In contrast, the neutral bits technique takes one right pair and generates many right pairs.

In addition to the data complexity reduction, the effect of these techniques on the time complexity should be examined. Beierle et al. [4] point out an advantage of the neutral bits technique: While usually the partitioning technique requires guessing key material which results in increasing the time complexity, the neutral bits technique is independent of the key. However, it depends on the attack details, and it is possible to achieve lower time complexity using the partitioning technique than using neutral bits (see, e.g., Sects. 5.2.2 and 5.2.3).

3.4 Combining Partitioning and Neutral Bits

When the two techniques refer to the same part of the DL characteristic, then the use of neutral bits may obviates the use of partition. For example, in the case of the two DL attacks [4,22] on Chaskey [29], Leurent [22] uses partitioning in both the differential characteristic and the linear approximation, and Beierle et al. [4] improve the attack by using neutral bits in the differential characteristic instead of partitioning. Beierle et al. do not apply neutral bits on top of the partitioning technique, but replace the partitioning technique on the differential part with neutral bits. However, we point out two situations in which it is possible to use the two techniques together on the differential part, which leads to an attack with lower complexities than can be achieved by using each technique separately.

---

[7] The probability should be significantly higher than the differential's probability.

1. In some cases each subset in the partitioning determines a good value for the non-neutral bits (i.e., an input with this determined value and any value for the neutral bits satisfies the differential part). In Sect. 4 we present the first DL distinguisher on 5-round Xoodoo [14], and then we apply this idea and show how a combination of the two techniques together allows us to attack 5-round Xoodyak [15].
2. In some cases it is possible to decompose the differential characteristic into two parts, and to perform the partitioning technique on the first part and the neutral bits technique on the second part, to take advantage of these two techniques.[8] We use this idea to improve the DL attack of [8] on round-reduced DES [1] in Sect. 5.

4   New DL Attacks on Round-Reduced Xoodyak

In this section we present the first DL distinguishers on 4- and 5-round Xoodoo [14], and use them to perform key-recovery attacks on 4- and 5-round Xoodyak [15]. We show that the key-recovery attacks are possible only by using the partitioning technique and the neutral bits idea together.

A Brief Description of Xoodyak. Xoodyak is a cryptographic primitive for hashing, authenticated encryption, and MAC computation, and is one of the finalists of the NIST LightWeight Cryptography (LWC) competition. Xoodyak relies on Xoodoo, a family of 384-bit to 384-bit permutations. A 384-bit state is represented by three *planes*, each consists of four 32-bit *lanes*. The lanes within a plane are indexed by x, the planes are indexed by y, and the bits within a lane are indexed by z. In addition, the i'th bit ($0 \leq i < 384$) of a state S is denoted by S_i. Given a state of three planes $S = (A_0, A_1, A_2)$, each round is defined by the following 5 steps:

$$
\begin{aligned}
\theta: \quad & P \leftarrow A_0 \oplus A_1 \oplus A_2 \\
& E \leftarrow P \lll (1,5) \oplus P \lll (1,14) \\
& A_y \leftarrow A_y \oplus E, y \in \{0,1,2\} \\
\rho_{west}: \quad & A_1 \leftarrow A_1 \lll (1,0) \\
& A_2 \leftarrow A_2 \lll (0,11) \\
\iota: \quad & A_0 \leftarrow A_0 \oplus C_i \\
\chi: \quad & B_y \leftarrow \overline{A_{y+1 \ (\mathrm{mod}\ 3)}} \wedge A_{y+2 \ (\mathrm{mod}\ 3)}, y \in \{0,1,2\} \\
& A_y \leftarrow A_y \oplus B_y, y \in \{0,1,2\} \\
\rho_{east}: \quad & A_1 \leftarrow A_1 \lll (0,1) \\
& A_2 \leftarrow A_2 \lll (2,8),
\end{aligned}
$$

where $A_y \lll (i,j)$ denotes the left rotation which moves the bit in (x,z) to the new position $(x + i \pmod 4, z + j \pmod{32})$, C_i is a round constant, and $\overline{A_y}$ denotes the bitwise complement of A_y. All operations but χ are affine.

Xoodyak uses two modes: hash mode and keyed mode. Here, we discuss the keyed mode, and in particular the initialization phase: The first plane is

---

[8] This idea was used in [20].

initialized by an 128-bit key, and the additional two planes by a 256-bit nonce. Then, Xoodoo is performed on the initialized state, and the first 192 bits are visible and XORed to the first block of the plaintext.

4.1   4-Round DL Attack on Xoodyak

We now present the first DL distinguisher[9] on 4-round Xoodoo, and then a DL attack that based on it. Recall that the first plane A_0 is initialized by an 128-bit key, and the last two planes A_1, A_2 are initialized by a 256-bit nonce. Therefore, to mount a DL attack on Xoodoo, the DL characteristic is restricted: the input difference can be only in the last two planes, and the active bits of the output mask can be only in the first 192 bits, which are visible.

4.1.1   Description of Our Distinguisher

To choose the input difference we examine the first two steps of the round function: θ and ρ_{west}. We note that given an input difference with two active bits in one column, then θ does not change the difference, and ρ_{west} shifts each bit by a different number of positions, resulting in two active S-boxes in the S-box layer χ (the constant addition does not change the difference). For comparison, if the input difference contains only one active bit then after θ, in addition to this active bit, there are three additional active bits at two columns, and ρ_{west} shifts each bit by a different number of positions, resulting in 7 active S-boxes in the first S-box layer. We thus consider an input difference of the form $(0, e_i, e_i), 0 \le i < 128$.

Following the rotation-invariant property of Xoodoo's characteristics, and for sake of clarity, we consider the input difference $(0, e_0, e_0)$, but this characteristic can be rotated (each word is rotated by the same amount of bits). This input difference leads to two active S-boxes before χ: S-box 11 with an input difference of 4 and S-box 32 with an input difference of 2. Denote the output differences (after χ) at S-box 11 by Ω_{11}, and the output differences (after χ) at S-box 32 by Ω_{32}. According to the DDT of χ we have: $\Omega_{11} \in \{4, 5, 6, 7\}, \Omega_{32} \in \{2, 3, 6, 7\}$ in a uniform distribution. We experimentally tested the bias of each DL characteristic with each of the 16 possible differences $(\Omega_{11}, \Omega_{32})$ after the first χ layer, and output mask of one or two active bits after 3.5 additional rounds of Xoodoo. The best result was obtained for the output mask[10] $(0, e_{15}, 0)$. The combination

---

[9] Liu et al. [24] present a 4-round rotational DL distinguisher, with the highest possible bias of $\frac{1}{2}$, without any attack that uses it. We give in the ePrint version the rotational DL distinguisher used by Liu et al. and recall that rotational DL distinguisher is not a DL distinguisher.

[10] In detail, for each $0 \le i < 128$, when the input difference is $(0, e_i, e_i)$, the best results occurs for the output mask $(0, e_{32 \cdot \lfloor \frac{i}{32} \rfloor + (15+i \pmod{32})}, 0)$. It should be noted that since the mask is in the second plane and only the first 64 bits of this plane are visible, we can not use all the 128 characteristics, but only the 64 characteristics for which $0 \le i < 64$. However, this fact does not impact our analysis.

$(\Omega_{11}, \Omega_{32}) = (4, 2)$ results in a bias of $+2^{-6}$, where as $(\Omega_{11}, \Omega_{32}) = (4, 6)$ results in a bias of $+2^{-8}$. The other differences have a bias of about zero. Summing all of these characteristics, we get the following DL characteristic:

$$(0, e_0, e_0) \xrightarrow[\text{4-round Xoodoo}]{\approx 2^{-9.68}} (0, e_{15}, 0).$$

The bias is calculated as follows: $\frac{1}{16} \cdot 2^{-6} + \frac{1}{16} \cdot 2^{-8} + \frac{14}{16} \cdot 0 \approx 2^{-9.68}$. In terms of state indexes, the input difference is $e_{128,256}$ and the output mask is e_{143}. We experimentally verified the bias, using 2^{28} pairs, observing a bias of about $2^{-9.7}$.

4.1.2   Attacking 4-Rounds Xoodyak

We now present an attack, which reveals four key bits of the initialized state. It is should be noted that in this case it is impossible to reveal key bits using a classical DL attack: Assume that we generate about $2^{21.3}$ nonce pairs (this number was calculated according to [31]) with the required input difference, and we compute the number of pairs that are the same on the output mask of the output. Indeed, about $2^{21.3} \cdot \left(\frac{1}{2} + 2^{-9.7}\right)$ pairs are expected to be equal on the output mask, but it does not tell us anything about the key as the question which pairs satisfy the DL characteristic is independent of the key (like in [24]). We show that using neutral bits and the partitioning technique, it is possible to reveal four key bits.

Finding The Neutral Bits. We now look for bits of the initial state, and in particular those initialized by the nonce, that *do not* influence the output of the two active S-boxes in the first χ: S-box 11 and S-box 32. Denote the initial state by S, and the state just before the S-box layer χ by T (i.e., $T = \iota \circ \rho_{west} \circ \theta(S)$). In these terms, the two non-active bits of the 11'th S-box are: T_{11}, T_{139}, and the two non-active bits of the 32'nd S-box are: T_{32}, T_{288}. Each of them could be represented as the XOR of 7 bits of the initial state, as follows:

$$
\begin{aligned}
T_{11} &= \bigoplus_{i \in I_{11}} S_i, \ I_{11} = \{11, 102, 125, 230, 253, 358, 381\}, \\
T_{139} &= \bigoplus_{i \in I_{139}} S_i, \ I_{139} = \{70, 93, 198, 221, 235, 326, 349\}, \\
T_{32} &= \bigoplus_{i \in I_{32}} S_i, \ I_{32} = \{18, 27, 32, 146, 155, 274, 283\}, \\
T_{288} &= \bigoplus_{i \in I_{288}} S_i, \ I_{288} = \{7, 16, 135, 144, 263, 272, 309\}.
\end{aligned}
\tag{1}
$$

It means that there are 28 bits of the initial state that influence the two active S-boxes (i.e., that influence the two non active bits of each active S-box), and 18 of them are initialized by the nonce. Therefore, we have $256 - 18 = 238$ neutral bits. By fixing all the 18 bits that influence these active S-boxes (i.e., all the non-neutral bits) in all of the nonces, we get the same values at the active S-boxes, which yields the same output difference. Hence, by generating about 2^4 sets of about $2^{13.34}$ nonce pairs (this number was calculated according to [31] for success rate of 95%), each is defined by another fixed value of the non-neutral bits, the good values (i.e., the values which satisfy $(\Omega_{11}, \Omega_{32}) = (4, 2)$) are expected to appear in about one set, which has the highest bias. To produce an attack using this characteristic, we need also the partitioning technique.

Using the Partitioning Technique. We now describe how the partitioning technique allows us to link between the good set (or, in other words, the good values for the non-neutral bits) and four key bits. As mentioned above, given a right pair (i.e., a pair that satisfies the first round) $S = K \parallel N, S' = K \parallel N'$ (where, K is the key, and N, N' are the nonces), we know that $(\Omega_{11}, \Omega_{32}) = (4, 2)$. According to the DDT of χ, the transition $4 \rightarrow 4$ occurs when the input values are 2 and 6 and the transition $2 \rightarrow 2$ occurs when the input values are 1 and 3. Thus, according to Eq. (1):

$$
\begin{aligned}
T_{11} &= T'_{11} = 0, \\
T_{139} &= T'_{139} = 1, \\
T_{32} &= T'_{32} = 1, \\
T_{288} &= T'_{288} = 0,
\end{aligned}
$$

where $T = \iota \circ \rho_{west} \circ \theta(S), T' = \iota \circ \rho_{west} \circ \theta(S')$. Therefore, we get the following four equations:

$$
\begin{aligned}
K_{11} \oplus K_{102} \oplus K_{125} &= N_{230} \oplus N_{253} \oplus N_{358} \oplus N_{381}, \\
K_{70} \oplus K_{93} &= N_{198} \oplus N_{221} \oplus N_{235} \oplus N_{326} \oplus N_{349} \oplus 1, \\
K_{18} \oplus K_{27} \oplus K_{32} &= N_{146} \oplus N_{155} \oplus N_{274} \oplus N_{283} \oplus 1, \\
K_7 \oplus K_{16} &= N_{135} \oplus N_{144} \oplus N_{263} \oplus N_{272} \oplus N_{309},
\end{aligned}
\tag{2}
$$

where the key bits are indexed by $0 \leq i < 128$ and the nonce bits are indexed by $128 \leq i \leq 383$. It means that there is a partitioning of the space to 16 subsets, depending on four key values: $K_{11} \oplus K_{102} \oplus K_{125}, K_{70} \oplus K_{93}, K_{18} \oplus K_{27} \oplus K_{32}, K_7 \oplus K_{16}$. Each value for these key values determines another subset of the non-neutral nonce bits, in which the characteristic has a bias of 2^{-6}, instead of $2^{-9.7}$ when the nonces are generated randomly without the use of these techniques. The data complexity required to find four key bit is about $2^4 \cdot 2^{13.34} \cdot 2 = 2^{18.34}$ chosen nonces, and the time complexity is about $2^{18.34}$ 4-round Xoodoo calls. We experimentally verified the attack using 100 different keys.[11] The observed success rate was 85%. Following the rotation-invariant property of Xoodoo's characteristics, it is possible to recover the entire key with data complexity of about $2^{23.34}$ chosen nonces and time complexity of about $2^{23.34}$ 4-round Xoodoo calls.

4.2   5-Round Related-Key DL Attack on Xoodyak

We now present the first DL distinguisher on 5-round Xoodoo, and then a related-key DL attack based on it. To construct our 5-round DL distinguisher we first construct a 4-round DL distinguisher and then prepend one round before it.

---

[11] All the experiments can be found in https://github.com/ArielWeizman/AW/blob/master/Xoodoo.

4.2.1 Description of Our Distinguisher

Similarly to the input difference $(0, e_i, e_i)$ of the 4-round DL characteristic that described in Sect. 4.1, the input differences of the form $(e_i, e_i, 0)$ and $(e_i, 0, e_i)$ are also good candidates, with an additional requirement: Due to the fact that there is an active bit in the first plane, initialized by a key, an attack using these characteristics requires related keys. Our experiments show that $(e_i, 0, e_i)$ offers better results than $(e_i, e_i, 0)$ and thus the reminder of our analysis concentrates on differences of this form.

Following the rotation-invariant property of Xoodoo's characteristics, and for sake of clarity, we consider the input difference $(e_0, 0, e_0)$, but this characteristic can be easily rotated. This input difference leads to two active S-boxes before χ: S-box 0 with an input difference of 1 and S-box 11 with an input difference of 4. Denote the output differences (after χ) at S-box 0 by Ω_0, and the output differences (after χ) at S-box 11 by Ω_{11}. According to the DDT of χ we have: $\Omega_0 \in \{1, 3, 5, 7\}, \Omega_{11} \in \{4, 5, 6, 7\}$ in a uniform distribution. We experimentally tested the bias of each DL characteristic with each of the 16 possible differences (Ω_0, Ω_{11}) after the first χ layer and output mask of one or two active bits after 3.5 more rounds of Xoodoo. The best result was obtained for the output mask $(e_0, 0, 0)$. The combinations $(\Omega_0, \Omega_{11}) \in \{(1, 4), (1, 6)\}$ result in a bias of -2^{-3}, the combinations $(\Omega_0, \Omega_{11}) \in \{(1, 5), (1, 7), (3, 4), (3, 6)\}$ result in a bias of -2^{-5}, and the combinations $(\Omega_0, \Omega_{11}) \in \{(3, 5), (3, 7)\}$ result in a bias of -2^{-7}. The other differences have a bias of about zero. Summing all of these characteristics, we get the following DL characteristic:

$$(e_0, 0, e_0) \xrightarrow[\text{4-round Xoodoo}]{\approx -2^{-5.36}} (e_0, 0, 0).$$

The bias is calculated as follows: $-\frac{2}{16} \cdot 2^{-3} - \frac{4}{16} \cdot 2^{-5} - \frac{2}{16} \cdot 2^{-7} + \frac{8}{16} \cdot 0 \approx -2^{-5.36}$. In terms of state indexes, the input difference is $e_{0,256}$ and the output mask is e_0. We experimentally verified the bias, using 2^{28} pairs.[12]

We now add one round at the beginning, by performing the inverse of the round function step by step. First, ρ_{east}^{-1} transforms $(e_0, 0, e_0)$ to $(e_0, 0, e_{88})$. Then χ^{-1} maintains this difference with probability of 2^{-4} (i.e., 2^{-2} for each S-box), which is not changed by ι^{-1}. Finally, the difference $(e_0, 0, e_{88})$ is transformed by $\theta^{-1} \circ \rho_{west}^{-1}$ to $\Omega_I = (\Omega A_0, \Omega A_1, \Omega A_2)$, where

$$\Omega A_0 = a8b23b19\ 98810919\ 52674513\ 95a876f3_x$$
$$\Omega A_1 = a8b23b18\ 98810919\ 52674513\ 95a876f3_x$$
$$\Omega A_2 = a8b23b18\ 98810919\ 52676513\ 95a876f3_x.$$

---

[12] In detail, for each $0 \le i < 128$, when the input difference is $(e_i, 0, e_i)$, the best results occur for the output mask $(e_i, 0, 0)$.

Therefore, the entire DL distinguisher for 5-round Xoodoo is:

$$(\Omega A_0, \Omega A_1, \Omega A_2) \xrightarrow[\text{5-round Xoodoo}]{-2^{-9.36}} (e_0, 0, 0).$$

4.2.2 Attacking 5-Round Xoodyak

The 5-round attack is quite similar to the 4-round attack and therefore we give here only a brief description of the attack. The two active S-boxes in the first χ layer are: S-box 0 with an input difference of 1 and S-box 88 with an input difference of 4. Denote the initial state by S and $T = \iota \circ \rho_{west} \circ \theta(S)$. In these term the two non-active bits of the 0'th S-box are T_{128}, T_{256} and the two non-active bits of the 88'th S-box are T_{88}, T_{216}. Each of them could be represented as follows:

$$
\begin{aligned}
T_{128} &= \bigoplus_{i \in I_{128}} S_i, \ I_{128} = \{82, 91, 210, 219, 224, 338, 347\}, \\
T_{256} &= \bigoplus_{i \in I_{256}} S_i, \ I_{256} = \{103, 112, 231, 240, 277, 359, 368\}, \\
T_{88} &= \bigoplus_{i \in I_{88}} S_i, \ I_{88} = \{42, 51, 88, 170, 179, 298, 307\}, \\
T_{216} &= \bigoplus_{i \in I_{216}} S_i, \ I_{216} = \{10, 19, 138, 147, 184, 266, 275\}.
\end{aligned}
\tag{3}
$$

The rest of the attack is very similar to that of 4-round Xoodyak, up to the following changing of Eq. (2):

$$
\begin{aligned}
K_{82} \oplus K_{91} &= N_{210} \oplus N_{219} \oplus N_{224} \oplus N_{338} \oplus N_{347}, \\
K_{103} \oplus K_{112} &= N_{231} \oplus N_{240} \oplus N_{277} \oplus N_{359} \oplus N_{368} \oplus 1, \\
K_{42} \oplus K_{51} \oplus K_{88} &= N_{170} \oplus N_{179} \oplus N_{298} \oplus N_{307}, \\
K_{10} \oplus K_{19} &= N_{138} \oplus N_{147} \oplus N_{184} \oplus N_{266} \oplus N_{275} \oplus 1.
\end{aligned}
\tag{4}
$$

It means that there is a partitioning of the space to 16 subsets, depending on four key values: $K_{82} \oplus K_{91}, K_{103} \oplus K_{112}, K_{42} \oplus K_{51} \oplus K_{88}, K_{10} \oplus K_{19}$. Each value for these key values determines another subset of the non-neutral nonce bits, in which the characteristic has the bias of $2^{-5.36}$, instead of $2^{-9.36}$ when the nonces are generated randomly. Algorithm 1 describes the attack. The data complexity required to reveal four key bits is about $2^4 \cdot 2^{12.04} \cdot 2 = 2^{17.04}$ chosen nonces, and the time complexity is about $2^{17.04}$ 5-round Xoodoo performances. We experimentally verified the attack using 100 random keys, and observed an 89% success rate. Following the rotation-invariant property of Xoodoo's characteristics, it is possible to recover the entire key with data complexity of about $2^{22.04}$ chosen nonces and time complexity of about $2^{22.04}$ 5-round Xoodoo encryptions.

5   Improved DL Attacks on Round-Reduced DES

In [8] Biham et al. present two attacks on round-reduced DES. The 8- and 9-round attacks are based on a 7-round DL distinguisher composed of a 4-round

---

Algorithm 1. DL Attack on 5-Round Xoodyak (Recovering 4 key bits).

Set an array *keyOptions* of 2^4 key values to zeroes. The *keyOptions* bits are defined as the XOR of the key bits from Eq. (4).

for all $k \in \{0,1\}^4$ **do**

　　Fix values for the non-neutral nonce bits, that satisfy Eq. (4).

　　for all $1 \leq i \leq 2^{12.04}$ **do**

　　　　Generate a nonce (according to the fixed bits) N_i, and set the pairs $(S = K \parallel N_i, S' = (K \parallel N_i) \oplus \Omega_I)$ as two initial states.

　　　　Request the output of these initial states after the first performance of Xoodoo, denoted by (O_i, O'_i).

　　　　if $O_{i_0} = O'_{i_0}$ **then**

　　　　　　Increment *keyOptions*[k].

　　　　end if

　　end for

end for

Output the key k such that *keyOptions*[k] = min{*keyOptions*[j]}.

---

differential characteristic and a 3-round linear approximation. We now show how to use the partitioning technique to decrease the attacks' complexity. Then we show an improvement of the 9-round attack using neutral bits. Finally, we show how to combine the partitioning technique and the neutral bits to get the best known attack against 9-round DES.

Brief Description of DES [1]. DES is a 64-bit block size, 56-bit key size block cipher, composed of 16 Feistel rounds. Each round is defined by

$$F_{K_r}(x, y) = (y, x \oplus P(S(E(y) \oplus K_r))),$$

where $E : \{0,1\}^{32} \rightarrow \{0,1\}^{48}$ is a linear expansion function, K_r is the round key, S is an S-box layer consisting of 8 different S-boxes $S_i : \{0,1\}^6 \rightarrow \{0,1\}^4$ ($1 \leq i \leq 8$) that performed in parallel on 8 different 6-bit parts, and $P : \{0,1\}^{32} \rightarrow \{0,1\}^{32}$ is a bit permutation.

5.1 Description of Biham et al.'s Attacks [8]

The 8-Round Attack [8]. To attack 8-round DES Biham et al. use the following distinguisher on 7-round DES and additional round after it covered by guessing some key bits. The distinguisher uses the decomposition of 7-round DES to $E_1 \circ E_0$, where E_0 consists of rounds 1–4 and E_1 consists of rounds 5–7. E_0 is covered by the truncated differential characteristic

$$\Omega_I = 00808200 \ 60000000_x \xrightarrow[E_0]{p = \frac{14}{64}} \Omega_M = 00W0XY0Z \ ????U???_x,$$

where $U \in \{0, 1, 2, \ldots, 7\}, W, X \in \{0, 8\}, Y, Z \in \{0, 2\}$, and ? is an unknown value. The linear approximation for E_1 is:

$$\lambda_M = 21040080 \; 00008000_x \xrightarrow[E_1]{\epsilon=0.195} \lambda_O = \lambda_M.$$

Hence, the bias of the full DL characteristic is about $2p\epsilon^2 = 2^{-5.9}$.

The 8-round attack of [8] is as follows: Ask for the encryption of $2^{12.82}$ plaintext pairs with input difference of $\Omega_I = 00808200 \; 60000000_x$, and initialize an array of 2^6 counters to zeros (corresponding to the six key bits entering to S_1 in the last round). Then, for each possible key, compute each ciphertext pair backwards by one round and check if the parity of the resulting pair is equal in the mask $\lambda_O = 21040080 \; 00008000_x$. If yes, increment the related entry in the array. The highest entry in the array should correspond to the six key bits. The data and time complexity of this attack both are about[13] $2^{13.82}$.

The 9-Round Attack [8]. To attack 9-round DES, an additional round preceding the distinguisher is used, covered by guessing additional key material. In order to minimize the number of actives S-boxes in this round, they replace the 4-round truncated differential. The main replacement is in the first round, where the new first round differential is:

$$40000000_x \xrightarrow[F]{p'=\frac{12}{64}} 00000202_x.$$

Using this characteristic, there are only two active S-boxes in the first round: S_6 and S_8. The bias of the new 7-round DL characteristic is thus $2p'\epsilon^2 \approx 2^{-6.13}$.

In [8], 2^7 structures each consisting of 2^9 plaintexts are generated as follows:

1. Select a plaintext P_0.
2. Select the plaintexts $P_1, \ldots P_{255}$ which differ from P_0 by all the possible subsets of the eight bits related to the output of S_6 and S_8 according to the P permutation of the round function (i.e., the bits masked by $18222828 \; 00000000_x$).
3. Select the plaintexts $P_{256}, \ldots P_{511}$ as $P_i = P_{i-256} \oplus 40000000 \; 00000202_x$.

Now, for each possible guess of 12 key bits related to S_6 and S_8 in the first round, find in each structure the 2^8 appropriate pairs such that the input difference for the second round is $00000202 \; 40000000_x$, and perform the 8-round attack on them. The data complexity of this attack is about 2^{16} chosen plaintexts. The time complexity is about $2^{16} \cdot 2^{18} \cdot \frac{3}{72} \approx 2^{29.42}$ 9-round DES encryptions (each parity computation takes about 3 S-boxes out of 72 in 9-round DES).

5.2   Our Improved Attacks on Round-Reduced DES

5.2.1   Improved 8-Round Attack, Using Partitioning

---

[13] We note that the time complexity is about $2^{12.82} \cdot 2 \cdot 2^6$ one S-box evaluations, which are equivalent to about $2^{13.82}$ 8-round encryptions.

We now revisit the 8-round attack of [8], based on the 4-round truncated differential $\Omega_I = 00808200\ 60000000_x \xrightarrow[E_0]{p=\frac{14}{64}} \Omega_M =????U???\ 00W0XY0Z_x$. Instead of using standard plaintext pairs with the difference Ω_I, i.e., randomly selected P and $P' = P \oplus \Omega_I$, we propose to use structures in a similar way to that of [20]: Fix two right half values $R, R' = R \oplus 60000000$ (60000000_x is the input difference of F in the first round). Now, generate a structure of 2^4 left halves $L_0, \ldots, L_{15}$, containing all the possible values in the four bits corresponding to the output of S_1 (i.e., bits 9, 17, 23, 31). The structure contains all the 2^5 plaintexts induced by the two right halves and the 2^4 left halves. We get that all the plaintext pairs (P, P') (from any structure) have the same input values for F in the first round (R, R', respectively), and thus have the same output difference of F in the first round. Denote this output difference by Ω_G. Obviously, Ω_G is key dependent.

We now partition the plaintext pairs according to the value of Ω_G (which has 10 possible values): Each time we concentrate only on plaintext pairs with difference Ω_G in the left half, i.e., pairs with zero difference at the beginning of the second round with probability of 1. For the correct subset, the probability of the differential characteristic is 1 instead of $\frac{14}{64}$, and the bias of the entire DL characteristic is $2 \cdot 1 \cdot (2 \cdot (-\frac{20}{64})^2)^2 \approx 2^{-3.71}$ instead of $2^{-5.9}$.

Our attack thus tries all the possible values of Ω_G, and for each such value tries to recover the 6 key bits entering S_1 in the last round (which is done as in [8]). Given the correct output difference Ω_G, we can also recover some key material for the first round.

The data complexity of this attack is about $2^{10.14}$ chosen plaintexts. This number was calculated according to [31] for a success rate of 75% (i.e., the right key, Ω_G combination has the highest bias). Note that since we run over all the 10 possible output differences in the first round and all 2^6 possible keys, the number of the possible keys in the formula of [31] is replaced by $2^6 \cdot 10 = 640$. The time complexity is mainly affected by checking the parities of the appropriate ciphertexts. Since there are about $2^{10.14}$ ciphertexts and we check it for each six key bits and for each output difference in the first round, the time complexity is about $2^{10.14} \cdot 640 \cdot \frac{1}{64} \approx 2^{13.46}$ 8-round DES encryptions (The parity of each plaintext should be checked about 640 times, each test takes about one S-box computation out of the 64 S-boxes of a full 8-round encryption). This improved attack was experimentally verified using 100 different keys with a success rate of 76%. Table 1 compares the previous attack and ours for a success rate of 75%.[14]

5.2.2   Improved 9-Round Attack, Using Partitioning

The idea of running over the output differences in the first round can also be extended to the 9-round attack. Instead of guessing the 12 key bits related to S_6 and S_8 in the first round, it is possible to partition the plaintext pairs according to the output difference of S_6 and S_8: Fix two right half values $P_r, P'_r = P_r \oplus$

---

[14] All the experiments can be found in https://github.com/ArielWeizman/AW/blob/master/DES..

00000202_x, and generate the structures as described in [8]. The input differences of S_6 and S_8 (after the expansion permutation of DES) are both 4. The fixing ensures that in all of the pairs, the differences in S_6 and S_8 are composed from the same values, which ensures that all the output differences are the same. Now, we guess the output differences in S_6 and S_8, and select the appropriate plaintext pairs from each structure according to that. For input difference of 4 in S_6 and S_8, there are 9 and 10 possible output differences, respectively. Hence, the plaintext pairs for the attack are selected from 90 possibilities, instead of 4096 as in [8]. The rest of the attack remains the same. Given the right output differences in the first round, we can also recover key material for the first round.

According to [31], since the right key is revealed from only $2^6 \cdot 90 \approx 2^{12.5}$ options (instead of 2^{18} in the original attack), about $2^{15.44}$ chosen plaintexts are needed to detect the right key with a success rate of 75%. The time complexity is about $2^{15.44} \cdot 2^6 \cdot 90 \cdot \frac{1}{72} \approx 2^{21.76}$ 9-round DES encryptions. This improved attack was experimentally verified using 100 different keys with a success rate of 78%.

A subtle point should be noted: In contrast to the analysis in Sect. 3.1 which claims for reducing the data complexity using the partitioning technique, in our case the main effect of this idea is reducing the time complexity. The reason is that Biham et al. [8] already used structures to ensure that enough pairs with the required input difference exist in the data, and the key guessing is needed to identify the structure. This idea affects the data complexity in the same way as the partitioning technique. However, there is a subtle difference between their structures and the partitioning technique: their structures heavily depend on the specific structure of DES, while the partitioning technique is more general. To emphasize this difference between the two ideas, consider a DES variant for which the P-permutation is an 8-bit key dependent permutation. For this variant, the structures of Biham et al. [8] are of size 2^{32} to ensure that indeed all the required pairs exist in the data, since the positions of the relevant bits after the P-permutation are unknown. However, most of these plaintexts are not going to be used in the attack. In comparison, the partitioning technique would define a structure of $2^{15.44}$ plaintexts for each of the 2^8 possible P-permutations, i.e., a total of $2^{23.44}$ plaintexts.

5.2.3   Improved 9-Round Attack, Using Neutral Bits

We now show how to use neutral bits in order to minimize the attack's complexity. The goal is to find a subspace $\mathcal{U} \subseteq \mathbb{F}_2^{64}$ such that if a pair (P, P') satisfies the differential characteristic, than $\forall u \in \mathcal{U} : (P \oplus u, P' \oplus u)$ also satisfies the differential characteristic. Recall that the differential characteristic covers rounds 2–5 (the first round is covered by guessing key material). The first round of the differential characteristic is

$$40000000_x \xrightarrow[F]{\frac{12}{64}} P(30000000_x) = 00000202_x$$

(the rest of the characteristic has probability 1). In the left half, all the bits that are masked by $07\mathrm{ffffe}_x$ do not affect the input values of S_1 in the second round, and thus they are neutral bits. In the right half, the six bits that affect the input values of S_1 in the second round come from six different S-boxes $(S_2, S_4, S_5, S_6, S_7, S_8)$, thus the bits that are masked by 60600000_x are also neutral bits. Note that since all these neutral bits do not affect S_1 in the second round, every linear combination of them is also neutral (unlike in [7]). Thus, all these neutral bits are a basis for the desired neutral subspace $\mathcal{U} \subseteq \mathbb{F}_2^{64}$ with 2^{30} neutral vectors. The bits masked by 18222828_x in the left half can be used to define the structures used in the attack. Each structure defines 4 different pairs entering S_1 in the second round, i.e., 4 subsets of 2^6 pairs each (since there are six bits that are masked by 00222828_x), such that either all of them satisfy the differential characteristic, or no one satisfies it. Using the other 24 neutral bits, it is possible to increase the size of these subsets up to 2^{30} right pairs.[15]

We now compute the data complexity. Since each structure (which is defined according to a fixed value) generates four subsets, and for each subset the probability of being a right subset is $\frac{12}{64}$, the probability that all of the four subsets are wrong is $\left(1 - \frac{12}{64}\right)^4$. Thus, the probability of having at least one right subset, given s structures, is $1 - \left(1 - \frac{12}{64}\right)^{4s}$. Therefore, using two structures we get a probability of about 0.81 to have a right subset. Hence, for a success rate of 75% of the entire attack, a success rate in each subset is needed to be about $\frac{0.75}{0.81} \approx 0.93$. Now, given such a subset of pairs such that all of them satisfy the differential characteristic, the bias of the DL approximation is about $2^{-3.71}$, as before. According to [31], about $2^{10.57}$ pairs are needed to detect the 18 key bits with success rate of 93%. Therefore, increasing each structure by $2^{4.57}$ plaintexts, using the neutral bits, is sufficient. Thus the data complexity is about $2^{13.57} \cdot 2 = 2^{14.57}$ chosen plaintexts. The time complexity is about $2^{14.57} \cdot 2^{18} \cdot \frac{3}{72} \approx 2^{28}$ 9-round DES encryptions. The improved attack was experimentally verified using 100 different keys with a success rate of 79%.

5.2.4   Improved 9-Round Attack, Using a Combination of Partitioning and Neutral Bits

We note that the main effect of the partitioning technique is on the time complexity, and that of the neutral bits is on the data complexity. Therefore, combining these two techniques together can reduce both. To do that, we fix two right half values $P_r, P_r' = P_r \oplus 00000202_x$, generate the structures as described in [8], and partition the data according to the output difference of S_6 and S_8 as described in Sect. 5.2.2. As described in Sect. 5.2.3, each structure defines 4 subsets of 2^6 pairs that satisfy together the differential characteristic. To increase the size of these subsets, note that since the right half is fixed in all of the inputs, the neutral bits are only those from the left half that are masked by $07\mathrm{ffffe}_x$. However, the

---

[15] For attacks that needed more plaintext pairs, we refer the reader to the chosen plaintext linear cryptanalysis techniques suggested Knudsen and Mathiassen [20].

Algorithm 2. Improved Attack on 9-Round DES (Recovering 6 key bits and the output difference Ω_G).

Fix a random right half value R.

Set[16] *max counter* $= 0$.

for all iteration $\in \{0, 1\}$ **do**

Fix a random value for all left half non-neutral bits L_{fixed}.

Generate $2^{4.1}$ structures S_i as follows:

for all Structure S_i **do**

Select A random left half value for all neutral bits L^i_{rand}.

Set $L^i_0 = L_{\text{fixed}} \oplus L^i_{\text{rand}}, P^i_0 = L^i_0 \parallel R$.

Select the plaintexts $P^i_1, \ldots, P^i_{255}$ which differ from P^i_0 by all the 255 possible subsets of the eight bits masked by $18222828\ 00000000_x$.

Set $P^i_j = P^i_{j-256} \oplus 40000000\ 00000202_x, \forall 256 \leq j \leq 511$.

end for

Request the ciphertexts of these plaintexts.

for all $K_1 \in \{0, 1\}^6$ (The subkey entering S_1 in the last round) **do**

for all Ω_G (The output difference of F in the first round, of two plaintexts P_i, P_j, such that $0 \leq i \leq 255, 256 \leq j \leq 511$). **do**

Select the pairs with difference Ω_G in the left half.

Partially decrypt all these pairs through S-box S_1 of the last round.

Check how many ciphertext pairs are equal in the parity of the five bits masked by $21040080\ 00008000_x$ and denote this number by c.

if $c > max$ *counter* **then**

Set *max counter* $= c, K_{\max} = K_1, \Omega_{\max} = \Omega_G$.

end if

end for

end for

end for

Output $K_{\max}, \Omega_{\max}$.

---

resulting neutral subspace is big enough for the attack. Algorithm 2 describes the improved attack[16].

Since the right key is detected from only $2^6 \cdot 90$ options (instead of 2^{18} in Sect. 5.2.3), about $2^{10.1}$ pairs are needed in each subset to detect the right key with a success rate of 93% (which leads to a success rate of 75% of the entire attack). Thus, the data complexity is about $2^{13.1} \cdot 2 = 2^{14.1}$ chosen plaintexts. The time complexity is about $2^{14.1} \cdot 2^6 \cdot 90 \cdot \frac{3}{72} \approx 2^{22}$ 9-round DES encryptions. This improved attack was experimentally verified using 100 different keys with a success rate of 77%. Table 1 compares the previous attacks and ours for a success rate of 75%.

---

[16] Since each plaintext pair passes the differential characteristic has zero difference in the bits masked by λ_M (i.e., $(P \oplus P') \cdot \lambda_M = \Omega_M \cdot \lambda_M = 0$), the sign of the bias is necessarily positive.

Table 1. Comparison of DL attacks on round-reduced DES.

Rounds		[8]^a	Partitioning	Neutral Bits	Combination
8	Data (CP)	$2^{13.82}$	$2^{10.14}$	–	–
	Time (Enc.)	$2^{13.82}$	$2^{13.46}$	–	–
	Recovered Key Bits	6	6	–	–
9	Data (CP)	2^{16}	$2^{15.44}$	$2^{14.57}$	$2^{14.1}$
	Time (Enc.)	$2^{29.42}$	$2^{21.76}$	2^{28}	2^{22}
	Recovered Key Bits	18	6	18	6

^{a} The values given here are calculated according to [31] for success rate of 75%, which differs a bit from [8].

6 Conclusions

In this paper we showed hot to combine the partitioning technique with the neutral bits to offer better DL attacks. The first is used to find a subset of the data for which the distinguisher has an higher bias and the second generates more right pairs given a single one.

When using neutral bits, two issues should be taken in account: First, the probability of each neutral bit: The basic definition of a neutral bit [7] is: if (P, P') is a right pair then $(P \oplus e_i, P' \oplus e_i)$ is also a right pair with probability of 1. But, in practice, it is possible to use almost neutral bits, which satisfy the condition with probability of $p < 1$ [4]. Second, the transition from t neutral bits to 2^t neutral vectors: Although all the vectors in the linear span of some neutral vectors are expected to be neutral, this is not always the case [7]. We note that for the three ciphers discussed in this paper are based on S-boxes, and in such ciphers all the neutral bits satisfy with probability of 1, and the transition to linear subspace works as expected.

We also point out a case in which a link between the partitioning and the neutral bits ideas allow us to perform the first DL attack on 5-round Xoodyak. We also showed that when these two techniques are performed on different parts of the DL characteristic, then it is possible to combine them to achieve the best results. We applied combinations of them to improve two DL attacks, on 9-round DES, and we significantly improve previous DL results.

References

1. Data Encryption Standard, Federal Information Processing Standards publications no. 46, 1977
2. Aumasson, J.-P., Fischer, S., Khazaei, S., Meier, W., Rechberger, C.: New features of Latin dances: analysis of salsa, ChaCha, and rumba. In: Nyberg, K. (ed.) FSE 2008. LNCS, vol. 5086, pp. 470–488. Springer, Heidelberg (2008). https://doi.org/10.1007/978-3-540-71039-4_30

3. Bar-On, A., Dunkelman, O., Keller, N., Weizman, A.: DLCT: a new tool for differential-linear cryptanalysis. In: Ishai, Y., Rijmen, V. (eds.) EUROCRYPT 2019. LNCS, vol. 11476, pp. 313–342. Springer, Cham (2019). https://doi.org/10.1007/978-3-030-17653-2_11

4. Beierle, C., Leander, G., Todo, Y.: Improved differential-linear attacks with applications to ARX ciphers. In: Micciancio, D., Ristenpart, T. (eds.) CRYPTO 2020. LNCS, vol. 12172, pp. 329–358. Springer, Cham (2020). https://doi.org/10.1007/978-3-030-56877-1_12

5. Bernstein, D.J.: The Salsa20 family of stream ciphers. In: Robshaw, M., Billet, O. (eds.) New Stream Cipher Designs. LNCS, vol. 4986, pp. 84–97. Springer, Heidelberg (2008). https://doi.org/10.1007/978-3-540-68351-3_8

6. Biham, E., Carmeli, Y.: An improvement of linear cryptanalysis with addition operations with applications to FEAL-8X. In: Joux, A., Youssef, A. (eds.) SAC 2014. LNCS, vol. 8781, pp. 59–76. Springer, Cham (2014). https://doi.org/10.1007/978-3-319-13051-4_4

7. Biham, E., Chen, R.: Near-collisions of SHA-0. In: Franklin, M. (ed.) CRYPTO 2004. LNCS, vol. 3152, pp. 290–305. Springer, Heidelberg (2004). https://doi.org/10.1007/978-3-540-28628-8_18

8. Biham, E., Dunkelman, O., Keller, N.: Enhancing differential-linear cryptanalysis. In: Zheng, Y. (ed.) ASIACRYPT 2002. LNCS, vol. 2501, pp. 254–266. Springer, Heidelberg (2002). https://doi.org/10.1007/3-540-36178-2_16

9. Biham, E., Dunkelman, O., Keller, N.: The rectangle attack — rectangling the serpent. In: Pfitzmann, B. (ed.) EUROCRYPT 2001. LNCS, vol. 2045, pp. 340–357. Springer, Heidelberg (2001). https://doi.org/10.1007/3-540-44987-6_21

10. Biham, E., Shamir, A.: Differential cryptanalysis of DES-like cryptosystems. J. Cryptol. **4**(1), 3–72 (1991)

11. Blondeau, C., Leander, G., Nyberg, K.: Differential-linear cryptanalysis revisited. J. Cryptol. **30**(3), 859–888 (2017)

12. Blondeau, C., Nyberg, K.: New links between differential and linear cryptanalysis. In: Johansson, T., Nguyen, P.Q. (eds.) EUROCRYPT 2013. LNCS, vol. 7881, pp. 388–404. Springer, Heidelberg (2013). https://doi.org/10.1007/978-3-642-38348-9_24

13. Chabaud, F., Vaudenay, S.: Links between differential and linear cryptanalysis. In: De Santis, A. (ed.) EUROCRYPT 1994. LNCS, vol. 950, pp. 356–365. Springer, Heidelberg (1995). https://doi.org/10.1007/BFb0053450

14. Daemen, J., Hoffert, S., Van Assche, G., Van Keer, R.: The design of Xoodoo and Xoofff. IACR Trans. Symmetric Cryptol. **2018**(4), 1–38 (2018)

15. Daemen, J., Hoffert, S., Peeters, M., Van Assche, G., Van Keer, R.: Xoodyak, a lightweight cryptographic scheme. IACR Trans. Symmetric Cryptol. **2020**(1), 60–87 (2020)

16. Daemen, J., Rijmen, V.: The wide trail design strategy. In: Honary, B. (ed.) Cryptography and Coding 2001. LNCS, vol. 2260, pp. 222–238. Springer, Heidelberg (2001). https://doi.org/10.1007/3-540-45325-3_20

17. Dey, S., Garai, H.K., Sarkar, S., Sharma, N.K.: Revamped differential-linear cryptanalysis on reduced round ChaCha. In: Dunkelman, O., Dziembowski, S. (eds.) Advances in Cryptology – EUROCRYPT 2022. EUROCRYPT 2022. LNCS, vol. 13277, pp. 86–114. Springer, Cham (2022). https://doi.org/10.1007/978-3-031-07082-2_4

18. Dunkelman, O., Keller, N., Shamir, A.: A practical-time related-key attack on the KASUMI cryptosystem used in GSM and 3G telephony. J. Cryptol. **27**(4), 824–849 (2014)

19. Kelsey, J., Kohno, T., Schneier, B.: Amplified boomerang attacks against reduced-round MARS and serpent. In: Goos, G., Hartmanis, J., van Leeuwen, J., Schneier, B. (eds.) FSE 2000. LNCS, vol. 1978, pp. 75–93. Springer, Heidelberg (2001). https://doi.org/10.1007/3-540-44706-7_6

20. Knudsen, L.R., Mathiassen, J.E.: A chosen-plaintext linear attack on DES. In: Goos, G., Hartmanis, J., van Leeuwen, J., Schneier, B. (eds.) FSE 2000. LNCS, vol. 1978, pp. 262–272. Springer, Heidelberg (2001). https://doi.org/10.1007/3-540-44706-7_18

21. Langford, S.K., Hellman, M.E.: Differential-linear cryptanalysis. In: Desmedt, Y.G. (ed.) CRYPTO 1994. LNCS, vol. 839, pp. 17–25. Springer, Heidelberg (1994). https://doi.org/10.1007/3-540-48658-5_3

22. Leurent, G.: Improved differential-linear cryptanalysis of 7-round Chaskey with partitioning. In: Fischlin, M., Coron, J.-S. (eds.) EUROCRYPT 2016. LNCS, vol. 9665, pp. 344–371. Springer, Heidelberg (2016). https://doi.org/10.1007/978-3-662-49890-3_14

23. Liu, F., Isobe, T., Meier, W., Yang, Z.: Algebraic Attacks on Round-Reduced Keccak/Xoodoo. IACR Cryptol. ePrint Arch., p. 346 (2020)

24. Liu, Y., Sun, S., Li, C.: Rotational cryptanalysis from a differential-linear perspective. In: Canteaut, A., Standaert, F.-X. (eds.) EUROCRYPT 2021. LNCS, vol. 12696, pp. 741–770. Springer, Cham (2021). https://doi.org/10.1007/978-3-030-77870-5_26

25. Liu, Z., Gu, D., Zhang, J., Li, W.: Differential-multiple linear cryptanalysis. In: Bao, F., Yung, M., Lin, D., Jing, J. (eds.) Inscrypt 2009. LNCS, vol. 6151, pp. 35–49. Springer, Heidelberg (2010). https://doi.org/10.1007/978-3-642-16342-5_3

26. Jiqiang, L.: A methodology for differential-linear cryptanalysis and its applications. Des. Codes Cryptogr. **77**(1), 11–48 (2015)

27. Matsui, M.: Linear cryptanalysis method for DES cipher. In: Helleseth, T. (eds.) Advances in Cryptology — EUROCRYPT '93. EUROCRYPT 1993. LNCS, vol. 765, pp. 386–397. Springer, Berlin, Heidelberg (1994). https://doi.org/10.1007/3-540-48285-7_33

28. Miyaguchi, S.: The FEAL cipher family. In: Menezes, A.J., Vanstone, S.A. (eds.) CRYPTO 1990. LNCS, vol. 537, pp. 628–638. Springer, Heidelberg (1991). https://doi.org/10.1007/3-540-38424-3_46

29. Mouha, N., Mennink, B., Van Herrewege, A., Watanabe, D., Preneel, B., Verbauwhede, I.: Chaskey: an efficient MAC algorithm for 32-bit microcontrollers. In: Joux, A., Youssef, A. (eds.) SAC 2014. LNCS, vol. 8781, pp. 306–323. Springer, Cham (2014). https://doi.org/10.1007/978-3-319-13051-4_19

30. Nyberg, K., Knudsen, L.R.: Provable security against differential cryptanalysis. In: Brickell, E.F. (ed.) CRYPTO 1992. LNCS, vol. 740, pp. 566–574. Springer, Heidelberg (1993). https://doi.org/10.1007/3-540-48071-4_41

31. Selcuk, A.A.: On probability of success in linear and differential cryptanalysis. J. Cryptol. **21**(1), 131–147 (2008)

32. Wagner, D.: The boomerang attack. In: Knudsen, L. (ed.) FSE 1999. LNCS, vol. 1636, pp. 156–170. Springer, Heidelberg (1999). https://doi.org/10.1007/3-540-48519-8_12

Cryptographic Primitives

Injective Rank Metric Trapdoor Functions with Homogeneous Errors

Étienne Burle[1], Philippe Gaborit[2], Younes Hatri[1], and Ayoub Otmani[1(✉)]

[1] LITIS, University of Rouen Normandie, Normandie Univ, Rouen, France
{Etienne.Burle,Younes.Hatri,Ayoub.Otmani}@univ-rouen.fr
[2] XLIM, Université de Limoges, Limoges, France
gaborit@unilim.fr

Abstract. In rank-metric cryptography, a vector from a finite dimensional linear space over a finite field is viewed as the linear space spanned by its entries. The rank decoding problem which is the analogue of the problem of decoding a random linear code consists in recovering a basis of a random noise vector that was used to perturb a set of random linear equations sharing a secret solution. Assuming the intractability of this problem, we introduce a new construction of injective one-way trapdoor functions. Our solution departs from the frequent way of building public key primitives from error-correcting codes where, to establish the security, ad hoc assumptions about a hidden structure are made. Our method produces a hard-to-distinguish linear code together with low weight vectors which constitute the secret that helps recover the inputs. The key idea is to focus on trapdoor functions that take sufficiently enough input vectors sharing the same support. Applying then the error correcting algorithm designed for Low Rank Parity Check (LRPC) codes, we obtain an inverting algorithm that recovers the inputs with overwhelming probability.

Keywords: Trapdoor function · Rank decoding problem · Rank support learning · Homogeneous matrix

1 Introduction

Trapdoor functions are informally cryptographic primitives that compute efficiently images but do not allow the recovering of pre-images unless a secret quantity called the trapdoor is known. This basic security property is also called one-wayness. A classical application of trapdoor functions is the construction of public-key encryption scheme [13]. However these two notions are not equivalent because not every public-key encryption scheme derives from a trapdoor function. This distinction comes from the fact that trapdoor functions require to recover the entire input while encryption functions only have to recover the plaintext, leaving out the randomness if need be. Trapdoor functions form an important building tool for achieving the standard notion of CCA2 security when

© The Author(s), under exclusive license to Springer Nature Switzerland AG 2024
B. Smith and H. Wu (Eds.): SAC 2022, LNCS 13742, pp. 139–158, 2024.
https://doi.org/10.1007/978-3-031-58411-4_7

we are concerned with confidentiality under active attacks. A generic transformation was proposed in [48] to obtain CCA2 security from an injective trapdoor function. There exist currently several trapdoor functions from different algorithmic assumptions: factoring hardness [63], difficulty of decoding a random linear code [53], DDH and LWE assumptions [60] and Computational Diffie-Hellman assumption [39].

In this work, we are interested in building rank-based trapdoor functions. Rank-based cryptography is close in spirit to code-based cryptography with the difference that the ambient linear space defined over a finite field is endowed with the rank metric, namely vectors are viewed as matrices. The support of vector is then the linear space spanned by its entries. The fundamental hard-to-solve problem is the Rank decoding problem which is directly inspired by the decoding problem of random linear codes with the Hamming distance. This latter problem is the core assumption on which relies the security of the McEliece cryptosystem [53]. Loosely speaking, the rank decoding problem consists in recovering a basis of a random "noise" vector that was used to perturb a set of random linear equations sharing a secret solution.

The first rank-metric public key encryption scheme was proposed in [33] by Gabidulin, Paramonov and Tretjakov. This scheme which can be seen as an analogue of the McEliece cryptosystem [53] is based on the class of Gabidulin codes [29]. Gibson showed the weakness of the system through a series of successful attacks [42,43] exploiting the algebraic structure of Gabidulin codes. Following these failures, new reparations were published [31,32], later broken [57–59] and then again other variants appeared[1]. But still new attacks are devised [15,36,56].

This break-and-then-repair cycle follows from the fact that the designers try to hide the secret structure with techniques that are not based on standard assumptions. Currently, the rank decoding problem and its generalization, the Rank Support Learning (RSL) problem [34], are believed to be hard and serve as building blocks for proving the security of the encryption schemes in [2,6,66]. However the schemes in [2,6] require to use ideal codes and therefore relies on the stronger assumption that the rank decoding problem restricted to structured codes is intractable. In addition, the scheme in [6] has to hide the algebraic structure of Low Rank Parity-Check (LRPC) codes [8].

Our Contribution. We introduce a new construction of a family of rank metric trapdoor functions provably hard to invert assuming the intractability of the RSL problem. As in [66], our solution departs from the recurrent way of building public key primitives from error-correcting codes that makes non-standard assumptions about a hidden structure [1,6,16,53], which in some cases turn out to be false [24,25,54] even leading to cryptanalysis [12,17–21,40,41,55]. The technique we propose is reminiscent of Alekhnovich's [5] and Ajtai's [4] constructions. [4] shows how to sample an essentially uniform integer matrix $\mathbf{A}$ along with short trapdoor set of vectors that are orthogonal to $\mathbf{A}$. Similarly, our mechanism generates a (public) matrix $\mathbf{G} \in \mathbb{F}_{q^m}^{k \times (n+L)}$ that is statistically

---

[1] See [8,26,28,30,50,52,61,62,65].

indistinguishable from a uniformly sampled matrix along with a trapdoor matrix $\mathbf{W} \in \mathbb{F}_{q^m}^{n \times (n+L)}$ where the rows of $\mathbf{W}$ are of relatively small weight and such that $\mathbf{GW}^\mathsf{T} = \mathbf{0}$. Moreover, under the assumption of the hardness of the (decision) Rank decoding problem, we also manage to get $\mathbf{G}$ computationally indistinguishable from a random matrix in the way of [5] with the Hamming metric. For a security parameter $\lambda \in \mathbb{N}$, we then introduce a family of injective functions $\mathcal{F}_\lambda \subseteq \left\{ f_\mathbf{G} \mid \mathbf{G} \in \mathbb{F}_{q^m}^{k \times (n+L)} \right\}$ such that $f_\mathbf{G}(\mathbf{X}, \mathbf{E}) \triangleq \mathbf{XG} + \mathbf{E}$ where $\mathbf{X}$ is an arbitrary matrix from $\mathbb{F}_{q^m}^{N \times k}$ and $\mathbf{E} \in \mathbb{F}_{q^m}^{N \times (n+L)}$ is an *homogeneous matrix of weight* t, that is to say all the entries of $\mathbf{E}$ generate over $\mathbb{F}_q$ a linear subspace of $\mathbb{F}_{q^m}$ of dimension t. As in [3,7,66] which use the "multiple syndromes approach", the core idea to invert $f_\mathbf{G}$ is to take input vectors $(\mathbf{X}, \mathbf{E})$ with sufficiently enough rows. Adapting then the error-correcting algorithm designed specifically for Low Rank Parity Check (LRPC) codes [6,8], it is possible with overwhelming probability to efficiently recover the inputs. We recall that LRPC codes are defined through homogeneous parity-check matrices and were introduced to solve the rank decoding problem. In our context, the task of inverting $f_\mathbf{G}$ boils down to solving an instance of the RSL problem. For that purpose we introduce the concept of semi-homogeneous parity-check matrices which is a generalization of LRPC codes. Thanks to the analysis described in [67], we also give in Theorem 2 an upper-bound on the probability that our algorithm fails.

2   Preliminary Definitions

2.1   Notation

The symbol $\triangleq$ is used to define the left-hand side object. $|\mathcal{S}|$ defines the cardinality of a set $\mathcal{S}$. We write $x \xleftarrow{\$} \mathcal{S}$ to express that x is sampled according to the uniform distribution over a set $\mathcal{S}$. We use the notation $\mathbb{P}\{E(x) \mid x \xleftarrow{\$} \mathcal{S}\}$ to give the probability that an event $E(x)$ occurs under the constraint that $x \xleftarrow{\$} \mathcal{S}$.

The finite field with q elements where q is a power of a prime number is written as $\mathbb{F}_q$. All vectors are regarded by default as row vectors and denoted by boldface letters like $\mathbf{a} = (a_1, \ldots, a_n)$. The linear space over a field $\mathbb{F}$ spanned by vectors $\mathbf{b}_1, \ldots, \mathbf{b}_k$ belonging to a vector space over a field containing $\mathbb{F}$ is written as $\langle \mathbf{b}_1, \ldots, \mathbf{b}_k \rangle_\mathbb{F}$. For $f \in \mathbb{F}$ and $\mathcal{U} \subseteq \mathbb{F}$, the set $\{fu \mid u \in \mathcal{U}\}$ is denoted by $f \cdot \mathcal{U}$. Given two arbitrary sets $\mathcal{A}, \mathcal{B}$ included in $\mathbb{F}_{q^m}$ where $m \geqslant 1$, we let $\mathcal{A} \cdot \mathcal{B} \triangleq \langle ab \mid a \in \mathcal{A}, b \in \mathcal{B} \rangle_{\mathbb{F}_q}$. The set of $r \times n$ matrices with entries in a set $\mathcal{V} \subseteq \mathbb{F}$ is denoted by $\mathcal{V}^{r \times n}$ and $\mathrm{GL}_n(\mathcal{V})$ is the subset of $\mathcal{V}^{n \times n}$ of invertible matrices. The transpose operation is denoted by the symbol T. For matrices $\mathbf{A}$ and $\mathbf{B}$ having the same number of rows, $[\mathbf{A} \mid \mathbf{B}]$ represents the matrix obtained by concatenating the columns of $\mathbf{A}$ followed by the columns of $\mathbf{B}$.

2.2   Rank Metric

We consider a finite field extension $\mathbb{F}_{q^m}/\mathbb{F}_q$ of degree $m \geqslant 1$. The *support* of $\mathbf{x}$ from $\mathbb{F}_{q^m}^L$ denoted by $\langle \mathbf{x} \rangle_{\mathbb{F}_q}$ is the vector subspace over $\mathbb{F}_q$ spanned by its entries namely $\langle \mathbf{x} \rangle_{\mathbb{F}_q} \triangleq \langle x_1, \ldots, x_L \rangle_{\mathbb{F}_q} \subseteq \mathbb{F}_{q^m}$. The *rank weight* of $\mathbf{x}$ is $|\mathbf{x}| \triangleq \dim\langle \mathbf{x} \rangle_{\mathbb{F}_q}$. Likewise, the support $\langle \mathbf{X} \rangle_{\mathbb{F}_q}$ of a matrix $\mathbf{X} = [x_{i,j}]$ is the vector subspace over $\mathbb{F}_q$ spanned by all its entries, and its weight is $|\mathbf{X}| \triangleq \dim\langle \mathbf{X} \rangle_{\mathbb{F}_q}$. We let $\mathbf{Gr}_w(q, m)$ be the set of all w-dimensional linear subspaces over $\mathbb{F}_q$ included in $\mathbb{F}_{q^m}$, and the *sphere* in $\mathbb{F}_{q^m}^L$ of radius w centered at $\mathbf{0}$ is denoted by $\mathbb{S}_w\left(\mathbb{F}_{q^m}^L\right)$. We recall that the cardinality of $\mathbf{Gr}_w(q, m)$ is the Gaussian coefficient,

$$\left|\mathbf{Gr}_w(q, m)\right| = \prod_{i=0}^{w-1} \frac{q^m - q^i}{q^w - q^i}.$$

The cardinality of $\mathbb{S}_w\left(\mathbb{F}_{q^m}^L\right)$ is equal to the number of $m \times L$ q-ary matrices of rank w which is [51]

$$\left|\mathbb{S}_w\left(\mathbb{F}_{q^m}^L\right)\right| = \left|\mathbf{Gr}_w(q, m)\right| \prod_{i=0}^{w-1} \left(q^L - q^i\right). \tag{1}$$

We can bound (see Lemma 1 in Appendix A) the cardinality of a sphere as follows provided that $w + 3 \leqslant \min\{L, m\}$,

$$q^{(L+m)w - w^2} \leqslant \left|\mathbb{S}_w\left(\mathbb{F}_{q^m}^L\right)\right| \leqslant e^{2/(q-1)} q^{(L+m)w - w^2} \tag{2}$$

Definition 1 (Semi-homogeneous matrix). *A matrix $\mathbf{M}$ with ℓ rows is semi-homogeneous with supports $\mathcal{W}_1, \ldots, \mathcal{W}_\ell$ if the support of its ith row is $\mathcal{W}_i \in \mathbf{Gr}_{w_i}(q, m)$ where $w_1, \ldots, w_\ell$ are positive integers. A semi-homogeneous matrix is of weight w if all w_i equal w. When the supports $\mathcal{W}_i$ are all equal to the same linear space $\mathcal{W} \in \mathbf{Gr}_w(q, m)$ then $\mathbf{M}$ is homogeneous of weight w and support $\mathcal{W}$.*

2.3   Statistical Indistinguishability and Pseudo-Randomness

For random variables X and Y taking values in a finite domain $\mathcal{D}$, the *statistical distance* $\Delta\left(X : Y\right)$ between X and Y is

$$\Delta\left(X : Y\right) \triangleq \frac{1}{2} \sum_{w \in \mathcal{D}} \left| \mathbb{P}\left\{X = w\right\} - \mathbb{P}\left\{Y = w\right\} \right|.$$

A random variable X taking values on $\mathcal{A}$ is said to be ε-*close to uniform over* $\mathcal{A}$ (or ε-*uniform over* $\mathcal{A}$) where ε is a positive real number if its statistical distance from the uniform distribution is at most ε. Two collections of random variables $(X_n)_{n \in \mathbb{N}}$ and $(Y_n)_{n \in \mathbb{N}}$ are *statistically close* if the statistical distance $\Delta(X_n : Y_n)$ is negligible as n tends to $+\infty$. When $(Y_n)_{n \in \mathbb{N}}$ is a collection of uniform random variables then $(X_n)_{n \in \mathbb{N}}$ is *statistically close to uniform*. Finally, $(X_n)_{n \in \mathbb{N}}$ and $(Y_n)_{n \in \mathbb{N}}$ of random variables are *computationally indistinguishable* if for every probabilistic polynomial time algorithm $\mathcal{D}$ and all sufficiently large n's, there exists a negligible function ε such that

$$\left| \mathbb{P}\left\{\mathcal{D}(X_n) = 1\right\} - \mathbb{P}\left\{\mathcal{D}(Y_n) = 1\right\} \right| < \varepsilon(n).$$

When $(Y_n)_{n \in \mathbb{N}}$ is a collection of uniform random variables then $(X_n)_{n \in \mathbb{N}}$ is said to be *pseudo-random*.

Proposition 1. *Let X and Y be two random variables taking values in $\mathcal{A}$, and $g : \mathcal{A} \to \mathcal{B}$ be an arbitrary function independent from X and Y. Then we have*

$$\Delta(g(X), g(Y)) \leqslant \Delta(X, Y).$$

2.4   Universal Hashing

A family of hash functions $\left\{ h_{\mathbf{k}} : \mathcal{A} \to \mathcal{B} \mid \mathbf{k} \in \mathcal{K} \right\}$ where $\mathcal{A}, \mathcal{B}, \mathcal{K} \subset \{0,1\}^*$ are finite sets, is *universal* if for all *distinct* a and a' from $\mathcal{A}$, the following property holds

$$\mathbb{P}\left\{ h_{\mathbf{k}}(a) = h_{\mathbf{k}}(a') \mid \mathbf{k} \xleftarrow{\$} \mathcal{K} \right\} \leqslant \frac{1}{|\mathcal{B}|}.$$

A classical and well-known example of universal hash functions is obtained by considering the mapping $\phi_{\mathbf{A}} : \mathbb{F}^n \to \mathbb{F}^r$ such that for every $\mathbf{x} \in \mathbb{F}^n$, $\phi_{\mathbf{A}}(\mathbf{x}) \triangleq \mathbf{x}\mathbf{A}$ where $\mathbb{F}$ is an arbitrary finite field, and $\mathbf{A}$ is matrix from $\mathbb{F}^{n \times r}$ with $r < n$.

Proposition 2. *The family of hash functions $\{\phi_{\mathbf{A}} \mid \mathbf{A} \in \mathbb{F}^{n \times r}\}$ is universal.*

Proof. Let us consider $\mathbf{x} = (x_1, \ldots, x_n)$ and $\mathbf{y} = (y_1, \ldots, y_n)$ in $\mathbb{F}^n$ such that $\mathbf{x} \neq \mathbf{y}$. Without loss of generality, we assume that $x_1 \neq y_1$. Note that $\phi_{\mathbf{A}}(\mathbf{x}) = \phi_{\mathbf{A}}(\mathbf{y})$ is equivalent to $\mathbf{a}_1 = -(x_1 - y_1)^{-1} \sum_{j=2}^{n} (x_j - y_j)\mathbf{a}_j$ where $\mathbf{a}_1, \ldots, \mathbf{a}_n$ are the rows of $\mathbf{A}$. We then have

$$\mathbb{P}\left\{ \phi_{\mathbf{A}}(\mathbf{x}) = \phi_{\mathbf{A}}(\mathbf{y}) \mid \mathbf{A} \xleftarrow{\$} \mathbb{F}^{n \times r} \right\} = \frac{1}{|\mathbb{F}|^r}$$

which proves the proposition.   □

With help of the celebrated Leftover Hash Lemma [46], universal families of hash functions give a very useful tool to bound the statistical distance between a couple of random variables $(K, h_K(X))$ where $K \xleftarrow{\$} \mathcal{K}$, $X \xleftarrow{\$} \mathcal{A}$ and a uniformly distributed random variable $(K, U) \xleftarrow{\$} \mathcal{K} \times \mathcal{B}$. In this work we use the following theorem which is a generalization of the Leftover Hash Lemma to multiple instances.

Theorem 1 (Theorem 8.38 in [64]). *Let $\{h_{\mathbf{k}} : \mathcal{A} \to \mathcal{B} \mid \mathbf{k} \in \mathcal{K}\}$ be a universal family of hash functions where $\mathcal{A}, \mathcal{B}, \mathcal{K} \subset \{0,1\}^*$ are finite sets. The random variable $(K, h_K(X_1), \ldots, h_K(X_n))$ is $\dfrac{n}{2}\sqrt{\dfrac{|\mathcal{B}|}{|\mathcal{A}|}}$-close to uniform over $\mathcal{K} \times \mathcal{B}^n$ for independent and uniformly distributed random variables $K \xleftarrow{\$} \mathcal{K}$, $X_1 \xleftarrow{\$} \mathcal{A}, \ldots, X_n \xleftarrow{\$} \mathcal{A}$.*

2.5   Injective Trapdoor Function

Consider natural numbers ℓ, d, m, n that are polynomial functions of the security parameter $\lambda \in \mathbb{N}$. An *injective trapdoor* function family with domain $\{0,1\}^m$ and range $\{0,1\}^n$ is given by three probabilistic polynomial-time algorithms $\mathcal{T} = (\mathsf{gen}, \mathsf{eval}, \mathsf{invert})$. The key generation algorithm $(\mathsf{pk}, \mathsf{tk}) \leftarrow \mathcal{T}.\mathsf{gen}(\mathbb{1}^\lambda)$ takes as input a security parameter λ and outputs a public key $\mathsf{pk} \in \{0,1\}^\ell$ and a trapdoor key $\mathsf{tk} \in \{0,1\}^d$. The evaluation algorithm $\mathbf{y} \leftarrow \mathcal{T}.\mathsf{eval}(\mathsf{pk}, \mathbf{x})$ on input pk and $\mathbf{x} \in \{0,1\}^m$ outputs $\mathbf{y} \in \{0,1\}^n$. The inversion algorithm $\mathcal{T}.\mathsf{invert}(\mathsf{pk}, \mathsf{tk}, \mathbf{y})$ takes as input $\mathbf{y} \in \{0,1\}^n$, pk, the trapdoor key tk, and outputs either an m-string $\mathbf{x}$ or $\perp \notin \{0,1\}^m$ to indicate that an error occurred. Additionally, it is required that the inversion algorithm fulfills the *perfect correctness* meaning that for every pair of keys $(\mathsf{pk}, \mathsf{tk}) \leftarrow \mathcal{T}.\mathsf{gen}(\mathbb{1}^\lambda)$, we should have

$$\forall \mathbf{x} \in \{0,1\}^m, \quad \mathcal{T}.\mathsf{invert}(\mathsf{pk}, \mathsf{tk}, \mathcal{T}.\mathsf{eval}(\mathsf{pk}, \mathbf{x})) = \mathbf{x}.$$

It is possible to relax this constraint to allow the inversion algorithm to fail for a negligible fraction of keys. This feature is called the "almost-all-keys" injectivity property. The trapdoor functions that will be presented in Sect. 5 do not satisfy nor this condition neither the perfect correctness because we will see that for every $(\mathsf{pk}, \mathsf{tk})$ there exists a fraction of the inputs that cannot be inverted. We will show that this fraction can be made arbitrary small. As there exist generic methods that transform a trapdoor function with decryption errors into a secure public-key encryption scheme [13,23,47], these issues are deferred to the full version of the paper. We now finish this part by recalling that a trapdoor function should be computationally hard to invert without the trapdoor key.

Definition 2. *An injective trapdoor function family* $(\mathsf{gen}, \mathsf{eval}, \mathsf{invert})$ *with domain* $\{0,1\}^m$ *and range* $\{0,1\}^n$ *is one-way if for every probabilistic polynomial-time adversary* $\mathcal{A}$, *there exists a negligible function* $\varepsilon : \mathbb{N} \to \mathbb{R}$ *such that for all sufficiently large* $\lambda \in \mathbb{N}$,

$$\mathbb{P}\left\{ \mathcal{A}(\mathsf{pk}, \mathcal{T}.\mathsf{eval}(\mathsf{pk}, \mathbf{x})) = \mathbf{x} \;\middle|\; (\mathsf{pk}, \mathsf{tk}) \leftarrow \mathcal{T}.\mathsf{gen}(\mathbb{1}^\lambda) \,;\, \mathbf{x} \xleftarrow{\$} \{0,1\}^m \right\} < \varepsilon(\lambda).$$

3   Intractability Assumptions

We gather in this section classical hard problems from rank-metric cryptography.

Definition 3 (Rank decoding). *Let q be a power of a prime number, and consider natural numbers m, n, $k < n$, $t < n$. The* rank decoding *problem asks to find $\mathbf{e}$ from the input $(\mathbf{R}, \mathbf{e}\mathbf{R}^\mathsf{T})$ when $\mathbf{R} \xleftarrow{\$} \mathbb{F}_{q^m}^{(n-k) \times n}$ and $\mathbf{e} \xleftarrow{\$} \mathbb{S}_t(\mathbb{F}_{q^m}^n)$.*

It is currently widely believed that the rank decoding problem is computationally hard to solve for both classical and quantum computers. Indeed, the generic decoding problem in Hamming metric is well-studied and there exists a reduction in [38] from it to the rank decoding problem. Currently, the nature of the algorithms that solve this problem is either "combinatorial" or "algebraic". For the rank decoding problem, the most efficient ones are described in [9] and [11] respectively. It is important to note that this problem can be solved if one can recover the support $\langle \mathbf{e} \rangle_q \in \mathbf{Gr}_t(q, m)$. As explained in [37], when an arbitrary basis $\varepsilon_1, \dots, \varepsilon_t$ of $\langle \mathbf{e} \rangle_{\mathbb{F}_q}$ is known, then with high chances one expect to fully compute $\mathbf{e}$ from $(\mathbf{R}, \mathbf{s})$ where $\mathbf{s} \triangleq \mathbf{e}\mathbf{R}^\mathsf{T}$ when $nt < m(n-k)$. Indeed the coordinates of $\mathbf{e} = [e_1, \dots, e_n]$ can be recovered by writing that $e_j = \sum_{d=1}^t x_{j,d}\varepsilon_d$ where each $x_{j,d}$ is viewed as an unknown that lies in $\mathbb{F}_q$. One then picks a basis of $\mathbb{F}_{q^m}$ over $\mathbb{F}_q$ and uses it to project the linear system $\mathbf{s} = \mathbf{e}\mathbf{R}^\mathsf{T}$ within it. It results in a linear system involving nt unknowns, namely the $x_{j,d}$ variables, and $m(n-k)$ linear equations defined with coefficients in $\mathbb{F}_q$. Consequently when the parameters are appropriately chosen, and assuming the linear equations are random, one expects to get a unique solution to the linear system. This particular feature of the rank metric has led the authors in [34] to introduce a new fundamental computational problem called the "Rank Support Learning" problem.

Definition 4 (Rank Support Learning (RSL) [34]). *Let q be a power of a prime number, and consider natural numbers m, n, $k < n$, $t < n$ and N. The* Rank Support Learning *problem asks to recover $\mathcal{V}$ from $(\mathbf{R}, \mathbf{V}\mathbf{R}^\mathsf{T})$ when $\mathbf{R} \xleftarrow{\$} \mathbb{F}_{q^m}^{(n-k) \times n}$, $\mathcal{V} \xleftarrow{\$} \mathbf{Gr}_t(q, m)$ and $\mathbf{V} \xleftarrow{\$} \mathcal{V}^{N \times n}$.*

Equivalently, RSL can be defined as the problem where an adversary has access to $\mathbf{R}$ and N instances $\mathbf{v}_1\mathbf{R}^\mathsf{T}, \dots, \mathbf{v}_N\mathbf{R}^\mathsf{T}$ and has to recover $\mathcal{V} \in \mathbf{Gr}_t(q, m)$ such that $\langle \mathbf{v}_i \rangle_q \subseteq \mathcal{V}$ for every $i \in \{1, \dots, N\}$. Notice that the matrix $\mathbf{V}$ that appears in the definition of the RSL problem is an homogeneous matrix of weight t. It is clear that the RSL problem is not harder than the rank decoding problem. Additionally, the rank decoding problem is a special case of the RSL problem with a single sample $N = 1$, hence showing that the RSL problem with $N = 1$ and the rank decoding problem are computationally equivalent. But the problem becomes easier when N increases. [34] gives a combinatorial polynomial-time algorithm when $N \geqslant nt$, then a sub-exponential algebraic attack was introduced in [22] when $N \geqslant kt$. Recently a new combinatorial polynomial-time algorithm has been devised in [14] when $N > ktm/(m-t)$. Finally [10] presents an algebraic attack, whose complexity is given in [14], that can be thwarted when $N < kt$. We can conclude from this discussion that the RSL problem is intractable when $N < kt$.

Assumption 1. *Let m be a natural number that is a polynomial function of a parameter $\lambda \in \mathbb{N}$, and assume that $q = O(1)$, $n = \Theta(m)$, $k = \Theta(n)$, $t = \Omega(n^\alpha)$ where α is a real number from $]0,1]$ and $N < kt$. There exists a negligible function $\varepsilon : \mathbb{N} \to \mathbb{R}$ such that for every probabilistic polynomial-time algorithm $\mathcal{A}$, and all sufficiently large $\lambda \in \mathbb{N}$,*

$$\mathbb{P}\left\{ \mathcal{A}(\mathbf{R}, \mathbf{V}\mathbf{R}^\mathsf{T}) = \mathcal{V} \;\middle|\; \mathbf{R} \xleftarrow{\$} \mathbb{F}_{q^m}^{(n-k) \times n} \;;\; \mathcal{V} \xleftarrow{\$} \mathbf{Gr}_t(q, m) \;;\; \mathbf{V} \xleftarrow{\$} \mathcal{V}^{N \times n} \right\} < \varepsilon(\lambda).$$

This assumption about the hardness of RSL enables us to establish the hardness of the search version of the rank decoding problem.

Proposition 3. *Let m be a natural number that depends polynomially from a parameter $\lambda \in \mathbb{N}$, and assume that $q = O(1)$, $n = \Theta(m)$, $k = \Theta(n)$, and $t = \Omega(n^\alpha)$ where α is a real number from $]0,1]$. Let h_λ be the mapping from $\mathbb{F}_{q^m}^{(n-k) \times n} \times \mathbb{S}_t(\mathbb{F}_{q^m}^n)$ into $\mathbb{F}_{q^m}^{(n-k) \times n} \times \mathbb{F}_{q^m}^{n-k}$ such that for every $\mathbf{R} \in \mathbb{F}_{q^m}^{(n-k) \times n}$ and $\mathbf{e} \in \mathbb{S}_t(\mathbb{F}_{q^m}^n)$,*

$$h_\lambda(\mathbf{R}, \mathbf{e}) \triangleq (\mathbf{R}, \mathbf{e}\mathbf{R}^\mathsf{T}).$$

Then if Assumption 1 holds, there exists a negligible function $\varepsilon : \mathbb{N} \to \mathbb{R}$ such that for every probabilistic polynomial time algorithm $\mathcal{A}$, and all sufficiently large $\lambda \in \mathbb{N}$,

$$\mathbb{P}\left\{ \mathcal{A}(\mathbf{R}, \mathbf{e}\mathbf{R}^\mathsf{T}) \in h_\lambda^{-1}\{(\mathbf{R}, \mathbf{e}\mathbf{R}^\mathsf{T})\} \mid \mathbf{R} \xleftarrow{\$} \mathbb{F}_{q^m}^{(n-k) \times n} ; \mathbf{e} \xleftarrow{\$} \mathbb{S}_t(\mathbb{F}_{q^m}^n) \right\} < \varepsilon(\lambda).$$

We now introduce another seemingly less difficult computational problem which consist in distinguishing in polynomial time between the distributions $(\mathbf{D}, \mathbf{e}\mathbf{D})$ and $(\mathbf{D}, \mathbf{u})$ when $\mathbf{D} \xleftarrow{\$} \mathbb{F}_{q^m}^{n \times (n-k)}$, $\mathbf{e} \xleftarrow{\$} \mathbb{S}_t(\mathbb{F}_{q^m}^n)$ and $\mathbf{u} \xleftarrow{\$} \mathbb{F}_{q^m}^{n-k}$. This problem is the *decision* version of the rank decoding problem, and is currently believed to be intractable. Notice that if the family $(h_\lambda)_{\lambda \in \mathbb{N}}$ is not one-way then $(\mathbf{D}, \mathbf{e}\mathbf{D})$ and $(\mathbf{D}, \mathbf{u})$ can be distinguished in polynomial-time. A less obvious result is to prove that the converse also holds, hence establishing the equivalence between both versions of the rank decoding problem. This can be achieved by devising a "search-to-decision" reduction. Such a reduction exists in [27,49] in the context of Hamming-metric binary codes ($q = 2$ and $m = 1$). The reduction relies on the Goldreich-Levin theorem [45]. The authors of [35] used this reduction to build rank-metric pseudo-random number generators. They gave on that occasion a reduction from the Hamming-metric version of the (decision) decoding problem to its rank-metric counterpart. Besides this result which only holds for binary codes, to the best of our knowledge, there does not exist a search-to-decision reduction valid for any field. However it is widely believed that the decision rank decoding problem is intractable as well.

Assumption 2 (Decision Rank Decoding). *Let m be a natural number that is a polynomial function of a parameter $\lambda \in \mathbb{N}$, and assume that $q = O(1)$, $n = \Theta(m)$, $k = \Theta(n)$ and $t = \Omega(n^\alpha)$ where α is a real number from $]0,1]$. There exists a negligible function $\varepsilon : \mathbb{N} \to \mathbb{R}$ such that for every probabilistic polynomial-time algorithm $\mathcal{A}$, and all sufficiently large $\lambda \in \mathbb{N}$,*

$$\left| \mathbb{P}\left\{ \mathcal{A}(\mathbf{R}, \mathbf{e}\mathbf{R}^\mathsf{T}) = 1 \mid \mathbf{R} \xleftarrow{\$} \mathbb{F}_{q^m}^{(n-k) \times n} ; \mathbf{e} \xleftarrow{\$} \mathbb{S}_t(\mathbb{F}_{q^m}^n) \right\} \right.$$

$$\left. - \mathbb{P}\left\{ \mathcal{A}(\mathbf{R}, \mathbf{u}) = 1 \mid \mathbf{R} \xleftarrow{\$} \mathbb{F}_{q^m}^{(n-k) \times n} ; \mathbf{u} \xleftarrow{\$} \mathbb{F}_{q^m}^{n-k} \right\} \right| < \varepsilon(\lambda)$$

From this assumption, we can prove that the pseudo-randomness of $(\mathbf{D}, \mathbf{eD})$ is still true when a polynomially bounded number of samples is considered.

Proposition 4 (Theorem 3.2.6 in [44]). *Under Assumption 2, there exists a negligible function $\varepsilon : \mathbb{N} \to \mathbb{R}$ such that for every probabilistic polynomial-time algorithm $\mathcal{A}$, all sufficiently large λ's, and for every natural number ℓ that is a polynomial function of $\lambda \in \mathbb{N}$,*

$$\left| \mathbb{P}\left\{ \mathcal{A}\left(\mathbf{R}, \mathbf{E}\mathbf{R}^{\mathsf{T}}\right) = 1 \;\middle|\; \mathbf{R} \xleftarrow{\$} \mathbb{F}_{q^m}^{(n-k)\times n} \;;\; \mathbf{E} \xleftarrow{\$} \left(\mathbb{S}_t(\mathbb{F}_{q^m}^n)\right)^\ell \right\} \right.$$

$$\left. - \mathbb{P}\left\{ \mathcal{A}(\mathbf{R}, \mathbf{U}) = 1 \;\middle|\; \mathbf{R} \xleftarrow{\$} \mathbb{F}_{q^m}^{(n-k)\times n} \;;\; \mathbf{U} \xleftarrow{\$} \mathbb{F}_{q^m}^{\ell \times (n-k)} \right\} \right| < \varepsilon(\lambda)$$

Remark 1. All the previous complexity assumptions can be equivalently expressed with generator matrices by considering the family of functions $(f_\lambda)_{\lambda \in \mathbb{N}}$ where f_λ is the mapping from $\mathbb{F}_{q^m}^{k \times n} \times \mathbb{F}_{q^m}^k \times \mathbb{S}_t\left(\mathbb{F}_{q^m}^n\right)$ into $\mathbb{F}_q^{k \times n} \times \mathbb{F}_{q^m}^n$ such that $f_\lambda(\mathbf{G}, \mathbf{x}, \mathbf{e}) \triangleq (\mathbf{G}, \mathbf{x}\mathbf{G} + \mathbf{e})$ for every $\mathbf{G} \in \mathbb{F}_q^{k \times n}$, $\mathbf{x} \in \mathbb{F}_{q^m}^k$ and $\mathbf{e} \in \mathbb{S}_t(\mathbb{F}_{q^m}^n)$. It is then not difficult to see that $(f_\lambda)_{\lambda \in \mathbb{N}}$ is one-way if and only if $(h_\lambda)_{\lambda \in \mathbb{N}}$ is one-way.

4   A Decoding Algorithm for Homogeneous Errors

This section is devoted to explaining how to efficiently solve the RSL problem and decode with a semi-homogeneous parity-check matrix. Throughout this section we consider a semi-homogeneous matrix $\mathbf{H} \in \mathbb{F}_{q^m}^{\ell \times n}$ of weight w and supports $(\mathcal{W}_1, \ldots, \mathcal{W}_\ell)$ where $\ell < n$, an integer t and a matrix $\mathbf{S} \in \mathbb{F}_{q^m}^{\ell \times N}$. The goal is then to find an homogeneous "error" matrix $\mathbf{E} \in \mathbb{F}_{q^m}^{n \times N}$ such that the following holds,

$$\begin{cases} \mathbf{S} = \mathbf{H}\mathbf{E}, \\ \langle \mathbf{E} \rangle_{\mathbb{F}_q} \in \mathbf{Gr}_t(q, m). \end{cases}$$

We provide a two-step procedure denoted by Φ that solves this problem with overwhelming probability provided that $n \leqslant \ell w$ and $tw \leqslant N$. Throughout this section we assume that a basis $f_1^{(r)}, \ldots, f_w^{(r)}$ of $\mathcal{W}_r$ was picked for each $r \in \{1, \ldots, \ell\}$. We will also denote by $\mathbf{s}_r$ the r-th row of $\mathbf{S}$. The main goal of the first step (Algorithm 1) is to compute a basis of $\langle \mathbf{E} \rangle_{\mathbb{F}_q}$. The idea is to find an index r in $\{1, \ldots, \ell\}$ such that $\mathcal{E}_r \triangleq \bigcap_{i=1}^{w} \left(f_i^{(r)}\right)^{-1} \cdot \langle \mathbf{s}_r \rangle_{\mathbb{F}_q}$ belongs to $\mathbf{Gr}_t(q, m)$. If such r exists then we have the equality $\mathcal{E}_r = \langle \mathbf{E} \rangle_{\mathbb{F}_q}$. This step then terminates by computing a basis $\varepsilon_1, \ldots, \varepsilon_t$ of $\langle \mathbf{E} \rangle_{\mathbb{F}_q} = \mathcal{E}_r$.

Next the second step aims at fully recovering the entries of the matrix $\mathbf{E}$. It starts by checking whether for each r in $\{1, \ldots, \ell\}$ the dimension of $\mathcal{E} \cdot \mathcal{W}_r$ over $\mathbb{F}_q$ is equal to tw. When this happens then as a basis of $\mathcal{E} \cdot \mathcal{W}_r$ is given by $f_i^{(r)} \varepsilon_j$ with $i \in \{1, \ldots, w\}$ and $j \in \{1, \ldots, t\}$, each entry of $\mathbf{S} = [s_{r,c}]$ is written as

---

Algorithm 1. Step I of $\Phi(\mathbf{H}, \mathbf{S})$ – Recovering the support.

1: $r \leftarrow 1$
2: $\mathcal{E} \leftarrow \{\mathbf{0}\}$
3: **while** $(\dim \mathcal{E} \neq t)$ **and** $(r \leqslant \ell)$ **do**
4:    $\mathcal{E} \leftarrow \bigcap\limits_{i=1}^{w} \left(f_i^{(r)} \right)^{-1} \cdot \langle \mathbf{s}_r \rangle_{\mathbb{F}_q}$ {$\mathbf{s}_r$ is the rth row of $\mathbf{S}$}
5:    $r \leftarrow r + 1$
6: **end while**
7: $\mathcal{B} \leftarrow \emptyset$
8: **if** $\dim \mathcal{E} = t$ **then**
9:    $\mathcal{B} \leftarrow \{\varepsilon_1, \ldots, \varepsilon_t\}$ where $\varepsilon_1, \ldots, \varepsilon_t$ is a basis of $\mathcal{E}$
10: **end if**
11: **return** $\mathcal{B}$

$s_{r,c} = \sum_{i,j} \sigma_{i,j}^{(r,c)} f_i^{(r)} \varepsilon_j$ where $\sigma_{i,j}^{(r,c)}$ lies in $\mathbb{F}_q$. Similarly each entry of $\mathbf{H} = [h_{r,d}]$ with $d \in \{1, \ldots, n\}$ is decomposed as $h_{r,d} = \sum_i \nu_i^{(r,d)} f_i^{(r)}$ with $\nu_i^{(r,d)}$ in $\mathbb{F}_q$. Lastly each entry $e_{d,c}$ of the unknown matrix $\mathbf{E}$ is written as $e_{d,c} = \sum_j x_j^{(d,c)} \varepsilon_j$ where $x_j^{(d,c)}$ are unknowns that are sought in $\mathbb{F}_q$ so that we have

$$s_{r,c} = \sum_{d=1}^{n} h_{r,d} e_{d,c} = \sum_{d=1}^{n} \left(\sum_{i=1}^{w} \nu_i^{(r,d)} f_i^{(r)} \right) \left(\sum_{j=1}^{t} x_j^{(d,c)} \varepsilon_j \right)$$

$$= \sum_{i=1}^{w} \sum_{j=1}^{t} \left(\sum_{d=1}^{n} \nu_i^{(r,d)} x_j^{(d,c)} \right) f_i^{(r)} \varepsilon_j.$$

The latter equality implies that for every $c \in \{1, \ldots, N\}$, we have a system of $\ell t w$ linear equations involving tn unknowns composed of the linear relations

$$\sigma_{i,j}^{(r,c)} = \sum_{d=1}^{n} \nu_i^{(r,d)} x_j^{(d,c)}$$

where (r, i, j) runs through $\{1, \ldots, \ell\} \times \{1, \ldots, w\} \times \{1, \ldots, t\}$. As we have taken $\ell w \geqslant n$ and since $\dim \mathcal{E} \cdot \mathcal{W}_r = tw$ we are sure to get a unique solution.

However, the decoding algorithm Φ we described previously may fail for different reasons. During the first step, Φ will not find $\langle \mathbf{E} \rangle_{\mathbb{F}_q}$ if one of the following two events occur:

1. either $\langle \mathbf{s}_r \rangle_{\mathbb{F}_q}$ is not equal to $\mathcal{E} \cdot \mathcal{W}_r$ for every $r \in \{1, \ldots, \ell\}$ which always happens when $N < wt$
2. or, for every r such that the equality $\langle \mathbf{s}_r \rangle_{\mathbb{F}_q} = \mathcal{E} \cdot \mathcal{W}_r$ holds, we nevertheless have $\mathcal{E} \subsetneq \bigcap_{i=1}^{w} \left(f_i^{(r)} \right)^{-1} \cdot \langle \mathbf{s}_r \rangle_{\mathbb{F}_q}$.

Lastly, the decoding algorithm may fail during the second step, that is $\mathbf{E}$ is not recovered, if there exists at least one r in $\{1, \ldots, \ell\}$ such that the dimension of $\mathcal{E} \cdot \mathcal{W}_r$ is not equal to tw. We provide in Theorem 2 an upper-bound of the decoding failure probability of Φ.

Theorem 2. *Consider natural numbers w, t, m, n, ℓ, N such that $\ell < n \leqslant \ell w$, $(2w-1)t < m$ and $N \geqslant tw$. For a randomly drawn semi-homogeneous parity-check matrix $\mathbf{H} \in \mathbb{F}_{q^m}^{\ell \times n}$ with supports $\mathcal{W}_1 \xleftarrow{\$} \mathbf{Gr}_w(q,m), \ldots, \mathcal{W}_\ell \xleftarrow{\$} \mathbf{Gr}_w(q,m)$ and a random error matrix $\mathbf{E} \xleftarrow{\$} \mathcal{E}^{n \times N}$ with $\mathcal{E} \xleftarrow{\$} \mathbf{Gr}_t(q,m)$, the probability that $\Phi(\mathbf{H}, \mathbf{HE}) \neq \mathbf{E}$ is at most $\mathbb{P}_I + \mathbb{P}_{II}$ where*

$$
\begin{cases}
\mathbb{P}_I & \leqslant \left(1 - \prod_{i=0}^{tw-1} \left(1 - q^{i-N} \right) + \dfrac{q^{(2w-1)t}}{q^m - q^{t-1}} \right)^\ell, \\[2em]
\mathbb{P}_{II} & \leqslant 1 - \left(1 - \dfrac{q^{tw}}{q^m - q^{t-1}} \right)^\ell.
\end{cases}
$$

Proof. See Appendix B.

5 Injective Trapdoor Functions

We describe in this section our constructions of injective trapdoor functions $\mathcal{F}_\lambda \subseteq \left\{ f_{\mathbf{G}} \mid \mathbf{G} \in \mathbb{F}_{q^m}^{k \times (n+L)} \right\}$ that benefit from the hardness of the RSL problem as recalled in Assumption 1. Throughout this section we assume that $q = O(1)$ is a power of prime number and k, n, L, m, t, w are natural numbers that are supposed to be polynomial functions of a security parameter $\lambda \in \mathbb{N}$ so that Assumption 2 holds. We also take $N \geqslant tw$ and $nw \geqslant n + L$.

Algorithm 2. $(\mathsf{tk}, \mathsf{pk}) \leftarrow \mathsf{gen}(\mathbb{1}^\lambda)$

1: **for** $i \in \{1, \ldots, n\}$ **do**
2:     $\mathcal{W}_i \xleftarrow{\$} \mathbf{Gr}_w(\mathbb{F}_{q^m},)$
3: **end for**
4: $\mathbf{W}_1 \xleftarrow{\$} \mathbb{F}_{q^m}^{n \times L}$ where $\mathbf{W}_1$ is a semi homogeneous with supports $(\mathcal{W}_1, \ldots, \mathcal{W}_n)$
5: $\mathbf{W}_2 \xleftarrow{\$} \mathrm{GL}_n(\mathbb{F}_{q^m})$ where $\mathbf{W}_2$ is a semi homogeneous with supports $(\mathcal{W}_1, \ldots, \mathcal{W}_n)$
6: $\mathsf{tk} \triangleq [\mathbf{W}_1 \mid \mathbf{W}_2]$
7: $\mathbf{R} \xleftarrow{\$} \mathbb{F}_{q^m}^{k \times L}$
8: $\mathsf{pk} \triangleq [\mathbf{R} \mid -\mathbf{R}\mathbf{W}_1^{\mathsf{T}}(\mathbf{W}_2^{-1})^{\mathsf{T}}]$
9: **return** $(\mathsf{tk}, \mathsf{pk})$

The algorithm gen of $\mathcal{F}_\lambda$ is described in Algorithm 2. The interesting property of gen is to output a public key pk that is a generator matrix $\mathbf{G} \in \mathbb{F}_{q^m}^{k \times (n+L)}$ which is (computationally or statistically) indistinguishable from a randomly drawn matrix from $\mathbb{F}_{q^m}^{k \times (n+L)}$, together with a trapdoor key tk that is a semi-homogeneous matrix $\mathbf{W} \triangleq [\mathbf{W}_1 \mid \mathbf{W}_2]$ in $\mathbb{F}_{q^m}^{n \times (n+L)}$ of weight w such that

$\mathbf{GW}^\mathsf{T} = \mathbf{0}$. Notice that the definition of eval is straightforward as it computes $\mathsf{eval}(\mathsf{pk}, \mathbf{X}, \mathbf{E}) \triangleq \mathbf{XG} + \mathbf{E}$ where $\mathbf{X} \in \mathbb{F}_{q^m}^{N \times k}$ and $\mathbf{E} \in \mathbb{F}_{q^m}^{N \times (n+L)}$ is homogeneous of weight t. The algorithm invert takes as input $\mathbf{C} \triangleq \mathbf{XG} + \mathbf{E}$, and then applies the decoding algorithm $\Phi(\mathbf{W}, \mathbf{WC}^\mathsf{T})$ that is described in Sect. 4. Note that $\mathbf{W}$ is not a parity-check matrix of the code generated by the public generator matrix $\mathbf{G}$. But as $\mathbf{W}$ is semi-homogeneous matrix of weight w such that $\mathbf{GW}^\mathsf{T} = \mathbf{0}$ and we have taken $N \geqslant tw$ and $nw \geqslant n + L$, we can still recover $(\mathbf{X}, \mathbf{E})$ with overwhelming probability. All these previous facts are gathered in the following.

Theorem 3. *Let* $\mathcal{W}_1 \xleftarrow{\$} \mathbf{Gr}_w(q, m), \ldots, \mathcal{W}_\ell \xleftarrow{\$} \mathbf{Gr}_w(q, m)$, *and* $\mathbf{R}$ *be uniformly random matrix from* $\mathbb{F}_{q^m}^{k \times L}$. *For a randomly chosen semi-homogeneous matrix* $\mathbf{W} = [\mathbf{W}_1 \mid \mathbf{W}_2]$ *from* $\mathbb{F}_{q^m}^{n \times (n+L)}$ *with supports* $\mathcal{W}_1, \ldots, \mathcal{W}_n$ *where* $\mathbf{W}_1 \xleftarrow{\$} \mathbb{F}_{q^m}^{n \times L}$ *and* $\mathbf{W}_2 \xleftarrow{\$} \mathrm{GL}_n(\mathbb{F}_{q^m})$, *the random matrix from* $\mathbb{F}_{q^m}^{k \times (n+L)}$ *defined as* $\mathbf{G} \triangleq \left[\mathbf{R} \mid -\mathbf{RW}_1^\mathsf{T} \left(\mathbf{W}_2^\mathsf{T} \right)^{-1} \right]$ *satisfies the following properties,*

1. $\mathbf{GW}^\mathsf{T} = \mathbf{0}$.
2. *Under Assumption 2,* $\mathbf{G}$ *is computationally indistinguishable from a uniformly random matrix.*
3. $\mathbf{G}$ *is* ε-*close to uniform over* $\mathbb{F}_{q^m}^{k \times (n+L)}$ *where* $\varepsilon \triangleq \frac{n}{2} \sqrt{q^{mk - (m+L)w + w^2}}$.

Proof. The fact that $\mathbf{GW}^\mathsf{T} = \mathbf{0}$ is straightforward. Furthermore, $\mathbf{G}$ is computationally indistinguishable from a uniformly random matrix if and only if $\mathbf{G}_0 \triangleq [\mathbf{R} \mid -\mathbf{RW}_1^\mathsf{T}]$ is so. But $\mathbf{W}_1$ is a semi-homogeneous matrix of weight w, and consequently we can use Proposition 4 and claim that $\mathbf{G}_0$ is pseudo-random.

Let us now consider a uniform random matrix $\mathbf{U} \xleftarrow{\$} \mathbb{F}_{q^m}^{k \times (n+L)}$. By Proposition 1 we have

$$\Delta \left(\left[\mathbf{R} \mid -\mathbf{RW}_1^\mathsf{T} \left(\mathbf{W}_2^\mathsf{T} \right)^{-1} \right], \mathbf{U} \right) \leqslant \Delta \left([\mathbf{R} \mid -\mathbf{RW}_1^\mathsf{T}], \mathbf{U} \right)$$

Thanks to Proposition 2 we can now apply Theorem 1. Namely we have the following inequality

$$\Delta \left([\mathbf{R} \mid -\mathbf{RW}_1^\mathsf{T}], \mathbf{U} \right) \leqslant \frac{n}{2} \sqrt{\frac{q^{mk}}{\left| \mathbb{S}_w \left(\mathbb{F}_{q^m}^L \right) \right|}}.$$

Using then (2) one sees that $\mathbf{G}$ is ε-close to uniform as claimed.   □

6   Parameters

We provide in this section the parameters we obtained for different security levels. All our parameters are chosen such that the probability of decoding failure as given in Theorem 2 is at most $2^{-\lambda}$ where λ is the security parameter. Additionally we require that the public matrix $\mathbf{G} \triangleq \left[\mathbf{R} \mid -\mathbf{RW}_1^\mathsf{T} \left(\mathbf{W}_2^\mathsf{T} \right)^{-1} \right]$ has to comply with the following security constraints:

1. It is computationally hard to distinguish $\mathbf{G} \in \mathbb{F}_{q^m}^{k \times (n+L)}$ from a random matrix. As the best known algorithm for this problem basically solves the search version of the Rank decoding problem, the parameters we compute take only into account the complexity of the best algorithms that solve this problem. We recall that in our case we have to solve n instances of the form $\left(\mathbf{R}, \mathbf{w}_j^{(1)} \mathbf{R}^{\mathsf{T}}\right)$ where $\mathbf{R} \in \mathbb{F}_{q^m}^{k \times L}$ and $\mathbf{w}_j^{(1)}$ is the jth row of $\mathbf{W}_1 \in \mathbb{F}_{q^m}^{L \times n}$ such that $\langle \mathbf{w}_j^{(1)} \rangle_{\mathbb{F}_q} \subseteq \mathcal{W}_j$. We denote by $\mathsf{RD}_{q,m}(L, L - k, w)$ the time complexity of the best algorithm that solves such an instance of the Rank decoding problem.

2. It is computationally hard to invert $f_{\mathbf{G}}(\mathbf{X}, \mathbf{E}) = \mathbf{X}\mathbf{G} + \mathbf{E}$ where $\mathbf{X} \xleftarrow{\$} \mathbb{F}_{q^m}^{N \times k}$ and $\mathbf{E} \in \mathbb{F}_{q^m}^{N \times (n+L)}$ is a (random) homogeneous matrix of weight t. It is clearly an instance of the Rank Support Learning problem with a linear code $\subset \mathbb{F}_{q^m}^{n+L}$ of dimension k and N noisy codewords where the support of each error vectors are included in $\langle \mathbf{E} \rangle_{\mathbb{F}_q} \in \mathbf{Gr}_t(q, m)$. We denote by $\mathsf{RSL}_{q,m}(n + L, k, t, N)$ the time complexity of the best algorithm for solving such an instance. Note that another way to invert $f_{\mathbf{G}}$ is to view the problem as solving N instances $(\mathbf{G}, \mathbf{x}_i \mathbf{G} + \mathbf{e}_i)$ of the Rank decoding problem where $\mathbf{x}_i$ and $\mathbf{e}_i$ are respectively the ith row of $\mathbf{X}$ and $\mathbf{E}$. The time complexity of the best algorithm for such instances is then $\mathsf{RD}_{q,m}(n + L, k, t)$.

The goal is then to find parameters such that the following holds

$$\min \left\{ \mathsf{RD}_{q,m}(L, L - k, w), \mathsf{RSL}_{q,m}(n + L, k, t, N), \mathsf{RD}_{q,m}(n + L, k, t) \right\} \geq 2^\lambda \quad (3)$$

Table 1 gives examples of parameters for a computationally indistinguishable matrix $\mathbf{G}$ at different values of λ. The last columns also indicates the sizes in KBytes of the public keys and the ciphertexts. We took $tw \leq N \leq tw + 3$. We have also computed parameters such that $\mathbf{G}$ is $2^{-\lambda}$-close to uniform. We recall that $\mathbf{G}$ is ε-close to uniform over $\mathbb{F}_{q^m}^{k \times (n+L)}$ where $\varepsilon \triangleq \frac{n}{2} \sqrt{q^{mk - (m+L)w + w^2}}$. Consequently, besides the constraints that we gave in (3) we now require that $\varepsilon < 2^{-\lambda}$. This last constraint imposes a high value for w that becomes close to k as it can be seen in Table 2.

Table 1. Parameters for $\mathbf{G}$ generated by Algorithm 2 to be computationally indistinguishable

λ (Security)	q	m	L	k	n	w	t	N	Public Key (KB)	Ciphertext (KB)
80	2	179	37	16	163	6	14	84	64	367
128	2	293	43	20	261	8	19	153	203	1,664
192	2	443	59	27	391	9	26	237	618	5,694
256	2	409	200	33	521	4	32	128	1,134	4,608

Table 2. Parameters for **G** generated by Algorithm 2 to be $2^{-\lambda}$-close to uniform

λ (Security)	q	m	L	k	n	w	t	N	Public Key (KB)	Ciphertext (KB)
80	2	499	59	17	163	16	13	208	212	2,813
128	2	907	130	21	261	19	20	380	860	16,450
192	2	1657	234	29	391	26	28	728	3,496	92,033
256	2	2707	129	36	521	35	35	1225	7,304	263,116

7 Conclusion

The main achievement of this work is to highlight the first construction of a rank-metric scheme with public keys that are statistically indistinguishable from a random code. The construction of (injective) trapdoor functions we propose represents a first step for building a public-key encryption scheme and a Key Encapsulation Mechanism (KEM). The sizes of the keys are not competitive compared to those in [2,6]. This difference is due to several reasons. We do not use structured matrices like ideal codes. Our public keys are computationally hard to distinguish which impact the performances. We impose a probability of decoding failure to be less than $2^{-\lambda}$ where λ is the security parameter and lastly, because the inversion algorithm requires to recover the whole input, our probability of failure is greater than in [6], especially because of the probability $\mathbb{P}_{II} \sim \ell q^{tw-m}$ which implies that $m \geqslant \lambda + tw$. Hence we do not exclude any drastic key size reduction if we get rid of the second step that recovers **E** as it is done in [6].

Acknowledgments. We are grateful to M. Bardet for providing computer programs that helped us compute complexities of the best existing attacks. E. Burle is supported by RIN100 program funded by Région Normandie. Y. Hatri is supported by RIN Label d'Excellence MINMACS funded by Région Normandie. P. Gaborit and A. Otmani are supported by the grant ANR-22-PETQ-0008 PQ-TLS funded by Agence Nationale de la Recherche within France 2030 program. A Otmani is supported by FAVPQC (EIG CONCERT-Japan & CNRS).

A Auxiliary Result

Lemma 1. *Let us assume that* $w + 3 \leqslant \min\{L, m\}$. *Then we have*

$$q^{(L+m)w-w^2} \leqslant \left| \mathbb{S}_w\left(\mathbb{F}_{q^m}^L\right) \right| \leqslant e^{2/(q-1)} \, q^{(L+m)w-w^2}$$

Proof. Using the expression of the cardinality of $\mathbb{S}_w\left(\mathbb{F}_{q^m}^L\right)$ from (1) we therefore have

$$\left| \mathbb{S}_w\left(\mathbb{F}_{q^m}^L\right) \right| = \prod_{i=0}^{w-1} \left(q^L - q^i\right) \frac{q^m - q^i}{q^w - q^i} = q^{(L+m-w)w} \prod_{i=0}^{w-1} \left(1 - q^{i-L}\right) \prod_{i=0}^{w-1} \frac{1 - q^{i-m}}{1 - q^{i-w}}$$

Exploiting the fact that for every $x \in [0, 1/2]$, $e^{-2x} \leqslant 1 - x \leqslant e^{-x}$ we can write that

$$
\left| \mathbb{S}_w \left(\mathbb{F}_{q^m}^L \right) \right| \geqslant q^{(L+m-w)w} \prod_{i=0}^{w-1} e^{-2q^{i-L}} \prod_{i=0}^{w-1} \frac{e^{-2q^{i-m}}}{e^{-q^{i-w}}}
$$

$$
\geqslant q^{(L+m-w)w} e^{\left(-2q^{-L} - 2q^{-m} + q^{-w} \right) \frac{q^w - 1}{q - 1}}
$$

Let us set $\gamma \triangleq q/(q-1)$. This means that $q^{w-1} \leqslant \frac{q^w - 1}{q - 1} \leqslant \gamma q^{w-1}$ which entails that

$$
\left| \mathbb{S}_w \left(\mathbb{F}_{q^m}^L \right) \right| \geqslant q^{(L+m-w)w} \, e^{-2\gamma q^{-L+w-1} - 2\gamma q^{-m+w-1} + q^{-1}}
$$

But the conditions $w + 3 \leqslant L$ and $q \geqslant 2$ enable us to write that $2\gamma q^{-L+w-1} \leqslant 2\gamma q^{-4} \leqslant \frac{1}{2q}$. By the same arguments we also have $2\gamma q^{-m+w-1} \leqslant \frac{1}{2q}$. This implies that

$$
e^{-2\gamma q^{-L+w-1} - 2\gamma q^{-m+w-1} + q^{-1}} \geqslant 1.
$$

We have hence proved that $\left| \mathbb{S}_w \left(\mathbb{F}_{q^m}^L \right) \right| \geqslant q^{(L+m-w)w}$. Next, by similar techniques, we can show that

$$
\left| \mathbb{S}_w \left(\mathbb{F}_{q^m}^L \right) \right| \leqslant q^{(L+m-w)w} \, e^{\left(-q^{-L} - q^{-m} + 2q^{-w} \right) \frac{q^w - 1}{q - 1}}
$$

$$
\leqslant q^{(L+m-w)w} \, e^{2q^{-w} \frac{q^w - 1}{q - 1}} \leqslant q^{(L+m-w)w} \, e^{2/(q-1)}
$$

which concludes the proof of the lemma. □

B Upper-Bound on the Decoding Failure Probability

We now turn to the question of proving Theorem 2 by bounding the probability $\mathbb{P} \left\{ \Phi(\mathbf{H}, \mathbf{HE}) \neq \mathbf{E} \right\}$ that Φ fails on a random input $(\mathbf{H}, \mathbf{HE})$. For that purpose we define by $\mathbb{P}_{\mathrm{I}}$ and $\mathbb{P}_{\mathrm{II}}$ the probability that Φ fails at the first and second step respectively. We then clearly have $\mathbb{P} \left\{ \Phi(\mathbf{H}, \mathbf{HE}) \neq \mathbf{E} \right\} = \mathbb{P}_{\mathrm{I}} + (1 - \mathbb{P}_{\mathrm{I}}) \mathbb{P}_{\mathrm{II}}$ which implies that $\mathbb{P} \left\{ \Phi(\mathbf{H}, \mathbf{HE}) \neq \mathbf{E} \right\} \leqslant \mathbb{P}_{\mathrm{I}} + \mathbb{P}_{\mathrm{II}}$. We have seen in Sect. 4 that the decoding algorithm Φ fail during the first step if one of the following two events occur: either $\langle \mathbf{s}_r \rangle_{\mathbb{F}_q}$ is not equal to $\mathcal{E} \cdot \mathcal{W}_r$ for every $r \in \{1, \ldots, \ell\}$, or each time we have the equality $\langle \mathbf{s}_r \rangle_{\mathbb{F}_q} = \mathcal{E} \cdot \mathcal{W}_r$, the strict inclusion $\mathcal{E} \subsetneq \bigcap_{i=1}^{w} \left(f_i^{(r)} \right)^{-1} \cdot \langle \mathbf{s}_r \rangle_{\mathbb{F}_q}$ holds. As by assumption the rows of $\mathbf{H}$ are drawn independently, we see that $\mathbb{P}_{\mathrm{I}}$ is at most

$$
\prod_{r=1}^{\ell} \left(\mathbb{P} \left\{ \langle \mathbf{s}_r \rangle_{\mathbb{F}_q} \neq \mathcal{E} \cdot \mathcal{W}_r \right\} + \mathbb{P} \left\{ \mathcal{E} \neq \bigcap_{i=1}^{w} \left(f_i^{(r)} \right)^{-1} \cdot \langle \mathbf{s}_r \rangle_{\mathbb{F}_q} \;\middle|\; \langle \mathbf{s}_r \rangle_{\mathbb{F}_q} = \mathcal{E} \cdot \mathcal{W}_r \right\} \right). \quad (4)
$$

The last failure case is although $\langle \mathbf{E} \rangle_{\mathbb{F}_q}$ has been correctly computed, it cannot compute the entries of $\mathbf{E}$ because for at least one r in $\{1, \ldots, \ell\}$, the dimension of $\mathcal{E} \cdot \mathcal{W}_r$ is not equal to tw. We see that we have

$$\mathbb{P}_{\text{II}} = 1 - \prod_{r=1}^{\ell} \mathbb{P}\left\{ \dim \mathcal{E} \cdot \mathcal{W}_r = tw \right\}. \tag{5}$$

The rest of this section is devoted to proving bounds for $\mathbb{P}_{\text{I}}$ and $\mathbb{P}_{\text{II}}$, mainly using results from LRPC decoding described in [67].

In order to bound $\mathbb{P}_{\text{I}}$ we bound $\mathbb{P}\left\{ \langle \mathbf{s}_r \rangle_{\mathbb{F}_q} \neq \mathcal{E} \cdot \mathcal{W}_r \right\}$ with Proposition 5 and $\mathbb{P}\left\{ \mathcal{E} \neq \bigcap_{i=1}^{w} \left(f_i^{(r)} \right)^{-1} \cdot \langle \mathbf{s}_r \rangle_{\mathbb{F}_q} \mid \langle \mathbf{s}_r \rangle_{\mathbb{F}_q} = \mathcal{E} \cdot \mathcal{W}_r \right\}$ in Theorem 4, and with (4) we get the result.

Proposition 5 (Proposition 3 in [67]). *Assume that $N \geqslant tw$. For a random homogeneous matrix $\mathbf{E} \xleftarrow{\$} \mathcal{E}^{n \times N}$ and a random vector $\mathbf{h} \xleftarrow{\$} \mathcal{W}^n$ where $\mathcal{E} \xleftarrow{\$} \mathbf{Gr}_t(q, m)$ and $\mathcal{W} \xleftarrow{\$} \mathbf{Gr}_w(q, m)$, the probability that $\langle \mathbf{hE} \rangle_{\mathbb{F}_q}$ is different from $\mathcal{E} \cdot \mathcal{W}$ is at most*

$$\mathbb{P}\left\{ \langle \mathbf{hE} \rangle_{\mathbb{F}_q} \neq \mathcal{E} \cdot \mathcal{W} \right\} \leqslant 1 - \prod_{i=0}^{tw-1} \left(1 - q^{i-N} \right)$$

Theorem 4 (Theorem 2 in [67]). *Let $\mathcal{U} \triangleq \mathcal{E} \cdot \mathcal{W}$ where $\mathcal{W} \in \mathbf{Gr}_w(q, m)$ and $\mathcal{E} \xleftarrow{\$} \mathbf{Gr}_t(q, m)$ with $(2w - 1)t < m$. Then for an arbitrary basis $f_1, \ldots, f_w$ of $\mathcal{W}$, we have*

$$\mathbb{P}\left\{ \mathcal{E} = \bigcap_{i=1}^{w} f_i^{-1} \cdot \mathcal{U} \mid \mathcal{E} \xleftarrow{\$} \mathbf{Gr}_t(q, m) \right\} \geqslant 1 - \frac{q^{(2w-1)t}}{q^m - q^{t-1}}.$$

For $\mathbb{P}_{\text{II}}$, we bound $\mathbb{P}\left\{ \dim \mathcal{E} \cdot \mathcal{W}_r = tw \right\}$ in Proposition 6 and use (5).

Proposition 6 (Proposition 4 in [67]). *For $\mathcal{W} \in \mathbf{Gr}_w(q, m)$ and assuming that $wt < m$, we have*

$$\mathbb{P}\left\{ \dim \mathcal{E} \cdot \mathcal{W} = tw \mid \mathcal{E} \xleftarrow{\$} \mathbf{Gr}_t(q, m) \right\} \geqslant 1 - \frac{q^{wt}}{q^m - q^{t-1}}.$$

References

1. Aguilar Melchor, C., et al.: BIKE. Round 3 Submission to the NIST Post-Quantum Cryptography Call, v. 4.2, September 2021
2. Aguilar Melchor, C., et al.: Rank quasi cyclic (RQC). Second Round submission to NIST Post-Quantum Cryptography call, April 2020

3. Aguilar-Melchor, C., Aragon, N., Dyseryn, V., Gaborit, P., Zemor, G.: LRPC codes with multiple syndromes: near ideal-size KEMs without ideals. In: Cheon, J.H., Johansson, T. (eds.) Post-Quantum Cryptography. PQCrypto 2022. LNCS, vol. 13512, pp. 45–68. Springer, Cham (2022). https://doi.org/10.1007/978-3-031-17234-2_3

4. Ajtai, M.: Generating hard instances of lattice problems (extended abstract). In: STOC '96 (1996)

5. Alekhnovich, M.: More on average case vs approximation complexity. In: 44th Symposium on Foundations of Computer Science (FOCS 2003), 11–14 October 2003, Cambridge, MA, USA, Proceedings, pp. 298–307. IEEE Computer Society (2003)

6. Aragon, N., et al.: ROLLO (merger of Rank-Ouroboros, LAKE and LOCKER). Second round submission to the NIST post-quantum cryptography call, March 2019

7. Aragon, N., et al.: LowMS: a new rank metric code-based kem without ideal structure. Cryptology ePrint Archive, Paper 2022/1596, 2022. https://eprint.iacr.org/2022/1596

8. Aragon, N., Gaborit, P., Hauteville, A., Ruatta, O., Zémor, G.: Low rank parity check codes: new decoding algorithms and applications to cryptography. IEEE Trans. Inform. Theory 65(12), 7697–7717 (2019)

9. Aragon, N., Gaborit, P., Hauteville, A., Tillich, J.P.: A new algorithm for solving the rank syndrome decoding problem. In: 2018 IEEE International Symposium on Information Theory, ISIT 2018, Vail, CO, USA, 17–22 June 2018, pp. 2421–2425. IEEE (2018)

10. Bardet, M., Briaud, P.: An algebraic approach to the rank support learning problem. In: Cheon, J.H., Tillich, J.-P. (eds.) PQCrypto 2021 2021. LNCS, vol. 12841, pp. 442–462. Springer, Cham (2021). https://doi.org/10.1007/978-3-030-81293-5_23

11. Bardet, M., Briaud, P., Bros, M., Gaborit, P., Tillich, J.P.: Revisiting algebraic attacks on minrank and on the rank decoding problem, 2022

12. Bardet, M., Mora, R., Tillich, J.P.: Polynomial time attack on high rate random alternant codes. CoRR, abs/2304.14757 (2023)

13. Bellare, M., Rogaway, P.: Random oracles are practical: a paradigm for designing efficient protocols. In: Dorothy, E., Denning, R.P., Ravi, G., Ravi, S.S., Victoria, A. (eds.) CCS '93, Proceedings of the 1st ACM Conference on Computer and Communications Security, Fairfax, Virginia, USA, 3–5 November 1993, pp. 62–73. ACM (1993)

14. Bidoux, L., Briaud, P., Bros, M., Gaborit, P.: RQC revisited and more cryptanalysis for rank-based cryptography. ArXiv, abs/2207.01410, 2022

15. Bombar, M., Couvreur, A.: Decoding supercodes of gabidulin codes and applications to cryptanalysis. In: Cheon, J.H., Tillich, J.-P. (eds.) PQCrypto 2021 2021. LNCS, vol. 12841, pp. 3–22. Springer, Cham (2021). https://doi.org/10.1007/978-3-030-81293-5_1

16. Courtois, N.T., Finiasz, M., Sendrier, N.: How to achieve a McEliece-based digital signature scheme. In: Boyd, C. (ed.) ASIACRYPT 2001. LNCS, vol. 2248, pp. 157–174. Springer, Heidelberg (2001). https://doi.org/10.1007/3-540-45682-1_10

17. Couvreur, A., Gaborit, P., Gauthier-Umaña, V., Otmani, A., Tillich, J.-P.: Distinguisher-based attacks on public-key cryptosystems using Reed-Solomon codes. Des. Codes Cryptogr. 73(2), 641–666 (2014)

18. Couvreur, A., Gaborit, P., Gauthier-Umana, V., Otmani, A., Tillich, J.P.: Distinguisher-Based Attacks on Public-Key Cryptosystems Using Reed-Solomon Codes. In: International Workshop on Coding and Cryptography - WCC 2013, pp. 181–193, Bergen, Norway, April 2013

19. Couvreur, A., Mora, R., Tillich, J.P.: A new approach based on quadratic forms to attack the mceliece cryptosystem. CoRR, abs/2306.10294, 2023

20. Couvreur, A., Otmani, A., Tillich, J.-P.: New identities relating wild Goppa codes. Finite Fields Appl. **29**, 178–197 (2014)

21. Couvreur, A., Otmani, A., Tillich, J.P.: Polynomial time attack on wild McEliece over quadratic extensions. IEEE Trans. Inform. Theory **63**(1), 404–427 (2017)

22. Debris-Alazard, T., Tillich, J.-P.: Two attacks on rank metric code-based schemes: ranksign and an IBE scheme. In: Peyrin, T., Galbraith, S. (eds.) ASIACRYPT 2018. LNCS, vol. 11272, pp. 62–92. Springer, Cham (2018). https://doi.org/10.1007/978-3-030-03326-2_3

23. Dwork, C., Naor, M., Reingold, O.: Immunizing encryption schemes from decryption errors. In: Cachin, C., Camenisch, J.L. (eds.) EUROCRYPT 2004. LNCS, vol. 3027, pp. 342–360. Springer, Heidelberg (2004). https://doi.org/10.1007/978-3-540-24676-3_21

24. Faugere, J.C., Gauthier-Umana, V., Otmani, A., Perret, L., Tillich, J.P.: A distinguisher for high rate McEliece cryptosystems. In: Proceedings of the IEEE Information Theory Workshop- ITW 2011, pp. 282–286, Paraty, Brasil, October 2011

25. Faugère, J.-C., Gauthier, V., Otmani, A., Perret, L., Tillich, J.-P.: A distinguisher for high rate McEliece cryptosystems. IEEE Trans. Inform. Theory **59**(10), 6830–6844 (2013)

26. Faure, C., Loidreau, P.: A new public-key cryptosystem based on the problem of reconstructing p-polynomials. In: Coding and Cryptography, International Workshop, WCC 2005, Bergen, Norway, 14–18 March 2005. Revised Selected Papers, pp. 304–315 (2005)

27. Fischer, J.-B., Stern, J.: An efficient pseudo-random generator provably as secure as syndrome decoding. In: Maurer, U. (ed.) EUROCRYPT 1996. LNCS, vol. 1070, pp. 245–255. Springer, Heidelberg (1996). https://doi.org/10.1007/3-540-68339-9_22

28. Gabidulin, E.M., Rashwan, H., Honary, B.: On improving security of GPT cryptosystems. In: Proceedings of the IEEE International Symposium on Information Theory - ISIT, pp. 1110–1114. IEEE (2009)

29. Gabidulin, E.M.: Theory of codes with maximum rank distance. Problemy Peredachi Informatsii **21**(1), 3–16 (1985)

30. Gabidulin, E.M.: Attacks and counter-attacks on the GPT public key cryptosystem. Des. Codes Cryptogr. **48**(2), 171–177 (2008)

31. Gabidulin, E.M., Ourivski, A.V.: Modified GPT PKC with right scrambler. Electron. Notes Discret. Math. **6**, 168–177 (2001)

32. Gabidulin, E.M., Ourivski, A.V., Honary, B., Ammar, B.: Reducible rank codes and their applications to cryptography. IEEE Trans. Inform. Theory **49**(12), 3289–3293 (2003)

33. Gabidulin, E.M., Paramonov, A.V., Tretjakov, O.V.: Ideals over a noncommutative ring and their applications to cryptography. In: Advances in Cryptology - EUROCRYPT'91, number 547 in LNCS, pp. 482–489, Brighton, April 1991

34. Gaborit, P., Hauteville, A., Phan, D.H., Tillich, J.-P.: Identity-based encryption from codes with rank metric. In: Katz, J., Shacham, H. (eds.) CRYPTO 2017.

LNCS, vol. 10403, pp. 194–224. Springer, Cham (2017). https://doi.org/10.1007/978-3-319-63697-9_7

35. Gaborit, P., Hauteville, A., Tillich, J.-P.: RankSynd a PRNG based on rank metric. In: Takagi, T. (ed.) PQCrypto 2016. LNCS, vol. 9606, pp. 18–28. Springer, Cham (2016). https://doi.org/10.1007/978-3-319-29360-8_2

36. Gaborit, P., Otmani, A., Talé-Kalachi, H.: Polynomial-time key recovery attack on the Faure-Loidreau scheme based on Gabidulin codes. Des. Codes Cryptogr. 86(7), 1391–1403 (2018)

37. Gaborit, P., Ruatta, O., Schrek, J.: On the complexity of the rank syndrome decoding problem. IEEE Trans. Inform. Theory 62(2), 1006–1019 (2016)

38. Philippe, G., Gilles, Z.: On the hardness of the decoding and the minimum distance problems for rank codes. IEEE IT, 2016

39. Garg, S., Hajiabadi, M.: Trapdoor functions from the computational Diffie-Hellman assumption. In: Shacham, H., Boldyreva, A. (eds.) CRYPTO 2018. LNCS, vol. 10992, pp. 362–391. Springer, Cham (2018). https://doi.org/10.1007/978-3-319-96881-0_13

40. Gauthier, V., Otmani, A., Tillich, J.P.: A distinguisher-based attack of a homomorphic encryption scheme relying on Reed-Solomon codes. CoRR, abs/1203.6686, 2012

41. Gauthier, V., Otmani, A., Tillich, J.P.: A distinguisher-based attack on a variant of McEliece's cryptosystem based on Reed-Solomon codes. CoRR, abs/1204.6459, 2012

42. Gibson, K.: Severely denting the Gabidulin version of the McEliece public key cryptosystem. Des. Codes Cryptogr. 6(1), 37–45 (1995)

43. Gibson, K.: The security of the gabidulin public key cryptosystem. In: Maurer, U. (ed.) EUROCRYPT 1996. LNCS, vol. 1070, pp. 212–223. Springer, Heidelberg (1996). https://doi.org/10.1007/3-540-68339-9_19

44. Goldreich, O.: The Foundations of Cryptography - volume 1, Basic Techniques. Cambridge University Press, Cambridge (2001)

45. Oded, G., Leonid, A.L.: A hard-core predicate for all one-way functions. In: Proceedings of the Twenty-First Annual ACM Symposium on Theory of Computing, pp. 25–32. ACM (1989)

46. Hastad, J., Impagliazzo, R., Levin, L.A., Luby, M.: A pseudorandom generator from any one-way function. SIAM J. Comput. 28(4), 1364–1396 (1999)

47. Hofheinz, D., Hövelmanns, K., Kiltz, E.: A modular analysis of the Fujisaki-Okamoto transformation. In: Kalai, Y., Reyzin, L. (eds.) TCC 2017. LNCS, vol. 10677, pp. 341–371. Springer, Cham (2017). https://doi.org/10.1007/978-3-319-70500-2_12

48. Hohenberger, S., Koppula, V., Waters, B.: Chosen ciphertext security from injective trapdoor functions. In: Micciancio, D., Ristenpart, T. (eds.) CRYPTO 2020. LNCS, vol. 12170, pp. 836–866. Springer, Cham (2020). https://doi.org/10.1007/978-3-030-56784-2_28

49. Impagliazzo, R., Naor, M.: Efficient cryptographic schemes provably as secure as subset sum. In: 30th Annual Symposium on Foundations of Computer Science, North Carolina, USA, 30 October–1 November 1989, pp. 236–241. IEEE Computer Society (1989)

50. Lavauzelle, J., Loidreau, P., Pham, B.D.: RAMESSES, a Rank Metric Encryption Scheme with Short Keys. working paper or preprint, January 2020

51. Pierre, L.: Properties of codes in rank metric, 2006

52. Loidreau, P.: A new rank metric codes based encryption scheme. In: Lange, T., Takagi, T. (eds.) PQCrypto 2017. LNCS, vol. 10346, pp. 3–17. Springer, Cham (2017). https://doi.org/10.1007/978-3-319-59879-6_1

53. Robert, J.M.: A Public-Key System Based on Algebraic Coding Theory, pp. 114–116. Jet Propulsion Lab, 1978. DSN Progress Report 44

54. Mora, R., Tillich, J.-P.: On the dimension and structure of the square of the dual of a goppa code. Des. Codes Cryptogr. **91**(4), 1351–1372 (2023)

55. Otmani, A., Kalachi, H.T.: Square code attack on a modified sidelnikov cryptosystem. In: El Hajji, S., Nitaj, A., Carlet, C., Souidi, E.M. (eds.) C2SI 2015. LNCS, vol. 9084, pp. 173–183. Springer, Cham (2015). https://doi.org/10.1007/978-3-319-18681-8_14

56. Otmani, A., Talé-Kalachi, H., Ndjeya, S.: Improved cryptanalysis of rank metric schemes based on Gabidulin codes. Des. Codes Cryptogr. **86**(9), 1983–1996 (2018)

57. Overbeck, R.: Extending Gibson's attacks on the GPT cryptosystem. In: Ytrehus, Ø. (ed.) WCC 2005. LNCS, vol. 3969, pp. 178–188. Springer, Heidelberg (2006). https://doi.org/10.1007/11779360_15

58. Overbeck, R.: A new structural attack for GPT and variants. In: Dawson, E., Vaudenay, S. (eds.) Mycrypt 2005. LNCS, vol. 3715, pp. 50–63. Springer, Heidelberg (2005). https://doi.org/10.1007/11554868_5

59. Overbeck, R.: Structural attacks for public key cryptosystems based on Gabidulin codes. J. Cryptol. **21**(2), 280–301 (2008)

60. Peikert, C., Waters, B.: Lossy trapdoor functions and their applications. In: Dwork, C., (ed.), Proceedings of the 40th Annual ACM Symposium on Theory of Computing, Victoria, British Columbia, Canada, 17–20 May 2008, pp. 187–196. ACM (2008)

61. Rashwan, H., Gabidulin, E.M., Honary, B.: A smart approach for GPT cryptosystem based on rank code. In: Proceedings of the IEEE International Symposium on Information Theory - ISIT, pp. 2463–2467. IEEE (2010)

62. Rashwan, H., Gabidulin, E., Honary, B.: Security of the GPT cryptosystem and its applications to cryptography. Secur. Commun. Netw. **4**(8), 937–946 (2011)

63. Rivest, R.L., Shamir, A., Adleman, L.M.: A method for obtaining digital signatures and public-key cryptosystems. Commun. ACM **21**(2), 120–126 (1978)

64. Shoup, V.: A Computational Introduction to Number Theory and Algebra, 2nd edn. Cambridge University Press, USA (2008)

65. Wachter-Zeh, A., Puchinger, S., Renner, J. : Repairing the Faure-Loidreau public-key cryptosystem. In: Proceedings of the IEEE International Symposium on Information Theory - ISIT, pp. 2426–2430 (2018)

66. Wang, L.-P.: Loong: a new IND-CCA-secure code-based KEM. In: 2019 IEEE International Symposium on Information Theory (ISIT), pp. 2584–2588 (2019)

67. Burle, É., Otmani, A.: An upper-bound on the decoding failure probability of the LRPC decoder. In: Quaglia, E.A. (eds.) Cryptography and Coding. IMACC 2023. LNCS, vol. 14421, pp. 3–16. Springer, Cham (2024). https://doi.org/10.1007/978-3-031-47818-5_1

PERKS: Persistent and Distributed Key Acquisition for Secure Storage from Passwords

Gareth T. Davies[1] and Jeroen Pijnenburg[2(✉)]

[1] Bergische Universität Wuppertal, Wuppertal, Germany
davies@uni-wuppertal.de
[2] Royal Holloway, University of London, Egham, UK
jeroen.pijnenburg.2017@live.rhul.ac.uk

Abstract. We investigate how users of instant messaging (IM) services can acquire strong encryption keys to back up their messages and media with strong cryptographic guarantees. Many IM users regularly change their devices and use multiple devices simultaneously, ruling out any long-term secret storage. Extending the end-to-end encryption guarantees from just message communication to also incorporate backups has so far required either some trust in an IM or outsourced storage provider, or use of costly third-party encryption tools with unclear security guarantees. Recent works have proposed solutions for password-protected key material, however all require one or more servers to generate and/or store per-user information, inevitably invoking a cost to the users.

We define *distributed key acquisition* (DKA) as the primitive for the task at hand, where a user interacts with one or more servers to acquire a strong cryptographic key, and both user and server store as little as possible. We present a construction framework that we call PERKS—Password-based Establishment of Random Keys for Storage—providing efficient, modular and simple protocols that utilize Oblivious Pseudorandom Functions (OPRFs) in a distributed manner with minimal storage by the user (just the password) and servers (a single global key for all users). Along the way we introduce a formal treatment of DKA, and provide proofs of security for our constructions in their various flavours.

1 Introduction

Passwords are ubiquitous as authentication tokens and yet constructing schemes based on passwords is notoriously difficult to get right. Users regularly re-use and/or forget their passwords, application servers store passwords incorrectly, and more and more physical and technical tools are needed to prevent attacks and misuse. We consider the general problem of converting a human-memorable password into a single cryptographic secret, with minimal storage and communication requirements.

Gareth T. Davies has been supported by the European Research Council (ERC) under the European Union's Horizon 2020 research and innovation programme, grant agreement 802823. The full version of this article is available at [19].

As a motivating case study, consider instant messaging (IM) applications: it is at present not clear what keying material should be used to encrypt messages and files that are stored on the user's device, and/or backed up to an external backup service or cloud storage provider (CSP)[1]. It is not clear what security properties are obtainable in the scenario where a user defends against potential loss of their device by backing up messages, never mind in each of the many other possible variations of the message storage scenario (long-term on-device encryption, temporary backup for 'device changeover', backup for immediate local deletion). Our solutions are targeted at this main scenario—where a user acquires a new phone and wants to recover their backed-up data using only their password—but with applications to the others[2]. In this setting a user may interact with their IM service, a CSP that stores messages and media, and potentially other services that contribute to keying material: the user would prefer not to (fully) trust all of these services (or their device) and additionally would like to draw entropy from each of these services in deriving a(n initial) key for data encryption. We refer to all of these n entities, potentially including the IM and outsourced storage providers, as *key-contributing servers*. Our key tool is an oblivious PRF (OPRF): a user, holding a secret input x, engages in a protocol with a server, holding a key sk, where at the end of the protocol the user learns $F(sk, x)$ for some keyed pseudorandom function F and the server learns nothing.

A number of primitives exist in the literature that attempt to solve this problem and provide secure and distributed key generation, however all require the storage of user-specific information with the key servers. This is infeasible at the multi-billion-user scale required for modern IM applications, and would most likely result in this feature becoming a costly paid service. In particular, securely storing this per-user key material would often be done using a hardware security module (HSM), introducing significant key management challenges and financial costs. Further, many schemes require the user to generate the high-entropy secret in the first place and then securely distribute it, imposing a trust requirement on the client device and its randomness generation. We summarize these primitives in Sect. 1.3.

1.1 Problem Statement

There are at present (at least) three major stumbling blocks for deployment of encrypted backup systems for IM services:

- **Storage Cost.** Using existing techniques for OPRF-based password hardening would invoke per-user data to be stored at each of the key-contributing servers. For this reason it is necessary to minimize the storage burden for every entity in the system.

---

[1] In commercial settings there may exist on-premise file/backup storage, but in our more general case the entity storing the ciphertexts is regarded as external.

[2] We do not explicitly consider the scenario where the user has two devices in their possession and wishes to locally transfer messages and/or media from one device to another without the help of outsourced storage, as our approach would be overkill.

- **Key Longevity.** For the system to function, it is essential that over a long period of time the key acquisition interaction is 'long lived', in the sense that the key production operation must be deterministic and any secret values given as input to the operation (by user or server) must not change.
- **Trust Distribution.** In the IM setting it is by now industry standard to expect end-to-end-encryption (E2EE) of messages, ensuring that the storage server cannot decrypt sent content. With this in mind, it would appear risky to rely on the IM provider to act as a single key-contributing server, or to use only the IM server and cloud storage provider. It is thus desirable to introduce additional parties to the picture, and distribute the trust such that the user has fine-grained control of what they are able to do if they learn/believe that one or more of these parties has become compromised.

In our work we aim to overcome all of these challenges simultaneously, supplementing our proposals with rigorous security analyses.

The concept of key longevity is at odds with modern approaches to forward security that involve (regular) key rotation, and so any operation that does support key rotation must also enable the user to update their ciphertexts when this rotation occurs, which is a considerable technical challenge. In Sect. 5 we describe how key rotation can be done securely and efficiently within our framework.

1.2 Contributions

We design a novel formal framework for outsourced (and on-device) storage that allows a user to generate and store a cryptographic key with the aid of n key-contributing servers, with the constraints discussed already. We call the required primitive *distributed key acquisition* (DKA) and describe its syntax and security properties. We introduce a correctness game and two key indistinguishability games for DKA. We explain how a DKA scheme can be used in conjunction with encryption and key rotation to neatly solve the IM backup problem.

We provide two concrete constructions for DKA using OPRFs in a framework that we call PERKS (Password-based Establishment of Random Keys for Storage): the n out of n setting for when the user expects the key-contributing servers to be available for the lifetime of the system, and a threshold t out of n scheme based on secret sharing that tolerates n − t servers being unavailable or compromised. Even in the event that n − t + 1 (or more, even all n) servers are corrupted by the same entity, all is not lost: this adversary must still perform an offline attack to recover the key. Our constructions are extremely simple but the analysis is certainly not: we introduce appropriate security properties for user and server privacy in our setting, and prove that our schemes—when instantiated using a variety of existing OPRFs with different features—meet the corresponding properties.

1.3 Related Primitives and Existing Literature

The existing primitive that is most closely related to our setting is (t, n) password-protected secret sharing (PPSS): a user that is already in possession of some secret value distributes it among n servers such that reconstruction is possible using only the password and interaction with t + 1 honest servers. Bagherzandi *et al.* [3] gave the first formal treatment and a scheme where the user needs to store/trust one or more public keys. Later schemes gave security in the presence of related passwords via the UC framework [15], and in the setting where servers learn nothing in the reconstruction phase [14] (by sending out an encryption of a randomized quotient of the password and not the password itself). In September 2021, WhatsApp announced [41] that they would soon begin beta testing of an encrypted backup service that uses HSMs and the envelope part of the OPAQUE protocol [28] in a manner that is conceptually similar to a $(1,1)$-PPSS. In Appendix A we explain the differences with our work.

Jarecki, Kiayias and Krawczyk [23] gave threshold PPSS (and threshold PAKE) with optimal round complexity, but with the same setup assumptions as the prior papers. In [24] the same authors and Xu gained improved efficiency compared to previous work, and in essence these savings come from foregoing some heavy duty tools required to achieve the UC verifiability property of the OPRF. The same authors then presented TOPPSS [25] using a Threshold OPRF, where the secret sharing performed on the level of the OPRF key, so derivation of the single OPRF output for a given input is an interactive protocol with $t + 1$ of the n servers. Abdalla *et al.* [1] defined robust PPSS, where a robust secret sharing scheme is used to detect cheating servers, also foregoing the need for a verifiable OPRF.

Password-Hardened Encryption (PHE) was introduced by Lai *et al.* [31] and uses an oblivious external party for key derivation to protect against offline brute-force attacks on a ciphertext encrypted under just the password. Recognizing the single point of failure, threshold PHE was introduced in [13]. The scheme requires a trusted third party to distribute all secret keys during initialization.

Other primitives exist that use a distributed OPRF service (i.e. the server stores, for each user, a sharing of an OPRF secret key) to derive a cryptographic secret, including Baum *et al.* [5] who use the OPRF to get a signature key pair for distributed single sign-on, and Das *et al.* [17] who use a similar trick to obtain a signature key pair, then per-file encryption keys are created by computing a so-called extended POPRF for a second private input, namely a randomized hash of the file.

2 Preliminaries

2.1 Notation and Security Games

We specify scheme algorithms and security games in pseudocode. In such code we write '$var \leftarrow exp$' for evaluating expression exp and assigning the result to variable var. Here, expression exp may comprise the invocation of algorithms. If var is a set variable and exp evaluates to a set, we write $var \overset{\cup}{\leftarrow} exp$ shorthand for $var \leftarrow var \cup exp$. Similarly, if var is an integer variable and exp evaluates to an integer, we write $var \overset{+}{\leftarrow} exp$ shorthand for $var \leftarrow var + exp$. Associative arrays implement the 'dictionary' data structure: Once the instruction $A[\cdot] \leftarrow exp$ initialized all items of array A to the default value exp, with $A[idx] \leftarrow exp$ and

$var \leftarrow A[idx]$ individual items indexed by expression idx can be updated or extracted. For a vector $\vec{v}$ we denote with size($\vec{v}$) the number of defined elements, i.e. elements that are not $\perp$, which may be less than the length of $\vec{v}$. Many algorithms take as input a security parameter λ, however for visual clarity we omit this wherever possible (further, this implicit representation is possible because we do not build any primitives from computational assumptions nor present any equational relationships that depend directly on λ).

Security games are parameterized by an adversary, and consist of a main game body plus zero or more oracle specifications. The adversary is allowed to call any oracle specified in the game at any time. The execution of a game starts with the main game body and terminates when a 'Stop with exp' instruction is reached, where the value of expression exp is taken as the outcome of the game. If the outcome of a game G is Boolean, we write $\Pr[G(\mathcal{A})]$ for the probability that an execution of G with adversary $\mathcal{A}$ results in 1. We define macros for specific game-ending instructions: We write 'Win' for 'Stop with 1' and 'Lose' for 'Stop with 0', and for a condition C we write 'Require C' for 'If $\neg C$: Lose' and 'Reward C' for 'If C: Win'. We finally draw attention to an important detail of our algorithm and game notation: algorithms are allowed to abort. Here, by abort we mean the case where an algorithm does not generate output according to its syntax specification, but outputs some error indicator instead, e.g. outputs $\perp$. We have prefaced algorithms that may abort with the 'Try' statement. If an oracle calls an algorithm that aborts, the oracle also immediately aborts.

2.2 Oblivious Pseudorandom Functions: Syntax

Following Everspaugh et al. [20] and Tyagi et al. [40] we define OPRFs as a tuple $F = (F.KG, F.Req, F.BlindEv, F.Finalize, F.Ev)$. The syntax captures two optional properties of OPRFs, namely partial obliviousness (user provides as input a public value in addition to its secret input, known as POPRFs) and verifiability (user is convinced that server has evaluated for a particular key, where the user learns a public commitment/representation of this key, known as VOPRFs), which both are useful but not essential in our constructions later on. In Sect. F we provide an overview of the prior work and how existing OPRF constructions can fit into our approach, with and without these additional properties. In Fig. 1 we depict the operation of a (P)OPRF with optional verifiability.

F.KG generates a key pair (pk, sk) (or just sk for non-verifiable OPRFs), taking as input a security parameter. To form a request, the user runs $F.Req(t, x)$ with secret input x (and in POPRFs, public input t) and outputs a request req and a local state st. The server then runs $F.BlindEv(sk, t, req)$ and outputs a response rep. The user finishes by running $F.Finalize(pk, rep, st)$, either outputting the function evaluation y, or $\perp$ if it does not accept the outcome. The unblinded evaluation algorithm $F.Ev(sk, t, x)$ outputs y or $\perp$. The server should not learn (anything about) the secret input x even after multiple interactions where x was provided as input, and the user should not learn (anything about) sk.

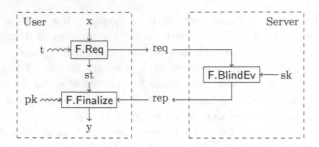

Fig. 1. OPRF operation diagram. Public input t is only present in POPRFs and verification public key pk is only present in VOPRFs.

Name	POPRF?	Assumption	F.Ev(sk, t, x)	req	rep
2HashDH [23]	✗	OM-Gap-DH	$H_2(x, H_1(x)^{sk})$	$H_1(x)^r$	$H_1(x)^{r \cdot sk}$
Pythia [20]	✓	OM-BCDH	$e(H_3(t), H_1(x))^{sk}$	$H_1(x)^r, t$	$e(H_3(t), H_1(x)^r)^{sk}$
3HashSDHI [40]	✓	OM-Gap-SDHI	$H_2(t, x, H_1(x)^{\frac{1}{H_3(t)+sk}})$	$H_1(x)^r, t$	$H_1(x)^{\frac{r}{H_3(t)+sk}}$

Fig. 2. Comparison of selected (partially) oblivious PRFs from the literature. Hash functions H_i are labelled for comparison purposes, but when used in protocols the domains and ranges will be different.

In Fig. 2 we detail the operation of three well-known OPRF protocols, all of which are reliant on Diffie-Hellman-like assumptions. In our constructions, the key-contributing servers will hold an OPRF secret key sk that they use for all users. User separation will either be done by employing a partially oblivious PRF with t = *uid*, or by deriving a per-user key in each protocol invocation. We will always use the password as the user's secret input, so hereon x = *pw*.

2.3 Oblivious Pseudorandom Functions: Security Notions

For *correctness* we require that honest OPRF evaluations consistently produce the same output when provided with equal inputs. The privacy games capture that a server cannot glean any information about users' private inputs, nor link transcripts of requests/responses to OPRF output values, even with knowledge of the OPRF secret key. Our security notions are based on the security models of Tyagi *et al.* [40]. Their *user privacy* notion has two flavours:

- POPRIV-1 essentially models an honest but curious server and so does not require verifiability. In the game the adversary has a transcript-generation oracle that provides the entire transcript.
- POPRIV-2 models a malicious server by allowing the adversary to separately engage with oracles for OPRF request generation and OPRF output generation (in our notation denoted Challenge and Finalize respectively).

Additionally they gave a pseudorandomness game for *server privacy* where an adversary interacts with a (blinded) evaluation oracle and tries to distinguish genuine operation from operation with a random function.

Game PRIV-$1^b(\mathcal{A})$
00 $b' \leftarrow \mathcal{A}()$
01 Stop with b'

Oracle Challenge(t, x_0, x_1)
02 $(\mathrm{req}_0, \mathrm{st}_0) \leftarrow \mathsf{F.Req}(t, x_0)$
03 $(\mathrm{req}_1, \mathrm{st}_1) \leftarrow \mathsf{F.Req}(t, x_1)$
04 Return $(\mathrm{req}_b, \mathrm{req}_{1-b})$

Game PRIV-$2^b(\mathcal{A})$
05 $i \leftarrow 0$
06 $\mathrm{ST}[\cdot] \leftarrow \perp$
07 $b' \leftarrow \mathcal{A}()$
08 Stop with b'

Oracle Challenge(t, x_0, x_1)
09 $i \stackrel{+}{\leftarrow} 1$
10 $(\mathrm{req}_0, \mathrm{st}_0) \leftarrow \mathsf{F.Req}(t, x_0)$
11 $(\mathrm{req}_1, \mathrm{st}_1) \leftarrow \mathsf{F.Req}(t, x_1)$
12 $\mathrm{ST}[i] \leftarrow (\mathrm{st}_0, \mathrm{st}_1)$
13 Return $(i, \mathrm{req}_b, \mathrm{req}_{1-b})$

Oracle Finalize$(j, \mathrm{pk}, \mathrm{rep}, \mathrm{rep}')$
14 Require $j \in [1 .. i]$
15 $(\mathrm{st}_0, \mathrm{st}_1) \leftarrow \mathrm{ST}[j]$
16 $y_b \leftarrow \mathsf{F.Finalize}(\mathrm{pk}, \mathrm{rep}, \mathrm{st}_b)$
17 $y_{1-b} \leftarrow \mathsf{F.Finalize}(\mathrm{pk}, \mathrm{rep}', \mathrm{st}_{1-b})$
18 If $y_0 = \perp$ or $y_1 = \perp$:
19   Return $(\perp, \perp)$
20 Return (y_0, y_1)

Game PRNG$^b(\mathcal{A}, n)$
21 $\mathrm{BE}[\cdot] \leftarrow 0; \mathrm{RE}[\cdot] \leftarrow 0$
22 For $i \in [1 .. n]$:
23      $(\mathrm{pk}_0^i, \mathrm{sk}_0^i) \leftarrow_\$ \mathsf{F.KG}$
24      $(\mathrm{pk}_1^i, \mathrm{sk}_1^i) \leftarrow_\$ \mathsf{F.KG}$
25      $G^i \leftarrow_\$ \{g \mid g : \mathcal{U} \times \mathcal{I} \to \mathcal{O}\}$
26 $b' \leftarrow \mathcal{A}(\vec{\mathrm{pk}_b})$
27 Stop with b'

Oracle Ev(t, x)
28 For $i \in [1 .. n]$:
29      $y_0 \leftarrow \mathsf{F.Ev}(\mathrm{sk}_0^i, t, x)$
30      $y_1 \leftarrow G^i(t, x)$
31 Return $\vec{y}_b$

Oracle BlindEv(t, req)
32 $\mathrm{BE}[t] \stackrel{+}{\leftarrow} 1$
33 For $i \in [1 .. n]$:
34      $\mathrm{rep}_0^i \leftarrow \mathsf{F.BlindEv}(\mathrm{sk}_0^i, t, \mathrm{req})$
35      $\mathrm{rep}_1^i \leftarrow \mathcal{S}.\mathsf{BlindEv}(\mathrm{sk}_1^i, t, \mathrm{req})$
36 Return $\vec{\mathrm{rep}}_b$

Oracle $H(x)$
37 $h_0 \leftarrow \mathsf{RO}(x)$
38 $h_1 \leftarrow \mathcal{S}.\mathsf{Ev}(x)$
39 Return h_b

Oracle RestrictedEv(t, x)
40 Require $\mathrm{RE}[t] < \mathrm{BE}[t]$
41 $\mathrm{RE}[t] \stackrel{+}{\leftarrow} 1$
42 $\vec{y} \leftarrow \mathrm{Ev}(t, x)$
43 Return $\vec{y}$

Fig. 3. OPRF Games for the multiple servers setting. For the meaning of instructions Stop with, Lose, Reward, and Require see Sect. 2.

Our PRIV-x games are adapted from the POPRIV-x games of Tyagi et al. [40]; due to space constraints we only detail our games and explain the differences. We remark we only return the request req and not the response rep nor the final output value y in PRIV-1. It should be obvious that the adversary can compute rep on its own because it holds the secret key to evaluate F.BlindEv, and in fact it can run this operation with arbitrary secret keys. Further, the adversary can run F.Ev on the values it has sent to Challenge using secret keys of its choosing, thus completing a full transcript. In PRIV-2 we do have a Finalize oracle, as the adversary is allowed to submit arbitrary responses and the correctness game makes no statement about this case. In Appendix D we show that PRIV-1 and POPRIV-1 are equivalent. Furthermore, the F.Req algorithm no longer takes a public key as input and is thus independent of the server. Instead, the F.Finalize algorithm, which uses the public key to verify the response, now takes in the public key directly, rather than it being passed via request state.

Definition 1 (PRIV-x Security). *The advantage of an adversary $\mathcal{A}$ in the* PRIV-x *security games defined in Fig. 3 for* $x \in \{1, 2\}$ *and OPRF* F *is*

$$\mathbf{Adv}_F^{\mathrm{PRIV-x}}(\mathcal{A}) := \left| \Pr\left[\mathsf{G}_F^{\mathrm{PRIV-x^1}}(\mathcal{A}) = 1 \right] - \Pr\left[\mathsf{G}_F^{\mathrm{PRIV-x^0}}(\mathcal{A}) = 1 \right] \right|.$$

Our PRNG^b game is in essence the POPRF game in [40] for verifiable POPRFs, but extended to our multi-server setting: the oracles now return vectors instead of single elements. The game is parameterized by a simulator $\mathcal{S}$ and creates an environment for an adversary to interact with n OPRF servers via an oracle for function evaluation (Ev) and in modelling malicious clients a blinded evaluation oracle (BlindEv). Initially the game creates 2n server key pairs (or just secret keys for OPRFs that are not verifiable): in the $b = 0$ case the real function is used with one of the secret keys, and in the $b = 1$ case a random function is used and the simulator is tasked with providing appropriate responses but given the other secret key. The Ev oracle returns either the output of the F.Ev algorithm or a random function. The adversary also has access to the BlindEv oracle, which either returns the output of the F.BlindEv algorithm or the response generated by the simulator $\mathcal{S}$.BlindEv. Queries to oracle H are either answered by a random oracle query or simulated by $\mathcal{S}$.Ev. Crucially, to maintain consistency between Ev and BlindEv queries, the simulator can obtain Ev outputs via its own $\mathcal{S}$-Oracle RestrictedEv. However, the simulator is restricted: the number of queries to RestrictedEv is bounded by the number of adversary queries to BlindEv, specific for each public input. This ensures that the adversary cannot compute more POPRF evaluations than the number of oracle queries it made. Moreover, restricting per public input means that querying with public input t_1 cannot help the adversary compute the evaluation for another public input $t_2 \neq t_1$. For a more detailed description of (the single server version of) this game motivating the modelling choices, see Section 3 of [40]: there are many subtleties discussed regarding the simulator and limited evaluation. For our purposes, it is sufficient to know we only build from secure (P)OPRFs.

Definition 2 (PRNG Security). *The advantage of an adversary $\mathcal{A}$ in the* PRNG *security game defined in Fig. 3 for OPRF* F *is*

$$\mathbf{Adv}_{F,\mathcal{S}}^{\mathrm{PRNG}}(\mathcal{A}, \mathrm{n}) := \left| \Pr\left[\mathsf{G}_{F,\mathcal{S}}^{\mathrm{PRNG^1}}(\mathcal{A}, \mathrm{n}) = 1 \right] - \Pr\left[\mathsf{G}_{F,\mathcal{S}}^{\mathrm{PRNG^0}}(\mathcal{A}, \mathrm{n}) = 1 \right] \right|.$$

3   DKA and Security Models

A distributed key acquisition scheme is an interactive protocol between parties, where the parties can either be users or servers. In this section we formally define the syntax of a distributed key acquisition scheme and define security via two games for key indistinguishability. The weaker KIND-1 security game effectively models an honest but curious adversary as it may call oracles for honest protocol executions for a user to learn its requests and responses. In the KIND-2 security game the adversary is in complete control of the servers and may choose arbitrarily how to respond to user requests.

3.1 Distributed Key Acquisition

SYNTAX. A distributed key acquisition scheme for a set S of n servers that are (initially) available to users consists of a secret key space $\mathcal{SK}$, a public key space $\mathcal{PK}$, a user identity space $\mathcal{UID}$, a dictionary $\mathcal{D}$, a key space $\mathcal{K}$, an output space $\mathcal{O}$, algorithms gen, init, acquire, recover and server.op.

The system is initialized by gen which assigns a key pair $(\text{sk}, \text{pk}) \in \mathcal{SK} \times \mathcal{PK}$ to each server $S_i \in S$, and public keys $\vec{\text{pk}} \in \mathcal{PK}^n$ are then distributed to users. A user $uid \in \mathcal{UID}$ with password $pw \in \mathcal{D}$ initializes itself in the system and acquires a key $k \in \mathcal{K}$ and possibly some setup values $\vec{\text{SV}} \in \mathcal{O}^n$ by running init$(uid, pw, \vec{\text{pk}}, S)$. We remark that $\vec{\text{SV}}$ is not secret, so it can be stored alongside the backed up data. The init procedure sends out a request req $\in \mathcal{RQ}$ to each server, who will run server.op$(\text{sk}_i, uid, \text{req})$ to respond with response rep $\in \mathcal{RP}$. An individual user's interaction with the system is defined by a threshold t $\in$ [1 .. n] which is the number of servers that are required to be honest and available in order for the user to reconstruct their secret. Later, a user can acquire output values $\vec{y} \in \mathcal{O}^n$ by running acquire$(uid, pw, \vec{\text{pk}}, S)$ and recover their key $k \in \mathcal{K}$ by subsequently running recover$(\vec{y}, C, \vec{\text{SV}})$, where the set of chosen servers C is a subset of S. Syntactically this takes as input all output values, but some may not be set, i.e. y_i may be $\bot$ if server S_i did not respond. With C, a user can indicate which output values to use for the key recovery.

We assume that passwords are selected uniformly at random from the set $\mathcal{D}$ throughout the rest of this chapter. However, similarly to the game-based PAKE literature, it is possible to cast the choosing of passwords according to (the min-entropy of) some distribution Dist [6,12].

3.2 A Unified Security Notion for DKA

We first describe the correctness game for DKA schemes depicted in Fig. 4. The correctness game initializes the secret and public keys for all servers and initializes several game variables to keep track of the game state. The adversary controls the honest executions of the protocol via its oracles Init, Acquire and Recover. It has complete control over the inputs, specifying which user identity uid, password pw and public keys $\vec{\text{pk}}$ to use in Init and Acquire, and the set of chosen servers C (for reconstruction) and setup values $\vec{\text{SV}}$ in the Recover oracle. The counter r is a game variable to associate the Recover query with the corresponding Acquire query. This gives the adversary more freedom as we do not require these oracles to be used in succession. Via the Corrupt oracle the adversary is allowed to corrupt up to $t - 1$ servers. Recall that the oracle immediately aborts if a procedure prefaced by 'Try' aborts. In particular, a correct construction can abort if it is fed garbage input (i.e. an empty set of chosen servers) as otherwise the adversary would trigger the 'Reward' line that wins the correctness game. The adversary wins the correctness game if it manages to create two different keys for a set of user id, password and setup values.

Next, we describe the security games for DKA schemes, KIND-x for $x \in \{1, 2\}$, provided in Fig. 5, which ultimately capture key indistinguishability:

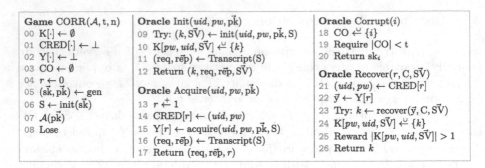

Fig. 4. Correctness game for DKA with algorithms gen, init, acquire and recover. Transcript is a special game procedure that records network requests sent by the DKA algorithms. For the meaning of instructions Lose, Reward, and Require see Sect. 2.

The task of the adversary is to distinguish real keys generated by the protocol from random. We remark that this implies other security properties such as privacy of the user's password: if the adversary learns (information about) a user's password it can compute the real key and compare this to the real or random key from the Challenge oracle to gain an advantage. Similarly to PRIV-x, the KIND-x game comes in two flavours: $x = 1$ corresponds to an adversary that may compromise servers but will subsequently follow the protocol honestly, and $x = 2$ which allows arbitrary server behaviour and thus intuitively security in this setting will require verifiable responses from the servers.

Initially, the game assigns passwords to all users in the user identity space $\mathcal{UID}$. An adversary can observe network traffic for executions of the protocol via its oracles Init and Acquire, and it specifies the user identity for these protocol runs. In the KIND-1 game for honest executions of the protocol, this is modelled by providing the adversary a transcript of the network requests to the servers S, handled by the game. For the KIND-2 game, the network requests are sent to the adversary directly, so the game does not need to record the transcript. The adversary may respond in any way it likes, in particular it may respond honestly. To aid the adversary in responding honestly without requiring it to corrupt a server, it can query the BlindEv oracle, which will return the honest response rep. Effectively, in the KIND-2 game the adversary becomes an active man-in-the-middle between the Init and Acquire oracles (representing the user) and the BlindEv oracle (representing the server).

We split the key reconstruction procedure into two processes to model the online communication (Acquire) between the user and the servers, and the key calculation done locally (Recover) by a user based on the servers it chooses to utilize and the public setup values. We allow the adversary to specify these setup values $\vec{SV}$ since the system's security should not rely on them being secret nor authentic. To model online attacks, i.e. login attempts for specific users, the adversary can call Reveal with a purported password and user identity, and if this guess is correct it receives the file encryption key for that user; if incorrect it receives nothing (this mimics the subsequent inability to decrypt files).

Definition 3 (KIND-x **Security**). *The advantage of an adversary* $\mathcal{A}$ *in the* KIND-x *games defined in Fig. 5 for* $x \in \{1, 2\}$ *and distributed key acquisition scheme* DKA *is*

$$\mathbf{Adv}_{\mathsf{DKA}}^{\mathrm{KIND}\text{-}x}(\mathcal{A}) := \left| \Pr\left[\mathsf{G}_{\mathsf{DKA}}^{\mathrm{KIND}\text{-}x^1}(\mathcal{A}) = 1 \right] - \Pr\left[\mathsf{G}_{\mathsf{DKA}}^{\mathrm{KIND}\text{-}x^0}(\mathcal{A}) = 1 \right] \right|.$$

As is natural in the password setting, it is necessary to consider the fact that passwords could be guessable and a successful guess that occurs before any rate-limiting has kicked in will result in an adversary compromising a particular user. The advantage statement needs to take into account the following generic attack, where the queries are all for a single user identity *uid*: the adversary runs Init, then makes q queries to Reveal for randomly chosen passwords in the password space, then queries Challenge. If any of the Reveal queries returned something other than $\perp$, then a user key was set for that user identity, and if this value is equal to the key provided by Challenge then the adversary outputs 0, and if it's different it outputs 1 (if it received $\perp$ for all Reveal queries then it just guesses). As a result, we regard a DKA scheme as being secure if

$$\mathbf{Adv}_{\mathsf{DKA}}^{\mathrm{KIND}\text{-}x}(\mathcal{A}) \leq \mathcal{O}\left(\frac{q}{|\mathcal{D}|} \right) + \delta,$$

where q is the number of queries made by the adversary to the Reveal oracle in the course of the experiment, $|\mathcal{D}|$ is the size of the password dictionary and δ is some negligible function in the security parameter λ.

4   Constructions

In this section we present two schemes, parameterized by an Oblivious PRF F = (F.KG, F.Req, F.BlindEv, F.Finalize, F.Ev), and prove their security in the models from Sect. 3. Our constructions follow a generic blueprint, portrayed in Fig. 6.

4.1   Generic Construction

There are four possibilities for OPRFs: verifiable or non-verifiable, and partially-oblivious or regular. In order to handle both partially-oblivious and regular oblivious PRFs, we desire that each server can derive a per-user key on the fly, see the Cli.SKG and Cli.PKG algorithms in Fig. 6. If the OPRF is partially oblivious then the auxiliary input *uid* creates domain separation in the key used by the OPRF server, and so the per-user key pair is just the single key pair created by F.KG, for all users. To work with verifiable (regular) OPRFs such that the servers are not required to store per-user data, we need the OPRF secret key sk to be a group element with public key g^{sk} for some generator g. Then, the server simply multiplies in the group its own OPRF secret key with a hash of

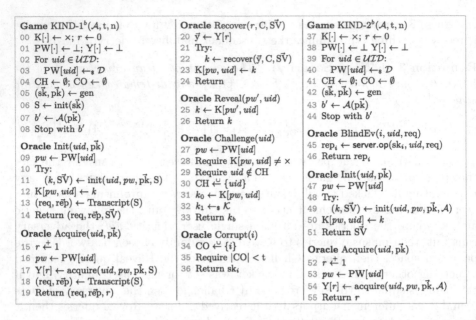

Game KIND-$1^b(\mathcal{A}, t, n)$
00 K$[\cdot] \leftarrow \times$; $r \leftarrow 0$
01 PW$[\cdot] \leftarrow \perp$; Y$[\cdot] \leftarrow \perp$
02 For $uid \in \mathcal{UID}$:
03   PW$[uid] \leftarrow_\$ \mathcal{D}$
04 CH $\leftarrow \emptyset$; CO $\leftarrow \emptyset$
05 $(\vec{sk}, \vec{pk}) \leftarrow$ gen
06 S $\leftarrow$ init$(\vec{sk})$
07 $b' \leftarrow \mathcal{A}(\vec{pk})$
08 Stop with b'

Oracle Init$(uid, \vec{pk})$
09 $pw \leftarrow$ PW$[uid]$
10 Try:
11      $(k, \vec{SV}) \leftarrow$ init$(uid, pw, \vec{pk}, S)$
12 K$[pw, uid] \leftarrow k$
13 $(req, \vec{rep}) \leftarrow$ Transcript(S)
14 Return $(req, \vec{rep}, \vec{SV})$

Oracle Acquire$(uid, \vec{pk})$
15 $r \xleftarrow{+} 1$
16 $pw \leftarrow$ PW$[uid]$
17 Y$[r] \leftarrow$ acquire$(uid, pw, \vec{pk}, S)$
18 $(req, \vec{rep}) \leftarrow$ Transcript(S)
19 Return $(req, \vec{rep}, r)$

Oracle Recover$(r, C, \vec{SV})$
20 $\vec{y} \leftarrow$ Y$[r]$
21 Try:
22      $k \leftarrow$ recover$(\vec{y}, C, \vec{SV})$
23 K$[pw, uid] \leftarrow k$
24 Return

Oracle Reveal(pw', uid)
25 $k \leftarrow$ K$[pw', uid]$
26 Return k

Oracle Challenge(uid)
27 $pw \leftarrow$ PW$[uid]$
28 Require K$[pw, uid] \neq \times$
29 Require $uid \notin$ CH
30 CH $\xleftarrow{\cup} \{uid\}$
31 $k_0 \leftarrow$ K$[pw, uid]$
32 $k_1 \leftarrow_\$ \mathcal{K}$
33 Return k_b

Oracle Corrupt(i)
34 CO $\xleftarrow{\cup} \{i\}$
35 Require $|$CO$| < t$
36 Return sk_i

Game KIND-$2^b(\mathcal{A}, t, n)$
37 K$[\cdot] \leftarrow \times$; $r \leftarrow 0$
38 PW$[\cdot] \leftarrow \perp$ Y$[\cdot] \leftarrow \perp$
39 For $uid \in \mathcal{UID}$:
40   PW$[uid] \leftarrow_\$ \mathcal{D}$
41 CH $\leftarrow \emptyset$; CO $\leftarrow \emptyset$
42 $(\vec{sk}, \vec{pk}) \leftarrow$ gen
43 $b' \leftarrow \mathcal{A}(\vec{pk})$
44 Stop with b'

Oracle BlindEv(i, uid, req)
45 $rep_i \leftarrow$ server.op(sk_i, uid, req)
46 Return rep_i

Oracle Init$(uid, \vec{pk})$
47 $pw \leftarrow$ PW$[uid]$
48 Try:
49      $(k, \vec{SV}) \leftarrow$ init$(uid, pw, \vec{pk}, \mathcal{A})$
50 K$[pw, uid] \leftarrow k$
51 Return $\vec{SV}$

Oracle Acquire$(uid, \vec{pk})$
52 $r \xleftarrow{+} 1$
53 $pw \leftarrow$ PW$[uid]$
54 Y$[r] \leftarrow$ acquire$(uid, pw, \vec{pk}, \mathcal{A})$
55 Return r

Fig. 5. Key indistinguishability games for DKA with algorithms gen, init, acquire, recover and server.op. The oracles in the middle column are equal for both games and hence only displayed once. Transcript is a special game procedure that records network requests sent by the DKA algorithms. Assuming $\times \notin \mathcal{K}$, we encode uninitialized keys with $\times$. For the meaning of instructions Stop with and Require see Sect. 2.

the user's identity to create the secret key component, and raises its own public key to the hash value to get the public key component; this public key component is provided to the user. If a verifiable OPRF is being used and it does not have this method of operation, and this includes all OPRFs built from non-DH assumptions, then another mechanism is required. For non-verifiable (non-DH) OPRFs, the server simply needs some way of generating per-user secret keys using its master secret key and the user's identity, e.g. a key derivation function.

The init algorithm allows the user to compute a random key using its password pw and a set of servers S that can be reconstructed later using pw and (a subset of) S. It creates an OPRF request and awaits the response for each server. We have used the 'Await' keyword in Fig. 6 to indicate this computation is not done locally. Computing the OPRF responses is done by server.op, which is a wrapper of the OPRF's blind evaluation function using the per-user key. The responses are finalized by init to obtain the OPRF output values, which are used by setup to compute the key and potentially some setup values. The setup algorithm is setting specific and will be discussed later.

The reconstruction of the key is similar, but split in two algorithms acquire and recover. This allows the user to choose which subset of servers C to use, after seeing the OPRF outputs (some servers may not respond). Indeed, this modularization allows any choice function from the OPRF output space to the

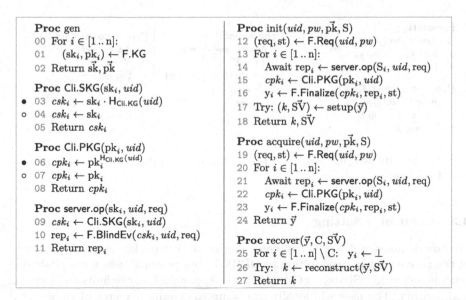

Proc gen
00 For $i \in [1 .. n]$:
01      $(\mathrm{sk}_i, \mathrm{pk}_i) \leftarrow$ F.KG
02 Return $\vec{\mathrm{sk}}, \vec{\mathrm{pk}}$

Proc Cli.SKG(sk_i, uid)
• 03 $csk_i \leftarrow \mathrm{sk}_i \cdot \mathsf{H}_{\mathrm{Cli.KG}}(uid)$
○ 04 $csk_i \leftarrow \mathrm{sk}_i$
05 Return csk_i

Proc Cli.PKG(pk_i, uid)
• 06 $cpk_i \leftarrow \mathrm{pk}_i^{\mathsf{H}_{\mathrm{Cli.KG}}(uid)}$
○ 07 $cpk_i \leftarrow \mathrm{pk}_i$
08 Return cpk_i

Proc server.op$(\mathrm{sk}_i, uid, \mathrm{req})$
09 $csk_i \leftarrow$ Cli.SKG(sk_i, uid)
10 $\mathrm{rep}_i \leftarrow$ F.BlindEv$(csk_i, uid, \mathrm{req})$
11 Return rep_i

Proc init$(uid, pw, \vec{\mathrm{pk}}, \mathrm{S})$
12 $(\mathrm{req}, \mathrm{st}) \leftarrow$ F.Req(uid, pw)
13 For $i \in [1 .. n]$:
14   Await $\mathrm{rep}_i \leftarrow$ server.op$(\mathrm{S}_i, uid, \mathrm{req})$
15      $cpk_i \leftarrow$ Cli.PKG(pk_i, uid)
16      $\mathrm{y}_i \leftarrow$ F.Finalize$(cpk_i, \mathrm{rep}_i, \mathrm{st})$
17 Try: $(k, \vec{\mathrm{SV}}) \leftarrow$ setup$(\vec{\mathrm{y}})$
18 Return $k, \vec{\mathrm{SV}}$

Proc acquire$(uid, pw, \vec{\mathrm{pk}}, \mathrm{S})$
19 $(\mathrm{req}, \mathrm{st}) \leftarrow$ F.Req(uid, pw)
20 For $i \in [1 .. n]$:
21   Await $\mathrm{rep}_i \leftarrow$ server.op$(\mathrm{S}_i, uid, \mathrm{req})$
22      $cpk_i \leftarrow$ Cli.PKG(pk_i, uid)
23      $\mathrm{y}_i \leftarrow$ F.Finalize$(cpk_i, \mathrm{rep}_i, \mathrm{st})$
24 Return $\vec{\mathrm{y}}$

Proc recover$(\vec{\mathrm{y}}, \mathrm{C}, \vec{\mathrm{SV}})$
25 For $i \in [1 .. n] \setminus \mathrm{C}$: $\mathrm{y}_i \leftarrow \perp$
26 Try: $k \leftarrow$ reconstruct$(\vec{\mathrm{y}}, \vec{\mathrm{SV}})$
27 Return k

Fig. 6. PERKS, a generic DKA protocol construction. The lines marked with • are executed iff a standard OPRF is used as building block. The lines marked with ○ are executed iff a POPRF is used as building block. Procedures setup and reconstruct are as in Fig. 7 for the n out of n setting and as in Fig. 8 for the t out of n setting. In a slight abuse of notation, we specify server.op on the user side with a server S_i as input, who will use its secret key sk_i to evaluate the procedure.

power set of S. The OPRF output values are computed by acquire, to be used subsequently by the local reconstruct algorithm inside recover to recompute the key. Similarly to setup, the reconstruct algorithm is setting specific.

We remark that the scheme stops working (in the sense that the user cannot decrypt their files) if one of the servers chosen for recover is not consistent with its responses. If the OPRF is verifiable, then the user can identify which server has replied inconsistently and exclude it from the servers chosen for recover, so it is recommended to use verifiable OPRFs when available. Alternatively, assuming the set of servers is small, the user could proceed by trying different subsets and rerunning recover until successful. In Sect. G we discuss how existing OPRF schemes from the literature can be used in PERKS.

4.2   n Out of n Setting

In Fig. 7 we provide the construction for the setting where all n key servers are required for key (re)production. The setup values $\vec{\mathrm{SV}}$ are effectively ignored in this setting, they are only present in the construction to be syntactically correct. The user derives their key as the XOR of the OPRF output values. The construction allows a user to generate a key even if it cannot produce randomness itself, and as long as at least one of the n servers is not malicious, the key produced will be pseudorandom.

Proc setup($\vec{y}$)
00 Assert size($\vec{y}$) = n
01 $k \leftarrow y_1 \oplus \ldots \oplus y_n$
02 Return $(k, \perp)$

Proc reconstruct($\vec{z}, \vec{SV}$)
03 Assert size($\vec{z}$) = n
04 $k \leftarrow z_1 \oplus \ldots \oplus z_n$
05 Return k

Proc setup($\vec{y}$)
00 Assert size($\vec{y}$) = n
01 $k \leftarrow_s \mathcal{K}$
02 $\vec{\alpha} \leftarrow$ SecShare(k, t, n)
03 $\vec{SV} \leftarrow \vec{\alpha} + \vec{y}$
04 Return $k, \vec{SV}$

Proc reconstruct($\vec{z}, \vec{SV}$)
05 Assert size($\vec{z}$) = t
06 $S = \emptyset$
07 For each $z_i \neq \perp$:
08     $\alpha_i \leftarrow \vec{SV}_i - z_i$
09     $\vec{\alpha}' \xleftarrow{\cup} \{\alpha_i\}$
10 $k \leftarrow$ SecCombine($\vec{\alpha}'$)
11 return k

Fig. 7. Construction for n out of n setting.

Fig. 8. Construction for t out of n setting.

4.3 t Out of n Setting

We now demonstrate how to use secret sharing to derive a key using only a subset of the active servers. In addition to OPRF F, the protocol uses a secret sharing scheme SSS = (SecShare, SecCombine), see Appendix C for definitions of syntax and security. The user will locally run setup to acquire a vector of values, that can be stored alongside its ciphertexts at the storage server, where each entry is an OPRF output summed with a secret sharing of the user's key. This idea was used by Everspaugh et al. [20] in the threshold version of their OPRF system. Later, the user can rederive the file encryption key by interacting with at least t servers. If reconstruction (or file decryption) fails, the user can retry with a different subset of servers. If F is verifiable then the user can identify if a server has not responded correctly, and omit that result from the reconstruct phase.

Conceptually this scheme is quite different to the n out of n scheme in Sect. 4.2. The file encryption key k is generated randomly by the user of the system, rather than as a function of the user password and the OPRF keys of the servers. This does not necessarily imply it has to be sampled on the device though. Indeed, we can bootstrap the procedure by first running an n' out of n' scheme for t ≤ n' ≤ n with an initially trusted subset of the servers to generate the random key k, and for most applications it would be prudent to do so.

4.4 Security Proofs

Theorem 4. Let PERKS be an n-out-of-n DKA scheme built using OPRF F according to Fig. 6 and Fig. 7. For any adversary $\mathcal{A}$ against the KIND-1 security of PERKS, there exist adversaries $\mathcal{B}$ and $\mathcal{C}$ against the PRIV-1 and PRNG security of F respectively, such that

$$\mathbf{Adv}_{\text{PERKS}}^{\text{KIND-1}}(\mathcal{A}, n, n) \leq n \cdot \left(2 \cdot \mathbf{Adv}_{\text{F}}^{\text{PRIV-1}}(\mathcal{B}) + \mathbf{Adv}_{\text{F}}^{\text{PRNG}}(\mathcal{C}, 1) + \frac{q}{|\mathcal{D}|}\right).$$

Proof Intuition. We will show a reduction from the KIND-1 to KIND'-1, where the server that may not be corrupted is fixed at the start of the game. Subsequently we will bound the KIND'-1 advantage using a sequence of game hops, starting with the $b = 0$ side where a real key is returned to the adversary and ending with the $b = 1$ side (random key). To provide a reduction to PRNG security we need to embed the PRNG challenge in one of the servers, which means that we will not be able to answer Corrupt queries for that index. To do this, we pick the server in the KIND'-1 game that may not be corrupted. The reduction from KIND-1 to KIND'-1 invokes a loss of $\frac{1}{n}$. Then, for the majority of this proof we will calculate the advantage of an adversary attempting to distinguish in which game it is playing, to bound the advantage of the KIND'-1 game.

Proof. In game KIND'-1, the environment is identical to KIND-1 except that it picks a random index j out of all n servers at the start of the game and the adversary loses if it calls Corrupt on index j. We simulate KIND-1 by simply forwarding all oracle queries to KIND'-1. Given that the adversary may corrupt up to $(n - 1)$ servers in the course of its execution and the index j in KIND'-1 is picked uniformly at random independently of the adversary, the probability that server j will be corrupted is bounded by $1 - \frac{1}{n}$. Thus, with probability at least $\frac{1}{n}$, game KIND'-1 will not abort and the simulation succeeds, as the games are identical in this case. As a result,

$$\mathbf{Adv}_{\mathsf{PERKS}}^{\mathsf{KIND\text{-}1}}(\mathcal{A}) \leq n \cdot \mathbf{Adv}_{\mathsf{PERKS}}^{\mathsf{KIND'\text{-}1}}(\mathcal{A}).$$

We proceed to bound $\mathbf{Adv}_{\mathsf{PERKS}}^{\mathsf{KIND'\text{-}1}}(\mathcal{A})$ using a sequence of games G_i, and define $\epsilon_i = \Pr\left[\mathsf{G}_{\mathsf{PERKS}}^{G_i}(\mathcal{A}) = 1\right]$. Game G_0 is the $b = 0$ side, i.e. with the key returned in the Challenge query being the key computed in the protocol (if it exists) of the KIND'-1 game, and consequently $\epsilon_0 = \Pr\left[\mathsf{G}_{\mathsf{PERKS}}^{\mathsf{KIND'\text{-}1}^0}(\mathcal{A}) = 1\right]$.

In game G_1, the environment is identical to G_0 except that for every user identity uid, the challenger will create two passwords: one will be used in Init, Acquire and Recover queries, and the other in Challenge and Reveal queries. Note that Reveal returns $\perp$ for any password that is not the selected password.

Intuitively, an adversary that can distinguish these games can infer information about the password or key from the req, rep values it sees from interacting with Init, Acquire and Recover, so it notices when a different password has been used in the Reveal and Challenge queries. From such an adversary we build a reduction with similar advantage against PRIV-1 of the underlying OPRF F.

The reduction $\mathcal{B}$ is detailed in Fig. 11. $\mathcal{B}$ plays the PRIV-1^b game and simulates the KIND'-1^0 game (G_0) or its two-password version (G_1) to $\mathcal{A}$. Let b' be the output bit of $\mathcal{A}$, i.e. its indication of which game $G_{b'}$ that $\mathcal{A}$ believes it is playing. To create the simulation, $\mathcal{B}$ selects pw_0, pw_1 for each uid and generates OPRF key pairs for each of the n key servers. When $\mathcal{A}$ calls Init or Acquire for some uid, the reduction will look up the two passwords pw_0, pw_1 associated with that user identity and call its own Challenge(uid, pw_0, pw_1) oracle and receive $(\mathrm{req}_b, \mathrm{req}_{1-b})$. $\mathcal{B}$ then uses secret keys for each OPRF server to produce rep_i values for req_b. Moreover, $\mathcal{B}$ computes OPRF outputs y_i for pw_0 and the user key k, to be used for Reveal and Challenge queries. Importantly, we already want to remark here that $\mathcal{B}$ will simulate G_0 if it is playing the PRIV-1^0 game (because the req, rep and k are all consistent with pw_0) and $\mathcal{B}$ will simulate G_1 if it is playing the PRIV-1^1 game (because k is derived from pw_0 and req and rep are derived from pw_1).

Acquire queries are handled similarly to Init queries, with the difference being that the OPRF output values y_i are simply stored by $\mathcal{B}$ in array Y indexed by reconstruct counter r, instead of being used to compute the key immediately. For Recover queries, the input given by the adversary is $(r, C, \vec{SV})$, and recall that in the n-out-of-n construction the $\vec{SV}$ are ignored and key reconstruction will fail if the chosen server set C is anything other than the full set of servers, i.e. $C = (S_1, \ldots, S_n)$. This means the only interesting input is r, but the adversary has no control over the (deterministic) operations involved that will reconstruct the user key for password pw_0 for the *uid* corresponding with reconstruct counter r.

For queries to Reveal of the form (pw', uid), the reduction simply returns $K[pw', uid]$. This will either be $\times$ if no value has been set or potentially user key k if $pw' = pw_0$ and $K[pw_0, uid]$ has already been set. For Challenge(uid) queries, $\mathcal{B}$ checks if the *uid* has been queried before, and if not it will return k. To answer a Corrupt query, $\mathcal{B}$ needs to check if the query is allowed and **abort** otherwise, but $\mathcal{A}$ would lose anyway as this would be an illegal oracle query in both games.

As we remarked above, if $\mathcal{B}$ is playing PRIV-1^0, it will provide req, rep and k values to $\mathcal{A}$ that are consistent with each other (and consistent with password pw_0), and thus this is a perfect simulation of G_0. If $\mathcal{B}$ is playing PRIV-1^1, then pw_0 governs Challenge and Reveal queries, while pw_1 governs Init and Reconstruct queries and thus this is a perfect simulation of G_1.

It is left to argue that $\mathcal{A}$'s success in distinguishing these games carries over to an advantage for $\mathcal{B}$. Intuitively, a win for $\mathcal{A}$ implies some way of linking (req, $\vec{rep}$) tuples to the user keys output by the protocol in the G_0 case, or noticing the absence of such a link in the G_1 case (to see this, consider n = 1 and a protocol where $k = pw$ and (req, $\vec{rep}$) information theoretically hide pw and k: an adversary has no way of distinguishing G_0 from G_1). This implies that $\mathcal{A}$ gains some information from its (req, $\vec{rep}$) values: if $b' = 0$ then $\mathcal{A}$ believes that its oracles are all running the same password, and thus (req$_b$, $\vec{rep}$) is linked to k, so $\mathcal{B}$ outputs 0; if $b' = 1$ then $\mathcal{A}$ thinks its oracles have been separated, and $\mathcal{B}$ outputs 1. To conclude, any advantage for $\mathcal{A}$ directly corresponds to the advantage for the reduction $\mathcal{B}$, thus we get: $\epsilon_0 - \epsilon_1 \leq \mathbf{Adv}_F^{PRIV-1}(\mathcal{B})$.

In game G_2, the environment is identical to G_1 except that the Reveal and Challenge oracles return a random element of the key space. For interactions with S_j, the reduction will replace the function $F.Ev(sk_j, \cdot, \cdot)$ by a random function of the same domain and range, where blinded evaluation queries are simulated. Recall S_j is the randomly picked server that the adversary may not corrupt. This invokes a reduction $\mathcal{C}$ to the PRNG security of OPRF F. We show that we can use an adversary $\mathcal{A}$ that distinguishes between G_1 and G_2 to win the PRNG game with the same advantage, i.e.: $\epsilon_1 - \epsilon_2 \leq \mathbf{Adv}_F^{PRNG}(\mathcal{C}, 1)$.

Let $\mathcal{C}$ play the PRNG game and simulate the KIND'-1 game (more specifically, either G_1 or G_2) to $\mathcal{A}$. The reduction is detailed in Fig. 12. Note that the reduction is displayed for the generalized t out of n case. We are in the special case t = n, thus the set of uncorrupted indices J consists of our single uncorrupted server S_j, i.e. $J = \{j\}$.

The reduction C receives a public key for its own $PRNG^b(C, 1)$ game, and then chooses two passwords for each user: pw_0 for Reveal and Challenge queries, and pw_1 for Init and Reconstruct queries. It is with the uncorrupted server S_j's interactions that C will embed its own queries. For any query to Init or Reconstruct, the reduction C needs to call its own Ev oracle with pw_0 to receive the session key share y_j that will be set for future Challenge and Reveal queries, and its own BlindEv oracle with pw_1 to acquire rep_j that the adversary A expects to receive. Note that the user key is only set for pw_0.

To answer a Corrupt query, C needs to check if the query is allowed and **abort** otherwise, but A would lose anyway as this would be an illegal oracle query in both games. For Reveal queries on (pw', uid), the reduction simply returns $K[pw', uid]$. This will either be $\times$ if no value has been set or potentially k if $pw' = pw_0$ and $K[pw_0, uid]$ has already been set. For Challenge(uid) queries, C first checks if the uid has been queried before, and if not it will return k. Eventually, C outputs to its own challenger whatever A outputs.

In the event that C is playing $PRNG^0$, the responses to its own queries will be the real F, and thus this perfectly simulates game G_1 for A. If C is playing $PRNG^1$ then req and the rep values lie in the correct space but for some other randomly chosen function, and the key share for server S_j is an output of this random function, so the user key returned in Challenge is an output of a random function XORed with 'genuine' key shares, which is equivalent to choosing a random element of the key space. Thus this is a perfect simulation of G_2 for A.

In game G_2 the Reveal and Challenge queries return a random element of the key space. Thus in G_3 we make a change to the Reveal oracle to use the key derived from pw_0 again. In all games up until this point the Reveal and Challenge oracles have been consistent with each other, but in G_3 they are not. Note that the adversary can only notice a difference between G_2 and G_3 if it queries Reveal on pw_0, as Reveal returns $\perp$ for all other passwords and the other oracles are identical. We remark that in both games Init and Reconstruct use pw_1 and Challenge simply samples a random key from the key space, so no information about pw_0 can be leaked from the oracle queries. Hence, the best any adversary can do is query the Reveal oracle for a randomly guessed password. As a result, we obtain $\epsilon_2 - \epsilon_3 \leq \frac{q}{|\mathcal{D}|}$.

In game G_4 we re-merge queries such that for a given user identity uid, queries to Init, Reconstruct and Reveal are all associated with a single password. In a very similar manner to the hop between G_0 and G_1, this invokes a PRIV-1 term. The reduction itself is almost identical to reduction B in Fig. 11, except that line 40 is replaced by selection of a random key from the key space. As a result, $\epsilon_3 - \epsilon_4 \leq \mathbf{Adv}_F^{\text{PRIV-1}}(B)$. Game G_4 is the $b = 1$ side, i.e. with the key returned in the Challenge query being a randomly chosen key, of the KIND'-1 game. Consequently $\epsilon_4 = \Pr\left[G_{\text{PERKS}}^{\text{KIND'-1}^1}(A)\right]$.

Collecting the terms results in the claimed bound.

Theorem 5. *Let* PERKS *be an* t-*out-of-*n DKA *scheme built using* OPRF F *according to Fig. 6 and Fig. 8 for* t *such that* $1 \leq t \leq n$. *For any adversary* $\mathcal{A}$ *against the* KIND-1 *security of* PERKS, *there exist adversaries* $\mathcal{B}$ *and* $\mathcal{C}$ *against the* PRIV-1 *and* PRNG *security of* F *respectively, such that*

$$\mathbf{Adv}_{\mathsf{PERKS}}^{\mathsf{KIND\text{-}1}}(\mathcal{A}, t, n) \leq \binom{n}{t-1} \cdot \left(2 \cdot \mathbf{Adv}_{\mathsf{F}}^{\mathsf{PRIV\text{-}1}}(\mathcal{B}) + \mathbf{Adv}_{\mathsf{F}}^{\mathsf{PRNG}}(\mathcal{C}, n - t + 1) + \frac{q}{|\mathcal{D}|} \right).$$

Proof Sketch. We remark Theorem 4 is the special case $t = n$ of this theorem and the game hops are very similar to that proof. For brevity we only provide the modifications to the proof here rather than duplicating the proof in its entirety. We also believe that only highlighting the steps where the proof needs to be generalized increases clarity.

For the first step, the success probability of the simulation now depends on t, as the reduction needs to select $n - t + 1$ uncorrupted servers. This success probability is lower bounded by $1/\binom{n}{t-1}$.

The reduction $\mathcal{B}$ in Fig. 11 from the indistinguishability between G_0 and G_1 to the PRIV-1 game is the same as in Theorem 4 with the trivial modification that it uses the t out of n setup and reconstruct procedures from Fig. 8 instead of the procedures from Fig. 7. We apply the same modification to the reduction $\mathcal{C}$ in Fig. 12 from the indistinguishability between G_1 and G_2 to the PRNG game.

We need to argue replacing XOR in the setup and reconstruct procedures with a key sharing scheme also simulates G_2, i.e. the selected key is a random element from the key space. It is clear the adversary can have at most $(t-1)$ 'genuine' key shares because $(n - t + 1)$ servers return a random element. By the security of the secret sharing scheme, with $(t-1)$ key shares, any $k \in \mathcal{K}$ can still be reconstructed. Thus, if key share $s_t \in \mathcal{K}$ is a random element of the key space, then so is the reconstructed key. It is clear this holds as s_t is the XOR of $\vec{SV}_t$ and y_t, where y_t is a random element of $\mathcal{K}$.

There is no modification to the hop from G_2 to G_3. The final hop from G_3 to G_4 is again the same as in Theorem 4 with the trivial modification that it uses the t out of n setup and reconstruct procedures from Fig. 8. Collecting the terms yields the claimed result.

We provide the theorems and proofs for KIND-2 security in Appendix E as the modifications are trivial. The theorems bound the advantage by $\mathbf{Adv}_{\mathsf{F}}^{\mathsf{PRIV\text{-}2}}(\mathcal{B})$ (instead of PRIV-1) and in the proof we only need to adapt the reductions to use the F.finalize procedure and the Finalize oracle in the PRIV-2 game to compute the OPRF output value (instead of using the F.ev procedure and the Ev oracle), since the response may now be maliciously formed.

5   Key Rotation in PERKS

Instant messaging apps are generally free to download and use, and users are often unwilling to pay for additional features. Thus, a service such as the one we propose needs to be extremely efficient in terms of bandwidth and storage to possibly be offered as a free service: this is why we aim to only use the most efficient OPRFs, and enforce minimal user and server storage. In particular, we envision OPRF services with multiple other roles in addition to PERKS, hence our system does not require the OPRF servers to be given a particular (share of a) key, as is done in many prior works [5,25,27].

Note that in the case of long-term encrypted backup, if a user's device is compromised and they wish to change their encryption key, they may still wish to recover messages stored under the old key (i.e. even if they believe that an adversary is already in possession of those messages). If the user wishes to rotate their file encryption key in PERKS then there are three possibilities:

1. Use an OPRF service that has automated key rotation, e.g. by using the Pythia OPRF [20]. Note that for the n out of n construction, just one OPRF server updating its sk_i value results in a change in file encryption key. If this is used, then the server will provide 'tokens' that work similarly to updatable encryption (UE) update tokens [33]: unblinded values provided under the old key can be efficiently modified to unblinded values under the new key, without the need to call the OPRF service under all the old inputs.
2. Use a different password or a different *uid* value (for the same user). This will result in new OPRF output values for all OPRF servers.
3. (t out of n construction only) Choose a new key k, essentially running setup again. This results in a new key share vector $\vec{\alpha}$ but the y_i values are unchanged so the user needs to publish a new public vector $\vec{SV}$.

A   WhatsApp Encrypted Backup Rollout

In September 2021, WhatsApp announced [41] that they would soon begin beta testing of an encrypted chat and media backup service that uses HSMs and the envelope part of the OPAQUE protocol [28] in a manner that is conceptually similar to a $(1,1)$-PPSS. In this subsection we discuss their system based on the details in the WhatsApp whitepaper and NCC Group's technical report [35] and explain the differences with our work.

OPAQUE is an asymmetric password-authenticated key exchange protocol that is a compiler of three components: an oblivious PRF to turn the user's password x into a strong secret value y, an 'envelope' mechanism whereby the user encrypts their AKE key material under y using symmetric encryption, and an AKE protocol. WhatsApp's approach uses the OPRF and a modified version of the envelope mechanism, but since no key exchange needs to occur the AKE component is dropped completely. In the WhatsApp system, at the point of registration (first ever backup), a client device generates a random 256-bit key k and then stores this as an encrypted record (envelope) in a 'HSM-based Backup Key Vault' so that it can later retrieve this key using only their password (PIN or passphrase): the HSM acts as the OPRF server and derives a per-user secret key sk_{uid} from a single master secret and *uid* when called. The envelope in the WhatsApp system is $PK.Enc_{pk.HSM}(SK.Enc_y(k))$, a public-key encryption of an encryption of k under the OPRF output value y. Later on when a user comes online to retrieve the contents of their envelope it is not apparent if this is sent encrypted under some user public key, and it would appear that this PKE scheme is not for protecting the channel, but rather so that the envelopes can be stored outside of the HSM. These envelopes are stored in an integrity-protected manner using a Merkle tree. No security analysis of the system has been provided for the WhatsApp approach, and the only analysis available is the report by NCC Group [35] that does not discuss any formal security requirements for the system.

Intuitively, the WhatsApp approach relies on the tamper-resistant properties of the HSM to make sure that the OPRF key sk (that is used to derive sk_{uid}) is not leaked to any party. If this key is leaked, then an offline adversary can attempt to recover the file encryption key that is contained within the registration envelope. Our approach avoids assuming a HSM on the server side, and instead distributes the trust among a number of servers. An adversary in possession of a stolen client device needs to guess the correct password while avoiding WhatsApp's rate-limiting mechanisms, and thus performing this type of online attack is similar in our system.

Further, the WhatsApp system requires that the client device generates the user file encryption key k using 'a built-in cryptographically secure pseudorandom number generator', however as already stated, this is of no use if the device's randomness generation is already compromised during registration.

B   Using **PERKS** as a Storage System

We now explain why our approach is well-suited to derivation of a backup key for outsourced storage systems, and particularly for instant messaging. Then, we describe how our construction can be used to build a feature rich file system for cloud storage, incorporating recent work analysing security of symmetric encryption schemes where a user encrypts 'to themself', deduplication, and efficient key rotation.

Instant messaging apps are generally free to download and use, and users are often unwilling to pay for additional features. This leaves very little room for manoeuvre when designing a secure backup service: users must use an internal solution like WhatsApp's (see Appendix A), where the protocol is potentially strong but not open source. A service such as the one we propose needs to be extremely efficient in terms of bandwidth and storage to possibly be offered as a free service: this is why we aim to only use the most efficient OPRFs, and enforce minimal user and server storage. In particular, we envision OPRF services with multiple other roles in addition to PERKS, hence our system does not require the OPRF servers to be given a particular (share of a) key, as is done in many prior works [5,25,27].

The constructions defined in Sect. 4 allow a user to derive a single symmetric key from a password. It remains to select a symmetric encryption primitive for encryption, a decision that is informed by the desired functionality and security properties.

Note that in the case of long-term encrypted backup, if a user's device is compromised and they wish to change their encryption key, they may still wish to recover messages stored under the old key (i.e. even if they believe that an adversary is already in possession of those messages). From this perspective, the user may wish to recover their messages after they have already chosen a new password for use with new messages, creating an overlap in the epochs of the system: this is a departure from the regular theoretical approach to key rotation via updatable encryption and we discuss this further below.

Encrypt-to-Self. Pijnenburg and Poettering [36] recently demonstrated that integrity protection can still be obtained in the event of user key corruption: if the user stores short file (ciphertext) hashes then even if the user knows that their key is corrupted they can check ciphertext integrity when downloading files and discard any where the hash does not match a local entry. In the same paper, the authors demonstrated a method to compute these hashes during encryption, to avoid making two passes over plaintext data.

Deduplication. If the user expects to upload some files many times, for example by backing up an entire disk periodically, and wants to avoid storing multiple copies of files then they can employ deduplication techniques such as convergent encryption [38]. File key derivation for a file F could be for example $k_F \leftarrow H(k||F)$ for some cryptographic hash function H.

Key Rotation. If the user wishes to rotate their file encryption key in PERKS then there are three possibilities:

1. Use an OPRF service that has automated key rotation, e.g. by using the Pythia OPRF [20]. Note that for the n out of n construction, just one OPRF server updating its sk_i value results in a change in file encryption key. If this is used, then the server will provide 'tokens' that work similarly to updatable encryption (UE) update tokens: unblinded values provided under the old key can be efficiently modified to unblinded values under the new key, without the need to call the OPRF service under all the old inputs.
2. Use a different password. This will result in new OPRF output values for all OPRF servers. (Note that another credential modification technique is possible via an OPRF service that supports tweaks, i.e. different *uid* input values for the same user: this will result in different OPRF output values for the OPRF servers offering this.)
3. (t out of n construction only) Choose a new key k, essentially running setup again. This results in a new key share vector $\vec{\alpha}$ but the y_i values are unchanged so the user needs to publish a new public vector $\vec{SV}$.

In all of these cases, the user can avoid downloading, decrypting, reencrypting and reuploading all of their files every time they update their file encryption key by utilizing updatable encryption [8,11,33], where the user can send a short update token to the ciphertext storage server (CSP) with which the underlying key for the ciphertexts can be rotated efficiently, without leaking information to the CSP. However the challenge is providing availability of key material in consecutive epochs. In the efficient (ciphertext-independent) UE schemes just mentioned, the update token calculation requires knowledge of an old key and a new key at the beginning of the new epoch. For user-initiated actions (items 2 and 3) this is trivial: the user runs the protocol to get their old key, then runs the protocol again using their new inputs, calculates the token, sends that to the file storage server and then deletes both keys locally. In the OPRF server key rotation setting (item 1) care is required: if a new epoch begins while the user does not have a local copy of the file encryption key available then the user would be locked out of access to their ciphertexts. To solve this issue the OPRF services could make a transition period available to users, where access is given to the OPRF functionality for the old and the new OPRF keys.

C   Secret Sharing Schemes

We define a secret sharing scheme SSS, that allows an entity to share some secret value k among n parties, such that any t of the shares enable reconstruction of k, while any set of t − 1 shares reveals nothing about k. The exposition here is adapted from Boneh and Shoup [9].

A secret sharing scheme SSS = (SecShare, SecCombine) over a finite set S_1 consists of two algorithms. Sharing algorithm SecShare(k, t, n) is probabilistic, taking as input $k \in S_1$ for $0 \le t \le n$ and returning shares $\vec{\alpha} = \{\alpha_1, \dots, \alpha_n\} \in S_2^n$. Reconstruction algorithm SecCombine($\vec{\alpha}'$) is deterministic, taking as input $\vec{\alpha}' = \{\alpha_1', \dots, \alpha_t'\} \in S_2^t$ and returning the reconstructed secret k.

Correctness asks that for every secret $k \in S_1$, every set of n shares $\vec{\alpha}$ output by SecShare(k, t, n), and every subset $\{\alpha_1', \dots, \alpha_t'\} = \vec{\alpha}' \subseteq \vec{\alpha}$ of size t, then SecCombine($\vec{\alpha}'$) = k.

Definition 6 (SSS   Security). *A   secret   sharing   scheme   (SecShare, SecCombine) over S_1 is secure if for every $k, k' \in S_1$, and every subset $\vec{\alpha}' \in S_2^{t-1}$, the distribution SecShare(k, t, n)[$\vec{\alpha}'$] is identical to the distribution SecShare(k', t, n)[$\vec{\alpha}'$].*

The most well known secret sharing scheme is due to Shamir [37] using polynomial interpolation and is suitable for our purposes. The scheme is fully specified elsewhere [9,37] and we refer to these sources for details. For the purposes of this paper, it is sufficient to know that Shamir's scheme is over $S_1 = \mathbb{F}_q$ with prime power $q > n$, where shares are elements of $S_2 = \mathbb{F}_q^2$. We choose S_1 such that it matches our key space $\mathcal{K}$, for example $S_1 = \mathbb{F}_{2^{256}}$ if we have a 256-bit key space.

D   OPRF Definition Relations

We now show the equivalence of our multi-server PRIV-x games and the single-server POPRIV-x games introduced by Tyagi et al. [40]. As stated earlier, our PRIV-2 game is identical to the POPRIV-2 game of Tyagi et al., and so we focus on showing PRIV-1 ⇔ POPRIV-1.

Theorem 7. *Let* F *be an oblivious pseudorandom function. For any adversary* $\mathcal{A}$ *against the* PRIV-1 *security of* F*, there exists an adversary* $\mathcal{B}$ *against the* POPRIV-1 *security of* F*, such that*

$$\mathbf{Adv}_F^{\mathrm{PRIV\text{-}1}}(\mathcal{A}) \leq \mathbf{Adv}_F^{\mathrm{POPRIV\text{-}1}}(\mathcal{B}).$$

Proof. The direct reduction is detailed in Fig. 9. $\mathcal{B}$ runs $\mathcal{A}$, and needs to respond to $\mathcal{A}$'s calls to Challenge. Note that $\mathcal{A}$'s calls to Challenge give (uid, x_0, x_1) as input, and $\mathcal{A}$ expects $(\mathrm{req}_b, \mathrm{req}_{1-b})$ in response, when it is playing PRIV-1^b. $\mathcal{B}$'s own oracle TRANS$_\mathcal{B}$ provides a more detailed response, and so $\mathcal{B}$ simply takes the $\mathrm{req}_b, \mathrm{req}_{1-b}$ that it receives and forwards this to $\mathcal{A}$.

Let b be the challenge bit in the experiment that $\mathcal{B}$ is playing, and let b' be the bit that is output by $\mathcal{A}$. $\mathcal{B}$ receives $(\mathrm{req}_b, \mathrm{rep}_b, y_0, \mathrm{req}_{1-b}, \mathrm{rep}_{1-b}, y_1)$ from its own call to TRANS$_\mathcal{B}$, and thus providing $(\mathrm{req}_b, \mathrm{req}_{1-b})$ to $\mathcal{A}$ simulates $\mathcal{A}$'s expected environment.

$\mathcal{B}$ perfectly simulates PRIV-1^b for $\mathcal{A}$, since the secret key vector is correctly distributed and the responses that $\mathcal{A}$ receives to its oracles calls are exactly as it would expect. The advantage of $\mathcal{A}$ directly corresponds to the advantage of $\mathcal{B}$. This concludes the proof.

Reduction $\mathcal{B}$ **playing** POPRIV-1^b	**Oracle** Challenge$_\mathcal{A}(uid, x_0, x_1)$
00 **receive** pk, sk	03 **call** TRANS$_\mathcal{B}(uid, x_0, x_1)$
01 $b' \leftarrow \mathcal{A}()$	04 **receive** $(\mathrm{req}_b, \mathrm{rep}_b, y_0, \mathrm{req}_{1-b}, \mathrm{rep}_{1-b}, y_1)$
02 **Return** b'	05 **Return** $(\mathrm{req}_b, \mathrm{req}_{1-b})$

Fig. 9. Reduction $\mathcal{B}$ for the proof of Theorem 7.

Theorem 8. *Let* F *be an oblivious pseudorandom function. For any adversary* $\mathcal{A}$ *against the* POPRIV-1 *security of* F*, there exists an adversary* $\mathcal{B}$ *against the* PRIV-1 *security of* F*, such that*

$$\mathbf{Adv}_F^{\mathrm{POPRIV\text{-}1}}(\mathcal{A}) \leq \mathbf{Adv}_F^{\mathrm{PRIV\text{-}1}}(\mathcal{B}).$$

Proof. The reduction is detailed in Fig. 10. In order to provide a sufficient response to $\mathcal{A}$, the reduction $\mathcal{B}$ must use the values $(\mathrm{req}_b, \mathrm{req}_{1-b})$ that it receives from TRANS$_\mathcal{A}$ and perform F.BlindEv on them to acquire $(\mathrm{rep}_b, \mathrm{rep}_{1-b})$. Producing y_0 and y_1 is straightforward, since $\mathcal{B}$ can simply compute the OPRF evaluation with sk$_j$ and the input values x_0 and x_1. $\mathcal{B}$ combines the values into output $(\mathrm{req}_b, \mathrm{rep}_b, y_0, \mathrm{req}_{1-b}, \mathrm{rep}_{1-b}, y_1)$ and returns it to $\mathcal{A}$. The reduction perfectly simulates the POPRIV-1^b environment for $\mathcal{A}$. This concludes the proof.

Reduction $\mathcal{B}$ playing PRIV-1^b	Oracle TRANS$_{\mathcal{A}}(uid, x_0, x_1)$
00 $(\text{pk}, \text{sk}) \leftarrow \text{F.KG}$	03 **call** Challenge$_{\mathcal{B}}(uid, x_0, x_1)$
01 $b' \leftarrow \mathcal{A}(\text{sk})$	04 **receive** $(\text{req}_b, \text{req}_{1-b})$
02 Return b'	05 $\text{rep}_b \leftarrow \text{F.BlindEv}(\text{sk}, uid, \text{req}_b)$
	06 $\text{rep}_{1-b} \leftarrow \text{F.BlindEv}(\text{sk}, uid, \text{req}_{1-b})$
	07 $y_0 \leftarrow \text{F.Ev}(\text{sk}, uid, x_0)$
	08 $y_1 \leftarrow \text{F.Ev}(\text{sk}, uid, x_1)$
	09 Return $(\text{req}_b, \text{rep}_b, y_0, \text{req}_{1-b}, \text{rep}_{1-b}, y_1)$

Fig. 10. Reduction $\mathcal{B}$ for the proof of Theorem 8.

E   Security Proofs

Theorem 9. *Let* PERKS *be an* n-*out-of-*n *DKA scheme built using OPRF* F *according to Fig. 6 and Fig. 7. For any adversary* $\mathcal{A}$ *against the* KIND-2 *security of* PERKS*, there exist adversaries* $\mathcal{B}$ *and* $\mathcal{C}$ *against the* PRIV-2 *and* PRNG *security of* F *respectively, such that*

$$\mathbf{Adv}_{\text{PERKS}}^{\text{KIND-2}}(\mathcal{A}, n, n) \leq n \cdot \left(2 \cdot \mathbf{Adv}_{\text{F}}^{\text{PRIV-2}}(\mathcal{B}) + \mathbf{Adv}_{\text{F}}^{\text{PRNG}}(\mathcal{C}) + \frac{q}{|\mathcal{D}|} \right).$$

Proof Sketch. The proof goes analogously to the proof of Theorem 4. We need to adapt the reductions as they cannot assume correctness and simply call the F.ev procedure or the Ev oracle, since the rep values may now be maliciously formed. Therefore, the reductions now use the F.finalize procedure and the Finalize oracle in the PRIV-2 game to compute the OPRF output value y (or receive ⊥). The modifications are trivial so we do not reproduce the reductions in full.

Theorem 10. *Let* PERKS *be an* t-*out-of-*n *DKA scheme built using OPRF* F *according to Fig. 6 and Fig. 8 for* t *such that* $1 \leq t \leq n$. *For any adversary* $\mathcal{A}$ *against the* KIND-2 *security of* PERKS*, there exist adversaries* $\mathcal{B}$ *and* $\mathcal{C}$ *against the* PRIV-2 *and* PRNG *security of* F *respectively, such that*

$$\mathbf{Adv}_{\text{PERKS}}^{\text{KIND-2}}(\mathcal{A}, t, n) \leq \binom{n}{t-1} \cdot \left(2 \cdot \mathbf{Adv}_{\text{F}}^{\text{PRIV-2}}(\mathcal{B}) + \mathbf{Adv}_{\text{F}}^{\text{PRNG}}(\mathcal{C}, n-t+1) + \frac{q}{|\mathcal{D}|} \right).$$

Proof Sketch. This proof effectively applies both the adaptations made in Theorem 5 and Theorem 9.

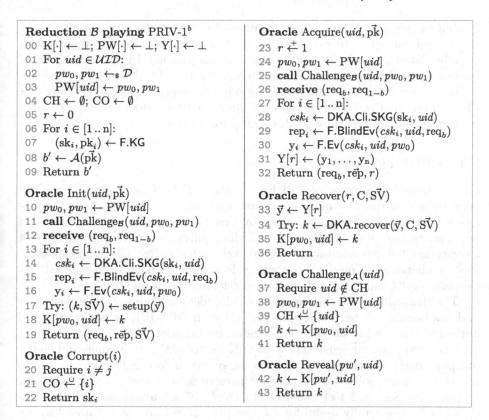

Reduction $\mathcal{B}$ playing PRIV-1^b
00 $K[\cdot] \leftarrow \perp; PW[\cdot] \leftarrow \perp; Y[\cdot] \leftarrow \perp$
01 For $uid \in \mathcal{UID}$:
02      $pw_0, pw_1 \leftarrow_s \mathcal{D}$
03      $PW[uid] \leftarrow pw_0, pw_1$
04 $CH \leftarrow \emptyset; CO \leftarrow \emptyset$
05 $r \leftarrow 0$
06 For $i \in [1..n]$:
07      $(sk_i, pk_i) \leftarrow F.KG$
08 $b' \leftarrow \mathcal{A}(\vec{pk})$
09 Return b'

Oracle Init$(uid, \vec{pk})$
10 $pw_0, pw_1 \leftarrow PW[uid]$
11 **call** Challenge$_\mathcal{B}(uid, pw_0, pw_1)$
12 **receive** (req_b, req_{1-b})
13 For $i \in [1..n]$:
14      $csk_i \leftarrow DKA.Cli.SKG(sk_i, uid)$
15      $rep_i \leftarrow F.BlindEv(csk_i, uid, req_b)$
16      $y_i \leftarrow F.Ev(csk_i, uid, pw_0)$
17 Try: $(k, \vec{SV}) \leftarrow setup(\vec{y})$
18 $K[pw_0, uid] \leftarrow k$
19 Return $(req_b, \vec{rep}, \vec{SV})$

Oracle Corrupt(i)
20 Require $i \neq j$
21 $CO \xleftarrow{\cup} \{i\}$
22 Return sk_i

Oracle Acquire$(uid, \vec{pk})$
23 $r \xleftarrow{\pm} 1$
24 $pw_0, pw_1 \leftarrow PW[uid]$
25 **call** Challenge$_\mathcal{B}(uid, pw_0, pw_1)$
26 **receive** (req_b, req_{1-b})
27 For $i \in [1..n]$:
28      $csk_i \leftarrow DKA.Cli.SKG(sk_i, uid)$
29      $rep_i \leftarrow F.BlindEv(csk_i, uid, req_b)$
30      $y_i \leftarrow F.Ev(csk_i, uid, pw_0)$
31 $Y[r] \leftarrow (y_1, \ldots, y_n)$
32 Return $(req_b, \vec{rep}, r)$

Oracle Recover$(r, C, \vec{SV})$
33 $\vec{y} \leftarrow Y[r]$
34 Try: $k \leftarrow DKA.recover(\vec{y}, C, \vec{SV})$
35 $K[pw_0, uid] \leftarrow k$
36 Return

Oracle Challenge$_\mathcal{A}(uid)$
37 Require $uid \notin CH$
38 $pw_0, pw_1 \leftarrow PW[uid]$
39 $CH \xleftarrow{\cup} \{uid\}$
40 $k \leftarrow K[pw_0, uid]$
41 Return k

Oracle Reveal(pw', uid)
42 $k \leftarrow K[pw', uid]$
43 Return k

Fig. 11. Reduction $\mathcal{B}$ for the proof of Theorem 4 and Theorem 5. Procedures setup and reconstruct as in Fig. 7 for Theorem 4 and as in Fig. 8 for Theorem 5.

F OPRFs and Their Variants

In the remaining sections we describe some of the properties of oblivious PRFs in the literature and explain how they can be used in our protocols. OPRFs can be *verifiable* or not, and independently, *partially oblivious* or not, meaning there are four categories of OPRF that we consider.

Verifiability. Verifiable OPRFs (VOPRFs) require the server to commit to the secret key that it uses, and allow the user to verify that the correct operation was performed by the server with this committed key (in a way that does not reveal the key to the user). Syntactically, the server includes a proof in rep that the user can verify using a server public key pk.

Note that verifiability does not guarantee that a server uses the same key over multiple protocol runs. In order to check *key consistency*, the user is forced to store pk, and this value must be deterministically generated (this is the case for DH-based OPRFs where $pk = g^{sk}$). However, this storage need not be local: all users use the same pk so it is sufficient for this value to be published somewhere.

Partial Obliviousness. In many applications for OPRFs the server needs to partition the input space to reduce the impact of active attacks, and this is often done by choosing a different key for each user identity *uid*. In practice this could be done by applying some key derivation function to *uid* and sk before the protocol is run (see below for a short discussion of this approach). Partially-oblivious PRFs (POPRFs) contain a (plaintext) input t that provides automated partitioning, thus the server only needs one key for all users.

F.1   OPRF Literature

For a thorough treatment of OPRFs, see the SoK by Casacuberta *et al.* [16]; here we summarize the most important literature for our approach. Oblivious PRFs were first formally defined by Freedman *et al.* [21]. A vast array of applications has arisen for OPRFs, including oblivious transfer and private set intersection [29], password-authenticated key exchange [28], Cloudflare's anonymous authentication mechanism Privacy Pass [18], checking compromised credentials [34,39] and Meta's 'de-identified telemetry' scheme [22].

The 2HashDH scheme by Jarecki *et al.* [23] (detailed in Fig. 2) is very efficient and has been suggested for use in TLS 1.3 with OPAQUE as password-based authentication, and is subject to a standardization effort [10].

There exist generic constructions of OPRFs from MPC techniques and homomorphic encryption that do not fit into the syntax in Sect. 2.2 since the communication does not follow a two-message pattern with the user sending the first message, see Section 2.4 of Casacuberta *et al.* [16] for a summary. These constructions are generally useful for gaining properties that are not useful in our setting such as input batching [30] for amortized efficiency gains.

POPRFs. To our knowledge, the only two (explicit) POPRFs are those by Everspaugh *et al.* [20] and Tyagi *et al.* [40], both of which are detailed in Fig. 2. The former requires a pairing which could be a hurdle in some practical applications, and the latter cannot support key rotation in a straightforward way.

Three works [17,26,32] obtain partial-obliviousness for 2HashDH in a generic way by applying a PRF to the server key and public input and using that value as the per-user key. In our generic construction in Fig. 6 we use a similar idea to turn any of the two non-PO, DH-based schemes in Fig. 2 into partially-oblivious variants, with the additional benefit of efficient computation of per-user public keys in the verifiable setting.

The approach in the (unpublished) work of JKR18 [26] actually works for any OPRF, and they present a non-updatable construction using 2HashDH and an updatable construction that uses HashDH, which is $H_2(H_1(x)^{sk})$: this is not an OPRF since a user can use one interaction to obtain multiple evaluations.

Post-quantum OPRFs. Boneh *et al.* [7] gave two constructions of OPRFs from isogenies: a VOPRF from SIDH with a 'one-more' assumption and an OPRF from CSIDH. A year later, Basso *et al.* [4] showed that the first construction's assumption does not hold and gave attacks on that OPRF; the second CSIDH-based scheme is unaffected by this work.

From lattices, Albrecht *et al.* [2] demonstrated that it is possible to build round-optimal (two messages in the online phase) VOPRFs from the Banerjee and Peikert PRF, but their protocols require large parameters and computation-heavy ZK proofs.

Kolesnikov *et al.* [30] sought to build multiple concurrent OPRF operations in a generic way from oblivious transfer (OT). OT can be built from post-quantum assumptions, however the PRF functionality requires 5 communication rounds and is only 'relaxed' (as defined by Freedman *et al.* [21]). Note that these special purpose OPRFs, where more than two rounds are required, do not fit the syntax in Sect. 2.2.

G   Use of Existing OPRFs in PERKS

As we have mentioned in Sect. 4, the DH-based VOPRFs in Fig. 2 allow the server to store one master key and compute private and public keys for users on the fly using *uid*: this operation is specified in Fig. 6. Remember that for non-verifiable OPRFs there is no public key and thus on-the-fly computation of per-user key material just needs to run a key derivation function from the server's (single) master key sk and *uid* to the same space as sk.

For non-DH VOPRFs, the DH group trick is not directly applicable, so either a similar trick using the structure of the public and secret keys needs to be found, or the server needs to store per-user key material. We regard finding such tricks in post-quantum VOPRFs as future work. The CSIDH-based scheme of Boneh *et al.* [7] is not defined as a VOPRF, however this would appear to be a good candidate for a VOPRF that could fit with our DH trick.

For key rotation, the Pythia OPRF has no 'outer hash' (that destroys algebraic structure) and so is eligible for simple key rotation. Note that the afore-mentioned HashDH scheme can provide key rotation but only if the user stores inner hash values, but this is undesirable in our setting and modelling security for this case is not trivial.

This invokes a tradeoff: the Pythia OPRF provides key rotation at a computational cost (due to the pairing operation), while 2HashDH and 3HashSDHI are fast but without key rotation. As a result, the system designer needs to judge if the 'user initiated' key rotation methods in Sect. 5 are viable for the system's users, and if so 2HashDH or 3HashSDHI can be used.

Note that each of the three OPRFs in Fig. 2 are proven secure in different models, and our theorems relate to the security games of the 3HashSDHI scheme. Thus it remains to formally prove that the other two schemes do in fact meet POPRIV-x and PRNG security, or by showing that the proven security properties of the other schemes—VOPRF UC functionality for 2HashDH, and one-more unpredictability and one-more PRF for Pythia—are at least as strong as POPRIV-x and PRNG.

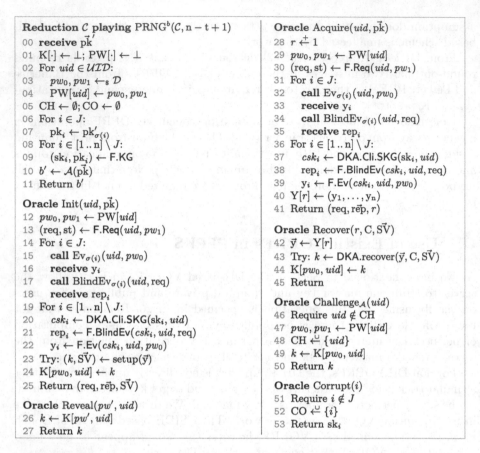

Reduction $\mathcal{C}$ playing $\mathrm{PRNG}^b(\mathcal{C}, \mathrm{n} - \mathrm{t} + 1)$

00 **receive** $\vec{\mathrm{pk}}'$
01 $\mathrm{K}[\cdot] \leftarrow \bot; \mathrm{PW}[\cdot] \leftarrow \bot$
02 For $uid \in \mathcal{UID}$:
03    $pw_0, pw_1 \leftarrow_\$ \mathcal{D}$
04    $\mathrm{PW}[uid] \leftarrow pw_0, pw_1$
05 $\mathrm{CH} \leftarrow \emptyset; \mathrm{CO} \leftarrow \emptyset$
06 For $i \in J$:
07    $\mathrm{pk}_i \leftarrow \mathrm{pk}'_{\sigma(i)}$
08 For $i \in [1 .. n] \setminus J$:
09    $(\mathrm{sk}_i, \mathrm{pk}_i) \leftarrow \mathrm{F.KG}$
10 $b' \leftarrow \mathcal{A}(\vec{\mathrm{pk}})$
11 Return b'

Oracle $\mathrm{Init}(uid, \vec{\mathrm{pk}})$
12 $pw_0, pw_1 \leftarrow \mathrm{PW}[uid]$
13 $(\mathrm{req}, \mathrm{st}) \leftarrow \mathrm{F.Req}(uid, pw_1)$
14 For $i \in J$:
15   **call** $\mathrm{Ev}_{\sigma(i)}(uid, pw_0)$
16   **receive** y_i
17   **call** $\mathrm{BlindEv}_{\sigma(i)}(uid, \mathrm{req})$
18   **receive** rep_i
19 For $i \in [1 .. n] \setminus J$:
20    $csk_i \leftarrow \mathrm{DKA.Cli.SKG}(\mathrm{sk}_i, uid)$
21    $\mathrm{rep}_i \leftarrow \mathrm{F.BlindEv}(csk_i, uid, \mathrm{req})$
22    $y_i \leftarrow \mathrm{F.Ev}(csk_i, uid, pw_0)$
23 Try: $(k, \vec{\mathrm{SV}}) \leftarrow \mathrm{setup}(\vec{y})$
24 $\mathrm{K}[pw_0, uid] \leftarrow k$
25 Return $(\mathrm{req}, \vec{\mathrm{rep}}, \vec{\mathrm{SV}})$

Oracle $\mathrm{Reveal}(pw', uid)$
26 $k \leftarrow \mathrm{K}[pw', uid]$
27 Return k

Oracle $\mathrm{Acquire}(uid, \vec{\mathrm{pk}})$
28 $r \stackrel{+}{\leftarrow} 1$
29 $pw_0, pw_1 \leftarrow \mathrm{PW}[uid]$
30 $(\mathrm{req}, \mathrm{st}) \leftarrow \mathrm{F.Req}(uid, pw_1)$
31 For $i \in J$:
32   **call** $\mathrm{Ev}_{\sigma(i)}(uid, pw_0)$
33   **receive** y_i
34   **call** $\mathrm{BlindEv}_{\sigma(i)}(uid, \mathrm{req})$
35   **receive** rep_i
36 For $i \in [1 .. n] \setminus J$:
37    $csk_i \leftarrow \mathrm{DKA.Cli.SKG}(\mathrm{sk}_i, uid)$
38    $\mathrm{rep}_i \leftarrow \mathrm{F.BlindEv}(csk_i, uid, \mathrm{req})$
39    $y_i \leftarrow \mathrm{F.Ev}(csk_i, uid, pw_0)$
40 $\mathrm{Y}[r] \leftarrow (y_1, \ldots, y_n)$
41 Return $(\mathrm{req}, \vec{\mathrm{rep}}, r)$

Oracle $\mathrm{Recover}(r, \mathrm{C}, \vec{\mathrm{SV}})$
42 $\vec{y} \leftarrow \mathrm{Y}[r]$
43 Try: $k \leftarrow \mathrm{DKA.recover}(\vec{y}, \mathrm{C}, \vec{\mathrm{SV}})$
44 $\mathrm{K}[pw_0, uid] \leftarrow k$
45 Return

Oracle $\mathrm{Challenge}_{\mathcal{A}}(uid)$
46 Require $uid \notin \mathrm{CH}$
47 $pw_0, pw_1 \leftarrow \mathrm{PW}[uid]$
48 $\mathrm{CH} \stackrel{\cup}{\leftarrow} \{uid\}$
49 $k \leftarrow \mathrm{K}[pw_0, uid]$
50 Return k

Oracle $\mathrm{Corrupt}(i)$
51 Require $i \notin J$
52 $\mathrm{CO} \stackrel{\cup}{\leftarrow} \{i\}$
53 Return sk_i

Fig. 12. Reduction $\mathcal{C}$ for the proof of Theorem 4 and Theorem 5. Procedures setup and reconstruct as in Fig. 7 for Theorem 4 and as in Fig. 8 for Theorem 5. J is a set of t indices that may not be corrupted. σ is a bijection of the uncorrupted indices in the KIND game to the indices in the underlying PRNG game.

References

1. Abdalla, M., Cornejo, M., Nitulescu, A., Pointcheval, D.: Robust password-protected secret sharing. In: Askoxylakis, I., Ioannidis, S., Katsikas, S., Meadows, C. (eds.) ESORICS 2016, Part II. LNSC, vol. 9879, pp. 61–79. Springer, Heidelberg (2016). https://doi.org/10.1007/978-3-319-45741-3_4
2. Albrecht, M.R., Davidson, A., Deo, A., Smart, N.P.: Round-optimal verifiable oblivious pseudorandom functions from ideal lattices. In: Garay, J.A. (ed.) PKC 2021, Part II. LNCS, vol. 12711, pp. 261–289. Springer, Heidelberg (2021). https://doi.org/10.1007/978-3-030-75248-4_10
3. Bagherzandi, A., Jarecki, S., Saxena, N., Lu, Y.: Password-protected secret sharing. In: ACM CCS 2011, pp. 433–444. ACM Press (2011)
4. Basso, A., Kutas, P., Merz, S.P., Petit, C., Sanso, A.: Cryptanalysis of an oblivious PRF from supersingular isogenies. In: Tibouchi, M., Wang, H. (eds.) ASIACRYPT

2021, Part I. LNCS, vol. 13090, pp. 160–184. Springer, Heidelberg (2021). https://doi.org/10.1007/978-3-030-92062-3_6

5. Baum, C., Frederiksen, T.K., Hesse, J., Lehmann, A., Yanai, A.: PESTO: proactively secure distributed single sign-on, or how to trust a hacked server. In: IEEE EuroS&P 2020, pp. 587–606. IEEE (2020)

6. Benhamouda, F., Pointcheval, D.: Verifier-based password-authenticated key exchange: new models and constructions. Cryptology ePrint Archive, Report 2013/833 (2013). https://eprint.iacr.org/2013/833

7. Boneh, D., Kogan, D., Woo, K.: Oblivious pseudorandom functions from isogenies. In: Moriai, S., Wang, H. (eds.) ASIACRYPT 2020, Part II. LNCS, vol. 12492, pp. 520–550. Springer, Heidelberg (2020). https://doi.org/10.1007/978-3-030-64834-3_18

8. Boneh, D., Lewi, K., Montgomery, H.W., Raghunathan, A.: Key homomorphic PRFs and their applications. In: Canetti, R., Garay, J.A. (eds.) CRYPTO 2013, Part I. LNCS, vol. 8042, pp. 410–428. Springer, Heidelberg (2013). https://doi.org/10.1007/978-3-642-40041-4_23

9. Boneh, D., Shoup, V.: A graduate course in applied cryptography (2020)

10. Bourdrez, D., Krawczyk, D.H., Lewi, K., Wood, C.A.: The OPAQUE asymmetric PAKE protocol. Internet-Draft draft-irtf-cfrg-opaque-08, Internet Engineering Task Force (2022). Work in Progress. https://datatracker.ietf.org/doc/html/draft-irtf-cfrg-opaque-08

11. Boyd, C., Davies, G.T., Gjøsteen, K., Jiang, Y.: Fast and secure updatable encryption. In: Micciancio, D., Ristenpart, T. (eds.) CRYPTO 2020, Part I. LNCS, vol. 12170, pp. 464–493. Springer, Heidelberg (2020). https://doi.org/10.1007/978-3-030-56784-2_16

12. Bresson, E., Chevassut, O., Pointcheval, D.: New security results on encrypted key exchange. In: Bao, F., Deng, R., Zhou, J. (eds.) PKC 2004. LNCS, vol. 2947, pp. 145–158. Springer, Heidelberg (2004). https://doi.org/10.1007/978-3-540-24632-9_11

13. Brost, J., Egger, C., Lai, R.W.F., Schmid, F., Schröder, D., Zoppelt, M.: Threshold password-hardened encryption services. In: ACM CCS 2020, pp. 409–424. ACM Press (2020)

14. Camenisch, J., Lehmann, A., Lysyanskaya, A., Neven, G.: Memento: How to reconstruct your secrets from a single password in a hostile environment. In: Garay, J.A., Gennaro, R. (eds.) CRYPTO 2014, Part II. LNCS, vol. 8617, pp. 256–275. Springer, Heidelberg (2014). https://doi.org/10.1007/978-3-662-44381-1_15

15. Camenisch, J., Lysyanskaya, A., Neven, G.: Practical yet universally composable two-server password-authenticated secret sharing. In: ACM CCS 2012, pp. 525–536. ACM Press (2012)

16. Casacuberta, S., Hesse, J., Lehmann, A.: SoK: oblivious pseudorandom functions. In: IEEE EuroS&P 2022. IEEE (2022)

17. Das, P., Hesse, J., Lehmann, A.: DPaSE: distributed password-authenticated symmetric-key encryption, or how to get many keys from one password. In: ASIACCS 2022, pp. 682–696. ACM Press (2022)

18. Davidson, A., Goldberg, I., Sullivan, N., Tankersley, G., Valsorda, F.: Privacy pass: bypassing internet challenges anonymously. In: PoPETs, vol. 2018, no. 3, pp. 164–180 (2018)

19. Davies, G.T., Pijnenburg, J.: PERKS: persistent and distributed key acquisition for secure storage from passwords. Cryptology ePrint Archive, Report 2022/1017 (2022). https://eprint.iacr.org/2022/1017

20. Everspaugh, A., Chatterjee, R., Scott, S., Juels, A., Ristenpart, T.: The Pythia PRF service. In: USENIX Security 2015, pp. 547–562. USENIX Association (2015)
21. Freedman, M.J., Ishai, Y., Pinkas, B., Reingold, O.: Keyword search and oblivious pseudorandom functions. In: Kilian, J. (ed.) TCC 2005. LNCS, vol. 3378, pp. 303–324. Springer, Heidelberg (2005). https://doi.org/10.1007/978-3-540-30576-7_17
22. Huang, S., et al.: DIT: deidentified authenticated telemetry at scale. Blog post, meta (2021). https://engineering.fb.com/2021/04/16/production-engineering/dit/
23. Jarecki, S., Kiayias, A., Krawczyk, H.: Round-optimal password-protected secret sharing and T-PAKE in the password-only model. In: Sarkar, P., Iwata, T. (eds.) ASIACRYPT 2014, Part II. LNCS, vol. 8874, pp. 233–253. Springer, Heidelberg (2014). https://doi.org/10.1007/978-3-662-45608-8_13
24. Jarecki, S., Kiayias, A., Krawczyk, H., Xu, J.: Highly-efficient and composable password-protected secret sharing (or: how to protect your bitcoin wallet online). In: IEEE European Symposium on Security and Privacy, EuroS&P 2016, pp. 276–291. IEEE (2016)
25. Jarecki, S., Kiayias, A., Krawczyk, H., Xu, J.: TOPPSS: cost-minimal password-protected secret sharing based on threshold OPRF. In: Gollmann, D., Miyaji, A., Kikuchi, H. (eds.) ACNS 2017. LNCS, vol. 10355, pp. 39–58. Springer, Heidelberg (2017). https://doi.org/10.1007/978-3-319-61204-1_3
26. Jarecki, S., Krawczyk, H., Resch, J.: Threshold partially-oblivious PRFs with applications to key management. Cryptology ePrint Archive, Report 2018/733 (2018). https://eprint.iacr.org/2018/733
27. Jarecki, S., Krawczyk, H., Resch, J.K.: Updatable oblivious key management for storage systems. In: ACM CCS 2019, pp. 379–393. ACM Press (2019)
28. Jarecki, S., Krawczyk, H., Xu, J.: OPAQUE: an asymmetric PAKE protocol secure against pre-computation attacks. In: Nielsen, J., Rijmen, V. (eds.) EUROCRYPT 2018, Part III. LNCS, vol. 10822, pp. 456–486. Springer, Heidelberg (2018). https://doi.org/10.1007/978-3-319-78372-7_15
29. Jarecki, S., Liu, X.: Efficient oblivious pseudorandom function with applications to adaptive OT and secure computation of set intersection. In: Reingold, O. (ed.) TCC 2009. LNCS, vol. 5444, pp. 577–594. Springer, Heidelberg (2009). https://doi.org/10.1007/978-3-642-00457-5_34
30. Kolesnikov, V., Kumaresan, R., Rosulek, M., Trieu, N.: Efficient batched oblivious PRF with applications to private set intersection. In: ACM CCS 2016, pp. 818–829. ACM Press (2016)
31. Lai, R.W.F., Egger, C., Reinert, M., Chow, S.S.M., Maffei, M., Schröder, D.: Simple password-hardened encryption services. In: USENIX Security 2018, pp. 1405–1421. USENIX Association (2018)
32. Lehmann, A.: ScrambleDB: oblivious (chameleon) pseudonymization-as-a-service. In: PoPETs, vol. 2019, no. 3, pp. 289–309 (2019)
33. Lehmann, A., Tackmann, B.: Updatable encryption with post-compromise security. In: Nielsen, J., Rijmen, V. (eds.) EUROCRYPT 2018, Part III. LNCS, vol. 10822, pp. 685–716. Springer, Heidelberg (2018). https://doi.org/10.1007/978-3-319-78372-7_22
34. Li, L., Pal, B., Ali, J., Sullivan, N., Chatterjee, R., Ristenpart, T.: Protocols for checking compromised credentials. In: ACM CCS 2019, pp. 1387–1403. ACM Press (2019)
35. NCC-Group: End-to-end encrypted backups security assessment: Whatsapp (version 1.2) (2021). https://research.nccgroup.com/wp-content/uploads/2021/10/NCC_Group_WhatsApp_E001000M_Report_2021-10-27_v1.2.pdf

36. Pijnenburg, J., Poettering, B.: Encrypt-to-self: securely outsourcing storage. In: Chen, L., Li, N., Liang, K., Schneider, S. (eds.) ESORICS 2020, Part I. LNCS, vol. 12308, pp. 635–654. Springer, Heidelberg (2020). https://doi.org/10.1007/978-3-030-58951-6_31

37. Shamir, A.: How to share a secret. Commun. Assoc. Comput. Mach. **22**(11), 612–613 (1979)

38. Storer, M.W., Greenan, K.M., Long, D.D.E., Miller, E.L.: Secure data deduplication. In: StorageSS 2008, pp. 1–10. ACM (2008)

39. Thomas, K., et al.: Protecting accounts from credential stuffing with password breach alerting. In: USENIX Security 2019, pp. 1556–1571. USENIX Association (2019)

40. Tyagi, N., Celi, S., Ristenpart, T., Sullivan, N., Tessaro, S., Wood, C.A.: A fast and simple partially oblivious PRF, with applications. In: Dunkelman, O., Dziembowski, S. (eds.) EUROCRYPT 2022, Part II. LNCS, vol. 13276, pp. 674–705. Springer, Heidelberg (2022). https://doi.org/10.1007/978-3-031-07085-3_23

41. WhatsApp: Security of end-to-end encrypted backups (2021). https://www.whatsapp.com/security/WhatsApp_Security_Encrypted_Backups_Whitepaper.pdf

Improved Circuit-Based PSI via Equality Preserving Compression

Kyoohyung Han, Dukjae Moon, and Yongha Son$^{(\boxtimes)}$

Samsung SDS, Seoul, Korea
{kh89.han,dukjae.moon,yongha.son}@samsung.com

Abstract. Circuit-based private set intersection (circuit-PSI) enables two parties with input set X and Y to compute a function f over the intersection set $X \cap Y$, without revealing any other information. State-of-the-art protocols for circuit-PSI commonly involves a procedure that securely checks whether two input strings are equal and outputs an additive share of the equality result. This procedure is typically performed by generic two party computation protocols, and its cost occupies quite large portion of the total cost of circuit-PSI. In this work, we propose *equality preserving compression* (EPC) protocol that compresses the length of equality check targets while preserving equality using homomorphic encryption (HE) scheme, which is secure against the semi-honest adversary. This can be seamlessly applied to state-of-the-art circuit-PSI protocol frameworks. We demonstrate by implementation that our EPC provides 10–40% speed-up for circuit-PSI with set size from 2^{16} to 2^{20}, on LAN network. We believe that EPC protocol itself can be independent interest, which can be applied to other application than PSI.

Keywords: Private Set Intersection · Circuit-based Private Set Intersection · Homomorphic Encryption

1 Introduction

A two-party functionality of private set intersection (PSI) enables two parties P_0 and P_1 having respective input set X and Y to compute the intersection $X \cap Y$, without revealing any other information beyond the original set cardinality $|X|$ and $|Y|$ to each other.

There are many real-world applications related to PSI, and some of them only requiring the intersection set may find an efficient solution from PSI alone. However, there is another variant of PSI that outputs only $f(X \cap Y)$ for some target function f rather than the intersection set $X \cap Y$, and this would be more desirable for other applications. One typical but a popular example is PSI-Cardinality that computes cardinality of the intersection, where $f(X \cap Y) = |X \cap Y|$. Indeed these kinds of PSI are receiving growing attention from industry, for example, Google [19] and Facebook [5] explored some variants PSI including PSI-Cardinality-with-Sum that computes the cardinality and the sum of associated values over the intersection set.

B. Smith and H. Wu (Eds.): SAC 2022, LNCS 13742, pp. 190–209, 2024.
https://doi.org/10.1007/978-3-031-58411-4_9

This PSI-with-computation notion is generalized to the *circuit-PSI* functionality, which outputs the intersection information in secret-shared form, instead of the intersection set itself. More precisely, for each element $x \in X$, circuit-PSI outputs each party random bits s_0 and s_1 respectively, such that $s_0 \oplus s_1 = 1$ if and only if $x \in X \cap Y$ (of course 0 otherwise). This is used as a general-purpose preprocessing, in the sense that two parties use the shares to perform target computation on the intersection. Notable example would be PSI-Threshold that only reveals whether the cardinality of $X \cap Y$ is larger than some threshold.

The work of Pinkas *et al.* [24] proposed a novel construction of circuit-PSI protocol which has linear communication complexity in the input set size. After that, several following works [6,27] have proposed improved instantiation of the framework and those works indeed shows the state-of-the-art performance for circuit-PSI.

To generate final bits s_0 and s_1 in circuit-PSI, the framework involves $O(N)$ times of private *equality share generation* (ESG) that takes an input string from each party and outputs Boolean shares of the equality result between two strings for $N = |X| = |Y|$. This is one of the main differences of circuit-PSI from plain PSI, where the latter one typically uses private *equality test* that simply outputs the equality result itself. For private equality test, there are many efficient methods such as *oblivious pseudo-random functions* (OPRFs) [14,21,27]. However it is not directly applicable for ESG, and the most of circuit-PSI protocols perform ESG by other costly methods such as generic two party computations (2PC).

Not too long ago, ESG occupied the largest part of circuit-PSI cost; about 96% and 91% of the total communication in circuit-PSI protocols of [24] and [6] respectively. Although such burden of ESG procedure is greatly reduced thanks to remarkable speed-up of OT extensions [10,30], it still takes quite large portion of circuit-PSI protocol, which is the main reason of performance gap of plain PSI and circuit-PSI.

1.1   Our Contribution

Our work starts with an observation that all known methods for *equality share generation* (ESG) have complexity linear in the input bit-length. Some works [24,27] simply exploited two party GMW protocol by evaluating equality check circuit composed of $\ell - 1$ AND gates, and it naturally results in complexity linear in ℓ. After then [6,13] proposed more efficient protocols that have improved communication burden, but it still suffered from linear complexity in ℓ.

- With a purpose of reducing workload of ESG, we propose a functionality what we call *equality preserving compression* (EPC) that converts two large integers into smaller integers, while preserving the equality condition. Then we construct a homomorphic encryption (HE) based efficient protocol realizing the EPC functionality with semi-honest security. Asymptotically it compresses ℓ-bit input integers into $O(\log \ell)$-bits, with $\tilde{O}(\ell)$ computational and communication complexity.

- We then combine our EPC into the circuit-PSI framework of [24]. Our EPC protocol *perfectly* preserve equality, in other words with zero failure probability, and hence the correctness analysis for previous circuit-PSI protocols remains exactly same. Moreover, it provides concrete improvement since it decreases the heavy ESG part input in the logarithmic scale. We check the concrete effect of EPC by implementation, and observe 10–40% speed-up over LAN network environment. See Table 1 for details.

1.2 Related Works

Circuit-PSI. Circuit-PSI was firstly proposed by [18] and then continuous improvements have been reported [9,23,25]. In particular [23] has a similarity with our paper, as their main idea called permutation-based hashing is to cut-off the length of item while preserving equality, with a purpose of reducing the cost for equality check. However, the technique is only applicable to the initial hashing routine (will be explained by cuckoo/simple hashing later), and not compatible with the currently best framework of circuit-PSI due to Pinkas *et al.* [24] based on *oblivious programmable PRF* (OPPRF). As OPPRF-based circuit-PSI framework shows the best performance, whose details are presented later in Sect. 3. We note that, despite the similarity of their names, construction of OPPRF is quite different from OPRF, and hence OPRF-based PSI protocol does not implies OPPRF-based circuit-PSI protocol. Indeed, we are aware of only one work [27] that constructs plain PSI and circuit-PSI from the same underlying idea. There is another concept of PSI-with-computation [13] different to circuit-PSI, which improves the efficiency of PSI-with-computation while additionally reveals the cardinality of intersection set as well as the desired function evaluation $f(X \cap Y)$.

HE in PSI Field. There are also HE-based PSI approaches [7,8], which mainly focused on extremely unbalance-sized set cases. The first work [8] considered plain PSI, and the main usage of HE is to solve the private set membership (PSM) problem by evaluating inclusion polynomial; $x \in Y$ is equivalent to $F(x) = \prod_{y \in Y}(x-y) = 0$, which is quite different to our use of HE. The following work [7] extended this protocol to PSI having associated value and strengthened the security to malicious setting, but HE is applied in the similar sense to the previous work. The authors of [7] leaved a short mention on circuit-PSI as a combination of their HE-based PSM protocol with the final equality share generation. As the circuit-PSI protocol was not the main interest of the paper, the authors merely mentioned that the final task can be done by a 2PC without detailed analysis.

1.3 Roadmap

In Sect. 2, we recall the preliminaries including oblivious transfer and homomorphic encryption, and in Sect. 3, we present the state-of-the-art circuit-PSI framework due to [24]. In Sect. 4, we propose an equality preserving compression functionality concept and efficient protocol for that. Then in Sect. 5, we combine our proposed EPC protocol with the OPPRF-based circuit-PSI protocol to improve efficiency, and provide experimental results in Sect. 6.

2   Preliminary

2.1   Notations

We write vectors as bold lowercase letters, and matrices as bold uppercase letters. For any real number x, we denote $\lfloor x \rceil$ by the round-off to integer. The i-th component of a vector $\mathbf{v}$ is denoted by v_i, and i,j-th entry of a matrix M is denoted by $m_{i,j}$. For an integer k, a set $\{1, \cdots, k\}$ is denoted by $[k]$. The logarithm function log is assumed to have base 2 unless specially denoted by $\log_w$ with base w. For any statement T that can be determined by true or false (Boolean), we denote $\mathbf{1}(T)$ be the truth value for the equality, i.e., it is 1 if T is true and 0 else.

2.2   Oblivious Transfers

A 1-out-of-n oblivious transfer (OT) of ℓ-bit input messages $(n, 1)$-OT_ℓ takes as input n messages $m_1, \cdots, m_n \in \{0, 1\}^\ell$ from the sender and a choice index $c \in [n]$ from the receiver, and outputs m_c to the receiver and nothing to the sender. We also use a notion of 1-out-of-2 *correlated-OT* (COT) of ℓ-bit input messages $(2, 1)$-COT_ℓ, where the sender inputs a correlation $d \in \{0, 1\}^\ell$ and the receiver inputs a choice bit $b \in \{0, 1\}$. Then the functionality outputs to the sender r and $d + r$ for a randomly chosen $r \in \{0, 1\}^\ell$, and to the receiver $b \cdot d + r$. We write m times of $(n, 1)$-$(\text{C})\text{OT}_\ell$ calls by $(n, 1)$-$(\text{C})\text{OT}_\ell^m$.

There are protocols called OT-extension (OTe) that efficiently extend small numbers of *base* OTs to large numbers of OTs. Assuming that such small numbers of base OTs are done, the most typical IKNP OTe protocols execute $(2, 1)$-OT_ℓ and $(2, 1)$-COT_ℓ with communication $\lambda + 2\ell$ [20] and $\lambda + \ell$ [2] bits per one call. Recently another breakthrough line of OT extensions [4,10,30] are proposed, which greatly reduces communication overhead of IKNP-style OT-extension, while preserving similar computational cost to IKNP. For sufficiently many OT and COT calls, for example more than 2^{20} calls, Silent OTe allows one to execute $(2, 1)$-OT_ℓ and $(2, 1)$-COT_ℓ with nearly $2\ell + 1$ and $\ell + 1$ bit communication per one call, respectively.

GMW Protocol or Gate Evaluation. For a bit $x \in \{0, 1\}$, we say $x_0 \in \{0, 1\}$ and $x_1 \in \{0, 1\}$ satisfying $x = x_0 \oplus x_1$ be 2-party additive Boolean shares, or simply Boolean shares of x. Consider two bits x and y are shared as x_i and y_i by two party P_0 and P_1. Then two parties can privately compute Boolean shares of gate evaluations on input x and y using OT. Note that Boolean shares for XOR $x \oplus y$ can be easily computed by $x_i \oplus y_i$ by each party's own. Boolean shares for AND gate can be evaluated by $(2, 1)$-COT_1^2 [11,16]. For the underlying idea, observe that $(2,1)$-COT_1 with the sender's input correlation bit d and the receiver's input choice bit b essentially computes Boolean shares of $b \wedge d$. To evaluate an AND gate, two parties execute a correlated-OT with input x_i and y_{1-i} to have Boolean shares of $a = x_i \wedge y_{1-i}$, and then with input y_i and x_{1-i} to have Boolean shares of $b = x_{1-i} \wedge y_{1-i}$. Then the party P_i outputs $x_i \wedge y_i \oplus a_i \oplus b_i$ and the other party P_{1-i} outputs $x_{1-i} \wedge y_{1-i} \oplus a_{1-i} \oplus b_{1-i}$, which are Boolean shares of $x \wedge y = (x_0 \oplus x_1) \wedge (y_0 \oplus y_1)$.

2.3 RLWE-Based Homomorphic Encryption

A homomorphic encryption (HE) scheme is an encryption scheme that supports a ring-structured plaintext $\mathcal{M}$, and homomorphic arithmetic operations between ciphertexts that acts on inner plaintext. We especially exploit a ring learning with errors (RLWE) based HE scheme, BFV scheme [12].

For simplicity, we restrict our description for RLWE-based HE using power-of-2 cyclotomic rings of integers, which is widely used in several HE libraries. Let $\mathcal{R} := \mathbb{Z}[X]/(X^n + 1)$ be a polynomial quotient ring where n is a power-of-2 integer. This scheme supports a plaintext space $\mathcal{R}_p := \mathcal{R}/p\mathcal{R} = \mathbb{Z}_p[X]/(X^n + 1)$ for some plaintext modulus prime integer p, and the corresponding ciphertext space is $\mathcal{R}_q^2$ for some $q \gg p$.

BFV Scheme. We will briefly review the BFV homomorphic encryption scheme. The IND-CPA security of BFV is based on the hardness assumption of the RLWE problem. For more details, we refer to [3,12].

Key Generation. Given a security parameter $\lambda > 0$, fix integers n, P (P be a positive integer that will be used in the evaluation key generation), and distributions $\mathcal{D}_{key}$, $\mathcal{D}_{err}$ and $\mathcal{D}_{enc}$ over $\mathcal{R}$ in a way that the resulting scheme is secure against any adversary with computational resource of $O(2^\lambda)$. Typically $\mathcal{D}_{key}$ is chosen by ternary coefficient polynomials in $\mathcal{R}$, and $\mathcal{D}_{err}$ and $\mathcal{D}_{enc}$ are chosen by a discrete Gaussian distribution of appropriate standard deviation σ.

1. Sample $a \leftarrow \mathcal{R}_q$, $s \leftarrow \mathcal{D}_{key}$, and $e \leftarrow \mathcal{D}_{err}$. Then the secret key is defined as $\mathsf{sk} = (1, s) \in \mathcal{R}^2$, and the corresponding public key is defined as $\mathsf{pk} = (b, a) \in \mathcal{R}_q^2$, where $b = [-a \cdot s + e]_q$.
2. Sample $a' \leftarrow \mathcal{R}_q$ and $e' \leftarrow \mathcal{D}_{err}$. Then the evaluation key is defined as $\mathsf{evk} = (b', a') \in \mathcal{R}_q^2$, where $b' = [-a' \cdot s + e' + Ps']_q$ for $s' = [s^2]_q$.

Encryption. Given a public key pk and a plaintext $m \in \mathcal{R}$, Sample $r \leftarrow \mathcal{D}_{\mathsf{Enc}}$ and $e_0, e_1 \leftarrow \mathcal{D}_{err}$. Then compute $\mathsf{Enc}(\mathsf{pk}, 0) = [r \cdot \mathsf{pk} + (e_0, e_1)]_q$ and $\mathsf{Enc}^{\mathsf{BFV}}(\mathsf{pk}, m) = [\mathsf{Enc}(\mathsf{pk}, 0) + (\Delta_{\mathsf{BFV}} \cdot [m]_p, 0)]_q$, where $\Delta_{\mathsf{BFV}} = \lfloor q/p \rfloor$.

Decryption. Given a secret key $\mathsf{sk} \in \mathcal{R}^2$ and a ciphertext $\mathsf{ct} \in \mathcal{R}_q^2$, $\mathsf{Dec}^{\mathsf{BFV}}$ $(\mathsf{sk}, \mathsf{ct}) = \left\lfloor \frac{p}{q} [\langle \mathsf{sk}, \mathsf{ct} \rangle]_q \right\rceil$.

The ciphertext of BFV scheme is $(b(x), a(x))$ satisfying $b(x) = -a(x) \cdot s(x) + e(x)$. The $e(x)$ part is called as *noise term* of ciphertext. We note that infinite norm of noise term of ct in decryption function should be bounded by $\frac{q}{2p}$ for correctness of decryption.

Addition. Given ciphertexts ct_1 and ct_2 in $\mathcal{R}_q^2$, their sum is defined as $ct_{Add} = [ct_1 + ct_2]_q$.

Multiplication. Given ciphertexts $ct_1 = (b_1, a_1)$ and $ct_2 = (b_2, a_2)$ in $\mathcal{R}_q^2$ and an evaluation key evk, their product is defined as $ct_{Mult} = [(d_0, d_1) + \lfloor P^{-1} \cdot d_2 \cdot evk \rceil]_q$, where (d_0, d_1, d_2) is defined by $\left[\left\lfloor \frac{p}{q}(b_1 b_2, a_1 b_2 + a_2 b_1, a_1 a_2) \right\rceil\right]_q$.

Batching. BFV scheme basically supports encryptions of plaintext ring $\mathcal{R}_p$ element, and homomorphic addition and multiplication over $\mathcal{R}_p$. As a useful notion for batching multiple data in one ciphertext, one can use a ring isomorphism $\mathcal{R}_p \cong \mathbb{F}_{p^d}^{n/d}$ where d is the smallest integer such that $p^d = 1 \mod 2n$ and $\mathbb{F}_{p^d}$ is a finite field of order p^d. Using this isomorphism, one can perform slot-wise encryption and operation of n/d elements in $\mathbb{F}_{p^d}$ by single instruction on the ciphertext. It is worth to note when the plaintext modulus p and the polynomial quotient n satisfies

$$p = 1 \mod 2n, \tag{1}$$

which provides n slots of $\mathbb{Z}_p$ element. This can be achieved only with somewhat restrictive parameters, but the underlying plaintext slot $\mathbb{Z}_p$ is much simpler than extension fields $\mathbb{F}_{p^d}$ so that one can fully enjoy the power of batching. In this regard, we refer this case by *full batch* and indeed our paper mainly focus on full batch HE parameters.

Security Notions. For security, we consider the standard IND-CPA security that requires two ciphertexts of different messages are (computationally) indistinguishable given an encryption oracle. The IND-CPA security of RLWE-based HE literally comes from the hardness of ring learning with errors (RLWE) problem. For concrete parameter setting of IND-CPA security, the bit-size of ciphertext modulus $\log q$ and polynomial ring dimension n, and error distribution $\mathcal{D}_{err}$ should be selected to secure against various lattice reduction attacks.

3   Circuit-Based PSI

The definition circuit-based PSI (circuit-PSI) functionality to generate Boolean additive shares is given as Fig. 1. After circuit-PSI, the results can be used for one's desired function evaluation. In the rest of this section, we describe the abstract framework of [24] which continues to the following improvements [6,27]. Then we especially review the equality share generation method of each work which occupies the largest part of the total cost, from which we can observe the input bit-length ℓ equality share generation plays the most crucial role for complexity.

Parameters: A receiver with an input set X of size N and a sender with an input set Y of size N.

Functionality: The functionality sends to the receiver an injective indexing function $\iota : X \to [M]$ for some $M \geq N$ and a vector $s_0 \in \{0,1\}^M$, and to the sender a vector $s_1 \in \{0,1\}^M$ such that $s_{0,i} \oplus s_{1,i} = \mathbf{1}(\iota^{-1}(i) \in X \cap Y)$ for $i \in \iota(X)$, and $s_{0,i} \oplus s_{1,i} = 0$ for $i \notin \iota(X)$.

Fig. 1. $\mathcal{F}_{\mathsf{CPSI}}$. (Ideal) Functionality of circuit-PSI

3.1 OPPRF-Based Circuit-PSI Framework

Let the receiver $\mathcal{R}$ holds a set X and the sender $\mathcal{S}$ holds a set Y of the same size N. The framework consists of the following three main stages.

Step 1. Hashing. For $\varepsilon > 0$, each party creates a hash table with $M = (1+\varepsilon) \cdot N$ bins, but with different hashing method. The receiver applies cuckoo hashing with d hash functions $h_1, \cdots, h_d : \{0,1\}^* \to [M]$ on input X. More precisely, for a suitable choice of ε, there is a cuckoo hashing algorithm that stores every element $x \in X$ in $h_j(x)$-th bin for some $j \in [d]$ with overwhelming probability, while ensuring that at most one element is stored in each bin. This yields a simple representation of the cuckoo hash table: $T_X[h_j(x)] = x$. Note that the mapping from $x \in X$ to $h_j(x)$ determines the indexing function ι in the circuit-PSI definition of Fig. 1.

On the other hand, the sender creates a simple hash table with the same hash functions on input Y, which stores each $y \in Y$ in every bin $h_j(x)$ for every $j \in [d]$. Naturally each bin can hold more than one element, and hence the i-th bin of the simple hash table $T_Y[i]$ is indeed a set. It is known that for $M = O(N)$ hash table size, the number of elements in each bin is $O(\log(N))$.

Since $h_j(x) \neq h_j(y)$ for some j implies $x \neq y$, two parties only need to compare each elements of the same bin of each hash tables. Since the cuckoo hash table T_X ensures at most one element of $x \in X$ per each bin, circuit-PSI reduces to the problem that securely outputs an additive share of $\mathbf{1}(T_X[i] \in T_Y[i])$ for each bin i, which is essentially a private set membership (PSM) problem. Here the receiver has to fill the empty bin in T_X with dummy value to prevent additional information leakage.

Step 2. Bin Tagging. This step further reduces the aforementioned PSM problem into an equality share generation (ESG) problem between two parties, where each party inputs a vector $\mathbf{v}$ and $\mathbf{v}^*$ of length M respectively, and is given as output a Boolean vector of additive share of $\mathbf{1}(v_i = v_i^*)$.

This is realized by a functionality called *oblivious programmable pseudo-random function* (OPPRF) [22] where the sender obliviously computes a PRF F on receiver's input while the sender can *program* F with values (y_i, z_i) so that $F(y_i) = z_i$. The formal definition of OPPRF is given as Fig. 2. [24] is the first work that applies OPPRF functionality for this purpose, and then [6] and [27] developed more efficient OPPRF protocols to improve the performance of circuit-PSI.

Parameters: A sender with input $L = \{(y_i, z_i)\}$ where $y_i \in \{0,1\}^*$ and $z_i \in \{0,1\}^\ell$, and a receiver with input $X = \{x_i\}$ with $x_i \in \{0,1\}^*$.

Functionality: The functionality samples a random function $F : \{0,1\}^* \to \{0,1\}^\ell$ such that $F(y) = z$ for each $(y, z) \in L$, and sends $F(X) := \{F(x) : x \in X\}$ to the receiver.
After then, upon an input y of the sender, the functionality outputs $F(y)$ to the sender.

Fig. 2. $\mathcal{F}_{\mathsf{OPPRF}}$. (Ideal) Functionality of oblivious programmable PRF

To convert PSM problem to ESG problem, two parties execute a protocol for OPPRF functionality with the following input. The sender who has a simple table samples a random tag value $v_i \in \{0,1\}^\ell$ for each i-th bin, and generate the input set L obtained by concatenating each $y \in Y$ with the tag of the bins where y is stored, namely

$$L = \left\{ (y \| h_j(y), v_{h_j(y)}) \right\}_{y \in Y, j \in [d]} = \{(y' \| i, v_i)\}_{i \in [M], y' \in T_Y[i]} .$$

The receiver feeds its input set by $\hat{T}_X = \{T_X[i] \| i\}_{i \in [M]}$. After the execution of OPPRF protocol, the receiver assigns

$$v_i^* = F\left(T_X[i] \| i\right) \in \{0,1\}^\ell$$

in each hash address i to construct a vector $\mathbf{v}^*$ of length M. From the definition of OPPRF functionality, it holds that $v_i = v_i^*$ if the element $T_X[i]$ is in the set $T_Y[i]$, otherwise v_i^* is a random element. Therefore the original PSM-related problem is translated into equality share generation problem between $\mathbf{v}$ from the sender and $\mathbf{v}^*$ from the receiver.

Remark 1 (Failure Probability). Note that there is a failure probability of $2^{-\ell}$ where the random element v_i^* is same to v_i despite $T_X[i]$ is not in $T_Y[i]$. The length of tag ℓ should be chosen so that the overall failure probability is smaller than $2^{-\sigma}$ where σ is statistical security parameter. Since there are M bins, it should hold that $2^{-\sigma} > 1 - (1 - 2^{-\ell})^M$, which is sufficient with

$$\ell > \sigma + \lceil \log M \rceil. \tag{2}$$

Step 3. Equality Share Generation. In this step two parties finally generate Boolean shares of $\mathbf{1}(v_i = v_i^*)$, whose definition is formally given as Fig. 3.

Parameters: A sender with an input string a and a receiver with an input string b.

Functionality: The functionality outputs bits s_0 and s_1 such that $s_0 \oplus s_1 = \mathbf{1}(a = b)$ to each party respectively.

Fig. 3. $\mathcal{F}_{\mathsf{ESG}}$. (Ideal) Functionality of equality share generation

There are several known methods [6,13] to perform this step in semi-honest model. Most of methods take an approach that evaluates the equality check circuit on ℓ-bit string, composed of $\ell - 1$ AND gate evaluations. One may exploit Yao's garbled circuit protocol for evaluation, and it requires $2\lambda = 256$ bits communication per one AND gate evaluation, with only a single round of interactions. Meanwhile, GMW protocol requires only 2 bits communication per one AND gate[1], at the cost of $\log(\ell)$ rounds of interactions. We consider the low communication benefit of GMW protocol is larger than the smaller round complexity of Yao's protocol. In the remaining of the paper, we implicitly assume that ESG is executed by GMW protocol.

4   Equality Preserving Compression

The final equality share generation procedure occupies the largest part of the total cost in circuit-PSI protocol, and the input bit-length ℓ of equality share generation plays an important role. In this section, we present a procedure that converts the equality share generation target inputs into another values whose size is asymptotically logarithm to the original input bit-length, while the equality results remain unchanged. More formally, we define the 2-party functionality *equality preserving compression* (EPC) $\mathcal{F}_{\mathsf{EPC}}$ that takes an integer $v \in \mathbb{Z}_t$ from the sender and another integer $v^* \in \mathbb{Z}_t$ from the receiver. The functionality outputs each party a random integer r and r^* in another modulus ring $\mathbb{Z}_p$, where it holds that $v = v^*$ in $\mathbb{Z}_t$ *if and only if* $r = r^*$ in $\mathbb{Z}_p$ for $p < t$.

4.1   A Basic Protocol

Our protocol starts from the following simple observation on word decomposition. For any base w, the w-base decomposition of v and v^* by $v = \sum_{i=0}^{u-1} v_i \cdot w^i$ and $v^* = \sum_{i=0}^{u-1} v_i^* \cdot w^i$ where $u := \lceil \log_w t \rceil$ and $v_i, v_i^* \in [0, w)$ satisfies

$$v = v^* \iff D := \sum_{i=0}^{u-1} (v_i - v_i^*)^2 = 0 \text{ in } \mathbb{Z}. \tag{3}$$

Note that $D \leq u \cdot (w-1)^2 \approx \log_w t \cdot (w-1)^2$, which has much smaller size than the original size t (Fig. 4).

---

[1] Thanks to recent improvements on OT extension [10,30].

> **Parameters:** A sender with an input $v \in \mathbb{Z}_t$ and a receiver with an input $v^* \in \mathbb{Z}_t$, and the target size p.
>
> **Functionality:** The functionality sends a random $r \in \mathbb{Z}_p$ and $r^* \in \mathbb{Z}_p$ to the sender and receiver respectively, such that $v = v^*$ in $\mathbb{Z}_t$ if and only if $r = r^*$ in $\mathbb{Z}_p$.

Fig. 4. $\mathcal{F}_{\mathsf{EPC}}$. (Ideal) Functionality of equality preserving compression

Based on this idea, we consider a simple protocol that privately computes D and output a random element $r \in \mathbb{Z}_p$ and $r^* := r + D \in \mathbb{Z}_p$ by Fig. 5. However, the correctness may fail without any condition on the word base w and p, since it may happen that $r = r^* \in \mathbb{Z}_p$ despite of $v \neq v^*$ if D is divisible by p. To avoid this, the word base w has to be chosen so that D is always less than p, namely

$$p > u \cdot (w - 1)^2. \tag{4}$$

We note that $u \cdot (w-1)^2 = O(\log t)$, this protocol asymptotically realizes $\mathcal{F}_{\mathsf{EPC}}$ for $p = O(\log t)$.

> **Parameters:** A sender with input $v \in \mathbb{Z}_t$ and a receiver with input $v^* \in \mathbb{Z}_t$ and the target size p.
>
> **Protocol:**
>
> 1. Sender generates a homomorphic encryption secret key sk, and decomposes in w-base $v \in \mathbb{Z}_t$ to $\{v_i\}_{0 \leq i < u}$ for $u = \lceil \log_w t \rceil$. After that sender encrypts each v_i using sk, and sends them to receiver.
> 2. Receiver picks a random integer $r \in \mathbb{Z}_p$, and decomposes $v^* \in \mathbb{Z}_t$ to $\{v_i^*\}_{0 \leq i < u}$. Then receiver homomorphically compute $r + \sum_{i=0}^{u-1}(v_i - v_i^*)^2$, and sends the resulting ciphertext back to sender.
> 3. Sender decrypts the received ciphertext using sk, to obtain $r^* = r + \sum_{i=0}^{u-1}(v_i - v_i^*)^2 \in \mathbb{Z}_p$.

Fig. 5. A basic protocol for $\mathcal{F}_{\mathsf{EPC}}$ functionalities

4.2   Optimizations and Full Protocol

Upon the basic protocol above, we specially focus on BFV scheme to utilize batching property. Furthermore, we achieve huge speed-up from a simple decomposition of $D = \sum(v_i - v_i^*)^2$ by totally removing homomorphic ciphertext multiplication. On security aspect, we use noise flooding to ensure function privacy of homomorphic encryption. A full protocol description that puts everything together is presented by Fig. 6, and below we provide some details for each technique.

Batching with RLWE-Based HE. As reviewed in Sect. 3, two parties have to perform $O(N)$-many times of equality checks in circuit-PSI. In this regard, we can exploit batch property of BFV scheme to perform multiple calls of $\mathcal{F}_{\mathsf{EPC}}$, on some conditions on target size p and HE parameters. To recall, for the given RLWE dimension n, we can encrypt n/d number of $\mathbb{F}_{p^d}$ elements in one ciphertext for the smallest integer d such that $p^d = 1 \bmod 2n$. This means that using smaller p gives better compression ratio, but makes the number of slots in a single ciphertext smaller. For example, $p > 2n$ is necessary to use full batch (i.e. n slots).

Removing Ciphertext Multiplications. In most of HE schemes, homomorphic multiplication takes much larger time than scalar multiplication. To remove homomorphic multiplications, we let the sender additionally sends one more ciphertext which is an encryption of $\sum_{i=0}^{u-1} v_i^2$. In this case, the receiver can compute D by

$$D = \sum_{i=0}^{u-1} v_i^2 - 2 \cdot \sum_{i=0}^{u-1} v_i \cdot v_i^* + \sum_{i=0}^{u-1} v_i^{*2}.$$

As the receiver knows v_i^* values, it can compute $\sum_{i=0}^{u-1} v_i^{*2}$ part and then the receiver only needs to perform scalar multiplications and additions to obtain an encryption of D.

Realizing Function Privacy. For the security proof, we need to ensure the function privacy from the return ciphertext from receiver to sender. For that we apply randomization and noise flooding method, whose detail will be presented in the next subsection. Concretely this can be realized by letting receiver randomize the resulting ciphertext by homomorphically adding a fresh encryption of zero, and add large enough error to apply noise flooding method before send the computation result back to sender.

4.3 Security and Cost Analysis

In this section, we will discuss about security of our protocol with correctness proof. We also analyze the computational and communication costs. Before that, we need to recall some details of RLWE-based HE scheme. We will focus on BFV scheme [12], but it does not mean that our method is restricted to this scheme.

Randomizing BFV Ciphertexts. Recall that a BFV encryption of a message $m(x)$ is of the form

$$\left(-a(x) \cdot s(x) + \frac{q}{p} \cdot m(x) + e(x), a(x) \right) \in \mathcal{R}_q^2.$$

As secret key owner can recover not only $m(x)$ but also $e(x)$. For this reason, we need to add additional noise $e^*(x)$ such that $|e_i^*| > 2^\sigma \cdot B$ for the function privacy

Parameters: A sender with input $\mathbf{v} \in \mathbb{Z}_t^M$ and a receiver with input $\mathbf{v}^* \in \mathbb{Z}_t^M$ and the target size p.

Protocol:

1. **[Setup]** Two parties agree on a proper HE parameter (n, q) that supports plaintext space $\mathbb{Z}_p^n$, and satisfies IND-CPA security. Then the sender samples a key pair $(\mathsf{sk}, \mathsf{pk})$, and sends the public key pk to the receiver. The sender pads $\mathbf{v}$ by 0 and the receiver pads $\mathbf{v}^*$ by 1, until they have length divisible by n, say $\gamma \cdot n$. Two parties also agree on word base w satisfying $p > \lceil \log_w t \rceil \cdot (w-1)^2$, and define $u = \lceil \log_w t \rceil$.

2. **[Encryption]** Sender performs the following for $0 \leq k < \gamma$:
   (a) Decompose each v_{nk+j} into $\sum_{i=0}^{u-1} v_{j,i} \cdot w^i$ for $1 \leq j \leq n$.
   (b) Batch them into $\mathbf{m}_{k,i} = (v_{j,i})_{1 \leq j \leq n} \in \mathbb{Z}_p^n$ for $0 \leq i < u$.
   (c) Define $\mathbf{m}_{k,u} = (\sum_{i=0}^{u-1} v_{j,i}^2)_{1 \leq j \leq n} \in \mathbb{Z}_p^n$
   (d) Encrypt $\{\mathbf{m}_{k,i}\}$ into $\{\mathsf{ctxt}_{k,i}\}$ using sk and send those ciphertexts to the receiver.

3. **[Compute D and Masking]** Receiver performs the following for $0 \leq k < \gamma$:
   (a) Decompose each v_{nk+j}^* into $\sum_{i=0}^{u-1} v_{j,i}^* \cdot w^i$ for $1 \leq j \leq n$.
   (b) Batch them into $\mathbf{m}_{k,i}^* = (v_{j,i}^*)_{1 \leq j \leq n} \in \mathbb{Z}_p^n$ for $0 \leq i < u$.
   (c) Define $\mathbf{m}_{k,u}^* = (\sum_{i=0}^{u-1} v_{j,i}^{*2})_{1 \leq j \leq n} \in \mathbb{Z}_p^n$
   (d) Compute a ciphertext $\mathsf{ctxt}_{k,d} = \mathsf{ctxt}_{k,u} \oplus \sum_{i=0}^{u-1} (\mathsf{ctxt}_{k,i} \odot 2\mathbf{m}_{k,i}^*) \oplus \mathbf{m}_{k,u}^*$
   (e) Sample a random vector $\mathbf{r}_k^* \in \mathbb{Z}_p^n$.
   (f) Generate an encryption $\mathsf{ctxt}_{fp,k}$ (using pk) of zero of error size B_{fp} which is large enough for function privacy.
   (g) Send back $\mathsf{ctxt}_k := \mathsf{ctxt}_{k,d} \oplus \mathsf{ctxt}_{fp,k} \oplus \mathbf{r}_k^*$ to the sender.

4. **[Decryption]** Sender decrypts ctxt_k to have $\mathbf{r}_k \in \mathbb{Z}_p^n$ for $0 \leq k < \gamma$.

5. **[Finalize]** Sender outputs $\mathbf{r} \in \mathbb{Z}_p^M$ by concatenating every $\mathbf{r}_k$ and cutting the last $\gamma \cdot n - M$ dummy elements. Receiver outputs $\mathbf{r}^* \in \mathbb{Z}_p^M$ by performing the same with $\mathbf{r}_k^*$.

Fig. 6. A full protocol Π_{BEPC} for M batch calls of $\mathcal{F}_{\mathsf{EPC}}$ functionalities

of homomorphic encryption scheme. Here B is upper bound of $e(x)$'s coefficients and σ is the statistical security parameter. This method is called *noise flooding* and this idea is firstly proposed by [15].

Noise Analysis. For the concrete choice of homomorphic encryption parameter, we need to analyze the noise term in our HE-based EPC protocol. Here we will consider the infinity norm $||f(x)||$ which is defined as $\max_i |f_i|$ and the expansion factor of ring $\mathcal{R}$ is defined as $\delta_R = \max\{||f(x) \cdot g(x)||/(||f(x)|| \cdot ||g(x)||) : f(x), g(x) \in \mathcal{R}\}$. In addition, we assume that the noise term of $\mathsf{ctxt}_{k,i}$ in Fig. 6 is bounded by B_{fresh}.

Lemma 1 (Noise growth during homomorphic scalar multiplication).
For the given BFV ciphertext $(b(x), a(x))$ with noise term $e(x)$ such that $\|e(x)\| < B$, the result ciphertext of homomorphic scalar multiplication has noise term $e^*(x)$ such that $\|e^*(x)\| < \delta_R \cdot p \cdot B + \delta_R \cdot p^2$.

Proof. Can be found in the full version [17].

Furthermore, homomorphic addition between two ciphertext with noise bound B_1 and B_2 returns ciphertext with noise bound $B_1 + B_2 + 2p$. Finally, homomorphic addition between ciphertext with noise bound B and plaintext returns ciphertext with noise bound $B + 2p$.

From now on, we can analyze the noise term in our HE-based EPC protocol. This analysis gives us concrete HE parameter choices. If we see Fig. 6, the receiver have to compute following (at 3-(d)):

$$\text{ctxt}_{k,d} = \text{ctxt}_{k,u} \oplus \sum_{i=0}^{u-1} \left(\text{ctxt}_{k,i} \odot 2\mathbf{m}^*_{k,i} \right) \oplus \mathbf{m}^*_{k,u}.$$

By Lemma 1, the noise term of output ciphertext $\text{ctxt}_{k,d}$ will be bounded by $B^* = 2u \cdot (\delta_R \cdot p \cdot B_{\text{fresh}} + \delta_R \cdot p^2) + B_{\text{fresh}} + 4p$. After that we need to add encryption of zero of error size $B_{fp} = 2^\sigma B^*$ for statistic security parameter σ for the function privacy. At last, receiver needs to add random vector $\mathbf{r}^*_k$ to the ciphertext. So, for the correct BFV decryption at the decryption phase, the ciphertext modulus q should satisfies the following inequality:

$$\frac{q}{p} > (2^\sigma + 1) \cdot \left(2u \cdot (\delta_R \cdot p \cdot B_{\text{fresh}} + \delta_R \cdot p^2) + B_{\text{fresh}} + 4p \right) + 2p.$$

Recall that we have $u = O(\log t)$ for the target size $p = O(\log t)$, and therefore we asymptotically have $q = O(\log^4 t)$ where t is input size.

Theorem 1. *The protocol Π_{BEPC} of Fig. 6 realizes M times of $\mathcal{F}_{EPC}$ functionality calls in a semi-honest model if*

$$q > p \cdot (B_{fp} + B^* + 2p)$$

where $B^* = 2u \cdot (\delta_R \cdot p \cdot B_{\text{fresh}} + \delta_R \cdot p^2) + B_{\text{fresh}} + 4p$ and $B_{fp} = 2^\sigma B^*$ for a statistical security parameter σ.

Proof. Can be found in the full version [17].

5   Application to Circuit-PSI Framework

Our equality preserving compression (EPC) of the previous section can be seamlessly augmented to the OPPRF-based circuit-PSI framework described in Sect. 3 as Fig. 7.

Parameters: A receiver with an input set X of size N and a sender with an input set Y of size N, and compression target bit-length ℓ_c.

Protocol:

1. [**Hashing**] Both parties agree on hash functions $h_1, \cdots, h_d$, and table size parameter ε. The receiver construct a cuckoo hash table T_X from X, and the sender constructs a simple hash table T_Y from Y using hash functions $h_1, \cdots, h_d$ into $M = (1 + \varepsilon) \cdot N$ bins. The receiver define the address mapping X to T_X by ι.
2. [**Bin Tagging**] The sender samples uniformly random tags $\mathbf{v} \in \mathbb{Z}_{2^\ell}^M$ and sends $L = \{(y'\|i, v_i)\}_{i \in [M], y' \in T_Y[i]}$ to $\mathcal{F}_{\mathsf{OPPRF}}$. The receiver sends $\tilde{T}_X = \{T_X[i]\|i\}_{i \in [M]}$ to $\mathcal{F}_{\mathsf{OPPRF}}$, and receives $\mathbf{v}^* \in \mathbb{Z}_{2^\ell}^M$ from $\mathcal{F}_{\mathsf{OPPRF}}$.
3. [**Equality Preserving Compression**] The sender sends $\mathbf{v}$ and the receiver sends $\mathbf{v}^*$ to $\mathcal{F}_{\mathsf{EPC}}$, and receives $\mathbf{r} \in \mathbb{Z}_{2^{\ell_c}}^M$ and $\mathbf{r}^* \in \mathbb{Z}_{2^{\ell_c}}^M$ from $\mathcal{F}_{\mathsf{EPC}}$ respectively.
4. [**Equality Share Generation**] For $1 \leq i \leq M$, the sender sends r_i and the receiver sends r_i^* to $\mathcal{F}_{\mathsf{ESG}}$, and receives $\mathbf{s}_{0,i} \in \{0,1\}$ and $\mathbf{s}_{1,i} \in \{0,1\}$ from $\mathcal{F}_{\mathsf{ESG}}$ respectively.

Fig. 7. Π_{CPSI}. Protocol of our circuit-PSI: OPPRF-based framework + EPC

Since EPC perfectly preserve equality (without failure probability), all previous works' analysis for correctness (or failure probability) are still valid. Moreover, as Theorem 1 shows that EPC is secure against semi-honest adversary, the semi-honest security Π_{CPSI} is also guaranteed.

Theorem 2. *The protocol Π_{CPSI} of Fig. 7 realizes the $\mathcal{F}_{CPSI}$ functionality in a semi-honest model in the hybrid model of $\mathcal{F}_{OPPRF}, \mathcal{F}_{EPC}$ and $\mathcal{F}_{ESG}$.*

Effect of EPC. In asymptotic complexity view, the overall cost remains same since EPC itself takes $\tilde{O}(\ell)$ complexities. Thus, we have to figure out concrete costs to see the effect of EPC. We already observe that known methods for ESG has linear cost in ℓ_c, and in particular GMW protocol requires about $2M\ell_c$ (correlated) OTs. For EPC from ℓ-bit to ℓ_c-bit, the word-size w should be maximally taken so that $2^{\ell_c} \approx \frac{(w-1)^2}{\log w} \cdot \ell$, and it determines the corresponding chunk size $u = \ell / \log w$. Then EPC takes u times homomorphic operations including encryption, scalar multiplication, decryption, and addition with communication of u number of ciphertext. We point that n times of EPC calls can be done at once, thanks to batching property. Thus, as ESG input bit-length reduces from ℓ to ℓ_c thanks to EPC, we can save $2n(\ell - \ell_c)$ the number of OTs from $\approx u$ times of HE operations. More precisely, we have the trade-off below:

$$2n(\ell - \ell_c) \times \text{correlated-OTs}$$
$$\updownarrow$$
$$u \times \text{HE encryptions, scalar-mults, additions, and Ciphertext Comm.}$$

One may think that HE operations are incomparably slow than OT, and hence this trade-off provides no benefit. However, we would like emphasize that our HE operations only consist of scalar multiplication and additions: HE scalar multiplication is just two polynomial multiplication with degree n which is quite fast compare to multiplication between encrypted data. For a concrete example, we may take $n = 4096$, $\ell = 61$, $\ell_c = 19$, and $u = 8$, which is one of exploited parameters in later experiment section. This reduces $344,064$ number of chosen-message OTs at the cost of 8 homomorphic scalar multiplication, 10 homomorphic additions, and 8 HE ciphertext communications.

Round Complexity. On round complexity view, one may think EPC requires additional one communication round than vanilla OPPRF-based framework. However, we remark that ESG stage takes $O(\log \ell)$ rounds for input length ℓ when performed by GMW protocol. Since EPC reduces ESG input length into $\ell_c = O(\log \ell)$, EPC indeed brings asymptotic improvement on the round complexity when GMW protocol is used.

6 Performance Evaluation

In this section, we evaluate the performance of several instantiation of our circuit-PSI protocol of Sect. 5. More precisely, we first discuss concrete parameter selections of sub-protocols, especially with respect to the compression target ℓ_c. Then we evaluate the performances of several combinations of our EPC protocol and previous ESG protocols. Finally, we provide full circuit-PSI protocol costs evaluation by attaching previous hashing and OPPRF steps, and some consequences of our protocols.

Throughout this section, we assume computational security parameter $\lambda = 128$ and statistical security parameter $\sigma = 40$. For experiments, we use a single machine equipped with 3.50 GHz Intel Xeon processors with 128 GBs of RAM. The network environments are simulated by `linux tc` command. LAN represents 5 Gbps bandwidth with 0.6 ms RTT, and WAN denotes 100 Mbps bandwidth with 80 ms RTT. All experiments are executed with a single thread on each party in order to be consistent with previous works. For implementation, we use SEAL [28] library for homomorphic encryption, libOTe library [26] for IKNP and Silver OTe [10], and emp-ot library [29] for Ferret OTe [30].

6.1 Parameter Selections

OPPRF Output Length ℓ. In our circuit-PSI framework, the output of OPPRF is directly fed into EPC or ESG. The OPPRF output length is taken by $\ell = \sigma + \lceil \log M \rceil$ to ensure failure probability less than $2^{-\sigma}$ (See Eq. 2) where $M = (1+\varepsilon) \cdot N$ is cuckoo/simple hash table size with d hash functions. We use $\varepsilon = 0.27$ and $d = 3$ by following previous works [24,27], and then OPPRF output length is given by $\ell = \sigma + 1 + \lceil \log N \rceil$.

HE Parameters. First of all, we fix HE ring dimension $n = 2^{12}$ which is the minimal one supporting depth-1 scalar multiplication. For the choice of HE plaintext modulus p, it is quite obvious that the full batch case would be the most efficient. Thus we take p to support full batch, whose concrete choice is a prime integer satisfying $p = 1 \mod 2n$. The minimal prime satisfying $p = 1 \mod 2n$ is $p = 40961$, and hence the minimal possible ℓ_c is $\lceil \log(40961) \rceil = 16$. For $\ell_c > 16$, there are several primes p such that $p = 1 \mod 2n$, and we choose maximal p among them for each ℓ_c. We then choose the word-base w by the maximal one satisfying the correctness condition $p > u \cdot (w-1)^2$, where $u = \lceil \ell / \log w \rceil$ is the number of chunks. Then we have several ℓ_c for the same chunk number u. Since EPC costs are mainly determined by u rather than ℓ_c, it is convenient to arrange parameters with respect to the chunk size u. To minimize the total cost, we choose the minimal ℓ_c for each u.

It remains to determine HE ciphertext modulus q. We first take an initial modulus q' by the minimal one where our protocol is correct, and then the final modulus q is augmented by σ-bit margin on q' for function privacy. It empirically holds that $\log q \approx \sigma + 2 \log p + \log n$. To finalize parameter selection, we have to consider concrete attack cost of resulting parameters. We found that small chunk number $u \leq 3$ leads too large ciphertext modulus q that makes the parameters has far less than $\lambda = 128$-level of security. Therefore, we only conduct experiments with chunk number $u \geq 4$. More detailed HE and EPC parameters are presented in Appendix A.

6.2   Choice of ℓ_c with ESG

First recall that state-of-the-art OTe like Silver [10] and Ferret [30] already have extremely low communication cost. As a consequence, combining EPC with ESG rather leads to larger communication cost than sole ESG. Thus, we have to weigh the gain from EPC on computational cost and the loss from EPC on communication cost. It clearly depends on the network environment, and hence we conduct several experiments for several ℓ_c over different network environments. Some results are visualized in Fig. 8. Generally, smaller ℓ_c leads to heavier EPC and lighter ESG, but the trade-off rate and the optimal point differ by network environment.

As expected, EPC effect is positive on LAN network as it reduces the computation burden, but negative in WAN network due to the communication cost growth. One can see that Silver [10] is always better than Ferret [30], but the both cases deserve to consider since the performance gain of Silver comes from so far non-standard assumption.

Another ESG Considerations. We also consider IKNP-OTe [20] for GMW protocol. It is obvious that IKNP is less competitive than Silver/Ferret for WAN, since it requires much larger communication; it requires more than 2500 MB communication for $N = 2^{20}$ [24], while Silver/Ferret requires only 38 MB. One may at least expect that it could be the best for LAN setting, but our internal

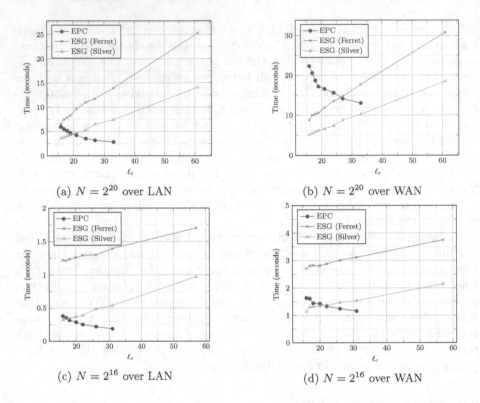

Fig. 8. Timing result of EPC and ESG on several network bandwidths and OTe protocols.

experiments show that IKNP and Silver have similar performance even on LAN environment. Thus we decide to omit IKNP results in tables.

6.3 Impact on Circuit-PSI

Toward a complete circuit-PSI protocol, we only have to attach hash step and OPPRF step before ESG. For that, we note that the choice of OPPRF has no relation with the post ESG and EPC phase. It implies that, regardless of the choice of OPPRF, the absolute amount of effect of EPC remains same. However, it is still important to consider full circuit-PSI cost; if ESG part occupies only a little portion of full circuit-PSI, our EPC leads to tiny improvement on circuit-PSI.

To argue that our EPC has a meaningful effect on circuit-PSI protocols, we implement one of state-of-the-art OPPRF protocols due to [6] as an example. The details are presented in Table 1. Our experiments indicates that EPC brings 10–40% speed-up over LAN environment, and small speed-up on WAN environment when ESG is done with Ferret OTe.

We end with a final remark. According to our implementation, OPPRF step occupies 20–60% of full circuit-PSI running time, as the rightmost column of Table 1 shows. Regarding this, we found further advances on OPPRF has been

Table 1. Resulting circuit-PSI performances obtained by attaching OPPRF protocol of [6] before ESG. Communications in MB, and timings in seconds.

Circuit-PSI $N = 2^{16}$	OTe	Ours (w/EPC)		Prev. (No EPC)		OPPRF [6]	
		Time	Comm.	Time	Comm.	Time	Comm.
LAN	Silver	**1.233**	21.96	1.549	12.21	0.576	9.87
	Ferret	**2.091**	20.69	2.278	12.09		
WAN	Silver	5.264	21.01	**4.703**	12.21	2.552	
	Ferret	6.770	20.89	**6.303**	12.09		

Circuit-PSI $N = 2^{20}$	OTe	Ours (w/EPC)		Prev. (No EPC)		OPPRF [6]	
		Time	Comm.	Time	Comm.	Time	Comm.
LAN	Silver	**16.65**	344.0	21.82	195.7	7.75	157.5
	Ferret	**20.17**	394.3	33.08	195.6		
WAN	Silver	45.39	327.0	**40.96**	195.7	22.46	
	Ferret	**50.48**	343.9	53.25	195.6		

reported, and hence OPPRF has smaller portion in total circuit-PSI [14,27]. Thus the relative benefit of EPC becomes larger, which makes our EPC technique more valuable.

A   HE and EPC Parameters

Below shows detailed parameter information that is used in our experiment. For all cases, ring dimension in HE scheme is fixed with 4096. And, this parameter satisfied 128 security based on homomorphic encryption standard document [1] (except the last row, as maximal possible $\log q$ for 4096 dimension is 109) (Table 2).

Table 2. HE and EPC parameters in our evaluations.

N	u	p	$\log q$	w	ℓ_c	N	u	p	$\log q$	w	ℓ_c
2^{16}	10	40961	84	65	16	2^{20}	10	114689	86	108	17
	9	114689	86	113	17		9	188417	88	145	18
	8	188417	88	154	18		8	417793	90	229	19
	7	1032193	92	385	20		7	2056193	94	542	21
	6	4169729	96	834	22		6	16760833	100	1672	24
	5	67094289	104	3663	26		5	134176769	106	5181	27
	4	2147377153	114	23170	31		4	8589852673	118	46341	33

References

1. Albrecht, M., et al.: Homomorphic encryption security standard. Technical report, HomomorphicEncryption.org, Toronto, Canada (2018)
2. Asharov, G., Lindell, Y., Schneider, T., Zohner, M.: More efficient oblivious transfer and extensions for faster secure computation. In: ACM CCS, pp. 535–548 (2013)
3. Bajard, J.-C., Eynard, J., Hasan, M.A., Zucca, V.: A full RNS variant of FV like somewhat homomorphic encryption schemes. In: Avanzi, R., Heys, H. (eds.) SAC 2016. LNCS, vol. 10532, pp. 423–442. Springer, Cham (2017). https://doi.org/10.1007/978-3-319-69453-5_23
4. Boyle, E., et al.: Efficient two-round OT extension and silent non-interactive secure computation. In: ACM CCS, pp. 291–308 (2019)
5. Buddhavarapu, P., Knox, A., Mohassel, P., Sengupta, S., Taubeneck, E., Vlaskin, V.: Private matching for compute. IACR Cryptology ePrint Archive 2020/599 (2020)
6. Chandran, N., Gupta, D., Shah, A.: Circuit-PSI with linear complexity via relaxed batch OPPRF. Cryptology ePrint Archive, Report 2021/034 (2021). https://eprint.iacr.org/2021/034
7. Chen, H., Huang, Z., Laine, K., Rindal, P.: Labeled PSI from fully homomorphic encryption with malicious security. In: ACM CCS, pp. 1223–1237 (2018)
8. Chen, H., Laine, K., Rindal, P.: Fast private set intersection from homomorphic encryption. In: ACM CCS, pp. 1243–1255 (2017)
9. Ciampi, M., Orlandi, C.: Combining private set-intersection with secure two-party computation. In: Catalano, D., De Prisco, R. (eds.) SCN 2018. LNCS, vol. 11035, pp. 464–482. Springer, Cham (2018). https://doi.org/10.1007/978-3-319-98113-0_25
10. Couteau, G., Rindal, P., Raghuraman, S.: Silver: silent VOLE and oblivious transfer from hardness of decoding structured LDPC codes. In: Malkin, T., Peikert, C. (eds.) CRYPTO 2021. LNCS, vol. 12827, pp. 502–534. Springer, Cham (2021). https://doi.org/10.1007/978-3-030-84252-9_17
11. Demmler, D., Schneider, T., Zohner, M.: ABY-A framework for efficient mixed-protocol secure two-party computation. In: NDSS (2015)
12. Fan, J., Vercauteren, F.: Somewhat practical fully homomorphic encryption. IACR Cryptology ePrint Archive 2012/144 (2012)
13. Garimella, G., Mohassel, P., Rosulek, M., Sadeghian, S., Singh, J.: Private set operations from oblivious switching. In: Garay, J.A. (ed.) PKC 2021. LNCS, vol. 12711, pp. 591–617. Springer, Cham (2021). https://doi.org/10.1007/978-3-030-75248-4_21
14. Garimella, G., Pinkas, B., Rosulek, M., Trieu, N., Yanai, A.: Oblivious key-value stores and amplification for private set intersection. In: Malkin, T., Peikert, C. (eds.) CRYPTO 2021. LNCS, vol. 12826, pp. 395–425. Springer, Cham (2021). https://doi.org/10.1007/978-3-030-84245-1_14
15. Gentry, C., et al.: A fully homomorphic encryption scheme. Ph.D. thesis, Standford University (2009)
16. Goldreich, O., Micali, S., Wigderson, A.: How to play ANY mental game. In: STOC, pp. 218–229. Association for Computing Machinery, New York (1987)
17. Han, K., Moon, D., Son, Y.: Improved circuit-based PSI via equality preserving compression. Cryptology ePrint Archive, Paper 2021/1440 (2021). https://eprint.iacr.org/2021/1440

18. Huang, Y., Evans, D., Katz, J.: Private set intersection: are garbled circuits better than custom protocols? In: NDSS (2012)
19. Ion, M., et al.: On deploying secure computing: private intersection-sum-with-cardinality. In: EuroS&P, pp. 370–389. IEEE (2020)
20. Ishai, Y., Kilian, J., Nissim, K., Petrank, E.: Extending oblivious transfers efficiently. In: Boneh, D. (ed.) CRYPTO 2003. LNCS, vol. 2729, pp. 145–161. Springer, Heidelberg (2003). https://doi.org/10.1007/978-3-540-45146-4_9
21. Kolesnikov, V., Kumaresan, R., Rosulek, M., Trieu, N.: Efficient batched oblivious PRF with applications to private set intersection. In: ACM CCS, pp. 818–829 (2016)
22. Kolesnikov, V., Matania, N., Pinkas, B., Rosulek, M., Trieu, N.: Practical multi-party private set intersection from symmetric-key techniques. In: ACM CCS, pp. 1257–1272 (2017)
23. Pinkas, B., Schneider, T., Segev, G., Zohner, M.: Phasing: private set intersection using permutation-based hashing. In: USENIX Security, Washington, D.C., pp. 515–530. USENIX Association (2015)
24. Pinkas, B., Schneider, T., Tkachenko, O., Yanai, A.: Efficient circuit-based PSI with linear communication. In: Ishai, Y., Rijmen, V. (eds.) EUROCRYPT 2019. LNCS, vol. 11478, pp. 122–153. Springer, Cham (2019). https://doi.org/10.1007/978-3-030-17659-4_5
25. Pinkas, B., Schneider, T., Weinert, C., Wieder, U.: Efficient circuit-based PSI via cuckoo hashing. In: Nielsen, J., Rijmen, V. (eds.) EUROCRYPT 2018. LNCS, vol. 10822, pp. 125–157. Springer, Cham (2018). https://doi.org/10.1007/978-3-319-78372-7_5
26. Rindal, P.: libOTe: an efficient, portable, and easy to use Oblivious Transfer Library. https://github.com/osu-crypto/libOTe
27. Rindal, P., Schoppmann, P.: VOLE-PSI: fast OPRF and circuit-PSI from vector-OLE. In: Canteaut, A., Standaert, F.X. (eds.) EUROCRYPT 2021. LNCS, vol. 12697, pp. 901–930. Springer, Cham (2021). https://doi.org/10.1007/978-3-030-77886-6_31
28. Microsoft SEAL (release 3.5). Microsoft Research, Redmond (2020). https://github.com/microsoft/SEAL
29. Wang, X., Malozemoff, A.J., Katz, J.: EMP-toolkit: efficient MultiParty computation toolkit (2016). https://github.com/emp-toolkit
30. Yang, K., Weng, C., Lan, X., Zhang, J., Wang, X.: Ferret: fast extension for correlated OT with small communication. In: Proceedings of the 2020 ACM SIGSAC Conference on Computer and Communications Security, pp. 1607–1626 (2020)

Isogeny-based Cryptography I

Revisiting Meet-in-the-Middle Cryptanalysis of SIDH/SIKE with Application to the $IKEp182 Challenge

Aleksei Udovenko[1]([⊠]) and Giuseppe Vitto[2]

[1] CryptoExperts, Paris, France
aleksei@affine.group
[2] SnT, University of Luxembourg, Esch-sur-Alzette, Luxembourg
giuseppe.vitto@uni.lu

Abstract. This work focuses on concrete cryptanalysis of the isogeny-based cryptosystems SIDH/SIKE under realistic memory/storage constraints. More precisely, we are solving the problem of finding an isogeny of a given smooth degree between two given supersingular elliptic curves. Recent works by Adj et al. (SAC 2018), Costello et al. (PKC 2020), Longa et al. (CRYPTO 2021) suggest that parallel "memoryless" golden collision search by van Oorschot-Wiener (JoC 1999) is the best realistic approach for the problem. We show instead that the classic meet-in-the-middle attack is still competitive due to its very low computational overhead, at least on small parameters.

As a concrete application, we apply the meet-in-the-middle attack with optimizations to the $IKEp182 challenge posed by Microsoft Research. The attack was executed on a cluster and required less than 10 core-years and 256 TiB of high-performance network storage (GPFS). Different trade-offs allow execution of the attack with similar time complexity and reduced storage requirements of only about 70 TiB.

Keywords: Isogenies · Cryptanalysis · SIDH · SIKE · Meet-in-the-Middle · Set Intersection

1 Introduction

Under the threat of quantum computers appearing in the near future, public-key cryptography has to evolve to keep modern communication protocols secure. To foster the evolution, NIST organizes a competition for Post-Quantum Cryptography Standardization (PQC) [13]. SIKE [9] (Supersingular Isogeny Key Encapsulation) is one of the alternate candidates of the ongoing 3rd round. It is based on

The work of Giuseppe Vitto was supported by the Luxembourg National Research Fund (FNR) project FinCrypt (C17/IS/11684537). The experiments presented in this paper were carried out using the HPC facilities of the University of Luxembourg [24] – see https://hpc.uni.lu.

the SIDH protocol (Supersingular Isogeny Diffie-Hellman) developed by De Feo and Jao [10] (and Plût [7]), following and improving the ideas of the constructions proposed by Couveignes, Rostovtsev and Stolbunov [6,15,19]. *Isogeny*-based cryptography only recently gained attention and started to develop rapidly.

In particular, for a specially shaped prime p, the security of SIKE relies on the hardness of finding an isogeny between two given supersingular elliptic curves defined over the finite field $\mathbb{F}_{p^2}$ (the so-called *computational supersingular isogeny* problem, CSSI). The classic meet-in-the-middle attack (MitM, also known as bidirectional search), applied in the isogeny setting by Galbraith [8], requires $\mathcal{O}(p^{1/4})$ time and memory/storage in the SIKE setting. Adj, Cervantes-Vazquez, Chi-Domínguez, Menezes and Rodríguez-Henríquez [1] observed that large amounts of storage are likely impossible to be achieved in practice due to fundamental physical constraints. They thus applied the classic low-memory van Oorschot-Wiener (vOW) golden collision search [23] to the isogeny setting by using less memory at the expense of more time, and conjectured that this attack represents the main threat to SIKE. Improved analysis of the application of van Oorschot-Wiener to SIKE with further optimizations was given by Costello, Longa, Naehrig, Renes and Virdia [5]. Based on this analysis, Longa, Wang and Szefer [11] estimated the real costs of mounting such attack at various security levels, concluded that previous security estimates were conservative, and proposed to revise parameters in order to improve efficiency. For example, they propose to replace SIKEp434 with SIKEp377, which is 40% faster, while still targeting to satisfy NIST Level 1 security requirements.

In order to motivate security analysis of SIKE, Microsoft recently published two challenges [12] with reduced-size instances of SIKE: \$IKEp182 and \$IKEp217. The classic security of the instances via the meet-in-the-middle attack amounts to only about 2^{45} and 2^{55} isogeny evaluations and storage units, respectively. However, such amount of memory (2^{45} storage units $\geq$ 256 TiB) is not trivial to manage efficiently.

In this work, we revisit the application of the classic MitM attack to the isogeny search problem. While it requires efficient usage of large amounts of memory/storage, it has much lower computational overhead than the vOW method, where, for example, a single step requires computing expensive isogenies (which can instead be amortized in MitM), and large penalties are paid to reduce the memory usage. We focus on optimizing the application of MitM to the SIKE cryptosystem and show how to efficiently use disk-based high-performance storage which is more practical than RAM memory. As a concrete application, we solve the \$IKEp182 challenge on a high-performance cluster. We estimate that the attack can in principle be executed in at most 9.5 core-years using about 70 TiB of high-performance storage. Our implementation is mainly written in SageMath [21] and C++, using parts of the SIDH library [22]. It will be publicly available at https://github.com/cryptolu/SIKE_MitM.

1.1   Our Approach

At the high level, we used the classic meet-in-the-middle approach for solving the isogeny path problem, in which the hardness of SIKE lies. We applied and improved several existing optimizations from both MitM and vOW settings in the literature, namely:

2-bit Leak from the Knowledge of the Final Curve. In [5], it was noted that the final curve (i.e., the image of the initial curve through a secret 2^e-isogeny) fully leaks the last 4-isogeny. This effectively reduces by a factor of 4 the set of j-invariants reachable from the final curve that need to be considered.

In addition, we show how to express this reduced set in the same form as the set of j-invariants reached from the initial curve. This simplifies conceptually the MitM application to SIKE, by unifying the representation of sets arising from the initial and the final curves.

1-bit Conjugation-Based Reduction. In SIKE, the initial Montgomery curve is $y^2 = x^3 + 6x^2 + x$, and by being defined over $\mathbb{F}_p$, almost all the curves ℓ-isogenous over $\mathbb{F}_{p^2}$ to it (through SIKE isogenies), have j-invariants which can be grouped in conjugate pairs. It is thus sufficient to search for a collision of e.g. half of the trace of the j-invariants in the middle, to effectively halve the size of the set arising from the initial curve. Recovering the full colliding j-invariant from such partial collision is easy due to the fact that paths to conjugate elements are element-wise conjugates. This technique was discovered and applied in the vOW setting in [5].

Depth-First Tree Exploration. A direct application of meet-in-the-middle with the (optimized) arithmetic from SIKE would recompute a lot of intermediate steps repeatedly (simply speaking, computing each entry in the middle would require following a full path from the root of a full binary tree to its leaf). It was shown in [1] how to perform depth-first tree exploration (denoted MITM-DFS) by maintaining a basis allowing to generate full current subtree. This idea was also partially used in the vOW attack in [5] for precomputing first levels of the tree.

In addition, we developed the following new optimizations:

Efficient Arithmetic for MITM-DFS. Whereas the work [1] relied on generic Vélu's formulas for computing isogenies on Weierstrass elliptic curves, we show how to adapt the MITM-DFS tree exploration method to the highly optimized x-only isogeny arithmetic on Montgomery elliptic curves used in SIKE.

Optimal Strategy for the Tree Variant of the Isogeny/Multiplication Trade-off. In the work proposing SIDH [7], the authors showed how to compute an optimal strategic trade-off between the number of ℓ-isogeny evaluations and point multiplications during an ℓ^e-isogeny computation. We show how an analogue of this strategy can be applied to explore the search tree more efficiently. This is an optimization of the MITM-DFS technique.

Disk-Based Storage and Sorting. It is much more feasible to obtain and use a large amount of disk-based storage, than a similar amount of RAM memory.

However, the classic meet-in-the-middle formulation uses a (hash-)table where the majority of queries follow a random access pattern, most suitable for RAM. When disk storage is used, latency represents the bottleneck of using hash-tables, and limits the application of parallelization. To counter this, we follow an alternative approach to implement the MitM attack: we generate the two large j-invariants sets arising from the starting and the final curves, and we intersect them using *sorting* and *merging* algorithms, which, instead, mostly perform local or sequential access patterns.

A similar idea was suggested by Bernstein [2] for searching collisions of hash functions using a 2-dimensional grid of devices (mesh sorting using an optimal algorithm by Schnorr and Shamir [16]); the authors of [1] also estimated performance of mesh sorting applied to the isogeny path problem, but considered only $p \geq 2^{448}$ and concluded that it is not competitive.

Storage-Collision Trade-off and Compression. Truncating intermediate entries (j-invariants representations) permits to reduce storage requirements at the cost of allowing false-positive collisions. By omitting all the auxiliary information (e.g. the path in the set to an entry), we can reduce the storage further at the cost of an extra recomputation step, where the two sets are recomputed (fully memoryless and in parallel) in order to retrieve the relevant auxiliary information for collisions found in the previous step. Furthermore, the resulting sets become *dense* due to the truncation of entries, and can be compressed (when sorted) by storing the differences between successive elements. In the case of \$IKEp182, we used 64-bit entries, which already at 32 GiB of sorted data (2^{32} truncated entries) have the expected difference of about 32 bits. This reduces the total storage requirements down to approximately $2^{44} \times 2 \times 4$ bytes $= 128$ TiB.

2   Preliminaries

2.1   Isogenies Between Supersingular Elliptic Curves

An *isogeny* of elliptic curves $\phi : E \to E'$ defined over $\mathbb{F}_q$ is a surjective morphism of curves that induces a group homomorphism $E(\overline{\mathbb{F}}_q) \to E'(\overline{\mathbb{F}}_q)$. When such a map is defined over $\mathbb{F}_q$, E and E' are said to be isogenous over $\mathbb{F}_q$. By Tate's Isogeny Theorem [20], two curves are isogenous over $\mathbb{F}_q$ if and only if they have the same number of points in $\mathbb{F}_q$.

In this work, we only consider *separable* isogenies, whose kernel has size equal to the degree of the respective rational map. We call an isogeny of degree ℓ an ℓ-isogeny. Separable isogenies $\phi : E(\overline{\mathbb{F}}_q) \to E'(\overline{\mathbb{F}}_q)$ (up to isomorphism) are in bijections with subgroups G of $E(\overline{\mathbb{F}}_q)$ so that $\ker(\phi) = G$ and ϕ is a $|G|$-isogeny: in such case, the curve E' as group is isomorphic to the group quotient E/G. When $p \nmid \ell$, the ℓ-torsion $E[\ell]$ of an elliptic curve E defined over a field of characteristic p has structure isomorphic to $\mathbb{Z}_\ell \times \mathbb{Z}_\ell$ and $\ell + 1$ cyclic subgroups of order ℓ if ℓ is prime.

For every separable degree-d isogeny $\phi : E \to E'$, there exists a dual degree-d isogeny $\hat{\phi} : E' \to E$ so that the maps $\phi \circ \hat{\phi} = [d]_E$ and $\hat{\phi} \circ \phi = [d]_{E'}$ are the multiplication-by-d endomorphisms on E and E', respectively.

If ℓ is composite, it is possible to decompose a ℓ-isogeny into a composition of isogenies of prime orders. This property allows, in practice, to compute efficiently high (smooth) degree isogenies. More precisely, if $\ell = p_0^{e_0} \cdot \ldots \cdot p_n^{e_n}$ and ϕ is a ℓ-isogeny, then there exists p_i-isogenies $\phi_j^{p_i}$ for $i \in [0, n], j \in [1, e_i]$, so that $\phi = \phi_1^{p_0} \circ \ldots \circ \phi_{e_0}^{p_0} \circ \ldots \circ \phi_1^{p_n} \circ \ldots \circ \phi_{e_n}^{p_n}$.

In the following, we will only consider separable isogenies over *Montgomery elliptic curves*, which are parametrized[1] by $A \in \mathbb{F}_q, A \neq 4$ and are defined by the equation $E_A \; : \; y^2 = x^3 + Ax^2 + x$

Two elliptic curves are $\overline{\mathbb{F}}_q$-isomorphic if they have the same j-invariant. The j-invariant of a Montgomery elliptic curve E_A is equal to $j(E_A) = \frac{256(A^2-3)^3}{A^2-4}$.

The trace t of an elliptic curve E defined over $\mathbb{F}_q$ is the integer satisfying $\#E(\mathbb{F}_q) = q + 1 - t$. An elliptic curve is called *supersingular* if it is defined over a field of characteristic p and has trace t congruent to 0 mod p. The j-invariant of a supersingular elliptic curve belongs to $\mathbb{F}_{p^2}$ (see [18, V.3 - Theorem 3.1.a]). In fact, any supersingular curve is isomorphic to an elliptic curve defined over $\mathbb{F}_{p^2}$. From Tate's Isogeny Theorem it follows that the set of supersingular elliptic curves is closed under isogenies. We conclude that the property of being supersingular is induced by curves' j-invariants: if there is a supersingular curve with j-invariant equal to j, then j is said to be a *supersingular j-invariant* and all curves having j as j-invariant are supersingular too. For any prime p, there exist approximately $\lfloor \frac{p+1}{12} \rfloor$ supersingular j-invariants [17, Theorem 4.6].

For any fixed j-invariant and a positive integer $\ell, p \nmid \ell$, any curve E with $j(E) = j$ has the same set of $\ell+1$ ℓ-isogenous curves (up to isomorphism), with the isogenies being defined by the distinct order-ℓ subgroups of the torsion $\mathbb{Z}_\ell \times \mathbb{Z}_\ell$. An order-$\ell^e$ kernel on a supersingular elliptic curve defines a decomposition of the respective ℓ^e-isogeny into e ℓ-isogenies, which we shall call a *walk*.

Definition 1 (Walk). *Let E_0 be a supersingular elliptic curve over $\mathbb{F}_{p^2}$, ℓ a prime distinct from p and let (P_0, Q_0) be two independent generators of $E_0[\ell^e] = \mathbb{Z}_{\ell^e} \times \mathbb{Z}_{\ell^e}$. Two values $a, b \in \mathbb{Z}_{\ell^e}$ not simultaneously divisible by ℓ, define a separable ℓ^e-isogeny $\phi = \phi_{e-1} \circ \ldots \circ \phi_0 : E_0 \to E_e$ over $\mathbb{F}_{p^2}$, where, for $i \in [0, e-1]$, $\phi_i : E_i \to E_{i+1}$ is an ℓ-isogeny with $\ker(\phi_i) = \langle [\ell^{e-1-i}] \cdot ([a]P_i + [b]Q_i) \rangle$ and $(P_{i+1}, Q_{i+1}) = (\phi_i(P_i), \phi_i(Q_i))$. We will often refer to such ϕ as the isogeny arising from $[a]P + [b]Q$.*

Remark 1. If $\ell \nmid a$, then $\langle [a]P + [b]Q \rangle = \langle P + [s]Q \rangle$, with $s = a^{-1}b \in \mathbb{Z}_{\ell^e}$, and such subgroups give rise to ℓ^e distinct isogenies. If instead $a = \ell \cdot c$, kernels can be written as $\langle [s\ell]P + Q \rangle$, with $s = b^{-1}c \in \mathbb{Z}_{\ell^e}$ and there exists at most ℓ^{e-1} such distinct subgroups. This brings the total number of walks that can be traversed from a starting curve F_0 to $\ell^{e-1}(\ell + 1)$, which in turn correspond to all walks obtained by iteratively exploring all $\ell+1$ neighbours of E_0 up to depth e (with no backtracking). Kernels of the form $\langle P + [s]Q \rangle$, with $s \in \mathbb{Z}_{\ell^e}$, are the ones employed by SIKE (Subsect. 2.2): we note that this choice restricts the possible

---

[1] More general Montgomery curves are given by $E_{A,B} = By^2 = x^3 + Ax^2 + x$, however the values of B are not relevant for our work.

isogeny-paths that can be walked, since only ℓ out of $\ell + 1$ neighbours of E_0 are explored.

Problem 1 (CSSI). Given two elliptic curves E and E' and integers ℓ, e such that there exists a separable isogeny $\phi : E \rightarrow E'$ of degree ℓ^e, compute ϕ (up to isomorphism) or, equivalently, find (a generator of) the subgroup G of $E[\ell^e]$ such that $E' \cong E/G$.

In practice, it suffices to find a composition of e ℓ-isogenies between the two curves, i.e., a length-e walk from E to E'. Then, a solution to Problem 1 can be efficiently recovered from the composition in a digit-by-digit (in base ℓ) manner.

2.2   SIDH and SIKE

Supersingular Isogeny Key Encapsulation (SIKE) [9] is a post-quantum key encapsulation mechanism (KEM) based on the difficulty of computing/finding an isogeny between two ℓ^e-isogenous elliptic curves (Problem 1). It is based on the Supersingular Isogeny Diffie-Hellman (SIDH) [10] key exchange. The public-key encryption and key encapsulation mechanisms in SIKE are derived from the basic key exchange protocol (SIDH), which we focus on.

In SIDH/SIKE, the prime p has the form $p = 2^{e_A} 3^{e_B} - 1$ with $2^{e_A} \approx 3^{e_B}$ and the working field is set to be $\mathbb{F}_{p^2} = \mathbb{F}_p[i]/(i^2 + 1)$. The parameters e_A and e_B are chosen so that the Montgomery curve $E = E_6$ over $\mathbb{F}_{p^2}$ is supersingular with $(p+1)^2$ rational points and torsions $E[\ell_A^{e_A}] = \mathbb{Z}_{\ell_A^{e_A}} \times \mathbb{Z}_{\ell_A^{e_A}} = \langle P_A, Q_A \rangle$ and $E[\ell_B^{e_B}] = \mathbb{Z}_{\ell_B^{e_B}} \times \mathbb{Z}_{\ell_B^{e_B}} = \langle P_B, Q_B \rangle$.

Once the public parameters $(p, E(\mathbb{F}_{p^2}), P_A, Q_A, P_B, Q_B)$ are generated, two parties, Alice and Bob, can agree on a common secret as follows:

- Alice picks secret $s_A \xleftarrow{\$} \mathbb{Z}_{2^{e_A}}$ and computes the 2^{e_A}-isogeny $\phi_A : E \rightarrow E_A$ with $\ker \phi_A = \langle P_A + [s_A]Q_A \rangle$. She then sends to Bob E_A and the points $\phi_A(P_B), \phi_A(Q_B)$.
- Bob picks secret $s_B \xleftarrow{\$} \mathbb{Z}_{3^{e_B}}$ and computes the 3^{e_B}-isogeny $\phi_B : E \rightarrow E_B$ with $\ker \phi_B = \langle P_B + [s_b]Q_B \rangle$. He then sends to Alice E_B and the points $\phi_B(P_A), \phi_B(Q_A)$.
- Alice computes the 2^{e_A}-isogeny $\phi_{\tilde{A}} : E_B \rightarrow E_{BA}$ with $\ker \phi_{\tilde{A}} = \langle \phi_B(P_A) + [s_A]\phi_B(Q_A) \rangle$ and sets the common secret to $j(E_{BA})$.
- Bob computes the 3^{e_B}-isogeny $\phi_{\tilde{B}} : E_A \rightarrow E_{AB}$ with $\phi_{\tilde{B}} = \langle \phi_A(P_B) + [s_B]\phi_A(Q_B) \rangle$ and sets the common secret to $j(E_{AB})$.

It easy to see that, since separable isogenies correspond to curve quotients, in this setting they commute, and so $j(E_{BA}) = j(E_{AB})$. For more details and proof of correctness of the above protocol we refer to [9,10].

The original version of SIDH [7] proposed to choose the kernel of the shape $\langle [s]P + [s']Q \rangle$ instead of $\langle P + [s]Q \rangle$. The latter version, adopted in SIKE and in the implementation of SIDH [22], reduces the number of possible kernels from $\ell^{e-1}(\ell + 1)$ to ℓ^e. In SIKE, it also avoids some technicalities introduced by adopting efficient 2-isogeny computation formulas: the order-2 point $(0,0)$ is not allowed to belong to the isogeny kernel $\langle P_A + [s]Q_A \rangle$ with $s \in \mathbb{Z}_{2^{e_A}}$. Thanks to a result of Renes [14, Corollary 2], this is guaranteed by choosing the generators P_A, Q_A of the torsion $E[2^{e_A}]$ so that $[2^{e_A-1}]Q_A = (0,0)$.

2.3 Efficient Isogeny Computation

In this section we provide an overview of how isogenies, and thus walks in the isogeny graph, can be practically and efficiently computed. We will focus on 2-isogenies, relevant for SIKE and for our attacks. Proofs that the following formulas define isogenies can be found, for example, in [3,14]. We shall distinguish isogenies based on these specific formulas as "SIKE 2-isogenies".

Proposition 1 (SIKE 2-isogeny). *Let $E_{A,B}$ be a Montgomery supersingular elliptic curve over $\mathbb{F}_{p^2}$ and let $R = (x_R, y_R) \in E(\mathbb{F}_{p^2})$ be an order 2 point not equal to $(0,0)$. Then,*

$$\phi : E_A \longrightarrow E_{A'}$$
$$(x,y) \longmapsto (f(x), yf'(x))$$

with

$$f(x) = x \frac{x \cdot x_R - 1}{x - x_R}$$

is a separable 2-isogeny between Montgomery elliptic curves with $\mathrm{ker}(\phi) = \langle R \rangle$ and $A' = 2 - 4x_R^2$.

Remark 2. The 2-isogeny defined in Proposition 1 fixes the point $(0,0)$, and thus cannot belong to its kernel.

An illustration of how the 6 possible curves in a given isomorphism class interact by SIKE 2-isogenies is given in the full version of this paper.

3 Meet-in-the-Middle Attack on SIKE

In this section we will provide an overview of the meet-in-the-middle attack to solve the CSSI problem and optimizations specific to isogeny arithmetic used in SIKE.

A high level description is as follows. In order to find a path of length e between two curves E_A and E_B in the supersingular isogeny graph (i.e., an ℓ^e-isogeny between E_A and E_B), an attacker can explore all length-$\lfloor e/2 \rfloor$ paths starting from E_A and all length-$\lceil e/2 \rceil$ paths starting from E_B looking for a non-trivial intersection: since isogenies are defined up to isomorphisms, we can identify the matching curve(s) *in-the-middle* by computing their j-invariants. The correctness of this approach follows from the fact that the last $\lceil e/2 \rceil$ steps of the actual walk from E_A to E_B can be reversed due to existence of dual isogenies. Thus, the j-invariant in-the-middle is the one visited by the original walk after $\lfloor e/2 \rfloor$ steps from E_A.

In SIDH/SIKE, MitM can be applied to attack either Alice's or Bob's public key: indeed, from Alice's public key we can easily recompute the curve E_A that is 2^{e_A}-isogenous to the starting curve E, and, similarly, Bob's public key reveals the curve E_B that is 3^{e_B}-isogenous to the starting curve E. Explicitly finding the secret isogeny $\phi_A : E \to E_A$ or $\phi_B : E \to E_B$, allows the attacker to reapply it to the other party's public key to ultimately obtain the shared secret key.

In SIKE, not all $(\ell+1)\ell^{e-1}$ isogenies are possible, because isogeny kernels are restricted to the shape $\langle P + [s]Q \rangle$, which excludes in the first ℓ-isogeny step the kernel $\langle [\ell^{e-1}]Q \rangle$, leaving only ℓ^e isogenies in total. Furthermore, in Sect. 3, we show that the isogeny formulas of Subsect. 2.3 can be used to walk from the curve E_A towards the starting curve E, by moving to an isomorphic curve $E_{A'}$ and finding appropriate torsion basis $\langle P', Q' \rangle = E_{A'}[\ell^e]$ with $[\ell^{e-1}]Q' = (0,0)$.

This refines the meet-in-the-middle into generating and intersecting the leaves of the two "trees" of j-invariants spanned by *walks* from the bases $P, Q \in E(\mathbb{F}_{p^2})$ and $P', Q' \in E_{A'}(\mathbb{F}_{p^2})$. The meet-in-the-middle trees structure for $\ell = 2$ is illustrated in the full version of this paper.

Definition 2 (SIKE-tree). *Given a curve E defined over $\mathbb{F}_{p^2}$ and a basis (P, Q) for its torsion $E[\ell^e]$, the tree spanned by (P, Q) of depth $d \leq e$ is the directed graph consisting of all length-d walks from E arising from $[\ell^{e-d}] \cdot (P + [s]Q)$ with $s \in \mathbb{Z}_{\ell^e}$.*

Remark 3. Since two different kernels may lead to the same image curve, the graph spanned by the ℓ^e-torsion generators (P, Q) may not always correspond to a tree. However, we can still obtain a tree by just distinguishing nodes arising from different paths, even if the respective image curves are the same. This approach will be of help when implementing our MitM attack.

Remark 4. In SIKE, a party computes a *full* ℓ^e-isogeny using an ℓ^e-torsion basis (P, Q). In other circumstances, like in the tree computation or in the meet-in-the-middle attack, we need to compute only the initial part of such full walks: thus, to keep Definition 1 consistent, such full torsion basis needs to be re-scaled, so that the path length matches the desired one. For a walk of length i, the re-scaling is done as $(P', Q') = ([\ell^{e-i}]P, [\ell^{e-i}]Q)$ so that all length-i walks arising from $P' + [t]Q'$ with $t \in [0, \ell^i - 1]$ will match the first i steps of length-e walks arising from $P + [s]Q$ with $s \in [0, \ell^e - 1]$. This can also be seen as an optimization, since computing ℓ^i-isogenies is much cheaper than computing the first i steps of ℓ^e-isogenies.

It follows that, to succeed in a meet-in-the-middle attack, it is crucial to be able to generate trees (more precisely, their leaves) from curves.

Problem 2 (Tree generation). Given a supersingular curve E defined over $\mathbb{F}_{p^2}$ and an ℓ^e-torsion basis (P, Q) for it, compute the set of j-invariants of curves appearing as leaves in the depth $d \leq e$ tree spanned by (P, Q).

Final Curve 2-bit Leak. In SIKE, the shared secret key is (computed from) the j-invariant of the image curve E_{AB} of the isogeny resulting from composing Alice's and Bob's walks in their respective torsions. To allow this, each party publishes the intermediate image curves[2] E_A and E_B.

As was further noticed in [5], the final value A leaks the j-invariant of the curve visited two 2-isogeny steps before reaching the final curve during her walk: more concretely, it can be shown that the order-4 points $\tilde{Q} = (1, \pm\sqrt{A+2})$ lie in the kernel of the dual of the isogeny $\phi : E_6 \to E_A$, and we can thus easily obtain the j-invariant $j' = j(E_{A'})$ of the curve $E_{A'} = E_A/\langle\tilde{Q}\rangle$ visited two steps before the end.

We note however that the exact curve visited two steps before the end remains undetermined (i.e., the j-invariant is known but the A-coefficient is not). On the other hand, we can choose one of the 6 curves with the given j-invariant based on the following condition: the kernel $\langle(0,0)\rangle$ must define an isogeny towards the penultimate j-invariant on the original path. Then, such a curve would span a SIKE-tree including a walk through the same j-invariants as the original path (excluding the last two steps). This allows to represent the meet-in-the-middle problem for SIKE (with the 2-bit leak incorporated) in terms of intersecting two SIKE-trees, as described before.

As an interesting observation, we note that such a curve $E_{A'}$ can be directly computed using the following simple formula[3] (the full statement with a proof is given in the full version of this paper):

$$A' = 2 - \frac{16}{A+2} \quad \text{(the case of two last 2-isogenies)}.$$

Storing Conjugation Representatives. In SIKE, the starting curve is chosen to be $E_6(\mathbb{F}_{p^2})$, and since $A = 6 \in \mathbb{F}_p$, the Frobenius map $\pi : (x, y) \mapsto (x^p, y^p)$ defines an automorphism for $E_6(\mathbb{F}_{p^2})$. As already noticed in [5], this implies that for any kernel $\langle R \rangle \subset E_6$, $j(E_6/\langle R\rangle)^p = j(E_6/\pi(\langle R\rangle))$, that is pairs of conjugate kernels give rise to paths to curves having conjugate j-invariants. By considering the intermediate A-coefficients and j-invariants modulo the conjugation (e.g., using the norm or the trace suffices), this property effectively allows to halve the size of the initial SIKE-tree. Once an intersection between the SIKE-trees is found, it is left to check both conjugate candidates, which can be done easily due to the respective paths being element-wise conjugate. We refer to [5] for theoretical and graphical description of this phenomenon.

4   Efficient Tree Generation

In this section, we focus on optimized generation of the leaves of the tree spanned by given torsion generators. We focus on the case of 2-isogenies but the discussion can be generalized to other values of ℓ as well.

---

[2] Even though the curves are not explicitly given, the torsion points needed by the other party are given, implicitly defining the concrete curve.

[3] In SIKE, if the last two steps were performed as a single 4-isogeny, then the sign of A has to be flipped due to specifics of the arithmetic.

A straightforward approach for generating a tree, is to enumerate all possible $s \in [0, 2^e - 1]$ and compute the respective isogeny's image curve, similarly as done in SIKE for a given private key s. In fact, such walk computation is performed (up to a precomputation of a fixed number of the first steps) as a *single step* in the low-memory van Oorschot-Wiener collision search applied to SIKE [1,5,11].

However, many intermediate curves will be visited multiple times for different values s in the kernel $\langle P + [s]Q \rangle$. To avoid the extra work, the authors of [1] developed a recursive method (called MITM-DFS) for computing the full tree in a depth-first traversal order, by efficiently maintaining a 2^{e-i}-torsion basis on each new visited curve at depth i.

In this section, we improve the MITM-DFS method in two ways. First, we show how to maintain the torsion basis in the case of SIKE isogenies, which allows to use the highly effective arithmetic of SIKE (including the available optimized implementation [22]). This requires careful choice of new generators so as to avoid the possibility of hitting the kernel $(0,0)$. Second, we show how to adapt the strategic trade-off between isogeny evaluations and scalar multiplications described in SIDH [7] to the tree generation.

4.1 Maintaining Torsion Basis for Efficient Isogeny Computations

We now describe a method which allows to maintain, during path traversals, a basis suitable for the efficient arithmetic formulas used by SIKE, i.e., the ones detailed in Subsect. 2.3. This extends a similar method for generic isogenies from [1]. The proof follows from the fact that the 2-isogeny formulas in SIKE (see Proposition 1) fix the point $(0,0)$ (see Remark 2). The idea is to base the DFS tree exploration on the parity of the possible value s defining the kernel $\langle P_i + [s]Q_i \rangle$ at the depth i. Indeed, this parity defines the two possible 2-isogeny choices, and the following proposition shows how to compute the right torsion basis for the codomains of each of the two isogenies. This allows to recursively run the exploration in each of the curves. Full proof and a pseudocode illustrating the use of this proposition are given in the full version of this paper.

Proposition 2. *Let $A \in \mathbb{F}_{p^2}$ and $e \geq 2$. Let $P, Q \in E_A(\mathbb{F}_{p^2})$ be a basis of $E_A[2^e]$ with $[2^{e-1}]Q = (0,0)$. Then, for a 2-isogeny $\phi : E_A \to E_{A'}$ arising from $[2^{e-1}](P + [s]Q)$ with $s \in [0, 2^e - 1]$, the pair $P', Q' \in E_{A'}(\mathbb{F}_{p^2})$ is a basis of $E_{A'}[2^{e-1}]$ with $[2^{e-2}]Q' = (0,0)$, where*

$$P' = \phi(P), \qquad Q' = \phi([2]Q), \quad \text{if } \ker \phi = \left\langle [2^{e-1}]P \right\rangle \text{ (i.e., } s \text{ is even);}$$
$$P' = \phi(P + Q), \quad Q' = \phi([2]P), \quad \text{if } \ker \phi = \left\langle [2^{e-1}](P + Q) \right\rangle \text{ (i.e., } s \text{ is odd).}$$

Proof. See the full version of this paper.   □

4.2 Optimal Strategies for the Doubling/Isogeny Evaluation Trade-Off

During evaluation of the isogeny walk arising from $P + [s]Q$, the order-ℓ kernel for the next step can be obtained through scalar multiplication as $[\ell^{e-1}](P + [s]Q)$.

To compute such kernels more efficiently, we can store some intermediate values $[\ell^{e_0-1}](P+[s]Q)$ with $e_0 < e$, and later push all such points through isogenies, to aid scalar multiplications on the subsequent curves arising in the walk. Indeed, this allows to compute the kernel of the next-step ℓ-isogeny with just $e - 1 - e_0$ point multiplications by ℓ using the maximum e_0 for which $[\ell^{e_0-1}](P+[s]Q)$ is stored, while storing and pushing smaller multiples is also useful for the later steps. It is then clear the relevance of finding good trade-offs between the number of multiplications by ℓ and the number of isogeny evaluations needed to traverse a walk: indeed, depending on the implementation adopted, these two operations have different costs.

In [7], De Feo, Jao and Plût describe how to derive an *optimal evaluation strategy* for the best trade-off between scalar multiplications and isogeny evaluations, using a dynamic programming-based algorithm.

We now provide a brief overview of how optimal evaluation strategies are found in [7]. Let $K_0 \in E_A[\ell^e]$, $\phi_i : E_{A_i} \to E_{A_{i+1}}, i \in [0, e - 1]$ be the sequence of isogenies on the length-e walk defined by K_0 and $K_i = \phi_{i-1}(K_{i-1})$ for $i \in [1, e - 1]$. The goal is to compute $\ker \phi_i = \langle [\ell^{e-1-i}]K_i \rangle$ for all $i \in [0, e - 1]$ in a minimum overall cost in terms of scalar multiplications and isogeny evaluations.

Aiming at this, we construct a directed graph with nodes

$$\left\{\, [\ell^i]K_j \mid j \in [0, e - 1], i \in [0, e - 1 - j]\,\right\},$$

connected by two types of edges, namely:

- "multiplication by $[\ell]$" edges of cost C_{mult}, connecting $[\ell^i]K_j$ to $[\ell^{i+1}]K_j$, for $i + j + 1 \le e - 1$;
- "isogeny evaluation" edges of cost C_{eval}, connecting $[\ell^i]K_j$ to $[\ell^i]K_{j+1}$ (through an ℓ-isogeny ϕ_j), for $i + j + 1 \le e - 1$.

A strategy for evaluating all the kernels $\ker \phi_i = \langle [\ell^{e-1-i}]K_i \rangle$ can then be described by a tree subgraph in this graph, rooted in K_0 and consisting of directed paths towards the goal leaf nodes $[\ell^{e-1-i}]K_i$ for $i \in [0, e - 1]$. The cost of a strategy is then the sum of the costs of the edges in it, counting only once edges traversed by multiple paths. It is then clear that best strategies are those ones in which paths to leaves overlap as much as possible. An example of such graph along with an optimal strategy is illustrated in Fig. 1.

In [7], it was shown that there exist minimal-cost strategies with recursive structures. The problem is decomposed into two subproblems, where the costs of the subgraph induced after following i multiplication edges (height $e - 1 - i$), and the subgraph induced after following $e - i$ isogeny evaluation edges (height $i - 1$) are taken into account. For $e \ge 2$, the minimal cost C_e for evaluating trees of height $e - 1$ is given by

$$C_e = \min_{1 \le i \le e-1} (i \cdot C_{\text{mult}} + (e - i) \cdot C_{\text{eval}} + C_{e-i} + C_i)$$

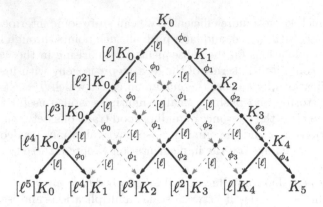

Fig. 1. An example of evaluation strategy graph. Multiplication by $[\ell]$ edges ($\nearrow$) and isogeny evaluation edges ($\searrow$) transform $K_0 \in E[\ell^6]$ to the leaf values $\{[\ell^{6-i-1}]K_i\}_{i \in [0,5]}$. In bold, an optimal evaluation strategy assuming $C_{\text{eval}} = 1.5 \cdot C_{\text{mult}}$.

This is possible due to the fact that, in paths towards leaves, the order of any two consecutive edges can be swapped (if it does not break strategy consistency), since multiplication commutes with isogenies and such swaps do not change the overall strategy cost. An optimal strategy can thus be obtained by evaluating all possible choices of i and solving recursively the induced subproblems. Since the subproblems are fully characterized by their size (and are independent from the root kernel chosen), their solutions can be cached and reused (dynamic programming).

Application to Tree Generation. We are interested in using best strategies during tree generation to make path computations faster.

The difference between the tree generation and a simple isogeny evaluation is that each isogeny evaluation edge creates ℓ new exploration nodes deeper in the tree. However, all the ℓ induced sub-trees differ only by curves and generators, and so all can follow the same sub-strategy. Effectively, an isogeny evaluation edge *multiplies* the number of nodes and edges being explored in the isogeny tree by ℓ (including the isogeny edge itself). To account for this, we can then set the weight of an isogeny evaluation edge ϕ_j to ℓ^{j+1}, while we assign to multiplication edges $[\ell^i]K_j \to [\ell^{i+1}]K_j$ a weight of ℓ^j, since in this case the overall number of nodes being explored doesn't change.

Once weights are assigned, the dynamic programming approach can be applied in order to find best strategies on these new graphs. However, in contrast to best strategies for single paths, sub-problems are not fully characterized by their size: edge weights depend, indeed, on where we currently are in the strategy graph. On the other hand, all weights at isogeny depth i are simply multiplied by a factor ℓ^i. Therefore, it is sufficient to find best strategies for trees of heights

$1, \ldots, e-1$ rooted at K_0. This leads to a simple 1-dimensional dynamic programming algorithm with complexity $\mathcal{O}(e^2)$, based on the new recursive expression:

$$
C_e = \min_{1 \le i \le e-1} \left(\underbrace{i \cdot C_{\mathrm{mult}}}_{i \text{ mult. edges}} + \underbrace{\left(\sum_{j=1}^{e-i} \ell^j \right) \cdot C_{\mathrm{eval}}}_{e-i \text{ isog. edges}} + \underbrace{C_{e-i}}_{\text{left subtree}} + \underbrace{\ell^{e-i} \cdot C_i}_{\text{right subtree}} \right)
$$

5 Set Intersection Using Sort and Merge

5.1 Hash-Tables or Sort and Merge?

A standard way to implement the final stage of a meet-in-the-middle attack, i.e., intersecting the two sets of values in-the-middle, is by using hash-tables: we fill one of such tables with entries from the first dataset, and we then lookup every element in the second one. In theory, the amortized cost of a hash-table lookup would be $\mathcal{O}(1)$, but in practice, *random* memory accesses get slower and slower as the table size grows and memory *latency* starts affecting the execution time.

An alternative approach is to *sort* the two datasets and perform a linear-time *merge* operation by keeping common elements only, an operation requiring *sequential* memory accesses. The drawback of this approach is that (in theory) the sorting step has quasilinear complexity $\mathcal{O}(n \log n)$ in the (biggest) dataset size n, and to complete it we need memory/storage access patterns which are not necessarily sequential.

The comparison of in-RAM set intersection using hash-tables and sort-and-merge is given in the full version of this paper. While even the toy $IKEp182 challenge requires out-of-RAM-scale data, this comparison illustrates the ideas on the small scale.

Sorting Big-Data. Sorting large amounts of data that cannot fit the main memory is known as *external sorting*. A well-known approach for external sorting is a hybrid sort-and-merge. First, the data is split into relatively small chunks that fit memory of the used machine and that are sorted in parallel using any standard algorithm (e.g., radix sort). Sorted chunks are written to the disk-based storage. The second stage is merging the sorted chunks into bigger sorted chunks. If the number of initial chunks is too large, this process can be performed in several layers, each merging every t sorted chunks into one bigger sorted chunk. This requires (parallel) sequential reading of the t chunks and a size-t heap (which exhibits random memory accesses but in a small memory range). For the purpose of set intersection, the last layer may merge chunks from both sets and compare elements on the fly, removing the need to write the full sorted dataset (which requires costly I/O operations).

Parallelization. When dataset sizes are large, efficient parallelization techniques are a requirement. The most straightforward approach for parallelizing intersection finding, consists in splitting the input datasets A and B in k (equally sized) chunks $(A_0, \ldots, A_k)$ and $(B_0, \ldots, B_k)$, and then intersect all k^2 distinct pairs $A_i \cap B_j$ independently in parallel. Clearly, this parallelization comes at the cost of k times more work than standard lookups/merges, but can be acceptable if k is small.

An advantage of this approach, is that each chunk can be preprocessed independently, so that each of the k^2 chunk pairs intersection takes preprocessed data as input. In our in-RAM experiments (see full version of this paper) we observed that already for $k = 2$, SortMerge (which requires a total number of 2 sort calls and k merges/intersections per chunk) outperforms the FastHash hash-set approach (which requires 1 chunk insertion and k chunks lookups per chunk).

5.2   Storage-Collisions Trade-Off and Compression

The large problem scale requires to reduce storage requirements as much as possible. We describe three techniques for this purpose.

Omitting Path Information. Basic MitM would store the paths associated to j-invariants in each tree in order to quickly reconstruct the isogeny path. This information can be omitted at the cost of an extra iteration of tree exploration, required to recover full j-invariants associated to colliding representations and the respective paths in the trees. This extra exploration can be considered memoryless, if the expected number of collisions is sufficiently small (for example, if it fits the local memory of a computing node).

Truncating j-invariants Representations. Storage reduction can be made by reducing the number of bits we use to represent j-invariants (modulo the conjugation), while allowing only a reasonable amount of false positive collisions. Since each tree has only approximately $2^{e_A/2} \approx p^{1/4}$ leaves, using n bits to represent j-invariants leads to approximately $c = (p^{1/4})^2/2^n$ collisions.

Sorted Set Compression. If the n-bit j-invariant representations are uniformly distributed, we can compress *sorted* chunks of 2^m such elements by noticing that any two consecutive elements are expected to differ, on average, by 2^{n-m} (as integers). We can then store only such reduced differences, reserving 1 *flag* bit for distinguishing a small difference from a full n-bit representation (in case two elements differ by more than 2^{n-m}).

This, in fact, reduces memory requirements from $n2^m$ bits to $\approx (n-m+1)2^m$ bits, with different implementation-specific word size trade-offs in the middle.

We note that by requiring the chunks to be sorted, this compression technique goes towards the SortMerge intersection finding approach we detailed in Sect. 5. Since the chunks can be decompressed on the fly without any overhead, the merge steps can be performed as usual.

6   Cryptanalysis of the \$IKEp182 Challenge

In this section we will detail how all the above ideas can be used to concretely break the \$IKEp182 challenge [12], a small-parameters specification-compliant SIKE instance generated by Microsoft in a live event during the 3rd NIST PQC Standardization conference.

In \$IKEp182, the field characteristic is equal to $p = 2^{91}3^{57} - 1$. According to specification, we have $\mathbb{F}_{p^2} = \mathbb{F}_p[i]/(i^2 + 1)$, $\#E_6(\mathbb{F}_{p^2}) = (p + 1)^2$ and $E_6[2^{91}] = \langle P_A, Q_A \rangle$, $E_6[3^{57}] = \langle P_B, Q_B \rangle$. The coordinates of the points P_A, Q_A, P_B, Q_B as well as all other values related to the attack in this section are reported in the full version of this paper.

Our meet-in-the-middle attack targets the 2^{91}-torsion in order to recover Alice's full 91-steps walk, followed by the private key recovery. After a quick Setup, the full attack consists of 5 main stages: Trees Traversal, k-way Merge, Compression, Sieving and Final Trees Traversal.

Setup. In the first step of the SIKE protocol (Subsect. 2.2), Alice sends to Bob a compressed representation of the points $\phi_A(P_B)$, $\phi_A(Q_B)$, consisting of the 3 x-coordinates $x_{\phi_A(P_B)}, x_{\phi_A(Q_B)}, x_{\phi_A(Q_B)-\phi_A(P_B)}$. Such compressed representation is justified by use of efficient implementations which exploits x-only arithmetic: we refer to [9] for more details.

If we denote the tuple $(x_{\phi_A(P_B)}, x_{\phi_A(Q_B)}, x_{\phi_A(Q_B)-\phi_A(P_B)})$ as (x_P, x_Q, x_{Q-P}) we obtain [4, Section 6] the A coefficient of the Montgomery curve E_A on which the points $\phi_A(P_B)$, $\phi_A(Q_B)$ lie, as

$$A = \frac{(1 - x_P x_Q - x_P x_{Q-P} - x_Q x_{Q-P})^2}{4 x_P x_Q x_{Q-P}} - x_P - x_Q - x_{Q-P}$$

To take advantage of the final 2-bit leak described in Sect. 3, we computed the coefficient A' such that $j(E_{A'})$ lies on the (secret) traversed path 2 steps before the final curve, and the SIKE-tree arising from A' does not go towards the final curve E_A. This can be achieved by using (3) to obtain the coefficient $A' = 2 + 16/(A - 2)$.

The Setup phase was implemented in SageMath [21].

Trees Traversal

We proceed by attacking the 89-steps path in the 2-isogeny graph between $j(E_6)$ and $j(E_{A'})$. Note that there may be no path in the SIKE-tree (Definition 2) between the exact *curves*, as we might chose a different representative curve, but there must exist a path in the 2-isogeny graph between $j(E_6)$ and $j(E_{A'})$, and the SIKE-trees arising from E_6 and $E_{A'}$ must contain paths following this path by j-invariants (from the opposite endpoints). In order to meet in the middle, we generate in a depth-first manner the SIKE-tree arising from E_6 (up to the depth 45) and the SIKE-tree arising from $E_{A'}$ (up to the depth 44), employing the optimal strategies detailed in Subsect. 4.2.

We note that, as discussed in Sect. 3, it suffices to explore only half of conjugate sub-branches of the tree expanded from E_6: this results in an almost equal number of leaves in-the-middle generated from both trees, with a total of $2^{44}+1$ leaves for the tree expanded from E_6, and 2^{44} leaves for the one expanded from $E_{A'}$.

Once the depth-first generation reaches a leaf, we compute the corresponding j-invariant and we store the least significant 64 bits of half of its trace. In our implementation, multiple jobs explore in parallel distinct branches of each tree: when a job collects 2 GiB of 64-bit j-invariant representations (which correspond to 2^{28} j-invariants visited), this chunk is sorted in-memory, written to disk, and then the job terminates. On the cluster we used, each of these job took approximately 17 minutes to complete on a single core of an Intel® Xeon® E5-2680v4 clocked at 2.4GHz with 4 GiB of RAM reserved. This sums up to a total of approximately 4.2 core-years and 256 TiB of disk space needed to explore both trees and store the truncated j-invariants.

Remark 5. By utilizing the Merge and Compression earlier, on the fly after a sufficient amount of chunks is generated, the storage requirement could be reduced to close to 128 TiB.

k-way Merge. We employed our custom *k-way merge* implementation optimized for 64-bit unsigned integers, to merge the 2 GiB sorted chunks generated from each tree: on a single core with 4 GiB of RAM, we needed approximately 2.5 core hours to merge 256 2 GiB chunks into a single 512 GiB sorted chunk. We note that, to keep memory requirements close to the ones needed to store all j-invariants representations, chunks can be merged at the same time with the depth-first traversal, as soon as enough new 2 GiB chunks from a certain tree are generated. Practicality of running multiple such merges in parallel depends, however, on storage architecture, cluster load and maximum disks I/O throughput: on our cluster we were able to run 4 nodes in parallel, running 28 merge jobs each, without degrading too much I/O performances. This merging stage took, overall, approximately 54 core days.

Compression. Since 512 GiB chunks contain already 2^{36} 64-bit elements each, at this point we ran single-core jobs to merge 4 chunks directly in compressed form (Subsect. 5.2), using 32 bits (including 1 flag bit) to encode elements differences. This resulted in a compression factor very close to $\frac{1}{2}$. In the same configuration as above (and under the same limitations), we needed roughly 5 core hours to complete one of such merge-to-compressed job (we ran only 2-3 nodes concurrently, each executing 28 such jobs), for a total of 27 core-days to complete all jobs.

We then finally obtained 64 compressed chunks of 1 TiB each from each tree, for a total of 128 TiB disk space used (all previous sub-chunks were deleted).

Sieving. At this point we proceed with finding elements shared by chunks from different trees. Since chunks are sorted already, we can use the parallel version of SortMerge with parameter $k = 64$ detailed at the end of Subsect. 5.1. This stage consists in merging tuples of (compressed) 1 TiB chunks and storing only the common elements. If ran in a single thread on the full data, this stage only requires sequential read of the 128 TiB of data. However, the heap operations in k-way merge dominate the performance and can not be parallelized. In our implementation, a sieving job consisted in merging at the same time 4 chunks from the first tree with 4 chunks from the second tree, by decompressing elements and storing only collisions: on a single core, it took approximately 1.1 core days to complete, for a total of 280 core-days for 256 such jobs. This trade-off results in 2 PiB of data read, which is acceptable to allow sufficient parallelization.

We expected $2^{44.2}/2^{64} = 2^{24} = 16\,777\,216$ 64-bit collisions among the two trees and we actually found $16\,777\,119$ of them: once such collisions were safely stored, we deleted all the 128 1 TiB chunks from previous stages.

Final Trees Traversal. With the collisions just found, we run the tree explorations again, similarly as in the first stage of the attack, but this time we store only full j-invariants in the middle that have the least 64 bits of half of their trace matching any of the collisions found, and their paths in the respective trees.

After the full collision is found, we reconstruct Alice's full walk from E_6 to E_A (and thus her secret) using the paths associated to the matching j-invariants, including the check for the conjugate path arising from E_6 (see Sect. 3). In our case, the colliding j-invariants in-the-middle obtained by expanding the trees from E_6 and $E_{A'}$ were, indeed, conjugate pairs. The respective values, j_0 and j_1, are reported in the full version of this paper.

Using the (implementation-dependent) path information we stored, we then reconstruct, in linear time, the Alice's private key as

$$s_A = \texttt{0x59d64d476da9487be414734}$$

which allows us to easily compute Alice's and Bob's shared secret from Bob's public key exchanged, as

$$j(E_{AB}) = \texttt{0x7a470546a24124f06f49bcbb855a6e3c1402ba1004bfc} +$$
$$\texttt{0x1a88f02557168dd75b64f8407a368aa4ff2bc03121fbaf} \cdot i$$

whose value is a correct pre-image for the publicly released SHA512 hash of the challenge shared secret [12].

We found the solution to the challenge after exploring approximately 44% of the tree expanded from E_6 (only conjugate-unique sub-branches) and 63% of the tree expanded from $E_{A'}$ (success probability of $\approx 28\%$). We remark that these percentages only correspond to the final tree regeneration step, the previous stages were fully completed.

This brings the total cost of our attack to approximately $4.2 + (54 + 27 + 280)/365 + 4.2 \cdot (0.63 + 0.44)/2 \leq 9.5$ core years and 256 TiB of disk memory.

We note, however, that we only decided to employ compression after the Trees Traversal phase was completed, in order to reduce the amount of not fully parallelizable disk reads needed for the parallel SortMerge. Thus, in fact, the whole attack can be executed in 9.5 core years with just slightly more than 128 TiB of disk memory available. The storage requirement can be reduced further by sacrificing parallelization and performing the main steps for a single group of the second tree at a time. In our case, we used 4-chunk groups (4 TiB) on each side and so only $64 + 4 = 68$ TiB of storage is sufficient for the (less-parallel) attack.

7   Discussion on Scalability

In this work, we showed how the $IKEp182 challenge can be broken in practice. A natural question is whether the $IKEp217 challenge is reachable for attacking using our method. More generally, on instances up to which size can the meet-in-the-middle attack compete with the van Oorschot-Wiener method?

($IKEp217). In $IKEp217, the prime p is equal to $2^{110}3^{67} - 1$, so that $e_A = 110$, leading to 192 PiB storage requirement if our attack on $IKEp182 is applied directly and 64-bit j-invariant representations are stored (which may produce a large but still manageable number of collisions, namely $2^{107-64} = 2^{43}$).

The computational cost should scale linearly with the sizes of the trees, resulting in $2^{(110-91)/2} \cdot 9.5 \approx 6900$ core-years. We remark though, that, on the cluster we used, the main limitation is the I/O performance upper bounded by about 20 GiB/s. Even if an unlimited storage is available, this maximum throughput limits the time needed to solve the instance, since full data must be read/written at least once. To read the 192 PiB of data on such a cluster, one would need at least 116 days. Since the full attack performs several I/O rounds, the attack would likely take more than a year.

Towards the other side of the memory-time trade-off, we could reuse the current attack setup on $IKEp182 with $\tilde{e}_A = 91$, by guessing $e_A - \tilde{e}_A = 19$ final steps on the path, leading to the estimation of $2^{19} \cdot 9.5 \approx 5$ million core-years for computations. This is a very "clean" upper-bound estimation in that it is based on a real experiment and it parallelizes perfectly (with the number of involved clusters similar to the one we used).

We can conclude that, depending on the physical feasibility of high-speed access to 192 PiB of storage, our attack on $IKEp217 may take between 6.9k and 5M core-years. We remark that we did not take into account possibilities of further optimization of the implementation or, more low-level implementations (GPU/FPGA/ASIC).

(SIKEp377). SIKEp377 is the smallest instance proposed in [11] based on detailed hardware-cost analysis of matching the NIST Security Level 1 (roughly equal to security of the block cipher AES). The respective prime p is equal to $2^{191}3^{117} - 1$.

As it is already unrealistic to consider $2^{(e_A-3)/2} = 2^{94}$ units of storage, we resort to the approach of [1,5] of bounding the memory units by 2^{80}, in order to obtain our attacker-optimistic estimation. Here, a unit may be, for example, a 128-bit integer (or a 64-bit integer after the difference-based compression). Then, after guessing 28 2-isogeny steps, the adversary would run the MitM attack on SIKE-trees of size $2^{(e_A-28-3)/2} = 2^{80}$ (we assume that the second tree is checked on-the-fly in chunks of negligible size; for example, using $2^{80} + 2^{77} = 2^{80.17}$ units results in slowdown of 2^3). The basic meet-in-the-middle analysis predicts the cost of $2^{28} \cdot 2 \cdot 2^{80} = 2^{119}$ tree-element (i.e., j-invariants) generations. On the other hand, for the storage of 2^{80} units, a realistic implementation of the sort-and-merge approach (repeated 2^{29} times) would clearly blow up the complexity beyond 2^{128} operations or even AES encryptions.

Similarly to \$IKEp217, we could also reuse the attack on \$IKEp182 to get an estimate for SIKEp377. Here, the multiplicative complexity factor is 2^{100}. In order to provide a comparison with the financial cost estimation given in [11] (based on the hardware implementation of the vOW method), we (optimistically) assume that our attack can be reproduced in 1 day on a device costing \$1000. Therefore, with a \$1 billion budget, we could use 1M such devices in parallel, leading to an estimate of 2^{71} years, compared to about 2^{40} years given in [11]. Even with an unlimited budget, we could use about 2^{35} such devices to fit the 2^{80} memory limit, leading to an estimate of $2^{100-35}/365 = 2^{56}$ years.

Conclusions. As we could see, the advantage of the Meet-in-the-middle attack over the van-Oorschot-Wiener method against SIKE decreases with the growth of the involved prime p. However, precise comparison of two methods is complicated by unclear physical limits of the set intersection problem. The estimation based on mesh sorting in [1] is too pessimistic at least for the toy instances \$IKEp182/\$IKEp217, where the required amount of memory is manageable and physical limitations do not yet have an effect. Our implementation of the attack on \$IKEp182 is relatively straightforward and only uses an existing computational architecture. According to our analysis, it has high potential to be applied to \$IKEp217 with sufficient amount of resources. However, already for the smallest non-toy instance SIKEp377, our implementation does not allow to straightforwardly beat the vOW-based estimation of [11] and it does not seem to threaten the claimed 128-bit security. On the other hand, we could not discard the possibility that a well-thought hardware-based architecture for the MitM attack could still compete with the vOW method on SIKEp377.

Acknowledgements. We thank the ULHPC cluster for providing the computational resources, and Teddy Valette from ULHPC for helping with the project setup. We also thank Microsoft Research for creating the challenge which inspired this work and the Isogeny-based Cryptography School (https://isogenyschool2020.co.uk/) for sparkling our interest in the topic.

References

1. Adj, G., Cervantes-Vázquez, D., Chi-Domínguez, J.J., Menezes, A., Rodríguez-Henríquez, F.: On the cost of computing isogenies between supersingular elliptic curves. In: Cid, C., Jacobson, M.J., Jr. (eds.) SAC 2018. LNCS, vol. 11349, pp. 322–343. Springer, Heidelberg (2019). https://doi.org/10.1007/978-3-030-10970-7_15

2. Bernstein, D.: Cost analysis of hash collisions : will quantum computers make SHARCS obsolete? In: SHARCS'09 Workshop Record (Proceedings 4th Workshop on Special-purpose Hardware for Attacking Cryptograhic Systems, Lausanne, Switserland, 9-10 September 2009), pp. 105–116 (2009)

3. Costello, C., Hisil, H.: A simple and compact algorithm for SIDH with arbitrary degree isogenies. In: Takagi, T., Peyrin, T. (eds.) ASIACRYPT 2017. LNCS, vol. 10625, pp. 303–329. Springer, Cham (2017). https://doi.org/10.1007/978-3-319-70697-9_11

4. Costello, C., Longa, P., Naehrig, M.: Efficient algorithms for supersingular isogeny Diffie-Hellman. In: Robshaw, M., Katz, J. (eds.) CRYPTO 2016. LNCS, vol. 9814, pp. 572–601. Springer, Heidelberg (2016). https://doi.org/10.1007/978-3-662-53018-4_21

5. Costello, C., Longa, P., Naehrig, M., Renes, J., Virdia, F.: Improved classical cryptanalysis of SIKE in practice. In: Kiayias, A., Kohlweiss, M., Wallden, P., Zikas, V. (eds.) PKC 2020. LNCS, vol. 12111, pp. 505–534. Springer, Cham (2020). https://doi.org/10.1007/978-3-030-45388-6_18

6. Couveignes, J.M.: Hard homogeneous spaces. Cryptology ePrint Archive, Report 2006/291 (2006)

7. Feo, L.D., Jao, D., Plût, J.: Towards quantum-resistant cryptosystems from supersingular elliptic curve isogenies. J. Math. Cryptol. 8(3), 209–247 (2014)

8. Galbraith, S.D.: Constructing isogenies between elliptic curves over finite fields. LMS J. Comput. Math. 2, 118–138 (1999)

9. Jao, D., et al.: Supersingular Isogeny Key Encapsulation. NIST Post-Quantum Cryptography Round 3 - Alternate Candidate (2020). https://sike.org/files/SIDH-spec.pdf

10. Jao, D., De Feo, L.: Towards quantum-resistant cryptosystems from supersingular elliptic curve isogenies. In: Yang, B.-Y. (ed.) PQCrypto 2011. LNCS, vol. 7071, pp. 19–34. Springer, Heidelberg (2011). https://doi.org/10.1007/978-3-642-25405-5_2

11. Longa, P., Wang, W., Szefer, J.: The cost to break SIKE: a comparative hardware-based analysis with AES and SHA-3. In: Malkin, T., Peikert, C. (eds.) CRYPTO 2021. LNCS, vol. 12827, pp. 402–431. Springer, Cham (2021). https://doi.org/10.1007/978-3-030-84252-9_14

12. Microsoft Research: SIKE Cryptographic Challenge (2021). https://www.microsoft.com/en-us/msrc/sike-cryptographic-challenge

13. National Institute of Standards and Technology (NIST): Post-Quantum Cryptography Standardization (2016–2022). https://csrc.nist.gov/projects/post-quantum-cryptography/post-quantum-cryptography-standardization

14. Renes, J.: Computing isogenies between Montgomery curves using the action of (0, 0). In: Lange, T., Steinwandt, R. (eds.) PQCrypto 2018. LNCS, vol. 10786, pp. 229–247. Springer, Cham (2018). https://doi.org/10.1007/978-3-319-79063-3_11

15. Rostovtsev, A., Stolbunov, A.: Public-Key Cryptosystem Based On Isogenies. Cryptology ePrint Archive, Report 2006/145 (2006)

16. Schnorr, C.P., Shamir, A.: An optimal sorting algorithm for mesh connected computers. In: Proceedings of the Eighteenth Annual ACM Symposium on Theory of Computing, pp. 255–263. STOC 1986, Association for Computing Machinery, New York, NY, USA (1986)

17. Schoof, R.: Nonsingular plane cubic curves over finite fields. J. Comb. Theory Ser. A 46(2), 183–211 (1987). https://www.sciencedirect.com/science/article/pii/0097316587900033

18. Silverman, J.: The Arithmetic of Elliptic Curves, vol. 106 (2009)

19. Stolbunov, A.: Constructing public-key cryptographic schemes based on class group action on a set of isogenous elliptic curves. Adv. Math. Commun. **4**(2), 215–235 (2010)
20. Tate, J.: Endomorphisms of abelian varieties over finite fields. Invent. Math. **2**(2), 134–144 (1966)
21. The Sage Developers: SageMath, the Sage Mathematics Software System (Version 9.4) (2021). https://www.sagemath.org
22. The SIDH Library Developers: SIDH v3.4 (C Edition) (2021). https://github.com/microsoft/PQCrypto-SIDH
23. van Oorschot, P.C., Wiener, M.J.: Parallel collision search with cryptanalytic applications. J. Cryptol. **12**(1), 1–28 (1999)
24. Varrette, S., Bouvry, P., Cartiaux, H., Georgatos, F.: Management of an academic HPC cluster: The UL experience. In: Proceedings of the 2014 International Conference on High Performance Computing & Simulation (HPCS 2014), pp. 959–967. IEEE, Bologna, Italy (2014)

Patient Zero & Patient Six: Zero-Value and Correlation Attacks on CSIDH and SIKE

Fabio Campos[1,3], Michael Meyer[2(✉)], Krijn Reijnders[3], and Marc Stöttinger[1]

[1] RheinMain University of Applied Sciences Wiesbaden, Wiesbaden, Germany
campos@sopmac.de, marc.stoettinger@hs-rm.de
[2] University of Regensburg, Regensburg, Germany
michael@random-oracles.org
[3] Radboud University, Nijmegen, The Netherlands
krijn@cs.ru.nl

Abstract. Recent works have started side-channel analysis on SIKE and show the vulnerability of isogeny-based systems to zero-value attacks. In this work, we expand on such attacks by analyzing the behavior of the zero curve E_0 and six curve E_6 in CSIDH and SIKE. We demonstrate an attack on static-key CSIDH and SIKE implementations that recovers bits of the secret key by observing via zero-value-based resp. exploiting correlation-collision-based side-channel analysis whether secret isogeny walks pass over the zero or six curve. We apply this attack to fully recover secret keys of SIKE and two state-of-the-art CSIDH-based implementations: CTIDH and SQALE. We show the feasibility of exploiting side-channel information for the proposed attacks based on simulations with various realistic noise levels. Additionally, we discuss countermeasures to prevent zero-value and correlation-collision attacks against CSIDH and SIKE in our attacker model.

Keywords: post-quantum cryptography · isogeny-based cryptography · CSIDH · SIKE · side-channel analysis · zero-value attacks · correlation attacks · countermeasures

1 Introduction

Isogeny-based cryptography is a promising candidate for replacing pre-quantum schemes with practical quantum-resistant alternatives. In general, isogeny-based schemes feature very small key sizes, while suffering from running times that are at least an order of magnitude slower than e.g. lattice- or code-based schemes. Therefore, they present a viable option for applications that prioritize bandwidth over performance. SIKE [27], a key encapsulation mechanism (KEM)

Author list in alphabetical order; see https://www.ams.org/profession/leaders/Cultu reStatement04.pdf. This work has been supported by the German Federal Ministry of Education and Research (BMBF) under the project QuantumRISC (ID 16KIS1039). Date of this document: 2024-04-04.

based on the key exchange SIDH [28], is the lone isogeny-based participant of the NIST post-quantum cryptography standardization process, and proceeded to the fourth round. In 2018, only after the NIST standardization process started, the key exchange scheme CSIDH was published [13]. Due to its commutative structure, a unique feature among the known post-quantum schemes, CSIDH allows for a non-interactive key exchange, which gained much attention among the research community. Together with its efficient key validation, which enables a static-static key setting, this makes CSIDH a promising candidate for a drop-in replacement of classical Diffie–Hellman-style schemes.

In this work, we focus on a side-channel attack against CSIDH and SIKE. We follow the main idea of [21], which reconstructs SIKE private keys through *zero-value* attacks. This attack approach tries to force zero values for some intermediate values of computations related to secret key bits. By recognizing these zero values via side-channel analysis (SCA), this allows an attacker to recover bits of the secret key. While *coordinate randomization* is an effective method to mitigate general *Differential Power Analysis* (DPA) and *Correlation Power Analysis* (CPA), it has no effect on zero values, such that forcing their occurrence bypasses this countermeasure, which is incorporated in SIKE [27]. Similar to [21], the recent *Hertzbleed attack* exploits zero values in SIKE [43].

While [21] focuses on forcing values connected to elliptic curve points becoming zero, we discuss the occurrence of zero values as curve parameters. This was first proposed in [29], yet [21] concludes that this idea is unlikely to be applicable in a realistic scenario, since curve representations in SIKE are such that they cannot produce a zero. In spite of this fact, we show that some curves in SIKE and CSIDH, as e.g. the zero curve, have a special correlation in these representations, which admits noticing their occurrence via side-channel analysis.

The secret isogeny computation in SIKE essentially consists of two phases: scalar multiplication and isogeny computation. In general, the first phase is believed to be more vulnerable to physical attacks, since private key bits are directly used there (see [17]). We propose the first passive implementation attack using side-channel analysis that exclusively targets the second phase of the SIKE isogeny computation. Notably, countermeasures like coordinate/coefficient randomization [17] or the *CLN test* [18,21] do not prevent this attack.

Our Contributions. In this work, we present zero-value and correlation attacks against state-of-the-art implementations of CSIDH and SIKE. For CSIDH, we use the fact that the zero curve E_0, i.e., the Montgomery curve with coefficient $a = 0$, represents a valid curve. Thus, whenever a secret isogeny walk passes over this curve, this can be detected via side-channel analysis. We present a passive adaptive attack that recovers one bit of the secret key per round by forcing the target to walk over the zero curve.

Some implementations, like SQALE and SIKE, represent the zero curve without using zero values. Nevertheless, in such a case there is often (with probability $1/2$ in SQALE and probability 1 in SIKE) a strong correlation between certain variables, which also occurs for the supersingular six curve E_6 with coefficient

$a = 6$. Via CPA, we exploit this correlation to detect these curves, and mount a similar adaptive attack.

Using these two approaches, we present a generic attack framework, and apply this attack to the state-of-the-art CSIDH implementations SQALE [15] and CTIDH [4] (Sect. 3), and to SIKE (Sect. 4). We explore the practical feasibility of the proposed attacks (Sect. 5), simulations (Sect. 6), and different types of countermeasures (Sect. 7). Our code is available in the public domain:

https://github.com/PaZeZeVaAt/simulation

Related Work. The analysis of physical attacks on isogeny-based schemes has only recently gained more attention, including both side-channel [21,24, 29,43,44] and fault attacks [1,9,10,23,30,40,41]. Introduced for classical elliptic curve cryptography (ECC) in [3,25,26], zero-value attacks were adapted to SIKE in [21], which applies t-tests to determine zero values within power traces [39].

An approach to identify certain structures within traces, similar to the ones occurring in non-zero representations of the zero curve and six curve in our case, are correlation-enhanced power analysis collision attacks [34], such as [5] for ECC. This attack combines the concept of horizontal side-channel analysis [36] with correlation-enhanced power analysis collision attacks to extract leakage from a single trace.

We note that from a constructive perspective, this attack follows the idea of steering isogeny paths over special curves, as proposed for the zero curve in [29]. Furthermore, the attack on SIKE uses the framework of [1] to produce suitable public keys. However, our attack is a *passive* attack that is much easier to perform in practice compared to the elaborate fault injection required for [1].

2   Preliminaries

We briefly introduce mathematical background related to isogeny-based cryptography, and the schemes CSIDH [13] and SIKE [27]. For more mathematical details, we refer to [20].

Mathematical Background. Let $\mathbb{F}_q$ with $q = p^k$ denote the finite field of order q, with a prime $p > 3$. Supersingular elliptic curves over $\mathbb{F}_q$ are characterized by the condition $\#E(\mathbb{F}_q) \equiv 1 \mod p$. Throughout this work, we will only encounter group orders that are multiples of 4, and hence elliptic curves E over $\mathbb{F}_q$ with $j(E) \in \mathbb{F}_q$ can be represented in Montgomery form:

$$E_a : y^2 = x^3 + ax^2 + x, \quad a \in \mathbb{F}_q. \tag{1}$$

Given two such elliptic curves E_a and $E_{a'}$, an isogeny is a morphism $\varphi : E_a \to E_{a'}$ such that $\infty_{E_a} \mapsto \infty_{E_{a'}}$ for the neutral elements of E_a and $E_{a'}$. In the context of isogeny-based cryptography, we are only interested in separable isogenies, which are characterized by their kernel (up to isomorphism): A finite subgroup $G \subset E_a(\overline{\mathbb{F}_q})$ defines a separable isogeny $\varphi : E_a \to E_a/G$ and vice versa. In such a case, the degree of φ is equal to the size of its kernel, $|G|$. For any isogeny $\varphi : E_a \to E_{a'}$, there is a unique isogeny $\hat{\varphi} : E_{a'} \to E_a$ such that $\hat{\varphi} \circ \varphi = [\deg(\varphi)]$ is the scalar point multiplication on E_a by $\deg(\varphi)$. We call $\hat{\varphi}$ the dual isogeny. Two elliptic curves E_a and $E_{a'}$ over $\mathbb{F}_q$ are isogenous, i.e., there exists an isogeny between them, if and only if $\#E_a(\mathbb{F}_q) = \#E_{a'}(\mathbb{F}_q)$.

2.1   CSIDH

In the context of CSIDH, we choose p of the form $p + 1 = h \cdot \prod_{i=1}^{n} \ell_i$ and work with supersingular elliptic curves over $\mathbb{F}_p$. Each ℓ_i is a small odd prime, and h is a suitable cofactor to ensure p is prime, with the additional requirement that $4 \mid h$. Usually, we pick p such that $p \equiv 3 \mod 8$ and work with the set $\mathcal{E}$ of supersingular elliptic curves with minimal endomorphism ring $\mathcal{O} \cong \mathbb{Z}[\sqrt{-p}]$. This ensures that the group order $p + 1$ is a multiple of 4, and any such supersingular elliptic curve can be represented uniquely in Montgomery form [13], as given by Equation (1) with $a \in \mathbb{F}_p$.

The main operation in CSIDH is the group action of the ideal class group of $\mathcal{O}$ acting on the set $\mathcal{E}$. We are interested in specific ideals $\mathfrak{l}_i$ of $\mathcal{O}$, whose action $\mathfrak{l}_i * E$ on some curve $E \in \mathcal{E}$ is given by an isogeny of degree ℓ_i that is defined by the kernel $G = E[\ell_i] \cap E[\pi - 1]$, where π denotes the Frobenius endomorphism, i.e., $\mathbb{F}_p$-rational points that have ℓ_i-torsion. For $E_a \in \mathcal{E}$ we get that $\#E_a = p + 1$, and $E_a(\mathbb{F}_p) \cong \mathbb{Z}_h \times \prod_{i=1}^{n} \mathbb{Z}_{\ell_i}$. This implies there are ℓ_i of such points $P \in E[\ell_i] \cap E[\pi - 1]$, and $\ell_i - 1$ of these (all but the point ∞_{E_a}) will generate G. The codomain $E_{a'}$ of such an isogeny is again supersingular and so $|E_{a'}(\mathbb{F}_p)| = p + 1$, which implies $\mathfrak{l}_i$ can also be applied to $E_{a'}$. This implies a group action of the ideals $\mathfrak{l}_i$ on the supersingular curves E_a over $\mathbb{F}_p$, which we denote by $[\mathfrak{l}_i] * E_a$. In particular, this group action is commutative: $[\mathfrak{l}_i\mathfrak{l}_j] * E_a \cong [\mathfrak{l}_i] * [\mathfrak{l}_j] * E_a \cong [\mathfrak{l}_j] * [\mathfrak{l}_i] * E_a \cong [\mathfrak{l}_j\mathfrak{l}_i] * E_a$. For each $\mathfrak{l}_i$ there exists an inverse $\mathfrak{l}_i^{-1}$, whose action on $E \in \mathcal{E}$ is given by an ℓ_i-isogeny that is defined by the kernel $G = E[\ell_i] \cap E[\pi + 1]$.

For reasons of brevity, in the following we will sometimes abuse notation and identify the ideals $\mathfrak{l}_i^{\pm 1}$ with the ℓ_i-isogenies that their action implies.

The CSIDH Scheme. The CSIDH scheme is based on the group action as described above: We apply each of the n different $\mathfrak{l}_i^{\pm 1}$ a number of times to a given curve E_a, and we denote this number by e_i. Hence, the secret key is some vector of n integers $(e_1, \ldots, e_n)$ defining an element $\mathfrak{a} = \prod_{i=1}^{n} \mathfrak{l}_i^{e_i}$ which we can apply to supersingular curves E_a over $\mathbb{F}_p$. There is some variation between different proposals on where e_i is chosen from: The original proposal of CSIDH-512 picks $e_i \in \{-m, \ldots, m\}$ with $m = 5$, but one can also define individual bounds $m_i \in \mathbb{Z}$ per e_i. The key space is of size $\prod(2m_i + 1)$. For the original CSIDH-512 proposal with $m_i = 5$ and $n = 74$, this gives roughly size 2^{256}.

The public key is the supersingular curve E_a corresponding to applying the secret key $\mathfrak{a}$ to the publicly known starting curve $E_0 : y^2 = x^3 + x$:

$$E_a = \mathfrak{a} * E_0 = \mathfrak{l}_1^{e_1} * \cdots * \mathfrak{l}_n^{e_n} * E_0. \tag{2}$$

To derive a shared secret between Alice and Bob with secret keys $\mathfrak{a}$ and $\mathfrak{b}$ and given public keys $E_a = \mathfrak{a} * E_0$ and $E_b = \mathfrak{b} * E_0$, Alice simply computes $E_{ab} = \mathfrak{a} * E_b$ and Bob computes $E_{ba} = \mathfrak{b} * E_a$. From the commutativity of the group action, we get $E_{ab} \cong E_{ba}$.

Security of CSIDH. The classical security relies mostly on the size of the keyspace $\prod(2m_i + 1)$, but the quantum security of CSIDH is heavily dependent on the size of the group generated by these elements $\mathfrak{l}_i$. It is heuristically assumed that the $\mathfrak{l}_i$ generate a group of size approximately $\sqrt{p}$. While the original CSIDH proposal considered a 512-bit prime p sufficient for NIST security level 1 [13], its exact quantum security is debated [7,8,15,38]. For instance, [15] claims that 4096-bit primes are required for level 1 security. Note that the key space is not required to cover the full group of size roughly $\sqrt{p}$, but can be chosen as a large enough subset, except for particularly bad choices like subgroups. At larger prime sizes, the number n of small primes ℓ_i grows, and therefore it becomes natural to pick secret key vectors from $\{-1, 0, 1\}^n$ resp. $\{-1, 1\}^n$ for primes sizes of at least 1792 resp. 2048 bits. This allows for a large enough key space for classical security, while increasing p for sufficient quantum security.

We note that the exact quantum security of CSIDH remains unclear, and thus work on efficient and secure implementations for both smaller and larger parameters continues to appear, e.g. in [4,15].

Constant-Time Implementations. CSIDH is inherently difficult to implement in constant time, as this requires that the timing of the execution is independent of the respective secret key $(e_1, \ldots, e_n)$. However, picking a secret key vector $(e_1, \ldots, e_n)$ translates to the computation of $|e_i|$ isogenies of degree ℓ_i, which directly affects the timing of the group action evaluation. One way to mitigate this timing leakage is by using dummy isogenies: We can keep the total number of isogenies per degree constant by computing m_i isogenies of degree ℓ_i, but discarding the results of $m_i - |e_i|$ of these, effectively making them dummy computations [31,32]. Several optimizations and different techniques have been proposed in the literature [14,16,37].

The latest and currently most efficient variant of constant-time implementations of CSIDH is CTIDH [4]. In contrast to sampling private key vectors such that $e_i \in \{-m_i, \ldots, m_i\}$, CTIDH uses a different key space that exploits the approach of batching the primes ℓ_i. We define *batches* $B_1, \ldots, B_N$ of consecutive primes of lengths $n_1, \ldots, n_N$, i.e., $B_1 = (\ell_{1,1}, \ldots, \ell_{1,n_1}) = (\ell_1, \ldots, \ell_{n_1})$, $B_2 = (\ell_{2,1}, \ldots, \ell_{2,n_2}) = (\ell_{n_1+1}, \ldots, \ell_{n_1+n_2})$, et cetera. We write $e_{i,j}$ for the (secret) coefficient associated to $\ell_{i,j}$. Instead of defining bounds m_i for each individual ℓ_i so that $|e_i| \leq m_i$, CTIDH uses bounds M_i for the batch B_i, i.e., we compute at most M_i isogenies of those degrees that are contained in B_i. That is, the key sampling requires $|e_{i,1}| + \cdots + |e_{i,n_i}| \leq M_i$. CTIDH then adapts the CSIDH algorithm such that the distribution of the M_i isogenies among degrees of batch B_i does not leak through the timing channel. Among other techniques, this involves Matryoshka isogenies, first introduced in [7], that perform the exact same sequence of instructions independent of its isogeny degree $\ell_{i,j} \in B_i$.

The main advantage of CTIDH is the ambiguity of the isogeny computations: From a time-channel perspective, a Matryoshka isogeny for B_i could be an $\ell_{i,j}$-isogeny for any $\ell_{i,j} \in B_i$. Thus, in comparison to the previous CSIDH algorithms, CTIDH covers the same key space size in fewer isogenies. For instance, the previously fastest implementation of CSIDH-512 required 431 isogenies in total [2] (including dummies), whereas CTIDH [4] requires only 208 isogenies (including dummies) for the same key space size. This leads to an almost twofold speedup.

Representation of Montgomery Coefficient. To decrease computational cost by avoiding costly inversions, the curve E_a is almost always represented using *projective* coordinates for $a \in \mathbb{F}_p$. The following two are used most in current CSIDH-based implementations:

- the Montgomery form $(A : C)$, such that $a = A/C$, with C non-zero,
- and the alternative Montgomery form $(A + 2C : 4C)$, such that $a = A/C$, with C non-zero.

The alternative Montgomery form is most common, as it is used in projective scalar point multiplication formulas. Hence, in most state-of-the-art implementations of CSIDH-based systems, the Montgomery coefficient a is mapped to alternative Montgomery form and remains in this form until the end, where it is mapped back to affine form for the public key resp. shared secret (e.g., in SQALE [15]). CTIDH [4] switches between both representations after each isogeny, and maps back to affine $a = A/C$ at the end. For most values of $(A : C)$ and $(A + 2C : 4C)$, $a = A/C$ represents either an ordinary or a supersingular curve. The exceptions are $C = 0$, which represents no algebraic object, and $A = \pm 2C$, which represents the singular curves $E_{\pm 2}$. Specifically the supersingular zero curve E_0 is represented as $(0 : C)$ in Montgomery form and $(2C : 4C)$ in alternative Montgomery form, where $C \in \mathbb{F}_p$ can be any non-zero value.

Isogeny Computation in Projective Form. When using projective representations to compute isogenies with domain E_a where a is represented as $(A : C)$, most implementations use projectivized versions of Vélu's formulas, described in [6,33,42]. To compute the action of $\mathfrak{l}_i^{\pm 1}$ on E_a, one finds a point P of order ℓ_i on E_a and computes the x-coordinates of the points $\{P, [2]P, \ldots, [\frac{\ell-1}{2}]P\}$. Let $(X_k : Z_k)$ denote the x-coordinate of $[k]P$ in projective form. Then, the projective Montgomery coefficient $(A' : C')$ of $E_{a'} = \mathfrak{l}_i * E_a$ using Montgomery form $(A : C)$ is computed by

$$B_z = \prod_{k=1}^{\frac{\ell-1}{2}} Z_k, \quad A' = (A + 2C)^\ell \cdot B_z^8, \tag{3}$$

$$B_x = \prod_{k=1}^{\frac{\ell-1}{2}} X_k, \quad C' = (A - 2C)^\ell \cdot B_x^8, \tag{4}$$

and when using alternative Montgomery form $(\alpha : \beta) = (A + 2C : 4C)$ by

$$B_z = \prod_{k=1}^{\frac{\ell-1}{2}} Z_k, \quad \alpha' = \alpha^\ell \cdot B_z^8, \tag{5}$$

$$B_x = \prod_{k=1}^{\frac{\ell-1}{2}} X_k, \quad \beta' = \alpha' - (\alpha - \beta)^\ell \cdot B_x^8, \tag{6}$$

where $(\alpha' : \beta')$ represents $E_{a'}$ in alternative Montgomery form. Note that the values $(A + 2C)$ in (3), $(A - 2C)$ in (4), α in (5) and $(\alpha - \beta)$ in (6) are never zero: In all cases, this implies $A/C = \pm 2$, i.e., the singular curves $E_{\pm 2}$.

Remark 1. So far, we know of no deterministic implementations based on the class group action. This is because in order to perform the isogenies, all current implementations sample a random point P on the curve and compute the scalar multiple of P required to perform isogenies. The projective coordinates $(X_k : Z_k)$ are then non-deterministic, and hence the output of Equations (3) to (6) is non-deterministic. This implies that the representation of a as $(A : C)$ or $(A + 2C : 4C)$ is non-deterministic after the first isogeny. A deterministic approach, e.g. as sketched in [7] using Elligator, ensures a deterministic representation of a, but has so far not been put into practice.

2.2   SIKE

In SIKE, we pick a prime of the form $p = 2^{e_A} \cdot 3^{e_B} - 1$ such that $2^{e_A} \approx 3^{e_B}$, and work with supersingular elliptic curves over $\mathbb{F}_{p^2}$ in Montgomery form. We choose to work with curves such that $E_a(\mathbb{F}_{p^2}) = (p+1)^2$, and we have $E_a(\mathbb{F}_{p^2}) \cong \mathbb{Z}_{2^{e_A}}^2 \times \mathbb{Z}_{3^{e_B}}^2$ for these curves. Thus, the full 2^{e_A}- and 3^{e_B}-torsion subgroups lie in $E_a(\mathbb{F}_{p^2})$. Any point R_A of order 2^{e_A} then uniquely (up to isomorphism) determines a 2^{e_A}-isogeny and codomain curve $E_{a'} = E_a/\langle R_A \rangle$ with kernel $\langle R_A \rangle$. For choosing an appropriate point, the SIKE setup defines basis points P_A and Q_A of the 2^{e_A}-torsion of the public starting curve. Picking an integer $\mathsf{sk}_A \in [0, 2^{e_A} - 1]$ and computing $R_A = P_A + [\mathsf{sk}_A]Q_A$ then results in choosing such a kernel generator R_A of order 2^{e_A}.

In practice, such a 2^{e_A}-isogeny is computed as a sequence of 2-isogenies of length e_A. This can be interpreted as a sequence of steps through a graph: For a prime ℓ with $\ell \neq p$, the ℓ-isogeny graph consists of vertices that represent (j-invariants of) elliptic curves, and edges representing ℓ-isogenies. Due to the existence of dual isogenies, edges are undirected. For supersingular curves, this graph is an $(\ell + 1)$-regular expander graph and contains approximately $p/12$ vertices. Hence, a sequence of 2-isogenies of length e_A corresponds to a walk of length e_A through the 2-isogeny graph. An analogous discussion applies to the case of 3^{e_B}-isogenies. Note that for reasons of efficiency, we often combine two 2-isogeny steps into one 4-isogeny.

The secret keys sk_A, sk_B can be decomposed as

$$\mathrm{sk}_A = \sum_{i=0}^{e_2-1} \mathrm{sk}_i \cdot 2^i \quad \mathrm{sk}_i \in \{0,1\}, \quad \mathrm{sk}_B = \sum_{i=0}^{e_3-1} \mathrm{sk}_i \cdot 3^i \quad \mathrm{sk}_i \in \{0,1,2\}.$$

We refer to these sk_i as the *bits* resp. the *trits* of the secret key sk_A resp. sk_B. For a given sk, we use $\mathrm{sk}_{<k}$ to represent the key up to the k-th bit/trit sk_{k-1}.

The SIKE Scheme. The main idea behind SIDH and SIKE is to use secret isogenies to set up a key exchange scheme resp. key encapsulation mechanism. SIDH fixes E_6 as starting curve, and torsion basis points P_A, Q_A and P_B, Q_B. It uses the following subroutines:

- KeyGen_A samples a secret key $\mathrm{sk}_A \in [0, 2^{e_A} - 1]$, computes $R_A = P_A + [\mathrm{sk}_A]Q_A$, and the secret isogeny $\phi_A : E_6 \rightarrow E_6/\langle R_A \rangle$. It outputs the key pair $(\mathrm{sk}_A, \mathrm{pk}_A)$, where $\mathrm{pk}_A = (\phi_A(P_B), \phi_A(Q_B), \phi_A(Q_B - P_B))$. We write $\mathrm{KeyGen}_A(\mathrm{sk})$ if KeyGen_A does not sample a secret key, but gets sk as input.
- KeyGen_B proceeds analogously with swapped indices A and B. The public key is $\mathrm{pk}_B = (\phi_B(P_A), \phi_B(Q_A), \phi_B(Q_A - P_A))$.
- Derive_A takes as input $(\mathrm{sk}_A, \mathrm{pk}_B) = (S_A, T_A, T_A - S_A)$. It computes the starting curve E_B from the points in pk_B, the secret point $R'_A = S_A + [\mathrm{sk}_A]T_A$, and the isogeny $\phi'_A : E_B \rightarrow E_B/\langle R'_A \rangle$.
- Derive_B proceeds analogously with input $(\mathrm{sk}_B, \mathrm{pk}_A)$, and computes the co-domain curve $E_A/\langle R'_B \rangle$.

When running this key exchange, both parties arrive at a curve (isomorphic to) $E_6/\langle R_A, R_B \rangle$, and (a hash of) its j-variant can serve as a shared secret.

SIKE uses the SIDH subroutines KeyGen and Derive to construct three algorithms KeyGen, Encaps, and Decaps. Furthermore, we define h and h' to be cryptographic hash functions.

- KeyGen generates a (static) key pair $(\mathrm{sk}, \mathrm{pk}) \leftarrow \mathrm{KeyGen}_B$.
- Encaps encapsulates a random value m in the following way:
  - Get an ephemeral key pair $(\mathrm{ek}, c) \leftarrow \mathrm{KeyGen}_A(\mathrm{ek})$ with $\mathrm{ek} = h(\mathrm{pk}, m)$.
  - Compute the shared secret $s \leftarrow \mathrm{Derive}_A(\mathrm{ek}, \mathrm{pk})$.
  - Compute the ciphertext $\mathrm{ct} = (c, h'(s) \oplus m)$.
- Decaps receives a ciphertext (c_0, c_1), and proceeds as follows:
  - Compute the shared secret $s' \leftarrow \mathrm{Derive}_B(\mathrm{sk}, c_0)$.
  - Recover $m' \leftarrow c_1 \oplus h'(s')$.
  - Recompute $\mathrm{ek}' = h(\mathrm{pk}, m')$.
  - Compute $(\mathrm{ek}', c') \leftarrow \mathrm{KeyGen}_A(\mathrm{ek}')$ and check if $c' = c_0$.

Passing this check guarantees that the ciphertext has been generated honestly, and $m' = m$ can be used to set up a session key.

Representation of Montgomery Coefficients. As in CSIDH, the curve E_a is almost always represented using projective coordinates, with the caveat that $a \in \mathbb{F}_{p^2}$. The following two representations are used throughout SIKE computations, although in different subroutines.

- The alternative Montgomery form $(A + 2C : 4C)$, such that $a = A/C$ with C non-zero. This representation is used for Alice's computations as it is the most efficient for computing 2-isogenies. It is often written as $(A_{24}^+ : C_{24})$ with $A_{24}^+ = A + 2C$ and $C_{24} = 4C$ so that $a = 2(2A_{24}^+ - C_{24})/C_{24}$.
- The form $(A + 2C : A - 2C)$, such that $a = A/C$, with C non-zero. This representation is used for Bob's computations as it is the most efficient for computing 3-isogenies. It is often written as $(A_{24}^+ : A_{24}^-)$ with $A_{24}^+ = A + 2C$ and $A_{24}^- = A - 2C$ so that $a = 2(A_{24}^+ + A_{24}^-)/(A_{24}^+ - A_{24}^-)$.

Note that the values A, C, A_{24}^+, A_{24}^- and C_{24} are in $\mathbb{F}_{p^2}$. When necessary, we write them as $\alpha + \beta i$ with $\alpha, \beta \in \mathbb{F}_p$ and $i^2 = -1$. Equal to CSIDH, both forms represent either an ordinary or a supersingular curve, with the exceptions $C = 0$, which represents no algebraic object, and $A = \pm 2C$, which represents the singular curves $E_{\pm 2}$. For the rest of the paper, we are interested in representations of the supersingular six curve E_6. Fortunately, E_6 is represented in *both* forms as $(8C : 4C)$, with $C = \alpha + \beta i \in \mathbb{F}_{p^2}$ any non-zero element. For the goal of the paper, this means that the analysis is similar for both forms.

Isogeny Computation in Projective Form. SIKE uses the above projective representations to compute the codomain $E_{\tilde{a}}$ of a 3- or 4-isogeny $\phi : E_a \to E_{\tilde{a}}$.

4-isogeny. Given a point P of order 4 on E_a with x-coordinate $x(P) = (X : Z)$, the codomain $E_{\tilde{a}} = E_a/\langle P \rangle$ with $\tilde{a}$ represented by $(\tilde{A}_{24}^+ : \tilde{C}_{24})$ is computed by

$$\tilde{A}_{24}^+ = 4 \cdot X^4, \qquad \tilde{C}_{24} = 4 \cdot Z^4. \tag{7}$$

3-isogeny. Given a point P of order 3 on E_a with x-coordinate $x(P) = (X : Z)$, the codomain $E_{\tilde{a}} = E_a/\langle P \rangle$ with $\tilde{a}$ represented by $(\tilde{A}_{24}^+ : \tilde{A}_{24}^-)$ is computed by

$$\tilde{A}_{24}^+ = (3X + Z)^3 \cdot (X - Z), \quad \tilde{A}_{24}^- = (3X - Z)^3 \cdot (X + Z). \tag{8}$$

3   Recovering CSIDH Keys with E_0 Side-Channel Leakage

In this section, we explore how side-channel information can leak information on secret isogeny walks. As shown in [21], it is possible to detect zero values in isogeny computations using side-channel information. In Sect. 3.1, we specifically explore how both representations of the zero curve E_0, i.e. $(0 : C)$ and $(2C : 4C)$, leak secret information, even though the value $C \in \mathbb{F}_p$ is assumed to be a uniformly random non-zero value. As E_0 is always a valid supersingular $\mathbb{F}_p$-curve in CSIDH, we can always construct a walk that potentially passes over E_0. This allows us to describe a generic approach to leak a given bit of information of the secret isogeny walk, hence, a general attack on the class group action as introduced in CSIDH. We apply this attack in more detail to the two current state-of-the-art cryptosystems based on this class group action: SQALE in Sect. 3.2 and CTIDH in Sect. 3.3. We discuss their practical feasibility in Sect. 5 and simulate these attacks in Sect. 6. We note that the proposed attack applies to all variants of CSIDH that we know of, e.g. from [13,14].

Throughout this work, we assume a static-key setting, i.e., that a long-term secret key $\mathfrak{a}$ is used, and that the attacker can repeatedly trigger key exchange executions on the target device using public key curves of their choice. Formally, this means that we adaptively feed curves E_{PK} and get side-channel information on the computations $\mathfrak{a} * E_{PK}$. We exploit this information to reveal $\mathfrak{a}$ bit by bit.

3.1 Discovering a Bit of Information on a Secret Isogeny Walk

Detecting E_0 in Montgomery form. As described in Remark 1, the representation of the Montgomery coefficient as $(A : C)$ or $(A + 2C : 4C)$ is non-deterministic after the first isogeny, so they effectively contain random $\mathbb{F}_p$-values, representing the affine Montgomery coefficient a. This makes it hard to get any information on E_a using side channels. However, in Montgomery form the curve E_0 is special: It is simply represented by $(0 : C)$ for some $C \in \mathbb{F}_p$. We define such a representation containing a zero a *zero-value representation*.

Definition 1. *Let E_a be an elliptic curve over $\mathbb{F}_p$. A zero-value representation is a representation of the Montgomery coefficient a in projective coordinates $(\alpha : \beta)$ such that either $\alpha = 0$ or $\beta = 0$.*

Clearly, a representation of E_0 in Montgomery form must be a zero-value representation. As is known for ECC and SIKE, an attacker can observe zero-value representations in several different ways using side-channel analysis [21]. We will expand on this in Sect. 5 to show that E_0 leaks secret information in implementations that use Montgomery form.

Detecting E_0 in alternative Montgomery form. Using the alternative Montgomery form, no non-singular curve has a zero-value representation, as $(A + 2C : 4C)$ can only be zero for $A = -2C$ corresponding to $a = -2$, which represents the singular curve E_{-2}. Thus, the alternative Montgomery form avoids the side-channel attack described above. Nevertheless, the representation of E_0 is still unusual: Whenever $2C$ is smaller than $p/2$, doubling $2C$ does not require a modular reduction, and hence the bit representation of $4C$ is precisely a bit shift of $2C$ by one bit to the left. Such strongly correlated values can be observed in several ways using side-channel analysis, as we detail later in Sect. 5.

Definition 2. *Let E_a be an elliptic curve over $\mathbb{F}_p$. A strongly-correlated representation is a representation of the Montgomery coefficient a in projective coordinates $(\alpha : \beta)$ such that the bit representations of α and β are bit shifts.[1]*

For E_0, for any non-zero value C with $2C \leq p/2$, the representation in alternative Montgomery form by $(2C : 4C)$ is a strongly-correlated representation. As C is effectively random during the computation of the class group action, in roughly 50% of the cases where we pass over E_0, the representation is strongly

---

[1] This definition may be expanded to cover other types of correlation, whenever such correlation can be distinguished from random values using side-channel information.

correlated. For random values of a, the values of $(A + 2C : 4C)$ are indistinguishable from random $(\gamma : \delta)$, and so an attacker can differentiate E_0 from such curves. From this, an attacker only needs a few traces to determine accurately whether a walk passes over E_0 or not, as discussed in Sect. 5.

Remark 2. Other curves have strongly-correlated representations too, e.g., the curve E_6 requires $A = 6C$ which gives $(8C : 4C)$ with $C \in \mathbb{F}_p$ random and non-zero, and so E_6 can be detected in precisely the same way as E_0. For simplicity, we focus on the zero curve in the CSIDH attack. We note that analyzing this attack to any curve with strongly-correlated representations is of independent interest for CSIDH and other isogeny-based schemes (such as SIKE).

Remark 3. In the case where $2C$ is larger than $p/2$, the modular reduction by p decreases the correlation between $2C$ and $4C$ significantly, which is why we disregard these cases. However, a modular reduction does not affect all bits, and so this correlation remains for unaffected bits. Especially for primes with large cofactor 2^k in $p + 1$, or primes close to a power of 2, the correlation between unaffected bits should be exploitable. For the primes used in the CSIDH instances in this work, this effect is negligible. However, the primes used in SIDH and SIKE do have this form and we exploit this in Sect. 4.

The idea is now to detect E_0 in a certain step k of the computation $\mathfrak{a} * E_{\text{PK}}$. In order to ensure that this happens the computation needs to be performed in a known order of isogeny steps $E \to \mathfrak{l}^{(k)} * E$. In general, by the way how isogenies are computed, such a step can fail with a certain probability. The following definition takes this into account.

Definition 3. *Let $\mathfrak{a}$ be a secret isogeny walk. An ordered evaluation of $\mathfrak{a} * E$ is an evaluation in a fixed order*

$$\mathfrak{l}^{(n)} * \ldots * \mathfrak{l}^{(1)} * E$$

of n steps, assuming that no step fails. We write $\mathfrak{a}_k * E$ for the first k steps of of such an evaluation,

$$\mathfrak{l}^{(k)} * \ldots * \mathfrak{l}^{(1)} * E.$$

We define $p_{\mathfrak{a}}$ resp. $p_{\mathfrak{a}_k}$ as the probability that $\mathfrak{a}$ resp. $\mathfrak{a}_k$ is evaluated without failed steps.

Generic Approach to Discover Isogeny Walks Using E_0. Given the ability to detect E_0 in a walk for both the Montgomery form and the alternative Montgomery form, we sketch the following approach to discover bits of a secret isogeny walk $\mathfrak{a}$ that has an ordered evaluation. Assuming we know the first $k - 1$ steps $\mathfrak{l}^{(k-1)} * \ldots * \mathfrak{l}^{(1)}$ in the secret isogeny walk $\mathfrak{a}$, denoted by $\mathfrak{a}_{k-1}$, we want to see if the k-th step $\mathfrak{l}^{(k)}$ equals $\mathfrak{l}_i$ or $\mathfrak{l}_i^{-1}$ for some i. We compute $E_a = \mathfrak{l}_i^{-1} * E_0$ and $E_{a'} = \mathfrak{l}_i^{-1} * E_a$, and as a public key we use $E_{\text{PK}} = \mathfrak{a}_{k-1}^{-1} * E_a$. Then, when applying the secret walk $\mathfrak{a}$ to E_{PK}, the k-th step either goes over E_0 or over $E_{a'}$. From side-channel information, we observe if the k-th step applies $\mathfrak{l}_i^e = \mathfrak{l}_i^1$ or $\mathfrak{l}_i^e = \mathfrak{l}_i^{-1}$, and set $\mathfrak{l}^{(k)} = \mathfrak{l}_i^e$, as shown in Fig. 1. Then we repeat with $\mathfrak{a}_k = \mathfrak{l}_i^e \cdot \mathfrak{a}_{k-1}$.

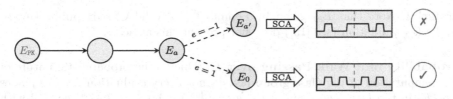

Fig. 1. Generic approach to discover secret bits using side-channel information.

If E_0 is not detected in the above setting, i.e. $e = -1$, we can confirm this by an additional measurement: We compute $\tilde{E}_a = \mathfrak{l} * E_0$ and $\tilde{E}_{a'} = \mathfrak{l} * \tilde{E}_a$, and use $\tilde{E}_{\text{PK}} = \mathfrak{a}_{k-1}^{-1} * \tilde{E}_a$ as public key. If $e = -1$, the isogeny walk now passes over E_0, which can be recognized via side-channel analysis. More formally, we get:

Lemma 1. *Let $\mathfrak{a}$ be any isogeny walk of the form $\mathfrak{a} = \prod \mathfrak{l}_i^{e_i}$. Assume the evaluation of $\mathfrak{a}$ is an ordered evaluation. Then, there exists a supersingular curve E_{PK} over $\mathbb{F}_p$ such that $\mathfrak{a} * E_{\text{PK}}$ passes over E_0 in the k-th step.*

After successfully detecting all steps $\mathfrak{l}^{(k)}$, the private key elements e_i can simply be recovered by counting how often $\mathfrak{l}_i$ resp. $\mathfrak{l}_i^{-1}$ appeared in the evaluation.

This generic approach has a nice advantage: If one detects the k-th step to walk over E_0, this confirms all previous steps were guessed correctly. In other words, guessing wrongly in a certain step will be noticed in the next step: Denote a wrong guess by $\mathfrak{a}_k^{\text{wrong}} = \mathfrak{l}^{-e} \cdot \mathfrak{a}_{k-1}$. The attacker computes E_a from E_0 so that $\mathfrak{l}' * E_a = E_0$ and gives the target E_{PK} such that $\mathfrak{a}_k^{\text{wrong}} * E_{\text{PK}} = E_a$. Due to the wrong guess, neither $e = 1$ nor $e = -1$ lead to E_0, as the *actual* secret walk $\mathfrak{a}$ leads to $E_{a'} = \mathfrak{a}_k * E_{\text{PK}}$, and the case $e = 1$ leads to $E_{\neg 0} = \mathfrak{l}' * E_{a'} = \mathfrak{l}^{-2e} * E_0$, as shown in Fig. 2.

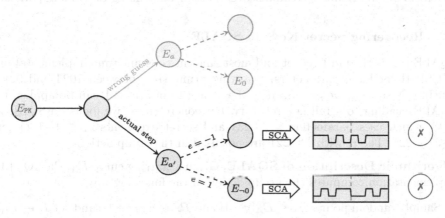

Fig. 2. Due to a wrong guess of the isogeny path $\mathfrak{a}_k$, an attacker miscomputes E_{PK} and the actual walk does not pass over E_0.

Remark 4. Note that E_{PK} given by Lemma 1 is a valid CSIDH public key, so public key validation (see [13]) does not prevent this attack.

Probability of a Walk Passing over E_0. Due to the probabilistic nature of the computation of the class group action, not every evaluation $\mathfrak{a} * E_{PK}$ passes over E_0 in the k-th step: One of the steps $\mathfrak{l}^{(j)}$ for $1 \leq j \leq k-1$ can fail with probability $1/\ell^{(j)}$, and if so, the k-th step passes over a different curve. With E_{PK} as given by Lemma 1, the probability that an ordered evaluation $\mathfrak{a} * E_{PK}$ passes over E_0 is then described by $p_{\mathfrak{a}_k}$, which we compute in Lemma 2.

Lemma 2. *Let $\mathfrak{a}$ be an isogeny walk computed as an ordered evaluation $\mathfrak{l}^{(n)} * \ldots * \mathfrak{l}^{(1)} * E_{PK}$. Then $p_{\mathfrak{a}_k}$, the probability that the first k isogenies succeed, is*

$$p_{\mathfrak{a}_k} := \prod_{j=1}^{k} \frac{\ell^{(j)} - 1}{\ell^{(j)}}$$

where $\ell^{(j)}$ is the degree of the isogeny $\mathfrak{l}^{(j)}$ in the j-th step.

As $p_{\mathfrak{a}_k}$ describes the chance that we pass over E_0 in the k-th step, $1/p_{\mathfrak{a}_k}$ gives us the estimated number of measurements of $\mathfrak{a} * E_{PK}$ we need in order to pass over E_0 in step k. We apply this more concretely in Sects. 3.2 and 3.3.

Remark 5. Instead of learning bit by bit starting from the beginning of the secret isogeny walk, we can also start at the end of the walk. To do so, we use the twist E_{-t} of the target's public key E_t, for which $\mathfrak{a} * E_{-t} = E_0$. As for the generic attack, we feed $E_{PK} = \mathfrak{l}^{-1} * E_{-t}$ and $\tilde{E}_{PK} = \mathfrak{l} * E_{-t}$. The computation then passes over E_0 in the *last* step instead of the *first*. This approach requires the same probability $p_{\mathfrak{a}_k}$ to recover the k-th bit, but assumes knowledge of all bits after k instead of before. Hence, we can discover starting and ending bits of $\mathfrak{a}$ in parallel.

3.2 Recovering Secret Keys in SQALE

SQALE [15] is the most recent and most efficient constant-time implementation of CSIDH for large parameters, featuring prime sizes between 1024 and 9216 bit. In this section, we explain how the attack from Sect. 3.1 can be applied to SQALE, leading to a full key recovery. For concreteness, we focus on SQALE-2048, which uses parameters $n = 231$ and secret exponents $e_i \in \{-1, 1\}$ for $1 \leq i \leq 221$. The ℓ_i with $i > 221$ are not used in the group action.

Algorithmic Description of SQALE. Given a starting curve E_A, the SQALE implementation computes the group action in the following way:

– Sample random points $P_+ \in E_A[\pi - 1]$ and $P_- \in E_A[\pi + 1]$, and set $E \leftarrow E_A$.
– Iterate through $i \in \{1, \ldots, n\}$ in ascending order, and attempt to compute $\phi : E \rightarrow \mathfrak{l}_i^{e_i} * E$ using P_+ resp P_-. Push both points through each ϕ.
– In case of point rejections, sample fresh points and attempt to compute the corresponding isogenies, until all $\mathfrak{l}_i^{e_i}$ have been applied.

In order to speed up computations, SQALE additionally pushes intermediate points through isogenies, which saves computational effort in following steps [16]. However, the exact design of the computational strategy inside CSIDH is not relevant for the proposed attack. Using the above description, we sketch the adaptive attack on SQALE-2048 to recover the secret key bit by bit. In case of no point rejections, the order of steps in which $\mathfrak{a} * E_{\text{PK}}$ is computed in SQALE is deterministic, and thus we can immediately apply Lemmas 1 and 2:

Corollary 1. *If no point rejections occur, the computation $\mathfrak{a} * E_{\text{PK}}$ in SQALE is an ordered evaluation with*

$$\mathfrak{l}^{(n)} * \ldots * \mathfrak{l}^{(1)} * E_{\text{PK}} = \mathfrak{l}_{221}^{e_{221}} * \ldots * \mathfrak{l}_{1}^{e_1} * E_{\text{PK}}.$$

Hence, $p_{\mathfrak{a}_k} = \prod_{i=1}^{k} \frac{\ell_i - 1}{\ell_i}$.

SQALE uses coefficients in alternative Montgomery form $(A + 2C : 4C)$, so that passing over the curve E_0 can be detected as described in Sect. 3.1.

Recovering the k-th bit. Recovering the k-th bit of a SQALE secret key works exactly as described in Fig. 1, as in a successful run SQALE performs each step $\mathfrak{l}_i^{\pm 1}$ in ascending order. Thus, the k-th step, in a run where the first k steps succeed, computes $E \to \mathfrak{l}_k^{\pm 1} * E$. For the attack, we assume knowledge of the first $k - 1$ bits of the secret to produce public keys E_{PK} resp. $\tilde{E}_{\text{PK}}$ that lead the target through E_0 via an application of $\mathfrak{l}_k^{-1}$ resp. $\mathfrak{l}_k$, as given by Lemma 1. For one of these cases, with probability $p_{\mathfrak{a}_k}$ (Lemma 2), the target passes over E_0 on the k-th step, and we learn the k-th secret bit e_k from side-channel information.

As k increases, $p_{\mathfrak{a}_k}$ decreases: In order for the target to pass over E_0 in one of the two cases, *all* previous isogenies have to succeed, for which Corollary 1 gives the probability $p_{\mathfrak{a}_k}$. Thus, the fact that SQALE first computes small-degree isogenies is slightly inconvenient for the attack, due to their low success probabilities. Nevertheless, attacking the last round of SQALE-2048 has a success probability of roughly $p_{\mathfrak{a}_{221}} = \prod_{j=1}^{221}(\ell_j - 1)/\ell_j \approx 19.3\%$, so that in about 1 in 5 runs, every isogeny succeeds and we pass over E_0 for the 221-th bit, compared to 2 in 3 runs to pass over E_0 for the first bit ($p_{\mathfrak{a}_1} = \frac{2}{3}$). This means that we need about three times as many measurements to discover the last bit, than the first bit. Nonetheless the required total number of measurements for all bits is very managable; we get with Lemma 2:

Corollary 2. *Assuming a pass over E_0 leaks the k-th bit when the representation is strongly correlated, the estimated number of measurements to recover a SQALE-2048 key is*

$$4 \cdot \sum_{k=1}^{221} \frac{1}{p_{\mathfrak{a}_k}} = 4 \cdot \sum_{k=1}^{221} \prod_{i=1}^{k} \frac{\ell_i}{\ell_i - 1} \approx 4 \cdot 1020.$$

Here, the factor 4 represents the fact that we need to feed both E_{PK} and $\tilde{E}_{\text{PK}}$, and that only half the time $(2C : 4C)$ is strongly-correlated. In practice, for more certainty, we increase the number of attempts per bit by some constant α, giving a total of $\alpha \cdot 4 \cdot 1020$ expected attempts. We detail this in Sect. 6.

3.3 Recovering Secret Keys in CTIDH

CTIDH [4] is the most efficient constant-time implementation of CSIDH to date, although the work restricts to the CSIDH-512 and CSIDH-1024 parameter sets. We note that techniques from CTIDH can be used to significantly speed up CSIDH for larger parameters too, yet this appears to require some modifications that have not been explored in the literature yet. In this section, we explain how zero-value curve attacks can be mounted on CTIDH, leading to a partial or full key recovery, depending on the number of measurements that is deemed possible. For concreteness, we focus on the CTIDH parameter set with a 220-bit key space, dubbed CTIDH-511 in [4], which uses 15 batches of up to 8 primes. The bounds satisfy $M_i \leq 12$.

Algorithmic Description of CTIDH. Given a starting curve E_A, CTIDH computes the group action by multiple rounds of the following approach:

- Set $E \leftarrow E_A$, sample random points $P_+ \in E[\pi - 1]$ and $P_- \in E[\pi + 1]$.
- Per batch B_i, (attempt to) compute $\phi : E \rightarrow \mathfrak{l}_{i,j}^{\mathrm{sign}(e_{i,j})} * E$ using P_+ resp P_- (or dummy when all $\mathfrak{l}_{i,j}^{e_{i,j}}$ are performed). Push both points through each ϕ.
- Repeat this process until all $\mathfrak{l}_{i,j}^{e_{i,j}}$ and dummy isogenies have been applied.

Furthermore, the following design choices in CTIDH are especially relevant:

- Per batch B_i, CTIDH computes real isogenies first, and (potential) dummy isogenies after, to ensure M_i isogenies are computed, independent of $(e_{i,j})$.
- Per batch B_i, CTIDH computes the actual $\ell_{i,j}$-isogenies in ascending order.
- Per batch B_i, CTIDH scales the point rejection probability to the largest value, $1/\ell_{i,1}$. This slightly changes the computation of $p_{\mathfrak{a}_k}$.
- The order in which batches are processed is deterministic.

Example 1. Let $B_1 = \{3, 5\}$ with $M_1 = 6$, and let $e_{1,1} = 2$ and $e_{1,2} = -3$. For B_1, we first try to compute $E \rightarrow \mathfrak{l}_1 * E$, until this succeeds twice. Then, we try to compute $E \rightarrow \mathfrak{l}_2^{-1} * E$, until this succeeds three times. After the real isogenies, we try to compute the remaining B_1-dummy isogeny. All B_1-isogenies, including dummies, have success probability $2/3$. If all six of the B_1-isogenies are performed but other B_i are unfinished, we skip B_1 in later rounds.

As for SQALE, the above description gives us that the order in which each $\mathfrak{l}$ is applied in CTIDH is deterministic, assuming that none of the steps fail, and so we get with Lemmas 1 and 2 again:

Corollary 3. *If no point rejections occur, the computation* $\mathfrak{a} * E$ *in CTIDH is an ordered evaluation* $\mathfrak{l}^{(n)} * \ldots * \mathfrak{l}^{(1)} * E$, *with* $n = \sum M_i$, *including dummy isogenies.*

Hence we can perform the adaptive attack on CTIDH-511 to recover the secret key bit by bit. The CTIDH implementation of [4] uses coefficients in alternative Montgomery form $(A + 2C : 4C)$, but passes over Montgomery form

$(A : C)$ after each isogeny. Hence, E_0 always has a zero-value representation and we detect E_0 as described in Sect. 3.1. We argue in Sect. 5 that zero-value representations are easier to detect than strongly-correlated representations.

Recovering the k-th bit. CTIDH introduces several difficulties for the attack, compared to SQALE. In particular, let $B_i = \{\ell_{i,1}, \ldots, \ell_{i,n_i}\}$ be the batch to be processed at step k. Then, since usually $n_i > 1$, we do not get a binary decision at each step as depicted in Fig. 1, but a choice between $2 \cdot n_i$ real isogeny steps $\mathfrak{l}_{i,j}^{\pm 1}$, or possibly a dummy isogeny. In practice, with high probability, we do not need to cover all $2 \cdot n_i + 1$ options, as the following example shows.

Example 2. As CTIDH progresses through the batch ascendingly from $\ell_{i,1}$ to ℓ_{i,n_i}, the first step of a batch can often be recovered as in Fig. 1, using public keys that are one $\ell_{i,1}$-isogeny away from E_0 respectively. If both do not pass over E_0, we deduce that $e_{i,1} = 0$, and we repeat this approach using an $\ell_{i,2}$-isogeny. In case of a successful attempt for $\ell_{i,j}$, we learn that the respective key element satisfies $e_{i,j} \leq -1$ resp. $e_{i,j} \geq 1$, depending on which of the binary steps was successful.[2] If we do not succeed in detecting E_0 after trying all $\ell_{i,j}^{\pm 1}$ in B_i, we learn that the target computes a B_i-dummy isogeny, and so all $e_{i,j} = 0$ for $\ell_{i,j} \in B_i$. We can easily confirm dummy isogenies: If the k-th step is a dummy isogeny, then using E_{PK} such that $\mathfrak{a} * E_{PK}$ passes over E_0 in step $k-1$, we do not move to a different curve in step k and so we observe E_0 using side-channel information after steps $k-1$ *and* k.

This approach to recover the k-th bit in CTIDH-511 only differs slightly from Sect. 3.2: Given the knowledge of the secret path up to step $k-1$, we recover the k-th step by iterating through the target batch $B_i = \{\ell_{i,1}, \ldots, \ell_{i,n_i}\}$, until we detect E_0 for a given degree $\ell_{i,j}$, or otherwise assume a dummy isogeny. This iteration becomes easier in later rounds of each batch:

- If a previous round found that some $e_{i,j}$ is positive, we only have to check for positive $\ell_{i,j}$-isogeny steps later on (analogously for negative).
- If a previous round computed an $\ell_{i,j}$-isogeny, we immediately know that the current round cannot compute an $\ell_{i,h}$-isogeny with $h < j$.
- If a previous round detected a dummy isogeny for batch B_i, we can skip isogenies for B_i in all later rounds, since only dummy isogenies follow.

Thus, knowledge of the previous isogeny path significantly shrinks the search space for later steps. As in SQALE, the probability p_{a_k} decreases the further we get: Batches containing small degrees ℓ_i appear multiple times, and steps with small ℓ_i have the most impact on p_{a_k}. For the last step $\mathfrak{l}^{(n)}$, the probability that *all* steps $\mathfrak{l}^{(k)}$ in CTIDH-511 succeed without a single point rejection, is roughly 0.3%. This might seem low at first, but the number of measurements required to make up for this probability does not explode; we are able to recover the full key with a reasonable amount of measurements as shown in Sect. 6. Furthermore, this

---

[2] Note that the $e_{i,j}$ are not limited to $\{-1, 1\}$ in CTIDH, in contrast to e_i in SQALE.

probability represents the absolute lower bound, which is essentially the worst-case scenario: It is the probability that for the worst possible key, with no dummy isogenies, all steps must succeed in one run. In reality, almost all keys contain dummy isogenies, and we can relax the requirement that none of the steps fail, as failing dummy isogenies do not impact the curves passed afterwards.

Example 3. Let $B_1 = \{3, 5\}$ with $M_1 = 6$ as in CTIDH-511. Say we want to detect some step in the eighth round of some B_i for $i > 1$; it is not relevant in which of the seven former rounds the six B_1-isogenies are computed, and thus we can effectively allow for one point rejection in these rounds. This effect becomes more beneficial when dummy isogenies are involved. For example, if three of these six B_1-isogenies are dummies, we only need the three actual B_1-isogenies to be computed within the first seven rounds. Furthermore, after detecting the first dummy B_1-isogeny, we do not need to attack further B_1-isogenies as explained above, and therefore save significant attack effort.

Remark 6. The generic attack requires that all first k steps succeed. This is not optimal: Assuming that some steps fail increases the probability of success of passing over E_0. For example, to attack isogenies in the sixth round and knowing that $e_{1,1} = 5$, it is better to assume that one or two out of these five fail and will be performed after the $\ell_{i,j}$-isogeny we want to detect, than it is to assume that all five of these succeed in the first five rounds. This improves the success probability of passing over E_0 per measurement, but makes the analysis of the required number of measurements harder to carry out. Furthermore, this optimal approach highly depends on the respective private key. We therefore do not pursue this approach in our simulations. A concrete practical attack against a single private key that uses this improved strategy should require a smaller number of measurements.

Remark 7. For CTIDH with large parameters, one would expect more large ℓ_i and fewer isogenies of low degrees, relative to CTIDH-511. This improves the performance of the attack, as the probability of a full-torsion path increases, and so we expect more measurements to pass over E_0. However, the details of such an attack are highly dependent on the implementation of a large-parameter CTIDH scheme. As we know of no such implementation, we do not analyze such a hypothetical implementation in detail.

Remark 8. At a certain point, it might be useful to stop the attack, and compute the remaining key elements via a simple meet-in-the-middle search. Especially for later bits, if some dummy isogenies have been detected and most of the key elements $e_{i,j}$ are already known, performing a brute-force attack may be faster than this side-channel attack.

4   Recovering SIKE Keys with Side-Channel Leakage of E_6

We now apply the same strategy from Sect. 3 to SIKE. In this whole section, we focus on recovering Bob's static key sk_B by showing side-channel leakage in

Derive_B, used in Decaps. In general, the idea would apply as well to recover Alice's key sk_A in static SIDH or SIKE with swapped roles, as we do not use any specific structure of 3-isogenies. One can easily verify that the attack generalizes to SIDH based on ℓ_A or ℓ_B-isogenies for *any* ℓ_A, ℓ_B. We repeat many of the general ideas from Sect. 3, with some small differences as SIKE operates in isogeny graphs over $\mathbb{F}_{p^2}$ instead of $\mathbb{F}_p$. Fortunately, these differences make the attack *easier*.

Detecting E_6 As remarked in Sect. 2, for both representations used in SIDH and SIKE, the curve E_6 is represented as $(8C : 4C)$, with $C = \alpha + \beta i \in \mathbb{F}_{p^2}$ non-zero. Similar to the CSIDH situation, whenever 4α or 4β is smaller than $p/2$, doubling $4C$ does not require a modular reduction for these values, and hence the bit representation of 8α resp. 8β of $8C$ is precisely a bit shift of 4α resp. 4β of $4C$ by one bit to the left. Such strongly-correlated values can be observed in several ways using side-channel analysis, as we detail later in Sect. 5. Different from the CSIDH situation are the following key observations:

- The prime used in SIKE is of the form $p = 2^{e_A} \cdot 3^{e_B} - 1$. As observed in Remark 3, this large cofactor 2^{e_A} in $p + 1$ implies a modular reduction does *not* affect the lowest $e_A - 1$ bits, except for the shift. Hence, even when 4α or 4β is larger than $p/2$, we see strong correlation between their lowest bits.
- C is now an $\mathbb{F}_{p^2}$ value, so we get strong correlation between 8α and 4α *and* between 8β and 4β. This implies at least $2 \cdot (e_A - 1)$ strongly-correlated bits in the worst case (25 %), up to $2 \cdot (\log_2(p) - 1)$ strongly-correlated bits in the best case (25%).

For random curves E_a, the representations of a are indistinguishable from random $(\alpha + \beta i : \gamma + \delta i)$, and so an attacker can differentiate E_6 from such curves. From this, an attacker only needs a few traces to determine accurately whether a walk passes over E_6 or not, as discussed in Sect. 5.

General Approach to Recover the k-th trit. Assuming we know the first $k - 1$ trits sk_i of a secret key sk, i.e. $\text{sk}_{<k-1} = \sum_{i=0}^{k-2} \text{sk}_i \cdot 3^i$, we want to find $\text{sk}_{k-1} \in \{0, 1, 2\}$. We construct three candidate secret keys, $\text{sk}^{(0)}, \text{sk}^{(1)}, \text{sk}^{(2)}$ as

$$\text{sk}^{(0)} = \text{sk}_{<k-1} + 0 \cdot 3^{k-1}, \quad \text{sk}^{(1)} = \text{sk}_{<k-1} + 1 \cdot 3^{k-1}, \quad \text{sk}^{(2)} = \text{sk}_{<k-1} + 2 \cdot 3^{k-1}.$$

We must have $\text{sk}_{<k} = \text{sk}^{(i)}$ for some $i \in \{0, 1, 2\}$. Thus, we use these three keys to construct (see Lemma 3) three public keys $\text{pk}^{(0)}, \text{pk}^{(1)}, \text{pk}^{(2)}$ such that $\text{Derive}_B(\text{sk}^{(i)}, \text{pk}^{(i)})$ computes E_6. When we feed these three keys to Bob, the computation $\text{Derive}_B(\text{sk}, \text{pk}^{(i)})$ will then pass over E_6 in the k-th step *if and only if* $\text{sk}_{k-1} = i$. By observing E_6 from side-channel information, we find sk_{k-1}.

In this attack scenario, another key observation makes the attack on SIDH and SIKE easier than the attack on CSIDH: The computation $\text{Derive}_B(\text{sk}, \text{pk}^{(i)})$ *always* passes over the same curves, as there are no "steps that can fail" as in CSIDH. We know *with certainty* that Bob will pass over E_6 in step k in precisely one of these three computations. Hence, the number of traces required reduces drastically, as we do not need to worry about probabilities, such as p_{a_k}, that we have for CSIDH.

Constructing $pk^{(i)}$ from $sk^{(i)}$ Using Backtracking. Whereas in CSIDH it is trivial to compute a curve E_{PK} such that $\mathfrak{a} * E_{PK}$ passes over E_0 in the k-th step (see Lemma 1), in SIDH and SIKE it is not immediatly clear how to construct $pk^{(i)}$ for $sk^{(i)}$. We follow [1, § 3.3], using *backtracking* to construct such a pk.[3] The main idea is that any $sk_{<k}$ corresponds to some *kernel point* R_B of order 3^k for some k, so to an *isogeny* $\phi^{(k)} : E_6 \to E^{(k)}$. Here, the trits sk_i determine the steps

$$E_6 = E^{(0)} \xrightarrow{sk_0} E^{(1)} \xrightarrow{sk_1} \dots \xrightarrow{sk_{k-1}} E^{(k)}.$$

The dual isogeny $\hat{\phi}^{(k)} : E^{(k)} \to E_6$ then corresponds to the kernel generator $\phi^{(k)}([3^{e_B-k}]Q_B)$ (see [35]). This leads to [1, Lemma 2].

Lemma 3 ([1]). Let sk be a secret key, and let $R_k = [3^{e_B-k}](P_B + [sk_{<k}]Q_B)$ so that $\phi : E_6 \to E^{(k)}$ is the corresponding isogeny for the first k steps. Let $T \in E^{(k)}[3^{e_B}]$ such that $[3^{e_B-k}]T \neq \pm[3^{e_B-k}]\phi(Q_B)$. Then

$$pk' = (\phi(Q_B) + [sk_{<k}]T, \ -T, \ \phi(Q_B) + [sk_{<k} - 1]T)$$

is such that $Derive_B(sk, pk')$ passes over E_6 in the k-th step.

It is necessary that such a pk' is not rejected by a SIKE implementation.

Corollary 4 ([1]). The points P' and Q' for a $pk' = (P', Q', Q' - P')$ as constructed in Lemma 3 form a basis for the 3^{e_B}-torsion of $E^{(k)}$. This implies they are of order 3^{e_B} and pass the CLN test.

Given Lemma 3 and $sk_{<k-1}$, we can therefore easily compute the $pk^{(i)}$ corresponding to $sk^{(i)}$ for $i \in \{0, 1, 2\}$. One of the three attempts $Derive_B(sk, pk^{(i)})$ will then pass over E_6 in the k-th step, while the other two will not. Only the representation of E_6 by $(8C : 4C)$ is then strongly-correlated, and by detecting this representation using side-channel information, we recover sk_{k-1}.

Remark 9. A straightforward attack computes $pk^{(0)}, pk^{(1)}$ and $pk^{(2)}$, and feeds all three to Bob, and so requires 3 traces to recover a single trit sk_{k-1}. Clearly, when we already detect E_6 in the trace of $Derive_B(sk, pk^{(0)})$, we do not need the traces of $pk^{(1)}$ and $pk^{(2)}$, similarly for $Derive_B(sk, pk^{(1)})$. This approach would require on average $\frac{1}{3} \cdot 1 + \frac{1}{3} \cdot 2 + \frac{1}{3} \cdot 3 = 2$ traces per trit. We can do even better: If we do not detect E_6 in both $Derive_B(sk, pk^{(0)})$ and $Derive_B(sk, pk^{(1)})$, we do not need a sample for $Derive_B(sk, pk^{(2)})$, as sk_{k-1} *must* equal 2. This gives $\frac{5}{3}$ samples per trit, giving a total of $\frac{5}{3} \cdot e_B$ traces.

5   Feasibility of Obtaining the Side-Channel Information

In this section, we discuss the practical feasibility of obtaining the required side-channel information.

---

[3] It is important that such a $pk = (P, Q, Q - P)$ passes the *CLN test* [18]: P and Q are both of order 3^{e_B} and $[3^{e_B-1}]P \neq [\pm 3^{e_B-1}]Q$, so that they generate $E[3^{e_B}]$.

Zero-Value Representations. For zero-value representations as in CTIDH, where E_0 is represented by $(0 : C)$ in Montgomery form, we exploit side-channel analysis methods to distinguish between the zero curve and others. In particular, as shown in [21], one can apply Welch's t-test [39] to extract the required information from the power consumption of the attacked device. Further, as mentioned in [21], one can use correlation-collision SCA methods to identify zero values using multiple measurements. Therefore, the attack scheme as demonstrated in [21] to SIKE can analogously be applied whenever zero-value representations occur.

Strongly-Correlated Representations. The attacks presented in Sects. 3.2 and 4 for implementations using strongly-correlated representations, such as SQALE and SIKE, are more challenging in practice, since no zero values occur. A naïve approach to mount the proposed attack for such instances would be to apply side-channel attacks like CPA or DPA, and estimate or guess the values of intermediate codomain curves. Revealing those intermediate values would require a fitting power model and a sufficiently high signal-to-noise ratio (SNR[4]).

By exploiting the pattern similarity in the strongly-correlated representation $(2C : 4C)$ for SQALE or $(8C : 4C)$ for SIKE, as mentioned in Sects. 3.1 and Sect. 4, we reduce the SNR required to successfully perform the attack. To achieve this, we apply the concept of correlation-collision attacks, so that there is no need to reveal the actual value of C via a sophisticated power model.

We exploit side-channel correlation-collision attacks [34] to find similar values by searching for strongly-correlated patterns versus non-correlated patterns. Instead of measuring *multiple* computations to identify similar or identical patterns, as in [34], we apply the concept of a horizontal side-channel attack as in [36]. That is, we extract the required side-channel information from a *single* segmented power trace. Such a segmented power trace contains the power values of the processed limbs (each limb is 64 bits), required to represent $\mathbb{F}_p$-values, which form a fingerprint characteristic of such a value. These fingerprints then serve as input to calculate the correlation between $2C$ and $4C$ for SQALE, or 4α, 4β, 8α and 8β for SIKE, from which we judge their similarity. For strongly-correlated representations of E_0 and E_6, this gives a higher correlation between the fingerprints than for representations of random curves E_a as either $(A + 2C : 4C)$ or $(A + 2C : A - 2C)$, with $A, C \neq 0$.

For both CSIDH attacks, we assume no point rejections prior to the respective isogeny computation, so that the specific isogeny steps are known in advance. For SIKE, there are no such probabilities involved in the isogeny computation, and so here too the specific isogeny steps are known in advance. This implies that an attacker will know where the values of interest are computed and used within the power trace, and can distinguish the relevant information from the rest of the trace. Thus, in all cases, the points of interest (position of the limbs) within the power trace are known in advance, and segmenting each power trace into vectors of the corresponding processed limbs for mounting the correlation-collision attack is easy.

---

[4] SNR is the ratio between the variance of the signal and the variance of noise. Too small SNR values make information and noise indistinguishable.

6   Simulating the Attacks on SQALE, CTIDH and SIKE

To demonstrate the proposed attacks, we implemented Python (version 3.8.10) simulations for our CTIDH-511[5] and SQALE-2048[6] attacks, and a C simulation of the attack on SIKE.[7] The C code for key generation and collecting the simulated power consumption were compiled with gcc (version 9.4.0). Security-critical spots of the attacked C code remained unchanged in both cases.

For the SQALE and CTIDH attacks, the implemented simulation works as follows: First, we generate the corresponding public keys E_{PK} and $\tilde{E}_{PK}$ for the current k-th step, as described in Sect. 3.1. Then we collect the bit values of the resulting codomain curve after the computation of the k-th step $E \leftarrow \mathfrak{l}^{(k)} * E$ in the group action $\mathfrak{a} * E_{PK}$ resp. $\mathfrak{a} * \tilde{E}_{PK}$ to simulate the power consumption.

We calculate the Hamming weight of these values and add a zero-mean Gaussian standard distribution to simulate noise in the measurement. We picked different values of the standard deviation to mimic realistic power measurements with different SNR values. By varying the SNR in such a way, we can determine up to which SNR the attacks are successful, and compare this to known SNR values achieved in physical attacks. For SQALE and CTIDH, we are only interested in power traces passing over E_0, and so we need the first k steps to succeed. We therefore take enough samples to ensure high probability that passing over E_0 happens multiple times for either E_{PK} or $\tilde{E}_{PK}$. Finally, based on the set of collected bit vectors for all these samples, we decide on which of the two cases contains paths over E_0, and therefore reveal the k-th bit of the secret key.

For the SIKE attack, we generate $pk^{(0)}, pk^{(1)}$ and $pk^{(2)}$ for the current k-th step, as described in Sect. 4, and collect the bit values of the resulting codomain curve in the computation of the k-th step of $\mathtt{Derive}_B$ in $\mathtt{Decaps}$. For simplicity, there is no noise in the simulation, as the results are exactly the same as for the SQALE situation after extracting the bit values. Deciding which sample has strongly-correlated values is easy, as is clear from Fig. 3.

As described in previous sections, due to the different representations, the decision step differs between CTIDH and SQALE. For SIKE, the probability to pass over E_6 is 100%, and so a single sample per $pk^{(i)}$ is enough to decide what the k-th trit sk_{k-1} is.

In order to reduce the running time of our simulations for SQALE and CTIDH, we terminate each group action run after returning the required bit values of the k-th step. Furthermore, we implemented a threaded version so that we collect several runs in parallel, which speeds up the simulation. All experiments were measured on AMD EPYC 7643 CPU cores.

Attacking CTIDH-511. As shown in [21, § 4] a practical differentiation between zero and non-zero values, even with low SNR, is feasible with a single trace containing the zero value. Hence, in CTIDH, where E_0 is represented by $(0 : C)$, a single occurrence of E_0 leaks enough information for the

---

[5] http://ctidh.isogeny.org/high-ctidh-20210523.tar.gz.

[6] https://github.com/JJChiDguez/sqale-csidh-velusqrt, commit `a95812f`.

[7] https://github.com/Microsoft/PQCrypto-SIDH, commit `ecf93e9`.

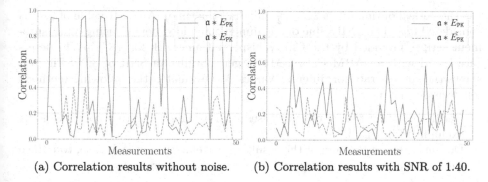

(a) Correlation results without noise.   (b) Correlation results with SNR of 1.40.

Fig. 3. Experimental results to discover bit $k = 1$: the correct hypothesis ($\mathfrak{a} * E_{PK}$) in blue and the wrong hypothesis ($\mathfrak{a} * \tilde{E}_{PK}$) in orange, for SQALE-2048. (Color figure online)

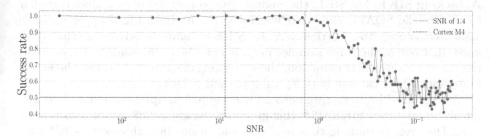

Fig. 4. Relation between SNR and success rate. Rate of 0.5 equals random guess.

decision in each step. Thus, the number of required attempts can be calculated as follows: Given $p_{\mathfrak{a}_k}$ from Lemma 2, the success probability of having *at least one* sequence that passes over E_0 in the k-th step in t_k attempts is $P_{exp}(X \geq 1) = 1 - (1 - p_{\mathfrak{a}_k})^{t_k}$. We can calculate t_k to achieve an expected success rate P_{exp} by $t_k = \log_{(1-p_{\mathfrak{a}_k})}(1 - P_{exp})$. For CTIDH-511, to achieve $P_{exp} \geq 99\%$ for all k, we get an estimate of $\sum t_k \approx 130,000$ attempts for full key recovery. In simulations, the required number of attempts for full key recovery was $\approx 85,000$ on average over 100 experiments, due to effects mentioned in Sect. 3.3. The average execution time was about 35 min (single core) or 5 min (120 threads). As described in Remark 8, finding the last few key bits by brute force drastically reduces the required measurements, as $p_{\mathfrak{a}_k}$ is low.

Attacking SQALE-2048. In this case, we simulate a correlation-collision attack as described in Sect. 5: We calculate the correlation between the 64-bit limbs that represent the $\mathbb{F}_p$-values, and apply the standard Hamming-weight model with noise drawn from a normal distribution. Even with an SNR as low as 1.40, strongly-correlated representations leak enough information to guess the k-th bit, as can be seen in Fig. 3 for $k = 1$. Both without noise and with SNR 1.40, we are able to determine the right bit in 74% of measurements (where 75% is the theoretical optimum, as $2C \leq \frac{p}{2}$ only half the time). An SNR value of 1.40 is considered *low*: The SNR value of a common embedded device, using a measurement script[8] provided by the ChipWhisperer framework for a ChipWhisperer-Lite board with an ARM Cortex-M4 target, obtains an SNR of 8.90. Figure 4 shows the success rate for different values. We evaluated the following methods for decision-making:

- Decide based on the number of cases with a higher resulting correlation, as exemplified in Fig. 3.
- Decide based on the sum of the resulting correlations for each case, to reduce the number of attempts required for a given success rate.

Empirical results show that the sum-based approach reduces the required number of attempts for key recovery by a factor 3 on average (from $\approx 24,819$ to $\approx 8,273$), which leads to an average execution time of 35 minutes (120 threads).

Attacking SIKE. For SIKE, the analysis after collecting the bit values is similar to that of the SQALE case, and hence the results from Fig. 3 apply to these simulated sampels too. Furthermore, for SIKE we have the advantage that i) we know that one of the three samples per trit must be an E_6-sample, ii) we know that even with modular reduction, there is strong correlation between the lowest limbs and iii) we can use both $\mathbb{F}_p$-values α and β for $C = \alpha + \beta i \in \mathbb{F}_{p^2}$.

As explained in Sect. 4, we need on average 5/3 samples per trit to find sk_i, for all e_B trits. For SIKEp434, this gives an average of 228 samples to recover sk_B. The average running time over 100 evaluations in each case was ≈ 4 s for SIKEp434, ≈ 8 s for SIKEp503, ≈ 17 s for SIKEp610, and ≈ 42 s for SIKEp751 respectively (Table 1).

Table 1. Required number of samples to reconstruct secret key in simulations.

Scheme	SQALE-2048	CTIDH-511	SIKEp434	SIKEp503	SIKEp610	SIKEp751
Samples	8,273	85,000	228	265	320	398

7   Countermeasures and Conclusion

We have shown that both CSIDH and SIKE are vulnerable to leakage of specific curves. For CSIDH, we have shown that both Montgomery form and alternative Montgomery form leak secret information when passing over E_0, and for SIKE we have shown that in both forms, the representation of E_6 by $(8C : 4C)$ leaks secret information. As described in Sect. 5, zero-value representations are easiest to detect, and accordingly one should prefer the alternative Montgomery form over the Montgomery form throughout the whole computation for CSIDH variants. However, more effective countermeasures are required to avoid strongly-correlated representations in CSIDH and SIKE.

---

[8] https://github.com/newaetech/chipwhisperer-jupyter/blob/master/archive/PA_Intro_3-Measuring_SNR_of_Target.ipynb, commit 44112f6.

7.1 Public Key Validation

As mentioned in Sect. 3, public keys in the proposed attacks on CSIDH variants consist of valid supersingular elliptic curves. Hence, the attack cannot be prevented by public key validation.

For the SIKE attack, the situation is different: Instead of containing valid points $(\phi_A(P_B), \phi_A(Q_B), \phi_A(Q_B - P_B))$ (see Sect. 2), we construct public keys differently, as described in Lemma 3. However, such public key points are not detected by partial validation methods contained in the current SIKE software, such as the CLN test (see Corollary 4). In general, the full validation of SIDH or SIKE public keys is believed to be as hard as breaking the schemes themselves [22]. It remains an open question if there is an efficient partial validation method to detect the specific public key points generated by our attack.

7.2 Avoiding E_0 or E_6

A straightforward way of mitigating the attacks is to avoid paths that lead over E_0 or E_6, or any other vulnerable curve. As argued in [1,21], avoiding them altogether seems difficult. We discuss techniques to achieve this.

Danger Zone. Similar to the rejection proposal from [1], it may appear intuitive to define a certain *danger zone* around vulnerable curves, e.g. for CSIDH, containing all curves $\mathfrak{l}_i^{\pm 1} * E_0$ for $1 \leq i \leq n$, and abort the execution of the protocol whenever an isogeny path enters this zone. In the SIKE attack, this zone could include the four curves that are 3-isogenous to E_6. However, the attacker can simply construct public keys that would or would not pass through this zone, and observe that the protocol aborts or proceeds. This leaks the same information as in the attack targeting only E_0 or E_6.[9]

Masking on Isogeny Level. One can fully bypass this danger zone by masking by a (small) isogeny before applying secret isogeny walks (see [1,29]). For CSIDH, for a masking isogeny $\mathfrak{z}$ and a secret $\mathfrak{a}$ we have that by commutativity, $\mathfrak{a} * E = \mathfrak{z}^{-1} * (\mathfrak{a} * (\mathfrak{z} * E))$, so this route avoids the danger zone when $\mathfrak{z}$ is sufficiently large. Drawing $\mathfrak{z}$ from a masking key space of k bits would require the attacker to guess the random ephemeral mask correctly in order to get a successful walk over E_0, which happens with probability 2^{-k}. Thus, a k-bit mask increases the number of samples needed by 2^k. Similarly, as detailed in [1], the secret isogeny in the SIKE attack can be masked by a 2^k-isogeny, where keeping track of the dual requires some extra cost. Although masking comes at a significant cost if the masking isogeny needs to be large, this appears to be the only known effective countermeasure that fully avoids the proposed attacks.

Randomization of Order (CSIDH). For CSIDH variants, intuitively, randomizing the order of isogenies, and as proposed in [30] the order of real and dummy isogenies, might seem beneficial to achieve this. However, we can then simply *always* attack the first step of the isogeny path, with a success probability

---

[9] Pun aficionados may wish to dub this scenario the *highway to the danger zone*.

of $1/n$. With enough repetitions, we can therefore statistically guess the secret key, where the exact success probabilities highly depend on the respective CSIDH variant. This countermeasure also significantly impacts performance, making it undesirable.

Working on the Surface (CSIDH).[10] An interesting approach to avoid vulnerable curves, specific to CSIDH, is to move to the *surface* of the isogeny graph. That is, we use curves E_A with $\mathbb{F}_p$-rational endomorphism ring $\mathbb{Z}[\frac{1+\pi}{2}]$ instead of $\mathbb{Z}[\pi]$, and use a prime $p = 7 \mod 8$. This idea was proposed in [12] and dubbed CSURF. We can still work with elliptic curves in Montgomery form, although Montgomery coefficients a are not unique in this setting. However, when following the setup described in [11], we are not aware of any vulnerable curves on the surface, but it seems difficult to prove that vulnerable curves do not exist there. More analysis is necessary to rule out such curves. Nevertheless, working on the surface offers other benefits, and we see no reason to work on the floor with known vulnerabilities, instead of on the surface.

Precomposition in SIKE. A potential countermeasure specific to SIKE is precomposing with a random isomorphism, as proposed in [29]. In our attack scenario, the isogeny walk then passes a curve isomorphic to E_6 instead of E_6, which may eliminate the leakage. However, as discussed in [19], each isomorphism class contains exactly six Montgomery curves, and the isomorphism class of E_6 also contains E_{-6}, which shares the same vulnerability as E_6. Thus, in $1/3$ of cases, leakage still occurs, only moderately increasing the number of required measurements. On the other hand, finding an isomorphism that guarantees the isogeny walk not to pass E_6 or E_{-6} only from public key information seems infeasible. Furthermore, the computation of isomorphisms usually contains expensive square root computations.

7.3 Avoiding Correlations

Another approach to mitigate the attacks is to ensure that vulnerable curves such as E_0 and E_6 do not leak information when passing over them. This requires adapting the representations of such curves.

Avoiding Correlations in alternative Montgomery form. As noted for CSIDH variants, the representation $(2C : 4C)$ leaks secret information whenever $2C < \frac{p}{2}$. In order to avoid this, we can try to represent the alternative Montgomery form $(A+2C : 4C)$ differently and use a *flipped* alternative Montgomery form $(A + 2C : -4C)$ instead, which we write as ǝʌᴉʇɐuɹǝʇlɐ Montgomery form for brevity. In the case of E_0, this means that the coefficients $2C$ and $-4C$ are *not* simple shifts of each other for $2C < \frac{p}{2}$, which prevents the correlation attack. In order to still achieve constant-time behavior, we should flip $4C$ for all curves, since otherwise E_0 would easily be detectable via side channels. The correctness of computations can be guaranteed by corresponding sign flips in computations

---

[10] We thank the anonymous reviewers of SAC 2022 for this suggestion.

that would normally include $4C$. Analogously, we can define a flipped representation of curves in SIKE. Although the ǝʌᴉʇɐuɹǝʇlɐ Montgomery form is effective in preventing leakage of E_0, it creates other vulnerable curves. It remains an open question to find a representation without both zero-value representations and strongly-correlated representations.

Masking a Single Value. Assuming we are working with the representations $(A_{24}^+ : A_{24}^-)$ or $(A_{24}^+ : C_{24})$ for either CSIDH or SIKE, masking is non-trivial, as it needs to respect the ratio A/C during the computation. However, it is possible to multiply by some random α during the computation of A_{24}^+, and to multiply by $1/\alpha$ in the next computations that use A_{24}^+. This requires a careful analysis and implementation, in order to guarantee that no leak of A_{24}^+ or some different correlation occurs at a given point in the computation.

Acknowledgements. We thank the anonymous reviewers of SAC 2022 for their helpful comments and suggestions.

References

1. Adj, G., Chi-Domínguez, J.J., Mateu, V., Rodríguez-Henríquez, F.: Faulty isogenies: a new kind of leakage. arXiv preprint: arXiv:2202.04896 (2022)
2. Adj, G., Chi-Domínguez, J., Rodríguez-Henríquez, F.: Karatsuba-based square-root Vélu's formulas applied to two isogeny-based protocols. Cryptology ePrint Archive, Paper 2020/1109 (2020)
3. Akishita, T., Takagi, T.: Zero-value point attacks on elliptic curve cryptosystem. In: Boyd, C., Mao, W. (eds.) Information Security. Lecture Notes in Computer Science, vol. 2851, pp. 218–233. Springer, Berlin (2003). https://doi.org/10.1007/10958513_17
4. Banegas, G., et al.: CTIDH: faster constant-time CSIDH. IACR Trans. Cryptogr. Hardw. Embed. Syst. **2021**(4), 351–387 (2021)
5. Bauer, A., Jaulmes, E., Prouff, E., Reinhard, J.R., Wild, J.: Horizontal collision correlation attack on elliptic curves. Cryptology ePrint Archive, Report 2019/321 (2019)
6. Bernstein, D.J., De Feo, L., Leroux, A., Smith, B.: Faster computation of isogenies of large prime degree. In: Galbraith, S.D. (ed.) ANTS 2020, pp. 39–55. Mathematics Sciences Publishers (2020)
7. Bernstein, D.J., Lange, T., Martindale, C., Panny, L.: Quantum circuits for the CSIDH: optimizing quantum evaluation of isogenies. In: Ishai, Y., Rijmen, V. (eds.) Advances in Cryptology – EUROCRYPT 2019. LNCS, vol. 11477, pp. 409–441. Springer, Cham (2019). https://doi.org/10.1007/978-3-030-17656-3_15
8. Bonnetain, X., Schrottenloher, A.: Quantum security analysis of CSIDH. In: Canteaut, A., Ishai, Y. (eds.) Advances in Cryptology - EUROCRYPT 2020. LNCS, vol. 12106, pp. 493–522. Springer, Cham (2020). https://doi.org/10.1007/978-3-030-45724-2_17
9. Campos, F., Kannwischer, M.J., Meyer, M., Onuki, H., Stöttinger, M.: Trouble at the CSIDH: protecting CSIDH with dummy-operations against fault injection attacks. In: FDTC 2020, pp. 57–65. IEEE (2020)

10. Campos, F., Krämer, J., Müller, M.: Safe-error attacks on SIKE and CSIDH. In: Batina, L., Picek, S., Mondal, M. (eds.) SPACE 2021. LNCS, vol. 13162, pp. 104–125. Springer, Cham (2021). https://doi.org/10.1007/978-3-030-95085-9_6

11. Castryck, W.: CSIDH on the surface (CSURF). Isogeny School 2020 (2021). https://homes.esat.kuleuven.be/~wcastryc/summer_school_csurf.pdf

12. Castryck, W., Decru, T.: CSIDH on the surface. In: Ding, J., Tillich, J.P. (eds.) Post-Quantum Cryptography. Lecture Notes in Computer Science(), vol. 12100, pp. 111–129. Springer, Cham (2020). https://doi.org/10.1007/978-3-030-44223-1_7

13. Castryck, W., Lange, T., Martindale, C., Panny, L., Renes, J.: CSIDH: an efficient post-quantum commutative group action. In: Peyrin, T., Galbraith, S.D. (eds.) Advances in Cryptology - ASIACRYPT 2018. LNCS, vol. 11274, pp. 395–427. Springer, Cham (2018). https://doi.org/10.1007/978-3-030-03332-3_15

14. Cervantes-Vázquez, D., et al.: Stronger and faster side-channel protections for CSIDH. In: Schwabe, P., Thériault, N. (eds.) LATINCRYPT 2019. LNCS, vol. 11774, pp. 173–193. Springer, Cham (2019). https://doi.org/10.1007/978-3-030-30530-7_9

15. Chávez-Saab, J., Chi-Domínguez, J., Jaques, S., Rodríguez-Henríquez, F.: The SQALE of CSIDH: square-root Vélu quantum-resistant isogeny action with low exponents. Cryptology ePrint Archive, Paper 2020/1520 (2020)

16. Chi-Domínguez, J.J., Rodríguez-Henríquez, F.: Optimal strategies for CSIDH. Cryptology ePrint Archive, Paper 2020/417 (2020)

17. Costello, C.: The case for SIKE: a decade of the supersingular isogeny problem. Cryptology ePrint Archive, Paper 2021/543 (2021)

18. Costello, C., Longa, P., Naehrig, M.: Efficient algorithms for supersingular isogeny Diffie-Hellman. In: Robshaw, M., Katz, J. (eds.) Advances in Cryptology - CRYPTO 2016. Lecture Notes in Computer Science(), vol. 9814, pp. 572–601. Springer, Berlin (2016). https://doi.org/10.1007/978-3-662-53018-4_21

19. Costello, C., Longa, P., Naehrig, M., Renes, J., Virdia, F.: Improved classical cryptanalysis of SIKE in practice. In: Kiayias, A., Kohlweiss, M., Wallden, P., Zikas, V. (eds.) Public-Key Cryptography - PKC 2020. LNCS, vol. 12111, pp. 505–534. Springer, Cham (2020). https://doi.org/10.1007/978-3-030-45388-6_18

20. De Feo, L.: Mathematics of isogeny based cryptography. CoRR abs/1711.04062 (2017). http://arxiv.org/abs/1711.04062

21. De Feo, L., et al.: SIKE Channels. Cryptology ePrint Archive, Paper 2022/054 (2022)

22. Galbraith, S.D., Vercauteren, F.: Computational problems in supersingular elliptic curve isogenies. Quantum Inf. Process. **17**(10), 265 (2018)

23. Gélin, A., Wesolowski, B.: Loop-abort faults on supersingular isogeny cryptosystems. In: Lange, T., Takagi, T. (eds.) PQCrypto 2017. LNCS, vol. 10346, pp. 93–106. Springer, Cham (2017). https://doi.org/10.1007/978-3-319-59879-6_6

24. Genêt, A., de Guertechin, N.L., Kaluđerović, N.: Full key recovery side-channel attack against ephemeral SIKE on the Cortex-M4. In: Bhasin, S., Santis, F.D. (eds.) COSADE 2021. LNCS, vol. 12910, pp. 228–254. Springer, Cham (2021). https://doi.org/10.1007/978-3-030-89915-8_11

25. Goubin, L.: A refined power-analysis attack on elliptic curve cryptosystems. In: Desmedt, Y. (ed.) Public Key Cryptography - PKC 2003. LNCS, vol. 2567, pp. 199–210. Springer, Cham (2003). https://doi.org/10.1007/3-540-36288-6_15

26. Izu, T., Takagi, T.: Exceptional procedure attack on elliptic curve cryptosystems. In: Desmedt, Y. (ed.) Public Key Cryptography - PKC 2003. LNCS, vol. 2567, pp. 224–239. Springer, Cham (2003). https://doi.org/10.1007/3-540-36288-6_17

27. Jao, D., Azarderakhsh, R., et al.: SIKE–Supersingular Isogeny Key Encapsulation (2017). https://sike.org/
28. Jao, D., De Feo, L.: Towards quantum-resistant cryptosystems from supersingular elliptic curve isogenies. In: Yang, B. (ed.) PQCrypto 2011. LNCS, vol. 7071, pp. 19–34. Springer, Cham (2011). https://doi.org/10.1007/978-3-642-25405-5_2
29. Koziel, B., Azarderakhsh, R., Jao, D.: Side-channel attacks on quantum-resistant supersingular isogeny Diffie-Hellman. In: Adams, C., Camenisch, J. (eds.) SAC 2017, pp. 64–81. Springer, Cham (2017). https://doi.org/10.1007/978-3-319-72565-9_4
30. LeGrow, J.T., Hutchinson, A.: (short paper) analysis of a strong fault attack on static/ephemeral CSIDH. In: Nakanishi, T., Nojima, R. (eds.) IWSEC 2021. LNCS, vol. 12835, pp. 216–226. Springer, Cham (2021). https://doi.org/10.1007/978-3-030-85987-9_12
31. Meyer, M., Campos, F., Reith, S.: On lions and Elligators: an efficient constant-time implementation of CSIDH. In: Ding, J., Steinwandt, R. (eds.) PQCrypto 2019. LNCS, vol. 11505, pp. 307–325. Springer, Cham (2019). https://doi.org/10.1007/978-3-030-25510-7_17
32. Meyer, M., Reith, S.: A faster way to the CSIDH. In: Chakraborty, D., Iwata, T. (eds.) Progress in Cryptology - INDOCRYPT 2018. LNCS, vol. 11356, pp. 137–152. Springer, Cham (2018). https://doi.org/10.1007/978-3-030-05378-9_8
33. Moody, D., Shumow, D.: Analogues of Vélu's formulas for isogenies on alternate models of elliptic curves. Math. Comput. **85**(300), 1929–1951 (2016)
34. Moradi, A., Mischke, O., Eisenbarth, T.: Correlation-enhanced power analysis collision attack. Cryptology ePrint Archive, Paper 2010/297 (2010)
35. Naehrig, M., Renes, J.: Dual isogenies and their application to public-key compression for isogeny-based cryptography. In: Galbraith, S.D., Moriai, S. (eds.) Advances in Cryptology - ASIACRYPT 2019. LNCS, vol. 11922, pp. 243–272. Springer, Cham (2019). https://doi.org/10.1007/978-3-030-34621-8_9
36. Nascimento, E., Chmielewski, L.: Horizontal clustering side-channel attacks on embedded ECC implementations (extended version). Cryptology ePrint Archive, Paper 2017/1204 (2017)
37. Onuki, H., Aikawa, Y., Yamazaki, T., Takagi, T.: (Short paper) A faster constant-time algorithm of CSIDH keeping two points. In: Attrapadung, N., Yagi, T. (eds.) IWSEC 2019. LNCS, vol. 11689, pp. 23–33. Springer, Cham (2019). https://doi.org/10.1007/978-3-030-26834-3_2
38. Peikert, C.: He gives C-Sieves on the CSIDH. In: Canteaut, A., Ishai, Y. (eds.) Advances in Cryptology - EUROCRYPT 2020. LNCS, vol. 12106, pp. 463–492. Springer, Cham (2020). https://doi.org/10.1007/978-3-030-45724-2_16
39. Schneider, T., Moradi, A.: Leakage assessment methodology - A clear roadmap for side-channel evaluations. In: Güneysu, T., Handschuh, H. (eds.) CHES 2015. LNCS, vol. 9293, pp. 495–513. Springer, Cham (2015). https://doi.org/10.1007/978-3-662-48324-4_25
40. Tasso, É., De Feo, L., Mrabet, N.E., Pontié, S.: Resistance of isogeny-based cryptographic implementations to a fault attack. In: Bhasin, S., Santis, F.D. (eds.) COSADE 2021. LNCS, vol. 12910, pp. 255–276. Springer, Cham (2021). https://doi.org/10.1007/978-3-030-89915-8_12
41. Ti, Y.B.: Fault attack on supersingular isogeny cryptosystems. In: Lange, T., Takagi, T. (eds.) PQCrypto 2017. LNCS, vol. 10346, pp. 107–122. Springer, Cham (2017). https://doi.org/10.1007/978-3-319-59879-6_7
42. Vélu, J.: Isogénies entre courbes elliptiques. Comptes Rendus de l'Académie des Sciences de Paris, Séries A **273**, 238–241 (1971)

43. Wang, Y., Paccagnella, R., He, E.T., Shacham, H., Fletcher, C.W., Kohlbrenner, D.: Hertzbleed: turning power side-channel attacks into remote timing attacks on x86 (2022)
44. Zhang, F., et al.: Side-channel analysis and countermeasure design on ARM-based quantum-resistant SIKE. IEEE Trans. Comput. **69**(11), 1681–1693 (2020)

An Effective Lower Bound
on the Number of Orientable
Supersingular Elliptic Curves

Antonin Leroux[1,2,3]($\boxtimes$)

[1] DGA, Paris, France
[2] LIX, CNRS, Ecole Polytechnique, Institut Polytechnique de Paris,
Palaiseau, France
antonin.leroux@polytechnique.org
[3] INRIA, Paris, France

Abstract. In this article, we prove a generic lower bound on the number of $\mathfrak{O}$-*orientable* supersingular curves over $\mathbb{F}_{p^2}$, i.e. curves that admit an embedding of the quadratic order $\mathfrak{O}$ inside their endomorphism ring. Prior to this work, the only known effective lower-bound is restricted to small discriminants. Our main result targets the case of fundamental discriminants and we derive a generic bound using the expansion properties of the supersingular isogeny graphs.

Our work is motivated by isogeny-based cryptography and the increasing number of protocols based on $\mathfrak{O}$-oriented curves. In particular, our lower bound provides a complexity estimate for the brute-force attack against the new $\mathfrak{O}$-uber isogeny problem introduced by De Feo, Delpech de Saint Guilhem, Fouotsa, Kutas, Leroux, Petit, Silva and Wesolowski in their recent article on the SETA encryption scheme.

1 Introduction

The link between quadratic imaginary orders and elliptic curves have always been of great importance to elliptic curve cryptography, and isogeny-based cryptography is no exception. This connection dates back to the very beginning of the field with the CRS scheme, discovered independently by Couveignes [Cou06] and Rostovtsev and Stolbunov [RS06]. Their original idea is based on isogenies between ordinary curves over finite fields, i.e. elliptic curves whose endomorphism ring is isomorphic to a quadratic imaginary order. However, for both security and efficiency reasons, ordinary curves were soon replaced by supersingular curves, i.e. curves whose endomorphism ring is isomorphic to a maximal order inside a quaternion algebra. With the CGL hash function [CLG09] and the SIDH key exchange [JDF11] leading the charge, it seemed like the quadratic orders were destined to slowly disappear from the picture. However, they claimed back a share of the spotlight with CSIDH [CLM+18], a revival of CRS in the setting of supersingular curves with the quadratic order obtained by restricting to endomorphisms defined over $\mathbb{F}_p$. In fact, quadratic orders were never really gone

© The Author(s), under exclusive license to Springer Nature Switzerland AG 2024
B. Smith and H. Wu (Eds.): SAC 2022, LNCS 13742, pp. 263–281, 2024.
https://doi.org/10.1007/978-3-031-58411-4_12

as quaternion orders actually contain an infinity of them. Isogeny experts only needed time to understand their place in the rapidly evolving picture of isogeny-based cryptography. In parallel to numerous schemes built upon CSIDH and its variants ([BKV19, ADFMP20] among others), several papers appeared trying to study the link between isogenies of supersingular curves and quadratic imaginary orders outside of the CSIDH framework. We can mention the OSIDH protocol by Colò and Kohel [CK19] for quadratic orders of smooth discriminant which introduced the terminology of orientations that we use in this paper and the work of Love and Boneh [LB20] on quadratic orders of small discriminant. More recently, Chenu and Smith [CS21] studied the case where the discriminant is a small integer times p. De Quehen et al. have highlighted in [QKL+21] the possibility to use the embedding of a specific quadratic order as a backdoor to break unbalanced variants of SIDH. The SETA encryption scheme [DFFDdSG+21] is built on the same principle. The set of SETA public keys is simply the set of $\mathfrak{O}$-orientable curves for some quadratic order $\mathfrak{O}$ and secret keys are concrete $\mathfrak{O}$-orientations. Additionally, the authors of SETA have introduced the "uber-isogeny assumption" as an attempt to provide a common framework for various security assumptions in isogeny-based cryptography. The formulation of the $\mathfrak{O}$-Uber Isogeny Problem ($\mathfrak{O}$-UIP) is explicitly parametrized by a quadratic imaginary order $\mathfrak{O}$ and it was shown in [DFFDdSG+21] how different variants of the $\mathfrak{O}$-UIP were related to the security of several isogeny-based protocols (including SIDH). Later [Wes21, ACL+22] have studied various algorithmic problems related to $\mathfrak{O}$-orientations and the $\mathfrak{O}$-UIP. Note that the recent attacks [CD22, MM22, Rob22] against SIDH do not apply to the $\mathfrak{O}$-UIP even if those attacks break SETA. It is because the attacks target the encryption mechanism of SETA but do not allow an attacker to perform a key recovery. Thus, the $\mathfrak{O}$-UIP remains an interesting subject of study.

Given the rich history that we have summarized above, it is important to study in more detail the link between quadratic orders and isogenies of supersingular curves. We denote by $\mathcal{E}_{\mathfrak{O}}(p)$ the set of $\mathfrak{O}$-orientable supersingular elliptic curves over $\mathbb{F}_{p^2}$. In this work, we study the cardinal $\#\mathcal{E}_{\mathfrak{O}}(p)$ of this set. The complexity of the brute force algorithm to solve the $\mathfrak{O}$-UIP is linear in $\#\mathcal{E}_{\mathfrak{O}}(p)$. Aiming at the cryptographic applications, we look for an effective bound in the cases where the discriminant of $\mathfrak{O}$ is polynomial in p and both have cryptographic size.

Related Works. The number of orientable supersingular curve is related to the number of optimal embeddings of quadratic orders inside maximal orders of the quaternion algebra ramified at p and ∞ and is also linked with the number of representations of integers by ternary quadratic forms. Both quantities have been studied in the literature but not with the same goal. As far as we know, prior to our work, an effective bound is only known for a restricted range of discriminants and is due to Kaneko [Kan89]. In [Voi21, Chapter 30], several formulas are given involving sums of these numbers (such as the Eichler class number formula) from which it seems hard to derive a bound. There are also asymptotic results on number of representations by ternary quadratic forms (see for instance [IK21,

Chapter 20]) but they rather target the case where d grows to infinity while p is fixed. Our work also shares some similarities with the trend of work started by Gross and Zagier [ZG85] on singular moduli and later enriched by Dorman, and Lauter and Viray [Dor87,LV15]. Their results cannot be directly applied to our case because they target simultaneous embeddings of quadratic orders of distinct discriminants while we are going to focus on simultaneous embeddings of quadratic orders with the same discriminant. Nonetheless, some of the techniques developed in these works have inspired part of our analysis.

Contributions. Our main result is Proposition 11, a lower bound on $\#\mathcal{E}_{\mathfrak{O}}(p)$ when $\mathfrak{O}$ is a maximal quadratic order. The proof is based on the study of $K_{\mathfrak{O}}(p)$, the number of quaternion orders obtained from pairs of distinct $\mathfrak{O}$-orientations. In the full version of the paper, we cover the case of non-maximal orders and a lower bound on $\#\mathcal{E}_{\mathfrak{O}}(p)$ can be derived for any quadratic order by combining with the fundamental discriminant case.

Asymptotically, our bound becomes trivial when the discriminant grows while the characteristic p stays fix. However, in the case where the discriminant is polynomial in p, our bound proves to be quite tight as we illustrate by using it to verify that the parameters proposed in [DFFDdSG+21] for the SETA encryption scheme reach the claimed level of security.

The remainder of this paper is organized as follows: Sect. 2 introduces the necessary notations and mathematical notions. Section 3 is where we present our main result, we treat the case of fundamental discriminants in Sect. 3.2. Finally, in Sect. 4, we apply our results to a concrete example corresponding to the parameters of SETA.

2   Mathematical Background

Notations. Throughout this document, we place ourselves in $B_{p,\infty}$, the definite quaternion algebra ramified at p and ∞ for some prime $p > 3$. We consider super-singular elliptic curves over $\mathbb{F}_{p^2}$ and write N_p for the number of isomorphism classes of such curves over the algebraic closure of $\mathbb{F}_p$.

We fix an imaginary quadratic field $\mathfrak{K}$ of discriminant $-d$ and ring of integers $\mathfrak{O}_{\mathfrak{K}}$. For any $\mathfrak{O} \subset \mathfrak{O}_{\mathfrak{K}}$, we write $f(\mathfrak{O})$ the conductor of $\mathfrak{O}$, i.e. the only integer such that $\mathfrak{O} = \mathbb{Z} + f(\mathfrak{O})\mathfrak{O}_{\mathfrak{K}}$ (when it is clear from the context we will simply write f). The class group of $\mathfrak{O}$ is $Cl(\mathfrak{O})$ and the class number is $h(\mathfrak{O})$. As a convention, we use $\mathcal{O}_*$ for quaternion orders in $B_{p,\infty}$ and $\mathfrak{O}_*$ for quadratic imaginary orders. We write $\mathbb{P}$ for the set of all primes. For any $d \in \mathbb{N}$, we define $\mathbb{P}_d = \{\ell \mid \ell \subset \mathbb{P} \text{ and } \ell \text{ divides } d\}$.

2.1   Quaternion Orders

For $a, b \in \mathbb{Z}^*$ we denote by $H(a, b) = \mathbb{Q} + i\mathbb{Q} + j\mathbb{Q} + k\mathbb{Q}$ the quaternion algebra over $\mathbb{Q}$ with basis $1, i, j, k$ such that $i^2 = a$, $j^2 = b$ and $k = ij = -ji$. The unique quaternion algebra (up to isomorphism) ramified exactly at p and ∞, is always isomorphic to $H(-q, -p)$ where q is a small integer relatively to p ($q = O(\log(p)^2)$). For instance, when $p \equiv 3 \mod 4$, we can always take $q = 1$. Every quaternion algebra has a canonical involution that sends an element $\alpha = a_1 + a_2i + a_3j + a_4k$ to its conjugate $\overline{\alpha} = a_1 - a_2i - a_3j - a_4k$. We define the *reduced trace* and the *reduced norm* by $tr(\alpha) = \alpha + \overline{\alpha}$ and $n(\alpha) = \alpha\overline{\alpha}$.

Quaternion orders of $B_{p,\infty}$ are lattices of rank 4 inside $B_{p,\infty}$ that are also rings. It can be shown that quaternion orders are integral, i.e. that norm and trace of all the elements are in $\mathbb{Z}$. Given a basis $\alpha_1, \alpha_2, \alpha_3, \alpha_4$ of $\mathcal{O}$, the *reduced discriminant* (or simply discriminant) of $\mathcal{O}$ is $\mathrm{disc}(\mathcal{O}) = \sqrt{\det(\alpha_i\alpha_j)_{i,j \in [1,4]}}$. For any $\mathcal{O} \subset B_{p,\infty}$, we have $p|\mathrm{disc}(\mathcal{O})$. The discriminant of a suborder $\mathcal{O}' \subset \mathcal{O}$ satisfies $\mathrm{disc}(\mathcal{O})|\mathrm{disc}(\mathcal{O}')$.

Maximal orders are the orders that admit no proper superorders and, in particular, their discriminant is equal to p. *Eichler* orders are equal to intersection of two maximal orders (not necessarily distinct). Every quaternion order admits the unique decomposition $\mathbb{Z} + f(\mathcal{O})\mathrm{Gor}(\mathcal{O})$ where $f(\mathcal{O}) \in \mathbb{N}$ is the *Brandt Invariant* and $\mathrm{Gor}(\mathcal{O})$ is the *Gorenstein closure*. We can define Gorenstein orders as orders whose Brandt Invariant is 1. As the name suggests, $\mathrm{Gor}(\mathcal{O})$ is always Gorenstein. An order is *Bass* when all its superorders are Gorenstein. Equivalently, Bass orders of $B_{p,\infty}$ are the orders containing a maximal order of a quadratic imaginary field (this was originally the definition of *basic* orders but the two notions were proven equivalent by Chari, Smertnig and Voight in [CSV21]).

We have a chain of proper implication between all those notions.

$$\text{maximal} \Rightarrow \text{Eichler} \Rightarrow \text{Bass} \Rightarrow \text{Gorenstein}.$$

We refer the reader to the book of John Voight for more background on quaternion algebras and quaternion orders [Voi21].

In this article, we will make use of *embedding numbers* of Bass orders, i.e. the number of distinct maximal orders containing a given order. This problem was studied by Eichler and Brzezinski [BE92, Brz83] and was more recently used in [EHL+20] to estimate the complexity of an algorithm to compute the endomorphism ring of a supersingular curve. For the rest of this section, we fix a Bass order $\mathcal{O}$ of discriminant D. Following [BE92], we denote by $e(\mathcal{O})$ the *embedding number of* $\mathcal{O}$. It turns out that $e(\mathcal{O})$ can be computed efficiently using the local-to-global principle with the formula $e(\mathcal{O}) = \prod_{\ell \in \mathbb{P}} e_\ell(\mathcal{O})$ where $e_\ell(\mathcal{O})$ is the analog of $e(\mathcal{O})$ over the ℓ-adics: $e_\ell(\mathcal{O})$ is the number of maximal orders in $B_{p,\infty} \otimes \mathbb{Q}_\ell$ containing $\mathcal{O}_\ell = \mathcal{O} \otimes \mathbb{Z}_\ell$. An easy preliminary observation is that, $e_\ell(\mathcal{O}) = 1$ when ℓ is coprime with D. Thus, we can rewrite the above formula as $e(\mathcal{O}) = \prod_{\ell \in \mathbb{P}_d} e_\ell(\mathcal{O})$. The value of $e_\ell(\mathcal{O})$ is in fact closely related to the Eichler symbol $(\mathcal{O}/\ell)$, a notion introduced by Eichler in [Eic36]. Let us write k for the residue field of $\mathbb{Q}_\ell$ and J for the Jacobson radical of $\mathcal{O}_\ell$. Then, we define the Eichler symbol as follows:

$$\left(\frac{\mathcal{O}}{\ell}\right) = \begin{cases} 1 & \text{if } \mathcal{O}_\ell/J \cong k \times k, \\ 0 & \text{if } \mathcal{O}_\ell/J \cong k, \\ -1 & \text{if } \mathcal{O}_\ell/J \text{ is a quadratic extension of } k. \end{cases} \tag{1}$$

The Eichler symbol is a very useful tool to understand the structure of an order $\mathcal{O}$ by the local-global principle. For instance, the order $\mathcal{O}_\ell$ is Eichler if and only if $(\mathcal{O}/\ell) = 1$. The Eichler symbol can be seen as a generalization of the Kronecker symbol, as becomes explicit with the reinterpretation presented in Proposition 1. For any quaternion element α, we write $\Delta(\alpha) = \mathrm{disc}(\mathbb{Z}[\alpha]) = \mathrm{tr}(\alpha)^2 - 4n(\alpha)$.

Proposition 1 [Voi21]. $\left(\frac{\mathcal{O}}{\ell}\right) = \varepsilon$ if and only if $\left(\frac{\Delta(\alpha)}{\ell}\right)$ takes all the values in $\{0, \varepsilon\}$ when α ranges over all the elements of $\mathcal{O}$.

Then, it was shown by Eichler in [Eic36] (see [Brz83] for an account in English of this result) how the value of the Eichler symbol is linked to $e_\ell(\mathcal{O})$. We write $v_\ell(n)$ for the ℓ-adic valuation of a integer n.

Proposition 2. Let $\mathcal{O}$ be a Bass order in $B_{p,\infty}$ of discriminant D and $\ell \in \mathbb{P}_D$:

$$e_\ell(\mathcal{O}) = \begin{cases} v_\ell(D) + 1 & \text{if } (\mathcal{O}/\ell) = 1, \\ 2 & \text{if } (\mathcal{O}/\ell) = 0 \text{ and } \ell \neq p, \\ 1 & \text{if } (\mathcal{O}/\ell) = -1 \text{ or } ((\mathcal{O}/\ell) = 0 \text{ and } \ell = p). \end{cases}$$

Remark 1. Note that $e_p(\mathcal{O})$ is always equal to 1. This follows from Proposition 2 and the fact that $(\mathcal{O}/p)$ cannot be 1.

2.2 Quadratic Orders and Oriented Supersingular Elliptic Curves

In this section, we recall the basic definition and properties about orientations of elliptic curves, inspired by Colò and Kohel in [CK19]. The notion of orientation in Definition 1 below corresponds to the one of *primitive orientations with a p-orientation* in [CK19] and it is equivalent under the Deuring correspondence to *optimal embeddings* of quadratic orders inside maximal orders of $B_{p,\infty}$ (see [LB20]). The same notion is referred to as *normalized optimal embeddings* in [Bel08].

Definition 1. *Let $\mathfrak{K}$ be a quadratic imaginary field. For any elliptic curve E, a $\mathfrak{K}$-orientation is a ring homomorphism $\iota : \mathfrak{K} \hookrightarrow \mathrm{End}(E) \otimes \mathbb{Q}$. A $\mathfrak{K}$-orientation induces an $\mathfrak{O}$-orientation if $\iota(\mathfrak{O}) = \mathrm{End}(E) \cap \iota(\mathfrak{K})$. In that case, the pair (E, ι) is called a $\mathfrak{O}$-oriented curve and E is an $\mathfrak{O}$-orientable curve.*

When $E/\mathbb{F}_{p^2}$ is supersingular, Deuring showed that $\mathrm{End}(E)$ is a maximal order of $B_{p,\infty}$ [Deu41] and so we have $\mathrm{End}(E) \otimes \mathbb{Q} \cong B_{p,\infty}$. We denote by $S_{\mathfrak{O}}(p)$ the set of $\mathfrak{O}$-oriented supersingular curves over $\mathbb{F}_{p^2}$ up to isomorphism and Galois conjugacy. Note that this does not exactly match the definition used in [Onu21, Wes21] where orientations are not considered up to Galois conjugacy. We took this convention because we can state precise results when working up to Galois conjugacy (the Frobenius, which is the only non-trivial element in the Galois group of $\mathbb{F}_{p^2}$, creates somewhat artificial duplicates of a given orientation). The following proposition was shown by Onuki [Onu21, Proposition 3.2] and gives a concrete criterion to determine when $S_{\mathfrak{O}}(p)$ is not empty.

Proposition 3. *The set $\mathcal{S}_{\mathfrak{O}}(p)$ is not empty if and only if p does not split in $\mathfrak{K}$ and does not divide the conductor of $\mathfrak{O}$.*

The value of $\#\mathcal{S}_{\mathfrak{O}}(p)$ can be easily computed from $p, \mathfrak{O}$. For instance, when p is inert in $\mathfrak{O}$, a consequence of [Onu21, Proposition 3.3, Theorem 3.4] is that $\#\mathcal{S}_{\mathfrak{O}}(p) = h(\mathfrak{O})$. When p ramified in $\mathfrak{O}$, the situation might be more complicated. In general we have that $\#\mathcal{S}_{\mathfrak{O}}(p) \in \{h(\mathfrak{O}), h(\mathfrak{O})/2\}$ by [ACL+22, Proposition 3.3].

In any case, the class group $\mathrm{Cl}(\mathfrak{O})$ acts on $\mathfrak{O}$-orientations through an operation that we write $\mathfrak{a} \star (E, \iota) = (E^{\mathfrak{a}}, \iota^{\mathfrak{a}})$.

Definition 2. $\mathcal{E}_{\mathfrak{O}}(p)$ *is the set of $\mathfrak{O}$-orientable curves (under isomorphism and Galois conjugacy).*

By definition of $\mathcal{E}_{\mathfrak{O}}(p)$, we have the obvious inequality $\#\mathcal{E}_{\mathfrak{O}}(p) \le \min(\#\mathcal{S}_{\mathfrak{O}}(p), N_p)$.

The recent article [DFFDdSG+21] introduced a new isogeny-based problem: the $\mathfrak{O}$-Uber Isogeny Problem ($\mathfrak{O}$-UIP). We describe below as Problem 1, the $\mathfrak{O}$-UBER variant introduced by Wesolowski in [Wes21]. We assume for Problem 1 that $\mathfrak{O}$ and p satisfy the constraint in Proposition 3.

Problem 1. ($\mathfrak{O}$-UBER) Given $(E, \iota) \in \mathcal{S}_{\mathfrak{O}}(p)$ and $F \in \mathcal{E}_{\mathfrak{O}}(p)$, find $\mathfrak{a} \in \mathrm{Cl}(\mathfrak{O})$, such that $F = E^{\mathfrak{a}}$.

The brute force method to solve Problem 1 consists in trying all ideal classes until a solution is found. The expected complexity of this algorithm is linear in $\#\mathcal{E}_{\mathfrak{O}}(p)$ (and not $\#\mathcal{S}_{\mathfrak{O}}(p)$ since we look for any class connecting E and F and not a specific class).

3   The Number of $\mathfrak{O}$-Orientable Supersingular Curves

In this section, we pursue the main goal of this article: finding a generic lower bound on the size of $\mathcal{E}_{\mathfrak{O}}(p)$. Henceforth, we assume that the Legendre symbol $(\mathrm{disc}(\mathfrak{O})/p) \ne 1$ and the conductor $f(\mathfrak{O})$ is coprime with p so we know by Proposition 3 that $\#\mathcal{E}_{\mathfrak{O}}(p) > 0$. We start with Sect. 3.1, where we introduce useful results from the literature and show a first lower bound when $\mathrm{disc}(\mathfrak{O}) \le p$. In Sect. 3.2, we prove our main lower bound in the case where $f(\mathfrak{O}) = 1$. We extend this result to the generic case using the expansion property of the isogeny graphs in the full version of the paper.

3.1   A First Result for Small Discriminants

The main result of this Section is Proposition 5 that was first proven by Kaneko in [Kan89]. This proposition allows us to derive interesting results on $\mathcal{E}_{\mathfrak{O}}(p)$ with Corollaries 1 and 2 (Corollary 1 being the only effective lower bound on $\#\mathcal{E}_{\mathfrak{O}}(p)$ prior to this work). Proposition 5 is obtained by studying the quaternion order generated by two integral elements in $B_{p,\infty}$. The study of these objects will prove to be very important for our results as well.

The Quaternion Order Generated by Two Non-commuting Elements. Let us take α_1, α_2, two integral elements in $B_{p,\infty}$. We want to look at the order $\mathcal{O}_{1,2} = \langle 1, \alpha_1, \alpha_2, \alpha_1\alpha_2 \rangle$. When α_1 and α_2 are not commuting, $\mathcal{O}_{1,2}$ is a quaternion order, i.e. has rank 4 as a $\mathbb{Z}$-module. In Proposition 4, we give the classical formula to compute $\mathrm{disc}(\mathcal{O}_{1,2})$. Proposition 5 is a consequence of this formula and was proven in [Kan89].

Proposition 4 [Koh96, *Chapter 7*] *Let $\mathfrak{O}_i$ be quadratic orders equal to $\mathbb{Z}[\alpha_i]$ for $i = 1, 2$ such that α_1, α_2 are not commuting. Let $D_i = \mathrm{disc}(\mathfrak{O}_i)$, $t_i = \mathrm{tr}(\alpha_i)$ for $i \in \{1, 2\}$ and $s = \mathrm{tr}(\alpha_1\alpha_2)$, then $\mathrm{disc}(\mathcal{O}_{1,2}) = (D_1 D_2 - (t_1 t_2 - 2s)^2)/4$.*

Proposition 5 [Kan89, *Theorem 2'*] *Let $\mathfrak{O}_i$ be quadratic orders equal to $\mathbb{Z}[\alpha_i]$ for $i = 1, 2$ such that α_1, α_2 are not commuting. If $\mathfrak{O}_1, \mathfrak{O}_2$ have respective discriminant $-f_i^2 d$ (where d is a fundamental discriminant) and are contained inside the same quaternion maximal order $\mathcal{O} \subset B_{p,\infty}$, we have that $p \leq f_i f_j d$.*

Remark 2. During the proof for Proposition 5 we showed that $t_1 t_2 - 2s \equiv \pm f_1 f_2 d$ mod p. This fact will be useful for what follows in Sect. 3.2.

Proposition 5 allows us to show interesting properties, including a lower bound on the size of $\mathcal{E}_{\mathfrak{O}}(p)$ (Corollary 1) and a bound on the minimal distance between two $\mathfrak{O}$-oriented curves (Corollary 2).

Corollary 1. *When $|\mathrm{disc}(\mathfrak{O})| < p$, $\#\mathcal{E}_{\mathfrak{O}}(p) = \#\mathcal{S}_{\mathfrak{O}}(p)$.*

Proof. If we assume that $\#\mathcal{E}_{\mathfrak{O}}(p) < \#\mathcal{S}_{\mathfrak{O}}(p)$, then there must be a curve E with two distinct $\mathfrak{O}$-orientations ι_1, ι_2. Under the Deuring correspondence, this implies that there are two distinct quadratic orders $\mathfrak{O}_1, \mathfrak{O}_2$ isomorphic to $\mathfrak{O}$ contained inside the maximal order $\mathcal{O} \cong \mathrm{End}(E)$. By Proposition 5, p must be smaller than d which contradicts our assumption.

Corollary 2. *Let ℓ be a prime different from p. If ℓ is inert in $\mathfrak{O}$ of discriminant d, then the shortest chain of ℓ-isogenies between two curves of $\mathcal{E}_{\mathfrak{O}}(p)$ has degree larger than p/d.*

Proof (sketch). Let us denote the two curves by E_1, E_2 and by $\mathcal{O}_1, \mathcal{O}_2$, their respective endomorphism rings. Let us take $\varphi : E_1 \to E_2$ the smallest chain of ℓ-isogenies connecting them. Let us write $\theta_i \in \mathcal{O}_i$ such that $\mathfrak{O} \cong \mathbb{Z}[\theta_i]$. Since ℓ is inert in $\mathfrak{O}$, it can be shown that $\alpha_1 = \theta_1$ and $\alpha_2 = \hat{\varphi} \circ \theta_2 \circ \varphi$ are two elements in $\mathcal{O}_1$ that are not commuting (otherwise, at least one of the isogenies composing φ would be commuting with θ which is impossible since $\ell \neq p$ and is inert in $\mathfrak{K}$). Since $\mathrm{disc}(\mathbb{Z}[\alpha_1]) = d$ and $\mathrm{disc}(\mathbb{Z}[\alpha_2]) = -\deg \varphi^2 d$, we obtain the desired bound by applying Proposition 5.

3.2   The Case of $\mathfrak{O}_{\mathfrak{K}}$.

In this section, we focus on the case where $\mathfrak{O} = \mathfrak{O}_{\mathfrak{K}}$ for a quadratic imaginary field $\mathfrak{K}$ of discriminant $-d$. Our main result is Proposition 11.

To improve the reader's understanding, we divide the proof of Proposition 11 into several lemmas and propositions. Next, we give a brief outline and some insights into the generic principle. Our starting point is the observation (already used to prove Corollary 1) that if $\#\mathcal{E}_{\mathfrak{O}}(p) < \#\mathcal{S}_{\mathfrak{O}}(p)$, then there are some curves admitting several $\mathfrak{O}$-orientations. Similarly to Proposition 5, our result is obtained through the analysis of the quaternion orders obtained by combining together the different pairs of orientations. More concretely, we bound the number of these quaternion orders in two very different ways. The first one is a lower bound depending on $\#\mathcal{E}_{\mathfrak{O}}(p)$ and $\#\mathcal{S}_{\mathfrak{O}}(p)$ (Proposition 7) while the second one is an upper-bound (Proposition 10) that involves an explicit quantity that can be computed from d and p. The combination of these two bounds yields Proposition 11.

Here are some notations that we will use throughout this section. For any given $E \in \mathcal{E}_{\mathfrak{O}}(p)$, we write $N_E \geq 1$ for the number of distinct $\mathfrak{O}$-orientations of E. We write $\iota_1, \ldots, \iota_{N_E}$ for these N_E orientations, they induce the existence of endomorphisms $\alpha_1, \ldots, \alpha_{N_E} \in \mathrm{End}(E)$ such that $(\iota_i(\mathfrak{O}))_{1 \leq i \leq N_E} = (\mathbb{Z}[\alpha_i])_{1 \leq i \leq N_E}$. Since $\mathfrak{O}$ is the maximal order of $\mathfrak{K}$, we can assume that α_i is either $\iota_i^{-1}(\sqrt{-q})$ or $\iota_i^{-1}((1 + \sqrt{-q})/2)$ where q is the squarefree integer such that $\mathfrak{K} = \mathbb{Q}(\sqrt{-q})$. Let $I_{\neq}^2(N_E)$ be the set of pairs of distinct unordered elements inside $\{1, \ldots, N_E\}$. We define an equivalence relation $\sim_E$ on $I_{\neq}^2(N_E)$ as

$$(i, j) \sim_E (l, m) \text{ iff } \langle 1, \alpha_i, \alpha_j, \alpha_i \alpha_j \rangle = \langle 1, \alpha_l, \alpha_m, \alpha_l \alpha_m \rangle.$$

Definition 3. *The set of equivalence classes under $\sim_E$ is denoted by $\mathcal{K}_E$. We write $K_E = \#\mathcal{K}_E$.*

Intuitively, $\mathcal{K}_E$ is the set of distinct quaternion orders obtained by combining two embeddings of $\mathfrak{O}$ inside $\mathrm{End}(E)$. By the results presented in Sect. 2.2, we have $\#\mathcal{S}_{\mathfrak{O}}(p) = \sum_{E \in \mathcal{E}_{\mathfrak{O}}(p)} N_E$. The quantity we propose to study is

$$K_{\mathfrak{O}}(p) = \sum_{E \in \mathcal{E}_{\mathfrak{O}}(p)} K_E \qquad (2)$$

The Link Between $\#\mathcal{E}_{\mathfrak{O}}(p)$ and $K_{\mathfrak{O}}(p)$. The number K_E is obviously related to N_E for every curve $E \in \mathcal{E}_{\mathfrak{O}}(p)$. Intuitively, we would like to say that every pair α_i, α_j generates a different quaternion order $\mathcal{O}_{i,j}$ with $1 \leq i < j \leq N_E$ (thus proving that $K_E = N_E(N_E - 1)/2$). However, even if this seems to be the case with good probability, it is not true in full generality. The correct statement is given in Proposition 6. Fortunately, Proposition 6 still allows us to derive Corollary 3 that lower-bounds K_E by $C N_E(N_E - 1)$ for some constant factor C, which is enough for our purpose.

Proposition 6. *Let $\mathbb{Z}[\alpha_1], \mathbb{Z}[\alpha_2], \mathbb{Z}[\alpha_3]$ be three distinct embeddings of the quadratic order of discriminant $-d$ (with $d > 10$) inside a maximal quaternion order $\mathcal{O}$. If $d \not\equiv 3 \mod 4$ or $d \not\equiv 0, 1 \mod p$, then $\alpha_3 \notin \mathcal{O}_{1,2} = \langle 1, \alpha_1, \alpha_2, \alpha_1 \alpha_2 \rangle$. When $d \equiv 0 \mod p$, either $\alpha_3 \notin \mathcal{O}_{1,2}$ or the trace of $\alpha_1 \alpha_2$ is equal to $4n(\alpha_1)$*

and α_3 is one of $\pm(\text{tr}(\alpha_1)/2 + \alpha_1 - \alpha_2)$. When $d \equiv 3 \mod 4$ and $d \equiv 1 \mod p$, either $\alpha_3 \notin \mathcal{O}_{1,2}$ or the trace of $\alpha_1\alpha_2$ is $(d-1)/2$ and α_3 is one of $((d-1)/4 + \alpha_2 - \alpha_1\alpha_2), ((d-1)/4 + \alpha_1 - \alpha_1\alpha_2), ((9-d)/4 - \alpha_2 + \alpha_1\alpha_2), ((9-d)/4 - \alpha_1 + \alpha_1\alpha_2)$.

Proof. Since all orders are isomorphic, we can assume that all α_i have the same trace and norm. Let us write $t = \text{tr}(\alpha_i), n = n(\alpha_i)$ for any $i = 1, 2, 3$. The proof is based on the following claim: any $\alpha_3 \in \mathcal{O}_{1,2}$ corresponds to a solution $x, y, z \in \mathbb{Z}[1/2]$ with $x - y, y - z \in \mathbb{Z}$ to the quadratic equation:

$$q = q(x^2 + y^2) + sxy + z^2(q^2 - s^2/4) \tag{3}$$

for some integers s, q that we will define below. We exclude the trivial solutions $(1, 0, 0)$ and $(0, 1, 0)$.

As a consequence, our proof can be divided in two parts: first, we prove the correspondence between the solutions to Eq. (3) and the $\alpha_3 \in \mathcal{O}_{1,2}$, then we find the solutions of Eq. (3) to identify all the possible α_3.

Proof of the Claim. If we assume that $\alpha_3 \in \mathcal{O}_{1,2}$, then there exists $v, x, y, z \in \mathbb{Z}$ such that $\alpha_3 = v + x\alpha_1 + y\alpha_2 + z\alpha_1\alpha_2$. The trace of α_3 implies the equation $t = 2v + t(x + y) + z\text{tr}(\alpha_1\alpha_2)$. Thus, we rewrite $\alpha_3 = t/2 + x(\alpha_1 - t/2) + y(\alpha_2 - t/2) + z(\alpha_1\alpha_2 - \text{tr}(\alpha_1\alpha_2)/2)$.

There are two different cases, depending on the value of $d \mod 4$. If $d \equiv 0 \mod 4$ then $d = 4q$ for some square-free $q \equiv 1 \mod 4$ and so we can assume w.l.o.g. that $t = 0$ and $\alpha_i = \omega_i$ with $\omega_i^2 = -q$. Else $d = q$ for some square-free $q \equiv 3 \mod 4$ and we can take $t = 1$, $\alpha_i = (1 + \omega_i)/2$ with $\omega_i^2 = -q$.

In both cases, let us write $s = \text{tr}(\omega_1\omega_2)$. If $d \equiv 0 \mod 4$, then we obtain the norm equation $q = n(\alpha_3) = q(x^2 + y^2) + sxy + z^2(q^2 - s^2/4)$. When $d \equiv q \equiv 3 \mod 4$, we have $\alpha_3 = (1 + \omega_3)/2 = 1/2 + x\omega_1/2 + y\omega_2/2 + (z/4)(1 + \omega_1 + \omega_2 + \omega_1\omega_2 - (1 + s/2))$. Then, we obtain $\omega_3 = (x + z/2)\omega_1 + (y + z/2)\omega_2 + z/2(\omega_1\omega_2 - s/2)$. Writing $x_2 = x + z/2$, $y_2 = y + z/2$, $z_2 = z/2$ and taking the norm, we obtain the equation $q = n(\omega_3) = q(x_2^2 + y_2^2) + sx_2y_2 + z_2^2(q^2 - s^2/4)$.

In conclusion, we need to find the solutions x, y, z in $\mathbb{Z}[1/2]$ and $x - y \in \mathbb{Z}, y - z \in \mathbb{Z}$ to the quadratic equation $q = q(x^2 + y^2) + sxy + z^2(q^2 - s^2/4)$ different from the trivial solutions $(1, 0, 0)$ and $(0, 1, 0)$. The end of the proof is dedicated to the enumeration of all possible solutions.

Finding the Solutions of Eq. (3). Throughout this search, we will use heavily the fact that $|s| < 2q$ (which comes from $\text{disc}(\mathbb{Z})[\omega_1\omega_2] = s^2 - 4q^2 < 0$). W.l.o.g. we can assume that $s \geq 0$. We can directly remove the case $x = y = 0$ as it is clearly impossible to find a z such that $q = z^2(q^2 - s^2/4)$.

Our first step is to find the possible values of z. Let us rewrite our equation as $q = q(x^2 + y^2) + sxy + z^2(q - s/2)(q + s/2)$. With the bound $(q - s/2)(q + s/2) \geq q/2$ we get that we must have $z \in \{0, \pm 1/2, \pm 1\}$. This implies that $s \equiv 0 \mod 2$ (otherwise $q(x^2 + y^2) + sxy + z^2(q - s/2)(q + s/2)$ would not be an integer). With that additional information, we can actually show that $q^2 - s^2/4 \geq q$. Thus, in fact we must have $z \in \{0, \pm 1/2\}$. We also have $q \geq q(x^2 + y^2) + sxy$.

Now that we have greatly reduced the number of possible z, we can look at the values x, y. We distinguish two cases, depending on the sign of x, y.

Let us assume that $xy \geq 0$. Then, we have $q \geq q(x^2 + y^2) + sxy$. Thus, we must have $x^2 + y^2 \leq 1$. Since we exclude $(x, y) \in \{(0,0), (0,1), (1,0)\}$, the only possibility respecting all our constraints is $(x, y, z) = (1/2, 1/2, \pm 1/2)$. Thus, we obtain $q = q/2 + s/4 + q^2/4 - s^2/16$ which leads to the equation $q^2 - 2q + s(1 - s/4) = 0$. The discriminant of the polynomial $X^2 - 2X + s(1 - s/4)$ is equal to $4 - 4s + s^2 = (s-2)^2$. The two possible solutions are $s/2$ and $(4-s)/2$. The first one is impossible by the bound $s < 2q$. Since $s \geq 0$ we obtain $(4-s)/2 < 2$ and this is incompatible with the bound $d > 10$.

We have seen that we have no solutions to Eq. (3) when $xy \geq 0$. Let us now consider the case $xy < 0$. W.l.o.g. we can assume that $x > 0$ and $y < 0$. Then, we have $q \leq q(x^2 + y^2) - s|xy|$, but the bound $s < 2q$ leads to the inequality $q(x^2 + y^2) - s|xy| > q(x^2 + y^2) - 2q|xy| = q(x+y)^2$. If we want to avoid a contradiction between these two bounds, then we must have $|x+y| < 1$. Since $x - y \in \mathbb{Z}$, the only possibility is $x = -y$.

When $x = -y$, we can rewrite Eq. (3) as

$$q = (q - s/2)(2x^2 + z^2(q + s/2)). \tag{4}$$

Let us study this new equation. Since we have only a few possibilities for z, we can simply see what happens with Eq. (4) for each value of z. Since the equation is in z^2 there are two cases: $z = 0$ and $z = \pm 1/2$.

If $z = 0$, we get $q = x^2(2q - s)$ where $x \in \mathbb{Z}$ and so the only solution is $x = 1$ and $s = q$ since q is square-free. However, looking at the discriminant of $\langle 1, \omega_1, \omega_2, \omega_1\omega_2 \rangle$ with Proposition 4, we get that p must divide q as it divides the discriminant of any maximal order in $B_{p,\infty}$. In that case, we have the solution $(x, y, z) = \pm(1, -1, 0)$.

If $z = \pm 1/2$, the requirement $x - z \in \mathbb{Z}$ implies that we can write $x = x'/2$ with $x' \equiv 1 \mod 2$. Putting all this in Eq. (4), we get $q = (q - s/2)x'^2/2 + 1/4(q - s/2)(q + s/2)$ (we recall that $s' := s/2$ is in $\mathbb{Z}$). It is clear that we must have $q \pm s' \equiv 0 \mod 2$ so let us write $q \pm s' = 2q_\pm$. Our equation becomes $q = q_- + q_+ = q_- x'^2 + q_+ q_-$ which implies that $q_+ \equiv 0 \mod q_-$. Thus, we must have $q_+ = kq_-$ for some $k \in \mathbb{Z}$ and Eq. 4 becomes $q = (k+1)q_- = q_-(x'^2 + kq_-)$ which can only be satisfied if $x' = 1$ and $q_- = 1$. In that case, the only possible solution (up to signs) is $(x, y, z) = (1/2, -1/2, \pm 1/2)$ when $s = 2q - 4$.

In summary, we have showed that our equations have the non-trivial solutions $\pm(1, -1, 0)$ when $d \equiv 0 \mod p$ and $s = q$ or $\pm(1/2, -1/2, \pm 1/2)$ when $d \equiv 3 \mod 4$ and $s = 2q - 4$ and none otherwise. We conclude the proof by computing what are the corresponding values of α_3, so we compute the concrete values $v, x, y, z \in \mathbb{Z}$ such that $\alpha_3 = v + x\alpha_1 + y\alpha_2 + z\alpha_1\alpha_2$ (note that these values x, y, z are not directly the solutions to Eq. (3) when $d = 3 \mod 4$, see the proof of our claim at the beginning of the proof).

For the first solution, selecting the value v to verify the trace equation we get that $\alpha_3 = \pm\text{tr}(\alpha_1) + \alpha_1 - \alpha_2$. It is easily verified that $\text{tr}(\alpha_1\alpha_2) = 4n(\alpha_1\alpha_2)$ when $s = q$. Otherwise, $\alpha_3 = v + x\alpha_1 + y\alpha_2 + z\alpha_1\alpha_2$ can only have a solution when $d \equiv q \equiv 3 \mod 4$ and $\text{tr}(\alpha_1\alpha_2) = 1/2 + 1/4(\text{tr}(\omega_1\omega_2)) = (d-1)/2$. By computing the discriminant of $\mathbb{Z}\langle 1, \alpha_1, \alpha_2, \alpha_1\alpha_2 \rangle$ with Proposition 4 when

$\operatorname{tr}(\alpha_1) = \operatorname{tr}(\alpha_2) = 1$ and $\operatorname{tr}(\alpha_1\alpha_2) = (q-1)/2$, we see that $\Delta = d-1$ and so p divides $d-1$. This proves that $d \equiv 1 \mod p$ is also a necessary condition for our equation to be satisfied.

The other possibilities for α_3 can easily be found by taking $(x + z/2, y + z/2, z/2) = \pm(1/2, -1/2, \pm1/2)$ and v be such that $\operatorname{tr}(\alpha_3) = 1$.

Corollary 3. $K_E \geq \frac{N_E(N_E-1)}{12}$.

Proof. From $\alpha_l \notin \mathcal{O}_{i,j}$ or $\alpha_m \notin \mathcal{O}_{i,j} \Rightarrow (i,j) \not\sim_E (l,m)$ for any i,j,m,l, we see from Proposition 6 that the cardinality of any equivalence class in $I^2_{\neq}(N_E)$ must be smaller than 6, as there at most four elements $\alpha_{i'}$ contained in $\mathcal{O}_{i,j}$ and we must choose two among the possible i' to get a full quaternion order. This bound combined with $\#I^2_{\neq}(N_E) = N(N-1)/2$ gives the result directly.

The bound obtained in Corollary 3 is the key ingredient to the inequality between $\#\mathcal{E}_\mathfrak{O}(p)$, $\#\mathcal{S}_\mathfrak{O}(p)$ and $K_\mathfrak{O}(p)$ in Proposition 7.

Proposition 7. $K_\mathfrak{O}(p) \geq \frac{1}{12}(\frac{\#\mathcal{S}_\mathfrak{O}(p)^2}{\#\mathcal{E}_\mathfrak{O}(p)} - \#\mathcal{S}_\mathfrak{O}(p))$

Proof. We have $\#\mathcal{S}_\mathfrak{O}(p) = \sum_{E\in\mathcal{E}_\mathfrak{O}(p)} N_E$. Using Corollary 3, we get $\sum_{E\in\mathcal{E}_\mathfrak{O}(p)} K_E \geq (1/12)\sum_{E\in\mathcal{E}_\mathfrak{O}(p)}(N_E^2 - N_E)$. Then, we can use the classical inequality $\sum_{i=1}^n x_i^2 \geq (1/n)(\sum_{i=1}^n x_i)^2$ to get the result.

A Generic Upper-Bound of $K_\mathfrak{O}(p)$. If (i,j) is a representative of a class $k \in \mathcal{K}_E$, we define t_k as the value of $\operatorname{tr}(\alpha_i\alpha_j)$ and $\mathcal{O}_k$ as the quaternion order equal to the image of $\langle 1, \alpha_i, \alpha_j, \alpha_i\alpha_j\rangle$ under the isomorphism between $B_{p,\infty}$ and $\operatorname{End}(E)\otimes\mathbb{Q}$ (by definition of $\mathcal{K}_E$, t_k and $\mathcal{O}_k$ are independent of a choice of i,j). The idea is to look at the embedding number of the different orders $\mathcal{O}_k$ for $k \in \mathcal{K}_E$ and $E \in \mathcal{E}_\mathfrak{O}(p)$ in order to rewrite $\sum_{E\in\mathcal{E}_\mathfrak{O}(p)} K_E$. With the notation from Sect. 2.1, we write this number $e(\mathcal{O}_k)$ for a given class k and we compute it in Proposition 8. Before proving this result, we need to understand a bit better the structure of the orders $\mathcal{O}_k$. This is the purpose of Lemma 1.

Lemma 1. *Let E be a curve in $\mathcal{E}_\mathfrak{O}(p)$ and $k \in \mathcal{K}_E$. The order $\mathcal{O}_k$ is a Bass order.*

Proof. One of the several equivalent definitions of Bass orders inside $B_{p,\infty}$ is that they contain a maximal order inside a commutative subalgebra of $B_{p,\infty}$ [Voi21, Section 24.5]. Since $\mathfrak{O}$ is the maximal order of $\mathfrak{K}$, and the property follows from the definition of $\mathcal{O}_k$.

With the knowledge that the $\mathcal{O}_k$ are Bass orders, we can use Proposition 1 and Proposition 2 to compute $e(\mathcal{O}_k)$.

Proposition 8. *Let $D_k = \operatorname{disc}(\mathcal{O}_k)/p$. The embedding number of $\mathcal{O}_k$ is*

$$e(\mathcal{O}_k) = \prod_{\ell\in\mathbb{P}_{D_k},(-d/\ell)=1} (v_\ell(D_k)+1) \prod_{\ell\in\mathbb{P}_{D_k},(-d/\ell)=0,\ell\neq p} 2.$$

Proof. If we show that when ℓ is a prime dividing D_k, $(\mathcal{O}/\ell) = (-d/\ell)$, then the result follows from Proposition 2 and Lemma 1. First, note that when $\ell = p$, the local embedding number $e_\ell(\mathcal{O})$ is always equal to 1 (it is a consequence of Propositions 1 and 2 and the fact that $(-d/p) \neq 1$). Then, it suffices to prove the result for the cases where $\ell \neq p$ is either split or ramified in $\mathfrak{K}$. The two results $(-d/\ell) = 1 \Rightarrow (\mathcal{O}/\ell) = 1$ and $(\mathcal{O}/\ell) = 0 \Rightarrow (-d/\ell) = 0$ are easily implied by Proposition 1. To conclude, it suffices to show $(\mathcal{O}/\ell) = 0 \Leftarrow (-d/\ell) = 0$, as $(\mathcal{O}/\ell) = 1 \Rightarrow (-d/\ell) \in \{0,1\}$. For that, we will show that ℓ divides the discriminant of every $\alpha \in \mathcal{O}_k$. We recall that there exists α_i, α_j with $\mathfrak{O} \cong \mathbb{Z}[\alpha_i] \cong \mathbb{Z}[\alpha_j]$ and $\mathcal{O}_k = \langle 1, \alpha_i, \alpha_j, \alpha_i\alpha_j \rangle$. By assumption, the property is satisfied for α_i, α_j. We recall the value of $D_k = (d^2 - (\varepsilon - 2t_k)^2)/4p$ where $\varepsilon = \mathrm{tr}(\alpha_i)\mathrm{tr}(\alpha_j)$. From $\ell \mid D_k$ and $\ell \mid d$, we get that ℓ must divide $2t_k - \varepsilon$ which implies that $\ell \mid \Delta(\alpha_i\alpha_j)$. Then, using $\ell \mid d$ and $\ell|(2t_k - \varepsilon)$, we can conclude that $\ell|\Delta(x + y\alpha_i + z\alpha_j + w\alpha_1\alpha_2)$ for any $x, y, z, w \in \mathbb{Z}^4$.

The value of $\mathrm{disc}(\mathcal{O}_k)$ is $(d^2 - (\mathrm{tr}(\alpha_i)\mathrm{tr}(\alpha_j) - 2t_k)^2)/4$ by Proposition 4. It can be shown that $\mathrm{tr}(\alpha_i)\mathrm{tr}(\alpha_j)$ is a constant that is either 0 or 1 depending only on the value of $d \mod 4$. Henceforth, we write this constant ε_d. Inspired by the formulation of Proposition 8, we define the functions

$$D : (t, d, p) \mapsto \frac{(d^2 - (\varepsilon_d - 2t)^2)}{4p}$$

and

$$e : (t, d, p) \mapsto \prod_{\ell \in \mathbb{P}_{D(t,d,p)}, (d/\ell)=1} (v_\ell(D(t, d, p)) + 1) \prod_{\ell \in \mathbb{P}_{D(t,d,p)}(d/\ell)=0, \ell \neq p} 2.$$

Let us define $T_\mathfrak{O}(p) = \{t_k | k \in \mathcal{K}_E \text{ for } E \in \mathcal{E}_\mathfrak{O}(p)\}$. For each $t \in T_\mathfrak{O}(p)$, the values $D(t, d, p)$ and $e(t, d, p)$ are well-defined, when p is prime and d is a fundamental discriminant coprime with p.

Proposition 9. *Let $\mathfrak{O}$ be the maximal quadratic order of discriminant $-d$. Then,*

$$\frac{1}{12} \sum_{t \in T_\mathfrak{O}(p)} e(t, d, p) \leq K_\mathfrak{O}(p) \leq \sum_{t \in T_\mathfrak{O}(p)} e(t, d, p)$$

Proof. By definition, we have that for every class k, there exists $t \in T_\mathfrak{O}(p)$ with $t = t_k$ and $e(\mathcal{O}_k) = e(t, d, p)$. Thus, each class k corresponds to at least one embedding of $\mathcal{O}_k$ inside a maximal order and so we must have $K_\mathfrak{O}(p) \leq \sum_{t \in T_\mathfrak{O}(p)} e(t, d, p)$.

The lower bound of $K_\mathfrak{O}(p)$ is more delicate to obtain. For that, we will need to quantify the maximum number of embedding that corresponds to the same class k. Let us take an element $t \in T_\mathfrak{O}(p)$. By definition of $T_\mathfrak{O}(p)$, there exists a curve $E \in \mathcal{E}_\mathfrak{O}(p)$ and a class $k \in K_E$ with $t_k = t$. By definition of the embedding number, there exist $e(t, d, p)$ distinct maximal orders containing $\mathcal{O}_k$. Each of these maximal orders $\mathcal{O}'$ corresponds to the isomorphism class (up to Galois conjugacy) of supersingular curve E' under the Deuring Correspondence. By definition there also exists a class $k' \in \mathcal{K}_{E'}$ such that $\mathcal{O}_{k'} \cong \mathcal{O}_k$.

We will provide an upper bound on the number of these $e(t, d, p)$ classes that are equal. Up to composition with the relevant isomorphisms, we can assume that all the orders $\mathcal{O}_{k'}$ are actually equal (and not simply isomorphic). Let us take $\mathcal{O}^1 \neq \mathcal{O}^2$, maximal orders with $\mathcal{O}_k \subset \mathcal{O}^i$ for $i = 1, 2$ and assume that these two embeddings of $\mathcal{O}_k$ lead to the same class k' and curve E'. We must have $\mathcal{O}^1 \cong \mathcal{O}^2 \cong \mathrm{End}(E)'$, so let us write $\sigma_i : \mathcal{O}^i \to \mathrm{End}(E)$ the corresponding isomorphisms. By definition of our equivalence relation, we must have $\sigma_1(\mathcal{O}_k) = \sigma_2(\mathcal{O}_k)$, which means that $\mathcal{O}_k$ is stable under the isomorphism $\sigma_1^{-1} \circ \sigma_2 : \mathcal{O}^2 \to \mathcal{O}^1$. This shows that our problem reduces to counting the number of isomorphisms that leave stable $\mathcal{O}_k$ but are not the identity. For that, it suffices to count the number of possible images of the two elements α_i, α_j such that $k = (i, j)$. Proposition 6 tells us that there are at most two other elements of same norm and trace as α_i, α_j. Thus, we have $3 \times 4 = 12$ possible image pair for α_i, α_j, and so we can conclude that each class k corresponds to at most 12 distinct embeddings of $\mathcal{O}_k$ inside distinct maximal orders. This proves the result.

With Proposition 9, we have all the necessary ingredients to prove our generic upper-bound of $K_{\mathfrak{O}}(p)$. We introduce in Definition 4, a final notation to simplify the formulation of Proposition 10.

Definition 4. *The function $\tau : \mathbb{N} \to \mathbb{N}$ is defined as $\tau(N) = \prod_{\ell \in \mathbb{P}_N} (v_\ell(N) + 1)$, and it computes the number of divisors of N.*

Proposition 10. $K_{\mathfrak{O}}(p) \leq \left\lceil \frac{d+1}{4p} \right\rceil \max_{0 \leq N \leq d^2/(4p)} \tau(N)$.

Proof. It is clear from the definition of the functions τ, D, e that $\tau(D(d, t, p)) \geq e(d, t, p)$. Since $0 \leq D(t, d, p) \leq d^2/(4p)$ we get that

$$\sum_{t \in T_{\mathfrak{O}}(p)} e(t, d, p) \leq \#T_{\mathfrak{O}}(p) \max_{0 \leq N \leq d^2/(4p)} \tau(N).$$

Next, we prove that $\#T_{\mathfrak{O}} \leq \lceil (d + 1)/4p \rceil$. If $t \in T_{\mathfrak{O}}$, we must have that $D(d, t, p) = \mathrm{disc}(\mathcal{O}_k)/p \in \mathbb{N}^*$ for some class k. The condition on the discriminant yields $d^2 - (\varepsilon_d - 2t)^2 \equiv 0 \mod 4p$ and $d^2 > (\varepsilon_d - 2t)^2$. When $t > 0$, we have $|2t| - \varepsilon_d > 0$ and so get the bound $(|d| + \varepsilon_d)/2 > |t|$. There are two possible values of $t \mod 4p$ and combining that with the $0 < |t| < (|d| + \varepsilon_d)/2$ we obtain at most $\lfloor (d + 1)/(4p) \rfloor$ possible values. Adding $t = 0$, we obtain the desired bound. The proof is concluded by Proposition 9.

We obtain a generic lower bound on $\#\mathcal{E}_{\mathfrak{O}}(p)$ in Proposition 11. It is a combination of Proposition 7 and Proposition 10.

Proposition 11. $\#\mathcal{E}_{\mathfrak{O}}(p) \geq \frac{AB}{A+B} \geq \frac{1}{2} \min(A, B)$ *where $A = \#\mathcal{S}_{\mathfrak{O}}(p)$ and $B = \frac{\#\mathcal{S}_{\mathfrak{O}}(p)^2}{3(4p+d+1)} \frac{p}{\max_{0 \leq N \leq d^2/4p} \tau(N)}$.*

Before proving Proposition 11, we prove Lemma 2 that will be useful.

Lemma 2. *For every 3 values $x, A, B > 0$ such that $x \geq \lambda A$ or $x \geq (1 - \lambda)B$ for every $0 < \lambda < 1$. Then, $x \geq \frac{AB}{A+B} \geq \frac{1}{2}\min(A, B)$.*

Proof. We are going to start with the intermediary result that $x \geq \lambda A$ or $x \geq (1 - \lambda)B$ for every $0 < \lambda < 1$ imply that $x \geq \max_{0<\lambda<1}\min(\lambda A, (1 - \lambda)B)$. The function $\lambda \mapsto \min(\lambda A, (1-\lambda)B)$ is increasing on $]0, \lambda_m]$ and decreasing on $[\lambda_m, 1[$ for the value λ_m such that $\lambda_m A = (1 - \lambda_m)B$. Thus, we get $\lambda_m = B/(A + B)$ and $\max_{0<\lambda<1}\min(\lambda A, (1 - \lambda)B) = \lambda_m A = AB/(A + B)$.

To conclude it is easy to verify that

$$\frac{AB}{A+B} \geq \frac{1}{2}\min(A, B).$$

Proof (Proposition 11). We will apply Lemma 2 with $x = \#\mathcal{E}_{\mathfrak{O}}(p)$ and the values A, B as in Proposition 11. Thus, we need to prove that either $\#\mathcal{E}_{\mathfrak{O}}(p) \geq \lambda A$ or $\#\mathcal{E}_{\mathfrak{O}}(p) \geq (1 - \lambda)B$ for any $0 < \lambda < 1$.

Note that when $\#\mathcal{E}_{\mathfrak{O}}(p) < \lambda\#\mathcal{S}_{\mathfrak{O}}(p)$ for some $\lambda \leq 1$, we must have $K_{\mathfrak{O}}(p) > 0$ because there is at least one curve with two distinct orientations. Thus, Proposition 7 proves that

$$\#\mathcal{E}_{\mathfrak{O}}(p) \geq \frac{\#\mathcal{S}_{\mathfrak{O}}(p)^2 - \#\mathcal{S}_{\mathfrak{O}}(p)\#\mathcal{E}_{\mathfrak{O}}(p)}{12K_{\mathfrak{O}}(p)}.$$

For any $\lambda \in [0, 1]$, if $\#\mathcal{E}_{\mathfrak{O}}(p) < \lambda\#\mathcal{S}_{\mathfrak{O}}(p)$, we have that

$$\#\mathcal{E}_{\mathfrak{O}}(p) > (1 - \lambda)\frac{\#\mathcal{S}_{\mathfrak{O}}(p)^2}{12K_{\mathfrak{O}}(p)}.$$

The proof is concluded by Proposition 10 and $\lceil (d + 1)/4p \rceil \leq 1 + (d + 1)/4p$.

Remark 3. Our bound becomes less and less tight when the size of d grows in comparison to p. Asymptotically, we have

$$\lim_{d\to\infty} \frac{\#\mathcal{S}_{\mathfrak{O}}(p)^2}{3(4p + d + 1)} \frac{p}{\max_{0\leq N\leq d^2/4p} \tau(N)} = 0$$

which is very far from the expected $\mathcal{E}_{\mathfrak{O}}(p) = N_p$ when $d \to \infty$. However, when the value of d is polynomial in p, classical analysis on the τ function detailed below shows that our bound will never be trivial even as p grows to infinity. This is typically the case needed for isogeny-based cryptography as illustrated by our numerical application in Sect. 4 for a prime $p \approx 2^{400}$ and a discriminant d satisfying $p < d < p^2$.

Remark 4. Note that we can derive a family of upper-bounds on the class number $h(\mathfrak{O})$ from Proposition 11. Indeed, since we have the trivial bound $p/12 + 1 \geq N_p \geq \#\mathcal{E}_{\mathfrak{O}}(p)$, in the cases where $A > B$ (which will happen when d is much bigger than p as explained in Remark 3), we obtain $p/12 + 1 \geq B/2$. When we replace $\#\mathcal{S}_{\mathfrak{D}}(p)$ by the correct value $ch(\mathfrak{D})$ (with $c \in \{1/2, 1\}$) in the formula for B we can obtain

$$h(\mathfrak{D})^2 < \frac{(p+12)(4p+d+1)}{2c^2 p} \max_{0 \leq N \leq d^2/4p} \tau(N) \tag{5}$$

Intuitively, the best bounds should be obtained when $d \approx p$. The estimates we provide on $\tau(N)$ below do not allow us to conclude that this would lead to an improvement on the state of the art upper bounds on class numbers.

Remark 5. When p divides d, it might be possible to get better bounds. For instance, when d/p is a prime smaller than $p/4$, a lower bound was proven in [EHL+20, Theorem 3.9], using the fact that a curve in $\mathcal{E}_{\mathfrak{D}}(p)$ must be d/p-isogenous to its Galois conjugate E^p. Another possibility, is to exploit the fact that when $d \equiv 0 \mod p$, the element $\omega_1\omega_2/p$ is integral (see the proof of Proposition 6 for the definition of ω_1, ω_2) and so we may be able to consider superorders of the $\mathcal{O}_k$ (which might give a better bound since the discriminants are smaller). While this idea seems promising, it does not appear trivial to obtain the analog of Proposition 6 and this is why we left the study of this special case open for future work.

Upper Bound on the Number of Divisors Function. The number of divisors function τ is well-studied and generic upper-bounds can be found in the literature. Since Wigert [Wig07], we know that $\tau(N) = O(N^\varepsilon)$ for any $\varepsilon > 0$. In 1983, Nicolas and Robin showed that

$$\tau(N) \leq 2^{\eta_1 \frac{\log(N)}{\log\log(N)}}, \text{ for any } N \geq 3 \tag{6}$$

where $\eta_1 = 1.53793986\ldots$

More recently De Konick and Letendre [DKL18] proved several new upper-bounds involving $\omega(N)$ the number of distinct prime factors of N. In particular they showed that for any composite $n \geq 2$

$$\tau(N) \leq \left(1 + \eta_3 \frac{\log(N)}{\omega(N)\log(\omega(N))}\right)^{\omega(N)} \tag{7}$$

where $\eta_3 = 1,1999953\ldots$

When $\omega(N) \geq 74$ they even prove that

$$\tau(N) \leq \left(1 + \frac{\log(N)}{\omega(N)\log(\omega(N))}\right)^{\omega(N)} \tag{8}$$

We will use this last bound in the numerical application we propose in Sect. 4.

4   A Numerical Application to the Parameters of SETA

In this section, we are going to use Proposition 11 to provide a lower bound on the complexity of the brute-force algorithm to solve the $\mathfrak{D}$-UBER problem where $\mathfrak{O}$ is the quadratic order used in the SETA encryption scheme. This will give a lower bound on the hardness of SETA key recovery (using brute-force) and answer the interrogations left open in [DFFDdSG+21, Section 5.3] on the concrete hardness of the uber isogeny problem. More precisely, with our new result, we are able to prove, under a few reasonable assumptions, that there exists a fitting choice of quadratic order $\mathfrak{O}$ such that the best brute force key recovery attack is hard enough for the claimed security level in [DFFDdSG+21].

The SETA Parameters. The set of SETA keys is $\mathcal{E}_{\mathfrak{O}}(p)$ where $\mathfrak{O} = \mathbb{Z}[\sqrt{-n}]$ where n is a solution of the quadratic equation $z^2 + nD^2 = N^2$ with $-n$ being a quadratic non-residue modulo all the prime divisors of D and p, where D, N and p are the three main parameters of SETA.

The authors of the SETA paper [DFFDdSG+21] provided an implementation of their protocol with given values for p, D, N. The characteristic p is a 400 bits primes equal to $2 \cdot 8426067021^{12} - 1$, and the two other parameters are:

$$D = 43^{12} \cdot 84719^{11},$$

$$N = 3^{21} \cdot 5 \cdot 7 \cdot 13 \cdot 17 \cdot 19 \cdot 23 \cdot 73 \cdot 257^{12} \cdot 313 \cdot 1009 \cdot 2857 \cdot 3733 \cdot 5519 \cdot 6961$$
$$\cdot 53113 \cdot 499957 \cdot 763369 \cdot 2101657 \cdot 2616791 \cdot 7045009 \cdot 11959093$$
$$\cdot 17499277 \cdot 20157451 \cdot 33475999 \cdot 39617833 \cdot 45932333.$$

The concrete value of n was not given in [DFFDdSG+21] but several solutions can be found quite easily. Below, we computed one such solution where n is easy to factor so that we could compute the conductor. For instance, we found the value:

$$n = 113 \cdot 337 \cdot 43913 \cdot 695221299145935547134666573552750006601852579089724 9$$
$$2522431413808553767205401453148081325894556965991428307754649539266$$
$$0333428750680260233706678307702253 0457.$$

Since, n is square free and equal to $1 \mod 4$, the order $\mathfrak{O} = \mathbb{Z}[\sqrt{-n}]$ is the ring of integers of $\mathfrak{K} = \mathbb{Q}(\sqrt{-n})$. Since p is inert in $\mathfrak{O}$, we have $\#\mathcal{S}_{\mathfrak{O}}(p) = h(\mathfrak{O})$. Under GRH, Littlewood [Lit28] proved the inequality

$$h(\mathfrak{O}) > \left(\frac{\pi}{12e^{\gamma}} + o(1)\right)\frac{\sqrt{4n}}{\log\log(4n)}$$

where γ is the Euler-Mascheroni constant with $e^{\gamma}/\pi \approx 0.56693$. To derive the concrete lower-bound in Corollary 4 from Proposition 11, we apply the classical lower bound on $h(\mathfrak{O})$ stated above and the upper-bound in Eq. (6) on the size of τ.

Corollary 4. *Let the values p, n be as above and $\mathfrak{O} = \mathbb{Z}[\sqrt{-n}]$. Assuming GRH, the size of $\mathcal{E}_{\mathfrak{O}}(p)$ is bigger than 2^{269}.*

Proof. Proposition 11 tells us that $\#\mathcal{E}_{\mathfrak{O}}(p)$ is bigger than $(1/2)\min(A, B)$ where:

$$A = h(\mathfrak{O}) \text{ and } B = \frac{h(\mathfrak{O})^2}{3(4p + 4n + 1)} \frac{p}{\max_{0 \leq N \leq 4n^2/p} \tau(N)}.$$

Assuming that our n is big enough for it to hold, we are going to use $A = h(\mathfrak{O}) > \frac{\pi}{24e^{\gamma}} \frac{\sqrt{4n}}{\log\log(4n)} > 2^{270}$. To get a lower bound on B, it remains to get an upper bound on $\max_{0 \leq N \leq 4n^2/p} \tau(N)$. We can compute this bound manually using Eq. (8). Indeed, it can be easily verified that $\omega(4n^2/p) \geq 98 \geq 74$ and so we can compute

$$\left(1 + \frac{\log(4n^2/p)}{k\log(k)}\right)^k \text{ for all } 1 \leq k \leq 98.$$

As expected, the maximum is obtained for $k = 98$ and we have that

$$\max_{0 \leq N \leq 4n^2/p} \tau(N) < 2^{105}.$$

Thus, using the bound on $h(\mathfrak{O})$, we get that $B > 2^{279}$. So, under GRH and the assumption that n is big enough so that our simplification of the Littlewood bound hold, we get that

$$\#\mathcal{E}_{\mathbb{Z}[\sqrt{-n}]}(p) > 2^{269}.$$

5   Conclusion and Open Problems

We have given a new generic lower bound on the size of $\mathcal{E}_{\mathfrak{O}}(p)$ and proven that our bound was useful in practice by applying it to a concrete example taken from isogeny-based cryptography. While our bound seems satisfying for the example we took, its behavior is a bit counter-intuitive as it tends to 0 when the discriminant of $\mathfrak{O}$ tends to infinity and p is fixed. It is an interesting question to see if this asymptotic behavior is intrinsic to our method or if we could derive a better bound. We have also observed that studying the case where p divides the discriminant of $\mathfrak{O}$ could lead to interesting improvements. Finally, it could be interesting to see if we could adapt our analysis to the case of embeddings of quadratic orders of distinct discriminants inside the same quaternion order and see how the resulting bound would compare with the results from the singular moduli literature (the ones from [LV15] for instance).

Acknowledgements.. We are very grateful to John Voight for some crucial comments regarding the results in Sect. 3.2 and Proposition 9 in particular. We would also like to thank Luca De Feo and some anonymous reviewers for useful comments on an earlier version of this work.

References

[ACL+22] Arpin, S., Chen, M., Lauter, K.E., Scheidler, R., Stange, K.E., Tran, H.T.N.: Orienteering with one endomorphism. arXiv preprint arXiv:2201.11079 (2022)

[ADFMP20] Alamati, N., De Feo, L., Montgomery, H., Patranabis, S.: Cryptographic group actions and applications. In: Moriai, S., Wang, H. (eds.) ASIACRYPT 2020. LNCS, vol. 12492, pp. 411–439. Springer, Cham (2020). https://doi.org/10.1007/978-3-030-64834-3_14

[BE92] Brzezinski, J., Eichler, M.: On the imbeddings of imaginary quadratic orders in definite quaternion orders (1992)

[Bel08] Belding, J.V.: Number theoretic algorithms for elliptic curves. University of Maryland, College Park (2008)

[BKV19] Beullens, W., Kleinjung, T., Vercauteren, F.: CSI-FiSh: efficient isogeny based signatures through class group computations. In: Galbraith, S.D., Moriai, S. (eds.) ASIACRYPT 2019. LNCS, vol. 11921, pp. 227–247. Springer, Cham (2019). https://doi.org/10.1007/978-3-030-34578-5_9

[Brz83] Brzezinski, J.: On orders in quaternion algebras. Commun. Algebra 11(5), 501–522 (1983)

[CD22] Castryck, W., Decru, T.: An efficient key recovery attack on SIDH (preliminary version). Cryptology ePrint Archive (2022)

[CK19] Colò, L., Kohel, D.: Orienting supersingular isogeny graphs. Number-Theoretic Methods in Cryptology 2019 (2019)

[CLG09] Charles, D.X., Lauter, K.E., Goren, E.Z.: Cryptographic hash functions from expander graphs. J. Cryptol. 22(1), 93–113 (2009)

[CLM+18] Castryck, W., Lange, T., Martindale, C., Panny, L., Renes, J.: CSIDH: an efficient post-quantum commutative group action. In: Peyrin, T., Galbraith, S. (eds.) ASIACRYPT 2018. LNCS, vol. 11274, pp. 395–427. Springer, Cham (2018). https://doi.org/10.1007/978-3-030-03332-3_15

[Cou06] Couveignes, J.-M.: Hard homogeneous spaces. Cryptology ePrint Archive, Report 2006/291 (2006)

[CS21] Chenu, M., Smith, B.: Higher-degree supersingular group actions. Math. Cryptol. (2021)

[CSV21] Chari, S., Smertnig, D., Voight, J.: On basic and bass quaternion orders. Proc. Am. Math. Soc. Ser. B 8(2), 11–26 (2021)

[Deu41] Deuring, M.: Die typen der multiplikatorenringe elliptischer funktionenkörper. Abh. Math. Semin. Univ. Hambg. 14(1), 197–272 (1941)

[DFFDdSG+21] De Feo, L., et al.: Séta: supersingular encryption from torsion attacks. In: Tibouchi, M., Wang, H. (eds.) ASIACRYPT 2021. LNCS, vol. 13093, pp. 249–278. Springer, Cham (2021). https://doi.org/10.1007/978-3-030-92068-5_9

[DKL18] De Koninck, J.-M., Letendre, P.: New upper bounds for the number of divisors function. arXiv preprint arXiv:1812.09950 (2018)

[Dor87] Dorman, D.R.: Global orders in definite quaternion algebras as endomorphism rings for reduced cm elliptic curves. Théorie des nombres (Quebec, PQ, 1987), pp. 108–116 (1987)

[EHL+20] Eisenträger, K., Hallgren, S., Leonardi, C., Morrison, T., Park, J.: Computing endomorphism rings of supersingular elliptic curves and connections to path-finding in isogeny graphs. Open Book Ser. 4(1), 215–232 (2020)

[Eic36] Eichler, M.: Untersuchungen in der zahlentheorie der rationalen quaternionenalgebren (1936)

[IK21] Iwaniec, H., Kowalski, E.: Analytic Number Theory, vol. 53. American Mathematical Society (2021)

[JDF11] Jao, D., De Feo, L.: Towards quantum-resistant cryptosystems from supersingular elliptic curve isogenies. In: Yang, B.-Y. (ed.) PQCrypto 2011. LNCS, vol. 7071, pp. 19–34. Springer, Heidelberg (2011). https://doi.org/10.1007/978-3-642-25405-5_2

[Kan89] Kaneko, M.: Supersingular j-invariants as singular moduli mod p (1989)

[Koh96] Kohel, D.: Endomorphism rings of elliptic curves over finite fields. Ph.D. thesis, University of California at Berkeley (1996)

[LB20] Love, J., Boneh, D.: Supersingular curves with small noninteger endomorphisms. Open Book Ser. 4(1), 7–22 (2020)

[Lit28] Littlewood, J.E.: On the class-number of the corpus p ($\sqrt{-k}$). Proc. London Math. Soc. 2(1), 358–372 (1928)

[LV15] Lauter, K., Viray, B.: On singular moduli for arbitrary discriminants. Int. Math. Res. Not. 2015(19), 9206–9250 (2015)

[MM22] Maino, L., Martindale, C.: An attack on SIDH with arbitrary starting curve. Cryptology ePrint Archive (2022)

[Onu21] Onuki, H.: On oriented supersingular elliptic curves. Finite Fields Appl. 69, 101777 (2021)

[QKL+21] de Quehen, V., et al.: Improved torsion-point attacks on SIDH variants. In: Malkin, T., Peikert, C. (eds.) CRYPTO 2021. LNCS, vol. 12827, pp. 432–470. Springer, Cham (2021). https://doi.org/10.1007/978-3-030-84252-9_15

[Rob22] Robert, D.: Breaking SIDH in polynomial time. Cryptology ePrint Archive (2022)

[RS06] Rostovtsev, A., Stolbunov, A.: Public-key cryptosystem based on isogenies. Cryptology ePrint Archive, Report 2006/145 (2006)

[Voi21] Voight, J.: Quaternion Algebras. Springer, Heidelberg (2021). https://doi.org/10.1007/978-3-030-56694-4

[Wes21] Wesolowski, B.: Orientations and the supersingular endomorphism ring problem. Cryptology ePrint Archive, Report 2021/1583 (2021). https://ia.cr/2021/1583

[Wig07] Wigert, C.S.: Sur l'ordre de grandeur du nombre des diviseurs d'un entier. Almqvist & Wiksell (1907)

[ZG85] Zagier, D., Gross, B.: On singular moduli. J. Fur Die Reine Angewandte Math. 191–220, 1985 (1985)

Block Ciphers

Finding All Impossible Differentials When Considering the DDT

Kai Hu[1], Thomas Peyrin[1], and Meiqin Wang[2,3,4]($\boxtimes$)

[1] School of Physical and Mathematical Sciences, Nanyang Technological University, Singapore, Singapore
{kai.hu,thomas.peyrin}@ntu.edu.sg
[2] School of Cyber Science and Technology, Shandong University, Qingdao, Shandong, China
mqwang@sdu.edu.cn
[3] Key Laboratory of Cryptologic Technology and Information Security, Ministry of Education, Shandong University, Qingdao, Shandong, China
[4] Quan Cheng Shandong Laboratory, Jinan, China

Abstract. Impossible differential (ID) cryptanalysis is one of the most important attacks on block ciphers. The Mixed Integer Linear Programming (MILP) model is a popular method to determine whether a specific difference pair is an ID. Unfortunately, due to the huge search space (approximately 2^{2n} for a cipher with a block size n bits), we cannot leverage this technique to exhaust all difference pairs, which is a well-known long-standing problem.

In this paper, we propose a systematic method to find all IDs for SPN block ciphers. The idea is to partition the whole difference pair space into lots of small disjoint sets, each of which has a representative difference pair. All difference pairs in one small set are possible if its representative pair is possible, and this can be conveniently checked by the MILP model. In this way, the overall search space is drastically reduced to a practical size by excluding the sets containing no IDs. We then examine the remaining difference pairs to identify all IDs (if some IDs exist). If our method cannot find any ID, the target cipher is proved free of ID distinguishers.

Our method works especially well for SPN ciphers with block size 64. We apply our method to SKINNY-64 and successfully find all 432 and 12 truncated IDs (we find all IDs but all of them can be assembled into certain truncated IDs) for 11 and 12 rounds, respectively. We also prove, for the first time, that 13-round SKINNY-64 is free of ID distinguishers even when considering the differential transitions through the Difference Distribution Table (DDT). Similarly, we find all 12 truncated IDs (all IDs are assembled into 12 truncated IDs) for 13-round CRAFT and prove there is no ID for 14 rounds. For SbPN cipher GIFT-64, we prove that there is no ID for 8 rounds.

For SPN ciphers with larger block sizes, we show that our idea is also useful to strengthen the current search methods. For example, if

---

The full version of this paper is https://eprint.iacr.org/2022/1034.pdf.

© The Author(s), under exclusive license to Springer Nature Switzerland AG 2024
B. Smith and H. Wu (Eds.): SAC 2022, LNCS 13742, pp. 285–305, 2024.
https://doi.org/10.1007/978-3-031-58411-4_13

we consider the Sbox to be ideal and only consider the branch number information of the diffusion matrix, we can find all 6,750 truncated IDs for 6-round Rijndael-192 in 1 s and prove that there is no truncated ID for 7 rounds. Previously, we need to solve approximately 2^{48} MILP models to achieve the same goal. For GIFT-128, we exhausted all difference patterns that have an active superbox in the plaintext and ciphertext and proved there is no ID of such patterns for 8 rounds.

Although we have searched for a larger or even full space for IDs, no longer ID distinguishers have been found. This implies the reasonableness of the intuition that a small number (usually one or two) of active bits/words at the beginning and end of an ID will be the longest.

Keywords: Impossible Differential · MILP · SKINNY · CRAFT · GIFT · Rijndael-192

1   Introduction

The impossible differential (ID) attack [5, 16] is one of the most important attacks for block ciphers. This attack exploits a pair of input and output differences (Δ_i, Δ_o) of a (round-reduced) cipher E_K that cannot be connected for any K. Namely, two plaintexts p, p' satisfying $p \oplus p' = \Delta_i$ never satisfy $E_K(p) \oplus E_K(p') = \Delta_o$. Such difference pair (Δ_i, Δ_o) is then called an ID. The ID attack has been one of the most powerful cryptographic attacks nowadays. For example, it is the first attack that could break 7 rounds of AES-128 [17] and remains the best attack on reduced SKINNY-64 under the single-tweakey setting [13].

In the early days, an ID (Δ_i, Δ_o) was detected by the miss-in-the-middle approach manually [6] and the details of the Sboxes are usually ignored. The first automated search attempt appeared in [5] with so-called *shrink* technique. It shrinks the word size to 3 bits and find impossible differentials of the global structure of the cipher by exhaustively testing all possible differences and values. This method is only applicable to those ciphers consisting of a small number of words with a big word size, so it doesn't work for many modern-day ciphers such as SKINNY [3], CRAFT [4] or GIFT [1], *etc.* In [15], Kim et al. presented a new automated tool called $\mathcal{U}$-method. To detect if (Δ_i, Δ_o) is impossible, one first propagates Δ_i forwards by r_1 rounds and checks the status of the difference of each output word (known active, active, inactive, or unknown). Then he/she propagates Δ_o backward by r_2 rounds and checks the status again. Finally, if any contradiction occurs, (Δ_i, Δ_o) is an $(r_1 + r_2)$-round ID. Several extensions of the $\mathcal{U}$-method have been done such as the UID-method by Luo et al. [18] and the method proposed by Wu and Wang [26]. Recently, a constraint-programming-aided version of the $\mathcal{U}$-method called $\mathcal{U}^*$-method has been developed by Sun *et al.* [22], which allows exhausting all possible plaintext and ciphertext difference patterns automatically. All these methods above focus on truncated IDs, *i.e.*, the contradictions inside the Differential Distribution Tables (DDT) of corresponding Sboxes are not considered. Consequently, we have no way of knowing if we would have gotten more if the information of the DDTs is taken into consideration.

Several attempts focus on the upper bound on the rounds of IDs. At EURO-CRYPT 2016, Sun et al. [21] used the *primitive index* of the characteristic matrix of the linear layer to give upper bounds on the length of IDs for some special Substitution-Permutation-Networks (SPN) block ciphers with the detail of the Sbox omitted. They proved that under some special conditions, the existence of IDs relies on the existence of low-weight IDs [21, Theorem 1]. In [25], by using linear algebra the authors gave a practical method that could give upper bounds on the length of IDs for any SPN block cipher when omitting the differential property of the Sboxes. Currently, all systematical methods for bounding the length of IDs are all without considering the Sbox details.

Another line of detecting IDs starts independently from [10,20]. The MILP model for searching for differential characteristics is simply modified by adding additional specific constraints on the plaintext and ciphertext differences. If the model is infeasible, the corresponding plaintext and ciphertext difference pair is an ID. Compared to the previous methods, this method can detect all kinds of contradictions (with the assumption that the round keys are uniformly random, which is a default assumption of this paper). However, since the constraints on the plaintext/ciphertext differences are fixed, the number of models we need to solve is equivalent to the number of difference pairs we want to check. Exhaustively checking all plaintext and ciphertext difference pairs is clearly computationally infeasible. Actually, for a cipher with block size n, the search space is as large as 2^{2n}. Based on the intuition that the longest IDs are usually caused by difference pairs with a small number of active bits or words in both plaintext and ciphertext ends, users of this model prefer to test only a small proportion of the difference pairs with one or two active bits or words for plaintext and ciphertext differences. Nowadays, the model has been very popular in measuring the security strength of newly designed ciphers against ID attacks. For example, the designers of GIFT [1] took it to prove that there does not exist any ID with one-active nibble against 7 rounds of GIFT-64. The designers of CRAFT searched for IDs with plaintext and ciphertext differences having at most two active nibbles and they found twelve 13-round IDs [4].

Apart from these works, it is worth mentioning that in [24] Wang and Jin proved that there is no ID for 5-round AES even with the information of the DDT based on some careful mathematical analyses. But unfortunately, this method is specifically designed for AES only. Generally speaking, the MILP method is much more convenient than other methods, since it only needs some slight modifications from the MILP models for searching for differential characteristics. However, as we mentioned, all current MILP models can check a small number of the difference pairs. How to tackle the huge search space has been a long-standing problem.

Contributions. In this paper, we propose a systematic method based on the MILP model to find all IDs in the whole search space. As mentioned above, to exhaust all input and output difference pairs requires a complexity of 2^{2n} which is infeasible. Our method delicately partitions the whole search space and efficiently excludes those containing no IDs. The search space is then reduced to a reasonable size. Finally, the remaining IDs (if they exist) can be detected with the plain MILP models. If our method finds no IDs for the r-round cipher, we know that there exists no ID for this r-round cipher. The provable security is thus achieved.

Our method is efficient for SPN ciphers with a block size equal to 64. For SKINNY-64, we find all IDs for 11 and 12 rounds in 4 and 1.5 h, respectively. Interestingly, all these IDs can be assembled into 432 and 12 truncated IDs for 11 and 12 rounds. We also prove, for the first time, that the 13-round SKINNY-64 is free of ID distinguishers *with considering the DDT information*. Similarly, we find all 2,700 IDs for 13-round CRAFT which is equivalent to 12 truncated IDs and prove there is no ID for 14 rounds. For Substitution Bit-Permutation Network (SbPN) cipher GIFT-64, we prove that there is no ID for 8 rounds.

Our method is also useful to improve the current search strategies for ciphers with large blocks. We show its usage in applications to Rijndael-192 and GIFT-128 as examples. For Rijndael-192, we search for IDs under the arbitrary Sbox/MC mode, *i.e.*, only the activeness of an Sbox and the branch number of the MixColumn operation would be considered (which is inspired by the arbitrary Sbox model [20]). In this scenario, we show that all 6,750 truncated IDs of 6-round Rijndael-192 can be identified in 1 s, and prove there is no truncated ID for 7 rounds. In previous methods, we need to solve approximately 2^{48} plain MILP models to achieve this. For GIFT-128, we search for IDs that have one active superbox in both plaintext and ciphertext differences. In previous methods, we need to solve 2^{38} plain MILP models, now with our new tool, we only need to handle 4,608 MILP models. We prove that there is no ID with one active superbox in both ends for 8-round GIFT-128. We list all our application results in Table 1 for readers' quick reference.

Implications of Finding All IDs. On the one hand, if our new model finds no ID for a (round-reduced) cipher, we achieve a more thorough security proof for the cipher against ID distinguishers compared to [20]. On the other hand, it is also useful to list all IDs for a (round-reduced) cipher. Firstly, different IDs would affect the concrete attacking phase as well as the data and time complexity. In terms of the ID distinguishers, more active bits in the output mean less data/time complexities. In terms of the key recovery attacks, IDs with good input and output difference patterns may have a better performance, *e.g.*, the ID attacks on AES were improved with alternative IDs [17]. Secondly, finding all IDs (with or without considering the DDT) is a long-standing challenge in cryptanalysis and cipher design. Finding out all IDs can help us understand better the structure of target ciphers and the ID attack itself.

We highlight that all IDs we discuss in this paper are under the assumption that the round keys are uniformly random. All source codes of this work are provided in the git repository https://github.com/hukaisdu/SearchForID.git to help readers understand our tool better.

Table 1. The application results of this paper. N in the #ID column means no IDs. #Space is the size of the whole search space with plain MILP models.

Cipher	#Space	#Round	#ID	Time	Remarks
SKINNY-64	2^{128}	11	432	4h	All IDs can be assembled into 432 truncated IDs
		12	12	1.5h	All IDs can be assembled into 12 truncated IDs
		13	N	4h	No IDs with the DDT considered
CRAFT	2^{128}	13	12	7d	All IDs can be assembled into 12 truncated IDs
		14	N	7d	No IDs with the DDT considered
GIFT-64	2^{128}	8	N	17h	No IDs with the DDT considered
Rijndael-192	2^{48}	6	6,750	1 s	Truncated IDs in arbitrary Sbox/MC model†
		7	N	1 s	No Truncated IDs in arbitrary Sbox/MC model
GIFT-128	2^{38}	8	N	30h	No IDs with one-active superbox with the DDT considered

† Arbitrary Sbox/MC model: we only consider the activeness of the Sbox and branch number of the MixColumn

Organization of the Remaining Paper. In Sect. 2, we introduce the notations and some global settings used in this paper. In Sect. 3, we show how to partition the whole search space and quickly exclude those containing no IDs and identify all IDs in the remaining candidates. Applications to SKINNY-64, CRYFT and GIFT-64 are presented in Sects. 4 and 5. In Sect. 6, we discuss how to apply our idea to enhance some traditional search strategies based on MILP for large-size ciphers. In Sect. 7 we conclude our paper and highlight two future works.

2   Preliminaries

2.1   Notations and Definitions

In this paper, we are only interested in the differences, so the differences are directly represented by lowercase letters such as x rather than conventional Δx. Consider a (round-reduced) cipher E, if (x, y) is an ID over E, we write it as $x \xrightarrow{E}\!\!\!\!/\ y$. Conversely, $x \xrightarrow{E} y$ means x can propagate to y over E, i.e., (x, y) is a possible pattern. We use uppercase letters to represent the sets of differences such as X and Y. $X \xrightarrow{E} Y$ means for all $(x, y) \in X \otimes Y$ we have $x \xrightarrow{E} y$. $x \xrightarrow{E} X$ is equivalent to $\{x\} \xrightarrow{E} X$. Similarly, $X \xrightarrow{E} y$ is equivalent to $X \xrightarrow{E} \{y\}$. $X \otimes Y$ (sometimes we use $X \bigotimes Y$ for a better looking of a complicated equation) is

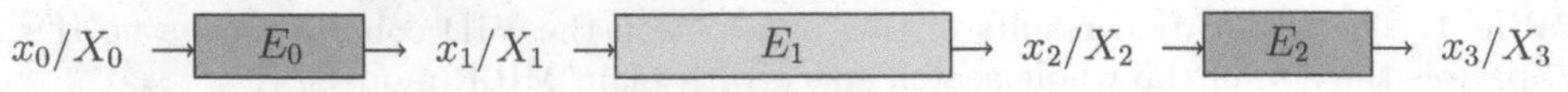

$x_0/X_0 \rightarrow \boxed{E_0} \rightarrow x_1/X_1 \rightarrow \boxed{E_1} \rightarrow x_2/X_2 \rightarrow \boxed{E_2} \rightarrow x_3/X_3$

Fig. 1. The global settings of our theoretical model.

defined as $\{(x, y) : x \in X, y \in Y\}$. If $X \cap Y = \varnothing$, we would write $X \cup Y$ as $X + Y$ to highlight $X \cap Y = \varnothing$. Generally, if $\bigcap_i X_i = \varnothing$, the union set of all X_i is written as $\sum_i X_i$. $X - Y$ is defined as $\{x \in X : x \notin Y\}$.

Global Settings. A modern block cipher usually iterates a simple round function many times with different round keys. So we can always decompose a (round-reduced) cipher into three parts, say $E = E_2 \circ E_1 \circ E_0$. We denote the input difference/set of E_0, E_1 and E_2 by $x_0/X_0, x_1/X_1$ and x_2/X_2 respectively, and output difference/set of E by x_3/X_3. See Fig. 1 for details of the settings. In the remaining paper, if we do not specify x_0, x_1, x_2, x_3 and X_0, X_1, X_2, X_3, they denote the difference or sets as defined here.

2.2   Current MILP Model for Detecting IDs

In [9,10,20], the MILP models for detecting IDs are independently proposed. This method is developed from the MILP models for searching for differential characteristics [19,23] by adding some additional constraints on the plaintext and ciphertext differences. To construct the MILP model for checking if a given difference pair (Δ_i, Δ_o) for a cipher E is impossible, we first declare a sequence of variables to represent input and output differences for all components of E such as Sboxes and linear layers. Next, we use inequalities to force these variables to be legal patterns that are compatible with the differential propagation rules of the corresponding components. Thus, any solutions satisfying these constraints are legal differential characteristics. Additionally, suppose the variables representing the differences of plaintext and ciphertext are u_0 and u_r, we add two more constraints as

$$u_0 = \Delta_i, \ u_r = \Delta_o.$$

If the overall MILP model is feasible, there is one differential characteristic propagating from Δ_i to Δ_o, i.e., (Δ_i, Δ_o) is a possible differential. Otherwise, (Δ_i, Δ_o) is an ID.

According to different methods in which we use inequalities to describe the differential propagations over an Sbox or linear layer, the capabilities to detect IDs of the corresponding MILP models are also different. For example, if details of the DDT and linear layers are all described, then all kinds of contradictions could be detected. This is the default mode we use in this paper. If only the information that an Sbox is active or not and the branch number of a linear layer is described in the MILP search model, truncated IDs could be detected. We refer to such a model as the *arbitrary Sbox/MC model*. In this paper, the application to Rijndael-192 is the only instance using this mode. We will assume that the readers of this paper have been familiar with the plain MILP models for detecting IDs. Or we refer the readers to [10,20] for more details of this topic.

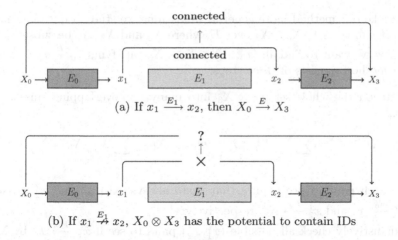

(a) If $x_1 \xrightarrow{E_1} x_2$, then $X_0 \xrightarrow{E} X_3$

(b) If $x_1 \overset{E_1}{\nrightarrow} x_2$, $X_0 \otimes X_3$ has the potential to contain IDs

Fig. 2. The illustration of Proposition 1 and the implication.

3 Finding All Impossible Differentials

Taking the MILP model in [10,20], we need to solve 2^{2n} models for a cipher with block size n bits to check all input and output difference pairs. The search space is obviously too large. So we partition the whole search space into many smaller sets and then process each set one by one to exclude those containing no IDs. For the remaining smaller sets that have the potential to contain IDs, we apply several methods to identify all IDs contained by them.

Main Idea. To determine if (x_0, x_3) is possible or not, we try to find a pair of (x_1, x_2) satisfying

$$x_0 \xrightarrow{E_0} x_1 \xrightarrow{E_1} x_2 \xrightarrow{E_2} x_3.$$

Obviously, if such (x_1, x_2) exists, (x_0, x_3) is possible. Further, if we have known $x_1 \xrightarrow{E_1} x_2$, then all (x_0, x_3) satisfying (1) $x_0 \xrightarrow{E_1} x_1$ (2) $x_2 \xrightarrow{E_1} x_3$ are possible. We have the following proposition (also illustrated by Fig. 2a),

Proposition 1. *Let $E = E_2 \circ E_1 \circ E_0$, $X_0 \subseteq \mathbb{F}_2^n$ be a set of differences satisfying $X_0 \xrightarrow{E_0} x_1$ and $X_3 \subseteq \mathbb{F}_2^n$ satisfying $x_2 \xrightarrow{E_2} X_3$. If $x_1 \xrightarrow{E_1} x_2$, then $X_0 \xrightarrow{E} X_3$.*

The proof is obvious from above analyses, so we omit it here. If $x_1 \overset{E_1}{\nrightarrow} x_2$, we cannot predict anything so we say $X_0 \otimes X_3$ has the potential to contain IDs, see Fig. 2b. We conclude it into a corollary of Proposition 1 for better understanding this fact.

Corollary 1. *With the same notations as Proposition 1, if $(x_0, x_3) \in X_0 \otimes X_3$ is an ID, then all x_1 and x_2 satisfying $X_0 \xrightarrow{E_0} x_1$ and $x_2 \xrightarrow{E_2} X_3$ cannot be connected, i.e., (x_1, x_2) must satisfy $x_1 \overset{E_1}{\nrightarrow} x_2$.*

To make our method more general, we assume we study a question how to find all IDs in the sets $X_0 \otimes X_3$ over E, where X_0 and X_3 can be subsets of $\mathbb{F}_2^n$. Thus, now we want to find all $(x_0, x_3) \in X_0 \otimes X_3$ satisfying $x_0 \xrightarrow{E} x_3$.

Our method consists of three steps:

(1) Partition the whole set $X_0 \otimes X_3$ into many non-overlapping smaller sets, i.e.,

$$X_0 \otimes X_3 = \sum_i \sum_j X_0^i \otimes X_3^j, \text{ where } X_0 = \sum_i X_0^i, \ X_3 = \sum_j X_3^j$$

For each pair i, j, we require that there always exist x_1^i and x_2^j satisfying $X_0^i \xrightarrow{E_0} x_1^i$ and $x_2^j \xrightarrow{E_2} X_3^j$, respectively;

(2) Exhaustively check all possible (x_1^i, x_2^j) pairs to see if $x_1^i \xrightarrow{E_1} x_2^j$ by MILP models introduced in [10,20]. $X_0^i \otimes X_3^j$ contains no IDs if $x_1^i \xrightarrow{E_1} x_2^j$, and otherwise has a potential to contain some IDs;

(3) Process those $X_0^i \otimes X_3^j$ that have the potential to contain IDs one by one to identify all IDs with specific strategies that we will introduce later.

3.1 Partition: A Theoretical Viewpoint

In this paper, we always assume that E_0 and E_2 are non-linear functions, so there exists an expansion property for the difference propagation over E_0 and E_2. Consequently, it is possible for us to find two smaller sets X_1 and X_2 satisfying

(1) $\forall x_0 \in X_0, \exists x_1 \in X_1 \ s.t. \ x_0 \xrightarrow{E_0} x_1$,

(2) $\forall x_3 \in X_3, \exists x_2 \in X_2 \ s.t. \ x_2 \xrightarrow{E_2} x_3$.

We call X_1 a *representative set* of X_0 over E_0 while X_2 a representative set of X_3 over E_2^{-1}. Suppose we have obtained one such representative set X_1, we know the following

$$\bigcup_{x_1 \in X_1} \left\{ x_0 \in X_0 : x_0 \xrightarrow{E_0} x_1 \right\} = X_0.$$

By removing the overlapping elements among $\left\{ x_0 \in X_0 : x_0 \xrightarrow{E_0} x_1 \right\}$ for all $x_1 \in X_1$, we get a partition of X_0 which can be stored in a hash table with the elements in X_1 as keys and sets after partitioning as values (similar to X_3 and X_2). We call such a hash table a *partition (hash) table* of X_0 over E_0. An intuitive algorithm for determining one representative set as well as the corresponding partition table for a non-linear function and its input difference set is given in Algorithm 1.

The basic idea of Algorithm 1 is to *select* representative for X one by one and exclude corresponding elements from X until X is reduced to an empty set. The complexity of Algorithm 1 is roughly limited by $\mathcal{O}(|X|)$ times of loops (line 3–10). The operations in line 5 and 8 determine the real time of this algorithm, whose complexity is at most $2^{2\log|X|}$ (the complexity of computing the whole DDT of

---

Algorithm 1: Determine a representative set and partition table of X over f

---

Data: $X \subseteq \mathbb{F}_2^n$ and $f : \mathbb{F}_2^n \to \mathbb{F}_2^n$
Result: A representative set S, a partition table H
1   Allocate $S \leftarrow \varnothing$
2   Allocate a hash table $H' \leftarrow \varnothing$
3   **while** X *is not empty* **do**
4     $x \xleftarrow{\mathcal{R}} X$ /* randomly select x from X */
5   compute Y s.t. $x \xrightarrow{f} Y$
6     $y \xleftarrow{\mathcal{R}} Y$ /* randomly select y from Y */
7     $S \leftarrow S \cup \{y\}$ /* y is chosen as a representative */
8   compute T s.t. $T \xrightarrow{f} y$ /* T has been represented by y */
9     $H'[y] \leftarrow T$
10    $X \leftarrow X - T$ /* Proceed with the remaining elements */

    /* remove overlapping elements   */
11   Allocate a hash table H
12   **for** $s \in S$ **do**
13   **for** $h \in H.keys$ **do**
14       $H[s] \leftarrow H'[s] - H[h]$ /* elements in $H[h]$ are recorded already */

15   **return** S, H

---

f). Thus the overall complexity of Algorithm 1 is bounded by $\mathcal{O}(2^{3\log|X|})$. Note that the actual complexity should be much less than this upper bound for the number of loops usually small. In applications of this paper, f will be at most a 16-bit-input function, so this algorithm is practical.

We first apply Algorithm 1 to X_0 to obtain its representative set X_1 and a partition table H_1 over E_0, *i.e.*,

$$X_0 = \sum_{x_1 \in X_1} H_1[x_1] \tag{1}$$

Similarly we get the representative set X_2 and partition table H_2 of X_3 over E_2^{-1}, *i.e.*,

$$X_3 = \sum_{x_2 \in X_2} H_2[x_2] \tag{2}$$

Then the whole search space $X_0 \otimes X_3$ has been partitioned into $|X_1| \times |X_2|$ smaller sets through combining Eqs (1) and (2), *i.e.*,

$$X_0 \otimes X_3 = \sum_{x_1 \in X_1} H_1[x_1] \bigotimes \sum_{x_2 \in X_2} H_2[x_2] = \sum_{x_1 \in X_1} \sum_{x_2 \in X_2} H_1[x_1] \otimes H_2[x_2] \tag{3}$$

Figure 3 demonstrates the partition of $X_0 \otimes X_3$. A partition of $X_0 \otimes X_3$ can be uniquely determined by a quartet (X_1, H_1, X_2, H_2). For simplicity of description, we define the partition of a (round-reduced) cipher.

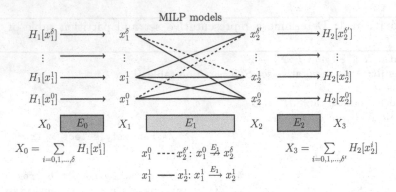

Fig. 3. The partitions of the input difference set X_0 and X_1. Since $x_1^0 \xrightarrow{E_1} x_2^{\delta'}$, $H_1[x_1^0] \otimes H_2[x_2^\delta]$ has potential to contain IDs. Since $x_1^1 \xrightarrow{E_1} x_2^1$, $H_1[x_1^1] \otimes H_2[x_2^1]$ contains no IDs.

Definition 1 (Partition). *For a (round-reduced) cipher $E = E_2 \circ E_1 \circ E_0$, a partition of its whole input and output difference spaces is a set of smaller sets as follows,*

$$\mathbb{P}(X_1, H_1, X_2, H_2) = \{H[x_1] \otimes H[x_2] : x_1 \in X_1, x_2 \in X_2\}$$

When there is no ambiguity, we just say $\mathbb{P}$ is a partition of E.

3.2 Partition: A Practical Viewpoint

If we apply directly Algorithm 1 to $\mathbb{F}_2^n$, the complexity is not affordable even for a 64-bit block cipher. However, an important observation is that SPN ciphers usually comprise several smaller parallel parts. The well-known examples include the superboxes used in AES-like ciphers such as SKINNY [3] and CRAFT [4]. Two continuous rounds can be represented by 4 parallel superboxes. Another example is GIFT [1] which follows a so-called Substitution bit-Permutation Network (SbPN) paradigm. All Sboxes of the i-th round of GIFT, denoted by $Sb_0^i, Sb_1^i, \ldots, Sb_s^i$ where $s = n/4$ and n is the block size, can be grouped in two different ways – the Quotient and Remainder groups, Qx and Rx, defined as

- $Qx = \{Sb_{4x}, Sb_{4x+1}, Sb_{4x+2}, Sb_{4x+3}\}$,
- $Rx = \{Sb_x, Sb_{x+q}, Sb_{x+2q}, Sb_{x+3q}\}$, where $q = \frac{s}{4}, 0 \leq x \leq q-1$.

Taking GIFT-64 as an instance, the 16-bit output of $Qx^i = \{Sb_{4x}^i, Sb_{4x+1}^i, Sb_{4x+2}^i, Sb_{4x+3}^i\}$ map to input bits of $Rx^{i+1} = \{Sb_x^{i+1}, Sb_{x+4}^{i+1}, Sb_{x+8}^{i+1}, Sb_{x+12}^{i+1}\}$. Then the interfacing two rounds of GIFT-64 can be also represented by 4 parallel superboxes. An illustration for GIFT-64 is shown in Fig. 4.

In the remaining part of this paper, we focus on these SPN or SbPN ciphers with superboxes. Suppose E_0 and E_2 comprise respectively of m

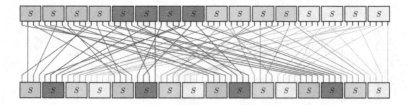

Fig. 4. The superbox representation of GIFT-64 based on the two groups (Quotient and Remainder) of Sboxes.

parallel superboxes, denoted by $E_0 = E_{0,0}||E_{0,1}||\cdots||E_{0,m-1}$ and $E_2 = E_{2,0}||E_{2,1}||\cdots||E_{2,m-1}$, where the size of input and output of $E_{i,j}, i \in \{0,2\}, j \in \{0,1,\ldots,m-1\}$ is $n/4$ bits. Then we apply Algorithm 1 to each $E_{i,j}$, which is a function with 16-bit block size.

For $i \in \{0,1,\ldots,m-1\}$, let $X_{1,i}$ and $H_{1,i}$ be representative sets and partition tables for $E_{0,i}$ of its input difference set $X_{0,i}$ while $X_{2,i}$ and $H_{2,i}$ the representative sets and partition tables for $E_{2,i}^{-1}$ of $X_{3,i}$. The Eqs. (1) and (2) can be re-written as

$$
X_0 = \bigotimes_{0 \leq j < m} X_{0,j} = \bigotimes_{0 \leq j < m} \left(\sum_{x_{1,j} \in X_{1,j}} H_{1,j}[x_{1,j}] \right)
$$

$$
= \sum_{x_{1,0} \in X_{1,0}} \cdots \sum_{x_{1,m-1} \in X_{1,m-1}} H_{1,0}[x_{1,0}] \otimes \cdots \otimes H_{1,m-1}[x_{1,m-1}].
$$

(4)

Similarly,

$$
X_3 = \bigotimes_{0 \leq j < m} X_{3,j} = \bigotimes_{0 \leq j < m} \left(\sum_{x_{2,j} \in X_{2,j}} H_{2,j}[x_{2,j}] \right)
$$

$$
= \sum_{x_{2,0} \in X_{2,0}} \cdots \sum_{x_{2,m-1} \in X_{2,m-1}} H_{2,0}[x_{2,0}] \otimes \cdots \otimes H_{2,m-1}[x_{2,m-1}].
$$

(5)

See Fig. 5 for a better understanding to Eq. (4).

Then we can accordingly rewrite Eq. (3) as

$$
X_0 \otimes X_3 = \bigotimes_{i=1,2} \left(\sum_{x_{i,0} \in X_{i,0}} \cdots \sum_{x_{i,m-1} \in X_{i,m-1}} H_{i,0}[x_{i,0}] \otimes \cdots \otimes H_{i,m-1}[x_{i,m-1}] \right)
$$

$$
= \sum_{x_{1,0} \in X_{1,0}} \cdots \sum_{x_{2,m-1} \in X_{2,m-1}} H_{1,0}[x_{1,0}] \otimes \cdots \otimes H_{2,m-1}[x_{2,m-1}]
$$

(6)

That is to say, considering the superbox effects, we can partition the whole difference space into $\prod_{i=1,2;j=0,1,\ldots,m-1} |X_{i,j}|$ smaller sets. A partition of E is consequently updated to

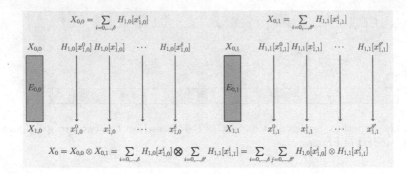

Fig. 5. The partition of the input difference set X_0 (the case $i = 0$ in Eq. (4)) based on 2 superboxes ($m = 2$).

$$\mathbb{P}(X_{1,0}, H_{1,0}, \ldots, X_{2,m-1}, H_{2,m-1})$$
$$= \{H[x_{1,0}] \otimes \cdots \otimes H[x_{2,m-1}] : x_{i,j} \in X_{i,j} \text{ for } i = 1, 2; 0 \leq j < m\}$$

which is related to a tuple with $4 \cdot m$ elements.

3.3   Solving MILP Models for E_1

Once we get a partition $\mathbb{P}(X_{1,0}, H_{1,0}, \ldots, X_{2,m-1}, H_{2,m-1})$ of E, we construct $\prod_{i=0,1;j=0,\ldots,m-1} |X_{i,j}|$ MILPs for each elements $(x_{1,0}, \ldots, x_{2,m-1}) \in X_{1,0} \otimes \cdots \otimes X_{2,m-1}$ to see whether $(x_{1,0}, \ldots, x_{1,m-1}) \xrightarrow{E_1} (x_{2,0}, \ldots, x_{2,m-1})$. If the MILP model for $(x_{1,0}, \ldots, x_{2,m-1})$ is feasible, we do not need to consider $H_{1,0}[x_{1,0}] \otimes \cdots \otimes H_{2,m-1}[x_{2,m-1}]$ any more. Otherwise, $H_{1,0}[x_{1,0}] \otimes \cdots \otimes H_{2,m-1}[x_{2,m-1}]$ has the potential to contain some IDs, we have to proceed with it in the next step.

3.4   Identify All IDs in Remaining $H_{1,0}[x_{1,0}] \otimes \cdots \otimes H_{2,m-1}[x_{2,m-1}]$

The final step is to handle the remaining $H_{1,0}[x_{1,0}] \otimes \cdots \otimes H_{2,m-1}[x_{2,m-1}] \in \mathbb{P}$ that survive the second step one by one. We mainly introduce two methods to find all IDs in each $H_{1,0}[x_{1,0}] \otimes \cdots \otimes H_{2,m-1}[x_{2,m-1}]$ in this subsection.

Direct Search. Considering the case when the size of $H_{1,0}[x_{1,0}] \otimes \cdots \otimes H_{2,m-1}[x_{2,m-1}]$ is small. Let $\sigma = \prod_{i=1,2;0\leq j<m} |H_{i,j}|$, for example, we say the size is small when $\sigma \leq 2^{28}$, we can just directly test every pattern with a MILP model as [10,20]. All IDs contained in $H_{1,0}[x_{1,0}] \otimes \cdots \otimes H_{2,m-1}[x_{2,m-1}]$ can be found naturally.

To enhance the efficiency of this step, we introduce the *fast reducing* technique. For a randomly chosen plaintext-ciphertext difference pair from $H_{1,0}[x_{1,0}] \otimes \cdots \otimes H_{2,m-1}[x_{2,m-1}]$, we construct the MILP model to see if this pair is an ID. If this pair is truly an ID, we continue checking whether it belongs to a truncated ID. If so, we will record this truncated ID and remove all related IDs that belong to this truncated ID from the search pool. If this ID doesn't belong to any truncated ID, we record it and proceed with another pair. If it is not an ID, then a difference characteristic will be returned by the MILP solver. We extract the values of $x_1^\star$ and $x_2^\star$ of this characteristic (this is easy with the interface of MILP solvers), and calculate two sets $X_0^\star$ and $X_3^\star$ satisfying $X_0^\star \xrightarrow{E_0} x_1^\star$ and $x_2^\star \xrightarrow{E_1} X_3^\star$. Thus all patterns in $X_0^\star \otimes X_3^\star$ are all possible, we only need to proceed with $H_{1,0}[x_{1,0}] \otimes \cdots \otimes H_{2,m-1}[x_{2,m-1}] \backslash X_0^\star \otimes X_3^\star$ until all patterns are determined as possible or impossible.

Partition Further. If σ is larger (e.g., $\sigma > 2^{28}$), exhausting all patterns is not a good idea. We can apply Algorithm 1 to sets in every $H_{i,j}, i \in \{1,2\}, j \in \{0,1,\ldots,m\}$ and repeatedly partition $H_{1,0}[x_{1,0}] \otimes \cdots \otimes H_{2,m-1}[x_{2,m-1}]$ into several smaller sets. We handle each smaller set according to its size recursively until the size is below the threshold and can be handled by a direct search.

The whole procedure for identifying all IDs among $X_0 \otimes X_3$ over E is demonstrated in Algorithm 2.

Algorithm 2: Find all IDs over a cipher E

Data: $E_0 = E_{0,1}||\cdots||E_{0,m-1}, E_2 = E_{2,1}||\cdots||E_{2,m-1}, E_1$
Result: a set I containing all IDs
/* step 1: partition the whole set   */
1 **for** *each $i \in \{1,2\}$* **do**
2   **for** *each $j \in \{0,1,\ldots,m-1\}$* **do**
3   apply Algorithm 1 to $H_{i,j}$ getting its representative set $X_{i,j}$ and partition table $H_{i,j}$

/* step 2: solve MILP Models for E_1 */
4 Allocate $J \leftarrow \varnothing$
5 **for** *each $(x_{1,0},\ldots,x_{2,m-1}) \in X_{1,0} \otimes \cdots \otimes X_{2,m-1}$* **do**
6   construct a MILP model for E_1 with the input/output difference with $(x_{1,0},\ldots,x_{1,m-1})$ and $(x_{2,0},\ldots,x_{2,m-1})$, respectively
7   **if** *model is infeasible* **then**
8          $J \leftarrow J \cup \{(x_{1,0},\ldots,x_{2,m-1})\}$

/* step 3: identify all IDs   */
9 Allocate $I \leftarrow \varnothing$
10 **for** *each $(x_{1,0},\ldots,x_{2,m-1}) \in J$* **do**
11   **if** $\prod_{i=1,2;j=0,1,\ldots,m-1} |H_{i,j}| > 2^{28}$ **then**
12   recursively recall Algorithm 2 to $H_{1,0} \otimes \cdots \otimes H_{2,m-1}$ and push all the IDs into I
13   **else**
14   construct MILP models to test every patterns in $H_{1,0} \otimes \cdots \otimes H_{2,m-1}$, and push those impossible ones into I
15 **return** I

---

4   Applications to AES-Like SPN Ciphers

One of the standard ways for designing a good round function from an Sbox and an MDS mapping is the one followed by the AES [12] and is known as the wide trail strategy [11]. Some newly proposed lightweight ciphers also follow the AES structure by replacing the MDS matrix with simple ones such as SKINNY [3] and CRAFT [4]. We say these ciphers are AES-like. In this section, we show how to apply our methods to SKINNY-64, the application to CRAFT is provided the full version.

The experiments are conducted by Gurobi Solver (version 9.1.1) on a workstation with 2×AMD EPYC 7302 16-core (32 siblings) Processor 3.3 GHz, (a total 64 threads), 256G RAM, and Ubuntu 20.10.

Application to SKINNY-64. Our first application is to SKINNY-64. The block cipher family SKINNY was presented at CRYPTO 2016 [3] designed under the TWEAKEY framework [14], whose goal is to compete with the NSA design SIMON [2] in terms of hardware/software performance. According to the length of block and tweakey, the SKINNY family consists of 6 different members represented as SKINNY-n-t, where $n = 64, 128$ and $t = n, 2n, 3n$, which respectively represent the sizes of the block and tweakey. We are only interested in the security of the 64-bit version of SKINNY in this paper, $i.e.$, SKINNY-64, under the single tweakey model. The round function of SKINNY-64 comprises five operations as SubCells (SC), AddConstants (AC), AddRoundTweakey (ART), ShiftRows (SR) and MixColumns (MC). Since we only consider the single-tweakey scenario, we can ignore the ART and AC operations and pay attention to the remaining three ones. Therefore, a round of SKINNY can be written as

$$R = \mathsf{MC} \circ \mathsf{SR} \circ \mathsf{SC}$$

When applying Algorithm 2 to r-round SKINNY-64, we rearrange the functions in the r rounds as

$$R^r = \underbrace{\mathsf{SC} \circ \mathsf{MC} \circ \mathsf{SC}}_{E_2} \circ \underbrace{\mathsf{SR} \circ R^{r-4} \circ \mathsf{MC} \circ \mathsf{SR}}_{E_1} \circ \underbrace{\mathsf{SC} \circ \mathsf{MC} \circ \mathsf{SC}}_{E_0}$$

As can be seen, the SR in the first round and MC ∘ SR in the last round are omitted for they do not affect our analysis. E_0 and E_2 consist of four parallel superboxes $E_{0,i}$ and $E_{2,i}$ for $i = 0, 1, 2, 3$, respectively.

We apply Algorithm 1 to the four superboxes of E_0 and the four inverse superboxes of E_2^{-1}. The representative sets we calculated in the experiment are listed in Table 2. Note that the four superboxes are identical as well as their representative sets and partition tables.

As is seen, each representative set of the superbox of $E_{0,i}$ and $E_{2,i}^{-1}$ contains only 7 values, so the sizes of X_1 and X_2 are both $7^4 - 1 = 2,400$ non-zero values. Considering the rotational symmetry of SKINNY-64, we can remove the rotationally-symmetric elements in X_1. After this treatment, only 615 elements remain in X_1. Therefore, the total number of MILP models we need to solve

Table 2. Representative sets of the superboxes $E_{0,i}$ and $E_{2,i}^{-2}$ for $i = 0,1,2,3$, of SKINNY-64

Representative set	Values (hexadecimal)
$X_{1,i}, i = 0,1,2,3$	0, b0, b000, b080, de9d, e0e4, ee0e
$X_{2,i}, i = 0,1,2,3$	0, a, 606, eee, f00, 3330, eeef

is $615 \times 2,400 = 147,600 \approx 2^{20.5}$. Since these MILP models are treated independently, we can solve them by a parallel strategy based on multi-threading programming.

11-Round. For 11-round SKINNY-64, We need to solve $2^{20.5}$ MILP models for $11 - 4 = 7$ rounds. These MILP models were solved in roughly 4 h. There are 618 infeasible patterns $(x_{1,0}, \ldots, x_{1,3}, x_{2,0} \ldots, x_{2,3}) \in X_{1,0} \otimes X_{1,1} \otimes X_{2,0} \cdots \otimes X_{2,3}$. We then try to identify all the IDs from the corresponding sets related to these 618 patterns. Finally, since every ID belongs to one certain truncated ID, we identified all 432 truncated IDs. All these IDs are provided in our git repository.

12-Round. For 12-round SKINNY-64, we need to solve $2^{20.5}$ MILP models for 8 rounds. Solving these MILP models cost about 1.5 hours in our cluster. Only 15 patterns out of them $(x_{1,0}, x_{1,1}, x_{2,0} \ldots, x_{2,3}) \in X_{1,0} \otimes X_{1,1} \otimes X_{2,0} \cdots \otimes X_{2,3}$ are infeasible. Among them, we extracted 2,700 IDs, which are assembled into 12 truncated IDs. These IDs are identical to those reported in previous works [3,22].

13-Round. We prove that there does not exist any ID for 13-round SKINNY-64 even with consideration of the details of Sboxes and linear layers.

5   Applications to SbPN Cipher GIFT-64

Substitution and bit-Permutation Network (SbPN) is a special SP network where the permutation layer takes a bit shuffle rather than a word-oriented diffusion. It was introduced by the first ultra-lightweight block cipher PRESENT at CHES 2007 [7], and recently refined by GIFT at CHES 2017 [1]. SbPN consists of a layer of Sboxes (denoted by S), a bit shuffle (denoted by P), and a layer of key/constant addition only, which can be very efficient, especially in hardware implementation. In this section, we show how to apply our methods to GIFT-64. This paper is only interested in the single-key scenario, we do not need to consider the key/constant addition. So a round function of GIFT-64 is viewed as $R - \mathsf{P} \circ \mathsf{S}$. As is mentioned in Sect. 3.2 and also shown in Fig. 6, two interfacing rounds of GIFT-64 can be viewed as four parallel superboxes. Then we have

$$\mathsf{S} \circ \mathsf{P} \circ \mathsf{S} = \mathsf{P}_2 \circ \mathsf{S} \circ \mathsf{P}_1 \circ \mathsf{S},$$

where P_1 consists of four identical small bit shuffles and P_2 is a word-oriented permutation. P_1 and P_2 in GIFT-64 are illustrated in Fig. 6. Let $\mathsf{P}_1 = \mathsf{P}_1' \| \mathsf{P}_1' \| \mathsf{P}_1' \| \mathsf{P}_1'$,

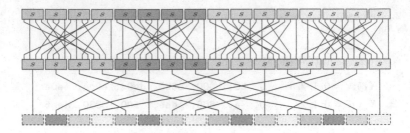

Fig. 6. An equivalent representation of the GIFT-64 round functions.

then P_1' and P_2 are as follows (inside each permutation, the 0-th is the leftmost unit),

$$P_1' = [12, 1, 6, 11, 8, 13, 2, 7, 4, 9, 14, 3, 0, 5, 10, 15],$$
$$P_2 = [0, 4, 8, 12, 1, 5, 9, 13, 2, 5, 10, 14, 3, 6, 11, 15].$$

We thus rearrange the round functions of an r-round GIFT-64 cipher as

$$R^r = \underbrace{S \circ P_1 \circ S}_{E_2} \circ \underbrace{R^{r-4} \circ P \circ P_2}_{E_1} \circ \underbrace{S \circ P_1 \circ S}_{E_0}$$

Again, we apply Algorithm 1 to superboxes of $E_{0,i}$ and $E_{2,i}^{-2}$ and get the representative sets as shown in Table 3. The number of elements in the representative sets of superboxes for $E_{0,i}$ are 10, and for $E_{2,i}^{-1}$ is 9, so the number of non-zero elements in $X_1 \otimes X_2$ is $(10^4 - 1) \times (9^4 - 1) = 65,593,440 \approx 2^{26}$. We then need to construct 2^{26} MILP models with these patterns for E_1.

In the specification, the designers showed that there do not exist any impossible differentials with 1-active nibble against 7 rounds of GIFT-64. We then check the 7-round GIFT-64 first, unfortunately, after the first step of Algorithm 2 costing about 12 h, there are too many (363,510) impossible patterns out of the 2^{26} patterns. We find that processing these bad inner patterns costs a significant amount of time, this may imply that 7 rounds is the borderline of whether IDs exist or not. Considering that GIFT-64 is a 28-round cipher, 7 round IDs (even if an ID exists) should not threaten its security, we do not pursue the exact security proof for 7 rounds.

For 8-round GIFT-64, these 2^{26} MILP models can be processed within 17 h, where only 236 are impossible. With another 4 min, all the 236 patterns can be processed and none of them imply IDs. In other words, 8-round GIFT-64 is free of any IDs.

6   Towards Large-Size Ciphers

Our tool works very well on 64-bit SPN and SbPN ciphers. However, its efficiency for ciphers with larger blocks is not high. Note that in the second step of Algorithm 2 (also introduced in Sect. 3.3), we still need to solve a set of MILP models

Table 3. The representative sets of superboxes $E_{0,i}$ and $E_{2,i}^{-1}$ for $i = 0, 1, 2, 3$, of GIFT-64

Representative set	Values (hexadecimal)
$X_{1,i}, i = 0, 1, 2, 3$	0, 50b, f39, 5a97, a9d9, b35f, b3d0, b706, d0b3, d5f0
$X_{2,i}, i = 0, 1, 2, 3$	0, ec, d90, e0f, 9b7b, cd7e, e00f, e7cf, fdd7

whose size can be larger than 2^{20}. For large-size ciphers, this step would take a lot of time. However, with some compromises between accuracy and efficiency, our method can be very useful to strengthen some existing search strategies for large-size ciphers. In this section, we show how to use our idea to enhance the search for the large-size cipher Rijndael-192. The application to GIFT-128 is provided in the full version.

Application to Rijndael-192. In [20], Sasaki and Todo also encountered similar problems with the efficiency when processing 8-bit Sbox ciphers, so they took a degenerated version of the MILP model called the *arbitrary Sbox mode* to boost the search efficiency. The arbitrary Sbox mode allows the model to ignore the details of the Sbox while mainly reflecting the property of the linear layers, thus the search time can be saved a lot. Despite this compromise, their MILP model still cannot work to search for all plaintext and ciphertext difference pairs. Let s be the number of Sboxes of a cipher, then the whole search space is 2^{2s}, e.g., for Rijndael-192 that has 24 Sboxes, the search space is approximately 2^{48} which is also very costly.

Inspired by their work, we can also boost our search efficiency by ignoring the details of Sboxes and even the linear layers. Different from Sasaki and Todo's tool, ours can exhaust all truncated difference pairs very fast. As is well known, Rijndael was designed by Daemen and Rijmen in 1998 and the 128 block size version was selected as the AES [12]. In this section, we take Rijndael-192 as an example and show how to identify all truncated IDs of 6-round Rijndael-192 within seconds. The state of Rijndael-192 is arranged as 4×6 matrix of bytes. Its round function comprises four operations, AddRoundKey (AK), SubBytes (SB), ShiftRows(SR) and MixColumns(MC). Without considering AK, r-round Rijndael-192 can be written similar to SKINNY-64,

$$R^r = \underbrace{\text{SB} \circ \text{MC} \circ \text{SB}}_{E_2} \circ \underbrace{\text{SR} \circ R^{r-4} \circ \text{MC} \circ \text{SR}}_{E_1} \circ \underbrace{\text{SB} \circ \text{MC} \circ \text{SB}}_{E_0},$$

Note that we also omit the SR of the first round and MC ∘ SR of the last round. Thus E_0 and E_2 of Rijndael-192 can be seen as 6 parallel superboxes, respectively.

In the arbitrary Sbox/MC mode, only being active or inactive for an Sbox would be considered instead of its detailed input and output differences. Thus, the difference of an Sbox can be labeled by one bit 0 or 1. Consequently, the differences of plaintexts, ciphertexts, and intermediate states are labeled by a

Table 4. The representative sets of superboxes $E_{0,i}$ and $E_{2,i}^{-1}$ for $i = 0, 1, 2, 3, 4, 5$, of Rijndael-192

Representative set	Values (hexadecimal)
$X_{1,i}, i = 0, 1, 2, 3, 4, 5$	0, f
$X_{2,i}, i = 0, 1, 2, 3, 4, 5$	0, f

binary vector $x \in \mathbb{F}_2^{24}$. Consequently, to apply our new tool with the arbitrary Sbox/MC mode, we adapt Algorithm 1 to compute the representative sets and partition tables for all truncated differences into a superbox. In terms of Rijndael-192, there are only 16 kinds of truncated IDs as input of a superbox (from 0b0000 to 0b1111). Since we only consider the branch number of MC, its representative set contains only 2 elements as shown in Table 4.

We first call Algorithm 2 to test 6-round Rijndael-192 (note that the MILP models here are in the arbitrary Sbox mode and only the branch number of MC are considered.). Within 1 s, we can find out all 6,750 IDs, which are provided with our codes in our git repository. Next, we test 7 rounds, no ID can be found. Therefore, we prove that there is no truncated ID for 7-round Rijndael-192.

7   Conclusion and Future Work

In this paper, we proposed a new method to detect all IDs based on MILP models with the DDT considered. The whole search space is partitioned into smaller ones and some of them can be quickly determined to contain no IDs. Thus the search space is significantly reduced, sometimes to a practical size. Then we could handle the remaining candidates to check if there are any IDs. With this novel strategy, we identified all IDs for 11-, and 12-round SKINNY-64 and prove there exists no ID for 13-round SKINNY-64. Similarly, we identified all IDs for 13-round CRAFT and prove there is no ID for 14 rounds. We also proved there is no ID for 8-round GIFT-64. The idea of our new method is also very useful to enhance the current MILP models for ciphers with large blocks. For example, we can partition the whole space of truncated differences for Rijndael-192 into smaller ones under the arbitrary Sbox mode. We quickly identified all truncated IDs for 6-round Rijndael-192 in 1 s and proved there is no truncated ID for 7 rounds. For GIFT-128, we searched in a smaller space where all differences have an active superbox in plaintext and ciphertext differences.

It is interesting to study if our method is also applicable to searching for all zero-correlation linear hull distinguishers [8] due to the dual property of the ID and zero-correlation linear hull. However, since the correlation of a linear hull is equivalent to the summation of the correlation of all its trails, in theory there might be a linear hull with the zero-correlation consisting some non-zero-correlation linear trails. Thus, our method cannot be directly used for zero-correlation linear hulls, or more assumptions might be necessary. This would be one of our future works. The representative sets and partition tables in our work are generated based on an intuitive algorithm (Algorithm 1) that is not very efficient. We guess there may be other methods to choose the representative sets and partition tables that could consider the property of E_1 simultaneously, such that we could reduce the number of MILP models we need to solve in the second step of Algorithm 2 and fewer impossible patterns for E_1 remains after it. This would be another interesting future work. Finally, our method currently works only for ciphers whose round functions are based on superboxes, it is also interesting to see how to generalize it to more types of ciphers.

Acknowledgment. The authors would like to thank the anonymous reviewers for their valuable comments and suggestions. Meiqin Wang is supported by the National Natural Science Foundation of China (Grant No. 62002201, Grant No. 62032014), the National Key Research and Development Program of China (Grant No. 2018YFA0704702, 2018YFA0704704), the Major Scientific and Technological Innovation Project of Shandong Province, China (Grant No. 2019JZZY010133), the Major Basic Research Project of Natural Science Foundation of Shandong Province, China (Grant No. ZR202010220025).

References

1. Banik, S., Pandey, S.K., Peyrin, T., Sasaki, Y., Sim, S.M., Todo, Y.: GIFT: a small present. In: Fischer, W., Homma, N. (eds.) Cryptographic Hardware and Embedded Systems - CHES 2017. Lecture Notes in Computer Science(), vol. 10529, pp. 321 345. Springer, Cham (2017). https://doi.org/10.1007/978-3-319-66787-4_16

2. Beaulieu, R., Shors, D., Smith, J., Treatman-Clark, S., Weeks, B., Wingers, L.: The SIMON and SPECK lightweight block ciphers. In: DAC 2015, pp. 1–6. ACM (2015)

3. Beierle, C., et al.: The SKINNY family of block ciphers and its low-latency variant MANTIS. In: Robshaw, M., Katz, J. (eds.) Advances in Cryptology - CRYPTO 2016. Lecture Notes in Computer Science(), vol. 9815, pp. 123–153. Springer, Berlin (2016). https://doi.org/10.1007/978-3-662-53008-5_5

4. Beierle, C., Leander, G., Moradi, A., Rasoolzadeh, S.: CRAFT: lightweight tweakable block cipher with efficient protection against DFA attacks. IACR Trans. Symmetric Cryptol. **2019**(1), 5–45 (2019)

5. Biham, E., Biryukov, A., Shamir, A.: Cryptanalysis of skipjack reduced to 31 rounds using impossible differentials. In: Stern, J. (ed.) Advances in Cryptology - EUROCRYPT '99. Lecture Notes in Computer Science, vol. 1592, pp. 12–23. Springer, Berlin (1999). https://doi.org/10.1007/3-540-48910-x_2

6. Biryukov, A.: Miss-in-the-middle attack. In: Encyclopedia of Cryptography and Security, 2nd ed., page 786. Springer, Cham (2011)

7. Bogdanov, A., et al.: PRESENT: an ultra-lightweight block cipher. In: Paillier, P., Verbauwhede, I. (eds.) Cryptographic Hardware and Embedded Systems - CHES 2007. Lecture Notes in Computer Science, vol. 4727, pp. 450–466. Springer, Berlin (2007). https://doi.org/10.1007/978-3-540-74735-2_31

8. Bogdanov, A., Rijmen, V.: Linear hulls with correlation zero and linear cryptanalysis of block ciphers. Des. Codes Crypt. **70**(3), 369–383 (2014)

9. Cui, T., Chen, S., Jia, K., Fu, K., Wang, M.: New automatic tool for finding impossible differentials and zero-correlation linear approximations. Sci. China Inf. Sci. **64**(2) (2021)

10. Cui, T., Chen, S., Jia, K., Fu, K., Wang, M.: New automatic search tool for impossible differentials and zero-correlation linear approximations. IACR Cryptol. ePrint Arch., 689 (2016)

11. Daemen, J., Rijmen, V.: AES and the Wide Trail Design Strategy. In: Knudsen, L.R. (ed.) Advances in Cryptology - EUROCRYPT 2002. Lecture Notes in Computer Science, vol. 2332, pp. 108–109. Springer, Berlin (2002). https://doi.org/10.1007/3-540-46035-7_7

12. Daemen, J., Rijmen, V.: The Design of Rijndael: AES - The Advanced Encryption Standard. ISC. Springer, Cham (2002). https://doi.org/10.1007/978-3-662-04722-4

13. Dunkelman, O., Huang, S., Lambooij, E., Perle, S.: Single tweakey cryptanalysis of reduced-round SKINNY-64. In: Dolev, S., Kolesnikov, V., Lodha, S., Weiss, G. (eds.) Cyber Security Cryptography and Machine Learning. Lecture Notes in Computer Science(), vol. 12161, pp. 1–17. Springer, Cham (2020). https://doi.org/10.1007/978-3-030-49785-9_1

14. Jean, J., Nikolic, I., Peyrin, T.: Tweaks and keys for block ciphers: the TWEAKEY framework. In: Sarkar, P., Iwata, T. (eds.) Advances in Cryptology - ASIACRYPT 2014. Lecture Notes in Computer Science, vol. 8874, pp. 274–288. Springer, Berlin (2014). https://doi.org/10.1007/978-3-662-45608-8_15

15. Kim, J., Hong, S., Sung, J., Lee, S., Lim, J., Sung, S.: Impossible differential cryptanalysis for block cipher structures. In: Johansson, T., Maitra, S. (eds.) Progress in Cryptology - INDOCRYPT 2003. Lecture Notes in Computer Science, vol. 2904, pp. 82–96. Springer, Berlin (2003). https://doi.org/10.1007/978-3-540-24582-7_6

16. Knudsen, L.: Deal-a 128-bit block cipher. Complexity **258**(2), 216 (1998)

17. Lu, J., Dunkelman, O., Keller, N., Kim, J.: New impossible differential attacks on AES. In: Chowdhury, D.R., Rijmen, V., Das, A. (eds.) Progress in Cryptology - INDOCRYPT 2008. Lecture Notes in Computer Science, vol. 5365, pp. 279–293. Springer, Berlin (2008). https://doi.org/10.1007/978-3-540-89754-5_22

18. Luo, Y., Lai, X., Wu, Z., Gong, G.: A unified method for finding impossible differentials of block cipher structures. Inf. Sci. **263**, 211–220 (2014)

19. Mouha, N., Wang, Q., Gu, D., Preneel, B.: Differential and linear cryptanalysis using mixed-integer linear programming. In: Wu, C.K., Yung, M., Lin, D. (eds.) Information Security and Cryptology. Lecture Notes in Computer Science, vol. 7537, pp. 57–76. Springer, Berlin (2011)

20. Sasaki, Y., Todo, Y.: New impossible differential search tool from design and cryptanalysis aspects. In: Coron, J.S., Nielsen, J. (eds.) Advances in Cryptology - EUROCRYPT 2017. Lecture Notes in Computer Science(), vol. 10212, pp. 185–215. Springer, Cham (2017). https://doi.org/10.1007/978-3-319-56617-7_7

21. Sun, B., Liu, M., Guo, J., Rijmen, V., Li, R.: Provable security evaluation of structures against impossible differential and zero correlation linear cryptanalysis. In: Fischlin, M., Coron, J.S. (eds.) Advances in Cryptology - EUROCRYPT 2016. Lecture Notes in Computer Science(), vol. 9665, pp. 196–213. Springer, Berlin (2016). https://doi.org/10.1007/978-3-662-49890-3_8

22. Sun, L., Gérault, D., Wang, W., Wang, M.: On the usage of deterministic (related-key) truncated differentials and multidimensional linear approximations for SPN ciphers. IACR Trans. Symmetric Cryptol. **2020**(3), 262–287 (2020)

23. Sun, S., Hu, L., Wang, P., Qiao, K., Ma, X., Song, L.: Automatic security evaluation and (related-key) differential characteristic search: application to SIMON, PRESENT, LBlock, DES(L) and other bit-oriented block ciphers. In: Sarkar, P., Iwata, T. (eds.) Advances in Cryptology – ASIACRYPT 2014. Lecture Notes in Computer Science, vol. 8873, pp. 158–178. Springer, Berlin (2014). https://doi.org/10.1007/978-3-662-45611-8_9
24. Wang, Q., Jin, C.: More accurate results on the provable security of AES against impossible differential cryptanalysis. Des., Codes Cryptograp. **87**(12), 3001–3018 (2019)
25. Wang, Q., Jin, C.: Bounding the length of impossible differentials for SPN block ciphers. Des., Codes Cryptograp. **89**(11), 2477–2493 (2021)
26. Wu, S., Wang, M.: Automatic search of truncated impossible differentials for word-oriented block ciphers. In: Galbraith, S., Nandi, M. (eds.) Progress in Cryptology - INDOCRYPT 2012. Lecture Notes in Computer Science, vol. 7668, pp. 283–302. Springer, Berlin (2012). https://doi.org/10.1007/978-3-642-34931-7_17

A Three-Stage MITM Attack on LowMC from a Single Plaintext-Ciphertext Pair

Lulu Zhang[1,2], Meicheng Liu[1,2(✉)], and Dongdai Lin[1,2(✉)]

[1] State Key Laboratory of Information Security, Institute of Information Engineering, Chinese Academy of Sciences, Beijing 100093, China
algebubu@163.com, {liumeicheng,ddlin}@iie.ac.cn
[2] School of Cyber Security, University of Chinese Academy of Sciences, Beijing 100049, China

Abstract. The block cipher LowMC was proposed by Albrecht et al. at EUROCRYPT 2015 for a low multiplicative complexity. Over the years, LowMC has been receiving widespread cryptanalytic attention. Recently, the digital signature scheme PICNIC3, an alternative third-round candidate in NIST's Post-Quantum Cryptography competition, has been proposed and utilized LowMC as the underlying block cipher. The security of PICNIC3 can be reduced to the security of underlying LowMC in a single plaintext-ciphertext scenario. However, this scenario results in inapplicability of conventional cryptanalysis method like differential or linear cryptanalysis, which require many chosen plaintexts or ciphertexts. At ASIACRYPT 2021, Banik et al. used a linearization technique of the LowMC SBox and gave a two-stage MITM attack on LowMC instances from a single plaintext-ciphertext pair. In this paper, we revisit the Banik et al.'s work and make a more precise analysis of the independence of multiple-round subkey bits, deriving the method of estimating the success probability of this attack. Then we generalize the two-stage MITM attack into a three-stage MITM attack on LowMC instances with partial SBoxes layers. We add one MITM phase to further filter the reduced candidate set and successfully screen out the full master key bits with lower computational complexity. As a result, we improve Banik et al.'s attack and give a higher-round cryptanalysis for these instances.

Keywords: LowMC · PICNIC3 · Three-Stage MITM · Key Recovery

1 Introduction

LowMC family [3] is a parameterizable Substitution-Permutation-Network (SPN) block cipher proposed at EUROCRYPT 2015 which aims at realizing low multiplicative complexity. Its design adopts the relatively new idea that the designers combined the very simple SBox and the random linear layer to guarantee security, meanwhile achieving the goal of low multiplicative complexity. Specially, the number of Sboxes in nonlinear layer is an optional term and the full rank matrix

© The Author(s), under exclusive license to Springer Nature Switzerland AG 2024
B. Smith and H. Wu (Eds.): SAC 2022, LNCS 13742, pp. 306–327, 2024.
https://doi.org/10.1007/978-3-031-58411-4_14

of linear layer is chosen randomly. So the users could choose their own instantiations. Due to these features, LowMC instances are widely utilized as underlying
block cipher or pseudorandom functions for FHE and MPC usage.

LowMC family has evolved several versions since it was proposed in 2015.
After its first publication, the higher-order differential attack and the interpolation attack on LowMC were presented in [9,10], both of which also required much
data. To resist both attacks, the designers proposed LowMCv2, which has a new
way of determining the number of rounds. So far, the latest updated source code
deciding the number of total rounds was shown in [2]. In ToSC 2018, Rechberger
et al. [13] demonstrated a kind of effective attack called difference enumeration
attack on LowMCv2 instances under one of the most useful settings, namely
with few applied SBoxes at each round and only low allowable data complexity.
Next, Liu et al.'s work [11] developed new algebraic techniques based on difference enumeration technique in [13] to achieve efficient key-recovery attacks with
data complexity 2. Based on this work, Liu et al. in [12] again presented a new
attack model called algebraic MITM attack and improved the cryptanalysis of
LowMC instances in [11].

Recently, the digital signature algorithm PICNIC3 [14], an alternative third-
round candidate in NIST's Post-Quantum Cryptography competition, has used
several LowMC instances with partial or full SBoxes layers. For the instances
with partial SBoxes layers, the recommended parameters for PICNIC3 are the
blocksize $n = 128, 192, 256$, the number of Sboxes $s = 10$, the size of the master
key $k = n$ and the number of rounds $r = 20, 30, 38$. For the instances with full
SBoxes layers, the recommended parameters are the blocksize $n = 129, 192, 255$,
the number of Sboxes $s = 43, 64, 85$, the size of the master key $k = n$ and the
number of rounds $r = 4$. Note that all parameters are computed in the scenario
that the attackers have access to only a single pair of plaintext-ciphertext.

To gain a deeper knowledge about the security of LowMC in PICNIC use-
case, the LowMC Challenge [1] was launched in 2020. The LowMC challenge
specifies the following 9 challenge scenarios for key recovery in a single plaintext-
ciphertext scenario, where the size of the master key is equal to its blocksize:

$$(n, s) = (128, 1); (n, s) = (128, 10); (n, s) = (129, 43);$$
$$(n, s) = (192, 1); (n, s) = (192, 10); (n, s) = (192, 64);$$
$$(n, s) = (256, 1); (n, s) = (256, 10); (n, s) = (255, 85).$$

The recommended number of attack rounds for instances with full SBoxes
layers are 2, 3 and 4, for instances with partial Sboxes layers are $0.8 \times \lfloor \frac{n}{s} \rfloor$, $\lfloor \frac{n}{s} \rfloor$
and $1.2 \times \lfloor \frac{n}{s} \rfloor$. Banik et al. in [5] used a linearization technique to mount two key-
recovery attacks on these LowMC instances using a single plaintext-ciphertext
pair. In [8], the authors showed a concretely efficient polynomial method-based
algorithm for solving multivariate equation systems over $\mathbb{F}_2$. They applied this
method to the cryptanalysis of LowMC instances with full SBoxes layers and
showed that 2 out of 3 new instances do not achieve their claimed security level.
And in [6] Banik et al. took the linearization technique again and also gave a
cryptanalysis for full SBoxes layers LowMC instances and their 2-round attacks

had better time complexity than [8]. Recently, in [4] Banik et al. combined the linearization techniques of [5,6] and the equation solving methods of [8] to cryptanalyze LowMC instances with full SBoxes layers with reduced memory complexity and quasi-equivalent time complexity compared with [8]. For instances with partial Sboxes layers, the best known attack is the two-stage MITM with Gray Code speedup techniques in [6].

Banik, Barooti, Vaudenay and Yan in [6] gave a novel theoretical technique to linearize the SBox of LowMC by guessing only one bit. In addition, they also adopted other two trivial linearized techniques to deal with the SBoxes in various parts, meanwhile took forward and backward transformations to transform the parts before and after the guessed part, respectively. Base on these techniques they devised the two-stage MITM attack and the main cost of their attack was up to the number of guessed bits.

Contributions. In this paper, we improve the attack for LowMC instances with partial SBoxes layers. Our work is based on the two-stage MITM attack framework and we generalize it into three-stage MITM attack to improve the cryptanalysis of LowMC instances with partial SBoxes layers. Our results are detailed as follows:

1. We make a precise discussion about independence of multiple-round subkey bits. From the description of LowMC, the same round subkey bits are linearly independent expressions in terms of the master key bits, since the randomly chosen binary matrix for generating round key must be full rank. But the subkey bits in different rounds do not always satisfy the condition of independent expressions intuitively, which may directly lead to inapplicability of two-stage MITM attack on LowMC. However, the authors implicitly assumed that it always holds. This motivates us to find a precise theoretical analysis on this problem to guarantee rationality of the attack. We show that for the parameters used in the attack, the condition of independent expressions holds in a large probability, and we could use it to estimate the success probability of the attack since this method can recover full key bits as long as the condition holds.
2. We generalize the two-stage MITM attack into three-stage MITM attack to improve the cryptanalysis of LowMC instances with partial SBoxes layers, which are the recommended instances in PICNIC3 and lowMC Challenge. Firstly, we split the whole LowMC into 5 sections instead of 4 sections. Then we add the third MITM phase to further filter the reduced candidate set, expecting to find a better trade-off between time and memory. In the added section, we introduce slightly fewer additional variables to replace subkey bits involved in these rounds so that we get an improved attack with almost the same memory complexity and lower time complexity. Specially, our attacks achieve up to $1.1 \times \lfloor \frac{n}{s} \rfloor$ rounds for $(n, s) = (128, 10)$ and $(192, 10)$, $(1.1 \times \lfloor \frac{n}{s} \rfloor - 1)$ rounds for $(n, s) = (256, 10)$. Table 1 presents our main results in details.
3. We also apply our analysis on independence of multiple-round subkey bits to our three-stage MITM attack. Fortunately, the condition holds also in a large

probability, which means that our attack has a large success probability. We give the final results in Table 1.

Let us give some intuitions for the improved cryptanalysis of LowMC instances with partial SBoxes layers. From Banik et al.'s works, we find that one way of improving the cryptanalysis is to reduce the guessed bits. Inspired by this, we add one more part after the guessed part to construct an almost symmetrical model. We introduce new variables to indicate the input and output bits of SBoxes in the added part. When involving additional new variables, the attack will be less efficient if we still use two-stage MITM attack. So we add one MITM phase to avoid increasing total time complexity. Under the optimal parameters[1], the number of rounds where guessing the majority bits of SBoxes in our three-stage MITM attack is less than that in the two-stage MITM attack, which allows us to reduce the total time complexity.

Organization. The rest of the paper is organized as follows. A brief introduction of LowMC is given in Sect. 2. We revisit the two-stage MITM attack in Sect. 3. Next, we discuss the linear independence of multiple-round subkey bits and give a theoretical analysis to estimate the success probability of these multiple-stage MITM attacks in Sect. 4. In Sect. 5, we generalize the two-stage MITM attack into three-stage MITM attack on partial SBoxes LowMC instances and estimate the success probability of the new attack by the theoretical method in last section. The experimental results on small variants of LowMC instances are reported in Sect. 6. Finally, we conclude this paper in Sect. 7.

2   Preliminaries

2.1   Notation

As there are many LowMC instances in this paper, we use the following notations to represent the parameters of LowMC.

- n represents the blocksize.
- s represents the number of Sboxes in each round.
- k represents the size of master key.
- K represents the k-bit master key.
  r represents the total number of rounds of LowMC instances.

2.2   Description of LowMC

LowMC [3] is a family of SPN-structure block cipher different from conventional block ciphers. LowMC round function consists of a nonlinear layer including s

---

[1] In this paper, our attack splits the LowMC into 5 parts, called the first r_1 rounds, following r_2 rounds, middle r_{guess} rounds, next r_3 rounds and the final r_4 rounds. The different parameters $(r_1, r_2, r_{guess}, r_3, r_4)$ will lead to different final results. Our improved results are all under optimal parameters.

Table 1. The results for LowMC with partial SBoxes layers

n	s	r_1	r_2	r_3	r_4	r_{guess}	$i \times \lfloor \frac{n}{s} \rfloor$	r	Complexity	Suc. Pro	Reference
128	1	5	5	-	5	88	$0.8 \times \lfloor \frac{n}{s} \rfloor$	103	$2^{100.7}$	1	[6]
		5	5	-	5	113	$\lfloor \frac{n}{s} \rfloor$	128	$2^{125.4}$	1	
		5	5	-	5	115	-	130*	$2^{127.4}$	1	
128	1	5	3	3	5	87	$0.8 \times \lfloor \frac{n}{s} \rfloor$	103	$2^{99.7}$	1	Sect. 5
		5	3	3	5	112	$\lfloor \frac{n}{s} \rfloor$	128	$2^{124.4}$	1	
		5	3	3	5	115	-	**131**	$2^{127.4}$	1	
192	1	5	5	-	5	139	$0.8 \times \lfloor \frac{n}{s} \rfloor$	154	$2^{151.2}$	1	[6]
		5	5	-	5	177	$\lfloor \frac{n}{s} \rfloor$	192	$2^{188.9}$	1	
		5	5	-	5	179	-	194*	$2^{190.9}$	1	
192	1	5	3	3	5	138	$0.8 \times \lfloor \frac{n}{s} \rfloor$	154	$2^{150.2}$	1	Sect. 5
		5	3	3	5	176	$\lfloor \frac{n}{s} \rfloor$	192	$2^{187.9}$	1	
		5	3	3	5	180	-	**196**	$2^{191.9}$	1	
256	1	5	5	-	5	190	$0.8 \times \lfloor \frac{n}{s} \rfloor$	205	$2^{201.9}$	1	[6]
		5	5	-	5	241	$\lfloor \frac{n}{s} \rfloor$	256	$2^{252.6}$	1	
		5	5	-	5	243	-	258*	$2^{254.6}$	1	
256	1	5	3	3	5	189	$0.8 \times \lfloor \frac{n}{s} \rfloor$	205	$2^{200.9}$	1	Sect. 5
		5	3	3	5	240	$\lfloor \frac{n}{s} \rfloor$	256	$2^{251.6}$	1	
		5	3	3	5	244	-	**260**	$2^{255.6}$	1	
128	10	1	1	-	1	7	$0.8 \times \lfloor \frac{n}{s} \rfloor$	10	$2^{90.8}$	1*	[6]
		1	1	-	1	9	$\lfloor \frac{n}{s} \rfloor$	12	$2^{110.6}$	1*	
		1	1	-	1	10	-	13*	$2^{120.5}$	1*	
128	10	1	1	1	1	6	$0.8 \times \lfloor \frac{n}{s} \rfloor$	10	$2^{82.3}$	1*	Sect. 5
		1	1	1	1	8	$\lfloor \frac{n}{s} \rfloor$	12	$2^{102.1}$	1*	
		1	1	1	1	10	$1.1 \times \lfloor \frac{n}{s} \rfloor$	**14**	$2^{121.9}$	1*	
192	10	1	1	-	1	13	$0.8 \times \lfloor \frac{n}{s} \rfloor$	16	$2^{149.0}$	1	[6]
		1	1	-	1	16	$\lfloor \frac{n}{s} \rfloor$	19	$2^{178.7}$	1	
		1	1	-	1	17	-	20*	$2^{188.7}$	1	
192	10	1	1	1	1	12	$0.8 \times \lfloor \frac{n}{s} \rfloor$	16	$2^{140.5}$	1	Sect. 5
		1	1	1	1	15	$\lfloor \frac{n}{s} \rfloor$	19	$2^{170.2}$	1	
		1	1	1	1	17	$1.1 \times \lfloor \frac{n}{s} \rfloor$	**21**	$2^{190.1}$	1	
256	10	1	1	-	1	17	$0.8 \times \lfloor \frac{n}{s} \rfloor$	20	$2^{187.8}$	1	[6]
		1	1	-	1	22	$\lfloor \frac{n}{s} \rfloor$	25	$2^{237.5}$	1	
		1	1	-	1	23	-	26*	$2^{247.5}$	1	
256	10	1	1	1	1	16	$0.8 \times \lfloor \frac{n}{s} \rfloor$	20	$2^{179.3}$	1	Sect. 5
		1	1	1	1	21	$\lfloor \frac{n}{s} \rfloor$	25	$2^{229.0}$	1	
		1	1	1	1	23	$1.1 \times \lfloor \frac{n}{s} \rfloor - 1$	**27**	$2^{248.9}$	1	

* We calculated the largest number of rounds that two-stage MITM attack in [6] can reach with the complexity below the exhaustive search.

* These indicate that the success probability is very close to 1, around $1 - \lambda$ where λ is a negligible number.

3-bit SBoxes where $3s \leq n$, an affine layer, an addition with an n-bit round constant and a following addition with an n-bit round key. Specifically, LowMC encryption starts with a key whitening and then iterates a round function by r times. We give the specific description of round function as follows:

1. SBoxLayer: A 3-bit SBox mapping as $(t_0, t_1, t_2) = (s_0 + s_1 \cdot s_2, s_0 + s_1 + s_0 \cdot s_2, s_0 + s_1 + s_2 + s_0 \cdot s_1)$ is applied to the first $3s$ bits of the state while an identical mapping is applied to the remaining $n - 3s$ bits.
2. LinearLayer: A randomly generated regular matrix $M_i \in \mathbb{F}_2^{n \times n}$ multiplies the n-bit state.
3. KeyAddition: The n-bit round key K_i is obtained by multiplying the k-bit master key by a randomly generated full-rank $n \times k$ binary matrix. Then the n-bit state is xored with K_i.
4. ConstantAddition: A randomly generated n-bit constants $C_i \in \mathbb{F}_2^n$ is xored to the n-bit state.

According to the above description and [6], we can know that the total number of bit operations required in performing a whole LowMC encryption is around $2rn^2$. Note that in this paper, all the computational complexity are recalculated in terms of number of encryptions and for all instances we study the size of the master key equals the blocksize, i.e., $k = n$.

3 Revisiting Banik, Barooti, Vaudenay and Yan's Attack

In this section, we briefly revisit the two-stage MITM attack in [6]. This attack was designed based on the following lemma, which can linearize a whole LowMC SBox by guessing only one bit of a balanced quadratic expression on its inputs.

Lemma 1 [5,6]. *Consider the LowMC SBoxes defined over the input bits s_0, s_1 and s_2. If we guess the value of any 3-variable quadratic Boolean function f which is balanced over the input bits of the SBoxes, then it is possible to re-write the SBoxes as an affine function of its input bits.*

The authors chose the majority function $f = s_0 \cdot s_1 + s_0 \cdot s_2 + s_1 \cdot s_2$ as the used balanced quadratic expression. Therefore, the LowMC SBox output bits can be expressed in the following form. The inverse of LowMC SBox also has a similar form (a detailed form is given in Appendix A).

$$
\begin{aligned}
t_0 &= s_0 + s_1 \cdot s_2 & &= f \cdot (s_1 + s_2 + 1) + s_0, \\
t_1 &= s_0 + s_1 + s_0 \cdot s_2 & &= f \cdot (s_0 + s_2 + 1) + s_0 + s_1, \\
t_2 &= s_0 + s_1 + s_2 + s_0 \cdot s_1 & &= f \cdot (s_0 + s_1 + 1) + s_0 + s_1 + s_2.
\end{aligned}
$$

Beyond the above linearization technique of the LowMC SBox, for lowMC instances with partial SBoxes layers the authors used a trick used in [5,6,13] to transform the initial and the final rounds of into the equivalent representations so that the total number of round key bits becomes $3s$ per round instead of n. The transformations are shown in Figs. 1 and 2, which show how to transform the first r_1 rounds and the final r_3 rounds, respectively. We briefly summarize the idea of the transformations that the affine layer and key addition are interchangeable. It is well-known that we have $\mathsf{Lin}(x) + K = \mathsf{Lin}(x + \mathsf{Lin}^{-1}(K))$ and $\mathsf{Lin}(x + K) = \mathsf{Lin}(x) + \mathsf{Lin}(K)$ when Lin is a linear function. Hence, the key addition can be moved before or after the affine layer as we needed, by multiplying the appropriate matrix. In fact, we can say that the key schedule is changed by a known conversion. We refer the interested readers to [5,6,13] for more details.

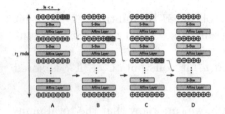

Fig. 1. The initial r_1 rounds forward-transformation. Figure taken from [5]

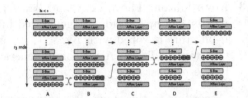

Fig. 2. The final r_3 rounds backward-transformation. Figure taken from [5]

Next, we summarize that the overall two-stage MITM attack process can be described as follows:

1. Split the LowMC into 4 parts as shown in Fig. 3, including the first $(r_1 + r_2)$ rounds which have been transformed as Fig. 1, the final r_3 rounds which have been transformed as shown in Fig. 2, and the remaining $r_{guess} = r - r_1 - r_2 - r_3$ rounds which lie in the middle.
2. Denote the output of the first r_1 rounds by X, the output of the following r_2 rounds by W and the input of the final r_3 rounds by Y. Denote the inputs/outputs of the SBoxes in the r_2 rounds by U/Z.
3. Denote the key bits involved in the first r_1 rounds, the following r_2 rounds and the final r_3 rounds by $K_{r_1} = [k_0, k_1, \cdots, k_{3sr_1-1}]$, $K_{r_2} = [k_{3sr_1}, k_{3sr_1+1}, \cdots, k_{3sr_1+3sr_2-1}]$ and $K_{r_3} = [k_{n-3sr_3}, k_{n-3sr_3+1}, \cdots, k_{n-1}]$, respectively.
4. Construct the remaining $n - 3s(r_1 + r_2 + r_3)$ key bits K_{rem} such that K_{r_1}, K_{r_2}, K_{r_3} and K_{rem} are linearly independent expressions of the master key K and so any master key bit can be expressed as a linear function of them. Hence, the key bits in the middle r_{guess} rounds also can be linearly represented by them.
5. According to Lemma 1, guess majority bits of the inputs of the SBoxes in the middle r_{guess} rounds to linearize the sr_{guess} SBoxes in the middle r_{guess} rounds.
6. For per guessed majority value do:
   First MITM:
   - Compute the relations $\mathsf{Affine}(Y, Z, x_{3s}, \cdots, x_{n-1}, K_{r_1}, K_{r_2}, K_{r_3}, K_{rem}) = 0$.
   - Eliminate K_{rem}, Z and K_{r_2} from above equations and rearrange the equations into the form of $\mathsf{Affine}_1(K_{r_1}, X) = \mathsf{Affine}_2(K_{r_3}, Y)$.

- For every guessed value of K_{r_1}, compute X with corresponding K_{r_1} and plaintext pt and construct a list L_1 of $\mathsf{Affine}_1(K_{r_1}, X)$.
- For every guessed value of K_{r_3}, compute Y and $\mathsf{Affine}_2(K_{r_3}, Y)$ with corresponding K_{r_3} and ciphertext ct. Find collisions between $\mathsf{Affine}_2(K_{r_3}, Y)$ and list L_1. Construct a list L_2 of (K_{r_1}, K_{r_3}) values satisfying the condition.

Second MITM:

- Compute the relations $\mathsf{Affine}(Y, Z, x_{3s}, \cdots, x_{n-1}, K_{r_1}, U, K_{r_3}, K_{rem}) = 0$ by taking the place of K_{r_2} by U.
- Eliminate K_{rem} from the above equations and rearrange the equations into the form of $\mathsf{Affine}_3(Z, U) = \mathsf{Affine}_4(K_{r_1}, K_{r_3}, X, Y)$.
- For every (K_{r_1}, K_{r_3}) in list L_2, compute $\mathsf{Affine}_4(K_{r_1}, K_{r_3}, X, Y)$ and make a list L_3 to store (K_{r_1}, K_{r_3}) indexed by corresponding values of $\mathsf{Affine}_4(K_{r_1}, K_{r_3}, X, Y)$.
- For every possible value of Z, obtain corresponding U by Z since the SBox is bijective and compute $\mathsf{Affine}_3(Z, U)$. Find the collisions with L_3 and keep a new list L_4 of (K_{r_1}, K_{r_3}, Z, U).
- For every (K_{r_1}, K_{r_3}, Z, U) in list L_4, compute K_{r_2} and K_{rem} from above equations.
- When $K_{r_1}, K_{r_2}, K_{r_3}, K_{rem}$ are known, check if they result in the corresponding guessed majority values. Otherwise, guess another majority values and try the attack procedure again.

As described above in step 4, it is worth noting that there are two implicit conditions:

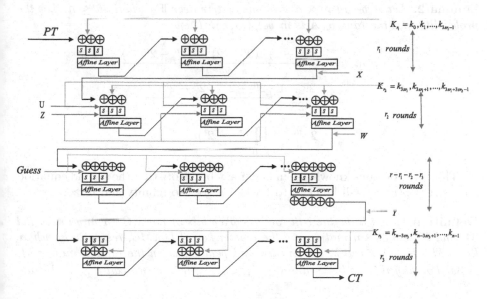

Fig. 3. Splitting LowMC into 4 parts

Condition 1. $n \geq 3 \cdot s \cdot (r_1 + r_2 + r_3)$.

Condition 2. $K_{r_1}, K_{r_2}, K_{r_3}$ are *linearly independent expressions in terms of the n-bit master key.*

Condition 1 restricts that r_1, r_2 and r_3 cannot reach too large value and LowMC cannot be separated into too many sections. There is a balance between the values of r_1, r_2, r_3 and the number of parts split. Moreover, Condition 2 is not always satisfied according to key schedule scheme. We will show the detailed discussion in Sect. 4 and observe that Condition 2 is correct with a large probability when n goes to infinity. As a result, we give the accurate probability of success of the two-stage MITM attack.

4 Discussion About Linear Independence of K_{r_1}, K_{r_2} and K_{r_3}

Note that all elements in K_{r_i} are expressions in terms of the n master key bits where $i = 1, 2, 3$. All linear expressions of $3s$ subkey bits in the same round of lowMC are linearly independent, since the matrix generating round subkey is full rank according to Sect. 2.2. For example, first all $3s$ bits $k_0, k_1, \cdots, k_{3s-1}$ are linearly independent expressions of the master key, and second all $3s$ bits $k_{3s}, k_{3s+1}, \cdots, k_{6s-1}$ are linearly independent and so forth. However, whether these $6s$ bits are linearly independent? Furthermore, what is the chance of Condition 2 being true?

To obtain the answer, we give a lemma as follows firstly:

Lemma 2. *Let A be an $m \times n$ random matrix over $\mathbb{F}_2$ where $m \leq n$. Let the probability that the rank of A is m be $p(m, n)$. Then*

$$p(m, n) = \frac{(2^n - 1) \cdot (2^n - 2) \cdots (2^n - 2^{m-1})}{2^{m \cdot n}}$$

$$= \frac{2^n - 1}{2^n} \cdot \frac{2^n - 2}{2^n} \cdots \frac{2^n - 2^{m-1}}{2^n}$$

$$= 2^{-m \cdot n} \cdot \prod_{i=0}^{m-1} (2^n - 2^i).$$

This is the obvious knowledge in linear algebra. Note that the second equation means that $p(m, n)$ will be close to 1 when n goes to infinity and $n \gg m$.

Definition 1. *Let $\hat{k}_i$ be the i-th round subkey bits of LowMC for any $i < r$. Let M_i and K be a $3s \times n$ matrix and the master key of LowMC, respectively, where $\hat{k}_i^T = M_i \cdot K^T$. We call $\hat{k}_i$ are linearly independent when the rank of matrix M_i is $3s$. For any integer $l \leq r$ and $0 \leq i_1 < \cdots < i_l < r$, we call $\hat{k}_{i_1}, \ldots, \hat{k}_{i_l}$ are* *linearly independent when the rank of matrix M is $3ls$, where matrix M has the following form:*

$$\begin{pmatrix} M_{i_1} \\ M_{i_2} \\ \cdots \\ M_{i_l} \end{pmatrix}.$$

Theorem 1. *Let $\hat{k}_i$ be the i-th round subkey bits of LowMC for any $i < r$. Then $\hat{k}_i$ are linearly independent for any $i < r$. Furthermore, for any integer $l \leq r$ and $0 \leq i_1 < \cdots < i_l < r$, the probability that $\hat{k}_{i_1}, \ldots, \hat{k}_{i_l}$ are linearly independent is*

$$pro(l) = \frac{p(3 \cdot l \cdot s, n)}{p(3 \cdot s, n)^l}. \tag{1}$$

By the description of LowMC, the $3s$ subkey bits in the same round of lowMC are linearly independent and the matrix generating round key in each round is randomly chosen independently. We have total $2^{3ls \cdot n} \cdot p(3s, n)^l$ possible $3ls \times n$ matrices and there are $2^{3ls \cdot n} \cdot p(3ls, n)$ matrices among them satisfying the condition that the rank is $3ls$.

Corollary 1. *Let K_{r_1}, K_{r_2}, K_{r_3} be the set of subkey bits involved in the first r_1, the following r_2 and the final r_3 rounds for two-stage MITM attack in [6], respectively. Then for any $i = 1, 2, 3$, the probability that K_{r_i} is linearly independent is*

$$pro(r_i) = \frac{p(3 \cdot r_i \cdot s, n)}{p(3 \cdot s, n)^{r_i}}. \tag{2}$$

Furthermore, the probability that K_{r_1}, K_{r_2}, K_{r_3} are linearly independent is

$$pro(r_1, r_2, r_3) = \frac{p(3 \cdot (r_1 + r_2 + r_3) \cdot s, n)}{p(3 \cdot s, n)^{(r_1 + r_2 + r_3)}}. \tag{3}$$

Moreover, $pro(r_1, r_2, r_3)$ is the probability of Condition 2 holding, which can also be seen as the success probability of the two-stage MITM attack.

Remark 1. $pro(r_1, r_2, r_3)$ approaches 1 when n goes to infinity and r_1, r_2, r_3 are small. For example, when $n = 128$, $s = 1$, $(r_1, r_2, r_3) = (5, 5, 5)$, $pro(5, 5, 5) = 1 - \lambda$ where λ is a negligible number. The probabilities for more LowMC instantiations with specific values of r_1, r_2, r_3 will be given in Table 1.

5   Improved Attacks on LowMC Instances with Partial SBoxes Layers

As mentioned in Sect. 3, in order to mount the two-stage MITM attack, Banik et al. separated LowMC into 4 sections. They dealt with the SBoxes (nonlinear parts) in three ways. In the first r_1 and the final r_3 rounds, SBox parts were calculated by plaintext pt or ciphertext ct and relevant guessed subkey bits. They did the initial filtering and collected (K_{r_1}, K_{r_3}) satisfying equations after first MITM. In the following r_2 rounds, the authors introduced $6sr_2$ new variables to indicate the input bits and output bits of SBoxes, dealing with nonlinear transmission. The SBoxes in the remaining rounds of LowMC were linearized by guessing all possible majority values. Therefore, they can obtain some required linear equations before the final r_3 rounds.

In this section, based on the two-stage MITM attack framework, we add one part denoted r_3 rounds after the parts in which we guess majority values. We introduce new variables to indicate the input bits and output bits of SBoxes for linearizing SBoxes as ways in the r_2 rounds. Hence, we establish an almost symmetrical model and generalize the two-stage MITM attack into three-stage MITM attack to improve the attacks on LowMC. In short, the total attack number of rounds r are divided into 5 sections, i.e., r_1, r_2, r_3, r_4 and the middle r_{guess} rounds. The original attacks in [6] can be seen as the case of $r_3 = 0$. The number of rounds where we guess the majority bits of SBoxes is less when $r_1 + r_2 + r_3 + r_4$ is larger.

To devise an improved attack, we maintain the hypothesis like Conditions 1 and 2, and estimate the success probabilities of various LowMC instances by Sect. 4. Denote the subkey bits involved in the first r_1 rounds, the following r_2 rounds, the next r_3 rounds and the final r_4 rounds by $K_{r_1} = [k_0, k_1, \cdots, k_{3sr_1-1}]$, $K_{r_2} = [k_{3sr_1}, k_{3sr_1+1}, \cdots, k_{3sr_1+3sr_2-1}]$, $K_{r_3} = [k_{n-3s(r_3+r_4)}, \cdots, k_{n-3sr_4-1}]$ and $K_{r_4} = [k_{n-3sr_4}, k_{n-3sr_4+1}, \cdots, k_{n-1}]$, respectively. Furthermore, we rewrite the conditions as follows:

Condition 3. $n \geq 3 \cdot s \cdot (r_1 + r_2 + r_3 + r_4)$.

Condition 4. $K_{r_1}, K_{r_2}, K_{r_3}, K_{r_4}$ are linearly independent expressions in terms of the n-bit master key.

5.1   The Three-Stage MITM Attack Framework

Based on Banik et al.'s attack framework, we improve the attack to recover the master key of higher-round LowMC instances. To mount this attack, let us separate the LowMC into 5 parts as shown in Fig. 4. Similarly, transform the first (r_1+r_2) rounds as Fig. 1 and the final (r_3+r_4) rounds as Fig. 2. The middle $r_{guess} = (r - r_1 - r_2 - r_3 - r_4)$ rounds keep in the middle.

Owing to the Conditions 3 and 4, we can construct the remaining $n - 3s(r_1 + r_2 + r_3 + r_4)$ key bits called K_{rem} such that $K_{r_1}, K_{r_2}, K_{r_3}, K_{r_4}$ and K_{rem} are linearly independent expressions of the master key and so any master key bit can be expressed as a linear function of them. Hence, the key bits in the middle r_{guess} rounds can be linearly represented by them.

Denote the outputs of the first r_1 rounds and the first (r_1+r_2) rounds by $X = [x_0, x_1, \cdots, x_{n-1}]$ and $W = [w_0, w_1, \cdots, w_{n-1}]$, respectively. Denote the inputs of the final r_4 rounds and the final $(r_3 + r_4)$ rounds by $Y = [y_0, y_1, \cdots, y_{n-1}]$

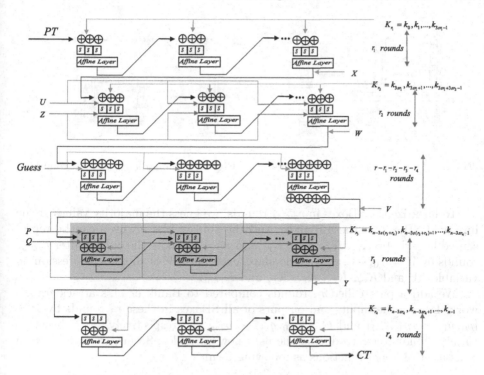

Fig. 4. Splitting LowMC into 5 parts

and $V = [v_0, v_1, \cdots, v_{n-1}]$, respectively. In the following r_2 rounds, we introduce $6sr_2$ new variables to indicate the input bits and output bits of SBoxes involved, called $U = [u_0, u_1, \cdots, u_{3sr_2-1}]$ and $Z = [z_0, z_1, \cdots, z_{3sr_2-1}]$. Let $A = [a_0, \cdots, a_{n-1}]$ and $B = [b_0, \cdots, b_{n-1}]$ be the output of the first round and second round in these r_2 rounds as shown in Fig. 5. Then there are such affine expressions $A = \mathsf{Aff}_1(z_0, z_1, \cdots, z_{3s-1}, x_{3s}, \cdots, x_{n-1})$ where Aff_1 denotes a set of n affine functions. Again, we can express B as a set of affine functions in terms of $(z_{3s}, z_{3s+1}, \cdots, z_{6s-1}, a_{3s}, \cdots, a_{n-1})$ which indicate that there are relations $B = \mathsf{Aff}_2(z_0, z_1, \cdots, z_{6s-1}, x_{3s}, \cdots, x_{n-1})$ as affine functions in terms of variables X and the first $6s$ z_i's. After iterating over the total r_2 rounds in this way, we can obtain the affine expressions of W which means that W can be written as a set of affine expressions in terms of whole Z and the last $(n - 3s)$ x_i's, i.e., $(Z, x_{3s}, x_{3s+1}, \cdots, x_{n-1})$.

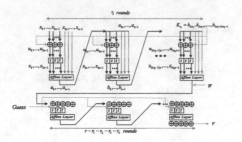

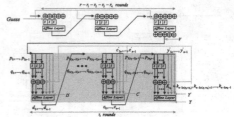

Fig. 5. The middle $r_2 + r_{guess}$ rounds. **Fig. 6.** The middle $r_{guess} + r_3$ rounds.

To linearize the SBoxes in r_{guess} rounds, we guess the majority values of the inputs of SBoxes in these rounds. And the subkey bits involved can be represented linearly by $K_{r_1}, K_{r_2}, K_{r_3}, K_{r_4}$ and K_{rem}. Denote the output after r_{guess} rounds by $V = [v_0, \cdots, v_{n-1}]$. Therefore, each bit of V is an affine expression on variables W and $K_{r_1}, K_{r_2}, K_{r_3}, K_{r_4}$ and K_{rem}.

We add a part called r_3 rounds compared to Banik et al.'s attack framework. Denote the inputs and outputs of all SBoxes in these r_3 rounds by $P = [p_0, p_1, \cdots, p_{3sr_3-1}]$ and $Q = [q_0, q_1, \cdots, q_{3sr_3-1}]$, respectively. So it becomes totally affine after introducing the $6sr_3$ new variables. So far, we have written Y as a set of linear functions as following form:

$$Y = \mathsf{Affine}(Z, x_{3s}, \cdots, x_{n-1}, K_{r_1}, K_{r_2}, K_{r_3}, K_{r_4}, K_{rem}, Q).$$

We can rewrite this form as:

$$\mathsf{Affine}(Y, Z, x_{3s}, \cdots, x_{n-1}, K_{r_1}, K_{r_2}, K_{r_3}, K_{r_4}, K_{rem}, Q) = 0. \qquad (4)$$

Before performing our three-stage MITM, we observe that K_{r_2} in Eq. (4) can be expressed by X, Z and U from Fig. 5 and K_{r_3} can be represented by Y, Q and $p_{3s}, \cdots, p_{3sr_3-1}$ from Fig. 6. Now we give specific description about this. Firstly, we can see that the following relations hold in the first three rounds for $\forall i \in [0, 3s - 1]$ by Fig. 6:

$$
\begin{aligned}
u_i &= x_i + k_{3sr_1+i}, \\
u_{3s+i} &= a_i + k_{3s(r_1+1)+i} \\
&= \mathsf{Aff}_{1,i}(z_0, z_1, \cdots, z_{3s-1}, x_{3s}, \cdots, x_{n-1}) + k_{3s(r_1+1)+i}, \\
u_{6s+i} &= b_i + k_{3s(r_1+2)+i} \\
&= \mathsf{Aff}_{2,i}(z_0, z_1, \cdots, z_{6s-1}, x_{3s}, \cdots, x_{n-1}) + k_{3s(r_1+2)+i},
\end{aligned}
$$

where $\mathsf{Aff}_{1,i}$ and $\mathsf{Aff}_{2,i}$ are the i-th affine functions of Aff_1 and Aff_2. After iterating over the entire r_2 rounds we can get a system of affine equations $U = \overline{\mathsf{L}}(Z, X) + K_{r_2}$, where $\overline{\mathsf{L}}$ is the set of $3sr_2$ affine expressions as above. Now we can rewrite the Eqs. (4) by taking place K_{r_2} by $U + \overline{\mathsf{L}}(Z, X)$ as

$$\text{Affine}(Y, Z, x_{3s}, \cdots, x_{n-1}, K_{r_1}, U + \overline{\text{L}}(Z, X), K_{r_3}, K_{r_4}, K_{rem}, Q)$$
$$= \text{Affine}'(Y, Z, X, K_{r_1}, U, K_{r_3}, K_{r_4}, K_{rem}, Q) = 0. \tag{5}$$

Next, for a more convenient narrative, we denote the inputs of affine layers in the first, the penultimate and the last rounds in this part by $D' = [d'_0, \cdots, d'_{n-1}]$, $C' = [c'_0, \cdots, c'_{n-1}]$ and $Y' = [y'_0, \cdots, y'_{n-1}]$, respectively, as seen in Fig. 6. Likely, denote the outputs in the first and penultimate rounds by $D = [d_0, \cdots, d_{n-1}]$ and $C = [c_0, \cdots, c_{n-1}]$. By Fig. 6, $Y' = \text{AL}_0(Y)$, $C' = \text{AL}_1(Y, p_{3s(r_3-1)}, \cdots, p_{3sr_3-1})$ and $D' = \text{AL}_2(Y, p_{3s}, \cdots, p_{3sr_3-1})$, where AL_0, AL_1 and AL_2 are affine functions. We can also get the following relations for $\forall i \in [0, 3s-1]$:

$$q_{3s(r_3-1)+i} = y'_i + k_{3s(r_3-1)+i} = \text{AL}_{0,i}(Y) + k_{3s(r_3-1)+i},$$
$$q_{3s(r_3-2)+i} = c'_i + k_{3s(r_3-2)+i} = \text{AL}_{1,i}(Y, p_{3s(r_3-1)}, \cdots, p_{3sr_3-1}) + k_{3s(r_3-2)+i},$$
$$\cdots$$
$$q_i \quad = d'_i + k_i = \text{AL}_{2,i}(Y, p_{3s}, \cdots, p_{3sr_3-1}) + k_i.$$

In this way, after backward iterating over the entire r_3 rounds we can get a system of affine equations $Q = \overline{\text{L}}'(Y, p_{3s}, \cdots, p_{3sr_3-1}) + K_{r_3}$, where $\overline{\text{L}}'$ is the set of $3sr_3$ affine expressions as above. Note that for expressing $3sr_3$ subkey bits in K_{r_3}, only additional $3sr_3 - 3s$ bits new variables $p_{3s}, \cdots, p_{3sr_3-1}$ have been introduced. This is different from the above r_2 rounds, since the r_3 rounds are transformed in slightly different ways from the r_2 rounds at the beginning of the attack. Now we can rewrite Eqs. (5) as the form that

$$\text{Affine}'(Y, Z, X, K_{r_1}, U, Q + \overline{\text{L}}'(Y, p_{3s}, \cdots, p_{3sr_3}), K_{r_4}, K_{rem}, Q)$$
$$= \text{Affine}''(Y, Z, X, K_{r_1}, U, p_{3s}, \cdots, p_{3sr_3-1}, , K_{r_4}, K_{rem}, Q) = 0. \tag{6}$$

First MITM. So far, we have obtained a linear function system (6) including n affine equations with $3n + 3s(r_2 + r_3 - 1)$ variables $X, Z, K_{r_1}, U, p_{3s}, \cdots, p_{3sr_3-1}$, K_{r_4}, K_{rem}, Q and Y. Firstly, we need to collect the reduced equation system only involving variables X, Y, K_{r_1} and K_{r_4} by eliminating $\theta_1 = 6sr_2 + 6sr_3 - 3s + n - 3s(r_1 + r_2 + r_3 + r_4) = n - 3s(r_1 - r_2 - r_3 + r_4 + 1)$ variables Z, Q, $U, p_{3s}, \cdots, p_{3sr_3-1}$ and K_{rem} from the above equation system. Like [6], we can write the equation system into a matrix form as $M \cdot v = a$ where v is the set of $3n + 3s(r_2 + r_3 - 1)$ variables, a is a constant vector, M is the coefficient matrix over $\mathbb{F}_2$ of all variables in v. Rearrange v so that the variables needed to be eliminated are the first θ_1 elements of v. Then sweep out at least the first θ_1 columns of M by Gaussian elimination. We collect the last $n - \theta_1$ rows of the matrix to get $n - \theta_1$ linear equations on X, Y, K_{r_1} and K_{r_4} by multiplying the vector v. Now we have around $n - \theta_1 - 3s(r_1 - r_2 - r_3 + r_4 + 1)$ equations after this phase. Note that we implicitly add a condition that $r_1 - r_2 - r_3 + r_4 + 1 > 0$ to make the first MITM be valid. The remaining equations can be rewritten as the form of $\text{Affine}_1(K_{r_1}, X) = \text{Affine}_2(K_{r_4}, Y)$ where Affine_1 and Affine_2 are the sets of affine functions in terms of variables X, K_{r_1} and Y, K_{r_4}, respectively.

Now we can start going to describe the first MITM phase. If K_{r_1} is guessed, the corresponding output X of the first r_1 rounds can be calculated from pt and

K_{r_1}. Then we make a list $List_1$ to store 2^{3sr_1} values of K_{r_1} indexed by the values of $\mathsf{Affine}_1(K_{r_1}, X)$, i.e., the $3s(r_1 - r_2 - r_3 + r_4 + 1)$-bit vector calculated by K_{r_1} and X. Similarly, we guess K_{r_4} and calculate Y from ct. Make a list $List_2$ again to store 2^{3sr_4} guessed values of K_{r_4} indexed by the values of $\mathsf{Affine}_2(K_{r_4}, Y)$, i.e., $3s(r_1 - r_2 - r_3 + r_4 + 1)$-bit vector. We find the collisions between $List_1$ and $List_2$. The expected number of collisions is $2^{3sr_1 + 3sr_4 - 3s(r_1 - r_2 - r_3 + r_4 + 1)} = 2^{3s(r_2 + r_3 - 1)}$. We store these $2^{3s(r_2 + r_3 - 1)}$ pairs of (K_{r_1}, K_{r_4}) in list L_1.

Second MITM. In this phase, our aim is to obtain a system of affine equations only in terms of variables X, Y, K_{r_1}, K_{r_4}, Z and U. Concretely, we get the required equations from above Eqs. (6) by Gaussian elimination. In other words, after eliminating $\theta_2 = n - 3s(r_1 + r_2 + r_3 + r_4)$ (for K_{rem}) $+ (3sr_3 - 3s)$ (for $p_{3s}, \ldots, p_{3sr_3 - 1}$) $+ 3sr_3$ (for Q) $= n - 3s(r_1 + r_2 - r_3 + r_4 + 1)$ variables from the original equation system, there are $3s(r_1 + r_2 - r_3 + r_4 + 1)$ remaining equations. Then we rearrange the equations to collect a new form as $\mathsf{Affine}_3(Z, U) = \mathsf{Affine}_4(K_{r_1}, K_{r_4}, X, Y)$ where Affine_3 and Affine_4 are the sets of affine functions in terms of variables Z, U and K_{r_1}, K_{r_4}, X, Y, respectively.

Similarly, if we guess Z, the corresponding U can be calculated by SBoxes since each SBox is bijective. Then the $3s(r_1 + r_2 - r_3 + r_4 + 1)$-bit vector of $\mathsf{Affine}_3(Z, U)$ is known and we store it as the index of each of 2^{3sr_2} pairs (Z, U) in a list called $List_3$. We make another list $List_4$ to store $2^{3s(r_2 + r_3 - 1)}$ values of (K_{r_1}, K_{r_4}) from previous list L_1 indexed with the corresponding $3s(r_1 + r_2 - r_3 + r_4 + 1)$-bit vector of $\mathsf{Affine}_4(K_{r_1}, K_{r_4}, X, Y)$. Now we look for all collisions between $List_3$ and $List_4$. We can expect around $2^{3sr_2 + 3s(r_2 + r_3 - 1) - 3s(r_1 + r_2 - r_3 + r_4 + 1)} = 2^{3s(-r_1 + r_2 + 2r_3 - r_4 - 2)}$ collisions and store these collisions (K_{r_1}, K_{r_4}, Z, U) in a list called L_2.

Third MITM. Like the second MITM, we need to obtain a system of affine functions only in terms of variables X, Y, K_{r_1}, K_{r_4}, Z, U, $p_{3s}, \ldots, p_{3sr_3 - 1}$ and Q. Similarly, we eliminate $\theta_3 = n - 3s(r_1 + r_2 + r_3 + r_4)$ variables K_{rem} by Gaussian elimination method from above Eqs. (6), remaining $3s(r_1 + r_2 + r_3 + r_4)$ equations required. Then we rearrange these equations into a set of affine equations as $\mathsf{Affine}_5(p_{3s}, \ldots, p_{3sr_3 - 1}, Q) = \mathsf{Affine}_6(K_{r_1}, K_{r_4}, X, Y, Z, U)$ where Affine_5 and Affine_6 are the sets of affine functions.

Note that we still guess each value of Q, getting value of P and store 2^{3sr_3} $(p_{3s}, \ldots, p_{3sr_3 - 1}, Q)$ with the corresponding $3s(r_1 + r_2 + r_3 + r_4)$-bit vector value of $\mathsf{Affine}_5(p_{3s}, \ldots, p_{3sr_3 - 1}, Q)$ in a new list $List_5$. For each suite of (K_{r_1}, K_{r_4}, Z, U) in L_2, we store it with its value of $\mathsf{Affine}_6(K_{r_1}, K_{r_4}, Z, U)$ in another list $List_6$. Now we find the collisions between $List_5$ and $List_6$. The expected number of collisions is $2^{3sr_3 + 3s(-r_1 + r_2 + 2r_3 - r_4 - 2) - 3s(r_1 + r_2 + r_3 + r_4)} = 2^{3s(-2r_1 + 2r_3 - 2r_4 - 2)}$. Note that when we guess the correct majority values, there must exist at least one collision after three-step filtrating.

Once found a candidate suite of $(K_{r_1}, K_{r_4}, Z, U, p_{3s}, \cdots, p_{3sr_3 - 1}, Q)$, we can compute X, Y from known plaintext pt and ciphertext ct. Furthermore, we obtain K_{r_2} from relations $U = \overline{\mathsf{L}}(Z, X) + K_{r_2}$ and compute K_{r_3} from relations $Q = \overline{\mathsf{L}}'(Y, p_{3s}, \cdots, p_{3sr_3 - 1}) + K_{r_3}$. While guessing one majority values in the middle r_{guess} rounds, we can recover K_{rem} from Eqs. (6) in which any variable except K_{rem} is known. So far, we have got one candidate equivalent key. As the suite of K_{r_1}, K_{r_2}, K_{r_3}, K_{r_4} and K_{rem} resulting in the same majority value as the real majority value, we have recovered the entire key. Otherwise, we try another majority value again and restart the attack. We expect that we need to perform such checks around $2^{s(r-r_1-r_2-r_3-r_4)+3s(-2r_1+2r_3-2r_4-2)} = 2^{s(r-6-7r_1-r_2+5r_3-7r_4)}$ times. Finally, We give the formal attack as follows:

1. Split LowMC into 5 parts, in order of the first r_1 rounds, following r_2 rounds, middle r_{guess} rounds, next r_3 rounds and final r_4 rounds.
2. Denote the output bits after the first r_1 rounds by $X = [x_0, \cdots, x_{n-1}]$, the output bits after $r_1 + r_2$ rounds by $W = [w_0, \cdots, w_{n-1}]$, the input bits of the next r_3 rounds by $V = [v_0, \cdots, v_{n-1}]$ and the input bits of the final r_4 rounds by $Y = [y_0, \cdots, y_{n-1}]$.
3. Denote the input and output bits of the SBoxes in the r_2 rounds by $U = [u_0, \cdots, u_{3sr_2-1}]$ and $Z = [z_0, \cdots, z_{3sr_2-1}]$, the input and output bits of the SBoxes in the r_3 rounds by $P = [p_0, \cdots, p_{3sr_3-1}]$ and $Q = [q_0, \cdots, q_{3sr_3-1}]$.
4. Guess the majority values of input bits of the SBoxes in the middle r_{guess} rounds.
5. For each majority value guessed do:
   - Obtain the equation system $\mathsf{Affine}(Y, Z, x_{3s}, \cdots, x_{n-1}, K_{r_1}, K_{r_2}, K_{r_3}, K_{r_4}, K_{rem}, Q) = 0$.
   - Replace K_{r_2} by U, K_{r_3} by $p_{3s}, \cdots, p_{3sr_3-1}$. Then get the equation system $\mathsf{Affine}''(Y, Z, X, K_{r_1}, U, p_{3s}, \cdots, p_{3sr_3-1,}, K_{r_4}, K_{rem}, Q) = 0$.

   First MITM:
   - Eliminate $Z, Q, U, p_{3s}, \cdots, p_{3sr_3-1}$ and K_{rem} from the above equations and rewrite the equations as the form of $\mathsf{Affine}_1(K_{r_1}, X) = \mathsf{Affine}_2(K_{r_4}, Y)$.
   - For every value of K_{r_1} guessed, compute X by K_{r_1} and pt, and construct a list $List_1$ to store 2^{3sr_1} values of K_{r_1} with the corresponding values of $\mathsf{Affine}_1(K_{r_1}, X)$.
   - For every value of K_{r_4} guessed, compute Y by K_{r_4} and ct, and make a list $List_2$ to store 2^{3sr_4} values of K_{r_4} with the corresponding values of $\mathsf{Affine}_2(K_{r_4}, Y)$.
   - Find all collisions between list $List_1$ and $List_2$. Construct a list L_1 to store these $2^{3s(r_2+r_3-1)}$ collisions as (K_{r_1}, K_{r_4}).

   Second MITM:
   - Eliminate $p_{3s}, \cdots, p_{3sr_3-1}, Q$ and K_{rem} and rearrange the equations into the form of $\mathsf{Affine}_3(Z, U) = \mathsf{Affine}_4(K_{r_1}, K_{r_4}, X, Y)$.
   - For every Z possible value, obtain the corresponding U by Z and compute $\mathsf{Affine}_3(Z, U)$. Construct a list $List_3$ to store each pair of (Z, U) with its value of $\mathsf{Affine}_3(Z, U)$.
   - For every (K_{r_1}, K_{r_4}) in list L_1, compute $\mathsf{Affine}_4(K_{r_1}, K_{r_4}, X, Y)$ and make a list $List_4$ to store (K_{r_1}, K_{r_4}) indexed by the corresponding values of $\mathsf{Affine}_4(K_{r_1}, K_{r_4}, X, Y)$.

- Find the collisions between $List_3$ and $List_4$, and make a new list L_2 to store collisions as (K_{r_1}, K_{r_4}, Z, U).

Third MITM:

- Eliminate K_{rem} from the above equations and rearrange the equations into the form of $\mathsf{Affine}_5(p_{3s}, \cdots, p_{3sr_3-1}, Q) = \mathsf{Affine}_6(K_{r_1}, K_{r_4}, X, Y, Z, U)$.
- For every Q possible value, obtain the corresponding P by Q and compute $\mathsf{Affine}_5(p_{3s}, \cdots, p_{3sr_3-1}, Q)$. Construct a list $List_5$ to store each pair of $(p_{3s}, \cdots, p_{3sr_3-1}, Q)$ with its value of $\mathsf{Affine}_5(p_{3s}, \cdots, p_{3sr_3-1}, Q)$.
- For every (K_{r_1}, K_{r_4}, Z, U) in list L_2, compute $\mathsf{Affine}_6(K_{r_1}, K_{r_4}, X, Y, Z, U)$ and construct a list $List_6$ to store each pair of (K_{r_1}, K_{r_4}, Z, U) indexed by the corresponding values of $\mathsf{Affine}_6(K_{r_1}, K_{r_4}, X, Y, Z, U)$.
- Find the collisions between $List_5$ and $List_6$. For each candidate suite of $(K_{r_1}, K_{r_4}, Z, U, p_{3s}, \cdots, p_{3sr_3-1}, Q)$, calculate K_{r_2} from U, Z and X, K_{r_3} from $p_{3s}, \cdots, p_{3sr_3-1}$, Q and Y, K_{rem} from the original equations.
- When $K_{r_1}, K_{r_2}, K_{r_3}, K_{r_4}, K_{rem}$ are known, check if they result in the corresponding guessed majority values. Otherwise, guess another majority value and try the attack procedure again.

Remark 2. In fact, constructing two different lists in every step is not necessary. We can instead insert each new collision of $List_2$ with $List_1$ into a single hash table. By the same logic, we deal with the collisions from $List_3$ and $List_4$, $List_5$ and $List_6$. In this way, the total memory complexity will be slightly reduced.

5.2 Complexity Analysis

In order to make a more effective and meaningful comparison with [6], we also give our complexity analysis to the same extent. We firstly state some analysis that matters (for details referring to [6]):

- Obtaining original Eqs. (4) is equivalent to $2n + 3s(r_2 + r_3 - 1)$ times $(r - r_1 - r_4)$-round encryptions, in other words, equivalent to $(2n + 3s(r_2 + r_3 - 1)) \cdot \frac{r - r_1 - r_4}{r}$ encryptions.
- Calculating U from X and K is equivalent to the encryption of $2n$ base vectors limited to r_2 rounds. Hence, it consumes around $2n \cdot \frac{r_2}{r}$ encryptions. Similarly, calculating Q from Y and K costs around $2n \cdot \frac{r_3}{r}$ encryptions.
- In the first MITM, eliminating $\theta_1 = n - 3s(r_1 - r_2 - r_3 + r_4 + 1)$ variables from an $n \times (3n + 3s(r_2 + r_3 - 1))$ matrix using the Gaussian Elimination consumes about $\frac{n \cdot \theta_1 \cdot (3n + 3s(r_2 + r_3 - 1))}{2rn^2}$ encryptions.
- Similarly, in the second MITM, eliminating $\theta_2 = n - 3s(r_1 + r_2 - r_3 + r_4 + 1)$ variables consumes around $\frac{n \cdot \theta_2 \cdot (3n + 3s(r_2 + r_3 - 1))}{2rn^2}$ encryptions. And in the third MITM, eliminating $\theta_3 = n - 3s(r_1 + r_2 + r_3 + r_4)$ variables costs around $\frac{n \cdot \theta_3 \cdot (3n + 3s(r_2 + r_3 - 1))}{2rn^2}$ encryptions.
- Solving the equation system to obtain K_{rem} requires one entire Gaussian Elimination which is equivalent to $\frac{(n - 3s(r_1 + r_2 + r_3 + r_4))^3}{2rn^2}$ encryptions.

Note that for every majority value guessed in the r_{guess} rounds, we need to perform all three MITM stages. It costs $2^{s(r-r_1-r_2-r_3-r_4)}$ times thereby. Now we analyze the costs of computing values from two sides of equations for every MITM. In order to evaluate $\mathsf{Affine}_1(K_{r_1}, X)$, we firstly need to compute X from pt and K_{r_1}, whose cost is equivalent to one r_1-round encryption. Furthermore, for values of $\mathsf{Affine}_1(K_{r_1}, X)$, we compute $3s(r_1-r_2-r_3+r_4+1)$ linear equations in terms of $(3sr_1 + n)$ bits of K_{r_1}, X, which requires about $3s(r_1 - r_2 - r_3 + r_4 + 1) \cdot (3sr_1 + n)$ bit operations. By the same logic, computing the values of $\mathsf{Affine}_2(K_{r_4}, Y)$ costs around $3s(r_1 - r_2 - r_3 + r_4 + 1) \cdot (3sr_4 + n)$ bit operations. As above, the time complexity in the first MITM is $Time_1 = 2^{3sr_1} \cdot (\frac{r_1}{r} + \frac{3s(r_1-r_2-r_3+r_4+1)\cdot(3sr_1+n)}{2rn^2}) + 2^{3sr_4} \cdot (\frac{r_4}{r} + \frac{3s(r_1-r_2-r_3+r_4+1)\cdot(3sr_4+n)}{2rn^2})$ encryptions. After this step, the number of pairs of (K_{r_1}, K_{r_4}) stored in L_1 is $2^{3s(r_2+r_3-1)}$.

Next we compute the values of $\mathsf{Affine}_3(Z, U)$ and $\mathsf{Affine}_4(K_{r_1}, K_{r_4}, X, Y)$ from the K_{r_1}, K_{r_4} in L_1 and Z. By the same perspective as above, the time complexity in the second MITM is $Time_2 = 2^{3sr_2} \cdot (\frac{r_2}{r} + \frac{3s(r_1+r_2-r_3+r_4+1)\cdot(6sr_2)}{2rn^2}) + 2^{3s(r_2+r_3-1)} \cdot (\frac{r_1+r_4}{r} + \frac{3s(r_1+r_2-r_3+r_4+1)\cdot(3s(r_1+r_4)+2n)}{2rn^2})$ encryptions. There remains about $2^{3s(-r_1+r_2+2r_3-r_4-2)}$ suites of (K_{r_1}, K_{r_4}, Z, U).

Finally, evaluating the values of $\mathsf{Affine}_5(p_{3s}, \cdots, p_{3sr_3-1}, Q)$ and $\mathsf{Affine}_6(K_{r_1}, K_{r_4}, X, Y, Z, U)$ costs around $Time_3 = 2^{3sr_3} \cdot (\frac{r_3}{r} + \frac{3s(r_1+r_2+r_3+r_4)\cdot(6sr_3-3s)}{2rn^2}) + 2^{3s(r_2+2r_3-r_1-r_4-2)} \cdot (\frac{r_1+r_2+r_4}{r} + \frac{3s(r_1+r_4+r_2+r_3)\cdot(3s(r_1+r_4)+2n+6sr_3)}{2rn^2})$ encryptions. The expected number of collisions in this process is $2^{3s(-2r_1+2r_3-2r_4-2)}$. Hence, the total time complexity T is

$$2^{s(r-r_1-r_2-r_3-r_4)} \times [Time_1 + Time_2 + Time_3 + 2^{3s(-2r_1+2r_3-2r_4-2)}$$
$$+ (2n + 3s(r_2 + r_3 - 1)) \cdot \frac{r - r_1 - r_4}{r} + \frac{n \cdot \theta_1 \cdot (3n + 3s(r_2 + r_3 - 1))}{2rn^2}$$
$$+ \frac{n \cdot \theta_2 \cdot (3n + 3s(r_2 + r_3 - 1))}{2rn^2} + \frac{n \cdot \theta_3 \cdot (3n + 3s(r_2 + r_3 - 1))}{2rn^2}$$
$$+ 2n \cdot (\frac{r_2}{r} + \frac{r_3}{r}) + \frac{(n - 3s(r_1 + r_2 + r_3 + r_4))^3}{2rn^2}].$$

Based on Condition 3, the values of r_1, r_2, r_3 and r_4 are limited not too large when $n = 128, 192, 256$. We find out optimal parameters by exhaustively searching all values satisfying the conditions for different LowMC instances. As for memory complexity, the total memory complexity in the three stages is not more than

$$3s(r_1 - r_2 - r_3 + r_4 + 1) \cdot (2^{3sr_1} + 2^{3sr_4})$$
$$+ 3s(r_1 + r_2 - r_3 + r_4 + 1) \cdot (2^{3sr_2} + 2^{3s(r_2+r_3-1)})$$
$$+ 3s(r_1 + r_2 + r_3 + r_4) \cdot (2^{3sr_3} + 2^{3s(-r_1+r_2+2r_3-r_4-2)}).$$

We take optimal parameters $r_1 = r_4 = 5$, $r_2 = r_3 = 3$ when $n = 128$, $s = 1$, $r = 103$, the time complexity is around $2^{99.7}$ encryptions with 2^{21} bits of memory, which is slightly faster than the two-stage MITM attack. For $n = 128$,

$s = 10$, $r = 10$, we take $r_1 = r_2 = r_3 = r_4 = 1$, which results in time complexity $2^{89.6}$ encryptions and memory 2^{38} bits. Note that our memory complexity is not more than the original attack under these parameters. However, our attacks are around $2^{1.3}$ times faster than the original attacks. For other LowMC instances, we also improve the previous results, as shown in Table 1.

5.3   Speedup for Cases of $r_1 = r_2 = r_3 = r_4 = 1$

Similar to [6], we also adopt the Gray Code tricks in [7] to speed up our attacks. From [7, Section 4], we know that evaluating a quadratic function using the algorithm (b) described in page 209 is faster than the naive evaluations when the degree of function is 2. A detailed description of the Gray Code can be referred to Appendix B.

For example, we need to compute $\mathsf{Affine}_1(K_{r_1}, X)$ for every guessed K_{r_1} and this is a quadratic function in terms of K_{r_1} since X is quadratic expressions on K_{r_1} when $r_1 = r_2 = r_3 = r_4 = 1$. Theorem 1 in [7] indicates that we can evaluate t-variable quadratic Boolean functions in $2 \cdot 2^t$ bit operations. Therefore, the time complexity of evaluating $\mathsf{Affine}_1(K_{r_1}, X)$ become $2^{3sr_1+1} \cdot \frac{3s(r_1-r_2-r_3+r_4+1)}{2rn^2}$ encryptions instead of $2^{3sr_1} \cdot (\frac{r_1}{r} + \frac{3s(r_1-r_2-r_3+r_4+1)\cdot(3sr_1+n)}{2rn^2})$. We can evaluate the Affine_2, Affine_3, Affine_4, Affine_5 and Affine_6 in same way. The time complexities of the three MITM stages are $T_{SP_1} = (2^{3sr_1+1} + 2^{3sr_4+1}) \cdot \frac{3s(r_1-r_2-r_3+r_4+1)}{2rn^2}$ encryptions, $T_{SP_2} = (2^{3sr_1+1} + 2^{3sr_4+1} + 2^{3sr_2+1}) \cdot \frac{3s(r_1+r_2-r_3+r_4+1)}{2rn^2}$ encryptions and $T_{SP_3} = (2^{3sr_1+1} + 2^{3sr_4+1} + 2^{3sr_2+1} + +2^{3sr_3+1}) \cdot \frac{3s(r_1+r_2+r_3+r_4)}{2rn^2}$ encryptions.

When $r_1 = r_2 = r_3 = r_4 = 1$, we have $T_{SP_1} + T_{SP_2} + T_{SP_3} < Time_1 + Time_2 + Time_3$. For $n = 128$, $s = 10$, $r = 10$ or 12, we improve the attack by a factor of $2^{8.5}$ than the original two-stage MITM attack. For all other instances we improve by a factor of around $2^{8.5}$ than the original attacks as presented in Table 1.

5.4   Success Probability

By discussions in Sect. 4, we can estimate the success probability of the three-stage MITM attack. When LowMC is divided into 5 sections: $r = r_1 + r_2 + r_{guess} + r_3 + r_4$, $pro(r_1, r_2, r_3, r_4)$ can be seen as the success probability of the attacks. The results of all instances are showed in Table 1. We can see that success probability is close to 1 as n goes to larger.

6   Experimental Verification

To verify the theoretical model of the three-stage MITM in this paper, we present practical attacks on several small variants of LowMC instances with partial SBoxes layers. All the experiments were implemented in Sage on a desktop computer with Intel Core i7-8700 CPU @ 3.20 GHz processor and 16 GB of memory. We ran every attack on 500 randomly generated LowMC instances and gave the average practical attack time divided by the time of one encryption.

We implemented the three-stage MITM attack described in Sect. 5 and tested the experiment of the two-stage MITM attack according to the source codes given in [6] on LowMC instances with $n = 12$, $s = 1$, $r = \lceil 0.8 \times \lfloor \frac{n}{s} \rfloor \rceil = 10$, whose one encryption time averagely is $2^{-9.00}$ seconds. We take the parameters of the two-stage and three-stage MITM attacks as $(r_1, r_2, r_3) = (1,1,1)$ and $(r_1, r_2, r_3, r_4) = (1,1,1,1)$, respectively. Furthermore, we also adopt the GrayCode tricks to speed up all these attacks. According to our experimental results, the two-stage MITM and three-stage MITM attacks cost around averagely 7.52 s and 4.46 s, equivalent to $2^{11.91}$ and $2^{11.16}$ encryptions respectively. The corresponding theoretical time complexities are $2^{11.60}$ and $2^{10.85}$ encryptions. For $n = 12$, $s = 1$, $r = \lfloor \frac{n}{s} \rfloor = 12$, whose average time for one encryption is $2^{-8.77}$ seconds, the two-stage MITM and three-stage MITM attacks take around averagely 29.18 s and 17.64 s, equal to $2^{13.64}$ encryptions[2] and $2^{12.91}$ encryptions, respectively. The corresponding theoretical time complexities are $2^{13.60}$ and $2^{12.83}$ encryptions.

We also implemented attacks on LowMC instances with $n = 16$, $s = 1$, $r = \lceil 0.8 \times \lfloor \frac{n}{s} \rfloor \rceil = 13$ and $(r_1, r_2, r_3, r_4) = (1,1,1,1)$ or $(2,1,1,1)$, where the time of one encryption we obtained is $2^{-8.41}$ seconds. Our experimental results indicate that $(2,1,1,1)$ are the better parameters with time cost 49.74 s than $(1,1,1,1)$ with 85.61 s, whose time complexities are equal to $2^{14.04}$ encryptions and $2^{14.83}$ encryptions, respectively. The corresponding theoretical time complexities are $2^{13.63}$ and $2^{14.24}$ encryptions. The two-stage MITM attack takes 90.07 s, i.e., $2^{14.90}$ encryptions, whose theoretical time complexity is $2^{15.02}$ encryptions.

Our experimental results show that the three-stage MITM attack can recover the full key bits successfully with better time complexity than the two-stage MITM attack. And the experimental results match well with the theoretical evaluations.

7   Conclusion

In this paper, we give a precise analysis for the independence of multiple-round subkey bits and derive the method estimating the success probability of multi-stage MITM attacks. We present an improved attack on LowMC instances with partial SBoxes layers, which is a generalization of the two-stage MITM attack. Our experiments on small variants of LowMC instances show that our attack is more effective for LowMC instances with partial SBoxes layers. However, our improved attack relies on the equivalent transformations of key schedule scheme of LowMC instances, so it is more suitable for cryptanalysis of instances with partial SBoxes layers than with full SBoxes layers. To get further analysis of

---

[2] For this instance, the authors in [6] obtained the time complexity as $2^{7.402}$ encryptions in [6], which has a striking difference with our result $2^{13.64}$ encryptions. The main reason is the different ways to capture the time of one encryption. We ran the whole 2^{13} times encryptions to obtain the total time divided by 2^{13} as the time of one encryption, while the authors in [6] performed only one encryption to get the time. In fact, our way to capture the time of one encryption is closer to the real situation, and it is more reasonable to convert time complexity using this time.

LowMC instances with full SBoxes layers, maybe we need to find new linear relations on variables.

Note that multi-stage MITM attacks depend on various linearized SBoxes techniques. Generalizing from two to three stages gave us better results, however we found that extending to more stages does not give us any further improvement. The main reason might be that even with more parts, only one part allows us to introduce fewer variables. But if we can find more ways to linearize SBoxes to construct more stages MITM model, maybe we can further reduce the total time complexity (but accompanied a slight increase in memory complexity). Studying how to linearize Sbox of LowMC more effectively is an important topic. We leave it as the future work.

Acknowledgement. This work was supported by the National Natural Science Foundation of China (Grant No. 61872359, 62122085 and 61936008), the National Key R&D Program of China (Grant No. 2020YFB1805402), and the Youth Innovation Promotion Association of Chinese Academy of Sciences.

A   The Inverse of LowMC SBox

Lemma 1 is true for the inverse of LowMC SBoxes. Let $f = t_0 \cdot t_1 + t_0 \cdot t_2 + t_1 \cdot t_2$, then it can be expressed as following form:

$$
\begin{aligned}
s_0 &= t_0 + t_1 + t_1 \cdot t_2 & &= f \cdot (t_1 + t_2 + 1) + t_0 + t_1, \\
s_1 &= t_1 + t_0 \cdot t_2 & &= f \cdot (t_0 + t_2 + 1) + t_1, \\
s_2 &= t_0 + t_1 + t_2 + t_0 \cdot t_1 & &= f \cdot (t_0 + t_1 + 1) + t_0 + t_1 + t_2.
\end{aligned}
$$

B   Gray Code Technique

A classical Gray Code is an ordering of the binary numeral system such that two successive values differ in only one bit (binary digit), which allows to derive each object from the preceding object by changing a small (constant) part. Due to this feature, Gray Code usually can be used to speed up certain computations in many scenarios. The techniques used in this paper are the same as in [6] so we refer the interested readers to page 9 in [6] for more details. We only give a simple introduction as follows:

Definition 2 [7]. *For $i \in \mathbf{N}$, $GaryCode(i) = i \oplus (i \gg 1)$, where $\oplus$ denotes addition in $\mathbf{F}_2$, and $i \gg k$ denotes binary right shift of the integer i by k bits.*

Note that hamming difference between $GrayCode(i)$ and $GrayCode(i+1)$ is always 1 for all values of i. The idea of the speedup technique is instead of ordering the majority guesses in lexicographic order, we choose the order defined by the Gray Code, i.e., in the i-th step the majority guess sequence is the binary string defined by the bits of $GrayCode(i)$.

References

1. LowMC challenge (2020). https://lowmcchallenge.github.io
2. Reference code, updated 2017. https://github.com/LowMC/lowmc/blob/master/determine_rounds.py
3. Albrecht, M.R., Rechberger, C., Schneider, T., Tiessen, T., Zohner, M.: Ciphers for MPC and FHE. In: Oswald, E., Fischlin, M. (eds.) EUROCRYPT 2015. LNCS, vol. 9056, pp. 430–454. Springer, Heidelberg (2015). https://doi.org/10.1007/978-3-662-46800-5_17
4. Banik, S., Barooti, K., Caforio, A., Vaudenay, S.: Memory-efficient single data-complexity attacks on LowMC using partial sets. IACR Cryptol. ePrint Arch. 688 (2022). https://eprint.iacr.org/2022/688
5. Banik, S., Barooti, K., Durak, F.B., Vaudenay, S.: Cryptanalysis of LowMC instances using single plaintext/ciphertext pair. IACR Trans. Symmetric Cryptol. **2020**(4), 130–146 (2020). https://doi.org/10.46586/tosc.v2020.i4.130-146
6. Banik, S., Barooti, K., Vaudenay, S., Yan, H.: New attacks on LowMC instances with a single plaintext/ciphertext pair. In: Tibouchi, M., Wang, H. (eds.) ASIACRYPT 2021. LNCS, vol. 13090, pp. 303–331. Springer, Cham (2021). https://doi.org/10.1007/978-3-030-92062-3_11
7. Bouillaguet, C., Chen, H.-C., Cheng, C.-M., Chou, T., Niederhagen, R., Shamir, A., Yang, B.-Y.: Fast exhaustive search for polynomial systems in $\mathbb{F}_2$. In: Mangard, S., Standaert, F.-X. (eds.) CHES 2010. LNCS, vol. 6225, pp. 203–218. Springer, Heidelberg (2010). https://doi.org/10.1007/978-3-642-15031-9_14
8. Dinur, I.: Cryptanalytic applications of the polynomial method for solving multivariate equation systems over GF(2). In: Canteaut, A., Standaert, F.-X. (eds.) EUROCRYPT 2021. LNCS, vol. 12696, pp. 374–403. Springer, Cham (2021). https://doi.org/10.1007/978-3-030-77870-5_14
9. Dinur, I., Liu, Y., Meier, W., Wang, Q.: Optimized interpolation attacks on LowMC. In: Iwata, T., Cheon, J.H. (eds.) ASIACRYPT 2015. LNCS, vol. 9453, pp. 535–560. Springer, Heidelberg (2015). https://doi.org/10.1007/978-3-662-48800-3_22
10. Dobraunig, C., Eichlseder, M., Mendel, F.: Higher-order cryptanalysis of LowMC. In: Kwon, S., Yun, A. (eds.) ICISC 2015. LNCS, vol. 9558, pp. 87–101. Springer, Cham (2016). https://doi.org/10.1007/978-3-319-30840-1_6
11. Liu, F., Isobe, T., Meier, W.: Cryptanalysis of full LowMC and LowMC-M with algebraic techniques. In: Malkin, T., Peikert, C. (eds.) CRYPTO 2021. LNCS, vol. 12827, pp. 368–401. Springer, Cham (2021). https://doi.org/10.1007/978-3-030-84252-9_13
12. Liu, F., Wang, G., Meier, W., Sarkar, S., Isobe, T.: Algebraic meet-in-the-middle attack on LowMC. IACR Cryptol. ePrint Arch. 19 (2022). https://eprint.iacr.org/2022/019
13. Rechberger, C., Soleimany, H., Tiessen, T.: Cryptanalysis of low-data instances of full LowMCv2. IACR Trans. Symmetric Cryptol **2018**(3), 163–181 (2018). https://doi.org/10.13154/tosc.v2018.i3.163-181
14. Zaverucha, G.: The picnic signature algorithm specifications, version 3.0. https://github.com/microsoft/Picnic/blob/master/spec/spec-v3.0.pdf

Collision-Based Attacks on White-Box Implementations of the AES Block Cipher

Jiqiang Lu[1,2,3]($\boxtimes$), Mingxue Wang[1], Can Wang[1], and Chen Yang[4]

[1] School of Cyber Science and Technology, Beihang University, Beijing, China
{lvjiqiang,wangmx,canwang}@buaa.edu.cn
[2] Guangxi Key Laboratory of Cryptography and Information Security, Guilin, China
[3] Hangzhou Innovation Institute, Beihang University, Hangzhou, China
[4] Institute of Software, Chinese Academy of Sciences, Beijing, China
yangchen@iscas.ac.cn

Abstract. Since Chow et al. introduced white-box cryptography with a white-box implementation of the AES block cipher in 2002, a few attacks and improvements on Chow et al.'s white-box AES implementation have been presented, particularly Lepoint et al. gave a collision-based attack with a time complexity of about 2^{22} in 2013. Lepoint et al.'s attack involves three phases at a high level: first defining a collision function to recover a round's keyed S-box transformations each from protected input by a white-box encoding to original output, then recovering the output encoding of this round, and finally recovering the round key bytes of the next round by testing every key candidate under a statistical distinguisher. In this paper, we give two extensions to Lepoint et al.'s collision-based attack, one is by executing Lepoint et al.'s first phase for two consecutive rounds and then recovering the round key of the latter round directly from the two recovered SubBytes outputs of the two rounds, and the other is by executing Lepoint et al.'s first phase for two consecutive rounds, then executing Lepoint et al.'s second phase for the former round and finally recovering the round key of the latter round directly from the recovered keyed S-box transformations of the latter round. Compared with Lepoint et al.'s approach, the two extensions avoid the last one or two phases and the associated prerequisites, and thus they can attack a broader range of white-box implementations, specifically, the first extension targets SPN ciphers, and the second extension targets both SPN and Feistel ciphers. As an example, we apply the first extension to attack Bai et al.'s white-box AES implementation with an expected time complexity of about 2^{20} S-box computations. Together with some previous work, our work indicates that all the previously published white-box AES implementations with external encodings are not practically secure, and white-box implementation designers should pay attention to these new collision-based approaches.

Keywords: White-box cryptography · Block cipher · AES · Collision attack

1   Introduction

In 2002, Chow et al. [14] introduced white-box cryptography and proposed a white-box implementation of the AES [31] block cipher. White-box cryptography works under the so-called white-box security model, which assumes an attacker has full access to the execution environment and execution details of a software implementation. At present, one research direction on white-box cryptography is the design and analysis of white-box implementations of existing (mostly standardised) cryptographic algorithms [2,6,12,13,15,17,21–23,25–27,29,33–35], the other research direction is the design and analysis of new dedicated white-box algorithms for a full security [7,10,11,20], and both the directions have their own pros and cons. The first research direction can be further classified into two categories: one is the traditional white-box cryptography with external encodings on both plaintext and ciphertext sides, like Chow et al.'s white-box AES implementation in 2002, and the other is the newly emerging white-box cryptography without external encodings (or without external encoding on plaintext or ciphertext side, or a similar assumption) [4,9,13,25,26,32], mainly starting with Bos et al.'s differential computation analysis (DCA) [13] in 2016. Generally speaking, it is understood that white-box implementation for an existing cryptographic algorithm is hardly possible to achieve the full security as in the black-box model, but it is expected to provide some realistic protection.

Our work is focused on white-box AES implementation with external encodings on both plaintext and ciphertext sides, which represents a conservative implementation deadline in some sense. Following Chow et al.'s work, a number of white-box AES implementation designs and attacks has been published [3,6,17,23,27–29,33,35], mainly as follows. In 2004, Billet et al. [6] attacked Chow et al.'s implementation for the first time, with a time complexity of about 2^{30} (to extract key). In 2008, Michiels et al. [29] gave an attack on white-box implementations of a generic class of so-called substitution linear transformation ciphers. In 2009, Xiao and Lai [35] proposed a white-box AES implementation by putting two S-boxes into a white-box table and expressing the ShiftRows operation as a matrix multiplication. In 2010, Karroumi [23] proposed a white-box AES implementation based on the dual cipher concept [5]. In 2012, De Mulder et al. [16] attacked Xiao and Lai's implementation with a time complexity of 2^{32} using Biryukov et al.'s affine equivalence technique [8]. In 2013, Lepoint et al. [27] improved Billet et al.'s attack and gave a collision-based attack, either of which broke Chow et al.'s and Karroumi's implementations with a time complexity of about 2^{22}. In 2014, Luo et al. [28] improved Xiao and Lai's implementation by performing the ShiftRows operation as a series of white-box tables and using both linear and non-linear white-box operations. In 2018, Bai et al. [3] attacked Luo et al.'s implementation with a time complexity of 2^{44} by combining Billet et al.'s, Michiels et al.'s and Tolhuizen's attacks [33], and proposed a white-box AES implementation by expressing an original state byte as two or more shares protected with different encodings, and got a lower security bound of over 2^{60} among a variety of attack methods including Billet et al.'s and Lepoint et al.'s attacks.

Being one of the best currently published attacks on Chow et al.'s white-box AES implementation, Lepoint et al.'s collision-based attack involves three phases at a high level: first defining a collision function to recover a round's keyed S-box transformations each from protected input by a white-box encoding operation to original output, then recovering the output encoding operation of this round, and finally recovering the correct round key bytes of the next round by testing every possible candidate under a distinguisher that is a variant of the collision function. In this paper, we give two extensions to Lepoint et al.'s attack, specifically, if we execute Lepoint et al.'s first phase for two consecutive rounds, we have two different ways to recover the round key easily, so that Lepoint et al.'s last one or two phases are not needed, particularly there is no need to test every key candidate in the last key-recovery phase. One way is to directly compute the round key (of the former or latter round, depending on round representation) at once from the recovered original outputs of the protected keyed S-boxes of the two rounds, which is feasible because a round key can be computed from the two original SubBytes outputs of two consecutive rounds for an substitution-permutation network (SPN) cipher. The other way is to further execute Lepoint et al.'s second phase for the former round to recover its output encoding operation, then recover the original input of a protected keyed S-box in the latter round by applying the inverse of the recovered output encoding (of the former round) to the protected input of the keyed S-box (of the latter round), and finally compute directly the key byte at once from the recovered original input-output pair of the keyed S-box. Clearly, both the extensions execute Lepoint et al.'s first phase twice, but avoid Lepoint et al.'s last one or two phases, particularly Lepoint et al.'s last key-recovery phase where a series of probabilistic exhaustive computations is replaced with a simple deterministic computation, thus the extensions are not restricted by those inherent prerequisites of Lepoint et al.'s last one or two phases, as a consequence they can attack a broader range of white-box AES implementations than Lepoint et al.'s approach. Finally, we apply the first extension to attack Bai et al.'s white-box AES implementations [3] for the first time, with an expected time complexity of about 2^{20} S-box computations. We do not find a good white-box implementation example for the second extension, but nevertheless it can clearly be applied to those already attacked by Lepoint et al.'s approach. All in all, the two extensions can attack a broader range of white-box implementations than Lepoint et al.'s approach, they are not limited to white-box AES implementations, the first extension is applicable to similar white-box implementations of SPN ciphers, the second extension is applicable to similar white-box implementations of both SPN and Feistel ciphers, and white-box implementation designers should pay attention to these new approaches, particularly the first extension, which does not need to recover the internal encodings and only needs to know whether an encoding produces different outputs for different inputs, which is the first such key-recovery attack on white-box AES implementation with external encodings, to the best of our knowledge. Besides, we also analyse the security of Xiao and Lai's and Luo et al.'s white-box AES implementations [28,35] against our extensions, and our small-scale experiments under different (encodings, round key) combinations show that the rank of the concerned linear system is much less than the number of the involved unknowns and thus they can resist our extensions, which suggests that building a white-box table with two S-boxes is preferable to building a white-box table with a single S-box in this sense, but nevertheless we leave it as an open problem whether there are such encodings that the rank of the corresponding linear system is slightly less than the number of the involved unknowns.

The remainder of the paper is organised as follows. In the next section, we describe the notation, the AES block cipher and Chow et al.'s white-box AES implementation. We describe the two extensions to Lepoint et al.'s attack in Sect. 3, apply the first extension to Bai et al.'s white-box AES implementation in Sect. 4, and discuss other applications and some related work in Sect. 5. Section 6 concludes this paper.

2 Preliminaries

In this section, we give the notation used throughout this paper, and briefly describe the AES block cipher and Chow et al.'s white-box AES implementation.

2.1 Notation

In all descriptions we assume that a number without a prefix expresses a decimal number, and a number with prefix $0x$ expresses a hexadecimal number. We use the following notation throughout this paper.

|| bit string concatenation
∘ functional composition
⊕ bitwise exclusive OR (XOR)
$\oplus_x$ XOR with a value x
⊗ polynomial multiplication modulo $x^8 + x^4 + x^3 + x + 1$ in $GF(2^8)$
$\lfloor x \rfloor$ the largest integer that is less than or equal to a value x

2.2 The AES Block Cipher

AES [31] is a 128-bit SPN cipher with a user key of 128, 192 or 256 bits and a total number of 10, 12 or 14 rounds, respectively. We focus on the 128-bit key version in this paper. AES uses the following four elementary operations to construct its round function.

- The AddRoundKey (ARK) operation XORs a 4×4 byte array with a 16-byte subkey.
- The SubBytes (SB) operation applies the same 8×8-bit bijective S-box (denoted below by **S**) 16 times in parallel to a 4×4 byte array.

- The ShiftRows (SR) operation cyclically shifts the i-th row of a 4×4 byte array to the left by i bytes, $(0 \leq i \leq 3)$.
- The MixColumns (MC) operation pre-multiplies a 4×4 byte array by the following fixed 4×4 byte matrix $\mathbf{M}$:

$$\mathbf{M} = \begin{pmatrix} 0x02 \ 0x03 \ 0x01 \ 0x01 \\ 0x01 \ 0x02 \ 0x03 \ 0x01 \\ 0x01 \ 0x01 \ 0x02 \ 0x03 \\ 0x03 \ 0x01 \ 0x01 \ 0x02 \end{pmatrix}.$$

The encryption procedure of AES takes as input a 128-bit plaintext, represented as a 4×4 byte array, XORs it with a 128-bit subkey K_0, and finally goes through 10 rounds iteratively, with the i-th round being ARK(MC ∘ SR ∘ SB$(\cdot), K_i$) for $i = 1, 2, \cdots, 9$, and the last round being ARK(SR ∘ SB$(\cdot), K_{10}$). Note that there are different equivalent representations for a round. We refer the reader to [31] for the detailed specifications of AES.

2.3   Chow et al.'s White-Box AES Implementation

Chow et al.'s implementation can be seen as being built by first implementing the original AES as a series of look-up tables (in the black-box model) and then adding white-box operations to protect both input and output of each table, given a user key.

First, implement the original AES as a series of look-up tables, where a round starts with an ARK operation. Let X_{r-1} represents the r-th round input ($r = 1, 2, \cdots, 10$, X_0 is plaintext), then an encryption round is MC ∘ SR ∘ SB$(X_{r-1} \oplus K_{r-1})$ for the first nine rounds or SR∘SB$(X_9 \oplus K_9) \oplus K_{10}$ for the last round. Since all the elementary operations are byte-oriented, the MC operation is column-wise on the input byte array and the SR operation is just a reordering of the input bytes, the effect of SR can be annihilated by determining the four S-boxes that constitute an input column of the MC operation. For each round, define 16 keyed S-boxes called T-boxes, as follows,

$$\mathbf{T}_i^r(x) = \mathbf{S}(x \oplus \hat{K}_{r-1,i}), \quad r = 1, 2, \cdots, 9, \quad i = 0, 1, \cdots, 15;$$
$$\mathbf{T}_i^{10}(x) = \mathbf{S}(x \oplus \hat{K}_{9,i}) \oplus \hat{K}_{10,i}, \quad i = 0, 1, \cdots, 15,$$

where $\hat{K}_{r-1,i}$ is the corresponding byte of K_{r-1} due to the SR operation. For the MC multiplication to an input column of four bytes, a table taking as input the whole input column takes a storage of $2^{32} \times 32 = 2^{37}$ bits, which is too costly. To reduce the storage complexity, it is preferable to split such an MC multiplication into four partial multiplications and finally summate them to obtain the original output, say,

$$\mathbf{M}(\mathbf{S}(x_0 \oplus \hat{K}_{r-1,0}), \mathbf{S}(x_1 \oplus \hat{K}_{r-1,1}), \mathbf{S}(x_2 \oplus \hat{K}_{r-1,2}), \mathbf{S}(x_3 \oplus \hat{K}_{r-1,3}))$$
$$= \mathbf{MC}_0(\mathbf{S}(x_0 \oplus \hat{K}_{r-1,0}) \oplus \mathbf{MC}_1(\mathbf{S}(x_1 \oplus \hat{K}_{r-1,1}) \oplus \mathbf{MC}_2(\mathbf{S}(x_2 \oplus \hat{K}_{r-1,2}) \oplus$$
$$\mathbf{MC}_3(\mathbf{S}(x_3 \oplus \hat{K}_{r-1,3}),$$

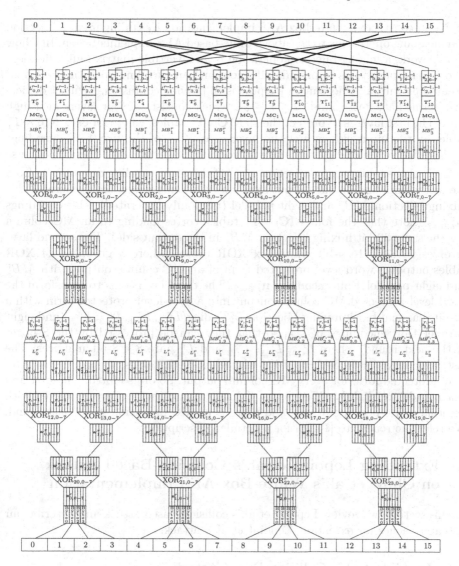

Fig. 1. A typical round of Chow et al.'s white-box AES implementation

where (x_0, x_1, x_2, x_3) represents an input of four bytes, and $\mathbf{MC}_l$ represents the corresponding 32×8-bit strip of the $\mathbf{M}$ matrix ($l = 0, 1, 2, 3$), i.e. $\mathbf{M} = (\mathbf{MC}_0 || \mathbf{MC}_1 || \mathbf{MC}_2 || \mathbf{MC}_3)$. Each $\mathbf{MC}_l \circ \mathbf{T}_i^r$ table is 8-bit to 32-bit, thus the four tables corresponding to an output column take a storage of $4 \times 2^8 \times 32 = 2^{15}$ bits, and there are a total of 16 such tables in a round. The XOR operations can be easily implemented with tables. This completes a table-based implementation of a typical round of AES, and the last round is simple, as there is no MC operation.

Next, construct a white-box AES implementation by adding mixing bijection and encoding operations to the above table-based AES implementation. In Chow et al.'s work, a mixing bijection operation is an invertible matrix multiplication, whose main purpose is to provide diffusion, and an encoding operation is a non-linear substitution, whose main purpose is to provide confusion. Figure 1 depicts an intermediate r-th round ($2 \leq r \leq 9$), which consists of four layers at a high level. The first layer is to protect the 16 $\mathbf{MC}_l \circ \mathbf{T}_i^r$ tables, where for each $\mathbf{MC}_l \circ \mathbf{T}_i^r$ table, on the input side is first the inverses $\mathbf{e}_{*,*}^{r-1,-1}$ of the two 4-bit encodings $\mathbf{e}_{*,*}^{r-1}$ of the corresponding output byte from the last round and then the inverse $L_{*,*}^{r-1,-1}$ of the 8-bit mixing bijection $L_{*,*}^{r-1}$ of the corresponding output byte from the last round, and on the output side is a (randomly generated) general 32-bit mixing bijection MB_*^r and eight parallel (randomly generated) 4-bit encodings $\mathbf{m}_{*,0-7}^r$ (note that the four $\mathbf{MC}_l \circ \mathbf{T}_i^r$ tables corresponding to an MC column use the same 32-bit mixing bijection MB_*^r in the output side). The second layer involves 96 8-bit to 4-bit white-box XOR tables, where a group of 24 XOR tables output a word-level protected form of an MC column output with MB_*^r and eight parallel 4-bit encodings $\mathbf{u}_{*,0-7}^r$. The third layer aims to transform the word-level protected MC column output into a byte-level protected form with a 32-bit diagonal block mixing bijection $L_*^r = \mathrm{diag}(L_{*,0}^r, L_{*,1}^r, L_{*,2}^r, L_{*,3}^r)$ and eight parallel 4-bit encodings $\mathbf{u}_{*,0-7}^r$, so that they can be processed by the S-boxes of the next round, where $L_{*,0}^r$, $L_{*,1}^r$, $L_{*,2}^r$ and $L_{*,3}^r$ are 8×8-bit matrices. The last layer involves 96 8-bit to 4-bit white-box XOR tables, to produce a byte-level protected form for every MC column output. So on, so forth. The first and last rounds are slightly different, as plaintext and ciphertext are protected with external white-box operations, and there is no MC operation in the last round. We refer the reader to [14,30] for a detailed description.

3   Extending Lepoint et al.'s Collision-Based Attack on Chow et al.'s White-Box AES Implementation

In this section, we review Lepoint et al.'s collision-based attack and describe our two approaches for extending Lepoint et al.'s attack.

3.1   Lepoint et al.'s Collision-Based Attack

Lepoint et al. [27] defined a collision function from the protected inputs of four keyed S-boxes to a protected MC column output in a round of Chow et al.'s implementation, say, the following collision function from the first column in the r-th round ($1 \leq r \leq 8$),

$$f^r(x_0, x_1, x_2, x_3) = \mathbf{e}_{0,0-7}^r \circ L_0^r \circ \mathbf{M} \circ (\mathbf{S}(L_{0,0}^{r-1,-1}(\mathbf{e}_{0,0-1}^{r-1,-1}(x_0)) \oplus \hat{K}_{r-1,0}),$$
$$\mathbf{S}(L_{1,1}^{r-1,-1}(\mathbf{e}_{0,2-3}^{r-1,-1}(x_1)) \oplus \hat{K}_{r-1,1}), \mathbf{S}(L_{2,2}^{r-1,-1}(\mathbf{e}_{0,4-5}^{r-1,-1}(x_2)) \oplus \hat{K}_{r-1,2}),$$
$$\mathbf{S}(L_{3,3}^{r-1,-1}(\mathbf{e}_{0,6-7}^{r-1,-1}(x_3)) \oplus \hat{K}_{r-1,3}))$$

$$= (Q_0^r, Q_1^r, Q_2^r, Q_3^r) \circ \mathbf{M} \circ (\mathbf{S}(P_0^r(x_0) \oplus \hat{K}_{r-1,0}), \mathbf{S}(P_1^r(x_1) \oplus \hat{K}_{r-1,1}),$$
$$\mathbf{S}(P_2^r(x_2) \oplus \hat{K}_{r-1,2}), \mathbf{S}(P_3^r(x_3) \oplus \hat{K}_{r-1,3})),$$
$$= (Q_0^r, Q_1^r, Q_2^r, Q_3^r) \circ \mathbf{M} \circ (\mathbf{S}_0^r(x_0), \mathbf{S}_1^r(x_1), \mathbf{S}_2^r(x_2), \mathbf{S}_3^r((x_3))), \tag{1}$$

where $Q_i^r = \mathbf{e}_{0,*}^r \circ L_{0,i}^r$ and $P_i^r = L_{i,i}^{r-1,-1} \circ \mathbf{e}_{0,*}^{r-1,-1}$ are 8-bit encodings, and $\mathbf{S}_i^r(x) = \mathbf{S}(P_i^r(x) \oplus \hat{K}_{r-1,i})$ $(i = 0, 1, 2, 3)$.

The first phase for Lepoint et al.'s attack is to recover the keyed S-box transformations $\mathbf{S}_i^r$ by exploiting internal collisions under f^r. Below is a group of 255 collisions for 255 pairs of inputs $\alpha \neq 0$ and $\beta \neq 0$, by varying x_0 and x_1 and fixing both x_2 and x_3 to zero:

$$Q_0^r(0x02 \otimes \mathbf{S}_0^r(\alpha) \oplus 0x03 \otimes \mathbf{S}_1^r(0) \oplus 0x01 \otimes \mathbf{S}_2^r(0) \oplus 0x01 \otimes \mathbf{S}_3^r(0))$$
$$= Q_0^r(0x02 \otimes \mathbf{S}_0^r(0) \oplus 0x03 \otimes \mathbf{S}_1^r(\beta) \oplus 0x01 \otimes \mathbf{S}_2^r(0) \oplus 0x01 \otimes \mathbf{S}_3^r(0)).$$

Since Q_0^r is a bijection, one gets $0x02 \otimes \mathbf{S}_0^r(\alpha) \oplus 0x03 \otimes \mathbf{S}_1^r(0) = 0x02 \otimes \mathbf{S}_0^r(0) \oplus 0x03 \otimes \mathbf{S}_1^r(\beta)$, that is, $0x02 \otimes (\mathbf{S}_0^r(\alpha) \oplus \mathbf{S}_0^r(0)) = 0x03 \otimes (\mathbf{S}_1^r(\beta) \oplus \mathbf{S}_1^r(0))$. As a result, a system of 4×255 linear equations with 510 unknowns $\mathbf{S}_0^r(\alpha) \oplus \mathbf{S}_0^r(0)$ and $\mathbf{S}_1^r(\beta) \oplus \mathbf{S}_1^r(0)$ can be obtained by considering other three collision positions, whose rank is 509 by a few experiments, and thus all possible solutions to the 510 unknowns can be obtained by solving the linear equations. Finally, Lepoint et al. used Lai's higher-order derivative concept [24] to distinguish out the correct solution by testing whether the 4th-order derivative of $\mathbf{S}^{-1} \circ \hat{\mathbf{S}}_0^r(\cdot)$ is constant or not for a possible solution $\hat{\mathbf{S}}_0^r$, because $\mathbf{S}^{-1} \circ \mathbf{S}_0^r(\cdot) = P_0^r(\cdot) \oplus \hat{K}_{r-1,0}$ has an algebraic degree at most 4 if the solution $\hat{\mathbf{S}}_0^r$ is correct, otherwise an algebraic degree greater than 4 with an overwhelming probability. Once $\mathbf{S}_0^r$ is recovered, $\mathbf{S}_1^r$ can be recovered from the linear equations by exhaustive search on $\mathbf{S}_1^r(0)$. Similarly for recovering $\mathbf{S}_2^r$ and $\mathbf{S}_3^r$.

The second phase for Lepoint et al.'s attack is to recover the encoding transformations Q_i^r's, which is easy by Eq. (1) after the $\mathbf{S}_i^r$'s transformations are recovered.

The last phase for Lepoint et al.'s attack is to use another distinguisher to recover a round key byte, based again on Lai's higher-order derivative concept. Define $f^{r+1} = (f_0^{r+1}, f_1^{r+1}, f_2^{r+1}, f_3^{r+1})$ for the $(r + 1)$-th round similarly. Since the encoding P_i^{r+1} is the inverse of some encoding Q_*^r in the r-th round, which has been recovered above, one can compute the output of the distinguisher $f_0^{r+1}(P_0^{r+1,-1}(\mathbf{S}^{-1}(x) \oplus \hat{K}_{r,0}), 0, 0, 0)$ after making a guess for $\hat{K}_{r,0}$; if the key guess is correct, $f_0^{r+1}(P_0^{r+1,-1}(\mathbf{S}^{-1}(x) \oplus \hat{K}_{r,0}), 0, 0, 0) = Q_0^{r+1}(0x02 \otimes x \oplus 0x03 \otimes \mathbf{S}_1^{r+1}(0) \oplus 0x01 \otimes \mathbf{S}_2^{r+1}(0) \oplus 0x01 \otimes \mathbf{S}_3^{r+1}(0))$ has an algebraic degree at most 4, otherwise an algebraic degree greater than 4 with an overwhelming probability.

The first phase for recovering the round's whole 16 keyed S-boxes has an expected time complexity of $4 \times (2^{20} + 3 \times 2^{12}) \approx 2^{22}$, the second phase has a negligible time complexity, and the last phase for recovering the whole round key bytes K_r has an expected time complexity of about $16 \times 2^{12} = 2^{16}$. Therefore, the attack has a total time complexity of about $4 \times (2^{20} + 3 \times 2^{12}) + 16 \times 2^{12} \approx 2^{22.03} \approx 2^{22}$.

3.2 First Extension to Lepoint et al.'s Attack

Lepoint et al.'s attack tests every possible key candidate under a statistical distinguisher in the last key recovery phase. We observe a simple but still efficient way to recover the round key bytes directly. We execute Lepoint et al.'s first phase for two consecutive rounds, and obtain the original outputs of the keyed S-boxes in two consecutive rounds for some arbitrary plaintext, say, we have such two outputs Y_r and Y_{r+1} of the r-th and $(r+1)$-th rounds under some plaintext in Chow et al.'s implementation,

$$Y_r = (\mathbf{S}(P_0^r(x_0) \oplus \hat{K}_{r-1,0}), \mathbf{S}(P_1^r(x_1) \oplus \hat{K}_{r-1,1}), \cdots, \mathbf{S}(P_{15}^r(x_{15}) \oplus \hat{K}_{r-1,15})),$$
$$Y_{r+1} = (\mathbf{S}(P_0^{r+1}(\hat{y}_0) \oplus \hat{K}_{r,0}), \mathbf{S}(P_1^{r+1}(\hat{y}_1) \oplus \hat{K}_{r,1}), \cdots, \mathbf{S}(P_{15}^{r+1}(\hat{y}_{15}) \oplus \hat{K}_{r,15})),$$

where $(x_0, x_1, \cdots, x_{15})$ denotes the input to the r-th round, and $(\hat{y}_0, \hat{y}_1, \cdots, \hat{y}_{15})$ denotes the corresponding input to the $(r+1)$-th round. Thus, we have $Y_{r+1} = \mathrm{SB} \circ \mathrm{SR}(\mathrm{MC}(Y_r) \oplus K_r)$. As a consequence, we can easily recover the round key K_r as $K_r = \mathrm{MC}(Y_r) \oplus \mathrm{SR}^{-1} \circ \mathrm{SB}^{-1}(Y_{r+1})$.

Clearly, this extension is feasible first because AES is an SPN cipher. It executes Lepoint et al.'s first phase twice, for both the r-th and $(r+1)$-th rounds, so the resulting total attack complexity is approximately $2 \times [4 \times (2^{20} + 3 \times 2^{12})] \approx 2^{23.01}$, about twice of Lepoint et al.'s attack complexity $2^{22.03}$, however, it does not need Lepoint et al.'s second and last phases, in particular it replaces a series of probabilistic exhaustive computations with a deterministic simple computation, does not need to recover the encoding Q_*^r or P_*^{r+1}, and does not assume the knowledge of the algebraic degree of the encoding Q_*^{r+1} that Lepoint et al.'s key recovery phase relies on. Thus, it can be applicable to a white-box AES implementation such that Lepoint et al.'s first phase is feasible while Lepoint et al.'s last two phases are infeasible, for which Lepoint et al.'s attack is not applicable, as we show on Bai et al.'s white-box AES implementation in Sect. 4.

It is worthy to note that this extension does not need to recover the internal encodings like Q_*^r or P_*^r, and only requires a little knowledge of the internal encoding, that is, whether the encoding produces different outputs for different inputs, which, to the best of our knowledge, is the first such attack on white-box AES implementation with external encodings on both plaintext and ciphertext sides.

3.3 Second Extension to Lepoint et al.'s Attack

We also observe that the round key bytes can be directly computed at once after executing Lepoint et al.'s first phase for two consecutive rounds and Lepoint et al.'s second phase for the former round. Specifically, suppose the keyed S-box $\mathbf{S}_i^{r+1}$ has been recovered in the first phase and the input encoding P_i^{r+1}

has been recovered as the inverse of some output encoding Q^r_* in the second phase (by the ShiftRows operation), then we can recover the key byte $\hat{K}_{r,i}$ as $\hat{K}_{r,i} = \mathbf{S}^{-1}(y) \oplus P^{r+1}_i(x)$ from an arbitrary pair of input and output $(x, y = \mathbf{S}^{r+1}_i(x) = \mathbf{S}(P^{r+1}_i(x) \oplus \hat{K}_{r,i}))$ of the keyed S-box $\mathbf{S}^{r+1}_i$. All the other 15 bytes of K_r can be recovered by this approach.

This extension also executes Lepoint et al.'s first phase twice, so the resulting total attack complexity is also about twice of Lepoint et al.'s attack complexity, but nevertheless it avoids Lepoint et al.'s last phase and thus removes the corresponding constraints such as the assumption on the knowledge of the algebraic degree of the encoding Q^{r+1}_*. In short, this extension can be applicable to a white-box AES implementation such that Lepoint et al.'s first two phases are feasible while Lepoint et al.'s last phase is infeasible, to which Lepoint et al.'s attack does not apply.

It is worthy to note that this extension is not limited to SPN ciphers, but can be applicable to Feistel ciphers as well. Nevertheless, we do not see a good published white-box implementation example, that is, a white-box implementation where Lepoint et al.'s first two phases are feasible while Lepoint et al.'s last phase is infeasible, although it can clearly be applied to those attacked by Lepoint et al.'s approach.

3.4   A Remark

Lepoint et al.'s approach is applicable to some white-box implementations of both SPN and Feistel ciphers. Compared with Lepoint et al.'s approach, the first extension can attack a broader range of white-box implementations of some SPN ciphers, due to the removal of Lepoint et al.'s last two phases, and the second extension can attack a broader range of white-box implementations of some SPN and Feistel ciphers, due to the removal of Lepoint et al.'s last phase. Thus, for the case of SPN ciphers, the two extensions intersect, and the first extension covers the second extension owing to the absence of Lepoint et al.'s second phase, but for the case of Feistel ciphers, the first extension is not applicable, because it is not possible to recover the round key, given only the outputs of the two SubBytes layers of two adjacent rounds, due to the existence of the unknown one or more branches not entering the S-box layer. Therefore, the two extensions intersect somewhere, but one cannot contain the other.

4   Collision-Based Attack on Bai et al.'s White-Box AES Implementation

Bai et al.'s white-box AES implementation uses a general 32×32-bit mixing bijection after each $\mathbf{MC}_l$ operation, which, together with other features, invalidates Lepoint et al.'s collision-based attack. In this section, we describe Bai et al.'s implementation and apply our first extension to it, showing for the first time that it is rather insecure.

4.1 Bai et al.'s White-Box AES Implementation

Bai et al.'s implementation [3] uses only affine mixing bijections (also called encodings), and consists of two types of white-box tables, namely 8-bit to 32-bit TD tables and 16-bit to 32-bit TR tables, plus 32-bit XOR operations. As depicted in Fig. 2, each of the first nine rounds involves 16 TD tables, 16 TR tables and 20 XOR operations, as follows.

First, a layer of 16 $\text{TD}^r_{i,j}$ tables ($1 \leq r \leq 9, 0 \leq i,j \leq 3$). Each $\text{TD}^r_{i,j}$ table takes as input a protected byte x^{r-1}_* from the last round output for $2 \leq r \leq 9$ or the protected plaintext for $r = 1$, and is constructed by sequentially applying the j-th 8×32-bit strip $(E^{r-1}_i)^{-1}_j$ of the inverse $(E^{r-1}_i)^{-1}$ of the non-singular

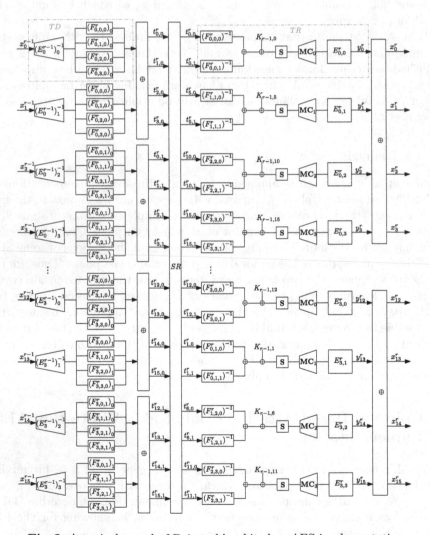

Fig. 2. A typical round of Bai et al.'s white-box AES implementation

32×32-bit affine encoding E_i^{r-1} (from the last round or protected plaintext) and four parallel non-singular 8×8-bit affine encodings $\left(F^r_{i,k,\lfloor \frac{i}{2} \rfloor \bmod 2}\right)_{j \bmod 2}$, where $(E_i^{r-1})^{-1} = ((E_i^{r-1})_0^{-1}, (E_i^{r-1})_1^{-1}, (E_i^{r-1})_2^{-1}, (E_i^{r-1})_3^{-1})$, $\left(F^r_{i,k,\lfloor \frac{i}{2} \rfloor \bmod 2}\right)_0$ and $\left(F^r_{i,k,\lfloor \frac{i}{2} \rfloor \bmod 2}\right)_1$ have the same linear part and their sum $\left(F^r_{i,k,\lfloor \frac{i}{2} \rfloor \bmod 2}\right)_0 \oplus \left(F^r_{i,k,\lfloor \frac{i}{2} \rfloor \bmod 2}\right)_1 = F^r_{i,k,\lfloor \frac{i}{2} \rfloor \bmod 2}$ is also a non-singular 8×8-bit affine encoding ($0 \leq k \leq 3$).

Then, a layer of eight 32-bit XOR operations, each of which XORs two TD outputs and produces 16 protected bytes denoted by $t^r_{*,*}$ each.

Next, a layer of 16 $\mathrm{TR}^r_{i,j}$ tables ($1 \leq r \leq 9, 0 \leq i,j \leq 3$). Each $\mathrm{TR}^r_{i,j}$ table takes as input two bytes $t^r_{*,0}$ and $t^r_{*,1}$ according to the effect of the SR operation, and is constructed by sequentially applying the inverses $(F^r_{i,j,0})^{-1}$ and $(F^r_{i,j,1})^{-1}$ of the corresponding encodings $F^r_{i,j,0}$ and $F^r_{i,j,1}$, an XOR operation, the keyed S-box $\mathbf{T}^r_{4 \times i+j}$, and finally a general non-singular 32×32-bit affine encoding $E^r_{i,j}$, where $\bigoplus_{j=0}^{3} E^r_{i,j} = E^r_i$ is also a general non-singular 32×32-bit affine encoding.

At last, a layer of twelve 32-bit XOR operations to produce sixteen protected bytes $x^r_0, x^r_1, \cdots, x^r_{15}$ finally, with three XOR operations for a column of four bytes. This completes the r-th white-box round.

Bai et al.'s implementation has a few features different from Chow et al.'s implementation, to name a few, it uses a 32-bit general affine matrix $E^r_{i,j}$ after each $\mathbf{MC}_l$ operation, instead of a 32-bit diagonal block matrix L^r_i; the four 8-bit affine encodings of $\mathrm{TD}^r_{i,0}(x_{4 \times i}) \oplus \mathrm{TD}^r_{i,0}(x_{4 \times i+1})$ and $\mathrm{TD}^r_{i,0}(x_{4 \times i+2}) \oplus \mathrm{TD}^r_{i,0}(x_{4 \times i+3})$ are different, and the XOR operation of two input shares is performed inside a TR table; the 8×8-bit blocks of E^r_i may be singular; the 32×32-bit block from the 128×128-bit matrix SR corresponding to an MC column is not invertible. As a consequence, Bai et al. concluded a lower security bound of 2^{69} after analysing its security against known cryptanalysis methods, including Billet et al.'s attack [6], Michiels et al.'s attack [29] and Lepoint et al.'s attacks [27]. In particular, they concluded that it is "not applicable" for Lepoint et al.'s collision-based attack, which should still require 2^{64} affine equivalence tests even one could invert a column of protected S-boxes. We refer the reader to [3] for detail.

4.2 Attacking Bai et al.'s White-Box AES Implementation

Lepoint et al.'s collision-based attack requires all the three phrases to hold, so it is not applicable to Bai et al.'s implementation owing to the above-mentioned design features. However, since AES is an SPN cipher, by our first extension given in Sect. 3.2, we only need Lepoint et al.'s first phase to hold, and we find that this is feasible for Bai et al.'s implementation, as follows.

4.2.1 Devising a Collision Function

We consider the r-th and $(r+1)$-th rounds ($1 \leq r \leq 8$), and define the first collision function as depicted in Fig. 3, that is, from the 8 input bytes $(t_{0,0}^r, t_{5,0}^r, t_{10,0}^r, t_{15,0}^r, t_{0,1}^r, t_{5,1}^r, t_{10,1}^r, t_{15,1}^r)$ of the four TR tables corresponding to the first MC column in the r-th round to the four 32-bit output words $(y_0^{r+1}, y_{13}^{r+1}, y_{10}^{r+1}, y_7^{r+1})$ of the four associated TR tables in the $(r+1)$-th round, denoted by f:

$$(y_0^{r+1}, y_{13}^{r+1}, y_{10}^{r+1}, y_7^{r+1})$$
$$= f(t_{0,0}^r, t_{5,0}^r, t_{10,0}^r, t_{15,0}^r, t_{0,1}^r, t_{5,1}^r, t_{10,1}^r, t_{15,1}^r)$$
$$= (f_0(t_{0,0}^r, t_{5,0}^r, \cdots, t_{15,1}^r), f_1(t_{0,0}^r, t_{5,0}^r, \cdots, t_{15,1}^r), f_2(t_{0,0}^r, t_{5,0}^r, \cdots, t_{15,1}^r),$$
$$f_3(t_{0,0}^r, t_{5,0}^r, \cdots, t_{15,1}^r)).$$

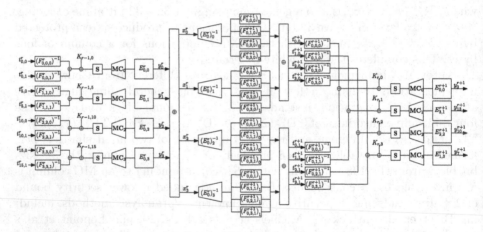

Fig. 3. Our collision function on Bai et al.'s white-box AES implementation

We define $\mathbf{S}_0^r$, $\mathbf{S}_1^r$, $\mathbf{S}_2^r$ and $\mathbf{S}_3^r$ functions as

$$\mathbf{S}_0^r(x,y) = \mathbf{S}((F_{0,0,0}^r)^{-1}(x) \oplus (F_{0,0,1}^r)^{-1}(y) \oplus K_{r-1,0}),$$
$$\mathbf{S}_1^r(x,y) = \mathbf{S}((F_{1,1,0}^r)^{-1}(x) \oplus (F_{1,1,1}^r)^{-1}(y) \oplus K_{r-1,5}),$$
$$\mathbf{S}_2^r(x,y) = \mathbf{S}((F_{2,2,0}^r)^{-1}(x) \oplus (F_{2,2,1}^r)^{-1}(y) \oplus K_{r-1,10}),$$
$$\mathbf{S}_3^r(x,y) = \mathbf{S}((F_{3,3,0}^r)^{-1}(x) \oplus (F_{3,3,1}^r)^{-1}(y) \oplus K_{r-1,15}),$$

where x and y are 8-bit variables. Then the above f function can be simplified and expressed as

$$(y_0^{r+1}, y_{13}^{r+1}, y_{10}^{r+1}, y_7^{r+1})$$
$$= f(t_{0,0}^r, t_{5,0}^r, t_{10,0}^r, t_{15,0}^r, t_{0,1}^r, t_{5,1}^r, t_{10,1}^r, t_{15,1}^r)$$
$$= (f_0(t_{0,0}^r, t_{5,0}^r, \cdots, t_{15,1}^r), f_1(t_{0,0}^r, t_{5,0}^r, \cdots, t_{15,1}^r), f_2(t_{0,0}^r, t_{5,0}^r, \cdots, t_{15,1}^r),$$
$$f_3(t_{0,0}^r, t_{5,0}^r, \cdots, t_{15,1}^r))$$
$$= (E_{0,0}^{r+1} \| E_{3,1}^{r+1} \| E_{2,2}^{r+1} \| E_{1,3}^{r+1}) \circ ((\mathbf{MC}_0 \circ \mathbf{S}) \| (\mathbf{MC}_1 \circ \mathbf{S}) \| (\mathbf{MC}_2 \circ \mathbf{S}) \| (\mathbf{MC}_3 \circ \mathbf{S})) \circ$$
$$\oplus_{(K_{r,0} \| K_{r,1} \| K_{r,2} \| K_{r,3})} \circ \mathbf{M} \circ \begin{bmatrix} \mathbf{S}((F_{0,0,0}^r)^{-1}(t_{0,0}^r) \oplus (F_{0,0,1}^r)^{-1}(t_{0,1}^r) \oplus K_{r-1,0}) \\ \mathbf{S}((F_{1,1,0}^r)^{-1}(t_{5,0}^r) \oplus (F_{1,1,1}^r)^{-1}(t_{5,1}^r) \oplus K_{r-1,5}) \\ \mathbf{S}((F_{2,2,0}^r)^{-1}(t_{10,0}^r) \oplus (F_{2,2,1}^r)^{-1}(t_{10,1}^r) \oplus K_{r-1,10}) \\ \mathbf{S}((F_{3,3,0}^r)^{-1}(t_{15,0}^r) \oplus (F_{3,3,1}^r)^{-1}(t_{15,1}^r) \oplus K_{r-1,15}) \end{bmatrix}$$

$$= (E_{0,0}^{r+1} \| E_{3,1}^{r+1} \| E_{2,2}^{r+1} \| E_{1,3}^{r+1}) \circ ((\mathbf{MC}_0 \circ \mathbf{T}_0^{r+1}) \| (\mathbf{MC}_1 \circ \mathbf{T}_9^{r+1}) \| (\mathbf{MC}_2 \circ \mathbf{T}_2^{r+1}) \|$$
$$(\mathbf{MC}_3 \circ \mathbf{T}_{11}^{r+1})) \circ \mathbf{M} \circ \begin{bmatrix} \mathbf{S}_0^r(t_{0,0}^r, t_{0,1}^r) \\ \mathbf{S}_1^r(t_{5,0}^r, t_{5,1}^r) \\ \mathbf{S}_2^r(t_{10,0}^r, t_{10,1}^r) \\ \mathbf{S}_3^r(t_{15,0}^r, t_{15,1}^r) \end{bmatrix}. \tag{2}$$

We can similarly define $\mathbf{S}_i^{r+1}(x,y)$ functions and collision functions starting with the $(r+1)$-th round.

4.2.2   Recovering the $\mathbf{S}_i^r(\cdot, 0)$ and $\mathbf{S}_i^{r+1}(\cdot, 0)$ Functions

Without loss of generality, we always set $t_{0,1}^r = t_{5,1}^r = t_{10,1}^r = t_{15,1}^r = 0$ and try to recover the $\mathbf{S}_i^r(\cdot, 0)$ functions in our attack. We first use the following collision form in order to recover $\mathbf{S}_0^r(\cdot, 0)$ and $\mathbf{S}_1^r(\cdot, 0)$:

$$f_0(\alpha, 0, 0, 0, 0, 0, 0, 0) = f_0(0, 0, \beta, 0, 0, 0, 0, 0), \tag{3}$$

where $\alpha, \beta \in \mathrm{GF}(2)^8$. Following the definition of f_0 in Eq. (2), we have the following equation by Eq. (3):

$$E_{0,0}^{r+1} \circ \mathbf{MC}_0 \circ \mathbf{T}_0^{r+1}(0x02 \otimes \mathbf{S}_0^r(\alpha, 0) \oplus 0x03 \otimes \mathbf{S}_1^r(0, 0) \oplus c)$$
$$= E_{0,0}^{r+1} \circ \mathbf{MC}_0 \circ \mathbf{T}_0^{r+1}(0x02 \otimes \mathbf{S}_0^r(0, 0) \oplus 0x03 \otimes \mathbf{S}_1^r(\beta, 0) \oplus c), \tag{4}$$

where $c = \mathbf{S}_2^r(0, 0) \oplus \mathbf{S}_3^r(0, 0)$ is an unknown 8-bit constant.

Observe that $E_{0,0}^{r+1} \circ \mathbf{MC}_0 \circ \mathbf{T}_0^{r+1}(\cdot)$ is an 8-bit to 32-bit function, although it is not bijective as the encoding operation in Lepoint et al.'s attack, it is injective, that is, if $x \neq y$, we have $E_{0,0}^{r+1} \circ \mathbf{MC}_0 \circ \mathbf{T}_0^{r+1}(x) \neq E_{0,0}^{r+1} \circ \mathbf{MC}_0 \circ \mathbf{T}_0^{r+1}(y)$. Thus, we can still determine an internal collision by Eq. (4), and it implies

$$0x02 \otimes \mathbf{S}_0^r(\alpha, 0) \oplus 0x03 \otimes \mathbf{S}_1^r(0, 0) = 0x02 \otimes \mathbf{S}_0^r(0, 0) \oplus 0x03 \otimes \mathbf{S}_1^r(\beta, 0),$$

which is

$$0x02 \otimes (\mathbf{S}_0^r(\alpha, 0) \oplus \mathbf{S}_0^r(0, 0)) = 0x03 \otimes (\mathbf{S}_1^r(\beta, 0) \oplus \mathbf{S}_1^r(0, 0)). \tag{5}$$

Subsequently, the remaining steps are pretty similar to those of Lepoint et al.'s attack, except that the $\mathbf{S}_i^r$ functions in our attack have two input parameters with the right one fixed to zero and that Bai et al.'s implementation uses affine encodings, and we briefly describe as follows. We refer the reader to [27] for some relevant explanations.

- First, obtain 255 equations of the form Eq. (5) for 255 pairs $(\alpha, \beta) \neq (0,0)$ under f_0, where every α value appears once and has a corresponding β value.
- Second, obtain 255×3 similar equations with three pairs of different coefficient combinations in $\{0x01, 0x02, 0x03\}$ by changing f_0 to f_1, f_2, f_3. By now, we obtain a system of 255×4 linear equations involving all the 512 unknowns $\mathbf{S}_0^r(\cdot, 0)$ and $\mathbf{S}_1^r(\cdot, 0)$, and it can be rewritten in terms of 510 unknowns $\mathbf{S}_0^r(\alpha, 0) \oplus \mathbf{S}_0^r(0,0)$ and $\mathbf{S}_1^r(\beta, 0) \oplus \mathbf{S}_1^r(0,0)$ with $\alpha \neq 0$ and $\beta \neq 0$, which has a rank of 509 by our experimental test under one hundred million different (encodings, round key) combinations (specifically, ten thousand sets of encodings under each of ten thousand round keys), and thus all the unknowns can be expressed in function of one unknown, and there exist coefficients a_i and b_i so that all the unknowns are linearly linked as

$$\mathbf{S}_0^r(\alpha, 0) = a_i \otimes (\mathbf{S}_0^r(0,0) \oplus \mathbf{S}_0^r(1,0)) \oplus \mathbf{S}_0^r(0,0),$$
$$\mathbf{S}_1^r(\beta, 0) = b_i \otimes (\mathbf{S}_1^r(0,0) \oplus \mathbf{S}_1^r(1,0)) \oplus \mathbf{S}_1^r(0,0). \qquad (6)$$

- Third, recover the $\mathbf{S}_0^r(\cdot, 0)$ function by exhaustive search on $(\mathbf{S}_0^r(0,0), \mathbf{S}_0^r(1,0))$ using Lai's higher-order derivative concept [24]. For the correct $(\mathbf{S}_0^r(0,0), \mathbf{S}_0^r(1,0))$, the function $\mathbf{S}^{-1} \circ \mathbf{S}_0^r(\cdot, 0)$ satisfies

$$\mathbf{S}^{-1} \circ \mathbf{S}_0^r(\cdot, 0) = (F_{0,0,0}^r)^{-1}(\cdot) \oplus (F_{0,0,1}^r)^{-1}(0) \oplus K_{r-1,0},$$

which has an algebraic degree of at most 1, as $(F_{0,0,0}^r)^{-1}$ is an affine encoding. For a wrong $(\mathbf{S}_0^r(0,0), \mathbf{S}_0^r(1,0))$, a wrong candidate $\hat{\mathbf{S}}_0^r(\cdot, 0)$ would be got as an affine equivalent to $\mathbf{S}_0^r(\cdot, 0)$, namely there exist an 8×8-bit matrix a and an 8-bit vector b such that $\hat{\mathbf{S}}_0^r(\cdot, 0) = a \cdot \mathbf{S}_0^r(\cdot, 0) \oplus b$, with $a \neq 0$ and $(a, b) \neq (0, 1)$, and thus the function $\mathbf{S}^{-1} \circ \hat{\mathbf{S}}_0^r(\cdot, 0)$ satisfies

$$\mathbf{S}^{-1} \circ \hat{\mathbf{S}}_0^r(\cdot, 0) = \mathbf{S}^{-1}\big(a \cdot \mathbf{S}^r\big((F_{0,0,0}^r)^{-1}(\cdot) \oplus (F_{0,0,1}^r)^{-1}(0) \oplus K_{r-1,0}\big) \oplus b\big),$$

which has an algebraic degree greater than 1 with an overwhelming probability. As a result, whether an $(\mathbf{S}_0^r(0,0), \mathbf{S}_0^r(1,0))$ candidate is correct or not can be distinguished by testing whether the first-order derivative of the resulting function $\mathbf{S}^{-1} \circ \hat{\mathbf{S}}_0^r(\cdot, 0)$ at some point say $0x01$ is constant or not with at most 2^7 inputs, since the first-order derivative function $\mathbf{S}^{-1} \circ \hat{\mathbf{S}}_0^r(x, 0) \oplus \mathbf{S}^{-1} \circ \hat{\mathbf{S}}_0^r(x \oplus 0x01, 0)$ is invariant for x and $x \oplus 0x01$.
- Finally, recover the $\mathbf{S}_1^r(\cdot, 0)$ function by exhaustive search on $\mathbf{S}_1^r(0,0)$ under Eq. (6). The $\mathbf{S}_2^r(\cdot, 0)$ and $\mathbf{S}_3^r(\cdot, 0)$ functions can be similarly recovered by solving similar linear equations.

So far, we have recovered the $\mathbf{S}_0^r(\cdot, 0)$, $\mathbf{S}_1^r(\cdot, 0)$, $\mathbf{S}_2^r(\cdot, 0)$ and $\mathbf{S}_3^r(\cdot, 0)$ functions corresponding to the first MC column in the r-th round. Likewise, by defining similar collision functions corresponding to the other three MC columns in the r-th round, we can recover all the other $\mathbf{S}_4^r(\cdot, 0), \cdots, \mathbf{S}_{15}^r(\cdot, 0)$ functions.

The $\mathbf{S}_i^{r+1}(\cdot, 0)$ functions for the $(r+1)$-th round can be recovered by performing a similar process as above.

4.2.3   Recovering the Round Key K_r

After all the $\mathbf{S}_i^r(\cdot, 0)$ and $\mathbf{S}_i^{r+1}(\cdot, 0)$ functions for the r-th and $(r+1)$-th rounds have been recovered ($i = 0, 1, \cdots, 15$), we can recover the $(r+1)$-th round key K_r, which is similar to but a bit more complex than that described in Sect. 3.2, because each of the $\mathbf{S}_i^r(\cdot, 0)$ and $\mathbf{S}_i^{r+1}(\cdot, 0)$ functions has the second input parameter fixed to zero, anyway it is feasible, as follows.

1. Choose a value $(x_2^{r+1}, x_3^{r+1}, x_6^{r+1}, x_7^{r+1}, x_{10}^{r+1}, x_{11}^{r+1}, x_{14}^{r+1}, x_{15}^{r+1})$ for the eight corresponding TD tables so that $t_{0,1}^{r+1} = t_{1,1}^{r+1} = \cdots = t_{15,1}^{r+1} = 0$ in the $(r+1)$-th round. Choose an arbitrary value $(x_0^{r+1}, x_1^{r+1}, x_4^{r+1}, x_5^{r+1}, x_8^{r+1}, x_9^{r+1}, x_{12}^{r+1}, x_{13}^{r+1})$ for the eight corresponding TD tables in the $(r+1)$-th round, and obtain the corresponding $(t_{0,0}^{r+1}, t_{1,0}^{r+1}, \cdots, t_{15,0}^{r+1})$.
2. Choose a value $(y_0^r, y_1^r, \cdots, y_{15}^r)$ that produces the above $(x_0^{r+1}, x_1^{r+1}, \cdots, x_{15}^{r+1})$ value after the XOR operations.
3. For each TR table corresponding to y_i^r in the r-th round ($i = 0, 1, \cdots, 15$), fix the input byte $t_{*,1}^r$ to zero, and determine the other input byte $t_{*,0}^r$ by y_i^r. For a possible y_i^r under the TR table, there is always a corresponding $t_{*,0}^r$, given the other input byte $t_{*,1}^r = 0$. Now, the set of sixteen bytes $(t_{0,0}^r, t_{1,0}^r, \cdots, t_{15,0}^r, t_{0,1}^r = 0, t_{1,1}^r = 0, \cdots, t_{15,1}^r = 0)$ in the r-th round results into the set of the above sixteen bytes $(t_{0,0}^{r+1}, t_{1,0}^{r+1}, \cdots, t_{15,0}^{r+1}, t_{0,1}^{r+1} = 0, t_{1,1}^{r+1} = 0, \cdots, t_{15,1}^{r+1} = 0)$ in the $(r+1)$-th round.
4. Since all the $\mathbf{S}_i^r(\cdot, 0)$ and $\mathbf{S}_i^{r+1}(\cdot, 0)$ functions have been recovered, let

$$Y_r = (\mathbf{S}_0^r(t_{0,0}^r, 0), \mathbf{S}_1^r(t_{5,0}^r, 0), \cdots, \mathbf{S}_{15}^r(t_{11,0}^r, 0)),$$
$$Y_{r+1} = (\mathbf{S}_0^{r+1}(t_{0,0}^{r+1}, 0), \mathbf{S}_1^{r+1}(t_{5,0}^{r+1}, 0), \cdots, \mathbf{S}_{15}^{r+1}(t_{11,0}^{r+1}, 0)),$$

where Y_r and Y_{r+1} are the two corresponding original 128-bit states immediately after the S-box layers of the r-th and $(r+1)$-th rounds, respectively. Thus, we have $Y_{r+1} = \mathrm{SB} \circ \mathrm{SR}(\mathrm{MC}(Y_r) \oplus K_r)$, and can recover the round key K_r as $K_r = \mathrm{MC}(Y_r) \oplus \mathrm{SR}^{-1} \circ \mathrm{SB}^{-1}(Y_{r+1})$.

4.2.4   Attack Complexity

In the phase of recovering $\mathbf{S}_0^r(\cdot, 0)$, there are 2^{16} candidates $(\mathbf{S}_0^r(0,0), \mathbf{S}_0^r(1,0))$ for exhaustive search, and we need to verify whether the first-order derivative function $\mathbf{S}^{-1} \circ \hat{\mathbf{S}}_0^r(x, 0) \oplus \mathbf{S}^{-1} \circ \hat{\mathbf{S}}_0^r(x \oplus 0x01, 0)$ is constant for at most 2^7 inputs. For a wrong candidate $(\mathbf{S}_0^r(0,0), \mathbf{S}_0^r(1,0))$, the probability that $\mathbf{S}^{-1} \circ \hat{\mathbf{S}}_0^r(x, 0) \oplus \mathbf{S}^{-1} \circ \hat{\mathbf{S}}_0^r(x \oplus 0x01, 0)$ is constant for a subsequent x is 2^{-8} roughly. Thus, the expected value of the test is $1 + 2^{-8} + \cdots + (2^{-8})^{2^7-1} \approx 1$. Hence, the expected time complexity of recovering $\mathbf{S}_0^r(\cdot, 0)$ is about $2^{16} \cdot 1 \cdot 2 = 2^{17}$ S (or $\mathbf{S}^{-1}$) computations.

Note that as mentioned by Lepoint et al. [27], the system of 255×4 linear equations is very sparse, and every equation involves only two variables, so the complexity of solving the linear system is negligible. The recovery of $\mathbf{S}_1^r(\cdot, 0)$, $\mathbf{S}_2^r(\cdot, 0)$ and $\mathbf{S}_3^r(\cdot, 0)$ takes an expected time complexity of $3 \cdot (2^8 \cdot 1 \cdot 2) = 3 \cdot 2^9$ **S** computations. Once the $\mathbf{S}_i^r(\cdot, 0)$ and $\mathbf{S}_i^{r+1}(\cdot, 0)$ functions are recovered, the time complexity for recovering K_r is negligible. Therefore, the attack has an expected time complexity of about $(2^{17} + 3 \cdot 2^9) \times 4 \times 2 \approx 2^{20}$ **S** computations in total.

5 Other Applications and Related Work

In this section, we discuss a few other applications and some related work about the two extensions.

5.1 Applications to Other White-Box Implementations

In [27], Lepoint et al. showed that Karroumi's white-box AES implementation [23] was the same as Chow et al.'s white-box AES implementation from a structural point of view, and so their attacks on Chow et al.'s implementation were applicable to Karroumi's implementation with the same time complexity. Thus, since our two extensions given in Sect. 3 only need the first one or two phases of Lepoint et al.'s attack, they also work on Karroumi's implementation with about twice of Lepoint et al.'s complexity.

In the category of DCA-driven white-box implementations, Boolean masks or 8-bit non-linear encodings (instead of two parallel 4-bit non-linear encodings) are often used to thwart DCA-type attacks, for example, Lee et al.'s white-box AES implementations [25,26] are built on Chow et al.'s white-box AES implementation by inserting a few Boolean masks. However, it is easy to see that Lee et al.'s schemes can be similarly broken from inner rounds by Lepoint et al.'s collision-based attack and our extensions, if the attacker knows the implementation details as generally assumed by white-box model.

5.2 Comparisons with Linear and Affine Equivalence Algorithms

There are a few general algorithms [1,8,18,19] for solving the linear or affine equivalence problem: given two n-bit non-linear bijections $\mathcal{S}_1$ and $\mathcal{S}_2$, find two invertible n-bit linear or affine (depending on the problem setting) transformations $\mathcal{A}$ and $\mathcal{B}$ such that $\mathcal{S}_2 = \mathcal{B} \circ \mathcal{S}_2 \circ \mathcal{A}$, if they exist.

In 2003, Biryukov et al. [8] proposed a solution algorithm when $\mathcal{S}_1$ and $\mathcal{S}_2$ are $n \times n$-bit S-boxes, which has a time complexity of $\mathcal{O}(n^3 \cdot 2^n)$ for the linear case and $\mathcal{O}(n^3 \cdot 2^{2n})$ for the affine case. In 2018, Dinur [19] gave an improved algorithm for the affine case when $\mathcal{S}_1$ and $\mathcal{S}_2$ are random permutations, which has a time complexity of $\mathcal{O}(n^3 \cdot 2^n)$ with a high probability.

Further, when $\mathcal{S}_1$ consists of k parallel m-bit S-boxes (that is, $n = k \cdot m$), in 2016 Baek et al. [1] proposed a solution algorithm for the affine case when $\mathcal{S}_1$ and $\mathcal{S}_2$ are $n \times n$-bit S-boxes, which has a time complexity of $\mathcal{O}(min(\frac{n^{m+4} \cdot 2^m}{m}, n \cdot$

$log(n) \cdot 2^{\frac{n}{2}}$); and in 2018, Derbez et al. [18] gave an improved algorithm with a time complexity of $\mathcal{O}((n^3 + m^2 \cdot n) \cdot 2^m + \frac{n^4}{m})$.

First, as mentioned by Derbez et al. [18], note that these linear and affine equivalence algorithms are not applicable to Chow et al.'s implementation due to the existence of those non-linear encodings, unless one can first peel off them somehow, for example, by using Billet et al.'s first attack phase.

Second, Derbez et al. [18] mentioned that Dinur's algorithm is for random permutation, and does not work for AES S-box, because AES S-box is self-affine equivalent, so Dinur gave a workaround [18], but Derbez et al. [18] reported that the workaround still failed on AES S-box. Our main focus is the first extension described in Sect. 3.2, and its main application example is Bai et al.'s implementation presented in Sect. 4, but Bai et al. used a few countermeasures [3] to resist affine equivalence algorithms, as partially mentioned in Sect. 4.1. Suppose Biryukov et al.'s, Baek et al.'s and Derbez et al.'s affine equivalence algorithms could apply on a whole state (i.e., $n = 128, m = 8, k = 16$) or a column (i.e., $n = 32, m = 8, k = 4$) of Bai et al.'s implementation, there would have a time complexity higher than ours, but anyway how to apply these algorithms under Bai et al.'s countermeasures is a problem.

5.3 Security of Xiao and Lai's Implementation Against Our Extensions

Xiao and Lai's white-box AES implementation uses the equivalent matrix form of the SR operation and puts two T-boxes and the corresponding 32×16-bit strip of the **M** matrix into a white-box table with a general 32×32-bit output mixing bijection. It has some features that make it infeasible to apply Lepoint et al.'s collision-based attack at a high level, and our investigation shows that collision functions can be defined for Xiao and Lai's implementation, however a small-scale experiment shows that the rank of the resulting linear system is much less than the number of unknowns, so it is resistant to our extensions, but nevertheless the number of tested encodings is very small compared with the whole space, and at present we are not clear about whether there are such encodings that the rank of the corresponding linear system is slightly less than the number of the involved unknowns, if this was the case, our first extension could attack it with an expected time complexity of about 2^{37} **S** computations. Below we briefly describe our investigation, and a detailed description is given in the full version of this paper.

5.3.1 Xiao and Lai's White-Box AES Implementation

Xiao and Lai's implementation [35] uses only linear mixing bijections (also called encodings), and consists of one type of white-box tables, namely 16-bit to 32-bit TMC tables, plus 128×128-bit matrix multiplications and 32-bit XOR operations. Each of the first nine rounds involves a 128×128-bit matrix multiplication M^r, 8 TMC tables and 4 XOR operations, as follows.

First, a 128×128-bit matrix multiplication M^r takes as input four 32-bit protected words $(X_0^{r-1}, X_1^{r-1}, X_2^{r-1}, X_3^{r-1})$, and outputs eight 16-bit values $(x_{0,0}^r, x_{0,1}^r, \ x_{1,0}^r, x_{1,1}^r, \cdots, x_{3,0}^r, x_{3,1}^r)$. It is constructed by sequentially applying a 128×128-bit diagonal block matrix $diag((R_0^{r-1})^{-1}, (R_1^{r-1})^{-1}, (R_2^{r-1})^{-1}, (R_3^{r-1})^{-1})$, the equivalent matrix form of the SR operation and a 128×128-bit diagonal block matrix $diag((L_0^r)^{-1}, (L_1^r)^{-1}, \cdots, (L_7^r)^{-1})$, where $(R_i^{r-1})^{-1}$ is the inverse of the 32×32-bit output encoding R_i^{r-1} of a TMC table corresponding to the i-th $\mathbf{M}$ column in the last round or protected plaintext, and $(L_j^r)^{-1}$ is the inverse of the 16×16-bit input encoding L_j^r of the corresponding TMC table in this round $(1 \leq r \leq 9, 0 \leq i \leq 3, 0 \leq j \leq 7)$.

Then, a layer of eight TMC_i^r tables $(0 \leq i \leq 7)$. Each TMC_i^r table takes as input a 16-bit value $x_{\lfloor \frac{i}{2} \rfloor, i \bmod 2}^r$ and outputs a 32-bit word $y_{\lfloor \frac{i}{2} \rfloor, i \bmod 2}^r$, which is constructed by sequentially applying a general 16×16-bit non-singular linear encoding L_i^r, two parallel T-boxes $\mathbf{T}_{2 \times i}^r$ and $\mathbf{T}_{2 \times i+1}^r$, the $(i \bmod 2)$-th 32×16-bit strip $\mathbf{MC}_{i \bmod 2}$ of $\mathbf{M}$, and a general 32×32-bit non-singular linear encoding $R_{\lfloor \frac{i}{2} \rfloor}^r$.

At last, a layer of four 32-bit XOR operations to produce four 32-bit protected words $(X_0^r, X_1^r, X_2^r, X_3^r)$. This completes the r-th white-box round.

5.3.2   Our Investigation

Represent the MC matrix $\mathbf{M}$ with two non-singular 16×16-bit matrices $\mathbf{M}_0$ and $\mathbf{M}_1$ as $\mathbf{M} = \begin{bmatrix} \mathbf{M}_0 & \mathbf{M}_1 \\ \mathbf{M}_1 & \mathbf{M}_0 \end{bmatrix}$. We consider the r-th and $(r + 1)$-th rounds $(1 \leq r \leq 8)$, and define the first collision function from the eight 16-bit input values $(x_{0,0}^r, x_{0,1}^r, \cdots, x_{3,1}^r)$ of the eight TMC tables in the r-th round to the four 16-bit output values $(x_{0,0}^{r+1}, x_{3,0}^{r+1}, x_{2,1}^{r+1}, x_{1,1}^{r+1})$ in the $(r + 1)$-th round, denoted by f: $((x_{0,0}^{r+1}, x_{3,0}^{r+1}), (x_{2,1}^{r+1}, x_{1,1}^{r+1})) = f(x_{0,0}^r, x_{0,1}^r, \ x_{1,0}^r, x_{1,1}^r, x_{2,0}^r, x_{2,1}^r, x_{3,0}^r, x_{3,1}^r) = (f_0(x_{0,0}^r, x_{0,1}^r, \cdots, x_{3,1}^r), f_1(x_{0,0}^r, x_{0,1}^r, \cdots, x_{3,1}^r))$.

We define $\mathbf{S}_i^r$ as $\mathbf{S}_i^r(x) = \begin{pmatrix} \mathbf{S} \\ \mathbf{S} \end{pmatrix} ((K_{r-1,j} || K_{r-1,(j+5) \bmod 16}) \oplus L_i^r(x))$, where $j = 0, 10, 4, 14, 8, 2, 12, 6$ respectively for $i = 0, 1, \cdots, 7$, and x is a 16-bit variable. Then, the above f function can be simplified and expressed as

$$((x_{0,0}^{r+1}, x_{3,0}^{r+1}), (x_{2,1}^{r+1}, x_{1,1}^{r+1}))$$
$$= f(x_{0,0}^r, x_{0,1}^r, x_{1,0}^r, x_{1,1}^r, x_{2,0}^r, x_{2,1}^r, x_{3,0}^r, x_{3,1}^r)$$
$$= (f_0(x_{0,0}^r, x_{0,1}^r, \cdots, x_{3,1}^r), f_1(x_{0,0}^r, x_{0,1}^r, \cdots, x_{3,1}^r))$$
$$= \Phi \circ M^{r+1} \circ \begin{bmatrix} R_0^r \circ \mathbf{MC}_0(\mathbf{S}_0^r(x_{0,0}^r)) \oplus R_0^r \circ \mathbf{MC}_1(\mathbf{S}_1^r(x_{0,1}^r)) \\ R_1^r \circ \mathbf{MC}_0(\mathbf{S}_2^r(x_{1,0}^r)) \oplus R_1^r \circ \mathbf{MC}_1(\mathbf{S}_3^r(x_{1,1}^r)) \\ R_2^r \circ \mathbf{MC}_0(\mathbf{S}_4^r(x_{2,0}^r)) \oplus R_2^r \circ \mathbf{MC}_1(\mathbf{S}_5^r(x_{2,1}^r)) \\ R_3^r \circ \mathbf{MC}_0(\mathbf{S}_6^r(x_{3,0}^r)) \oplus R_3^r \circ \mathbf{MC}_1(\mathbf{S}_7^r(x_{3,1}^r)) \end{bmatrix}, \qquad (7)$$

where Φ represents the operation of taking the four 16-bit values $(x_{0,0}^{r+1}, x_{3,0}^{r+1}, x_{2,1}^{r+1}, x_{1,1}^{r+1})$ from a 128-bit output of M^{r+1}. Similarly define $\mathbf{S}_i^{r+1}(x)$ functions and collision functions starting with the $(r + 1)$-th round.

We first set $x_{1,0}^r = x_{1,1}^r = x_{2,0}^r = x_{2,1}^r = x_{3,0}^r = x_{3,1}^r = 0$ and use the following collision form to recover the $\mathbf{S}_0^r$ and $\mathbf{S}_1^r$ functions:

$$f_0(\alpha, 0, 0, 0, 0, 0, 0, 0) = f_0(0, \beta, 0, 0, 0, 0, 0, 0), \tag{8}$$

where $\alpha, \beta \in \mathrm{GF}(2)^{16}$. By f definition, we have the following equation by Eq. (7):

$$\Phi_0 \circ M^{r+1} \circ \begin{bmatrix} R_0^r \circ \mathbf{MC}_0(\mathbf{S}_0^r(\alpha)) \oplus R_0^r \circ \mathbf{MC}_1(\mathbf{S}_1^r(0)) \\ R_1^r \circ \mathbf{MC}_0(\mathbf{S}_2^r(0)) \oplus R_1^r \circ \mathbf{MC}_1(\mathbf{S}_3^r(0)) \\ R_2^r \circ \mathbf{MC}_0(\mathbf{S}_4^r(0)) \oplus R_2^r \circ \mathbf{MC}_1(\mathbf{S}_5^r(0)) \\ R_3^r \circ \mathbf{MC}_0(\mathbf{S}_6^r(0)) \oplus R_3^r \circ \mathbf{MC}_1(\mathbf{S}_7^r(0)) \end{bmatrix}$$

$$= \Phi_0 \circ M^{r+1} \circ \begin{bmatrix} R_0^r \circ \mathbf{MC}_0(\mathbf{S}_0^r(0)) \oplus R_0^r \circ \mathbf{MC}_1(\mathbf{S}_1^r(\beta)) \\ R_1^r \circ \mathbf{MC}_0(\mathbf{S}_2^r(0)) \oplus R_1^r \circ \mathbf{MC}_1(\mathbf{S}_3^r(0)) \\ R_2^r \circ \mathbf{MC}_0(\mathbf{S}_4^r(0)) \oplus R_2^r \circ \mathbf{MC}_1(\mathbf{S}_5^r(0)) \\ R_3^r \circ \mathbf{MC}_0(\mathbf{S}_6^r(0)) \oplus R_3^r \circ \mathbf{MC}_1(\mathbf{S}_7^r(0)) \end{bmatrix}, \tag{9}$$

where Φ_0 represents the operation of taking the two 16-bit values $(x_{0,0}^{r+1}, x_{3,0}^{r+1})$ from a 128-bit output of M^{r+1}.

By the construction of the white-box M^{r+1} operation as described above, M^{r+1} shifts one of the first two bytes of the original first MC output column (i.e. $(R_0^r)^{-1}(X_0^r)$) into the $x_{0,0}^{r+1}$ value, and shifts the other of the first two bytes of the original first MC output column into the $x_{3,0}^{r+1}$ value; and the $x_{0,0}^{r+1}$ value also involves a byte from another original MC output column (of the r-th round), and the $x_{3,0}^{r+1}$ value also involves a byte from another original MC output column (of the r-th round), but the two original bytes are fixed in our above setting $x_{1,0}^r = x_{1,1}^r = x_{2,0}^r = x_{2,1}^r = x_{3,0}^r = x_{3,1}^r = 0$. Thus, if the first 16-bit half of the original first MC output column is identical for both sides of Eq. (8), the 32-bit value $(x_{0,0}^{r+1}, x_{3,0}^{r+1})$ should be identical. As a consequence, we can distinguish an internal collision by Eq. (9), which implies $\mathbf{MC}_0(\mathbf{S}_0^r(\alpha)) \oplus \mathbf{MC}_1(\mathbf{S}_1^r(0)) = \mathbf{MC}_0(\mathbf{S}_0^r(0)) \oplus \mathbf{MC}_1(\mathbf{S}_1^r(\beta))$, that is

$$\mathbf{M}_0(\mathbf{S}_0^r(\alpha) \oplus \mathbf{S}_0^r(0)) = \mathbf{M}_1(\mathbf{S}_1^r(\beta) \oplus \mathbf{S}_1^r(0)). \tag{10}$$

And we have $2^{16} - 1 = 65535$ equations of the form Eq. (10) for 65535 pairs of $(\alpha, \beta) \neq (0, 0)$.

Likewise, by considering the other collision form $f_1(\alpha, 0, 0, 0, 0, 0, 0, 0) = f_1(0, \beta, 0, 0, 0, 0, 0, 0)$, where M^{r+1} shifts one of the last two bytes of the original first MC output column into the $x_{2,1}^{r+1}$ value and shifts the other of the last two bytes of the original first MC output column into the $x_{1,1}^{r+1}$ value, we obtain

$$\mathbf{M}_1(\mathbf{S}_0^r(\alpha) \oplus \mathbf{S}_0^r(0)) = \mathbf{M}_0(\mathbf{S}_1^r(\beta) \oplus \mathbf{S}_1^r(0)). \tag{11}$$

And we have $2^{16} - 1 = 65535$ equations of the form Eq. (11) for 65535 pairs of $(\alpha, \beta) \neq (0, 0)$.

Finally, we obtain a system of $65535 \times 2 = 131070$ linear equations involving all the $2 \times 2^{16} = 131072$ unknowns $\mathbf{S}_0^r(\cdot)$ and $\mathbf{S}_1^r(\cdot)$, and it can be rewritten in terms of $2 \times (2^{16} - 1) = 131070$ unknowns $\mathbf{S}_0^r(\alpha) \oplus \mathbf{S}_0^r(0)$ and $\mathbf{S}_1^r(\beta) \oplus \mathbf{S}_1^r(0)$ with $\alpha \neq 0$ and $\beta \neq 0$.

5.3.2.1 A Small-Scale Experimental Result

Subsequently, one may similarly think that the linear system with (10) and (11) would have a rank of $131070 - 1 = 131069$ and thus the remaining steps were similar as we did in Sect. 4.2, except that each of the $\mathbf{S}_i^r$ functions is a parallel concatenation of two S-boxes and that Xiao and Lai's implementation uses linear encodings. The size of the linear system is very large, an experimental test on the rank of the linear system under a single (encodings, round key) combination takes about an hour on a workstation (Intel(R)Xeon(R) Platinum 8280 CPU @ 270 GHz(56 CPUs), 2.7 GHz), and we have experimentally tested 15 different (encodings, round key) combinations, but the rank is always 130814, which is much less than the number 131070 of unknowns, meaning that there are too many solutions for $(\mathbf{S}_0^r(\alpha) \oplus \mathbf{S}_0^r(0), \mathbf{S}_1^r(\beta) \oplus \mathbf{S}_1^r(0))$. As a consequence, it is not efficient to recover $(\mathbf{S}_0^r(\alpha) \oplus \mathbf{S}_0^r(0), \mathbf{S}_1^r(\beta) \oplus \mathbf{S}_1^r(0))$ by this way. Thus, this small-scale experiment shows that our extension cannot apply to Xiao and Lai's implementation. But nevertheless, we leave it as an open problem to theoretically investigate the distribution of the ranks under all encodings.

5.3.2.2 A Supposed Case

Below we suppose there are encodings such that the resulting linear system with (10) and (11) has a rank of 131069. In such a linear equation system, all the unknowns can be expressed in function of one unknown, and there exist coefficients a_i and b_i so that all the unknowns are linearly linked as

$$\mathbf{S}_0^r(\alpha) = a_i \otimes (\mathbf{S}_0^r(0) \oplus \mathbf{S}_0^r(1)) \oplus \mathbf{S}_0^r(0), \mathbf{S}_1^r(\beta) = b_i \otimes (\mathbf{S}_1^r(0) \oplus \mathbf{S}_1^r(1)) \oplus \mathbf{S}_1^r(0). (12)$$

Similarly, we exhaustively search on $(\mathbf{S}_0^r(0), \mathbf{S}_0^r(1))$ to recover the $\mathbf{S}_0^r(\cdot)$ function by testing whether the first-order derivative $(\mathbf{S}^{-1}\|\mathbf{S}^{-1}) \circ \hat{\mathbf{S}}_0^r(x) \oplus (\mathbf{S}^{-1}\|\mathbf{S}^{-1}) \circ \hat{\mathbf{S}}_0^r(x \oplus 0x0101)$ is constant for at most 2^{15} inputs, because the function $(\mathbf{S}^{-1}\|\mathbf{S}^{-1}) \circ \hat{\mathbf{S}}_0^r(\cdot)$ has an algebraic degree of at most 1 for the solution $\mathbf{S}_0^r(\cdot)$ from the correct $(\mathbf{S}_0^r(0), \mathbf{S}_0^r(1))$, and has an algebraic degree greater than 1 with an overwhelming probability for the solution $\hat{\mathbf{S}}_0^r(\cdot)$ from a wrong $(\mathbf{S}_0^r(0), \mathbf{S}_0^r(1))$. After $\mathbf{S}_0^r(\cdot)$ is recovered, we recover the $\mathbf{S}_1^r(\cdot)$ function by exhaustive search on $\mathbf{S}_1^r(0)$ under Eq. (12). The other $\mathbf{S}_2^r(\cdot), \cdots, \mathbf{S}_7^r(\cdot)$ functions similarly recovered. The $\mathbf{S}_i^{r+1}(\cdot)$ functions for the $(r+1)$-th round can also be recovered similarly.

After all the $\mathbf{S}_i^r(\cdot)$ and $\mathbf{S}_i^{r+1}(\cdot)$ functions for the r-th and $(r+1)$-th rounds have been recovered $(i = 0, 1, \cdots, 7)$, we can recover the $(r+1)$-th round key K_r in the way described in Sect. 3.2. Specifically, we choose an arbitrary value for $(x_{0,0}^r, x_{0,1}^r, \cdots, x_{3,0}^r)$, obtain the corresponding value for $(x_{0,0}^{r+1}, x_{0,1}^{r+1}, \cdots, x_{3,0}^{r+1})$, and by the recovered $\mathbf{S}_i^r(\cdot)$ and $\mathbf{S}_i^{r+1}(\cdot)$ functions we have $Y_r = (\mathbf{S}_0^r(x_{0,0}^r), \mathbf{S}_1^r(x_{0,1}^r), \cdots, \mathbf{S}_7^r(x_{3,1}^r))$ and $Y_{r+1} = (\mathbf{S}_0^{r+1}(x_{0,0}^{r+1}), \mathbf{S}_1^{r+1}(x_{0,1}^{r+1}), \cdots, \mathbf{S}_7^{r+1}(x_{3,1}^{r+1}))$ and recover the round key $K_r = \text{MC}(Y_r) \oplus \text{SR}^{-1} \circ \text{SB}^{-1}(Y_{r+1})$ from $Y_{r+1} = \text{SB} \circ \text{SR}(\text{MC}(Y_r) \oplus K_r)$, where Y_r and Y_{r+1} denote the two corresponding original 128-bit states immediately after the S-box layers of the r-th and $(r+1)$-th rounds, respectively.

As a result, in case of such encodings that make the resulting linear system have a rank of 131069, our first extension can apply to Xiao and Lai's implementation with an expected time complexity of about $((2^{16})^2 \cdot 1 \cdot 2 \cdot 2 + 2^{16} \cdot 1 \cdot 2 \cdot 2) \times 4 \times 2 \approx 2^{37}$ **S** computations.

5.4 Security of Luo et al.'s Implementation Against Our Extensions

Luo et al.'s implementation [28] improved Xiao and Lai's implementation by performing the ShiftRows operation as a series of white-box tables and using both linear and non-linear white-box operations. Our investigation shows that the case for Luo et al.'s implementation is similar to the case for Xiao and Lai's implementation, specifically, collision functions can be defined from the 32 4-bit inputs of the 8 nTMC tables of Stage 3 of the r-th round to the concerned 16 4-bit output values of the TXOR3 tables of the $(r+1)$-th round, but likewise the rank of the resulting linear system is much less than the number of unknowns, and thus our extensions cannot apply to Luo et al.'s implementation.

6 Conclusions

In this paper, we have given two extensions to Lepoint et al.'s collision-based attack on Chow et al.'s white-box AES implementation, which avoid Lepoint et al.'s last one or two phases and can attack a broader range of white-box implementations, and we have applied the first extension to attack Bai et al.'s white-box AES implementation with an expected time complexity of about 2^{20} S-box computations. White-box implementation designers should pay attention to these collision-based attack approaches, particularly the first extension, which does not need to recover internal encodings and only needs to know whether an encoding produces different outputs for different inputs, which is the first such key-recovery attack on white-box AES implementation with external encodings to the best of our knowledge. Besides, our cryptanalysis suggests to some extent that for white-box AES implementation, building a white-box table with two S-boxes is preferable to building a white-box table with a single S-box in the sense of their security against collision-based attacks, but nevertheless we leave it as an open problem whether there are such encodings that the rank of the corresponding linear system is slightly less than the number of the involved unknowns. A possible future research topic on white-box AES implementation is to investigate the distribution of the ranks under all encodings and learn whether they produce the same rank.

Acknowledgement. The authors are grateful to several anonymous referees for their comments. This work was supported by Guangxi Key Laboratory of Cryptography and Information Security (No. GCIS202102). Jiqiang Lu was Qianjiang Special Expert of Hangzhou.

References

1. Baek, C.H., Cheon, J.H., Hong, H.: White-box AES implementation revisited. J. Commun. Netw. **18**(3), 273–287 (2016)
2. Bai, K., Wu, C.: A secure white-box SM4 implementation. Secur. Commun. Netw. **9**(10), 996–1006 (2016)
3. Bai, K., Wu, C., Zhang, Z.: Protect white-box AES to resist table composition attacks. IET Inf. Secur. **12**(4), 305–313 (2018)
4. Banik, S., Bogdanov, A., Isobe, T., et al.: Analysis of software countermeasures for whitebox encryption. IACR Trans. Symmetric Cryptol. **2017**(1), 307–328 (2017)
5. Barkan, E., Biham, E.: In how many ways can you write Rijndael? In: Zheng, Y. (ed.) ASIACRYPT 2002. LNCS, vol. 2501, pp. 160–175. Springer, Heidelberg (2002). https://doi.org/10.1007/3-540-36178-2_10
6. Billet, O., Gilbert, H., Ech-Chatbi, C.: Cryptanalysis of a white box AES implementation. In: Handschuh, H., Hasan, M.A. (eds.) SAC 2004. LNCS, vol. 3357, pp. 227–240. Springer, Heidelberg (2004). https://doi.org/10.1007/978-3-540-30564-4_16
7. Biryukov, A., Bouillaguet, C., Khovratovich, D.: Cryptographic schemes based on the ASASA structure: black-box, white-box, and public-key (extended abstract). In: Sarkar, P., Iwata, T. (eds.) ASIACRYPT 2014. LNCS, vol. 8873, pp. 63–84. Springer, Heidelberg (2014). https://doi.org/10.1007/978-3-662-45611-8_4
8. Biryukov, A., De Cannière, C., Braeken, A., Preneel, B.: A toolbox for cryptanalysis: linear and affine equivalence algorithms. In: Biham, E. (ed.) EUROCRYPT 2003. LNCS, vol. 2656, pp. 33–50. Springer, Heidelberg (2003). https://doi.org/10.1007/3-540-39200-9_3
9. Biryukov, A., Udovenko, A.: Attacks and countermeasures for white-box designs. In: Peyrin, T., Galbraith, S. (eds.) ASIACRYPT 2018. LNCS, vol. 11273, pp. 373–402. Springer, Cham (2018). https://doi.org/10.1007/978-3-030-03329-3_13
10. Bogdanov, A., Isobe, T.: White-box cryptography revised: space-hard ciphers. In: ACM CCS 2015, pp. 1058–1069. ACM (2015)
11. Bogdanov, A., Isobe, T., Tischhauser, E.: Towards practical whitebox cryptography: optimizing efficiency and space hardness. In: Cheon, J.H., Takagi, T. (eds.) ASIACRYPT 2016. LNCS, vol. 10031, pp. 126–158. Springer, Heidelberg (2016). https://doi.org/10.1007/978-3-662-53887-6_5
12. Bringer, J., Chabanne, H., Dottax, E.: White box cryptography: another attempt. IACR Cryptol. ePrint Arch. **2006**, 468 (2006)
13. Bos, J.W., Hubain, C., Michiels, W., Teuwen, P.: Differential computation analysis: hiding your white-box designs is not enough. In: Gierlichs, B., Poschmann, A.Y. (eds.) CHES 2016. LNCS, vol. 9813, pp. 215–236. Springer, Heidelberg (2016). https://doi.org/10.1007/978-3-662-53140-2_11
14. Chow, S., Eisen, P., Johnson, H., Van Oorschot, P.C.: White-box cryptography and an AES implementation. In: Nyberg, K., Heys, H. (eds.) SAC 2002. LNCS, vol. 2595, pp. 250–270. Springer, Heidelberg (2003). https://doi.org/10.1007/3-540-36492-7_17
15. Chow, S., Eisen, P., Johnson, H., van Oorschot, P.C.: A white-box DES implementation for DRM applications. In: Feigenbaum, J. (ed.) DRM 2002. LNCS, vol. 2696, pp. 1–15. Springer, Heidelberg (2003). https://doi.org/10.1007/978-3-540-44993-5_1
16. De Mulder, Y., Roelse, P., Preneel, B.: Cryptanalysis of the Xiao – Lai white-box AES implementation. In: Knudsen, L.R., Wu, H. (eds.) SAC 2012. LNCS, vol.

7707, pp. 34–49. Springer, Heidelberg (2013). https://doi.org/10.1007/978-3-642-35999-6_3

17. De Mulder, Y., Wyseur, B., Preneel, B.: Cryptanalysis of a perturbated white-box AES implementation. In: Gong, G., Gupta, K.C. (eds.) INDOCRYPT 2010. LNCS, vol. 6498, pp. 292–310. Springer, Heidelberg (2010). https://doi.org/10.1007/978-3-642-17401-8_21

18. Derbez, P., Fouque, P., Lambin, B., Minaud, B.: On recovering affine encodings in white-box implementations. IACR Trans. Cryptogr. Hardw. Embed. Syst. **2018**(3), 121–149 (2018)

19. Dinur, I.: An improved affine equivalence algorithm for random permutations. In: Nielsen, J.B., Rijmen, V. (eds.) EUROCRYPT 2018. LNCS, vol. 10820, pp. 413–442. Springer, Cham (2018). https://doi.org/10.1007/978-3-319-78381-9_16

20. Fouque, P.-A., Karpman, P., Kirchner, P., Minaud, B.: Efficient and provable white-box primitives. In: Cheon, J.H., Takagi, T. (eds.) ASIACRYPT 2016. LNCS, vol. 10031, pp. 159–188. Springer, Heidelberg (2016). https://doi.org/10.1007/978-3-662-53887-6_6

21. Goubin, L., Masereel, J.-M., Quisquater, M.: Cryptanalysis of white box DES implementations. In: Adams, C., Miri, A., Wiener, M. (eds.) SAC 2007. LNCS, vol. 4876, pp. 278–295. Springer, Heidelberg (2007). https://doi.org/10.1007/978-3-540-77360-3_18

22. Jacob, M., Boneh, D., Felten, E.: Attacking an obfuscated cipher by injecting faults. In: Feigenbaum, J. (ed.) DRM 2002. LNCS, vol. 2696, pp. 16–31. Springer, Heidelberg (2003). https://doi.org/10.1007/978-3-540-44993-5_2

23. Karroumi, M.: Protecting white-box AES with dual ciphers. In: Rhee, K.-H., Nyang, D.H. (eds.) ICISC 2010. LNCS, vol. 6829, pp. 278–291. Springer, Heidelberg (2011). https://doi.org/10.1007/978-3-642-24209-0_19

24. Lai, X.: Higher order derivatives and differential cryptanalysis. In: Blahut, R.E., Costello, D.J., Maurer, U., Mittelholzer, T. (eds.) Communications and Cryptography. The Springer International Series in Engineering and Computer Science, vol. 276, pp. 227–233. Springer, Boston (1994). https://doi.org/10.1007/978-1-4615-2694-0_23

25. Lee, S., Kim, M.: Improvement on a masked white-box cryptographic implementation. IEEE Access **8**, 90992–91004 (2020)

26. Lee, S., Kim, T., Kang, Y.: A masked white-box cryptographic implementation for protecting against differential computation analysis. IEEE Trans. Inf. Forensics Secur. **13**(10), 2602–2615 (2018)

27. Lepoint, T., Rivain, M., De Mulder, Y., Roelse, P., Preneel, B.: Two attacks on a white-box AES implementation. In: Lange, T., Lauter, K., Lisoněk, P. (eds.) SAC 2013. LNCS, vol. 8282, pp. 265–285. Springer, Heidelberg (2014). https://doi.org/10.1007/978-3-662-43414-7_14

28. Luo, R., Lai, X., You, R.: A new attempt of white-box AES implementation. In: Proceedings of IEEE International Conference on Security, pp. 423–429. IEEE (2014)

29. Michiels, W., Gorissen, P., Hollmann, H.D.L.: Cryptanalysis of a generic class of white-box implementations. In: Avanzi, R.M., Keliher, L., Sica, F. (eds.) SAC 2008. LNCS, vol. 5381, pp. 414–428. Springer, Heidelberg (2009). https://doi.org/10.1007/978-3-642-04159-4_27

30. Muir, J.A.: A tutorial on white-box AES. In: Kranakis, E. (ed.) Advances in Network Analysis and its Applications. Mathematics in Industry, vol. 18, pp. 209–229. Springer, Heidelberg (2013). https://doi.org/10.1007/978-3-642-30904-5_9

31. National Institute of Standards and Technology (NIST): Advanced Encryption Standard (AES), FIPS-197 (2001)
32. Seker, O., Eisenbarth, T., Liskiewicz, M.: A white-box masking scheme resisting computational and algebraic attacks. IACR Trans. Cryptogr. Hardw. Embed. Syst. **2021**(2), 61–105 (2021)
33. Tolhuizen, L.: Improved cryptanalysis of an AES implementation. In: Proceedings of the 33rd WIC Symposium on Information Theory in the Benelux, pp. 68–71 (2012)
34. Wyseur, B., Michiels, W., Gorissen, P., Preneel, B.: Cryptanalysis of white-box DES implementations with arbitrary external encodings. In: Adams, C., Miri, A., Wiener, M. (eds.) SAC 2007. LNCS, vol. 4876, pp. 264–277. Springer, Heidelberg (2007). https://doi.org/10.1007/978-3-540-77360-3_17
35. Xiao, Y., Lai, X.: A secure implementation of white-box AES. In: Proceedings of the Second International Conference on Computer Science and its Applications, pp. 1–6. IEEE (2009)

Differential Cryptanalysis II

Advancing the Meet-in-the-Filter Technique: Applications to CHAM and KATAN

Alex Biryukov[1], Je Sen Teh[1,2], and Aleksei Udovenko[1(✉)]

[1] University of Luxembourg, Esch-sur-Alzette, Luxembourg
{alex.biryukov,jesen.teh,aleksei.udovenko}@uni.lu
[2] University Sains Malaysia, Gelugor, Malaysia
jesen_teh@usm.my

Abstract. Recently, Biryukov et al. presented a new technique for key recovery in differential cryptanalysis, called *meet-in-the-filter* (MiF). In this work, we develop theoretical and practical aspects of the technique, which helps understanding and simplifies application. In particular, we show bounds on MiF complexity and conditions when the MiF-enhanced attack may reach them. We present a method based on trail counting which allows to estimate filtering strength of involved rounds and perform consequent complexity analysis with pen and paper, compared to the computer-aided approach of the original work. Furthermore, we show how MiF can be combined with plaintext structures for linear key schedules, allowing to increase the number of attacked rounds or to reduce the data complexity.

We illustrate our methods on block cipher families CHAM and KATAN and show best-to-date single-key differential attacks for these ciphers.

Keywords: Symmetric-key · Differential cryptanalysis · ARX · NLFSR · CHAM · KATAN

1 Introduction

In over a decade or so, there has been a shift towards portable computing devices such as smart devices and wearable systems. Although these devices have greatly eased the lives of many, they also came with new security challenges, one being the design of cryptographic solutions that are not only efficient and secure, but also have minimal computational requirements (e.g. low memory and energy). Finding a balance between these requirements has been the focus of researchers in the field of *lightweight cryptography*. Many lightweight primitives have been proposed over the years to address this need, including symmetric-key block ciphers such as CHAM [10,12] and KATAN [5]. Differential cryptanalysis is one of the main techniques for assessing the security of various cryptographic primitives. Resistance to differential attacks has become one of the basic requirements

The work was supported by the Luxembourg National Research Fund's (FNR) and the German Research Foundation's (DFG) joint project APLICA (C19/IS/13641232).

of a modern block cipher. Many variants of the attack have since been introduced. Recently, a new differential cryptanalysis tool called *meet-in-the-filter* (MiF) was proposed by Biryukov et al. [4]. Using MiF, an attacker can append a large number of rounds for key recovery. When applied to SPECK [2], some of the best differential attacks were reported. However, its application to other block ciphers has yet to be investigated. In this paper, we apply MiF to attack CHAM-64 [10,12] and the KATAN family of block ciphers [5]. The choices of both CHAM and KATAN were motivated by their slow diffusion (slower than SPECK) which allows to append a large number of rounds for key recovery. We report the best differential attacks on both ciphers in the single-key setting using MiF as summarized in Table 1. A comparison with prior differential attacks on KATAN is provided in the full version of the paper.

Table 1. Key Recovery Attacks on CHAM-64 and the KATAN family.

Cipher	Rounds	Time	Data	Memory	Ref.
CHAM-64-128	52	2^{114}	2^{61}	2^{54}	Section 4.2
KATAN-32-80	124	2^{76}	2^{31}	2^{38}	Section 5.3
KATAN-48-80	130	2^{73}	2^{45}	2^{51}	Section 5.4
KATAN-64-80	110	2^{73}	2^{57}	2^{65}	Section 5.5

In addition to new cryptanalysis results for CHAM and KATAN, this paper revisits the practical and theoretical aspects of MiF. We describe theoretical bounds on its complexity and show how simple time complexity estimates can be obtained for MiF-enhanced differential attacks. We also introduce an approach for estimating trail weight distributions which is useful to determine the filtering strength of rounds involved in key recovery, which allows to perform complexity analysis with pen and paper. In addition, we show that MiF can be combined with plaintext structures to increase the number of attacked rounds for ciphers with linear key schedules (e.g. CHAM).

The outline of the paper is as follows. Section 2 provides a brief introduction to the MiF tool. Section 3 present new techniques and theories related to MiF that are used in our attacks. Finally, detailed descriptions of our attacks on CHAM-64 and the entire KATAN family are reported in Sect. 4 and 5.

2 The Meet-in-the-Filter Technique

A typical differential attack relies on a differential distinguisher over r rounds of a cipher with probability p to which k key-recovery rounds are appended. After guessing the last k round keys, an attacker performs partial decryptions to obtain the output difference after r rounds. If this difference matches the output difference of the r-round distinguisher, then the round key guesses are likely to be correct. Generally, an attacker would try to maximize r to obtain the best attack possible.

MiF [4] is a differential cryptanalysis tool that allows to also maximize k. If a cipher has a relatively slow diffusion an attacker can potentially add a large number of k rounds. MiF produces a set of full k-round trails that are used for key recovery by first splitting k into two parts, $k = s + t$, then processing each part separately to find a meeting point (matching difference in the middle). An illustration of MiF is provided in Fig. 1.

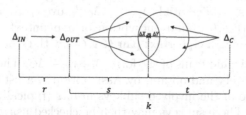

Fig. 1. MiF with an r-round differential and $k = s + t$ key recovery rounds.

Offline, a Matsui-like search is performed in the forward direction over s rounds starting from the output difference of the r-round differential, Δ_{OUT} to an intermediate difference ΔX. The set of these s-round trails (the *MiF cluster*) will be stored. In the online phase, plaintext pairs with difference Δ_{IN} are encrypted over $r + k$ rounds to obtain a ciphertext difference, ΔC. For each ciphertext pair (C_1, C_2), we then perform a reverse search on t rounds in search of a match in the cluster. The set of trails over t rounds is called the *MiF filter*.

Ciphertext pairs that result in a match are candidate *right pairs*, i.e., pairs whose plaintexts have followed the initial r-round differential ($\Delta_{\text{IN}} \xrightarrow{r} \Delta_{\text{OUT}}$), and come with a set of suggested k-round trails. The latter will be used in the key-recovery phase which involves guessing round keys and checking if the partial decryption of ciphertext pairs conforms to the suggested trails. Key recovery relies on the following formulation of the Markov assumption:

Assumption 1. *For a differential trail $\Delta P \to \Delta C$ with a weight w (and possibly truncated intermediate differences), the average fraction of pairs of ciphertexts (C_1, C_2) and subkeys for which the partial decryption of (C_1, C_2) follows the trail is equal to 2^{-w}.*

In the end, the attacker is left with a set of candidate keys that are tested with trial decryptions. Optimizing the key recovery phase requires deeper analysis and may vary depending on the target cipher.

3   New Theoretical Analysis of Meet-in-the-Filter Technique and Extensions

3.1   Performance Gain of MiF Key Recovery over Exhaustive Search

We first analyze the theoretical power and limits of MiF with respect to the weights of involved trails or differentials. Indeed, the MiF attack has several parameters and the trade-off between the time and data complexities is not very clear. For the purpose of this subsection, we will assume that the key recovery procedure is perfect: given a trail or even a *differential* over k rounds, it enumerates (without any extra overhead) all the candidate subkeys that satisfy the trail/differential. This is a strong condition and, although it can often be reached in basic MiF attacks, advanced attacks would require more precise analysis of the intermediate costs. We will focus on the following MiF-like setting.

An attacker uses a differential $\Delta_{\text{IN}} \xrightarrow{r} \Delta_{\text{OUT}}$ over r rounds with a weight w and queries an $(r + k)$-round encryption of a plaintext pair (P_1, P_2) with $P_1 \oplus P_2 = \Delta_{\text{IN}}$, obtaining a ciphertext pair (C_1, C_2) with $C_1 \oplus C_2 = \Delta C$. The MiF tool suggests a set of valid trails of the form $\Delta_{\text{OUT}} \xrightarrow{k} \Delta C$. The attacker may run the perfect key recovery and obtain, by Assumption 1, a list of 2^{K_s-w} subkeys, where K_s is the size of the involved subkeys in bits (typically equal to the size of the master key). These subkeys may then be checked using trial decryptions. Questions then arise: What are the chances to hit the correct master key? Should the attacker attempt the key recovery, or, perhaps, it is better to try another pair?

The key insight to answering these questions lies in studying the probability that the right subkey is among the suggested subkeys *posterior to observing the output difference ΔC*. Indeed, if the suggested subkeys are not better than fully randomly guessed subkeys, then the attack is not useful at all. On the other hand, if the suggested subkeys are g times more likely to match the right subkey ($g > 1$), then on average, the attacker would need to test g times fewer subkeys to find the right one, effectively reducing the time complexity (more precisely, of the trial decryption stage) by the factor g. This idea is similar to the classic definition of signal/noise ratio (S/N) by Biham and Shamir [3], and our theory specializes it based on the MiF trail $\Delta_{\text{OUT}} \xrightarrow{r+k} \Delta C$.

In the following, consider two differentials

$$\tau_r = \Delta_{\text{IN}} \xrightarrow{r} \Delta_{\text{OUT}}, \quad \tau_k = \Delta_{\text{OUT}} \xrightarrow{k} \Delta C, \tag{1}$$

with probabilities $\Pr[\tau_r] = p$ and $\Pr[\tau_k] = q$ respectively. Let $\tilde{p}$ be the probability of the full differential $\Delta_{\text{IN}} \xrightarrow{r+k} \Delta C$.

Definition 1. *Define the* gain *g of the pair (τ_r, τ_k) as*

$$g = \frac{\Pr[\kappa \text{ is the right key} \mid \kappa \text{ satisfies } \Delta_{\text{OUT}} \xrightarrow{k} \Delta C]}{2^{-K_s}}, \tag{2}$$

where the probability is over the encryptions of plaintext pairs.

Theorem 1. *The gain g is equal to*

$$g = \frac{\Pr[\Delta_{\text{IN}} \xrightarrow{r} \Delta_{\text{OUT}}]}{\Pr[\Delta_{\text{IN}} \xrightarrow{r+k} \Delta C]} = \frac{p}{\tilde{p}}. \tag{3}$$

Proof. For κ to be the right subkey, the encryption must have followed the path $\Delta_{\text{IN}} \xrightarrow{r} \Delta_{\text{OUT}} \xrightarrow{k} \Delta C$ (given $\Delta_{\text{IN}} \xrightarrow{r+k} \Delta C$) and κ is one of the subkeys satisfying the transition $\Delta_{\text{OUT}} \xrightarrow{k} \Delta C$ (which has expected size $2^{K_s}q$, where q is the transition probability over k rounds). Therefore,

$$g = \frac{\frac{pq}{\tilde{p}} \cdot \frac{1}{2^{K_s}q}}{2^{-K_s}} = \frac{p}{\tilde{p}}.$$

$\square$

Perhaps counter-intuitively, the proposition shows that the gain does not directly depend on the probability q of trail/differential $\Delta_{\text{OUT}} \xrightarrow{k} \Delta C$, except that it is included in the full differential when concatenated with $\Delta_{\text{IN}} \xrightarrow{r} \Delta_{\text{OUT}}$. The explanation for that in terms of a differential attack is that *the probability q of the transition τ_k is proportional to the number $2^{K_s}q$ of surviving keys and inversely proportional to the required number $1/(pq)$ of encryptions*: A lower probability transition yields fewer keys to check but requires more encryptions to actually hit it, while a higher probability transition yields more key candidates but happens more often.

The trivial bound $\tilde{p} \geq pq$ translates to the following bound on the gain.

Proposition 1. *The gain g is upper-bounded by $1/q$.*

This is also clear from the fact that the set of (on average) $2^{K_s}q$ subkeys is smaller than all 2^{K_s} keys precisely by the factor of $1/q$. However, this bound is tight only in the case $\tilde{p}=pq$, i.e., when all trails in the differential $\Delta_{\text{IN}} \xrightarrow{r+k} \Delta C$ are going through Δ_{OUT} after the first r rounds. In this case, getting *one* encryption pair with such ΔC is sufficient for the attack to succeed with gain $1/q$, since the right key has to be in those $2^{K_s}q$ suggested keys. In typical attacks, however, the gain would be much smaller. It is as close to $1/q$ as big is the fraction of trails $\Delta_{\text{IN}} \xrightarrow{r+k} \Delta C$ going through Δ_{OUT} (in terms of the total probability).

Usually, we expect all output differences to be equally possible, as described in the following assumption.

Assumption 2. *The probability[1] of any differential $\Delta_{\text{IN}} \xrightarrow{r+k} \Delta C$ over the full cipher is equal to $2^{-|C|}$ up to a negligible error, where $|C|$ is the ciphertext size.*

Corollary 1. *Under Assumption 2, the gain g is equal to $2^{|C|}p$.*

Interestingly and counter-intuitively, the gain does not depend on the differential in the MiF part (unless Assumption 2 does not hold and there is a full-round (improbable) differential distinguisher). Note however that here we only consider the final number of key candidates for trial decryptions. Other

---

[1] Here, we consider probability over all intermediate (long) keys. Therefore, the limitation of a fixed-key permutation to have minimum nonzero differential probability $2^{-|C|+1}$ (over plaintexts/ciphertexts) does not affect this assumption.

attack complexities which include the data complexity, the MiF complexity and the intermediate key recovery complexity do depend on the MiF part. For attacks where the trial decryption dominates, the corollary provides a simple time complexity estimate of $2^{K_s}/(2^{|C|}p)$. We further investigate Theorem 1 experimentally[2] and the details can be found in the full version of the paper.

Remark 1. In principle, the filtering in accordance with the trail does not necessarily need to filter *keys* for each given ciphertext pair: filtering by ciphertext values works as well, since it reduces the total number of trail-subkey candidates.

Remark 2. Our definition of *gain* specializes the S/N ratio to concrete output differences ΔC. Indeed, [3] compute $S/N = \frac{2^{K_s}p}{w}$, where w is the average number of subkey candidates suggested by a pair (including a possible filtration factor). A given ciphertext difference ΔC defines the differential $\Delta_{OUT} \xrightarrow{k} \Delta C$ with probability q, so that $w = 2^{K_s}q$ and the S/N value is specialized into simply $\frac{p}{q}$. This is correct as long as the probability of the actual encryption following the differential $\Delta_{IN} \xrightarrow{r} \Delta_{OUT}$ is equal to p; in particular, this is true if we average the S/N value over all possible ciphertext differences. However, for a given ciphertext difference, the actual probability is equal to $\frac{pq}{\tilde{p}}$ (see above), yielding the posterior factor $\frac{q}{\tilde{p}}$. Note that even Assumption 2 (fixing $\tilde{p}$ to $2^{|C|}$) does not make the gain match the S/N definition, since the MiF trails defining the probability q still vary depending on the observed ciphertext difference (but the gain will average to S/N over all possible differences). We conclude that the gain theory is more fine-grained than the S/N formula of [3], giving more insights into the MiF attack.

Trails or Differentials? In order to provide final complexity estimates for the trial decryption step, there are two cases depending on whether a trail is used for an attack or a differential. We will assume that the recovered subkey can be used to obtain all other subkeys using the cipher's decryption procedure. If only a part of the subkey is recovered, the rest can be recovered by exhaustive search.

In a *differential*-based attack, the recovered subkey is simply used to decrypt one r-round (partially decrypted) ciphertext and checked against the known plaintext. We assume the cost of this is equal to r rounds of the primitive, or, $r/(r+k)$ full primitive decryptions.

In a *trail*-based attack, a surviving pair can be decrypted round-by-round and checked for conformance to the trail. The expected number of round decryptions can be computed by using the trail's round weights $(w_1, w_2, \ldots, w_r)$ as

$$c = 1 + 2^{-w_r} \cdot \left(1 + 2^{-w_{r-1}} \cdot (\ldots)\right). \tag{4}$$

Since both values have to be decrypted to test the difference, the cost has to be doubled so that the final cost is equal to $2c/(r+k)$ full primitive decryptions.

---

[2] Codes and other relevant information are available at github.com/cryptolu/MeetInTheFilter_CHAM_KATAN.

Since the final number of candidates is proportional to the probability of the trail/differential, the final complexity can be expressed as

$$\min \left(\frac{2c}{r+k} \cdot \frac{1}{p_{\text{trail}}}, \frac{r}{r+k} \cdot \frac{1}{p_{\text{diff}}} \right)$$

full primitive decryptions.

We remark that a mix of the two methods is possible by fixing several final rounds of a differential to the same trail. The associated cost c can be computed as in (4), applied to the last $t \le r$ rounds with the additional cost of $(r-t)2^{-w_r-w_{r-1}-\cdots-w_{r-t+1}}$ single-round decryptions (i.e., for a pair surviving all t last rounds of the trail, we need to decrypt only one text up to the plaintext to check). We will use this method in the attack on CHAM (Sect. 4.2).

3.2 MiF-Like Key Recovery Applied to Plaintext Structures

When the attacked cipher has a simple (e.g., linear) key schedule, MiF-like key recovery can be also performed at the first round of the cipher, combined with a standard technique in differential cryptanalysis - *plaintext structures*. The latter allows to construct a compact set of plaintexts containing many pairs satisfying one of the given differences.

The standard approach is to start with a single difference Δ_{IN}, propagate it backward by a few rounds in all possible ways to determine the set of possibly active bits, and construct a structure consisting of plaintexts with active bits taking all possible values and inactive bits set to any constant. After the whole structure is encrypted, the attacker enumerates all pairs in the structure and analyzes conditions on which the pair would reach the difference Δ_{IN} after the initial rounds. Typically, there is a strong filter quickly discarding many such pairs. If the main differential $\Delta_{\text{IN}} \xrightarrow{r} \Delta_{\text{OUT}}$ requires more pairs, the process is repeated for the same structure but using different constants for inactive bits.

We recall that the core idea of MiF is to find a trail connecting the differences, and to use it to recover candidates for the intermediate subkey bits. This methodology can be directly applied to plaintext structures as well. Since the attacker needs to bound the activity pattern after propagating Δ_{IN} backward, we will assume that all t trails over these initial rounds can be explicitly enumerated. Then, during the attack, the attacker would simply enumerate these trails and choose accordingly pairs from the structure instead of enumerating all pairs. Note that a structure with n active bits contains 2^n plaintexts and distinct 2^{n-1} pairs of plaintexts satisfying a chosen difference fitting the pattern. Therefore, $t2^{n-1}$ pairs are enumerated instead of all 2^{2n-1} pairs, per one structure.

Then, for each plaintext-trail pair, the attacker can also apply MiF-like key recovery in addition to the ciphertext-side key recovery. This stage can in fact be precomputed offline. A necessary constraint is that it should be possible to combine the subkey bits recovered from the plaintext and ciphertext sides, which is typically the case for linear key schedules (at a reasonable cost).

3.3 Computing or Estimating the Average Trail Probability

We propose the following very simple but powerful theorem that relates the average probability of a trail to the total number of trails, where we only consider trails starting with a fixed difference.

Theorem 2. *Let Δ be a state difference of a cipher. Let T be the set of all possible l-round trails starting at Δ. Then, the average probability of a trail from T is equal to $1/|T|$.*

Proof. Follows from the fact that all trails starting from a single fixed difference must have probabilities summing to 1. □

For ARX ciphers, counting the number of valid output differences for a single ADD operation can be done efficiently using bit-based dynamic programming.

Lemma 1. *Let α, β be fixed differences for the n-bit inputs of ADD or SUB. Then, the number of differences γ such that $(\alpha, \beta) \to \gamma$ is a valid differential transition through the chosen operation can be computed in time $\mathcal{O}(n)$.*

Proof. The idea is to iterate an index i from the least significant bit to the most significant bit and keep 3 counters for the numbers of differences γ (defined up to the current bit) such that: (a) $\alpha_i = \beta_i = \gamma_i = 0$, (b) $\alpha_i = \beta_i = \gamma_i = 1$, (c) $\neg(\alpha_i = \beta_i = \gamma_i)$. Since the new bit of γ is defined by one of the three cases, and all bits of α and β are given, it is easy to update the counters. In particular, case (c) creates both possibilities for the new difference bit (branching factor 2), while cases (a) and (b) define the new difference bit deterministically. See Algorithm 1 for details. □

Algorithm 1. Counting differential trail extensions through single ADD or SUB

Input: $\alpha, \beta \in \mathbb{F}_2^n$
Output: $|\{\gamma \in \mathbb{F}_2^n \mid (\alpha, \beta) \to \gamma \text{ is valid through ADD/SUB}\}|$
1: **if** $\alpha_0 = \beta_0 = 0$ **then**
2:     $(c_0, c_1, c_{\neq}) \leftarrow (1, 0, 0)$
3: **else**
4:     $(c_0, c_1, c_{\neq}) \leftarrow (0, 0, 1)$
5: **end if**
6: **for** $i \in \{1, \ldots, n-1\}$ **do**
7:     **if** $\alpha_i = \beta_i = 0$ **then**
8:         $(c_0, c_1, c_{\neq}) \leftarrow (c_0 + c_{\neq}, 0, c_1 + c_{\neq})$
9:     **else if** $\alpha_i = \beta_i = 1$ **then**
10:         $(c_0, c_1, c_{\neq}) \leftarrow (0, c_1 + c_{\neq}, c_0 + c_{\neq})$
11:     **else if** $\alpha_i \neq \beta_i$ **then**
12:         $(c_0, c_1, c_{\neq}) \leftarrow (0, 0, c_0 + c_1 + 2c_{\neq})$
13:     **end if**
14: **end for**
15: **return** $c_0 + c_1 + c_{\neq}$

Theorem 2 and Lemma 1 allow to compute the average trail probability for a given cipher and a chosen difference for a relatively large number of rounds. The idea is to explicitly enumerate all possible trails for l rounds and then use Algorithm 1 on each trail to extend by 1 or more rounds implicitly, depending on the cipher's structure. For example, Speck allows only 1-round extension in both directions, while CHAM allows 3-round extension forwards and 1-round extension backwards. Furthermore, typically, after a few rounds, the round's branching factor (multiplier to the number of trails) converges to the branching factor of a random difference transition which is usually known (for example, it is about $2^{12.1}$ for a 16-bit ADD [4]). The latter estimation method is relevant also for non-ARX primitives, for which Algorithm 1 is non-applicable. Therefore, these techniques allow to count or to estimate the number of trails over any number of cipher's rounds.

3.4 Estimating the Truncated Trail Weight Distribution

For complexity analysis, we need to compute the probability of each round's differential transition, averaged over a given set of trails. For this, we employ the following assumption.

Assumption 3. *Let T_i be the set of all trails over i rounds of a cipher. Then, the probability of differential transitions at round $j \leq k$ averaged over the trails from T_k can be estimated as $|T_{j-1}|/|T_j|$, letting $|T_0| = 1$.*

Example 1. In CHAM64, the difference $(2000, 1000, 2810, 0020)$ spans forward $2^{19.55}$ trails over 4 rounds and $2^{29.89}$ trails over 5 rounds. Therefore, we assume that the average probability of a differential transition over the 5th round is equal to $2^{-10.34}$ (see Table 2b).

The intuition for this assumption is based on Theorem 2. Indeed, the average probability of all trails over the first $j - 1$ rounds is equal to $1/|T_{j-1}|$, and over the first j rounds it is equal to $1/|T_j|$. Since for a single trail the probabilities over rounds are multiplied, it is natural to use such a product rule for *average* probabilities of trails in order to estimate the single round's average probability. The possibility of approximation error comes from the fact that extending trails over j rounds to k rounds may change the distribution of the j-round prefixes (by changing their multiplicities).

Furthermore, the approximation error is limited by the fact that the average round probabilities computed in such way do multiply to the correct average trail probability $1/|T_k|$. Therefore, the actual average probabilities may only shift filtration power from one round to another, unlikely to significantly affect complexity analysis of our attacks. Our experiments on KATAN-32 in show that estimates using Assumption 3 closely approximates the actual average trail weights (see full version of the paper).

Eichlseder and Kales [8] adopted a similar approach to estimate the differential probability for semi-truncated differential characteristics. Rather than enumerating all possible trails, they calculate the sum of probabilities of all compatible differential characteristics for a fixed input difference, averaged over all compatible input differences.

4 Cryptanalysis of Round-Reduced CHAM

4.1 CHAM Revisited

CHAM is a family of lightweight block ciphers based on the ARX construction [10,12]. It consists of 3 members, CHAM-64-128 (to which we refer to as CHAM-64 in the rest of the paper), CHAM-128-128 and CHAM-128-256 with 88, 112 and 120 rounds respectively, where CHAM-n-k refers to a variant with an n-bit block and k-bit secret key. Each block is processed as $m = \frac{n}{4}$-bit words using three main operations: bitwise XOR, addition modulo 2^m and bitwise rotation. The two consecutive rounds of CHAM are depicted in Fig. 2. CHAM has a linear key schedule that generates $\frac{2k}{m}$ m-bit words defined as

$$RK[i] = K[i] \oplus ROL_1(K[i]) \oplus ROL_8(K[i]), \tag{5}$$

$$RK[i + \frac{k}{m} \oplus 1] = K[i] \oplus ROL_1(K[i]) \oplus ROL_{11}(K[i]). \tag{6}$$

Note that the master key words can be calculated from round subkeys by inverting these linear maps, for example, by precomputed lookup tables.

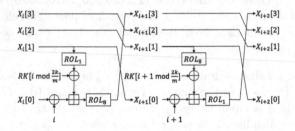

Fig. 2. Two consecutive rounds of CHAM starting from an even i-th round

The following observations on CHAM are used in our attack:

Observation 1. *In any 4 rounds of CHAM, the input and the output difference together determine the full 4-round differential trail (efficiently). Consequently, 4 rounds of CHAM do not have any trail clustering.*

Observation 2. *The addition in the i-th round of CHAM takes as inputs the outputs of additions in the $(i-3)$-rd and $(i-4)$-th rounds. The subtraction (in decryption) in the i-th round of CHAM takes as inputs the outputs of the subtractions in the $(i+1)$-st and $(i+4)$-th rounds.*

Prior differential cryptanalysis findings on CHAM only involved identifying the best differential trails. Apart from attacks briefly described by the designers, no other key recovery attacks have been proposed so far.

Details of the CHAM differentials used in our paper are given in the full version. While experimentally verifying the validity of these differentials, we also found that CHAM's differentials are highly key-dependent. This key-dependency is further investigated in the full version of the paper.

4.2 Attack on 52-Round CHAM-64

We use a differential over 40 rounds of CHAM having probability $p = 2^{-60.05}$ (with the first and last 4 rounds having fixed differences), and an attack split $4 + 40 + 4 + 4$. The main 40-round differential can be extended 4 rounds backward in $2^{35.67}$ possible ways (see Table 2a), with 10 least significant bits of the last word never active in the plaintext difference. This list of differences can be precomputed.

We encrypt $2^{7.05}$ structures of 2^{54} plaintexts ($2^{61.05}$ encryptions). After extracting pairs with one of $2^{35.67}$ possible plaintext differences in each structure, we obtain $2^{61.05+35.67-1} = 2^{95.72}$ plaintext-ciphertext pairs for analysis, each accompanied by a candidate trail in the first $4 + 40$ rounds. Note that we expect to find 1 right pair following the main 40-round differential in this set (by the linearity of expectation), since the sum of probabilities of all trails in the 4 prefix rounds is equal to 1, and we consider $2^{60.05}$ such sets. Each such pair is processed by MiF, getting a list of candidate trails for the last 8 rounds. From Table 2b we can see that each ciphertext difference induces $2^{64.84-64} = 2^{0.84}$ trails[3] on average, resulting in $2^{96.56}$ full 52-round trails (with associated plaintext and ciphertext pairs) for analysis. This can be done by expanding the difference Δ_{OUT} forward by $2^{19.55}$ possible 4-round trails and checking the validity of differential transitions through ADD in the bottom 4 rounds, leading to a time complexity of about $2^{19.55}$ one-round encryptions of CHAM per pair ($2^{116.11}$ total).

Using methodology from Sect. 3.3, we computed the filtering probabilities for each round of the first and last 8 rounds, see Table 3 (computed from Table 2a and Table 2b). Now, we will guess the subkeys in a carefully chosen order, cross-checking the top and bottom subkeys as soon as possible. The order must satisfy Observation 2, namely, guessing or verifying round r at the top must have rounds $r-3, r-4$ guessed (can skip 2 rounds); guessing or verifying round r at the bottom must have rounds $r + 1, r + 4$ guessed (cannot skip rounds). The timeline of the procedure is given in Table 4.

The procedure uses 2 main actions: computing a representation of the set of candidates for a subkey of one of the rounds, filtering a set of candidates for some subkey by a round from the other side. Both filters are based on one known incoming value into the addition/subtraction and the known differential transition.

---

[3] When extending 8 rounds forward, there are $2^{64.84}$ possible trails. Since there are only 2^{64} possible ciphertext differences, each ciphertext difference suggests $2^{0.84}$ trails on average.

Table 2. CHAM-64 trail statistics. Weight is defined as the $-\log_2$ of the probability.

(a) Backward extension from difference $\Delta_{\text{IN}} = (0020, 0010, 1020, 2800)$.

Round	#Trails	Avg. Weight (this round)
-1	$2^{4.17}$	4.17
-2	$2^{11.89}$	7.72
-3	$2^{23.8}$	11.91
-4	$2^{35.67}$	11.87

(b) Forward extension from difference $\Delta_{\text{OUT}} = (2000, 1000, 2810, 0020)$.

Round	#Trails	Avg. Weight (this round)
1	$2^{1.58}$	1.58
2	$2^{8.12}$	6.54
3	$2^{15.46}$	7.34
4	$2^{19.55}$	4.09
5	$2^{29.89}$	10.34
6	$2^{39.95}$	10.06
7	$2^{52.57}$	12.62
8	$2^{64.84}$	12.27

Table 3. Filter strength (top and bottom 8 rounds) in the 52-round attack on CHAM-64. Rounds 1–4 correspond to the 4-round backwards extension at the top; rounds 5–8 correspond to the first 4 rounds of the main differential trail; rounds 45–52 correspond to the 8-round forward extension (MiF) at the bottom.

Master key word	Round	Subkey	Filter	Round	Subkey	Filter	Total
$K[0]$	1	$RK[0]$	$2^{-11.87}$	49	$RK[0]$	$2^{-10.34}$	$2^{-22.21}$
$K[1]$	2	$RK[1]$	$2^{-11.91}$	50	$RK[1]$	$2^{-10.06}$	$2^{-21.97}$
$K[2]$	3	$RK[2]$	$2^{-7.72}$	51	$RK[2]$	$2^{-12.62}$	$2^{-20.34}$
$K[3]$	4	$RK[3]$	$2^{-4.17}$	52	$RK[3]$	$2^{-12.27}$	$2^{-16.44}$
$K[4]$	5	$RK[4]$	$2^{-1.00}$	46	$RK[13]$	$2^{-6.54}$	$2^{-7.54}$
$K[5]$	6	$RK[5]$	$2^{-2.00}$	45	$RK[12]$	$2^{-1.58}$	$2^{-3.58}$
$K[6]$	7	$RK[6]$	$2^{-3.00}$	48	$RK[15]$	$2^{-4.09}$	$2^{-7.09}$
$K[7]$	8	$RK[7]$	$2^{-2.00}$	47	$RK[14]$	$2^{-7.34}$	$2^{-9.34}$
all	1–8	$RK[0\text{–}7]$	$2^{-43.68}$	43–50	$RK[0\text{–}3, 12\text{–}15]$	$2^{-64.84}$	$2^{-108.52}$

Attack Complexity. The final time complexity (based on Table 4) is dominated by $2 \cdot 2^{117.63}$ one-round key recovery analyses per candidate subkey, and the cost to verify the $2^{116.05}$ final subkey candidates. We assume a 2-round cost for enumerating a subkey candidate. Since the last 4 rounds of the differential are fixed to a trail with round weights $(1, 2, 3, 2)$, we can test a key candidate with

$$1 + 2^{-2}(1 + 2^{-3}(1 + 2^{-2}(1 + 2^{-1})))$$

one-round decryptions on average and 2^{-8} 40-round decryptions, totalling to $1.45 = 2^{0.54}$ one-round decryptions. We obtain the final estimation of

$$2^{116.05+0.54} + 2^{118.63} \times 2 = 2^{119.80}$$

Table 4. Guessing procedure in the 52-round attack on CHAM-64. Time is measured in one-round key recovery analysis cost per key candidate.

Step	Guess subkey	Verify subkey	Filter	Time	Trail-key pairs remaining
0	initial (after MiF)				$2^{96.56}$
1	R52 : $K[3]$		$2^{-12.27}$	$2^{100.29}$	$2^{100.29}$
2	R51 : $K[2]$		$2^{-12.62}$	$2^{103.67}$	$2^{103.67}$
3		R3 : $K[2]$	$2^{-7.72}$	$2^{103.67}$	$2^{95.95}$
4	R2 : $K[1]$		$2^{-11.91}$	$2^{100.04}$	$2^{100.04}$
5		R50 : $K[1]$	$2^{-10.06}$	$2^{100.04}$	$2^{89.98}$
6	R1 : $K[0]$		$2^{-11.87}$	$2^{94.11}$	$2^{94.11}$
7		R49 : $K[0]$	$2^{-10.34}$	$2^{94.11}$	$2^{83.77}$
8		R4 : $K[3]$	$2^{-4.17}$	$2^{83.77}$	$2^{79.60}$
9	R48 : $K[6]$		$2^{-4.09}$	$2^{91.51}$	$2^{91.51}$
10		R7 : $K[6]$	$2^{-3.00}$	$2^{91.51}$	$2^{88.51}$
11	R47 : $K[7]$		$2^{-7.34}$	$2^{97.17}$	$2^{97.17}$
12	R46 : $K[4]$		$2^{-6.54}$	$2^{106.63}$	$2^{106.63}$
13		R5 : $K[4]$	$2^{-1.00}$	$2^{106.63}$	$2^{105.63}$
14		R8 : $K[7]$	$2^{-2.00}$	$2^{105.63}$	$2^{103.63}$
15	R6 : $K[5]$		$2^{-2.00}$	$2^{117.63}$	$2^{117.63}$
16		R45 : $K[5]$	$2^{-1.58}$	$2^{117.63}$	$2^{116.05}$

one-round encryptions, equal to $2^{114.10}$ 52-round CHAM encryptions. The data complexity is $2^{61.05}$ chosen-plaintext encryptions. The 2^{54} 64-bit blocks required to store plaintexts in a structure dominate memory complexity.

5   Cryptanalysis of Round-Reduced KATAN

5.1   KATAN Revisited

The KATAN family of block ciphers comprises three variants denoted as KATAN-b, where the block size b is 32, 48 or 64 [5]. KATAN consists of two nonlinear feedback shift registers (NLFSR) that store and update the plaintext and an LFSR to generate round subkeys. All variants of KATAN have an 80-bit key, the same key schedule and 254 rounds. They differ by register lengths, bit positions that enter the feedback functions, and the number of *steps*, which is the number of times the round function is repeated using the same subkey each round. Figure 3 depicts one round of KATAN where L_1 and L_2 are two NLFSRs while k_a and k_b are two round key bits. Given an 80-bit master key K, the subkey of round i is $k_a \| k_b = k_{2 \cdot i} \| k_{2 \cdot i+1}$ where

$$k_i = \begin{cases} K_i, & \text{for } i = 0, \dots, 79, \\ k_{i-80} \oplus k_{i-61} \oplus k_{i-50} \oplus k_{i-13}, & \text{otherwise.} \end{cases}$$

The L_1 and L_2 registers are updated by two nonlinear feedback functions, f_b and f_a respectively, defined as follows:

$$f_a(L_1) = L_1[x_1] \oplus L_1[x_2] \oplus (L_1[x_3] \wedge L_1[x_4]) \oplus (L_1[x_5] \wedge IR) \oplus k_a, \qquad (7)$$

$$f_b(L_2) = L_2[y_1] \oplus L_2[y_2] \oplus (L_2[y_3] \wedge L_2[y_4]) \oplus (L_2[y_5] \wedge L_2[y_6]) \oplus k_b,$$

where IR is the irregular update bit depending on the round. The selection of x_i and y_i bits differ for each variant of KATAN. During each *step*, LSBs of L_1 and L_2 are updated by f_b and f_a respectively. For KATAN-48 and -64, each round has two and three steps respectively. Table 5 defines the register lengths and bit positions that enter the feedback functions for all variants.

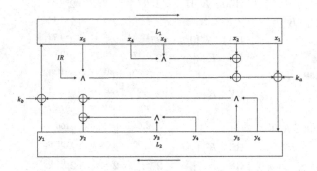

Fig. 3. One round of KATAN

Table 5. Parameters for the KATAN-b family of block ciphers

b	$|L_1|$	$|L_2|$	x_1	x_2	x_3	x_4	x_5	y_1	y_2	y_3	y_4	y_5	y_6
32	13	19	12	7	8	5	3	18	7	12	10	8	3
48	19	29	18	12	15	7	6	28	19	21	13	15	6
64	25	39	24	15	20	11	9	38	25	33	21	14	9

The most successful attacks on all variants of KATAN are multidimensional meet-in-the-middle attacks that span up to 206, 148 and 129 rounds for KATAN-32, 48 and 64 respectively [11]. As the goal of this paper is to use MiF to improve differential cryptanalysis, we will compare our results against the best single-key and related-key differential attacks.

In the single-key setting, Albrecht and Leander proposed a 115-round attack with time complexity $T = 2^{78}$ that exploits the full difference distribution of KATAN-32 [1]. Their attack was not computationally feasible for larger variants. A 117-round amplified boomerang attack with $T = 2^{79.3}$ was later introduced by Chen et al. [6]. The best single-key differential attacks on KATAN-48 and 64 were reported by Knellwolf et al. [9] using an approach known as conditional differential cryptanalysis. The latter is applicable to ciphers with NLFSR-based constructions. Using this approach, around 2 bits of subkey information could be recovered after 70 and 68 rounds of KATAN-48 and KATAN-64 respectively.

5.2   Key Recovery Observations

The differential propagation through AND is the basic block for constructing trails over the KATAN structure.

Fact 1. *Let $(\alpha, \beta) \rightarrow \gamma$ be a valid differential transition through AND (2-to-1 bit). Then, $\alpha = \beta = 0$ implies $\gamma = 0$ (probability 1); otherwise, the transition has probability $1/2$ (for both cases $\gamma = 0$ and $\gamma = 1$).*

The structure of KATAN's step allows to easily derive the average branching factor of differential trails, i.e., how many 1-step trails does a random difference span on average. This is useful for estimating the MiF complexity. Note that this factor does not depend on the version of KATAN.

Proposition 2. *Let α be a uniformly random state difference in KATAN. Then, it is expected to span $217/64 \approx 2^{1.76}$ 1-step trails (in any chosen direction).*

Proof. The L_2 register has 2 ANDs applied to it, but their outputs are XORed together. The transition we consider includes the full step and does not specify the intermediate output difference of the ANDs. The output difference of the two XORed ANDs is either fully determined (when both ANDs are inactive, i.e., have zero difference in all input and output bits), which happens with probability $1/16$, or can be equal to 0 or 1, which happens with probability $15/16$. For the single AND applied to the L_1 register, the situation is similar but simpler: the transition has a single extension if the AND is inactive (happens in $1/4$ of the cases), or 2 extensions otherwise (in $3/4$ of the cases). We obtain the expected number of 1-step extensions is equal to

$$\frac{15}{16} \cdot \frac{3}{4} \cdot 4 + \frac{1}{16} \cdot \frac{3}{4} \cdot 2 + \frac{15}{16} \cdot \frac{1}{4} \cdot 2 + \frac{1}{16} \cdot \frac{1}{4} \cdot 1 = \frac{217}{64}.$$ □

Our experiment on KATAN-32 supports the validity of Proposition 2 (see full version of the paper for details).

The key recovery behaviour of AND (with respect to a given differential transition) is illustrated in Table 6a and Table 6b. The tables show that an active differential transition through AND is conditioned by an affine function of the involved *values*. More precisely, if one of the input bits is active, then we learn the value of the other (inactive) bit (which has to be the same for both texts since it is inactive). If both input bits are active, then we learn the value of the difference between the input bits (which, again, has to be the same for both texts even though they have to be different).

Table 6. Differential properties of AND.

(a) Output differences $\Delta(xy)$ of transitions through AND.

(x, y)	$(\Delta x, \Delta y)$			
	$(0,0)$	$(0,1)$	$(1,0)$	$(1,1)$
$(0,0)$	0	0	0	1
$(0,1)$	0	0	1	0
$(1,0)$	0	1	0	0
$(1,1)$	0	1	1	1

(b) Conditions and output values induced by differential transitions through AND.

Diff. transition $(\Delta x, \Delta y) \to \Delta(xy)$	Condition	Output xy
$(0,0) \to 0$	-	xy
$(0,1) \to 0$	$x = 0$	0
$(0,1) \to 1$	$x = 1$	y
$(1,0) \to 0$	$y = 0$	0
$(1,0) \to 1$	$y = 1$	x
$(1,1) \to 0$	$x \oplus y = 1$	0
$(1,1) \to 1$	$x \oplus y = 0$	$x = y$

Proposition 3. *In the encryption mode, the key addition k_b (resp. k_b) going into the L_1 (resp. L_2) register does not affect an AND operation during $x_4 + 1$ (resp. $y_6 + 1$) encryption steps. The concrete numbers of steps are 6/8/12 (resp. 4/7/10) for 32-/48-/64-bit versions of* KATAN.

Proposition 4. *In the decryption mode, the key addition k_a going into the L_1 register affects an AND operation only after $x_1 - x_3$ decryption steps[4], equal to 4/3/4 for 32-/48-/64-bit versions of* KATAN *respectively. The key addition k_b going into the L_2 register affects an AND operation only after $y_1 - y_3$ decryption steps, equal to 6/7/5 for 32-/48-/64-bit versions of* KATAN *respectively.*

In our attacks, we guess key bits only when they are input to an AND being currently decrypted (bits x_3 and y_3). Note that the XOR feed takes as input a bit placed after the first AND input bit. In this way, we always guess concrete subkey bits and not linear functions of them.

5.3 Attack on 124-Round KATAN-32

Details of the KATAN differentials used in our attacks are given in the full version of the paper. We attack rounds 124 rounds of KATAN-32 after skipping the first 29 rounds (i.e., rounds 30–153). This skip is motivated by rounds 34–107 having a local minimum in the fraction of rounds with IR=1, leading to slower diffusion. The rounds are split as follows:

- Rounds 30–33 (4): free rounds at the top (key-independent transitions);
- Rounds 34–107 (74): main differential(s): 40028200 → 21000004/21000006;
- Rounds 108–149 (42): MiF and key recovery (involves 80 distinct key bits);
- Rounds 150–153 (4): free rounds at the bottom (key-independent transitions).

---

[4] In a decryption step, due to the register shift, the taps $x_2, \ldots, x_5, y_2, \ldots, y_6$ are increased by 1 in order to match the same bits used in the encryption. This explains why Proposition 3 has an extra step compare to Proposition 4.

Using the Trail(s). The two best 74-round differential trails covering rounds 34–107 both have the same weight 31 and differential probability $2^{-30.23}$. Since the differential effect is weak, we choose to use the best *trail* (rather than differentials), as it allows to verify the subkey candidates round-by-round by checking conformance to the trail (thus avoiding full cipher decryption). This allows to save a few bits in the time complexity since the number of rounds is large.

Free Rounds. We choose 2^{30} random inputs pairs at round 34, conforming to the difference 40028200. Each value is then decrypted by 4 rounds using zero subkey bits. These bits do not affect the differential propagation, so that the difference 40028200 will be satisfied at round 34 during actual encryption with real subkey bits. These 2^{30} pairs are than encrypted by the oracle.

Similarly, the last 4 rounds can be decrypted without involving the key material. Although the rounds actually perform key additions, they are effectively delayed until the first AND operation, which takes 4 rounds for the L1 register and 6 rounds for the L2 register.

MiF Trail Enumeration. We effectively end up with 2^{30} pairs of encryptions covering rounds 34–149, candidates for satisfying one of the two differentials in rounds 34–107.

For each of the two differences Δ_{OUT}, we run the MiF procedure and generate possible trails connecting Δ_{OUT} and the (partially decrypted) ciphertext difference. For each trail, we run the key recovery procedure (described below). The time complexity of MiF can be estimated as follows. By exhaustive trail enumeration, we observe that the two differences span respectively $2^{30.36}$ and $2^{32.87}$ trails ($2^{33.10}$ total) over 23 rounds (108–130). These trails form the MiF cluster. Then, for each ciphertext difference, we enumerate all possible trails backwards over 19 rounds (131–149), leading to $(2^{1.76})^{19} = 2^{33.44}$ trails on average (by Proposition 2)[5]. Each of the obtained differences is checked against the cluster. This requires $2^{30} \times 2^{33.44} = 2^{63.44}$ lookups (each may return several trails), which is negligible compared to the key recovery complexity (see below).

For the record, we expect to check in total over $2^{30+64.46-32} + 2^{30+66.97-32} = 2^{65.20}$ trails. Here, $2^{64.46}$ and $2^{66.97}$ are the number of 42-round trails spanned by the two chosen differences respectively (computed iteratively using dynamic programming).

Key Recovery. Each generated trail is passed through the basic round-by-round key recovery procedure, using the associated trail as a filter. By the gain analysis (Sect. 3.1), we expect the final number of key candidates to be around $2^{80-(32-\Pr T)} = 2^{79}$, which provides an estimate for the attack's complexity, given that the available differential filter can be efficiently used. This can be ensured by the simple structure of the cipher. Indeed, the total number of key candidates is only growing with the recursion depth, since the average trail probability per

---

[5] Experimentally, we obtained an average of $2^{33.49}$ trails which closely matches the estimates obtained by Proposition 2.

step is $2^{-1.76}$ and 2 subkey bits are involved per step, yielding an expansion factor $2^{0.24}$ per step (after the first few key recovery rounds where subkey material use is sparse/delayed[6]). Therefore, a few deepest (closest to Δ_{OUT}) key recovery rounds dominate the complexity. The enumeration of the subkey bits satisfying the transitions can be done very efficiently, since, by Table 6b, a transition gives a direct constraint on the input bit, yielding the subkey bit value or discarding the trail if the relevant input bit is constant. Pessimistically, we estimate the time complexity as 2 round decryptions per each of the final candidates, i.e., 2^{80} single-round KATAN-32 decryptions equal to $2^{73.04}$ full-round decryptions.

The final verification of the 2^{79} subkeys can be done by doing round-by-round decryption and checking conformance to the trail. Let

$$w_1, w_2, \ldots = (0, 1, 0, 0, 1, 0, 0, 0, 0, 0, 0, 1, 0, 1, 0, 1, 1, 0, 1, 0, 1, \ldots)$$

be the weights of transitions in the 74-round trail, starting from the last round. Then, on average, we would need to decrypt each pair for $1 + 2^{-w_1} \cdot (1 + 2^{-w_2} \cdot (\ldots)) \leq 5.71$ rounds, resulting in 11.42 single-round decryptions or $2^{-3.44}$ full decryptions per a full candidate subkey. The final complexity is thus $2^{75.56}$ full KATAN-32 decryptions. The total key recovery complexity is $2^{73.04} + 2^{75.56} = 2^{75.80}$ full decryptions.

Attack Complexity. The attack requires 2^{31} chosen-plaintext encryptions, $2^{33.10} \cdot 23 = 2^{37.62}$ memory blocks (for the MiF Cluster), and has time complexity of about $2^{75.80}$ full KATAN-32 decryptions. The success rate is $1 - 1/e \approx 63.2\%$ (defined solely by the main 74-round differential). It can be increased if needed by scaling the queried data.

5.4   Attack on 130-Round KATAN-48

We use four 87-round differential trails with weight 46 starting with the difference Δ_{IN} = 000001008000 at the beginning of round 35. It can be verified that this difference allows 7 free rounds backward.

In KATAN-48, the two round subkey bits are used in two consecutive steps. This makes the MiF filter part weaker: rounds modeled as random suggest $2^{3.52}$ candidate trails (Proposition 2) if we directly construct the MiF filter from differences, whereas the "actual" branching factor is 2^2 simply due to 2 key bits used. This may create a problem for the gain potential, since most of the valid trails would suggest no correct subkeys (by counting reasons) and the process of discarding these trails may dominate over the subkey verification stage in terms of complexity. We resolve this problem by replacing the MiF filter with simple guessing (similar to Dinur's attack on SPECK [7]).

The attack procedure is as follows:

1. Precompute the 17.5-round forward MiF cluster from the 4 output differences Δ_{OUT} (estimated size $2^{46.93}$).

---

[6] Subkey dependency matrices are provided in the supporting code repository.

2. Select 2^{44} pairs of texts with difference $\Delta_{\text{IN}} = 000001008000$.
3. Decrypt each text for 7 rounds using zero subkeys, and query the respective ciphertext after 130 rounds (2^{45} queries).
4. For each pair of ciphertexts, decrypt 19 rounds involving 34 distinct subkey bits by recursive guessing. We expect to obtain $2^{44+34} = 2^{78}$ candidate decryptions, with estimated time complexity of about 2^{78} single-round pair decryptions ($2^{78} \cdot 2/130 = 2^{71.98}$ full-round decryptions).
5. Match the difference in the cluster to get valid trails (expecting $2^{44+34+46.93-48} = 2^{76.93}$ key-trails in total). The naive approach requires 2^{78} memory lookups in the cluster of $2^{46.93}$ trails, which can be expensive in practice. However, one can easily reduce this workload due to slow diffusion in KATAN: for example, decrypting 14 rounds (instead of 19) produces $2^{44+24}=2^{68}$ candidates with already $48 - 5 \times 4 = 28$ bits of the final (19-round decrypted) difference available. This allows to localize memory accesses (e.g., by pooling intermediate 14-round decryptions before the other 5 rounds), dominated by 2^{78} memory accesses in clusters of size $2^{46.93-28} = 2^{18.93}$. We estimate the lookup cost to be equal to single-round decryption per pair ($2^{70.98}$ full-round decryptions).
6. Proceed with MiF round-by-round key recovery; the few first average round weights of trails as processed by MiF would be about 3.52, leading to a quick reduction in the number of surviving key-trail pairs (since, again, there are only 2 subkey bits per round), before it would start increasing up to the final number.
7. By the gain theory (or weight-based calculations), we expect to arrive at $2^{-2} \cdot 2^{17.2+34+2}=2^{68}$ candidates for the 70 involved subkey bits after processing 17.5 rounds of MiF (the last MiF half-round uses extra 2 subkey bits).
8. Then, we continue to recursively guess subkey bits and check conformance to the trail; the last 5 rounds of the trail have weight 4, so we expect about $2^{68+5\cdot2-4} = 2^{74}$ candidates for the 80 subkey bits. Let

$$w_{82}, w_{81}, w_{80}, w_{79} \ldots = (0,0,0,1,0,0,1,0,0,1,1,0,0,0,1,0,0,0,0,1,1,0,\ldots)$$

be the weights of transitions in the 87-round trail, starting from the 82nd round backward. Then, on average, we would need to decrypt each pair for $1 + 2^{-w_{82}} \cdot (1 + 2^{-w_{81}} \cdot (\ldots)) \le 2^3$ single-round decryptions of pairs, leading to complexity $2^{74} \cdot 2^3 \cdot 2/130 = 2^{70.98}$ full-round decryptions.

Attack Complexity. The attack requires 2^{45} chosen plaintext encryptions, $2^{46.24} \cdot 17 = 2^{50.33}$ memory blocks and time complexity of $2^{71.98} + 2^{70.98} + 2^{70.98} = 2^{72.98}$ full (130-round) KATAN-48 decryptions.

5.5   Attacks on 110-Round KATAN-64

We use 16 differential 79-round trails with weight 60 starting with the difference $\Delta_{\text{IN}}=0080402010000000$ at the beginning of round 34. It can be verified that this difference allows 5 free rounds backward. Since KATAN-64 uses the two round subkey bits in three consecutive steps, we will proceed using a similar strategy to our attack on KATAN-48 to limit the branching factor to 2^2.

The attack procedure is as follows:

1. Precompute the 14-round forward MiF cluster from the 16 output differences Δ_{OUT} (estimated size $2^{60.86}$).
2. Select 2^{56} pairs of texts with difference Δ_{IN} = 0080402010000000.
3. Decrypt each text for 5 rounds using zero subkeys and query the respective ciphertext after 108 rounds (2^{57} queries).
4. For each pair of ciphertexts, decrypt 12 rounds (which includes 1 free round) involving 22 distinct subkey bits by recursive guessing (total time complexity $2^{56+22} = 2^{78}$ one-round pair decryptions or $2^{78} \cdot 2/110 = 2^{72.22}$ full-round decryptions).
5. Match the difference in the cluster to get valid trails (expecting $2^{56+22+60.86-64} = 2^{74.86}$ key-trails in total). Similarly to the attack on KATAN48, we assume the cost of 1 round decryption per lookup ($2^{71.22}$ full-round decryptions)
6. Proceed with MiF round-by-round key recovery which will quickly reduce the number of surviving key-trail pairs.
7. By the gain theory, we expect to have $2^{-4}2^{14.2+22} = 2^{46}$ candidates for the 2^{50} involved subkey bits.
8. Then, we continue to recursively guess subkey bits and check if the key-trail pairs conform to the last 15 rounds of the trail, which have weight 12. We expect around $2^{46+15\cdot2-12} = 2^{64}$ candidates for the 80 subkey bits. Let

$$w_{64}, w_{63}, w_{62} \ldots = (1,1,1,0,1,0,0,1,0,1,0,0,1,1,1,1,2,1,1,2,2,\ldots)$$

be the weights of transitions in the 79-round trail, starting from the 64th round backward. Then, on average, we would need to decrypt each pair for $1 + 2^{-w_1} \cdot (1 + 2^{-w_2} \cdot (\ldots)) \leq 2^{1.21}$ single-round decryption of pairs, leading to complexity $2^{64} \cdot 2^{1.21} \cdot 2/110 = 2^{59.43}$ full-round decryptions.

Attack Complexity. The attack requires 2^{57} chosen plaintext encryptions, $2^{60.86} \cdot 14 = 2^{64.67}$ memory blocks and time complexity is dominated by recursive guessing, which requires $2^{72.22} + 2^{71.22} = 2^{72.80}$ full KATAN-64 decryptions. Success rate is ≈63.2%.

References

1. Albrecht, M.R., Leander, G.: An all-in-one approach to differential cryptanalysis for small block ciphers. In: Knudsen, L.R., Wu, H. (eds.) SAC 2012. LNCS, vol. 7707, pp. 1–15. Springer, Heidelberg (2013). https://doi.org/10.1007/978-3-642-35999-6_1
2. Beaulieu, R., Shors, D., Smith, J., Treatman-Clark, S., Weeks, B., Wingers, L.: The SIMON and SPECK families of lightweight block ciphers. Cryptology ePrint Archive, Report 2013/404 (2013)

3. Biham, E., Shamir, A.: Differential Cryptanalysis of the Data Encryption Standard. Springer, Heidelberg (1993). https://doi.org/10.1007/978-1-4613-9314-6
4. Biryukov, A., dos Santos, L.C., Teh, J.S., Udovenko, A., Velichkov, V.: Meet-in-the-filter and dynamic counting with applications to speck. Cryptology ePrint Archive, Paper 2022/673 (2022). https://eprint.iacr.org/2022/673, https://eprint.iacr.org/2022/673
5. De Cannière, C., Dunkelman, O., Knežević, M.: KATAN and KTANTAN—a family of small and efficient hardware-oriented block ciphers. In: Clavier, C., Gaj, K. (eds.) CHES 2009. LNCS, vol. 5747, pp. 272–288. Springer, Heidelberg (2009). https://doi.org/10.1007/978-3-642-04138-9_20
6. Chen, J., Teh, J., Liu, Z., Su, C., Samsudin, A., Xiang, Y.: Towards accurate statistical analysis of security margins: New searching strategies for differential attacks. IEEE Trans. Comput. **66**(10), 1763–1777 (2017)
7. Dinur, I.: Improved differential cryptanalysis of round-reduced speck. In: Joux, A., Youssef, A. (eds.) SAC 2014. LNCS, vol. 8781, pp. 147–164. Springer, Cham (2014). https://doi.org/10.1007/978-3-319-13051-4_9
8. Eichlseder, M., Kales, D.: Clustering related-tweak characteristics: application to MANTIS-6. IACR Trans. Symmetric Cryptol. **2018**(2), 111–132 (2018)
9. Knellwolf, S., Meier, W., Naya-Plasencia, M.: Conditional differential cryptanalysis of NLFSR-based cryptosystems. In: Abe, M. (ed.) ASIACRYPT 2010. LNCS, vol. 6477, pp. 130–145. Springer, Heidelberg (2010). https://doi.org/10.1007/978-3-642-17373-8_8
10. Koo, B., Roh, D., Kim, H., Jung, Y., Lee, D.-G., Kwon, D.: CHAM: a family of lightweight block ciphers for resource-constrained devices. In: Kim, H., Kim, D.-C. (eds.) ICISC 2017. LNCS, vol. 10779, pp. 3–25. Springer, Cham (2018). https://doi.org/10.1007/978-3-319-78556-1_1
11. Rasoolzadeh, S., Raddum, H.: Multidimensional meet in the middle cryptanalysis of KATAN. IACR Cryptol. ePrint Arch. 77 (2016)
12. Roh, D., Koo, B., Jung, Y., Jeong, I.W., Lee, D.-G., Kwon, D., Kim, W.-H.: Revised version of block cipher CHAM. In: Seo, J.H. (ed.) ICISC 2019. LNCS, vol. 11975, pp. 1–19. Springer, Cham (2020). https://doi.org/10.1007/978-3-030-40921-0_1

Improved the Automated Evaluation Algorithm Against Differential Attacks and Its Application to WARP

Jiali Shi, Guoqiang Liu[✉], and Chao Li

College of Science, National University of Defense Technology, Changsha, China
jiali00@126.com, liuguoqiang87@hotmail.com, lichao_nudt@sina.com

Abstract. This paper presents a heuristic approach to searching the key recovery-friendly distinguishers for block ciphers, which aims to attack more rounds with lower complexities. Firstly, we construct an SAT model to search for a set of distinguishers with the minimum number of active input-output words (and optimal probability). Subsequently, based on the discovered distinguishers, we select the advantageous distinguisher with fewer key bits involved in the key recovery phase. Finally, the guess-and-check for the key recovery attack is performed using the manual approach to compute the attack parameters accurately. By applying our new technique to WARP proposed in SAC 2020, we identify some 19-round and 20-round advantageous differentials. Simultaneously, the high-probability chain of Sbox leads to a stronger clustering effect of the differential trails for WARP, so we effectively improve the probability of the advantageous distinguisher. Also, the first 25-round differential attacks are performed by extending a 19-round distinguisher and a 20-round distinguisher, respectively. The results cover 2 more rounds than the previous known differential attacks.

Keywords: Differential Attack · SAT/SMT Model · Clustering Effect · WARP

1 Introduction

The differential attack was introduced by Biham and Shamir [5]. The goal of a differential attack is to attack more rounds with a lower complexity. There are generally two phases to achieve this goal, i.e., constructing a distinguisher and then launching a key recovery attack upon the distinguisher. Nowadays, most automated models focus on searching for differential trials with optimal probabilities, such as branch and bound method [12], CP [18], MILP [13,19], SAT [11,16], SMT [8]. However, a good differential attack is affected by many factors. In addition to the probability of the distinguisher, the cryptanalyst also needs to consider the input and output differences of the distinguisher, the number of rounds extended by the distinguisher, the number of key bits involved in the key recovery phase, etc. These factors influence and constrain each other, so how to trade off these factors is the key to executing better attacks.

© The Author(s), under exclusive license to Springer Nature Switzerland AG 2024
B. Smith and H. Wu (Eds.): SAC 2022, LNCS 13742, pp. 376–396, 2024.
https://doi.org/10.1007/978-3-031-58411-4_17

Table 1. Summary of cryptanalytic results on WARP

Approach	Rounds	Data	Time	Memory	Ref
Differential Attack	21 (2+16+3)	2^{113}	2^{113}	2^{72}	[9]
	23 (2+18+3)	$2^{106.62}$	$2^{106.68}$	$2^{106.62}$	[21]
	25 (3+19+3)	$2^{117.92}$	$2^{114.27}$	$2^{117.92}$	Sect. 4.2
	25 (2+20+3)	$2^{123.71}$	$2^{120.06}$	$2^{123.71}$	Sect. 4.3
Rectangle Attack	24 (1+21+2)	$2^{126.06}$	$2^{122.49}$	$2^{127.06}$	[21]
	26 (1+22+3)	$2^{120.6}$	$2^{115.9}$	$2^{120.6}$	[10]
Integral Attack	32 (1+22+9)	2^{127}	2^{127}	2^{108}	[7]

To search for an advantageous distinguisher, Zong et al. [23] studied the key-recovery-attack friendly differentials and performed the first 27-round differential attack on GIFT-128 [3]. At SAC 2021, to facilitate a 20-round attack on GIFT-64, Sun et al. [17] identified the advantageous distinguisher by exhaustively checking all the 13-round differential trails with probabilities no less than 2^{-64}. Motivated by this observation, we improve the automated evaluation algorithm against differential attacks on block ciphers.

WARP was proposed by Banik et al. at SAC 2020 [1]. It is a lightweight block cipher with a 128-bit block and key. The design goal of WARP is the small-footprint circuit in the field of 128-bit block ciphers. Its structure is a variant of the 32-branch Type-II generalized Feistel network (GFN). The designers [1] evaluated the resistance of WARP to the differential, linear, integral, impossible differential, and meet-in-the-middle attacks. For the differential attack, the designers provided the minimum number of active Sboxes for the first 19-round trails. Then, a 23-round differential attack and 24-round rectangle attack for WARP were proposed by Teh and Biryukov in [21]. This work has not yet determined the minimum active Sbox and optimal probability for the 20-round trail.

Our Contributions. Compared with Zong's method [23], our method is more efficient and general. Zong et al. first found the initial set containing the input-output differences of such distinguisher: extend more rounds and fewer keys involved in the key recovery phase, then identified the valid distinguisher from the initial set. Using this method, Zong et al. performed a 27-round differential attack on GIFT-128, one more round than the existing results. However, this method requires a lot of computational resources, and the probability of the distinguisher constructed from the input-output differences in the initial set may not be optimal. Therefore, we first search for the distinguisher with the optimal probability and then deduce the advantageous distinguisher that involves fewer key bits in the key recovery phase. In more detail, our contributions includes:

- We provide a two-step strategy to search for the differentials that have advantages in the distinguishing phase and key recovery phase. Firstly, an SAT model constructed is used to enumerate all the input-output differential patterns of the trail with optimal probability and the minimum number of active words (bytes/nibbles/bits) for its input-output differences. Secondly, for each input-output differential pattern of these distinguishers, we utilize the SMT model to describe the differential propagation in the extended rounds and count the number of key bits involved in the key recovery phase. These experimental results guide us to identify advantageous distinguishers that lead to attacking more rounds with a lower complexity.

- We apply this new technique to search for the advantageous distinguishers of WARP. With the observations in WARP, we provide some tips such as reducing constraints and reducing the search space to accelerate the search of differential trails. By using this model, the 19-round and 20-round advantageous distinguishers efficiently are identified.
- The first 25-round key recovery attacks on WARP are proposed. Notice that the strong clustering effect of the trails benefits from the high probability chain of the S-box. Hence, by enumerating 34566 trails with probabilities 2^{-132} sharing the same input-output differences, the probability of a 19-round distinguisher is improved from 2^{-132} to $2^{-116.92}$. Then, based on this distinguisher, a 25-round key recovery attack of WARP is launched by extending 3 rounds forward and 3 rounds backward. Similarly, a 20-round advantageous distinguisher can also be used to perform an effective 25-round key recovery attack. The results cover 2 more rounds than the existing differential attacks, as are summarized in Table 1.

Outline. The structure of WARP, and its observations and property are introduced in Sect. 2. We provide details about the SAT and SMT models for searching the advantageous distinguishers in Sect. 3. In Sect. 4, we find some advantageous distinguishers and perform the 25-round key recovery attacks on round-reduced WARP. Section 5 concludes the paper.

2   Preliminaries

2.1   Specification of WARP

WARP was proposed by Banik et al. at SAC 2020 [1]. WARP is a 128-bit block cipher with a 128-bit key, and its round number is 41. The structure of WARP is a variant of Type-II GFN. The round function is shown in Fig. 1, where the 32-nibble input state of the $(r + 1)$th round is denoted as $X^r = X_0^r || X_1^r || \dots || X_{31}^r$, and The 32-nibble input state of the shuffle operation in the $(r + 1)$th round is written as $Y^r = Y_0^r || Y_1^r || \dots || Y_{31}^r$, $0 \le r \le 40$. In each round function, three operations are performed in sequence, i.e. 4-bit Sbox, nibble XOR, and shuffle operation. The shuffle operation π in the 41st round is omitted.

- Sbox. To implement a lightweight threshold circuit, WARP applies the Sbox of Midori [2].
- Nibble XOR. The output nibble of the Sbox is xored to the subkey and the internal state.
- Shuffle operation. The shuffle operation π is worked on 32 nibbles, mapping the ith nibble to the $\pi(i)$th nibble.

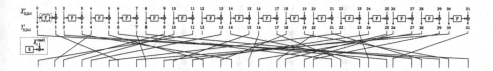

Fig. 1. The round function of WARP

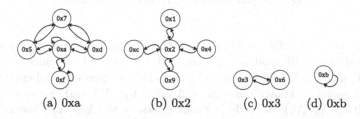

(a) 0xa   (b) 0x2   (c) 0x3   (d) 0xb

Fig. 2. The high-probability chains centered at 0xa, 0x2, 0x3, 0xb of the Sbox

Key Schedule. The 128-bit master key Mk is divided into two 64-bit keys $Mk = Mk^0 || Mk^1$. Let Mk_i^j denote one nibble, where $j \in \{0, 1\}$, $i \in \{0, 15\}$. i.e. $Mk^0 = Mk_0^0 || Mk_1^0 || \ldots || Mk_{15}^0$, $Mk^1 = Mk_0^1 || Mk_1^1 || \ldots || Mk_{15}^1$. The $(r+1)$th 64-bit subkey is given as $K^r = Mk^{r \mod 2}$, where $0 \leq r \leq 40$.

In addition, there are two nibbles of constants that are xored to the 1st and 3rd nibbles of the state. Since the differential attack does not consider the effect of constants, the introduction of constants is ignored. The details of WARP can be found in [1].

2.2 The Observations and Property of WARP

For block ciphers with Type-II GFN such as TWINE [20] and WARP, the differential distribution of the S-box has a significant impact on the differential behavior of these ciphers. There are some observations and properties of WARP that can be used to improve the automated models or optimize the key recovery attacks.

Observation 1 ([22]). *The Sbox has a high-probability chain*

$$(\Delta S_0, \Delta S_1, \ldots, \Delta S_L).$$

For all $i \in \{0, 1, \ldots, L\}$, $0 < L$, if $\Delta S_i \xrightarrow{Sbox} \Delta S_{i+1}$ is a high-probability transition. For the Sbox of WARP, there are several high-probability chains that have the iterative property illustrated in Fig. 2. The high-probability chain centered at 0xa in Fig. 2(a) is as follows.

$$\left. \begin{array}{l} 0x5 \xrightarrow{Sbox} 0xa \\ 0xf \xrightarrow{Sbox} 0xf \end{array} \right\} \xrightarrow{Sbox} 0xa \xrightarrow{Sbox} 0xd \xrightarrow{Sbox} 0x7 \xrightarrow{Sbox} 0x5. \qquad (1)$$

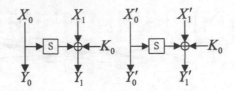

Fig. 3. A pair nibbles of the Feistel-subround

Property 1 ([21]). As illustrated in Fig. 3, the Feistel-subround performs on two nibbles, and the XOR 4-bit key is executed after the Sbox. Since the key K_0 has no influence on the differences ΔX_1 and ΔY_1, it allows partial encryption or decryption based on known differences $\Delta X_0 || \Delta X_1$, ΔY_1 and checks if the given pairs $(X_0 || X_1, X_0' || X_1')$ are valid without guessing the key K_0. The same goes for the decryption direction. This property can be used to filter wrong pairs in the key recovery phase.

Observation 2 *When encrypting, we can detect whether the input pair is valid without guessing the key according to Property 1. A similar situation exists in the decryption direction. Therefore,*

- *for the 25-round key recovery attack based on a 19-round distinguisher, without guessing the subkey, the following 14 nibbles in the 1st and 25th rounds can be used to directly filter the wrong pairs. That is* $\Delta Y_{1,3,13,15,19,29}^0 = \Delta X_{1,9,11,25,27}^{24} = 0x0$, $\Delta X_{23,31}^{24} = 0xa$.
- *Similarly, for the 25-round differential attack by extending a 20-round distinguisher, there are the following 16 nibbles in the 1st and 25th rounds to directly check whether the pairs are right. That is* $\Delta X_7^{24} = 0x5$, $\Delta X_{15}^{24} = 0xa$, $\Delta X_{9,11,15,17,25,27}^{24} = 0x0$, $\Delta Y_{21}^0 = 0xa$, $\Delta Y_{3,13,15,17,19,29,31}^0 = 0x0$,.

3   Improved the Automated Evaluation Algorithm Against Differential Attacks

To search for an advantageous distinguisher, Zong et al. [23] first found the initial set δ_{ini} containing the input-output differences of distinguishers with fewer involved key bits in the key recovery phase. Then, the advantageous differential was deduced from the initial set δ_{ini}. However, this method requires a lot of computational resources. In addition, for some ciphers, especially the Feistel-structured ciphers, the probability of a differential constructed from the input-output differences in δ_{ini} may not be optimal. To overcome this obstacle, we are motivated to improve the automated evaluation algorithm against differential attacks on block ciphers. We first introduce the basic strategy of differential attacks and then provide the SAT and SMT models used in the attack.

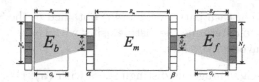

Fig. 4. Differential attack on block ciphers

3.1 The Strategy Towards Advantageous Distinguishers

For the differential attack shown in Fig. 4, an R-round cipher E is decomposed into three consecutive keyed permutations $E = E_f \circ E_m \circ E_b$. The block/key size is n/k-bit. Generally, the analyst uses an R_m-round distinguisher dominated by a differential trail with optimal probability P_{opt} and launch the key recovery attack by extending R_b-round forward and R_f-round backward.

However, multiple factors affect differential attacks, such as the number R_m of rounds and the probability of the distinguisher (α, β), the input and output differences of the distinguisher (the minimum number of active bits for the differences α, β is denoted as N_α, N_β, respectively), the number of key bits to be guessed in the key recovery phase (there are G_b/G_f key bits involved in the E_b/E_f part), and the number of active bits for the differences of the plaintexts and ciphertexts (similarly, the number of active bits for their differences are represented as N_b, N_f). These factors influence and restrict each other, e.g., the distinguisher with a minimum number of active bits for differences α, β can filter wrong pairs more effectively during data collection, so such a distinguisher has more advantages in the key recovery phase. Therefore, we need to trade off these factors and explore a longer attack with a lower complexity.

To execute longer attacks, we focus on such advantageous distinguishers (α, β): **(a)** the trail with long rounds $(R_m)_{max}$ and optimal probability P_{opt}. **(b)** the minimum number $(N_\alpha + N_\beta)_{min}$ of active words (bytes/nibbles/bits) for its input and output differences α, β. **(c)** more rounds $(R_b + R_f)_{max}$ are extended by the distinguisher. **(d)** fewer key bits are involved in the extended rounds (the minimum total number of the involved key bits is denoted as $(G_b + G_f)_{min}$). Currently, most works focus on constructing differential trails with P_{opt}. Few works have been devoted to deducing advantageous distinguishers for performing better key recovery attacks. In FSE 2022, Zong et al. searched for the key recovery-friendly distinguishers with high probability, **(c)** and **(d)**. Inspired by this work, we improve the automatic search algorithm against differential attacks, and provide the SAT and SMT models to search for the advantageous distinguishers with **(a)**, **(b)**, **(c)** and **(d)**, to launch better key recovery attacks. Specifically, we adopt the following two-step strategy to achieve this goal.

- **Step 1.** The SAT model is utilized to search for the differential trail with $(R_m)_{max}$, P_{opt} and $(N_\alpha + N_\beta)_{min}$. All input-output differential patterns of such differential (α, β) are denoted as $(\mathcal{A}_\alpha, \mathcal{A}_\beta)$.
- **Step 2.** The SMT model is used to describe the differential propagation in the extended rounds and count the number of involved key bits in the key

recovery phase. For each pattern $(\mathcal{A}_\alpha, \mathcal{A}_\beta)$ obtained in the **Step 1**, we apply the SMT model to determine the distinguisher with $(R_b + R_f)_{max}$ rounds and $(G_b + G_f)_{min}$ involved key bits.

In this way, the advantageous distinguishers with **(a)**, **(b)**, **(c)** and **(d)** can be found. Also, for the obtained distinguisher, we employ the strong clustering effect of differential trails to improve the probability of the distinguisher, thereby achieving a better key recovery attack. The process of the key recovery attack summarized in [14] is as follows.

- Data collection. We construct $2^t = 2 \cdot 2^{-N_b} \frac{N_e}{P_{opt}}$ structures and each structure includes N_b bits traversed, where N_e is the expected number of right pairs.
- $(n - N_f)$ bits inactive differences of the ciphertexts are used to filter wrong pairs. There are $2^{t+2N_b-1-(n-N_f)}$ pairs remaining.
- Set $2^{G_b+G_f}$ empty counters for counting correct partial subkey values. Continue guessing to filter the remaining pairs to determine the correct candidate key bits. The time complexity of this process is abbreviated as σ.

Once these parameters: $P_{opt}, N_b, N_f, G_b, G_f$ are found, the data complexity 2^{t+N_b} and the time complexity $2^t \cdot 2^{2N_b-1-(n-N_f)} \cdot \sigma \approx 2 \cdot \frac{N_e}{P_{opt}} \cdot 2^{N_b+N_f-n} \cdot \sigma$ can be calculated. The data complexity and time complexity are constrained by the block size and key size, respectively, i.e.

$$\begin{cases} 2^{t+N_b} < 2^n, \\ 2 \cdot \frac{N_e}{P_{opt}} \cdot 2^{N_b+N_f-n} \cdot \sigma < 2^k. \end{cases} \tag{2}$$

Since the round function of WARP performs on nibbles, for the above parameters, we mainly focus on the nibble-oriented parameters, such as $\frac{N_\alpha}{4}$, $\frac{N_\beta}{4}$, $\frac{N_b}{4}$, $\frac{N_f}{4}$, $\frac{G_b}{4}$, and $\frac{G_f}{4}$ nibbles.

Remarks. The Differential attack is affected by multiple factors, and the difficulty is how to trade off these parameters to construct a longer attack. In this paper, the advantageous distinguishers are identified by considering more parameters, but the obtained distinguisher is not necessarily globally optimal. Recently, some research work has also been continuously considering more factors to find advantage distinguishers. For instance, some distinguishers [14] used to improve the boomerang attack on SKINNY [4] have fewer active nibbles for their input-output differences than the distinguishers utilized in [6].

3.2   SAT Model for Searching Advantageous Differentials

In this section, the SAT model is used for searching all input-output differential patterns of the trails with more rounds $(R_m)_{max}$, optimal probability P_{opt} and $(\frac{N_\alpha+N_\beta}{4})_{min}$ nibbles. Specifically, the automated model is as follows.

- Step 1. The SAT model $\mathcal{M}_1$ is used to search for the differential trail with $(R_m)_{max}$ and P_{opt}. We construct this model to describe the differential propagation of the round function and set an objective function of the optimal probability P_{opt}. Besides, according to the property of WARP, we accelerate the search of the differential trail with P_{opt} by reducing the codomain of each nibble variable and reducing the number of constraints of the Sbox. After that, the solver returns a differential trial with the input and output differences α_0, β_0. We take the total number of active nibbles of the differences α_0, β_0 as the initial value $(\frac{N_{\alpha_0}+N_{\beta_0}}{4})_{ini}$.

- Step 2. The SAT model $\mathcal{M}_2$ is applied to search for the trails with $(R_m)_{max}$, P_{opt} and $(\frac{N_\alpha+N_\beta}{4})_{min}$. Based on the model $\mathcal{M}_1$ and the value $(\frac{N_{\alpha_0}+N_{\beta_0}}{4})_{ini}$, we add the constraints of the active nibbles of the differences α, β of the distinguisher and the objective function of minimizing the total number of active nibbles $(\frac{N_\alpha+N_\beta}{4})_{min}$. Then, we call the Cryptominisat5[1] solver until it returns a trail with P_{opt} and the minimum value $(\frac{N_\alpha+N_\beta}{4})_{min}$. The input-output differential pattern of the differences α, β is written as $\mathcal{A}_{\alpha,i}$, $\mathcal{A}_{\beta,i}$, where $\mathcal{A}_{\alpha,i}, \mathcal{A}_{\beta,i} \in \{0,1\}$, $0 \le i < 32$. That is, if the ith nibble of the input differences α is active, then $\mathcal{A}_{\alpha,i} = 1$, otherwise $\mathcal{A}_{\alpha,i} = 0$. The activeness of the output differences β is also expressed in the same way.
- Step 3. We utilize the model $\mathcal{M}_2$ to enumerate all the input-output differential patterns of the distinguisher (α, β) with $(R_m)_{max}$, P_{opt} and $(\frac{N_\alpha+N_\beta}{4})_{min}$. For every discovered pattern, we add a blocking clause that contains only $\mathcal{A}_{\alpha,0}, \ldots, \mathcal{A}_{\alpha,31}$, $\mathcal{A}_{\beta,0}, \ldots, \mathcal{A}_{\beta,31}$ to the model, and solve it again until the model has no solution, which means we have found all the solutions.

For the constraints of basic operations such as XOR and branching, please refer to [16] for more details. Thereafter, we introduce the constraints and objective functions used in the model.

Constraints Describing the Codomain of a Nibble. Let a nibble difference be $\Delta x_0 || \Delta x_1 || \Delta x_2 || \Delta x_3$. Due to the iterative property of the high-probability chain of the Sbox, the trails with optimal probability can be constructed by using the chain centered on 0xa given in Eq. (1). At this time, the codomain of the input and output differences for the Sbox is $\delta_N = \{0x0, 0x5, 0x7, 0xa, 0xd, 0xf\}$. In order to reduce the search space, the codomain of a nibble of all state variables in the round function is constrained to be δ_N. The following constraints represented as CN_1 are used to describe the codomain of a nibble.

$$\begin{cases} \Delta x_2 \vee \neg \Delta x_0 & = 1, \\ \neg \Delta x_2 \vee \Delta x_0 & = 1, \\ \Delta x_3 \vee \neg \Delta x_1 \vee \Delta x_0 & = 1, \\ \neg \Delta x_3 \vee \Delta x_1 \vee \Delta x_0 & = 1. \end{cases} \tag{3}$$

To compare the effectiveness of the model under different constraints, we also provide another constraint denoted as CN_2 that reduces the search space. From Observation 1, it can be seen that there is no high-probability 2^{-2} transition for the differential with the input or output differences 0x8. Therefore, to

---

[1] https://github.com/msoos/cryptominisat.

reduce the search space, remove 0x8 from the codomain of the nibble, that is, $\Delta x_0 || \Delta x_1 || \Delta x_2 || \Delta x_3 \neq$ 0x8. The corresponding constraint CN_2 is as follows.

$$\neg \Delta x_0 \vee \Delta x_1 \vee \Delta x_2 \vee \Delta x_3 = 1. \tag{4}$$

Constraints on the Differential Propagation with High-Probability Chain Centered on 0xa of the Sbox. The high-probability chain centered on 0xa has iterative property, so the trails with optimal probability can be constructed by using these chains. Therefore, we describe these valid differential propagation in Eq. (1) with CNF constraints. The input and output differences of the Sbox are represented as $\Delta X = \Delta x_0 || \Delta x_1 || \Delta x_2 || \Delta x_3$ and $\Delta Y = \Delta y_0 || \Delta y_1 || \Delta y_2 || \Delta y_3$ respectively. The differential probability written as DP belongs to $\{0, 2^{-2}, 1\}$. An additional variable $2 \cdot p_0$ describes the weight of the differential (Weight is the negative value of the binary logarithm of the differential probability).

$$p_0 = \begin{cases} 1, & \text{if } DP(\Delta X, \Delta Y) = 2^{-2}, \\ 0, & \text{if } DP(\Delta X, \Delta Y) = 1. \end{cases}$$

The differential propagation with probability dp_0 is denoted as $a_0 || a_1 || a_2 || a_3 \rightarrow b_0 || b_1 || b_2 || b_3$, then enumerate valid combinations of $(9 \cdot m)$-bit vectors

$$a_0^{(i)} || a_1^{(i)} || a_2^{(i)} || a_3^{(i)} || b_0^{(i)} || b_1^{(i)} || b_2^{(i)} || b_3^{(i)} || dp_0^{(i)}.$$

The original differential model of the Sbox consists of the following m clauses.

$$\bigvee_{j=0}^{3} (\Delta x_j \oplus a_j^{(i)}) \vee \bigvee_{j=0}^{3} (\Delta y_j \oplus b_j^{(i)}) \vee (p_0 \oplus dp_0^{(i)}) = 1, 0 \leq i \leq m-1.$$

Thereafter, the 9-bit Boolean function is defined as

$$f(\Delta X || \Delta Y || p_0) = \begin{cases} 1, & \text{if } \Delta X \rightarrow \Delta Y \text{ in Eq. (1)}, \\ 0, & \text{otherwise.} \end{cases}$$

After that, Logic Friday[2] is used to simplify the CNF expressions. As a result, for all valid differentials with probability 2^{-2}, the constraints CS_{vd4} are made up of 27 clauses with 9 variables. Similarly, the high-probability chain centered on 0xa is described by the constraints $CS_{vd4,a}$ which include 16 clauses with 9 variables ($\Delta x_0, \ldots, \Delta x_3, \Delta y_0, \ldots, \Delta y_3, p_0$).

Furthermore, to analyze the efficiency of searching for models under different constraints, different constraints are also utilized to describe the differential propagation of Sboxes. Generally, for searching the trail with optimal probability, the constraints CS_{vd} used to describe all valid differentials of the Sbox are composed of 57 clauses with 11 variables ($\Delta x_0, \ldots, \Delta x_3, \Delta y_0, \ldots, \Delta y_3, p_0, p_1, p_2$), where p_0, p_1, p_2 are used to represent the weight of the differential.

---

[2] https://web.archive.org/web/20131022021257/http:/www.sontrak.com/.

The Objective Function for Searching the Trails with Optimal Probability P_{opt}. For the r-round trail, the probability variable of the jth Sbox in the ith round is $p_0^{(i,j)}$ by using the constraints $CS_{vd4,a}$, where $0 \leq i < r, 0 \leq j < 16$. The prospective value of differential weight is w_{DT} ($P_{opt} = 2^{-w_{DT}}$), then the objective function is

$$\sum_{i=0}^{r-1}\sum_{j=0}^{15} 2 \cdot p_0^{(i,j)} \leq w_{DT}. \tag{5}$$

Constraints on the Activeness of Each Nibble for the Input-Output Differences α, β **of a Distinguisher.** The 4-bit difference is denoted as Δx_0, Δx_1, Δx_2, Δx_3, an extra binary variable t is required to represent whether the nibble is active or not. If $\Delta x_0 \| \Delta x_1 \| \Delta x_2 \| \Delta x_3 \neq \text{0x0}$, the nibble is active, that is, $t = 1$, otherwise, $t = 0$. The corresponding clauses are as follows.

$$\begin{cases} \neg \Delta x_0 \vee t & = 1, \\ \neg \Delta x_1 \vee t & = 1, \\ \neg \Delta x_2 \vee t & = 1, \\ \neg \Delta x_3 \vee t & = 1, \\ \Delta x_3 \vee \Delta x_2 \vee \Delta x_1 \vee \Delta x_0 \vee \neg t & = 1. \end{cases}$$

The Objective Function for Minimizing the Number of the Active Nibbles $(\frac{N_\alpha + N_\beta}{4})_{min}$ **of the input-output differences** α, β. For a differential (α, β), let the i-nibble of the input/output differences α/β be $\mathcal{A}_{\alpha,i}/ \mathcal{A}_{\beta,i}$, where $0 \leq i < 32$. We aim at minimizing the number of active nibbles for the differences α, β. The prospective value of $\frac{N_\alpha + N_\beta}{4}$ is $(\frac{N_\alpha + N_\beta}{4})_{min}$. Accordingly, the objective functions are as follows.

$$\sum_{i=0}^{31}(\mathcal{A}_{\alpha,i} + \mathcal{A}_{\beta,i}) \leq (\frac{N_\alpha + N_\beta}{4})_{min}. \tag{6}$$

In some cases, to execute a better differential attack, it may be necessary to constrain the minimum number of active nibbles of the input and output differences of the distinguisher, respectively. Hence, assuming that the prospective value of $\frac{N_\alpha}{4}$ and $\frac{N_\beta}{4}$ is $(\frac{N_\alpha}{4})_{min}$ and $(\frac{N_\beta}{4})_{min}$, the objective function is

$$\sum_{i=0}^{31}\mathcal{A}_{\alpha,i} \leq (\frac{N_\alpha}{4})_{min}, \sum_{i=0}^{31}\mathcal{A}_{\beta,i} \leq (\frac{N_\beta}{4})_{min}. \tag{7}$$

The essential form of Eq. (5), (6) and (7) is $\sum_{i=0}^{m-1} x_i \leq t$. We apply the sequential encoding approach [15] to convert this function into CNF formulas.

Finally, to illustrate the search efficiency of the SAT model, the time consumed is compared by searching the 18-round trails with optimal probability 2^{-122} under different constraints. All the experiments deploy a server with Intel(R) Xeon(R) E5-2680 CPU*2 with 2.50 GHZ, 256 GB RAM. The search

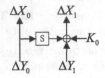

Fig. 5. The differential propagation of the Feistel-subround

time for the SAT model with CS_{vd} is 12605 s. On this basis, after only replacing the constraints CS_{vd} by CS_{vd4}, the search time is 4513 seconds, Furthermore, in order to reduce the search space, the SAT model with CS_{vd4} and CN_2 takes 913 s. Lastly, the SAT model with $CS_{vd4,a}$ and CN_1 returns a valid solution after 558 s. As a result, we verified that the optimal probability for 20 rounds trail is 2^{-140}, which was not confirmed in [21].

3.3   SMT Model Oriented to Key Recovery

In this section, for WARP, an SMT model constructed is utilized to describe differential propagation in the extended rounds and count the number of the master key nibbles involved in the key recovery phase. Based on the distinguisher (α, β), we extend R_b rounds forward from input differences α and R_f rounds backward from output differences β. Then, we mark the subkeys that need to be guessed in the extended rounds and count the total number $\frac{G_b + G_f}{4}$ of the involved master key nibbles by considering the key schedule of WARP.

There are two types of differences in the extended rounds: constant difference, and unknown difference. For each nibble variable, an extra variable x_{con} is introduced to describe whether the nibble difference ΔX is known. The constant difference and the unknown difference can be expressed as follows.

- Constant difference. Let a nibble difference ΔX be a constant δ, where $\delta \in \{0x0, 0x1, \dots, 0xf\}$. It is written as $\Delta X = \delta, x_{con} = 0$.
- Unknown difference. If a nibble difference ΔX is unknown, it is denoted as $\Delta X = 0xf, x_{con} = 1$.

Constraints on the Differential Propagation in the E_b and E_f Parts. Since the differential propagation in the E_b and E_f parts is similar, we only take Feistel-subround shown in Fig. 5 as an example to introduce the differential propagation in the E_b part. Given $\Delta Y_0, y_{con,0}$ and $\Delta Y_1, y_{con,1}$, $\Delta X_0, x_{con,0}$ and $\Delta X_1, x_{con,1}$ are derived. The details are as follows.

- For the left branch, the expressions describing the differential propagation are written as $\Delta X_0 = \Delta Y_0, x_{con,0} = y_{con,0}$.
- For the right branch, the input difference ΔX_1 will be affected by the output difference ΔY_0. The relations can be described with the following equations.

$$\begin{cases} \Delta Y_0 = 0x0 \Rightarrow \Delta X_1 = \Delta Y_1, x_{con,1} = y_{con,1}, \\ \Delta Y_0 \neq 0x0 \Rightarrow \Delta X_1 = 0xf, x_{con,1} = 1. \end{cases}$$

Constraints Describing the Subkeys Involved in the E_b and E_f Parts.
In [21], a 23-round key recovery attack was proposed by extending 2 rounds
forward and 3 rounds backward the 18-round distinguisher. Therefore, we choose
$R_b, R_f \in \{2, 3\}$ to deduce a better key recovery attack for a given distinguisher.
Next, for WARP, we take $R_b = 3$ as an example to illustrate how to mark the
subkey nibbles involved in the extended rounds.

- In the 3rd round, there is no need to guess the subkeys according to Property 1, then $K_i^2 = 0$, where $0 \le i < 16$.
- The following subkey nibbles that need to be guessed in the 2nd round are
  determined based on the nibbles that need to calculate the values in the 3rd
  round. $(0 \le i < 16)$

$$K_i^1 = \begin{cases} 1, & \text{if } \Delta Y_{2i+1}^1 \ne 0, \\ 0, & \text{otherwise.} \end{cases}$$

- The following subkey nibbles involved in the 1st round are determined based
  on the nibble values to be calculated in the 2nd and 3rd rounds. $(0 \le i < 16,$
  $j = \lfloor \frac{\pi^{-1}(2i)}{2} \rfloor)$

$$K_j^0 = \begin{cases} 1, & \text{if } \Delta X_{2i+1}^1 \ne 0, \\ 0, & \text{otherwise.} \end{cases}$$

**Constraints on Counting the Total Number $\frac{G_b + G_f}{4}$ of the Master
Key Nibbles Involved in the E_b and E_f Parts.** We obtain the corresponding relations between the subkeys and the master keys according to
the key schedule of WARP. The 128-bit master key is divided into 32 nibbles
$Mk = Mk_0^0|| \ldots ||Mk_{15}^0||Mk_0^1|| \ldots ||Mk_{15}^1$. If all subkeys K_i^r corresponding to the
master key nibble $Mk_i^{r \mod 2}$ do not need to be guessed, then $Mk_i^{r \mod 2} = 0$,
otherwise, $Mk_i^{r \mod 2} = 1$, where $r \in [0, R_b) \cup [R_b + R_m, R_b + R_m + R_f)$,
$0 \le i < 16$. Let $t = r \mod 2$, where $t \in \{0, 1\}$. The expression is specified
as follows.

$$Mk_i^t = \begin{cases} 0, \text{if } \sum_{r=0}^{R_b-1} K_i^r + \sum_{r=R_b+R_m}^{R_b+R_m+R_f-1} K_i^r = 0, \\ 1, \text{otherwise.} \end{cases}$$

The total number of the master key nibbles involved in the extended rounds is
$\sum_{i=0}^{15} (Mk_i^0 + Mk_i^1) = \frac{G_b + G_f}{4}$.

4   Differential Attack on WARP

In this section, we propose the 25-round key recovery attacks on WARP by extending the 19-round and the 20-round distinguishers, respectively. To find advantageous distinguishers, all input-output differential patterns of the trail with
$(R_m)_{max}$, P_{opt} and $(\frac{N_\alpha + N_\beta}{4})_{min}$ have obtained by utilizing the SAT model. For

Table 2. The experimental results for differential trails of WARP

Round	1	2	3	4	5	6	7	8	9	10
$\#AS$	0	1	2	3	4	6	8	11	14	17
P_{opt}	1	2^{-2}	2^{-4}	2^{-6}	2^{-8}	2^{-12}	2^{-16}	2^{-22}	2^{-28}	2^{-34}
$(\frac{N_\alpha+N_\beta}{4})_{ran}$	2	3	4	5	6	8	10	13	16	17
$(\frac{N_\alpha+N_\beta}{4})_{min}$	2	3	4	5	6	8	10	11	14	17
Round	11	12	13	14	15	16	17	18	19	20
$\#AS$	22	28	34	40	47	52	57	61	66	70
P_{opt}	2^{-44}	2^{-56}	2^{-68}	2^{-80}	2^{-94}	2^{-104}	2^{-114}	2^{-122}	2^{-132}	2^{-140}
$(\frac{N_\alpha+N_\beta}{4})_{ran}$	22	28	24	26	29	21	14	18	21	19
$(\frac{N_\alpha+N_\beta}{4})_{min}$	22	22	24	23	29	21	14	18	15	19

each pattern, we choose the input-output differences (α, β) belonging to the pattern to count the number of master keys involved in the extended rounds and try to identify the input-output patterns of the distinguishers with fewer involved master keys. Eventually, we find the 19-round and 20-round advantageous distinguishers which can be used to launch the 25-round differential attacks.

4.1 The Differential Friendly to Key Recovery Attacks

As far as we know, solvers like STP[3], and Gurobi[4] can be regarded as a black box that returns a valid solution according to the constructed model. Usually, there is only one objective function P_{opt} for the SAT model $\mathcal{M}_1$ given in Sect. 3.2 when searching for the trails. The solver returns a trail with P_{opt}. However, the number of active nibbles for their input and output differences is random. Then, we use the model $\mathcal{M}_2$ which adds another objective function $(\frac{N_\alpha+N_\beta}{4})_{min}$ (Eq. (6)) to minimize the total number of active nibbles for the input-output differences (α, β), and get a trail with P_{opt} and $(\frac{N_\alpha+N_\beta}{4})_{min}$.

With the help of the SAT model, the experimental results for the first 20 rounds are obtained and illustrated in Table 2. $\#AS$ denotes the minimum number of active Sboxes for the trail. $(\frac{N_\alpha+N_\beta}{4})_{min}/(\frac{N_\alpha+N_\beta}{4})_{ran}$ represents the minimum/random number of active input-output nibbles of the trail with optimal probability P_{opt} by using the model $\mathcal{M}_2/\mathcal{M}_1$. For instance, the number $(\frac{N_\alpha+N_\beta}{4})_{ran}$ of a 19-round trail with P_{opt} returned by the model $\mathcal{M}_1$ is 21-nibble, and the minimum number $(\frac{N_\alpha+N_\beta}{4})_{min}$ searched by the model $\mathcal{M}_2$ is 15 nibbles. The latter filters wrong pairs more effectively during the data collection.

In Table 3, two input-output patterns of the 18/19/20-round trials are found by utilizing the model $\mathcal{M}_2$. As in [21], Teh et al. applied an 18-round distinguisher whose input-output differences belong to the pattern $(\mathcal{A}_{\alpha_0}^{18}, \mathcal{A}_{\beta_0}^{18})$ to perform a

---

[3] https://github.com/stp/stp.
[4] http://www.gurobi.com.

Table 3. The input-output differential patterns of the differential trails with P_{opt} and $(\frac{N_\alpha+N_\beta}{4})_{min}$ of WARP

Round	Input pattern	Output pattern
18	$\mathcal{A}^{18}_{\alpha_0}$ = 0b0000 0000 1111 0001 0000 1100 1101 0000	$\mathcal{A}^{18}_{\beta_0}$ = 0b0010 0000 1000 0011 0000 0110 0001 1000
	$\mathcal{A}^{18}_{\alpha_1}$ = 0b0000 1100 1101 0000 0000 0000 1111 0001	$\mathcal{A}^{18}_{\beta_1}$ = 0b0000 0110 0001 1000 0010 0000 1000 0011
19	$\mathcal{A}^{19}_{\alpha_0}$ = 0b1100 0000 0001 0000 0001 0000 0011 0000	$\mathcal{A}^{19}_{\beta_0}$ = 0b1001 0000 0001 0010 1011 0000 1010 0000
	$\mathcal{A}^{19}_{\alpha_1}$ = 0b0001 0000 0011 0000 1100 0000 0001 0000	$\mathcal{A}^{19}_{\beta_1}$ = 0b1011 0000 1010 0000 1001 0000 0001 0010
20	$\mathcal{A}^{20}_{\alpha_0}$ = 0b0000 1100 1101 0000 0000 0000 11110001	$\mathcal{A}^{20}_{\beta_0}$ = 0b1001 0000 0001 0010 1011 0000 1010 0000
	$\mathcal{A}^{20}_{\alpha_1}$ = 0b0000 0000 1111 0001 0000 1100 1101 0000	$\mathcal{A}^{20}_{\beta_1}$ = 0b1011 0000 1010 0000 1001 0000 0001 0010

Table 4. The total number of master keys involved in the extended rounds based on the differential of WARP

Differential Pattern	R_b	R_f	$(\frac{G_b+G_f}{4})$
$\mathcal{A}^{18}_\alpha, \mathcal{A}^{18}_\beta$	2	3	18
$\mathcal{A}^{19}_\alpha, \mathcal{A}^{19}_\beta$	2	3	16
	3	2	15
	3	3	20
$\mathcal{A}^{20}_\alpha, \mathcal{A}^{20}_\beta$	2	3	17

23-round differential attack. Referring to this attack, we choose $R_b, R_f \in \{2, 3\}$. Then, for each input-output pattern shown in Table 3, we apply the SMT model to deduce the minimum number $(\frac{G_b+G_f}{4})_{min}$ of master keys involved in the extended rounds. The results show that the two input-output patterns of 18/19/20 rounds distinguishers involve the same number of master keys by extending the same rounds. As illustrated in Table 4, it can be seen that the 19-round distinguisher involves fewer master keys than the 18-round distinguisher in the key recovery phase. For instance, by extending $R_b = 2$, $R_f = 3$ rounds, the number $\frac{G_b+G_f}{4}$ of the 18-round, 19-round and 20-round distinguishers are 18, 16, and 17 nibbles, respectively. When $R_b = R_f = 3$, the number of master keys involved in the 19-round distinguisher is 20-nibble. When $R_b = 2$, $R_f = 3$, the number for the 20-round distinguisher is 17-nibble. However, the optimal probability of the 19/20-round trail is $2^{-132}/2^{-140}$. So if we can improve the probability of the 19-round or the 20-round distinguisher, then it is possible to perform an efficient key recovery attack based on this distinguisher.

With the help of SAT model, the probability of the distinguishers can be improved by utilizing the clustering effect of the trails. The results are listed in Table 5. the symbol "‡" means that we have found some trails with optimal probability sharing the same input and output differences, but not all of them. When searching for trails with the same input and output differences, we focus on the trials with optimal probability. So compared to the result in [21], the clustering effect of the trails starts from the 8th round instead of the 10th round, and we obtain a higher probability of the distinguisher by exploiting the clustering effect of fewer trails. E.g. for the following 19-round differential $(\alpha^{19}, \beta^{19})$,

Table 5. The experimental results for the differentials of WARP

Round	Input difference	Output difference	P_{opt}	#Trail	DP	Ref
8	0x0000 0000 00aa 0000 0000 da00 000a 0000	0x0a00 0000 0000 a000 f00a 0a00 00a0 0000	2^{-22}	4	2^{-20}	Sect. 4.1
9	0x0000 da00 000a 0000 0000 0000 00a5 0000	0xa00a 00a0 0700 5050 0000 5050 0000 000a	2^{-28}	6	$2^{-26.68}$	Sect. 4.1
10	0x0000 0000 2100 0400 0000 0024 2100 0004	0x2004 0020 0100 2020 0000 2020 0000 0004	2^{-34}	4	2^{-32}	Sect. 4.1
	0x0000 0000 ee00 0e00 0000 00ee ee00 000e	0xe00e 00e0 0e00 e0e0 0000 e0e0 0000 000e	2^{-34}	7	$2^{-33.19}$	[21]
11	0x0212 0002 0000 4200 1200 0002 0000 1292	0x0000 2020 0000 0004 2001 0020 0400 2020	2^{-44}	4	2^{-42}	Sect. 4.1
	0x2400 0001 0000 2121 0921 0001 0000 2100	0x4002 0010 0200 1010 0000 1010 0000 0002	2^{-44}	7	$2^{-43.19}$	[21]
12	0x7500 a5da 0a00 0000 0005 da00 000a 0a00	0x00a0 0000 0fa0 00a0 fa00 000d 0000 aaf0	2^{-56}	24	$2^{-52.68}$	Sect. 4.1
	0x0424 0004 0000 2100 2400 0004 0000 2121	0x0100 0404 2120 2001 0020 2120 2020 0020	2^{-56}	5	$2^{55.42}$	[21]
13	0x0002 4200 0002 0200 4200 9292 0200 0000	0x0000 0004 2020 0100 2024 0004 0120 0021	2^{-68}	2240	$2^{-62.15}$	Sect. 4.1
	0x1200 1212 0200 0000 0002 4200 0002 0200	0x2021 0004 0420 0021 0000 0001 2020 0200	2^{-68}	1600	$2^{-62.37}$	[21]
14	0xaa00 575a 0a00 0000 000a da00 0007 0a00	0x0050 00a0 a000 5000 a00a 500a 5000 0a0a	2^{-80}	1824	$2^{-70.38}$	Sect. 4.1
	0x000c 2400 0001 0100 2100 2921 0100 0000	0x2024 200c 2000 0c04 2024 0020 2001 0000	2^{-80}	21528	$2^{-72.14}$	[21]
15	0xaa00 aa75 0500 0000 000a 5700 000a 0500	0x0050 5000 5000 a0aa 0a00 5750 5a5a 5a50	2^{-94}	632	$2^{-84.70}$	Sect. 4.1
	0x0005 7500 0005 0a00 a500 a5a5 0a00 0000	0x0aa0 a750 5a55 5aa0 0070 000a 500a 005a	2^{-94}	497248	$2^{-85.54}$	[21]
16	0x0000 aa00 aa0a 0000 0000 0000 5a5a 000a	0x500a 5500 0aa0 5a00 0000 a000 a000 00a0	2^{-104}	13581‡	$2^{-90.27}$	Sect. 4.1
	0x0000 a500 a50a 0000 0000 0000 aaa5 000a	0xaa005 a500 05a0 5700 0000 a000 a000 00a0	2^{-104}	800152	$2^{-90.52}$	[21]
17	0xff00 0000 000a 0000 000a 0000 00aa 0000	0x0000 05a0 000d 7000 0070 0000 a000 00a5	2^{-114}	13280‡	$2^{-100.30}$	Sect. 4.1
	0x0007 0000 005a 0000 5700 0000 000a 0000	0x00a0 0000 a000 00aa 0000 0550 0005 a000	2^{-114}	734494	$2^{-95.66}$	[21]
18	0x0000 0000 57aa 000a 0000 a500 fa0a 0000	0x00a0 0000 a000 00a5 0000 0aa0 0005 a000	2^{-122}	626723	$2^{-104.62}$	[21]
19	0xaa00 0000 000a 0000 000a 0000 005a 0000	0x500a 0000 000a 0050 a05a 0000 50a0 0000	2^{-132}	34566‡	$2^{-116.92}$	Sect. 4.1
	0x0000 5a00 aa07 0000 0000 0000 a55a 0005	0xa000 7005 a00a 5a00 00a0 0a00 0500 0050	2^{-132}	594111	$2^{-118.07}$	[21]
20	0x0000 0000 faa5 000f 0000 7500 aa05 0000	0xa05f 0000 a050 0000 a005 0000 000a 00a0	2^{-140}	545054	$2^{-122.71}$	[21]

$$\alpha^{19} = 0\text{x}0000\ 5\text{a}00\ \text{aa}07\ 0000\ 0000\ 0000\ \text{a}55\text{a}\ 0005,$$

$$\beta^{19} = 0\text{xa}000\ 7005\ \text{a}00\text{a}\ 5\text{a}00\ 00\text{a}0\ 0\text{a}00\ 0500\ 0050,$$

Teh et al. improved the probability of $(\alpha^{19}, \beta^{19})$ from 2^{-132} to $2^{-118.07}$ by enumerating 594111 trails [21]. While we find another 19-round differential $(\alpha_0^{19}, \beta_0^{19})$

$$\alpha_0^{19} = 0\text{xaa}00\ 0000\ 000\text{a}\ 0000\ 000\text{a}\ 0000\ 005\text{a}\ 0000,$$

$$\beta_0^{19} = 0\text{x}500\text{a}\ 0000\ 000\text{a}\ 0050\ \text{a}05\text{a}\ 0000\ 50\text{a}0\ 0000,$$

which belonging to $(\mathcal{A}_{\alpha_0}^{19}, \mathcal{A}_{\beta_0}^{19})$, and use 34566 differential trails with 2^{-132} to improve the probability of $(\alpha_0^{19}, \beta_0^{19})$ from 2^{-132} to $2^{-116.92}$. The strong clustering effect of WARP benefits from the high-probability chain of the Sbox, which also makes it more effective in improving the probability of the distinguisher. In addition, it can be observed that the following 20-round differential $(\alpha_1^{20}, \beta_1^{20})$ given by Teh et al. [21]. belongs to the pattern $(\mathcal{A}_{\alpha_1}^{20}, \mathcal{A}_{\beta_1}^{20})$, and its probability is improved from 2^{-140} to $2^{-122.71}$ using 545054 trails.

$$\alpha_1^{20} = 0\text{x}0000\ 0000\ \text{faa}5\ 000\text{f}\ 0000\ 7500\ \text{aa}05\ 0000,$$

$$\beta_1^{20} = 0\text{xa}05\text{f}\ 0000\ \text{a}050\ 0000\ \text{a}005\ 0000\ 000\text{a}\ 00\text{a}0.$$

After obtaining the parameter information of P_{opt}, N_b, N_f and G_b, G_f, and substituting into Eq. (2) in Sect. 3.1, we can estimate the complexity of the differential attack. Lastly, we execute an effective 25-round key recovery attacks based on the 19-round, and 20-round distinguishers, respectively.

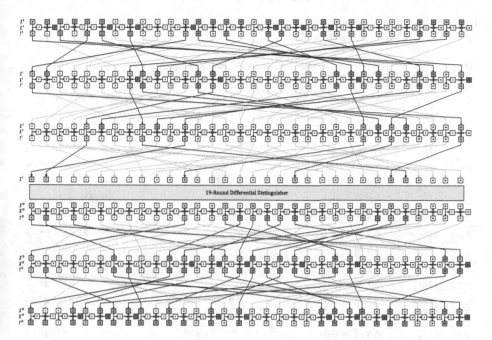

Fig. 6. The 25-round key recovery attack on WARP based on the 19-round differential. The nibble with zero difference is marked in white, the nibble with a nonzero difference is marked in grey, the nibble of unknown difference is marked in blue, and the subkeys involved in the extended rounds are marked in red. (Color figure online)

4.2 The 25-Round Key Recovery Attack on WARP Based on the 19-Round Distinguisher

In this section, based on the 19-round distinguisher $(\alpha_0^{19}, \beta_0^{19})$ with probability $2^{-116.92}$, we perform the 25-round key recovery attack by extending 3 rounds at the top and 3 rounds in the bottom. The 25-round key recovery attack is shown in Fig. 6. The attack procedures are as follows.

Data Collection. For WARP, there is no whitening key at the input, we can construct structures at the position of X^0. By traversing $N_f = 17 \times 4$ bits values of $X^0_{1,\ldots,5,7,12,\ldots,15,17,18,19,21,28,29,31}$, and the remaining 60 bits are fixed differences, each structure includes 2^{135} pairs. Construct 2^t structures, we obtain 2^{t+135} pairs.

Key Recovery

Step 1. By utilizing inactive bits in the output differences ΔX^{25}, we filter the wrong pairs. For each pair, the corresponding pair of ciphertexts $(X^{25}, X^{25'})$ are obtained by querying the oracle. There are 44 inactive bits for ΔX^{25}. In addition, according to Observation 2, 14 nibbles allow an immediate check of whether the given pair is valid. Then, the number of valid pairs would be reduced to $2^{t+135-44-56} = 2^{t+35}$. Let $2^m = 2^{t+35}$.

Table 6. Detailed computation of complexity for the 25-round key recovery attack based on the 19-round distinguisher

step	GMK	Condition on the difference	#{*Remaining pairs*}	Time complexity
2.1	Mk_3^0	$\Delta Y_9^1 = 0\mathrm{xa}, \Delta X_{31}^{23} = 0\mathrm{x}0$	$2^m \cdot 2^{-8}$	$2 \cdot 2^m \cdot 2^4 \cdot 4$
2.2	Mk_2^0	$\Delta Y_{13}^1 = 0\mathrm{xa}, \Delta X_{23}^{23} = 0\mathrm{x}5$	$2^{m-8} \cdot 2^{-8}$	$2 \cdot 2^{m-8} \cdot 2^4 \cdot 2^4 \cdot 4$
2.3	Mk_{11}^0	$\Delta Y_{25}^1 = 0\mathrm{x}0, \Delta X_{15}^{23} = 0\mathrm{xa}$	$2^{m-16} \cdot 2^{-8}$	$2 \cdot 2^{m-16} \cdot 2^8 \cdot 2^4 \cdot 4$
2.4	Mk_{10}^0	$\Delta Y_{29}^1 = 0\mathrm{x}0, \Delta X_7^{23} = 0\mathrm{x}0$	$2^{m-24} \cdot 2^{-8}$	$2 \cdot 2^{m-24} \cdot 2^{12} \cdot 2^4 \cdot 4$
2.5	Mk_8^0	$\Delta Y_{23}^1 = 0\mathrm{x}0$	$2^{m-32} \cdot 2^{-4}$	$2 \cdot 2^{m-32} \cdot 2^{16} \cdot 2^4 \cdot 2$
2.6	Mk_{11}^1	$\Delta Y_{25}^2 = 0\mathrm{xa}, \Delta X_{15}^{22} = 0\mathrm{x}0$	$2^{m-36} \cdot 2^{-8}$	$2 \cdot 2^{m-36} \cdot 2^{20} \cdot 2^4 \cdot 8$
2.7	Mk_5^0	$\Delta Y_1^1 = 0\mathrm{x}0$	$2^{m-44} \cdot 2^{-4}$	$2 \cdot 2^{m-44} \cdot 2^{24} \cdot 2^4 \cdot 2$
2.8	Mk_{15}^0	$\Delta X_1^{23} = 0\mathrm{x}0$	$2^{m-48} \cdot 2^{-4}$	$2 \cdot 2^{m-48} \cdot 2^{28} \cdot 2^4 \cdot 2$
2.9	Mk_1^0	$\Delta X_{11}^{23} = 0\mathrm{x}5$	$2^{m-52} \cdot 2^{-4}$	$2 \cdot 2^{m-52} \cdot 2^{32} \cdot 2^4 \cdot 2$
2.10	Mk_7^0	$\Delta X_{17}^{23} = 0\mathrm{x}0$	$2^{m-56} \cdot 2^{-4}$	$2 \cdot 2^{m-56} \cdot 2^{36} \cdot 2^4 \cdot 2$
2.11	Mk_6^0	$\Delta X_{19}^{23} = 0\mathrm{xa}$	$2^{m-60} \cdot 2^{-4}$	$2 \cdot 2^{m-60} \cdot 2^{40} \cdot 2^4 \cdot 2$
2.12	Mk_6^1	$\Delta Y_5^2 = 0\mathrm{x}0$	$2^{m-64} \cdot 2^{-4}$	$2 \cdot 2^{m-64} \cdot 2^{44} \cdot 2^4 \cdot 4$
2.13	Mk_{15}^1	$\Delta X_1^{22} = 0\mathrm{x}0$	$2^{m-68} \cdot 2^{-4}$	$2 \cdot 2^{m-68} \cdot 2^{48} \cdot 2^4 \cdot 4$
2.14	Mk_7^1	$\Delta X_{17}^{22} = 0\mathrm{x}0$	$2^{m-72} \cdot 2^{-4}$	$2 \cdot 2^{m-72} \cdot 2^{52} \cdot 2^4 \cdot 4$
2.15	Mk_{12}^0	$\Delta X_{19}^{22} = 0\mathrm{xa}$	$2^{m-76} \cdot 2^{-4}$	$2 \cdot 2^{m-76} \cdot 2^{56} \cdot 2^4 \cdot 4$
2.16	Mk_5^1	$\Delta X_{25}^{22} = 0\mathrm{x}0$	$2^{m-80} \cdot 2^{-4}$	$2 \cdot 2^{m-80} \cdot 2^{60} \cdot 2^4 \cdot 4$
2.17	Mk_9^1	$\Delta X_{27}^{22} = 0\mathrm{x}0$	$2^{m-84} \cdot 2^{-4}$	$2 \cdot 2^{m-84} \cdot 2^{64} \cdot 2^4 \cdot 4$
2.18	Mk_9^0	$\Delta Y_{27}^2 = 0\mathrm{x}0$	$2^{m-88} \cdot 2^{-4}$	$2 \cdot 2^{m-88} \cdot 2^{68} \cdot 2^4 \cdot 4$
2.19	Mk_3^1, Mk_0^0	$\Delta Y_9^2 = 0\mathrm{x}0$	$2^{m-92} \cdot 2^{-4}$	$2 \cdot 2^{m-92} \cdot 2^{72} \cdot 2^4 \cdot 4$
Total				$2^{m+7.10}$

Step 2. We guess the value of a nibble master key Mk_3^0 and check the 8-bit difference $\Delta Y_9^1 = 0\mathrm{xa}$, $\Delta X_{31}^{23} = 0\mathrm{x}5$. The remaining 2^{m-8} pairs will participate in the following process. This guess-and-check procedure is repeated for all the 18 parts until all the 80-bit master keys are traversed. The time complexity and the number of remaining pairs in each step are detailed in Table 6. Where "GMK" means that the nibble master key needs to be guessed.

Complexity Analysis. We set $N_e = 1$ pairs remaining for the right key guess, then construct $2^t = 2 \cdot 2^{-68} \cdot \frac{N_e}{p} \approx 2^{49.92}$ structures. The data complexity is $2^{t+68} = 2^{117.92}$. There are about $2^{m-96} = 2^{-11.08}$ pairs remaining for the wrong key guess. The memory complexity is $2^{49.92+68} + 2^{80} \cdot \frac{80}{128} = 2^{117.92}$ 128-bit blocks, and the time complexity is about $2^{t+68} \cdot \frac{2}{25} = 2^{t+68} \cdot 2^{-3.65} \approx 2^{114.27}$ 25-round encryptions.

4.3 The 25-Round Key Recovery Attack on WARP Based on the 20-Round Distinguisher

We launch a 25-round key recovery attack by extending the 20-round distinguisher $(\alpha_1^{20}, \beta_1^{20})$ with probability $2^{-122.71}$ given in Sect. 4.1. The whole attack

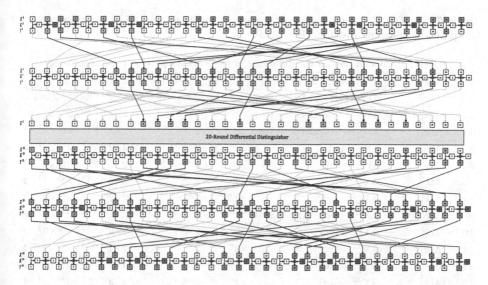

Fig. 7. The 25-round key recovery attack on WARP based on the 20-round differential.

details are demonstrated in Fig. 7. In the key recovery attack, we prepare 2^t structures and each structure includes 14 nibbles traversed. Then, we obtain 2^{t+111} pairs. For each pair, there are 11-nibble fixed differences for the ciphertexts and 16-nibble fixed differences in the 1st and 25th rounds (Observation 2). Thus, the remaining 2^{t+13} pairs will participate in the following processes. Let $2^m = 2^{t+13}$. For each pair, we repeat the guess-and-check procedure for the 17-nibble master key involved in the extended rounds. The time complexity and the number of remaining pairs in each step are detailed in Table 7.

Complexity Analysis. For the right key guess, there are $N_e = 1$ pairs remaining. We collect $2^t = 2 \cdot 2^{-14.4} \frac{N_e}{p} \approx 2^{67.71}$ structures. The data complexity is $2^{t+56} = 2^{123.71}$. There are about $2^{m-80} = 2^{-0.71}$ pairs remaining for the wrong key guess. The memory complexity is $2^{t+56} + 2^{68} \cdot \frac{68}{128} = 2^{123.71}$ 128-bit blocks, and the time complexity is about $2^{67.71+56} \cdot \frac{2}{25} \approx 2^{120.06}$ 25-round encryptions.

Table 7. The Detailed computation of complexity for the 25-round key recovery attack based on the 20-round distinguisher

step	GMK	Condition on the difference	#{Remaining pairs}	Time complexity
1	Mk_3^0	$\Delta Y_9^1 = $ 0x0, $\Delta X_{31}^{23} = $ 0xa	$2^m \cdot 2^{-8}$	$2 \cdot 2^m \cdot 2^4 \cdot 4$
2	Mk_2^0	$\Delta Y_{13}^1 = $ 0x0, $\Delta X_{23}^{23} = $ 0x0	$2^{m-8} \cdot 2^{-8}$	$2 \cdot 2^{m-8} \cdot 2^4 \cdot 2^4 \cdot 4$
3	Mk_{10}^0	$\Delta Y_{29}^1 = $ 0x7, $\Delta X_6^{23} = $ 0xa	$2^{m-16} \cdot 2^{-8}$	$2 \cdot 2^{m-16} \cdot 2^8 \cdot 2^4 \cdot 4$
4	Mk_{11}^0	$\Delta Y_{25}^1 = $ 0x0, $\Delta X_{15}^{23} = $ 0xa	$2^{m-24} \cdot 2^{-8}$	$2 \cdot 2^{m-24} \cdot 2^{12} \cdot 2^4 \cdot 2$
5	Mk_0^0	$\Delta Y_7^1 = $ 0xf	$2^{m-32} \cdot 2^{-4}$	$2 \cdot 2^{m-32} \cdot 2^{16} \cdot 2^4 \cdot 2$
6	Mk_{13}^0	$\Delta Y_{17}^1 = $ 0x0	$2^{m-36} \cdot 2^{-4}$	$2 \cdot 2^{m-36} \cdot 2^{20} \cdot 2^4 \cdot 2$
7	Mk_{15}^0	$\Delta X_1^{23} = $ 0xf	$2^{m-40} \cdot 2^{-4}$	$2 \cdot 2^{m-40} \cdot 2^{24} \cdot 2^4 \cdot 2$
8	Mk_{14}^0	$\Delta X_3^{23} = $ 0xf	$2^{m-44} \cdot 2^{-4}$	$2 \cdot 2^{m-44} \cdot 2^{28} \cdot 2^4 \cdot 2$
9	MK_7^0	$\Delta X_{17}^{23} = $ 0x0, $\Delta Y_9^1 = $ 0x0	$2^{m-48} \cdot 2^{-4}$	$2 \cdot 2^{m-48} \cdot 2^{32} \cdot 2^4 \cdot 2$
10	Mk_9^0	$\Delta X_{27}^{23} = $ 0xa	$2^{m-52} \cdot 2^{-4}$	$2 \cdot 2^{m-52} \cdot 2^{36} \cdot 2^4 \cdot 2$
11	Mk_{15}^1	$\Delta X_1^{22} = $ 0x0	$2^{m-56} \cdot 2^{-4}$	$2 \cdot 2^{m-56} \cdot 2^{40} \cdot 2^4 \cdot 4$
12	Mk_{13}^1	$\Delta X_9^{22} = $ 0x0	$2^{m-60} \cdot 2^{-4}$	$2 \cdot 2^{m-60} \cdot 2^{44} \cdot 2^4 \cdot 4$
13	Mk_1^1	$\Delta X_{11}^{22} = $ 0x0	$2^{m-64} \cdot 2^{-4}$	$2 \cdot 2^{m-64} \cdot 2^{48} \cdot 2^4 \cdot 4$
14	Mk_7^1	$\Delta X_{17}^{22} = $ 0x0	$2^{m-68} \cdot 2^{-4}$	$2 \cdot 2^{m-68} \cdot 2^{52} \cdot 2^4 \cdot 4$
15	Mk_3^1	$\Delta X_{31}^{22} = $ 0x0	$2^{m-72} \cdot 2^{-4}$	$2 \cdot 2^{m-72} \cdot 2^{56} \cdot 2^4 \cdot 4$
16	Mk_{14}^1, Mk_4^0	$\Delta X_3^{22} = $ 0xf	$2^{m-76} \cdot 2^{-4}$	$2 \cdot 2^{m-76} \cdot 2^{60} \cdot 2^8 \cdot 4$
Total				$2^{m+7.09}$

5   Conclusions

We provide an algorithm to search for the distinguishers that have advantages in both the distinguishing phase and the key recovery phase. This new technique is widely applicable and easy to implement for block ciphers. Taking WARP as an illustration, we propose the SAT model to search for the differential trail with optimal probability and a minimum number of active nibbles for its input-output differences. Subsequently, for each input and output differential pattern of these discovered distinguishers, the SMT model is used to describe the differential propagation and amount the number of master key bits involved in the extended rounds. Later, the 19-round and 20-round advantageous distinguishers are obtained. Furthermore, by utilizing the clustering effect of the differential trail, the probability of the distinguishers can be improved. At last, the 25-round key recovery attacks are launched based on a 19-round distinguisher and a 20-round distinguisher. The results cover 2 more rounds than the previous differential attacks.

Acknowledgements. The authors would like to thank the reviewers for their valuable comments. This work is supported by the National Natural Science Foundation of China (No. 61702537, No. 62172427).

References

1. Banik, S., et al.: WARP: Revisiting GFN for lightweight 128-bit block cipher. In: Dunkelman, O., Jr., M.J.J., O'Flynn, C. (eds.) SAC 2020. LNCS, vol. 12804, pp. 535–564. Springer, Heidelberg (2020). https://doi.org/10.1007/978-3-030-81652-0_21
2. Banik, S., et al.: Midori: a block cipher for low energy. In: Iwata, T., Cheon, J.H. (eds.) ASIACRYPT 2015. LNCS, vol. 9453, pp. 411–436. Springer, Heidelberg (2015). https://doi.org/10.1007/978-3-030-81652-0_21
3. Banik, S., Pandey, S.K., Peyrin, T., Sasaki, Y., Sim, S.M., Todo, Y.: GIFT: a small present - towards reaching the limit of lightweight encryption. In: Fischer, W., Homma, N. (eds.) CHES 2017. LNCS, vol. 10529, pp. 321–345. Springer, Heidelberg (2017). https://doi.org/10.1007/978-3-319-66787-4_16
4. Beierle, C., et al.: The SKINNY family of block ciphers and its low-latency variant MANTIS. In: Robshaw, M., Katz, J. (eds.) CRYPTO 2016. LNCS, vol. 9815, pp. 123–153. Springer, Heidelberg (2016). https://doi.org/10.1007/978-3-662-53008-5_5
5. Biham, E., Shamir, A.: Differential cryptanalysis of des-like cryptosystems. In: Menezes, A., Vanstone, S.A. (eds.) CRYPTO'90. LNCS, vol. 537, pp. 2–21. Springer, Heidelberg (1990). https://doi.org/10.1007/BF00630563
6. Hadipour, H., Bagheri, N., Song, L.: Improved rectangle attacks on SKINNY and CRAFT. IACR Trans. Symm. Cryptol. 2021(2), 140–198 (2021)
7. Hadipour, H., Eichlseder, M.: Integral cryptanalysis of WARP based on monomial prediction. IACR Trans. Symm. Cryptol. 2022(2), 92–112 (2022)
8. Kölbl, S., Leander, G., Tiessen, T.: Observations on the SIMON block cipher family. In: Gennaro, R., Robshaw, M. (eds.) CRYPTO 2015. LNCS, vol. 9215, pp. 161–185. Springer, Heidelberg (2015). https://doi.org/10.1007/978-3-662-47989-6_8
9. Kumar, M., Yadav, T.: MILP based differential attack on round reduced WARP. In: Batina, L., Picek, S., Mondal, M. (eds.) SPACE 2021. LNCS, vol. 13162, pp. 42–59. Springer, Heidelberg (2021). https://doi.org/10.1007/978-3-030-95085-9_3
10. Lallemand, V., Minier, M., Rouquette, L.: Automatic search of rectangle attacks on feistel ciphers: application to WARP. IACR Trans. Symm. Cryptol. 2022(2), 113–140 (2022)
11. Liu, Y., Wang, Q., Rijmen, V.: Automatic search of linear trails in ARX with applications to SPECK and chaskey. In: Manulis, M., Sadeghi, A., Schneider, S.A. (eds.) ACNS 2016. LNCS, vol. 9696, pp. 485–499. Springer, Heidelberg (2016). https://doi.org/10.1007/978-3-319-39555-5_26
12. Matsui, M.: Linear cryptanalysis method for DES cipher. In: Helleseth, T. (ed.) EUROCRYPT '93. LNCS, vol. 765, pp. 386–397. Springer, Heidelberg (1993). https://doi.org/10.1007/3-540-48285-7_33
13. Mouha, N., Wang, Q., Gu, D., Preneel, B.: Differential and linear cryptanalysis using mixed-integer linear programming. In: Wu, C., Yung, M., Lin, D. (eds.) Inscrypt 2011. LNCS, vol. 7537, pp. 57–76. Springer, Heidelberg (2011). https://doi.org/10.1007/978-3-642-34704-7_5
14. Qin, L., Dong, X., Wang, X., Jia, K., Liu, Y.: Automated search oriented to key recovery on ciphers with linear key schedule applications to boomerangs in SKINNY and forkskinny. IACR Trans. Symm. Cryptol. 2021(2), 249–291 (2021)
15. Sinz, C.: Towards an optimal CNF encoding of boolean cardinality constraints. In: van Beek, P. (ed.) CP 2005. LNCS, vol. 3709, pp. 827–831. Springer, Heidelberg (2005). https://doi.org/10.1007/11564751_73

16. Sun, L., Wang, W., Wang, M.: Accelerating the search of differential and linear characteristics with the SAT method. IACR Trans. Symm. Cryptol. **2021**(1), 269–315 (2021)
17. Sun, L., Wang, W., Wang, M.: Improved attacks on GIFT-64. In: AlTawy, R., Hülsing, A. (eds.) SAC 2021. LNCS, vol. 13203, pp. 246–265. Springer, Heidelberg (2021). DOI: https://doi.org/10.1007/11564751_73
18. Sun, S., Gérault, D., Lafourcade, P., Yang, Q., Todo, Y., Qiao, K., Hu, L.: Analysis of aes, skinny, and others with constraint programming. IACR Trans. Symm. Cryptol. **2017**(1), 281–306 (2017)
19. Sun, S., Hu, L., Wang, P., Qiao, K., Ma, X., Song, L.: Automatic security evaluation and (related-key) differential characteristic search: Application to simon, present, lblock, DES(L) and other bit-oriented block ciphers. In: Sarkar, P., Iwata, T. (eds.) ASIACRYPT 2014. LNCS, vol. 8873, pp. 158–178. Springer, Heidelberg (2014). https://doi.org/10.1007/978-3-662-45611-8_9
20. Suzaki, T., Minematsu, K., Morioka, S., Kobayashi, E.: Twine: a lightweight block cipher for multiple platforms. In: Knudsen, L.R., Wu, H. (eds.) SAC 2012. LNCS, vol. 7707, pp. 339–354. Springer, Heidelberg (2012). https://doi.org/10.1007/978-3-642-35999-6_22
21. Teh, J.S., Biryukov, A.: Differential cryptanalysis of WARP. IACR Cryptol. ePrint Arch., p. 1641 (2021)
22. Todo, Y., Sasaki, Y.: Designing s-boxes providing stronger security against differential cryptanalysis for ciphers using byte-wise XOR. In: AlTawy, R., Hülsing, A. (eds.) SAC 2021. LNCS, vol. 13203, pp. 179–199. Springer, Heidelberg (2021). https://doi.org/10.1007/978-3-030-99277-4_9
23. Zong, R., Dong, X., Chen, H., Luo, Y., Wang, S., Li, Z.: Towards key-recovery-attack friendly distinguishers: application to GIFT-128. IACR Trans. Symm. Cryptol. **2021**(1), 156–184 (2021)

Isogeny-based Cryptography II

Faster Cryptographic Hash Function from Supersingular Isogeny Graphs

Javad Doliskani[1]([⊠]), Geovandro C. C. F. Pereira[2], and Paulo S. L. M. Barreto[3]

[1] Ryerson University, Toronto, Canada
javad.doliskani@ryerson.ca
[2] Institute for Quantum Computing, University of Waterloo, Waterloo, Canada
geovandro.pereira@uwaterloo.ca
[3] University of Washington Tacoma, Tacoma, USA
pbarreto@uw.edu

Abstract. We propose a variant of the CGL hash algorithm [5] that is significantly faster than the original algorithm, and prove that it is preimage and collision resistant. For $n = \log p$ where p is the characteristic of the finite field, the performance ratio between CGL and the new proposal is $(5.7n + 110)/(13.5 \log n + 46.4)$. This gives an exponential speed up as the size of p increases. Assuming the best quantum preimage attack on the hash algorithm has complexity $O(p^{\frac{1}{4}})$, we attain a concrete speed-up for a 256-bit quantum preimage security level by a factor 33.5. For a 384-bit quantum preimage security level, the speed-up is by a factor 47.8.

1 Introduction

A provably secure hash function is a hash function in which finding collisions is efficiently reducible from a computationally hard problem. The first proposals for provably secure hash functions were based on number theoretic problems such as integer factorization and discrete logarithm which are widely believed to be hard. The Very Smooth Hash (VSH) proposed by Contini et al. [8] is a provably secure hash algorithm based on an assumption related to integer factorization. The idea behind VSH is similar to the one introduced in the earlier work of Chaum [6] on undeniable signatures. A variant of VSH, called VSH-DL, is based on a problem related to the discrete logarithm problem. VSH is very fast and can be used in schemes like the Cramer-Shoup signature [11] to improve the performance without sacrificing any security.

Security of the schemes based on these classical number theoretic problems, however, is threatened by the emergence of quantum computers. A quantum computer can perform the *Fourier Transform* on an exponential number of amplitudes in polynomial time [7,22]. This leads to polynomial time quantum algorithms for phase estimation and order-finding, and consequently factoring and computing discrete logarithms [27,29].

Modern provably secure hash functions are based on less standard assumptions but are believed to resist quantum attacks. Inspired by Ajtai's seminal

B. Smith and H. Wu (Eds.): SAC 2022, LNCS 13742, pp. 399–415, 2024.
https://doi.org/10.1007/978-3-031-58411-4_18

work [1] on average-case to worst-case reduction of standard lattice problems, Micciancio [19] proposed an efficient hash function whose security is based on certain approximation problems on ideal lattices.

A class of provably secure hash functions are based on expander graphs. An expander graph is, informally, a graph with low degree and high connectivity. The use of expander graphs for hashing started with the works of Zémor and Tillich [33, 38, 39] on particular expander graphs called Cayley graphs. In 2009, Charles et al. [5] proposed an expander hash algorithm, called CGL, which is based on the isogeny graph of supersingular elliptic curves over finite fields. Supersingular isogeny graphs are excellent expander graphs with asymptotically optimal expansion constant [24]. The security of CGL is based on the hardness of computing isogenies of large degree between supersingular elliptic curves. Since the introduction of CGL, supersingular isogeny problems have attracted considerable attention in cryptography, and the best known attacks on them have exponential complexity. The main drawback of CGL is efficiency. For a finite field of characteristic p, the algorithm requires roughly $2 \log p$ modular multiplications per bit of the input. This makes CGL far less efficient than other provably secure hash algorithms.

Our Contributions. We exploit primes of the form $p = 2^n f \pm 1$, where $f > 0$ is a small integer, as the characteristic of the finite field. Instead of consuming a bit of the input at a time, we use a block of length $n \approx \log p$ bits at once to generate the kernel of a cyclic smooth isogeny of degree 2^n. The isogeny is then computed efficiently using the technique of [13] to get the next curve in the graph. We show that this does not sacrifice any security and reduces the complexity of the original CGL hash algorithm from $5.7 \log p + 110$ to $13.5 \log \log p + 46.4$ modular multiplications per bit of the input. As the size of the prime p increases, this gives an exponential speed up.

Organization of the Paper. In Sect. 2 we review some background on elliptic curves, isogenies and the CGL hash algorithm. Our new hash algorithm and the proofs of its preimage and collision resistance are given in Sect. 3. In Sect. 4 we perform a detailed operation count on CGL and the new hash algorithm, and compare the runtime complexities.

2   Preliminaries

Let $\mathbb{F}_q$ be a finite field of q elements where $q = p^n$ for some prime $p > 3$ and integer $n \geq 1$. An elliptic curve $E/\mathbb{F}_q$ is an abelian variety of dimension 1 which also has genus 1; that is, a nonsingular projective curve of genus 1 which is also an abelian group. A morphism $E_1 \to E_2$ of elliptic curves that preserves the group structure is called an isogeny. An isogeny from an elliptic curve E to itself is called an endomorphism. The set of all such endomorphisms, denoted by $\mathrm{End}(E)$, form a ring under addition and composition.

Any isogeny $\phi : E_1 \to E_2$ induces an inclusion $\phi^* : \mathbb{F}_q(E_2) \hookrightarrow \mathbb{F}_q(E_1)$ of function fields. We say that ϕ is separable if ϕ^* is separable. Also the degree of

ϕ, denoted by $\deg(\phi)$, is defined to be the degree of ϕ^*. We will call an isogeny of degree m an m-isogeny. For a separable isogeny ϕ we have $\deg(\phi) = |\ker \phi|$ [35]. For any integer m, the multiplication-by-m endomorphism $[m] : E \to E$ is separable. The kernel of $[m]$, denoted by $E[m]$, is the m-torsion subgroup of E. It can be shown that $E[m] \cong \mathbb{Z}/m\mathbb{Z} \oplus \mathbb{Z}/m\mathbb{Z}$ for any m such that $p \nmid m$. We have $E[p] = 0$ or $\mathbb{Z}/p\mathbb{Z}$. The curve E is called ordinary if $E[p] = \mathbb{Z}/p\mathbb{Z}$, and supersingular otherwise. This is equivalent to saying that $\mathrm{End}(E)$ is an order in an imaginary quadratic extension or a quaternion algebra over $\mathbb{Q}$ [28, §V.3].

Two curves $E_1/\mathbb{F}_q$ and $E_2/\mathbb{F}_q$ are called isogenous if there exists an isogeny between them. For any isogeny $\phi : E_1 \to E_2$ there exists an isogeny $\hat{\phi} : E_2 \to E_1$ such that $\phi \circ \hat{\phi} = [m]$ where $m = \deg(\phi)$. Therefore, being isogenous is an equivalence relation between curves defined over $\mathbb{F}_q$. Two isogenous curves are either both ordinary or both supersingular. This means the isogeny classes of ordinary and supersingular curves are disjoint. As a consequence of Tate's isogeny theorem [32], E_1 and E_2 are $\mathbb{F}_q$-isogenous if and only if $|E_1(K)| = |E_2(K)|$ for any finite extension $K/\mathbb{F}_q$. This implies that all curves in the same isogeny class have the same number of $\mathbb{F}_q$-rational points.

2.1 Isogeny Graphs

It can be shown that every supersingular elliptic curve can be defined over $\mathbb{F}_{p^2}$, that is, it is isomorphic to a curve defined over $\mathbb{F}_{p^2}$. For a prime $\ell \neq p$, the set of isomorphism classes of elliptic curves over $\mathbb{F}_{p^2}$ and the degree-ℓ isogenies between them form a graph called the graph of ℓ-isogenies. The graph consists of ordinary and supersingular components that, according to above remarks, are disconnected. The ordinary components, which we will not discuss here, are called isogeny volcanoes [30].

There is only one supersingular component in the isogeny graph, which we denote by G_ℓ [17]. The nodes in G_ℓ are usually represented by the j-invariants. In this paper, we interchangeably use curves and j-invariants to refer to the vertices of G_ℓ. For $p = 3$ we have $|G_\ell| = 1$ and for $p \geq 5$ we have $|G_\ell| \approx [p/12]$. We consider the edges of G_ℓ to be isomorphism classes of ℓ-isogenies: two ℓ-isogenies $\phi : E_1 \to E_2$ and $\psi : E_1' \to E_2'$ are isomorphic if there are isomorphisms $\theta_1 : E_1 \to E_1'$ and $\theta_2 : E_2 \to E_2'$ such that $\theta_2\phi = \psi\theta_1$. Another way to look at the edges in G_ℓ is through the modular polynomial $\Phi_\ell(x, y) \in \mathbb{Z}[x, y]$ [36, §69]. The modular polynomial is symmetric in the sense that $\Phi_\ell(x, y) = \Phi_\ell(y, x)$, and is of degree $\ell + 1$ in both x, y. It is well known that there is an ℓ-isogeny between two curves E_1, E_2 with j-invariants j_1, j_2 if and only if $\Phi_\ell(j_1, j_2) = 0$. Therefore, the neighbors of each $E \in G_\ell$ are exactly the curves with j-invariants a root of the univariate polynomial $\Phi_\ell(x, j(E))$. Since all the j-invariants are in $\mathbb{F}_{p^2}$, we see that G_ℓ is an $(\ell + 1)$-regular graph.

2.2 Computational Problems

In this subsection, we review the hard problems [5] on which the security of our hash function will be based. Let n, which is the main security parameter, be a positive integer and let p be a prime of size $\approx n$ bits. For a prime $\ell \neq p$, denote by G_ℓ the graph of supersingular elliptic curves over $\mathbb{F}_{p^2}$.

Problem 1. Given a curve $E \in G_\ell$, find an endomorphism $\phi \in \mathrm{End}(E) \setminus \mathbb{Z}$ of degree ℓ^{rn} for some integer $r > 0$. By ϕ not being in $\mathbb{Z}$ we mean when rn is even, ϕ is not $\psi \circ [\ell^{rn/2}]$ for some automorphism ψ of E.

Problem 2. Given curves $E_1, E_2 \in G_\ell$, find an isogeny $\phi : E_1 \to E_2$ of degree ℓ^{rn} for some integer $r > 0$.

Problem 1 can be reduced to Problem 2 by taking a random walk ϕ of length rn from a curve E_1 to a curve E_2 in G_ℓ, and using the solver for Problem 2 to find another path $\psi : E_1 \to E_2$ of length sn for some $s \geq 1$. These two paths will be distinct with high probability. So the composition $\hat{\psi} \circ \phi$ is an endomorphism of E_1.

Attacks. Problem 2 is known as the *Supersingular Isogeny Problem*, and was first introduced in [16]. As noted in [5], a variation of the Pollard-rho attack would give an algorithm of complexity $O(\sqrt{p}\log^2 p)$ for this problem.

Another attack is known as the *claw finding* attack. The claw finding problem is as follows. Given sets X, Y, Z and functions $f : X \to Y$ and $g : Z \to Y$ as an oracle, find at least one pair $(x, y) \in X \times Z$ such that $f(x) = g(z)$. A naive algorithm can solve this in time $O(|X| + |Z|)$. Therefore, setting X and Z to be all the isogenies of length $n/2$ starting from E_1 and E_2, respectively, we get an attack of complexity $O(\sqrt{p})$ on Problem 2. Using a quantum computer, the claw finding problem can be solved in time $O(\sqrt[3]{|X||Z|})$ which is optimal for black-box claw algorithm [31,40]. This gives a quantum attack of complexity $O(\sqrt[3]{p})$.

The best known attack on Problem 2 is due to Biasse et al. [4]. Given curves E_1, E_2 over $\mathbb{F}_{p^2}$, the idea is to generate random isogenies $E_1 \to E_1'$ and $E_2 \to E_2'$ until E_1' and E_2' are both defined over $\mathbb{F}_p$. Using Grover's algorithm, this can be done in $O(p^{1/4})$ quantum operations. Computing an isogeny between E_1' and E_2' can then be done in subexponential time. The total complexity of the algorithm is thus $O(p^{1/4})$. However, this attack does not compute an isogeny of degree ℓ^{nr} for some integer r. So it is unclear that this algorithm actually solves Problem 2.

Another computational problem related to supersingular isogeny graphs is the *endomorphism ring problem* which is: given $E \in G_\ell$, compute the endomorphism ring $\mathrm{End}(E)$. In a recent work by Petit and Lauter [23], it is shown that the endomorphism ring problem is polynomially equivalent to Problem 2 under some plausible heuristic assumptions. Petit and Lauter also give an algorithm that can efficiently compute an endomorphism for a special j-invariant in the isogeny graph. This leads to a backdoor attack on the CGL hash algorithm which can easily be detected if a collision is produced. Later, Eisentraeger et al. [15] showed that the endomorphism ring problem reduces to Problem 2 if in addition to a chain of ℓ-isogenies, the representation of the ℓ-power isogeny by a left ideal in a maximal order is given.

2.3   The CGL Hash Algorithm

In this subsection, we review the original hash function construction proposed in [5]. Let us first recall some definitions. For a family of hash functions $\mathcal{H} = \{h : \{0,1\}^{L(n)} \to S\}$, where $L(n) = \text{poly}(n)$, we always assume that

- $2^{L(n)} > |S|$, and
- any $h \in \mathcal{H}$ is efficiently computable.

A hash function is called collision resistant if it is computationally infeasible to find two messages that hash to the same value for any member $h \in \mathcal{H}$.

Definition 1. *A hash function h is called provable collision resistant if there exists a computational hard problem that is polynomially reducible to any algorithm that can find collisions in h.*

A hash function is called preimage resistant if given an output y of the function, it is computationally infeasible to find a message that hashes to y.

Definition 2. *A hash function h is called provable preimage resistant if there exists a computational hard problem that is polynomially reducible to any algorithm that can find preimages of h.*

Let $G_\ell = G_\ell(\mathbb{F}_{p^2})$ be the graph of ℓ-isogenies over $\mathbb{F}_{p^2}$. For simplicity we only consider the case $\ell = 2$, i.e., the graph of 2-isogenies. The whole scheme can be easily generalized for any prime ℓ. Let $E \in G_\ell$ be a fixed starting curve. Since G_ℓ is 3-regular, there are three isogenies from E to the neighboring curves. One of these isogenies is ignored once and for all. Given an n-bit message $M = b_1 b_2 \ldots b_n$, the process starts by choosing an isogeny from E according to the bit b_1 to arrive at a curve E_1. If we don't allow backtracking, then there are two isogenies out of E_1, one of which can be chosen according to b_2. Continuing the same process, the message M determines a unique path of length n in G_ℓ. Note that it is required to make a convention for the ordering of the isogenies at each curve so that the hash is well defined. That is, the same output is produced for the same messages.

The output of the hash function is the j-invariant of the curve at the end of the path. The j-invariants are of the form $ax + b$ where x is a generator of the extension $\mathbb{F}_{p^2}/\mathbb{F}_p$. As suggested in [5], the output of the hash function can be represented in $\log p$ bits by applying a linear congruential operator to the resulting j-invariant.

From this scheme, we see that selecting a different starting curve $E \in G_\ell$ gives a different hash function. This way, we get a family of hash functions $\mathcal{H} = \{h_j\}_{j \in G_\ell}$ indexed by the supersingular j-invariants. Assume the hash functions accept inputs of length a multiple of n. Then the above hash function family is provably collision and preimage resistant.

Theorem 1 ([5], **Theorem 1**). *If there is polynomial-time algorithm for finding collisions in the hash function family $\mathcal{H} = \{h_j\}_{j \in G_\ell}$, then there is a polynomial-time algorithm for Problem 1 when $\ell = 2$.*

Algorithm 1. $h(E, m, T)$

Input:
- An n-bit message m,
- A supersingular curve $E \in G_\ell$ as the starting vertex,
- The generator T of the backtrack 2-isogeny from E

Output:
- $E' \in G_\ell$
- The generator T' of the kernel of the backtrack 2-isogeny from E'

1: Obtain generators P, Q of $E[2^n]$ deterministically (e.g., Alg. 3.1 of [37])
2: If $T = $ NULL then go to Step 8
3: **if** $2^{n-1}P = T$ **then**
4:     Swap P and Q
5: **else if** $2^{n-1}Q \neq T$ **then**
6:     $Q := P + Q$
7: **end if**   ▷ Now the basis P, Q never leads to backtrack
8: Compute $R = P + mQ$
9: Compute an isogeny $\phi : E \rightarrow E'$ with kernel $\langle R \rangle$
10: Obtain the 2-torsion point T' on E' that backtracks on ϕ
11: **return** (E', T')

Theorem 2 ([5], **Theorem 2**). *If there is a polynomial-time algorithm for finding preimages in the hash function family $\mathcal{H} = \{h_j\}_{j \in G_\ell}$, then there is a polynomial-time algorithm for Problem 2 when $\ell = 2$.*

By a polynomial-time algorithm we mean an algorithm that runs in $O(\text{poly} (\log p))$ time.

3 The New Hash Algorithm

In this section, we propose a new hash algorithm based on supersingular isogeny graphs G_ℓ. For simplicity, we assume $\ell = 2$, but the scheme can easily be generalized for any prime $\ell \geq 2$. To be able to compute smooth degree isogenies, i.e. isogenies of degree 2^n, using the optimal strategy technique of [13], we choose $p = 2^n f \pm 1$ where f is small. Then we can assume that the curves in G_ℓ have order $(p \mp 1)^2 = (2^n f)^2$. This follows from the fact that the group of $\mathbb{F}_{p^2}$-rational points on a supersingular elliptic curve over $\mathbb{F}_{p^2}$ is of the form $(\mathbb{Z}/(p \mp 1)\mathbb{Z})^2$. From this group structure we see that for each $E \in G_\ell$, the whole 2^n-torsion subgroup $E[2^n]$ is contained in $E(\mathbb{F}_{p^2})$. Let $P, Q \in E[2^n]$ denote a set of generators of the 2^n-torsion. Given any n-bit message m, we obtain a hash of m as follows.

First, we compute $R = P + mQ$ which determines a cyclic subgroup $H = \langle R \rangle \subset E$ of order 2^n. Then we compute an isogeny $E \rightarrow E'$ with kernel H, which is also of degree 2^n, and return the j-invariant of E' as the hash. This way, taking E as the starting vertex, we have mapped an n-bit message to a vertex $E' \in G_\ell$.

Algorithm 2. $H(E, m)$

Input: A message m, a supersingular curve $E \in G_\ell$ as the starting vertex
Output: A supersingular curve $E' \in G_\ell$
1: Pad the message m to get $m = m_1 \| m_2 \| \dots \| m_k$ where each block m_i is n bits
2: $T_1 = \text{NULL}$
3: $E_1 := E$
4: **for** $i = 1$ to k **do**
5: $\quad (E_1, T_1) := h(E_1, m_i, T_1)$
6: **end for**
7: $E' := E_1$
8: **return** E'

The function $h(E, m)$ computed using Algorithm 1 is a compression function: it accepts a j-invariant and a message m, and returns a j-invariant. Therefore, we can apply the Merkle-Damgård construction [12,18] to hash messages of arbitrary length using h.

Remark 1. In Step 1 of Algorithm 1, the generators P, Q of the 2^n-torsion should be obtained canonically so that the hash is well-defined. For example, one could use a predefined initial value as the starting index of the table T_1 (or T_2) in the entangled basis algorithm of [37].

Since the starting vertex can be any $E \in G_\ell$, Algorithm 2 gives a hash function family $\mathcal{H} = \{H_j\}_{j \in G_\ell}$ indexed by the curves in G_ℓ. So a hash can be selected from the family by providing a curve $E \in G_\ell$. Note that as in the original CGL algorithm, we need to prevent backtracking.

Proposition 1. *For any given input message m, the isogeny path computed by Algorithm 2 contains no backtracks. In particular, the isogeny computed by Algorithm 2 is cyclic.*

Proof. We have the following:
An ℓ-power isogeny is cyclic if and only if there is no backtracking in the isogeny path.
This is essentially proved by Proposition 1 in [5]. More precisely, they prove that if an isogeny is not cyclic then it contains a backtrack. The other direction is easy to prove.
This implies that there will never be a backtracking in the cyclic isogeny computed in Step 9 of Algorithm 1. In other words, there is no backtracking for individual message blocks. So to ensure that there is no backtracking in the long isogeny corresponding to the input message m of Algorithm 2 we only need to prove that consecutive message blocks do not produce backtracking. For this, it is enough to select the current kernel in a way that the first 2-isogeny of the current block is not dual to the last 2-isogeny of the previous block.
The construction of the basis points P, Q through Steps 1–7 ensures that the new P, Q are also a basis, and we always have $2^{n-1}Q = T$. This implies that

$2^{n-1}R = 2^{n-1}P + m2^{n-1}Q = 2^{n-1}P + mT \neq T$, where the last inequality is because $2^{n-1}P$ is linearly independent from T. This proves the proposition.

Note that backtrack prevention eliminates the possibility of simple attacks such as the following : compute two random isogenies $\phi_1 : E \to E_1$ and $\phi_2 : E \to E_2$ using two random message blocks m_1 and m_2. Then compute the duals $\hat{\phi}_1, \hat{\phi}_2$ corresponding to some message blocks t_1, t_2 respectively. This gives a collision $h(E, m_1\|t_1) = h(E, m_2\|t_2)$.

3.1   Preimage and Collision Resistance

We assume $p = 2^n f \pm 1$ as above, and assume that the length of the input is kn for some integer $k \geq 1$. Let $\mathcal{H} = \{H_j\}_{j \in G_\ell}$ be the hash function family computed using Algorithm 2. Following the notation of [5], given an isogeny $\phi : E \to E'$ of degree 2^n, we say that the two factorizations

$$E = E_0 \xrightarrow{\phi_1} E_1 \xrightarrow{\phi_2} E_2 \xrightarrow{\phi_3} \cdots \xrightarrow{\phi_n} E_n = E',$$
$$E = E_0 \xrightarrow{\phi'_1} E'_1 \xrightarrow{\phi'_2} E'_2 \xrightarrow{\phi'_3} \cdots \xrightarrow{\phi'_n} E_n = E'$$

are isomorphic if there exist isomorphisms $\epsilon_i : E_i \xrightarrow{\sim} E'_i$ such that $\phi'_i \circ \epsilon_{i-1} = \epsilon_i \circ \phi_i$ for all $1 \leq i \leq n$. In [5] it is proved that isomorphic isogenies correspond to the same input messages. That is indeed easy to see in their construction, since the decomposition of a long isogeny into 2-isogenies is directly determined by the bits of the message. Proving the same statement in our settings requires a bit of extra work.

Calim. Algorithm 2 never produces isomorphic isogenies for inputs with different number of blocks.

Proof. Since the isogenies are cyclic, they have unique decompositions into sequences of 2-isogenies. Since the degrees are different, the kernels have different sizes and the isogenies will not be isomorphic.

Lemma 1. *Let ϕ, ϕ' be two isogenies generated by Algorithm 2 on inputs m, m', respectively. If ϕ and ϕ' are isomorphic, then $m = m'$.*

Proof. By Claim 3.1 m and m' must have the same number of blocks. We proceed by induction on the number of blocks. Since there is a one-to-one correspondence between n-bit integers $m \in \{0, 1\}^n$ and kernels $P + mQ$ constructed in Algorithm 1, the lemma is true for a single block. Suppose m, m' have k blocks. Write $\phi = \psi_k \circ \psi$ and $\phi' = \psi'_k \circ \psi'$ where ψ, ψ' are the isogenies corresponding to the first $k-1$ blocks of m, m', and ψ_k, ψ'_k are the isogenies corresponding to the last blocks m_k, m'_k of m, m', respectively.

By the induction hypothesis ψ and ψ' correspond to the same $k-1$ blocks. Since ϕ, ϕ' are isomorphic, they must have the same cyclic kernels, that is $\ker(\psi_k \circ \psi) = \ker(\psi'_k \circ \psi')$. From this we have $\ker(\psi_k) = \ker(\psi'_k)$, or equivalently $\langle P + m_k Q \rangle = \langle P + m'_k Q \rangle$ which implies $m_k = m'_k$ by the above correspondence for single blocks.

Theorem 3 (Preimage Resistance). *If there is a polynomial-time algorithm for finding preimages for the hash function family $\mathcal{H}$, then there is a polynomial-time algorithm for Problem 2.*

Proof. Let $H \in \mathcal{H}$ be a hash function corresponding to an initial vertex $E \in G_\ell$. Given an output $E_1 \in G_\ell$ of H, a preimage for E_1 is a message $m = m_1\|m_2\|\ldots\|m_k$, where each m_i is n bits. By construction, the message m corresponds to an isogeny $E \to E_1$ of degree 2^{kn}. This means finding a preimage for H is equivalent to finding a 2^{kn}-isogeny between the two given curves E, E_1.

Remark 2. By Merkle-Damgård Theorem, collision resistance of the compression function implies the collision resistance of the hash function. A compression function $h(a,b)$ is said to be collision resistant if it is hard to find two pairs $(a_1, b_1) \neq (a_2, b_2)$ such that $h(a_1, b_1) = h(a_2, b_2)$. Therefore, we only need to prove that the compression function $h(E, m)$ of Algorithm 1 is collision resistant. But $h(E, m)$ is not collision resistant. In fact, we can easily find curves $E_1, E_2 \in G_\ell$ and n-bit messages m_1, m_2 such that $h(E_1, m_1) = h(E_2, m_2)$ as follows. Let $E \in G_\ell$ be any curve and let $P, Q \in E[2^n]$ be a basis generated by Algorithm 1. For any integer $0 \leq t_1 < 2^n$ we can construct an isogeny $\phi_1 : E \to E_1$ with kernel $\langle P + t_1 Q \rangle$. Now, the kernel of $\hat{\phi}_1 : E_1 \to E$ is of the form $\langle P_1 + m_1 Q_1 \rangle$ for a basis $P_1, Q_1 \in E_1[2^n]$. We can efficiently find m_1 from ϕ. Repeating the process for another $t_2 \neq t_1$, we get an isogeny $\hat{\phi}_2 : E_2 \to E$ with kernel $\langle P_2 + m_2 Q_2 \rangle$. Clearly, the pairs (E_1, m_1) and (E_2, m_2) give a collision in h.

This, however, does not imply that the hash function $H(E, m)$ is not collision resistant. On the contrary, we prove in the following that Problem 1 is efficiently reducible to finding collisions in $H(E, m)$. This means, the collision resistance condition on the compression function might not be required in some concrete instantiations of the Merkle-Damgård paradigm. In other words, the condition is sufficient but not necessary.

Theorem 4 (Collision Resistance). *If there is a polynomial-time algorithm for finding collisions in the hash function family $\mathcal{H}$, then there is a polynomial-time algorithm for Problem 1.*

Proof. Let $H \in \mathcal{H}$ be a hash function corresponding to an initial vertex $E \in G_\ell$ and let $H(E, m) = j(E') = H(E, m')$ for two distinct messages m, m'. Let ϕ, ϕ' be the isogenies computed by Algorithm 2 on inputs m and m', respectively. Since m and m' are distinct, the isogenies ϕ and ϕ' are not isomorphic by Lemma 1. Therefore, $\hat{\phi} \circ \phi'$ is a valid solution to Problem 1.

4 Complexity

In this section, we compare the running time complexity of the original CGL hash algorithm with the one proposed in Sect. 3. We will count the number of operations in $\mathbb{F}_p$, and denote multiplication, squaring, and inversion by **m**, **s**, and **i**, respectively. As the size of p increases, addition becomes negligible compared to multiplication, so we shall ignore addition in the subsequent complexity estimations. The costs of multiplication, squaring, and inversion in $\mathbb{F}_{p^2}$ are $3\mathbf{m}$, $2\mathbf{m}$, $1\mathbf{i} + 2\mathbf{m} + 2\mathbf{s}$, respectively. To get a more precise operation count we fix the following parameters:

- The prime $p = 2^n f - 1$, where f is a small positive integer,
- The prime $\ell = 2$ so that we work on the 2-isogeny graph G_ℓ,
- The length kn of the input message, where k is a positive integer.

We assume the curves in G_ℓ have order $(p+1)^2 = (2^n f)^2$. The assumption on the length of the input message means we have already padded the input message so that it is k blocks of size n bits.

The special shape $p = 2^n f - 1$ of our prime leads to a more precise operation count for exponentiations. This is because most of the bits in the binary representation of p are 1's. Let $a \in \mathbb{F}_{p^2}$ be any given element. We shall use the following operation counts in the next subsections:

- Testing if a is a quadratic residue amounts to raising the norm of a to the $(p+1)/4$, which takes $\approx \log p \mathbf{s}$.
- Taking a square root of a using the method of [26], requires 1 inversion in $\mathbb{F}_p$, and raising to $(p+1)/4$ twice in $\mathbb{F}_p$, respectively. Therefore, $\sqrt{a}$ is computed using $\approx 2 \log p \mathbf{s} + 1\mathbf{i}$.

4.1   Moving Around in the Isogeny Graph

The complexities of both hash algorithms clearly depend on the cost of walking around in G_ℓ. The standard approach is to use the Vélu formulas [34]. This involves operations such as point addition and scalar multiplication, and small degree isogeny computation and evaluation. So we need to choose a curve model that is most optimized for these operations. The three well-known models that are widely used for computations are the Weierstrass model, the Montgomery model [20], and the twisted Edwards model [2,14].

The short Weierstrass model is written as $y^2 = x^3 + ax + b$. Using projective coordinates, one point addition in this model takes $40\mathbf{m}$ and one doubling takes $27\mathbf{m}$ [3]. If we assume one of the points is scaled to have $Z = 1$, then addition and doubling are done using $22\mathbf{m}$ and $19\mathbf{m}$, respectively.

The Montgomery model is written as $by^2 = x^3 + ax^2 + x$. Using the X, Z coordinates, which is called the Kummer line, one differential addition in this model costs $12\mathbf{m}$, and one doubling costs $10\mathbf{m}$. If one of the points is scaled to have $Z = 1$, then a differential addition costs $13\mathbf{m}$, and a doubling costs $7\mathbf{m}$.

The twisted Edwards model is written as $ax^2 + y^2 = 1 + dx^2y^2$. Using projective coordinates, one addition in this model costs $32\mathbf{m}$, and one doubling costs $17\mathbf{m}$. If one of the points is scaled to have $Z = 1$, then an addition and doubling cost $20\mathbf{m}$ and $14\mathbf{m}$.

Unfortunately, there is not much literature on efficient computation and evaluation of small degree isogenies. Analogues of the Vélu formulas for twisted Edwards curves are given in [21], and the ones for Montgomery curves are given in [13]. Note that since the order of curves in G_ℓ is $(2^n f)^2$, all curves have points of order 2, so any of the above models can be used for our algorithm. However, based on the above operation counts and the advice of [13], we choose to work with the Montgomery model in this paper.

Montgomery Curves. As mentioned above, a Montgomery curve over $\mathbb{F}_{p^2}$ has equation

$$E_{a,b} : by^2 = x^3 + ax^2 + x$$

where $a, b \in \mathbb{F}_{p^2}$. The projective equation of $E_{a,b}$ is $bY^2Z = X^3 + aX^2Z + XZ^2$. The projection $x : E_{a,b} \setminus \{0\} \to \mathbb{P}^1$ defined by $(X : Y : Z) \mapsto (X : Z)$ is a morphism of order 2 that induces a bijection $E_{a,b}/\langle 1, -1 \rangle \cong \mathbb{P}^1$. This map provides efficient arithmetic in $E_{a,b}/\langle 1, -1 \rangle$, done entirely in the X, Z coordinates. The line $\mathbb{P}^1$ can be considered as the Kummer variety of $E_{a,b}$, and is called the Kummer line of $E_{a,b}$. Since the map x takes both P and $-P$ to $x(P)$ for all $P \in E_{a,b}$, we cannot add two distinct points P, Q on the Kummer line unless the difference $P - Q$ is already known. This particular addition, that takes $P - Q$ as an input, is called differential addition.

Efficient formulas for the following operations on the Kummer line were given in [20].

- Doubling: $\{x(P), a\} \mapsto x(2P)$,
- Differential addition: $\{x(P), x(Q), x(P - Q)\} \mapsto x(P + Q)$,
- Double and add: $\{x(P), x(Q), x(P - Q), a\} \mapsto \{x(2P), x(P + Q)\}$,
- Ladder: $\{x(P), a, m\} \mapsto x(mP)$.

The last operation, known as the Montgomery ladder, is done using doubling and differential addition.

Isogenies of Montgomery Curves. Computing 2-isogenies between Montgomery curves can also be done entirely on the Kummer line. Efficient formulas for 2 and 4-isogenies were derived in [13]. Later, it was observed by Costello et al. [9] that computing an isogeny of degree 2^n is more efficiently done using 4-isogenies. To avoid many inversions in computing small degree isogenies, it was proposed in [10] to consider "projective" coefficients for the curve $E_{a,b}$ as well. That is to write $E_{a,b}$ as $E_{(A:B:C)} : By^2 = Cx^3 + Ax^2 + Cx$ for some $C \neq 0$, with $b = B/C$ and $a = A/C$. Like the arithmetic on the Kummer line, this leads to an isogeny arithmetic in which curves and their quadratic twists are identified by working only with the coefficients $(A : C) \in \mathbb{P}^1$. Following [9] we also use $(A_{24} : C_{24})$ to denote the Montgomery curve constant $(a - 2)/4$.

The projective versions of the 4-isogeny formulas in [13] can be written as follows [9]. Let $P = (X_4 : Z_4) \in E_{(A:C)}$ be a point of order 4 and denote by $\phi : E_{(A_{24}:C_{24})} \to E_{(A'_{24}:C'_{24})}$ the 4-isogeny with kernel $\langle P \rangle$. The target curve of ψ is given by

$$(A'_{24} : C'_{24}) = (X_4^4 - Z_4^4 : Z_4^4),$$

and an evaluation $(X' : Z') = \phi(X : Z)$ is given by

$$(X' : Z') = (X(2X_4Z_4Z - X(X_4^2 + Z_4^2))(X_4X - Z_4Z)^2 :$$
$$Z(2X_4Z_4X - Z(X_4^2 + Z_4^2))(Z_4X - X_4Z)^2).$$

We shall also need computing and evaluating 2-isogenies for backtrack prevention, see Algorithm 1. For a point $P = (X_2, Z_2)$ of order 2, using the formulas in [25] the target curve of the isogeny ϕ with kernel $\langle P \rangle$ is given

$$(A' + 2 : 4) = (-X_2^2 : Z_2^2).$$

An evaluation $(X' : Z') = \phi(X : Z)$ is given by

$$(X' : Z') = (X(XX_2 - ZZ_2) : Z(XZ_2 - ZX_2)).$$

The costs of point and isogeny arithmetics on Montgomery curves, taken from [10,25], are summarized in Table 1.

Table 1. Costs of different operations for Montgomery curves

operation	input	output	m
doubling	$x(P), a$	$x(2P)$	16
differential addition	$x(P), x(Q), x(P-Q)$	$x(P+Q)$	13
double and add	$x(P), x(Q), x(P-Q), a$	$x(2P), x(P+Q)$	26
ladder	$x(P), a, m$	$x(mP)$	$23n$
compute 2-isogeny	$x(P)$	A', C'	4
evaluate 2-isogeny	$x(P)$	A', C'	12
compute 4-isogeny	$x(P)$	A', C'	8
evaluate 4-isogeny	$x(Q)$	$x(\phi(Q))$	22

4.2   Complexity of CGL

For hashing a message in the original CGL algorithm, 2-torsion points and the Vélu formulas are used. This requires obtaining two 2-torsion points at each curve by eliminating the point corresponding to the arriving isogeny, and using Vélu to compute the next curve. The 2-torsion can be computed using $f(x)$ from the equation $y^2 = f(x)$ of the curve. The polynomial $f(x)$ is cubic, but a linear factor corresponding to one of the 2-torsion points is eliminated. This means we always have a quadratic equation to factor. Therefore, hashing each bit of the message needs: 1 isogeny computation, 1 isogeny evaluation, and 1 square root computation.

Modular Polynomials. Since we only need to work with j-invariants, a more efficient approach is to use the modular polynomial $\Phi_2(x, y)$. For any curve $E \in G_\ell$, the univariate polynomial $\Phi_2(x, j(E))$ is a cubic with roots the j-invariants of the curves 2-isogenous to E. Eliminating one of the linear factors corresponding to the j-invariant of the previous curve, we are left with a quadratic equation. Now, computing a square root gives the j-invariant of the next curve. This way, isogeny computation and evaluation is avoided altogether. For each bit of the input we need to do the following:

- Evaluate the modular polynomial for the current curve. The modular polynomial is

$$\Phi_2(x,y) = x^3 + y^3 - x^2y^2 + 1488(x^2y + y^2x) - 162000(x^2 + y^2)$$
$$40773375xy + 8748000000(x + y) - 157464000000000.$$

The evaluation $\Phi_2(x, j(E))$ requires 5**m** and a few scalar multiplications.
- Obtain a quadratic equation $g(x)$ from $\Phi_2(x, j(E))$ by factoring out a linear factor. This needs only 3**m**.
- Solve the quadratic equation. This needs 2**m** and 1 square root computation. The square root computation takes $5 \log p\mathbf{m} + \log p\mathbf{s} + 1\mathbf{i}$.

In summary, we need $(5 \log p + 10)\mathbf{m} + \log p\mathbf{s} + 1\mathbf{i}$ for each bit, and hence

$$kn((5 \log p + 10)\mathbf{m} + \log p\mathbf{s} + 1\mathbf{i}) \tag{1}$$

for a message of length kn bits.

4.3   Complexity of the New Hash Algorithm

For each n-bit block m of the input message Algorithm 2 performs the following:

- Obtain generators P, Q of the group $E[2^n]$ of the current curve E. This can be efficiently done using the *entangled basis* technique of [37]. An entangled basis computation takes, on average, 2 quadratic residuosity tests, 1 square root finalization and 24**m**. A quadratic residuosity test in $\mathbb{F}_{p^2}$ takes $\log p\mathbf{s}$, and the square root finalization can be done in $\log p\mathbf{s} + 1\mathbf{i}$. The total cost of basis generation is thus $24\mathbf{m} + 3 \log p\mathbf{s} + 1\mathbf{i}$.
- Compute $2^{n-1}P, 2^{n-1}Q$. The value $2^{n-1}P$ is always computed, but the value $2^{n-1}Q$ is computed 2/3 of the time on average. The total cost on average is then $\approx 1.67n$ point doublings which is $26.7n\mathbf{m}$.
- Compute $R = P + mQ$. For this, we first compute mQ using the usual Montgomery ladder which takes $23n\mathbf{m}$, and then add P at the cost of a few multiplications.
- Compute an isogeny $\phi : E \to E'$ with kernel $\langle R \rangle$. For this, we use the optimal strategy approach of [13]. Using this strategy, computing a 2^n-isogeny takes $\frac{1}{2}n \log n$ point doublings and 2-isogeny computations. As mentioned above, we can use 4-isogenies instead of 2-isogenies. Using this strategy, obtaining the target curve E' takes $\frac{n}{2}$ 4-isogeny computations and $\frac{n}{4} \log \frac{n}{2}$ point quadrupling and 4-isogeny evaluations. According to Table 1, all these together take

$$\left(\frac{27}{2}n \log n - \frac{19}{2}n\right) \mathbf{m}.$$

- Compute the backtrack 2-torsion point. For this we only need to compute the last 4-isogeny as 2-isogenies, and then compute the image of a 2-torsion point that is not in the kernel of the last 2-isogeny. If the kernel is not $\langle (0,0) \rangle$ then we can simply use $(0,0)$ as the desired point. Otherwise, we need to take a square root to obtain a 2-torsion that is not in the kernel. The latter case happens with probability $\approx 1/3$. The total cost of this is step is then $\approx (2 \log p\mathbf{s} + 1\mathbf{i})/3$.

Replacing $\log p$ by n, the total complexity of Algorithm 2 for an input of length kn bits is then

$$\left(\frac{27}{2}n\log n + 40.2n\right)k\mathbf{m} + \frac{10}{3}nk\mathbf{s} + \frac{4}{3}k\mathbf{i}. \tag{2}$$

Performance Comparison. Comparing the complexity of the new hash algorithm, Eq. (2), with CGL, Eq. (1), we immediately see that the new algorithm is significantly faster. Asymptotically, the runtime of the new hash algorithm is quasi-linear in n while the runtime of CGL is quadratic in n. For a concrete performance comparison, we can replace the squaring and inversion operations $\mathbf{s}$ and $\mathbf{i}$ by a factor of multiplication $\mathbf{m}$. A frequently used convention is to set $\mathbf{s} = 0.67\mathbf{m}$ and $\mathbf{i} = 100\mathbf{m}$. From this, we get the estimations

$$kn(5.7n + 110)\mathbf{m}$$

for complexity of the CGL hash algorithm, and

$$kn(13.5\log n + 42.4)\mathbf{m}$$

for complexity of the new hash algorithm. This leads to the performance ratio

$$\frac{5.7n + 110}{13.5\log n + 42.4} \tag{3}$$

which is asymptotically $c\frac{n}{\log n}$ for the constant $c = 5.7/13.5$. Figures 1a and 1b compare the performances of CGL and the new hash algorithm for different parameter sizes.

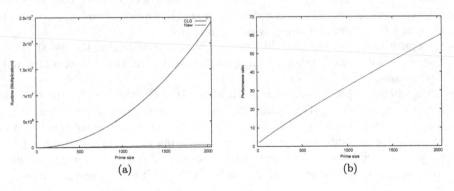

(a)   (b)

Fig. 1. (a) Number of multiplications in $\mathbb{F}_{p^2}$ for CGL and this work. (b) Performance ratio between CGL and this work

Figure 1a shows the quadratic versus quasi-linear behaviors of the algorithms. From Fig. 1b and Eq. (3) we see that for $n = 1024$, i.e., a prime of size ≈ 1024 bits, the new algorithm is 33.5 times faster than the original CGL algorithm. Given that the best attack on the isogeny problem, and hence on both hash algorithms, has quantum complexity $O(p^{1/4})$, this corresponds to 256-bit quantum security level. For a 384-bit quantum security level, we get a performance ratio of 47.8.

Remark 3. Although our hash algorithm is significantly faster asymptotically, for short messages, it suffers from the computational overhead of the extra block of padding. For example, in the extreme case of hashing only one block of size $n = 1024$, the performance ratio drops to $(5.7 \times 1024 + 110)/(2 \times (13.5 \times 10 + 42.5)) \approx 16.8$.

References

1. Ajtai, M.: Generating hard instances of lattice problems. In: Proceedings of the Twenty-Eighth Annual ACM Symposium on Theory of Computing, pp. 99–108. ACM (1996)
2. Bernstein, D.J., Birkner, P., Joye, M., Lange, T., Peters, C.: Twisted Edwards curves. In: Vaudenay, S. (ed.) AFRICACRYPT 2008. LNCS, vol. 5023, pp. 389–405. Springer, Heidelberg (2008). https://doi.org/10.1007/978-3-540-68164-9_26
3. Bernstein, D.J., Lange, T.: Explicit formulas database (2007). http://www.hyperelliptic.org/EFD/index.html
4. Biasse, J.-F., Jao, D., Sankar, A.: A quantum algorithm for computing isogenies between supersingular elliptic curves. In: Meier, W., Mukhopadhyay, D. (eds.) INDOCRYPT 2014. LNCS, vol. 8885, pp. 428–442. Springer, Cham (2014). https://doi.org/10.1007/978-3-319-13039-2_25
5. Charles, D.X., Lauter, K.E., Goren, E.Z.: Cryptographic hash functions from expander graphs. J. Cryptol. **22**(1), 93–113 (2009)
6. Chaum, D., van Heijst, E., Pfitzmann, B.: Cryptographically strong undeniable signatures, unconditionally secure for the signer. In: Feigenbaum, J. (ed.) CRYPTO 1991. LNCS, vol. 576, pp. 470–484. Springer, Heidelberg (1992). https://doi.org/10.1007/3-540-46766-1_38
7. Cleve, R., Ekert, A., Macchiavello, C., Mosca, M.: Quantum algorithms revisited. In: Proceedings of the Royal Society of London A: Mathematical, Physical and Engineering Sciences, vol. 454, pp. 339–354. The Royal Society (1998)
8. Contini, S., Lenstra, A.K., Steinfeld, R.: VSH, an efficient and provable collision-resistant hash function. In: Vaudenay, S. (ed.) EUROCRYPT 2006. LNCS, vol. 4004, pp. 165–182. Springer, Heidelberg (2006). https://doi.org/10.1007/11761679_11
9. Costello, C., Hisil, H.: A simple and compact algorithm for SIDH with arbitrary degree isogenies. In: Takagi, T., Peyrin, T. (eds.) ASIACRYPT 2017. LNCS, vol. 10625, pp. 303–329. Springer, Cham (2017). https://doi.org/10.1007/978-3-319-70697-9_11
10. Costello, C., Longa, P., Naehrig, M.: Efficient algorithms for supersingular isogeny Diffie-Hellman. In: Robshaw, M., Katz, J. (eds.) CRYPTO 2016. LNCS, vol. 9814, pp. 572–601. Springer, Heidelberg (2016). https://doi.org/10.1007/978-3-662-53018-4_21
11. Cramer, R., Shoup, V.: Signature schemes based on the strong RSA assumption. ACM Trans. Inf. Syst. Secur. (TISSEC) **3**(3), 161–185 (2000)
12. Damgård, I.B.: A design principle for hash functions. In: Brassard, G. (ed.) CRYPTO 1989. LNCS, vol. 435, pp. 416–427. Springer, New York (1990). https://doi.org/10.1007/0-387-34805-0_39
13. De Feo, L., Jao, D., Plût, J.: Towards quantum-resistant cryptosystems from supersingular elliptic curve isogenies. J. Math. Cryptol. **8**(3), 209–247 (2014)

14. Edwards, H.: A normal form for elliptic curves. Bull. Am. Math. Soc. **44**(3), 393–422 (2007)
15. Eisentraeger, K., Hallgren, S., Morrison, T.: On the hardness of computing endomorphism rings of supersingular elliptic curves. Cryptology ePrint Archive, Report 2017/986 (2017). https://eprint.iacr.org/2017/986
16. Galbraith, S.D.: Constructing isogenies between elliptic curves over finite fields. LMS J. Comput. Math. **2**, 118–138 (1999)
17. Kohel, D.R.: Endomorphism rings of elliptic curves over finite fields. Ph.D. thesis, University of California, Berkeley (1996)
18. Merkle, R.C.: A certified digital signature. In: Brassard, G. (ed.) CRYPTO 1989. LNCS, vol. 435, pp. 218–238. Springer, New York (1990). https://doi.org/10.1007/0-387-34805-0_21
19. Micciancio, D.: Generalized compact knapsacks, cyclic lattices, and efficient one-way functions. Comput. Complex. **16**(4), 365–411 (2007)
20. Montgomery, P.L.: Speeding the pollard and elliptic curve methods of factorization. Math. Comput. **48**(177), 243–264 (1987)
21. Moody, D., Shumow, D.: Analogues of vélu's formulas for isogenies on alternate models of elliptic curves. Math. Comput. **85**(300), 1929–1951 (2016)
22. Nielsen, M.A., Chuang, I.: Quantum Computation and Quantum Information. AAPT (2002)
23. Petit, C., Lauter, K.: Hard and easy problems for supersingular isogeny graphs. Cryptology ePrint Archive, Report 2017/962 (2017). https://eprint.iacr.org/2017/962
24. Pizer, A.K.: Ramanujan graphs and Hecke operators. Bull. Am. Math. Soc. **23**(1), 127–137 (1990)
25. Renes, J.: Computing isogenies between montgomery curves using the action of (0, 0). In: Lange, T., Steinwandt, R. (eds.) PQCrypto 2018. LNCS, vol. 10786, pp. 229–247. Springer, Cham (2018). https://doi.org/10.1007/978-3-319-79063-3_11
26. Scott, M.: Implementing cryptographic pairings. In: Takagi, T., et al. (eds.) Pairing 2007. LNCS, vol. 4575, pp. 177–196. Springer, Heidelberg (2007). https://doi.org/10.1007/978-3-540-73489-5
27. Shor, P.W.: Polynomial-time algorithms for prime factorization and discrete logarithms on a quantum computer. SIAM Rev. **41**(2), 303–332 (1999)
28. Silverman, J.H.: The Arithmetic of Elliptic Curves, vol. 106. Springer, Heidelberg (2009). https://doi.org/10.1007/978-0-387-09494-6
29. Simon, D.R.: On the power of quantum computation. SIAM J. Comput. **26**(5), 1474–1483 (1997)
30. Sutherland, A.: Isogeny volcanoes. Open Book Ser. **1**(1), 507–530 (2013)
31. Tani, S.: Claw finding algorithms using quantum walk. Theoret. Comput. Sci. **410**(50), 5285–5297 (2009)
32. Tate, J.: Endomorphisms of abelian varieties over finite fields. Invent. Math. **2**(2), 134–144 (1966)
33. Tillich, J.-P., Zémor, G.: Group-theoretic hash functions. In: Cohen, G., Litsyn, S., Lobstein, A., Zémor, G. (eds.) Algebraic Coding 1993. LNCS, vol. 781, pp. 90–110. Springer, Heidelberg (1994). https://doi.org/10.1007/3-540-57843-9_12
34. Vélu, J.: Isogénies entre courbes elliptiques. Comptes-Rendus l'Acad. Sci. **273**, 238–241 (1971)
35. Washington, L.C.: Elliptic Curves: Number Theory and Cryptography. CRC Press, Boca Raton (2008)
36. Weber, H.: Lehrbuch der algebra, vol. 3, 3rd edn. Chelsea, New York (1908). 1961

37. Zanon, G.H.M., Simplicio Jr., M.A., Pereira, G.C.C.F., Doliskani, J., Barreto, P.S.L.M.: Faster isogeny-based compressed key agreement. Cryptology ePrint Archive, Report 2017/1143 (2017). https://eprint.iacr.org/2017/1143
38. Zémor, G.: Hash functions and graphs with large girths. In: Davies, D.W. (ed.) EUROCRYPT 1991. LNCS, vol. 547, pp. 508–511. Springer, Heidelberg (1991). https://doi.org/10.1007/3-540-46416-6_44
39. Zémor, G.: Hash functions and Cayley graphs. Des. Codes Crypt. 4(3), 381–394 (1994)
40. Zhang, S.: Promised and distributed quantum search. In: Wang, L. (ed.) COCOON 2005. LNCS, vol. 3595, pp. 430–439. Springer, Heidelberg (2005). https://doi.org/10.1007/11533719_44

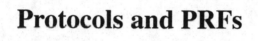

Protocols and PRFs

From Plaintext-Extractability
to IND-CCA Security

Ehsan Ebrahimi[(✉)] [iD]

Department of Computer Science, University of Luxembourg, Esch-Sur-Alzette,
Luxembourg
ehsan.ebrahimi@uni.lu

Abstract. We say a public-key encryption is plaintext-extractable in
the random oracle model if there exists an algorithm that given access
to the input/output of all queries to the random oracles can simulate the
decryption oracle. We argue that the plaintext-extractability is enough to
show the indistinguishably under chosen ciphertext attack (IND-CCA) of
OAEP+ transform (Shoup, Crypto 2001) when the underlying trapdoor
permutation is one-way.

We extend the result to the quantum random oracle model (QROM)
and show that OAEP+ is IND-CCA secure in QROM if the underlying
trapdoor permutation is quantum one-way.

Keywords: Post-quantum Security · OAEP+ · Quantum Random
Oracle Model

1 Introduction

The OAEP transform was proposed by Bellare and Rogaway [4] to transfer a
trapdoor permutation into a public-key encryption scheme using two random
oracles. It was believed that the OAEP-cryptosystem is provable secure in the
random oracle model based on the one-wayness of trapdoor permutation, but
Shoup [14] showed it is an unjustified belief.

In [4], the technique to show the IND-CCA security is introducing a notion
of plaintext-awareness (PA1) that guarantees the existence of an algorithm Ext
that can simulate the decryption oracle given access to the inputs/outputs of
the random oracle queries. Then, given this extractor Ext, we may reduce the
IND-CCA security to the one-wayness of the underlying trapdoor permutation.
A stronger definition of plaintext-awareness (PA2) was introduced in the random
oracle model [1], in which, the adversary is able to eavesdrop some valid ciphertexts (through an oracle $\mathcal{E}_{pk}^H$) and the extractor, given access to these ciphertexts
and the random oracle queries made by the adversary (and not the random ora-
cle queries used by $\mathcal{E}_{pk}^H$), should be able to decrypt any ciphertext outputted by
the adversary. In [1], it was shown that an encryption scheme that is PA2 and
IND-CPA secure, is IND-CCA secure.

However, Shoup [14] argued that PA1 might not be sufficient to show the IND-
CCA security of OAEP because the adversary might be able to turn the challenge

ciphertext c^* into a new valid ciphertext for which Ext is not able to decrypt (since Ext does not have access to the random oracles queries used to obtain c^*). And it has not been proven that the OAEP transform is PA2. Therefore, the IND-CCA security of OAEP under the one-wayness assumption of the underlying permutation remains an open question. Shoup [14] even made an argument that the existence of a IND-CCA security proof is unlikely under the one-wayness assumption. Alternatively, Shoup [14] presented the OAEP+ transform along with a IND-CCA security proof based on the one-wayness of the permutation.

The IND-CCA security of the OAEP transform was proven in [11], however, based on a stronger assumption, namely, the partial-domain one-wayness of the underlying permutation. This result is extended to the quantum random oracle model [9,15] under the quantum partial-domain one-wayness of the underlying permutation. Since in the real world applications, a random oracle will be substituted with a cryptographic hash function and the code of this hash function is public, to claim the post-quantum security, one needs to prove the security in the quantum random oracle model in which a quantum adversary is able to make superposition queries to the random oracles. To date, the post-quantum security of OAEP+ has not been investigated. In fact, this post-quantum security proof is needed since the existence of a quantum partial-domain one-way trapdoor permutation implies the existence of a quantum one-way trapdoor permutation and not other way around. To use the result in [9,15], one needs a quantum-secure trapdoor permutation with a stronger security requirement than the quantum one-wayness.

Note that this has not been problematic so far since this does not affect the instantiation of OAEP with the RSA function (RSA-OAEP) [4]. In more details, since the partial-domain one-wayness of the RSA function is equivalent to its (full-domain) one-wayness, it follows that the security of RSA-OAEP can actually be proven under the sole RSA assumption [11]. However, RSA assumption does not hold in the post-quantum setting due to Shor's quantum algorithm [13]. And we are not aware of a quantum-hard assumption for which these two security definitions (partial-domain one-wayness and one-wayness assumptions) are equivalent. So we need a quantum partial-domain one-way trapdoor permutation to use in the OAEP transform. In contrast, if the post-quantum security of OAEP+ exists, we can use a quantum one-way trapdoor permutation that is a weaker assumption.

In this paper, we fill this gap. We show that OAEP+ is secure in the quantum random oracle model. Our proof technique is to define a notion of plaintext-extractability, show that OAEP+ is plaintext-extractable and use it to prove IND-CCA security in the quantum random oracle model.

OAEP+ Transform. We informally present how OAEP+ encrypts a message m. Let G, H, H' be random oracles and f be a trapdoor permutation. To encrypt m, it chooses a random element r and computes a ciphertext c as follows:

$$s = \underbrace{(G(r) \oplus m)}_{[s]^n} \| \underbrace{H'(r, m)}_{[s]_{k_1}}, \ t = r \oplus H(s), \ c = f(s, t).$$

1.1 Our Contribution

We investigate the security of OAEP+ in the quantum random oracle model. We define a notion of plaintext-extractability in the (quantum) random oracle model. Our notion is different from PA1 since the adversary is given the possibility of eavesdropping some valid ciphertexts (through an oracle $\mathcal{E}_{pk}^{H}$) in contrast to PA1. It is not PA2 either because the extractor Ext is given access to the inputs/outputs of all queries to the random oracles (including random oracle queries used by $\mathcal{E}_{pk}^{H}$) in contrast to PA2.

We informally discuss why our plaintext-extractability notion is sufficient to prove the IND-CCA security of OAEP+ under the one-wayness of the underlying permutation. Our argument is classical but it would be extended to the quantum random oracle model in Sect. 4.

We start with IND-CCA game (**Game 0**) in which the adversary given access to the random oracles and decryption oracle outputs two messages m_0, m_1. The challenger chooses a random bit b and encrypts m_b and sends this challenge ciphertext c^* to the adversary. The adversary is allowed to make decryption queries, except for the challenge ciphertext, and random oracle queries. Finally, the adversary outputs a bit b' and wins if $b' = b$.

Then, we define a game (**Game 1**) in which the challenger instead of using the secret key (f^{-1}) to answer decryption queries, it uses the extractor algorithm Ext. Note that in this game, the challenger simulates the decryption queries, therefore, Ext has access to all queries to the random oracles. The indistinguishably of these two games hold due to the plaintext-extractability of OAEP+.

We define another game (**Game 2**) in which the challenger aborts and return a random bit if the adversary submits the randomness r^* (that has been used to compute c^*) as a query to either G or H'. Obviously, the probability of the abort event is negligible before the challenge query since r^* has not been used yet. We show that if r^* is queried after the challenge query, this breaks the one-wayness of the underlying permutation.

Let $\mathcal{A}$ be an adversary that distinguishes **Game 1** and **Game 2**, that is, $\mathcal{A}$ queries r^* as a post-challenge query with a non-negligible probability. Now it comes to the reduction adversary $\mathcal{B}$. Note that the input of the adversary $\mathcal{B}$ is a value c^* that is an image of f on some random values s^*, t^*. In other words, c^* is generated without any queries to the random oracles. Therefore, the adversary $\mathcal{B}$ chooses random oracles G, H and H', a random bit b, runs $\mathcal{A}$ and answers to its decryption queries using Ext. Upon receiving the challenge query m_0, m_1 from $\mathcal{A}$, the adversary sends c^* as the challenge query.

The adversary $\mathcal{B}$ guesses, randomly, the first query in which the randomness r^* (that is used to generate c^*) will be submitted to G or H'. Therefore, the adversary $\mathcal{B}$ can find r^* with a non-negligible probability. It outputs $s^* := (G(r^*) \oplus m_b) \| H'(r^*, m_b)$ and $t^* := r^* \oplus H(s^*)$ as the pre-image of f on c^*.

Back to **Game 2**, when r^* is not submitted as a query to G and H', the values of $G(r^*)$ and $H'(r^*, m_b)$ are distributed uniformly at random. Therefore, the adversary is able to guess b only with a probability of $1/2$ and this finishes the proof.

Difference with the Implication PA2+IND-CPA ⟹ IND-CCA [1,2].
Note that in the sketch above, the extractor algorithm knows all the random oracle queries and in the reduction, the adversary $\mathcal{B}$ possess a value that is obtained by computing f on some random values s^*, t^* and without any random oracle queries. Therefore, we do not need the strong security requirement PA2 to conclude the IND-CCA security. This is of course different when we want to show IND-CCA security from IND-CPA and a plaintext-awareness notion. In this general implication, the reduction adversary $\mathcal{B}$ attacking CPA security gets its challenge ciphertext c^* through an encryption oracle (the challenger of CPA game) and the adversary $\mathcal{B}$ does not know the random oracle queries that have been used to compute c^*. For this general implication, indeed, we need PA2 notion in which the extractor Ext is not given access to the random oracle queries used to compute the challenge ciphertext c^*. However, in our case, c^* is generated without making any random oracle query. Note that both the actual decryption algorithm and the extractor return $\bot$ if c^* is submitted as a decryption query.

2 Preliminaries

Notations. The notation $x \xleftarrow{\$} X$ means that x is chosen uniformly at random from the set X. For a natural number n, $[n]$ means the set $\{1, \cdots, n\}$. $\Pr[P : G]$ is the probability that the predicate P holds true where free variables in P are assigned according to the program in G. The function $\mathsf{negl}(\eta)$ is any non-negative function that is smaller than the inverse of any non-negative polynomial $p(\eta)$ for sufficiently large η. For a function f, f_x denotes the evaluation of f on the input x, that is $f(x)$. For a bit-string x of size more-than-equal k, $[x]_k$ are the k least significant bits of x and $[x]^k$ are the k most significant bits of x. For two bits b and b', $[b = b']$ is 1 if $b = b'$ and it is 0 otherwise. QPT is a quantum polynomial-time algorithm.

2.1 Quantum Computing

We present basics of quantum computing in this subsection. The interested reader can refer to [12] for more information. For two vectors $|\Psi\rangle = (\psi_1, \psi_2, \cdots, \psi_n)$ and $|\Phi\rangle = (\phi_1, \phi_2, \cdots, \phi_n)$ in $\mathbb{C}^n$, the inner product is defined as $\langle \Psi, \Phi \rangle = \sum_i \psi_i^* \phi_i$ where ψ_i^* is the complex conjugate of ψ_i. Norm of $|\Phi\rangle$ is defined as $\||\Phi\rangle\| = \sqrt{\langle \Phi, \Phi \rangle}$. The n-dimensional Hilbert space $\mathcal{H}$ is the complex vector space $\mathbb{C}^n$ with the inner product defined above. A quantum system is a Hilbert space $\mathcal{H}$ and a quantum state $|\psi\rangle$ is a vector $|\psi\rangle$ in $\mathcal{H}$ with norm 1. A unitary operation over $\mathcal{H}$ is a transformation $\mathbb{U}$ such that $\mathbb{U}\mathbb{U}^\dagger = \mathbb{U}^\dagger\mathbb{U} = \mathbb{I}$ where $\mathbb{U}^\dagger$ is the Hermitian transpose of $\mathbb{U}$ and $\mathbb{I}$ is the identity operator over $\mathcal{H}$. Norm of an operator $\mathbb{U}$ is $\|\mathbb{U}\| = \max_{|\psi\rangle} \|\mathbb{U}|\psi\rangle\|$. The computational basis for $\mathcal{H}$ consists of $\log n$ vectors $|b_i\rangle$ of length $\log n$ with 1 in the position i and 0 elsewhere.

An orthogonal projection $\mathbb{P}$ over $\mathcal{H}$ is a linear transformation such that $\mathbb{P}^2 = \mathbb{P} = \mathbb{P}^\dagger$. A measurement on a Hilbert space is defined with a family of projectors that are pairwise orthogonal. An example of measurement is the computational basis measurement in which any projection is defined by a basis vector. The output of computational measurement on a state $|\Psi\rangle$ is i with the probability $\|\langle b_i, \Psi\rangle\|^2$ and the post measurement state is $|b_i\rangle$. For a general measurement $\{\mathbb{P}_i\}_i$, the output of this measurement on a state $|\Psi\rangle$ is i with the probability $\|\mathbb{P}_i|\Psi\rangle\|^2$ and the post measurement state is $\frac{\mathbb{P}_i|\Psi\rangle}{\|\mathbb{P}_i|\Psi\rangle\|}$.

For two operators $\mathbb{U}_1$ and $\mathbb{U}_2$, the commutator is $[\mathbb{U}_1, \mathbb{U}_2] = \mathbb{U}_1\mathbb{U}_2 - \mathbb{U}_2\mathbb{U}_1$. For two quantum systems $\mathcal{H}_1$ and $\mathcal{H}_2$, the composition of them is defined by the tensor product and it is $\mathcal{H}_1 \otimes \mathcal{H}_2$. For two unitary $\mathbb{U}_1$ and $\mathbb{U}_2$ defined over $\mathcal{H}_1$ and $\mathcal{H}_2$ respectively, $(\mathbb{U}_1 \otimes \mathbb{U}_2)(\mathcal{H}_1 \otimes \mathcal{H}_2) = \mathbb{U}_1(\mathcal{H}_1) \otimes \mathbb{U}_2(\mathcal{H}_2)$. In this paper, QFT over an n-qubits system is $\mathbb{H}^{\otimes n}$.

If a system is in the state $|\Psi_i\rangle$ with the probability p_i, we interpret this with a quantum ensemble $E = \{(|\Psi_i\rangle, p_i)\}_i$. Different outputs of a quantum algorithm can be represented as a quantum ensemble. The density operator corresponding with the ensemble E is $\rho = \sum_i p_i |\Psi_i\rangle\langle\Psi_i|$ where $|\Psi_i\rangle\langle\Psi_i|$ is the operator acting as $|\Psi_i\rangle\langle\Psi_i| : |\Phi\rangle \rightarrow \langle\Psi_i, \Phi\rangle|\Psi_i\rangle$. The trace distance of two density operators ρ_1, ρ_2 is defined as $\mathrm{TD}(\rho_1, \rho_2) := \frac{1}{2}\mathrm{tr}|\rho_1 - \rho_2|$ where tr is the trace of a square matrix (the sum of the entries on the main diagonal) and $|\rho_1 - \rho_2| := \sqrt{(\rho_1 - \rho_2)^\dagger(\rho_1 - \rho_2)}$. Note that the trace distance of two pure states $|\Psi\rangle, |\Phi\rangle$ is defined as $\mathrm{TD}(|\Psi\rangle\langle\Psi|, |\Phi\rangle\langle\Phi|)$.

Any classical function $f : X \rightarrow Y$ can be implemented as a unitary operator $\mathbb{U}_f$ in a quantum computer where $\mathbb{U}_f : |x, y\rangle \rightarrow |x, y \oplus f(x)\rangle$ and it is clear that $\mathbb{U}_f^\dagger = \mathbb{U}_f$. A quantum adversary has standard oracle access to a classical function f if it can query the unitary $\mathbb{U}_f$.

2.2 Definitions

We define a public-key encryption scheme, the IND-CCA security notion in the quantum random oracle model and the quantum (partial-domain) one-wayness.

Definition 1. *A scheme $\mathcal{E}$ with three polynomial-time (in the security parameter η) algorithms* Gen, Enc, Dec) *is called a public-key encryption scheme if:*

1. *The key generation algorithm* Gen *is a probabilistic algorithm which on input 1^η outputs a pair of keys, $(\mathsf{pk}, \mathsf{sk}) \leftarrow \mathrm{Gen}(1^\eta)$, called the public key and the secret key for the encryption scheme, respectively.*
2. *The encryption algorithm* Enc *is a probabilistic algorithm which takes as input a public key* pk *and a message m and outputs a ciphertext $c \leftarrow \mathrm{Enc}_{\mathsf{pk}}(m)$.*
3. *The decryption algorithm is a deterministic algorithm that takes as input a secret key* sk *and a ciphertext c and returns the message $m := \mathrm{Dec}_{\mathsf{sk}}(c)$. It is required that the decryption algorithm returns the original message, i.e., $\mathrm{Dec}_{\mathsf{sk}}(\mathrm{Enc}_{\mathsf{pk}}(m)) = m$, for every $(\mathsf{pk}, \mathsf{sk}) \leftarrow \mathrm{Gen}(1^\eta)$ and every m. The algorithm* Dec *returns $\bot$ if ciphertext c is not decryptable.*

In the following, we define the IND-CCA security notion in the quantum random oracle model. The IND-CCA security notion for a public-key encryption scheme allows the adversary to make quantum random oracle queries but the challenge query and decryption queries are classical. We define Dec' as:

$$\mathrm{Dec}'(c) \rightarrow \begin{cases} \bot & \text{if } c^* \text{ is defined } \wedge c = c^* \\ \mathrm{Dec}_{sk}(c) & \text{otherwise} \end{cases},$$

where c^* is the challenge ciphertext and $\bot$ is a value outside of the output space. We say that a quantum algorithm A has quantum access to the random oracle H if A can submit queries in superposition and the oracle H answers to these queries by applying a unitary transformation that maps $|x, y\rangle$ to $|x, y \oplus H(x)\rangle$.

Definition 2 (IND-CCA in the quantum random oracle model). *A public-key encryption scheme $\Pi = (\mathrm{Gen}, \mathrm{Enc}, \mathrm{Dec})$ is IND-CCA secure if for any QPT adversary A*

$$\Pr\left[b = 1 : b \leftarrow \mathsf{Exp}_{A,\mathcal{E}}^{CCA,qRO}(\eta)\right] \leq 1/2 + \textit{negl}(\eta),$$

where $\mathsf{Exp}_{A,\mathcal{E}}^{CCA,qRO}(\eta)$ game is define as:
$\mathsf{Exp}_{A,\mathcal{E}}^{CCA,qRO}(\eta)$ *game:*

Key Gen: *The challenger runs $\mathrm{Gen}(1^\eta)$ to obtain a pair of keys $(\mathsf{pk}, \mathsf{sk})$ and chooses random oracles.*

Query: *The adversary A given the public key pk, the oracle access to Dec' and the **quantum** access to the random oracles, chooses two **classical** messages m_0, m_1 of the same length and sends them to the challenger. The challenger chooses a random bit b and responds with $c^* \leftarrow \mathrm{Enc}_{\mathsf{pk}}(m_b)$.*

Guess: *The adversary A continues to query the decryption oracle and the random oracles. Finally, the adversary A produces a bit b'. The output of the game is $[b = b']$.*

Definition 3 (Quantum one-way function). *We say a permutation $f : \{0,1\}^{n+k_1} \times \{0,1\}^{k_0} \rightarrow \{0,1\}^m$ is quantum one-way if for any QPT adversary A,*

$$\Pr\left[(\tilde{s}, \tilde{t}) = (s,t) : s \xleftarrow{\$} \{0,1\}^{n+k_1}, \ t \xleftarrow{\$} \{0,1\}^{k_0}, \ (\tilde{s}, \tilde{t}) \leftarrow A(f(s,t))\right] \leq \textit{negl}(\eta).$$

Definition 4 (Quantum partial-domain one-way function). *We say a permutation $f : \{0,1\}^{n+k_1} \times \{0,1\}^{k_0} \rightarrow \{0,1\}^m$ is quantum partial-domain one-way if for any QPT adversary A,*

$$\Pr\left[\tilde{s} = s : s \xleftarrow{\$} \{0,1\}^{n+k_1}, \ t \xleftarrow{\$} \{0,1\}^{k_0}, \ \tilde{s} \leftarrow A(f(s,t))\right] \leq \textit{negl}(\eta).$$

We use the 'gentle-measurement lemma' [16] in the proof. Informally, it states that if an output of a measurement is almost certain for a quantum state, the measurement does not disturb the state much.

Lemma 1 (gentle-measurement lemma). *Let $\mathbb{M} = \{\mathbb{P}_i\}_i$ is a measurement. For any state $|\Psi\rangle$, if there exists an i such that $\|\mathbb{P}_i|\Psi\rangle\|^2 \geq 1 - \epsilon$, then $\mathrm{TD}(|\Psi\rangle, \mathbb{M}|\Psi\rangle) \leq \sqrt{\epsilon} + \epsilon.$*

2.3 Compressed Standard Oracle

Generally, it is not possible to copy a quantum state due to no-cloning theorem and destructive nature of quantum measurements. However, in a recent work, Zhandry showed that for quantum queries to a random oracle, a sort of recording is possible. Note that the conventional way to query a random oracle in superposition is to choose a uniformly at random function H and answers to the query with the unitary $\mathbb{U}_H$. However, one can consider another approach in which the oracle starts with a private state that keeps a uniform superposition of all functions and the query is answered as:

$$|x,\ y\rangle \sum_H \frac{1}{\sqrt{|\Omega_H|}}|H\rangle \to \sum_H \frac{1}{\sqrt{|\Omega_H|}}|x,\ y \oplus H(x)\rangle|H\rangle,$$

where Ω_H is the set of all functions H. Following the perspective above, Zhandry [18] developed the CStO that its private register can be implemented efficiently, symmetrically stores the inputs/outputs of the adversary's queries in its private register and it is perfectly indistinguishable from the standard oracle (StO).

Lemma 2 (Lemma 4 in [18]). CStO *and* StO *are perfectly indistinguishable.*

We import the representation of CStO from [8]. Let $\mathfrak{D} = \otimes_{x \in X}\mathfrak{D}_x$ be the oracle register. The state space of $\mathfrak{D}_x$ is generated with vectors $|y\rangle$ for $y \in Y \cup \{\perp\}$. Let $F_{\mathfrak{D}_x}$ be a unitary acting on $\mathfrak{D}_x$ that maps $|\perp\rangle$ to $\mathsf{QFT}|0\rangle$ and vice versa. And for any vector orthogonal to $|\perp\rangle$ and $\mathsf{QFT}|0\rangle$, F is identity. We define CStO to be the following unitary acting on the input register, the output register and the $\mathfrak{D}$ register.

$$\mathsf{CStO} = \sum_x |x\rangle\langle x| \otimes F_{\mathfrak{D}_x} CNOT_{Y\mathfrak{D}_x} F_{\mathfrak{D}_x},$$

where $CNOT_{Y\mathfrak{D}_x}|y, y_x\rangle = |y \oplus y_x, y_x\rangle$ for $y, y_x \in Y$ and it is identity on $|y, \perp\rangle$. The initial state of $\mathfrak{D}$ register is $\otimes_{x \in X}|\perp\rangle$.

In the following, we present preliminaries for Theorem 3.1 in [8]. For a fixed relation $R \subset X \times Y$, Γ_R is the maximum number of y's that fulfill the relation R where the maximum is taken over all $x \in X$:

$$\Gamma_R = \max_{x \in X} |\{y \in Y | (x, y) \in R\}|.$$

We define a projector $\Pi_{\mathfrak{D}_x}^x$ that checks if the register $\mathfrak{D}_x$ contains a value $y \neq \perp$ such that $(x, y) \in R$:

$$\Pi_{\mathfrak{D}_x}^x := \sum_{y \ s.t. \ (x,y) \in R} |y\rangle\langle y|_{\mathfrak{D}_x}.$$

Let $\bar{\Pi}_{\mathfrak{D}_x}^x = \mathbb{I}_{\mathfrak{D}_x} - \Pi_{\mathfrak{D}_x}^x$. We define the measurement $\mathbb{M}$ to be the set of projectors $\{\Sigma^x\}_{x \in X \cup \{\emptyset\}}$ where

$$\Sigma^x := \bigotimes_{x' < x} \bar{\Pi}_{\mathfrak{D}_{x'}}^{x'} \otimes \Pi_{\mathfrak{D}_x}^x \text{ for } x \in X \text{ and } \Sigma^\emptyset := \mathbb{I} - \sum_x \Sigma^x. \tag{1}$$

Informally, the measurement $\mathbb{M}$ checks for the smallest x for which $\mathfrak{D}_x$ contains a value $y \neq \bot$ such that $(x,y) \in R$. If no register $\mathfrak{D}_x$ contains a value $y \neq \bot$ such that $(x,y) \in R$, the outcome of $\mathbb{M}$ is $\emptyset$. We define a purified measurement $\mathbb{M}_{\mathfrak{D}P}$ corresponding to $\mathbb{M}$ that XORs the outcome of the measurement to an ancillary register:

$$\mathbb{M}_{\mathfrak{D}P}|\phi, z\rangle_{\mathfrak{D}P} \rightarrow \sum_{x \in X \cup \{\emptyset\}} \Sigma^x |\phi\rangle_{\mathfrak{D}} |z \oplus x\rangle_P.$$

The following lemma states that CStO and $\mathbb{M}_{\mathfrak{D}P}$ almost commute if Γ_R is small proportional to the size of Y.

Lemma 3 (Theorem 3.1 in [8]). *For any relation R and Γ_R defined above, the commutator $[\text{CStO}, \mathbb{M}_{\mathfrak{D}P}]$ is bounded as follows:*

$$\|[\text{CStO}, \mathbb{M}_{\mathfrak{D}P}]\| \leq 8 \cdot 2^{-n/2} \sqrt{2\Gamma_R}.$$

3   Plaintext-Extractability

We define "plaintext-extractable" notion below in the random oracle model and quantum random oracle model. Our notion lies between the plaintext-awareness notions PA1 and PA2[1]. Our notion is stronger than PA1 notion [4] because the adversary is allowed to eavesdrop some ciphertexts in contrast to PA1 in which the adversary is not able to eavesdrop. Our notion is weaker than PA2 [1] because in our notion the extractor has access to all random oracle queries, in contrast, in PA2 notion the adversary does not know the random oracle queries that have been used to generate the eavesdropped ciphertexts.

3.1   Random Oracle Model

The random oracle model [3] is a powerful model in which the security of a cryptographic scheme is proven assuming the existence of a truly random function that is accessible by all parties including the adversary.

Informally, we say a public-key encryption scheme is plaintext-extractable if there exists an extractor algorithm Ext that given access to the list of all queries to the random oracle can simulate the decryption oracle.

Let $\mathcal{E}_{\text{pk}}^H$ indicates an encryption oracle that upon receiving a query m_0, m_1 from the adversary, it chooses a random bit b, encrypts m_b and sends the resulting ciphertext to the adversary. All ciphertexts obtained from $\mathcal{E}_{\text{pk}}^H$ are stored in **List** and for any $c \in$ **List**, the decryption oracle Dec_{sk}^H returns $\bot$.

Definition 5. *Let $\mathfrak{L}_H$ be the list of inputs/outputs of all queries to the random oracle H and* **List** *be the list of ciphertexts obtained from $\mathcal{E}_{\text{pk}}^H$. Let η be the security parameter. We say a public-key encryption scheme $\Pi_H = (\text{Gen}, \text{Enc}, \text{Dec})$*

---

[1] Recently, the classical plaintext-awareness notions PA0, PA1 and PA2 are adopted to the post-quantum setting, however, in the standard model [10].

is plaintext-extractable in the random oracle model if there exists an algorithm Ext *such that for any polynomial-time distinguisher* $\mathcal{D}$, *the following holds:*

$$|\Pr\left[\mathcal{D}^{\mathsf{Dec}^H_{\mathsf{sk},\mathbf{List}},H,\mathcal{E}^H_{\mathsf{pk}}}(\mathsf{pk})=1:(\mathsf{pk},\mathsf{sk})\leftarrow\mathsf{Gen}(1^\eta),H\xleftarrow{\$}\Omega_H\right]-$$
$$\Pr\left[\mathcal{D}^{\mathsf{Ext}(\mathsf{pk},\mathfrak{L}_H,\mathbf{List}),H,\mathcal{E}^H_{\mathsf{pk}}}(\mathsf{pk})=1:(\mathsf{pk},\mathsf{sk})\leftarrow\mathsf{Gen}(1^\eta),H\xleftarrow{\$}\Omega_H\right]|\leq \mathit{negl}(\eta).$$

In the definition above, the random oracle H can consist of several random oracles $\{H_i\}_i$ and is defined as $H(i,x):=H_i(x)$. (This remark has been made since OAEP+ uses three random oracles).

Remark. The definition above can be generalized to any oracle $\mathcal{E}^H_{\mathsf{pk}}$ that upon receiving a query M from the adversary, it randomly generates a message m (note that m may depend on M), encrypts it and sends the resulting ciphertext to the adversary. In more details, we say an encryption scheme is plaintext-extractable if there exists an extractor that works for any $\mathcal{E}^H_{\mathsf{pk}}$ defined above. (This generalization is not needed in our paper but it might be needed in other context. For instance this extension is crucial to prove the implication PA2+IND-CPA $\Longrightarrow$ IND-CCA in [2]).

3.2 Quantum Random Oracle Model

We define the plaintext-extractability in the quantum random oracle model [6] in which queries to the random oracles are quantum (superposition of inputs). This is necessary in the post-quantum setting since a quantum adversary attacking a scheme based on a real hash function is necessarily able to evaluate that function in superposition. Hence the random oracle model must reflect that ability if one requests post-quantum security.

In the definition below, an oracle with quantum access is differentiated with an underline (and an oracle without an underline is accessed classically).

Definition 6. *Let* $\mathfrak{D}_H$ *be a database of* CStO_H. *Let* η *be the security parameter. We say a public-key encryption scheme* Π_H *is plaintext-extractable in the quantum random oracle model if there exists an algorithm* Ext *such that for any* QPT *distinguisher* $\mathcal{D}$, *the following holds:*

$$|\Pr\left[\mathcal{D}^{\mathsf{Dec}^{\mathsf{CStO}_H}_{\mathsf{sk},\mathbf{List}},\underline{\mathsf{CStO}_H},\mathcal{E}^{\mathsf{CStO}_H}_{\mathsf{pk}}}(\mathsf{pk})=1:(\mathsf{pk},\mathsf{sk})\leftarrow\mathsf{Gen}(1^\eta),H\xleftarrow{\$}\Omega_H\right]-$$
$$\Pr\left[\mathcal{D}^{\mathsf{Ext}(\mathsf{pk},\mathfrak{D}_H,\mathbf{List}),\underline{\mathsf{CStO}_H},\mathcal{E}^{\mathsf{CStO}_H}_{\mathsf{pk}}}(\mathsf{pk})=1:(\mathsf{pk},\mathsf{sk})\leftarrow\mathsf{Gen}(1^\eta),H\xleftarrow{\$}\Omega_H\right]|\leq \mathit{negl}(\eta).$$

In the definition above, the random oracle H can consist of several random oracles $\{H_i\}_i$ and $H(i,x):=H_i(x)$. However, the first component of a quantum query (the index i) is restricted to be a classical value. In other words, the adversary is not allowed to query all oracles simultaneously by submitting $\sum_{i,x}\alpha_{i,x}|i,k\rangle$. (This restriction is not limiting since in OAEP+, the adversary is allowed to query the random oracles G,H,H' separately).

4   Security of OAEP+

We define OAEP+ transformation below.

Definition 7 (OAEP+). Let $G : \{0,1\}^{k_0} \rightarrow \{0,1\}^n$, $H : \{0,1\}^{n+k_1} \rightarrow \{0,1\}^{k_0}$ and $H' : \{0,1\}^{n+k_0} \rightarrow \{0,1\}^{k_1}$ be random oracles. The encryption scheme $OAEP+ = (\text{Gen}, \text{Enc}, \text{Dec})$ is defined as:

1. Gen: Specifies an instance of the injective function f and its inverse f^{-1}. Therefore, the public key and secret key are f and f^{-1} respectively.
2. Enc: Given a message $m \in \{0,1\}^n$, the encryption algorithm computes

$$ s := (G(r) \oplus m) \| H'(r, m) \quad and \quad t := r \oplus H(s), $$

where $r \xleftarrow{\$} \{0,1\}^{k_0}$, and outputs the ciphertext $c := f(s, t)$.
3. Dec: Given a ciphertext c, the decryption algorithm does the following: Compute $f^{-1}(c) = (s, t)$, query the random oracle H on input s, query the random oracle G on input $t \oplus H(s)$ and compute $m' := [s]^n \oplus G(t \oplus H(s))$. Then, if $H'(t \oplus H(s), m') = [s]_{k_1}$, it returns m', otherwise, it returns $\perp$.

Note that k_0 and k_1 depend on the security parameter n.

We prove that OAEP+ is IND-CCA secure in the quantum random oracle model. First, we show that OAEP+ is plaintext-extractable and use it to show the IND-CCA security.

To show the plaintext-extractability, the overall strategy is to start with a game in which the adversary has access to the actual decryption oracle, define some indistinguishable intermediate games and reach the last game for which the challenger does not use the secret key for decryption.

In the following, the algorithm $\text{Dec}_{f^{-1}}$ is the decryption algorithm of OAEP+ except for the challenge ciphertext c^* that outputs $\perp$. The number of queries to the random oracles G, H, H' is shown by $q_G, q_H, q_{H'}$, respectively, and q_D is the number of decryption queries.

Theorem 1. OAEP+ is plaintext-extractable in the quantum random oracle model.

Proof. **Game 0.** We start with Game 0 in which the quantum polynomial-time distinguisher $\mathcal{D}$ has classical access to the decryption oracle $\text{Dec}_{f^{-1}}$, quantum access to the random oracles G, H, H' and classical access to the encryption oracle $\mathcal{E}_f^{G,H,H'}$.

Game 1. We replace the random oracles G, H, H' with the compressed standard oracles $\text{CStO}_G, \text{CStO}_H, \text{CStO}_{H'}$, respectively. These changes are indistinguishable for the adversary by Lemma 2. Let $\mathfrak{D}_G$, $\mathfrak{D}_H$ and $\mathfrak{D}_{H'}$ denote the databases of these oracles.

Game 2. We modify the decryption oracle $\text{Dec}_{f^{-1}}$ to a decryption oracle $\text{Dec}_{f^{-1}}^{(1)}$ that works as follows. Let $\mathfrak{D}_{H'}$ denotes the database of $\text{CStO}_{H'}$. We define the relation $R_c^{H'}$ to be the set of all $((r, m), H'_{(r,m)})$ such that

$$[[f^{-1}(c)]^{n+k_1}]_{k_1} = H'_{(r,m)}. \tag{2}$$

Given the relation $R_c^{H'}$, the projectors $\Sigma_c^{(r,m)}$ for $(r, m) \in \{0, 1\}^{n+k_0}$ and $\Sigma_c^{\emptyset}$ are defined similar to Eq. (1). Now the measurement

$$\mathbb{M}^{H'} = \{\Sigma_c^{(r,m)}\}_{(r,m) \in \{0,1\}^{n+k_0} \cup \{\emptyset\}}$$

checks if there exists a pair in $\mathfrak{D}_{H'}$ satisfying the relation $R_c^{H'}$ or not. If there is more than one pair satisfying the relation $R_c^{H'}$, the smallest (r, m) will be the output of $\mathbb{M}^{H'}$[2]. If there is no such a pair the output of $\mathbb{M}^{H'}$ is $\emptyset$. Let $\mathbb{M}_{\mathfrak{D}_{H'}, P_{H'}}^c$ be the following purified measurement corresponding to $\mathbb{M}^{H'}$:

$$\mathbb{M}_{\mathfrak{D}_{H'}, P_{H'}}^c |\phi, z\rangle_{\mathfrak{D}_{H'} P_{H'}} \rightarrow \sum_{(r,m) \in \{0,1\}^{n+k_0} \cup \{\emptyset\}} \Sigma_c^{(r,m)} |\phi\rangle_{\mathfrak{D}_{H'}} |z \oplus (r, m)\rangle_{P_{H'}}.$$

Note that $\mathbb{M}_{\mathfrak{D}_{H'}, P_{H'}}^c$ is an involution, that is, $\mathbb{M}_{\mathfrak{D}_{H'}, P_{H'}}^c \mathbb{M}_{\mathfrak{D}_{H'}, P_{H'}}^c = \mathbb{I}$. For each decryption query on an input c, the decryption algorithm $\text{Dec}_{f^{-1}}^{(1)}$ first applies the $\mathbb{M}_{\mathfrak{D}_{H'}, P_{H'}}^c$ unitary with the $P_{H'}$ register initiated with 0. Then it executes $\text{Dec}_{f^{-1}}$. Finally it applies the $\mathbb{M}_{\mathfrak{D}_{H'}, P_{H'}}^c$ again.

$$\text{Dec}_{f^{-1}}^{(1)} = \mathbb{M}_{\mathfrak{D}_{H'}, P_{H'}}^c \text{Dec}_{f^{-1}} \mathbb{M}_{\mathfrak{D}_{H'}, P_{H'}}^c.$$

We show that Game 1 and Game 2 are indistinguishable. Note that we measure the database $\mathfrak{D}_{H'}$ and this measurement might be detectable to the adversary. In order to undo this measurement we apply the measurement again, however, after applying $\text{Dec}_{f^{-1}}$. Since $\text{Dec}_{f^{-1}}$ queries H', the measurement on $\mathfrak{D}_{H'}$ does not commute with $\text{Dec}_{f^{-1}}$, trivially. Therefore, we use Lemma 3 to show that these two almost commute and therefore this measurement is not detectable to the adversary.

Recall that $\Gamma_{R_c^{H'}}$ is the maximum values of $H'_{(r,m)}$ that satisfies the relation (2) where the maximum is taken over inputs (r, m). Since $[f^{-1}(c)]^{n+k_1}$ is a single value given c, $\Gamma_{R_c^{H'}} = 1$. By Lemma 3, $\mathbb{M}_{\mathfrak{D}_{H'}, P_{H'}}^c$ almost commutes with $\text{Dec}_{f^{-1}}$ and the adversary can distinguish these two games with a probability at most $q_D 2^{-k_1/2 + 7/2}$.

Game 3. We modify the decryption oracle $\text{Dec}_{f^{-1}}^{(1)}$ to a decryption oracle $\text{Dec}_{f^{-1}}^{(2)}$ that works as follows. It first applies $\mathbb{M}_{\mathfrak{D}_{H'}, P_{H'}}^c$, if the register $P_{H'}$ is empty, it returns $\perp$, otherwise, it executes $\text{Dec}_{f^{-1}}$. Finally it applies $\mathbb{M}_{\mathfrak{D}_{H'}, P_{H'}}^c$. To show

---

[2] Outputting the smallest (r, m) is a convention to have a correct definition of the projector. Since a random oracle is quantum collision-resistance [17], only with a negligible probability there will be more than one pair satisfying the relation (2).

that these two games are indistinguishable, we show that when the register $P_{H'}$ is empty, the decryption oracle $\text{Dec}_{f^{-1}}^{(1)}$ (or $\text{Dec}_{f^{-1}}$) returns $\perp$ with a high probability. Let assume the adversary submits a decryption query c for which the register $P_{H'}$ is empty, that is, there is no pair $((r,m), H'_{(r,m)})$ in $\mathfrak{D}_{H'}$ such that the relation (2) holds. Let $f^{-1}(c) = (s_c, t_c)$. The decryption algorithm $\text{Dec}_{f^{-1}}$ checks if $H'\left(t_c \oplus H(s_c), [s_c]^n \oplus G(t_c \oplus H(s_c))\right) = [s_c]_{k_1}$ and this equality holds with a probability at most $1/2^{k_1}$ because H' is a random oracle and $\left(t_c \oplus H(s_c), [s_c]^n \oplus G(t_c \oplus H(s_c))\right)$ has not been queried to H' by the adversary since $P_{H'}$ is empty. Overall, the adversary can distinguish these two games with a probability at most $q_D/2^{k_1}$.

Game 4. Let $\mathfrak{D}_G$ denotes the database of CStO_G. We modify the decryption oracle $\text{Dec}_{f^{-1}}^{(2)}$ to a decryption oracle $\text{Dec}_{f^{-1}}^{(3)}$ that on the input c works as follows. It first applies $\mathbb{M}_{\mathfrak{D}_{H'},P_{H'}}^c$, if the register $P_{H'}$ is empty, it returns $\perp$. Otherwise if the register $P_{H'}$ contains a pair (r', m'), it applies a purified measurement $\mathbb{M}^G$ on the database $\mathfrak{D}_G$ that returns 1 if there exists a pair $(r', G_{r'}) \in \mathfrak{D}_G$ such that

$$[[f^{-1}(c)]^{n+k_1}]^n \oplus m' = G_{r'} \tag{3}$$

and returns 0 otherwise. The output of this measurement is stored in the register P_G that starts with $|0\rangle$. Then it applies $\text{Dec}_{f^{-1}}$, $\mathbb{M}^G$ and $\mathbb{M}_{\mathfrak{D}_{H'},P_{H'}}^c$ respectively. (Note that $\mathbb{M}^G$ is defined similar to $\mathbb{M}_{\mathfrak{D}_{H'},P_{H'}}^c$ in Game 2).

In order to show that these two games are indistinguishable, we show that $\text{Dec}_{f^{-1}}$ and $\mathbb{M}^G$ almost commutes. (Then $\mathbb{M}^G$ will cancel out with its second application). By Lemma 3, these two games are indistinguishable with a probability at most $q_D 2^{-n+7/2}$.

Game 5. We modify the decryption oracle $\text{Dec}_{f^{-1}}^{(3)}$ to a decryption oracle $\text{Dec}_{f^{-1}}^{(4)}$ that on the input c works similar to $\text{Dec}_{f^{-1}}^{(3)}$ unless if the output of $\mathbb{M}^G$ is 0, it returns $\perp$.

$$\text{Dec}_{f^{-1}}^{(4)}(c) = \begin{cases} \perp & \text{if } P_{H'} \text{ is empty} \\ \perp & \text{if } P_G \text{ contains } 0 . \\ \text{Dec}_{f^{-1}}(c) & \text{otherwise} \end{cases}$$

In order to show that these two games are indistinguishable, we need to show that the decryption algorithms $\text{Dec}_{f^{-1}}^{(3)}$ and $\text{Dec}_{f^{-1}}^{(4)}$ return the same output with a high probability. If P_G contains 1, both algorithms return $\text{Dec}_{f^{-1}}(c)$. We prove that when P_G contains 0, $\text{Dec}_{f^{-1}}(c)$ is $\perp$ with a high probability. Let $f^{-1}(c) = (s_c, t_c)$. Note that $\text{Dec}_{f^{-1}}$ checks if

$$H'\left(t_c \oplus H(s_c), [s_c]^n \oplus G(t_c \oplus H(s_c))\right) = [s_c]_{k_1}$$

or not. We show that since P_G is 0, the query $\left(t_c \oplus H(s_c), [s_c]^n \oplus G(t_c \oplus H(s_c))\right)$ will be submitted to H' only with a negligible probability. Note that when P_G

is 0 the value $t_c \oplus H(s_c)$ has not been queried to the random oracle G. This means that the adversary has obtained the value $G(t_c \oplus H(s_c))$ without querying $t_c \oplus H(s_c)$ to G. This holds with a probability $1/2^n$.

When $(t_c \oplus H(s_c), [s_c]^n \oplus G(t_c \oplus H(s_c)))$ has not been queried to H', $\text{Dec}_{f^{-1}}$ returns $\perp$ with a probability at least $1 - 1/2^{k_1}$ because H' is a random oracle. Overall, the adversary can distinguish these two games with a negligible probability.

Game 6. Let $\mathfrak{D}_H$ denotes the database of CStO_H. We modify the decryption oracle $\text{Dec}_{f^{-1}}^{(4)}$ to a decryption oracle $\text{Dec}_{f^{-1}}^{(5)}$ that on the input c works as follows. The decryption oracle $\text{Dec}_{f^{-1}}^{(5)}$ is similar to $\text{Dec}_{f^{-1}}^{(4)}$ except if the register $P_{H'}$ is not empty and P_G is not zero it sets $s' = (G_{r'} \oplus m') || H'_{(r',m')}$. Then it applies a purified measurement M^H on the database $\mathfrak{D}_H$ that returns 1 if there exists a pair $(s', H_{s'}) \in \mathfrak{D}_H$ such that

$$H_{s'} = [f^{-1}(c)]_{k_0} \oplus r'. \tag{4}$$

Otherwise it returns 0. The output of this measurement is stored in the register P_H that starts with $|0\rangle$. Note that the measurement M^H is applied again after $\text{Dec}_{f^{-1}}$. By Lemma 3, these two games are indistinguishable with a probability at most $q_D 2^{-k_0+7/2}$. (Note that M^H is defined similar to $\mathsf{M}^c_{\mathfrak{D}_{H'},P_{H'}}$ in Game 2).

Game 7. We modify the decryption oracle $\text{Dec}_{f^{-1}}^{(5)}$ to a decryption oracle $\text{Dec}_{f^{-1}}^{(6)}$ that on the input c works similar to $\text{Dec}_{f^{-1}}^{(5)}$ unless if the output of M^H is 0, it returns $\perp$.

$$\text{Dec}_{f^{-1}}^{(6)}(c) = \begin{cases} \perp & \text{if } P_{H'} \text{ is empty} \\ \perp & \text{if } P_G \text{ contains } 0 \\ \perp & \text{if } P_H \text{ contains } 0 \\ \text{Dec}_{f^{-1}}(c) & \text{otherwise} \end{cases}.$$

In order to show that these two games are indistinguishable, we need to show that the decryption algorithms $\text{Dec}_{f^{-1}}^{(4)}$ and $\text{Dec}_{f^{-1}}^{(5)}$ return the same output with a high probability. If P_H contains 1, both algorithms return $\text{Dec}_{f^{-1}}(c)$. We prove that when P_H contains 0, $\text{Dec}_{f^{-1}}(c)$ is $\perp$ with a high probability. Let $f^{-1}(c) = (s_c, t_c)$. By the relations (2) and (3), we can write

$$s_c = (G_{r'} \oplus m') || H'_{(r',m')} = s'.$$

Since P_H is 0, s_c has not been queried to the random oracle H and therefore $H(s_c)$ remains a uniformly random value from the adversary's perspective. This means that the equality

$$H'\Big(t_c \oplus H(s_c), [s_c]^n \oplus G(t_c \oplus H(s_c))\Big) = [s_c]_{k_1}$$

holds with a probability at most $1/2^{k_1}$. Overall, the adversary is able to distinguish these two games with a probability at most $q_D/2^{k_1}$.

Game 8. In this game, we change $\mathrm{Dec}_{f^{-1}}^{(6)}$ to a decryption oracle $\mathrm{Dec}_f^{(7)}$ that does not use f^{-1} to decrypt. Note that the decryption oracle $\mathrm{Dec}_{f^{-1}}^{(6)}$ uses f^{-1} in the measurements $\mathrm{M}_{\mathfrak{D}_{H'},P_{H'}}^c, \mathrm{M}^G$ and M^H. So instead of applying these measurements, we search over all pairs in $\mathfrak{D}_{H'}$. Namely, for each pair $(r',m') \in \mathfrak{D}_{H'}$, the decryption oracle $\mathrm{Dec}_f^{(7)}$ checks if $(r', G_{r'})$ is in $\mathfrak{D}_G$. If yes, it sets $s' = (G_{r'} \oplus m') \| H'_{(r',m')}$. Then it checks if $(s', H_{s'}) \in \mathfrak{D}_H$. If yes, $\mathrm{Dec}_f^{(7)}$ checks if $c = f(s', r' \oplus H_{s'})$. If the equality holds, it returns m' and aborts. If there is no pair $(r', m') \in \mathfrak{D}_{H'}$ that make the decryption aborts, the output of $\mathrm{Dec}_f^{(4)}$ will be $\perp$.

We show that these decryption algorithms $\mathrm{Dec}_{f^{-1}}^{(6)}$ and $\mathrm{Dec}_f^{(7)}$ are indistinguishable. It is clear that if $P_{H'}$ is empty or one of P_G or P_H registers contain 0 for a ciphertext c, both decryption algorithms return $\perp$. If for a ciphertext c, $P_{H'}$ is not empty and P_G and P_H registers contain 1, this means that the relations (2), (3) and (4) hold for $f^{-1}(c) = (s_c, t_c)$ and a pair $((r', m'), H_{(r',m')}) \in \mathfrak{D}_{H'}$. That is,

$$s' = (G_{r'} \oplus m') \| H_{(r',m')}, \ [s_c]_{k_1} = H'_{(r',m')}, \ [s_c]^n = m' \oplus G_{r'} \text{ and } t_c = H_{s'} \oplus r'.$$

It is clear that $s' = s_c$ and $r' = t_c \oplus H(s_c)$. In this case, $\mathrm{Dec}_f^{(7)}$ returns m'. On the other hand, the decryption algorithm $\mathrm{Dec}_{f^{-1}}$ checks if

$$H'\Big(t_c \oplus H(s_c), [s_c]^n \oplus G(t_c \oplus H(s_c))\Big) = [s_c]_{k_1}$$

and if this equality holds, it returns $[s_c]^n \oplus G(t_c \oplus H(s_c))$. Now it is obvious that $\mathrm{Dec}_{f^{-1}}^{(6)}$ return m' as well. This finishes the proof because $\mathrm{Dec}_f^{(7)}$ does not use f^{-1} to decrypt. □

We use $\mathrm{Dec}_f^{(7)}$ to prove the IND-CCA security of OAEP+ in the quantum random oracle model. The overall strategy is to start with the IND-CCA game, define some indistinguishable intermediate games and reach the last game for which the adversary's success probability is $1/2$.

Theorem 2. *If the underlying permutation is quantum one-way, then the OAEP+ scheme is IND-CCA secure in the quantum random oracle model.*

Proof. We reduce an adversary that attacks in the IND-CCA sense to an adversary $\mathcal{B}$ that inverts the permutation f. Note that in all games below, $\mathrm{CStO}_G, \mathrm{CStO}_H, \mathrm{CStO}_{H'}$ denote the compressed oracles corresponding the random oracles G, H, H', respectively, b is a random bit chosen by the challenger, m_0, m_1 are challenge messages submitted by the adversary, r^* is a uniformly at random element, c^* is the challenge ciphertext that is computed as: $c^* = f(s^*, t^*)$ where $s^* = (G(r^*) \oplus m_b) \| H'(r^*, m_b)$ and $t^* = H(s^*) \oplus r^*$.

Game 0: We start with IND-CCA game in the quantum random oracle model in which the adversary $\mathcal{A}$ wins if it guesses the challenge bit b. Note that we use compressed oracles in this game.

Game 1: We replace the decryption algorithm $\mathrm{Dec}_{f^{-1}}$ with $\mathrm{Dec}_f^{(7)}$ constructed in Theorem 1.

Game 2: This is identical to Game 1, except the challenger measures all the queries to CStO_G and $\mathrm{CStO}_{H'}$ with the projective measurements

$$\mathbb{M}_{r^*} = \{P_1 = |r^*\rangle\langle r^*|, \ P_0 = \mathbb{I} - |r^*\rangle\langle r^*|\}.$$

If the output of $\mathbb{M}_{r^*}$ is 1, it aborts and returns a random bit.

Let q_{G1} and $q_{H'1}$ be the total number of queries submitted to G and H' before the challenge query. Let q_{G2} and $q_{H'2}$ be the total number of queries submitted to G and H' after the challenge query.

If there is no query to CStO_G and $\mathrm{CStO}_{H'}$ with a non-negligible weight on the state $|r^*\rangle$, we can use Lemma 1 (gentle-measurement lemma) to show that these two games are indistinguishable. In more details, let ρ_i is the state of the i-th query and let $\mathbb{M}_{r^*}(\rho_i)$ returns 1 with the probability ϵ_i. By the gentle-measurement lemma, the trace distance between $\mathbb{M}_{r^*}(\rho_i)$ and ρ_i is at most $\sqrt{\epsilon_i} + \epsilon_i$. So overall, these two games are distinguishable with the advantage of at most $2(q_G + q_{H'})\sqrt{\max_i\{\epsilon_i\}}$. Therefore, if $\max_i\{\epsilon_i\}$ is negligible, two games are indistinguishable.

Since r^* is a random value that has not been used before the challenge query $\mathbb{M}_{r^*}(\rho_i)$ returns 1 with a probability at most $1/2^{k_0}$ for any $i \in [q_{G1}+q_{H'1}]$. So the measurements before the challenge query are distinguishable with a probability at most $2(q_{G1} + q_{H'1})\sqrt{2^{-k_0}}$ that is negligible.

It is left to show that the measurements after the challenge query are indistinguishable. Let assume $\mathcal{A}$ makes a query to CStO_G or $\mathrm{CStO}_{H'}$ after the challenge query with a non-negligible weight on $|r^*\rangle$ with a probability ϵ. We can construct an adversary $\mathcal{B}$ that breaks the quantum one-wayness of f. The adversary $\mathcal{B}$ on input $c^*(\ := f(s^*, t^*)$ for uniformly random $s^*, t^*)$, runs $\mathcal{A}$ and guesses randomly in which query r^* will be submitted. The adversary $\mathcal{B}$ chooses a random bit b, chooses i from $[q_{G2} + q_{H'2}]$ uniformly at random and simulates the random oracle queries and decryption oracle queries right until this query. Upon receiving the challenge query from $\mathcal{A}$, the adversary $\mathcal{B}$ sends c^*. We describe $\mathcal{B}$ in more details.

H-Queries. For H-queries, the adversary $\mathcal{B}$ uses CStO_H where H is a random oracle.

Let Find be an operator that on inputs $r, c^*, \mathfrak{D}_H$, checks if there exists a pair (s, H_s) in $\mathfrak{D}_H$ such that $c^* = f(s, r \oplus H_s)$. If there exists such a pair it returns $(1, s)$. Otherwise, it returns $(0, 0^{n+k_1})$. Note that since f is a permutation, the Find unitary either returns $(0, 0^{n+k_1})$ or returns $(1, s^*)$.

G-Queries. Let $\tilde{G}$ be a random oracle with the same domain and co-domain as G. For each query to G, $\mathcal{B}$ first applies Find operator with an ancillary register $Q_{b'}Q_s$ of $(1 + n + k_1)$ qubits initiated with zero. Then, if the query is conducted before the challenge query or the $Q_{b'}$ is set to 0, it forwards the query to $\mathrm{CStO}_{\tilde{G}}$, otherwise, it XORs $m_b \oplus [s^*]^n$ to the output register:

$$G : |r, y\rangle|\mathfrak{D}_H\rangle \rightarrow \begin{cases} |r, y \oplus \tilde{G}(r)\rangle & \text{if } m_b \text{ is not defined} \\ |r, y \oplus \tilde{G}(r)\rangle & \text{if } \mathsf{Find}(r, c^*, \mathfrak{D}_H) = (0, 0^{n+k_1}) \\ |r, y \oplus (m_b \oplus [s^*]^n)\rangle & \text{if } \mathsf{Find}(r, c^*, \mathfrak{D}_H) = (1, s^*) \end{cases}.$$

And finally it applies the Find operator again. Since f is a permutation, there exists only one r such that $c^* = f(s^*, r \oplus H_{s^*})$ and that is r^*. For any $r \neq r^*$ the oracle G and the random oracle $\tilde{G}$ are the same. Recall that the adversary $\mathcal{B}$ guesses that a query with a non-negligible weight on $|r^*\rangle$ occurs in the i-th query. (This holds with a non-negligible probability $\epsilon/(q_{G2} + q_{H'2})$). Therefore, the simulation of G-queries is indistinguishable from a random oracle $\tilde{G}$ right before the i-th query.

H'-Queries. Let $\tilde{H}$ be a random oracle with the same domain and co-domain as H'. For each query $|r, m\rangle$, $\mathcal{B}$ first applies Find operator with an ancillary register $Q_{b'}Q_s$ of $(1 + n + k_1)$ qubits initiated with zero. Then, if the query is conducted before the challenge query or the $Q_{b'}$ is set to 0 or $m \neq m_b$, it forwards the query to $\mathsf{CStO}_{\tilde{H}}$, otherwise, it XORs $[s^*]_{k_0}$ to the output register:

$$H' : |r, m, y\rangle|\mathfrak{D}_H\rangle \rightarrow \begin{cases} |r, m, y \oplus \tilde{H}(r, m)\rangle & \text{if } m_b \text{ is not defined} \\ |r, m, y \oplus \tilde{H}(r, m)\rangle & \text{if } \mathsf{Find}(r, c^*, \mathfrak{D}_H) = (0, 0^{n+k_1}) \\ |r, m, y \oplus \tilde{H}(r, m)\rangle & \text{if } \mathsf{Find}(r, c^*, \mathfrak{D}_H) = (1, s^*) \wedge m \neq m_b \\ |r, m, y \oplus [s^*]_{k_1}\rangle & \text{if } \mathsf{Find}(r, c^*, \mathfrak{D}_H) = (1, s^*) \wedge m = m_b \end{cases}.$$

Similar to above, the simulation of H'-queries is indistinguishable from $\tilde{H}$ for queries right before the i-th query.

The Challenge Query. Upon receiving m_0 and m_1 from $\mathcal{A}$, the adversary $\mathcal{B}$ returns c^* as the challenge ciphertext. Note that the way we simulate G-queries and H'-queries, $G(r^*) := m_b \oplus [s^*]^n$, $H'(r^*, m_b) = [s^*]_{k_1}$ and $c^* = f(s^*, r^* \oplus H_{S^*})$ that is a perfect simulation of the challenge query.

Decryption Queries. $\mathcal{B}$ uses the oracle $\mathsf{Dec}_f^{(7)}$ on inputs $\mathfrak{D}_H$, $\mathfrak{D}_{\tilde{G}}$ and $\mathfrak{D}_{\tilde{H}}$ for the decryption queries. Note that we reprogram G and H' only on the input r^* for which $c^* = (s^*, r^* \oplus H_{s^*})$. Since $\mathsf{Dec}_f^{(4)}$ on input c^* does not use its database and returns $\perp$, the simulation of the decryption queries is perfect.

Output of $\mathcal{B}$. The adversary $\mathcal{B}$ measures the i-th random oracle query to CStO_G or $\mathsf{CStO}_{H'}$ with $\mathbb{M}_{r^*}$. Then, the adversary searches over the database $\mathfrak{D}_H$ to find a pair (s^*, H_{s^*}) such that $c^* = f(s^*, r^* \oplus H_{s^*})$. If it finds such a pair, it returns $(s^*, r^* \oplus H_{s^*})$ as the inverse of f on c^* and aborts. Otherwise, it returns $s^* = (\tilde{G}(r^*) \oplus m_b)||\tilde{H}(r^*, m_b)$ and $r^* \oplus H(s^*)$ as the inverse of f on the input c^*. Note that when there is no pair (s^*, H_{s^*}) in $\mathfrak{D}_H$ such that $c^* = f(s^*, r^* \oplus H_{s^*})$, that is $\mathsf{Find}(r^*, c^*, \mathfrak{D}_H) = (0, 0^{n+k_1})$, the G-queries and H'-queries are answered with the random oracle $\tilde{G}$ and $\tilde{H}$, respectively. Therefore, the equation $c^* = f(x, r^* \oplus H(x))$ holds for $x = (\tilde{G}(r^*) \oplus m_b)||\tilde{H}(r^*, m_b)$. Overall, the adversary $\mathcal{B}$ can break the one-wayness of f with probability at least $\epsilon/(q_{G2} + q_{H'2})$. Since f is quantum one-way, ϵ is negligible and this means Game 1 and Game 2 are indistinguishable.

Now, it is clear that Game 2 returns 1 with the probability $1/2$ because if one of the measurements returns 1, the output of the game is a random bit. If none of the measurements return 1, $G(r^*)$ and $H'(r^*, m_b)$ remain an uniformly random value for $\mathcal{A}$ and consequently $m_b \oplus G(r^*)$ is an uniformly random value for $\mathcal{A}$. So the probability that $\mathcal{A}$ guesses b is $1/2$. Finally, since each two consecutive games are indistinguishable, the probability that $\mathcal{A}$ guesses b in Game 0 is $1/2 + \mathsf{negl}(n)$ and this finishes the proof of the theorem. $\qquad\Box$

5   Conclusion and Future Direction

In this paper, we show that a weaker notion than PA2 (our plaintext-extractability notion) is sufficient to show the IND-CCA security when the reduction adversary tries to invert an injective function. We show the IND-CCA security of OAEP+ in QROM by first showing that OAEP+ is plaintext-extractable in QROM.

We argue that OAEP+ might even satisfy a stronger notion of plaintext-extractability, namely, the post-quantum PA2 introduced in [10]. Our high-level argument is that since the random oracle H' is used to sew the randomness and the message inside of the ciphertext, an adversary to attack PA2 might fail to output a valid ciphertext for which its corresponding plaintext is unknown to the adversary due to unpredictability of H'. We leave detailed investigation of this claim as a future work.

In addition, we leave investigating the security of OAEP+ with respect to a quantum IND-CCA notion that allows quantum challenge queries [7] as a future direction. (Note that the IND-qCCA scrutiny [5] of OAEP+ will follow with minor modification to our proof. The IND-qCCA is a notion with classical challenge queries and quantum decryption queries).

Acknowledgment. We would like to thank anonymous reviewers for their useful comments and suggestions.

References

1. Bellare, M., Desai, A., Pointcheval, D., Rogaway, P.: Relations among notions of security for public-key encryption schemes. In: Krawczyk, H. (ed.) CRYPTO 1998. LNCS, vol. 1462, pp. 26–45. Springer, Heidelberg (1998). https://doi.org/10.1007/BFb0055718
2. Bellare, M., Palacio, A.: Towards plaintext-aware public-key encryption without random oracles. In: Lee, P.J. (ed.) ASIACRYPT 2004. LNCS, vol. 3329, pp. 48–62. Springer, Heidelberg (2004). https://doi.org/10.1007/978-3-540-30539-2_4
3. Bellare, M., Rogaway, P.: Random oracles are practical: a paradigm for designing efficient protocols. In: Denning, D.E., Pyle, R., Ganesan, R., Sandhu, R.S., Ashby, V. (eds.) Proceedings of the 1st ACM Conference on Computer and Communications Security, CCS 1993, Fairfax, Virginia, USA, 3–5 November 1993, pp. 62–73. ACM (1993)

4. Bellare, M., Rogaway, P.: Optimal asymmetric encryption. In: De Santis, A. (ed.) EUROCRYPT 1994. LNCS, vol. 950, pp. 92–111. Springer, Heidelberg (1995). https://doi.org/10.1007/BFb0053428

5. Boneh, D., Zhandry, M.: Secure signatures and chosen ciphertext security in a quantum computing world. In: Canetti, R., Garay, J.A. (eds.) CRYPTO 2013. LNCS, vol. 8043, pp. 361–379. Springer, Heidelberg (2013). https://doi.org/10.1007/978-3-642-40084-1_21

6. Boneh, D., Dagdelen, Ö., Fischlin, M., Lehmann, A., Schaffner, C., Zhandry, M.: Random oracles in a quantum world. In: Lee, D.H., Wang, X. (eds.) ASIACRYPT 2011. LNCS, vol. 7073, pp. 41–69. Springer, Heidelberg (2011). https://doi.org/10.1007/978-3-642-25385-0_3

7. Chevalier, C., Ebrahimi, E., Vu, Q.H.: On security notions for encryption in a quantum world. In: Isobe, T., Sarkar, S. (eds.) INDOCRYPT 2022. LNCS, vol. 13774, pp. 593–613. Springer, Cham (2022). https://doi.org/10.1007/978-3-031-22912-1_26

8. Don, J., Fehr, S., Majenz, C., Schaffner, C.: Online-extractability in the quantum random-oracle model. In: Dunkelman, O., Dziembowski, S. (eds.) EUROCRYPT 2022. LNCS, vol. 13277, pp. 677–706. Springer, Cham (2022). https://doi.org/10.1007/978-3-031-07082-2_24

9. Ebrahimi, E.: Post-quantum security of plain OAEP transform. In: Hanaoka, G., Shikata, J., Watanabe, Y. (eds.) PKC 2022. LNCS, vol. 13177, pp. 34–51. Springer, Cham (2022). https://doi.org/10.1007/978-3-030-97121-2_2

10. Ebrahimi, E., van Wier, J.: Post-quantum plaintext-awareness. In: Cheon, J.H., Johansson, T. (eds.) PQCrypto 2022. LNCS, vol. 13512, pp. 260–285. Springer, Cham (2022). https://doi.org/10.1007/978-3-031-17234-2_13

11. Fujisaki, E., Okamoto, T., Pointcheval, D., Stern, J.: RSA-OAEP is secure under the RSA assumption. J. Cryptol. 17(2), 81–104 (2004)

12. Nielsen, M.A., Chuang, I.L.: Quantum Computation and Quantum Information, 10th Anniversary edn. Cambridge University Press (2016)

13. Shor, P.W.: Polynomial-time algorithms for prime factorization and discrete logarithms on a quantum computer. SIAM J. Comput. 26(5), 1484–1509 (1997)

14. Shoup, V.: OAEP reconsidered. In: Kilian, J. (ed.) CRYPTO 2001. LNCS, vol. 2139, pp. 239–259. Springer, Heidelberg (2001). https://doi.org/10.1007/3-540-44647-8_15

15. Targhi, E.E., Unruh, D.: Post-quantum security of the Fujisaki-Okamoto and OAEP transforms. In: Hirt, M., Smith, A. (eds.) TCC 2016. LNCS, vol. 9986, pp. 192–216. Springer, Heidelberg (2016). https://doi.org/10.1007/978-3-662-53644-5_8

16. Winter, A.J.: Coding theorem and strong converse for quantum channels. IEEE Trans. Inf. Theory 45(7), 2481–2485 (1999)

17. Zhandry, M.: A note on the quantum collision and set equality problems. Quantum Inf. Comput. 15(7&8), 557–567 (2015)

18. Zhandry, M.: How to record quantum queries, and applications to quantum indifferentiability. In: Boldyreva, A., Micciancio, D. (eds.) CRYPTO 2019. LNCS, vol. 11693, pp. 239–268. Springer, Cham (2019). https://doi.org/10.1007/978-3-030-26951-7_9

Farasha: A Provable Permutation-Based Parallelizable PRF

Najwa Aaraj[1], Emanuele Bellini[1], Ravindra Jejurikar[1(✉)], Marc Manzano[2,3], Raghvendra Rohit[1], and Eugenio Salazar[1]

[1] Cryptography Research Centre, Technology Innovation Institute, Abu Dhabi, UAE
{najwa.aaraj,emanuele.bellini,ravindra.jejurikar,raghvendra.rohit,
eugenio.salazar}@tii.ae
[2] SandboxAQ, Palo Alto, CA, USA
marc@sandboxaq.com
[3] Electronics and Computing Department, Faculty of Engineering,
Mondragon Unibertsitatea, Mondragon, Spain

Abstract. The pseudorandom function Farfalle, proposed by Bertoni *et al.* at ToSC 2017, is a permutation based arbitrary length input and output PRF. At its core are the public permutations and feedback shift register based rolling functions. Being an elegant and parallelizable design, it is surprising that the security of Farfalle has been only investigated against generic cryptanalysis techniques such as differential/linear and algebraic attacks and nothing concrete about its provable security is known. To fill this gap, in this work, we propose Farasha, a new permutation-based parallelizable PRF with provable security. Farasha can be seen as a simple and provable Farfalle-like construction where the rolling functions in the compression and expansion phases of Farfalle are replaced by a uniform almost xor universal (ΛXU) and a simple counter, respectively. We then prove that in the random permutation model, the compression phase of Farasha can be shown to be an uniform AXU function and the expansion phase can be mapped to an Even-Mansour block cipher. Consequently, combining these two properties, we show that Farasha achieves a security of $\min\{$keysize, permutation size$/2\}$. Finally, we provide concrete instantiations of Farasha with AXU functions providing different performance trade-offs. We believe our work will bring new insights in further understanding the provable security of Farfalle-like constructions.

Keywords: Pseudo random function · Farfalle · Almost xor universal function

1 Introduction

Designing a cryptographic primitive which is parallelizable and at the same time offers provable security bounds requires a holistic approach. The simplest example of such a design is Parallelizable Message Authentication Code (PMAC),

B. Smith and H. Wu (Eds.): SAC 2022, LNCS 13742, pp. 437–458, 2024.
https://doi.org/10.1007/978-3-031-58411-4_20

proposed by Black and Rogaway, which is based on the Hash-then-PRF design paradigm [14]. The same design principle with variations is later adopted in authenticated encryption (AE) modes based on (tweakable) block ciphers. Some of the examples include OCB [38], GCM [26,33], SIV [39], OCB-3 and ΘCB-3 [32], OTR [34], Deoxys-II [31] and SCT [37], to name a few.

Although parallelizable and provable, the aforesaid AE modes based on (tweakable) block ciphers employ a (tweakable) secret permutation as the core primitive. In order to have a mode which depends on an unkeyed cryptographic permutation rather than a (tweakable) secret permutation, Bertoni et al. introduced sponge functions [10].

Initially, the sponge construction was proposed for the Keccak hash function [11], but later gained popularity because of its versatility in providing multiple cryptographic functionalities such as hash, authenticated encryption with associated data (AEAD), MAC or pseudo random number generator (PRNG) [8,9,12] using a single permutation. As such, researchers focused on designing unkeyed cryptographically secure permutations (the so-called permutation-based crypto) rather than designing an individual mode. Numerous cryptographic primitives based on sponge construction have thus been proposed, with their security thoroughly analyzed. Examples of hash functions include Photon [30], Spongent [15] and Quark [1], while Ascon [23], Norx [2], Ketje [6], Gimli [5], Subterranean-AE [22], Xoodyak [20] and Elephant [13] are few examples of AEAD schemes.

Albeit versatile, the sponge-based primitives are inherently sequential and therefore not able to exploit available parallelism on high-end CPUs. At ToSC 2017, Bertoni et al. [7] proposed Farfalle, a parallel counterpart of sponge functions. It is an arbitrary length input and output pseudo random function (also referred to as a deck function [19]) by design and modes have been built on top of it. Figure 1a shows the high level description of Farfalle that uses public permutations denoted as p_b, p_c, p_d and p_e for the different stages of the construction. It takes a secret key K and a sequence of data blocks $M_{1,1}, \cdots, M_{1,\ell_{M_1}}$ as inputs (corresponding to message M_1) and outputs a sequence of keystream blocks $Z_{1,1}, \cdots, Z_{1,\ell_{Z_1}}$. The feedback shift register based rolling functions $roll_c$ and $roll_e$ (denoted by a circular arc within a square in Fig. 1a) are used for parallelism in the compression and expansion phases. An output block is computed by masking the permutation p_e output with a rolled key K''.

While the designers of Farfalle provided its security analysis based on unpredictability of state values and generating affine subspaces at the input of p_c, periodicity of rolling functions, differential/linear cryptanalysis and meet-in-the-middle attacks, a security proof for the construction is missing. Very recently, Dobraunig et al. [24] proposed a construction resembling Farfalle, but again it lacks a security proof. Thus, it is worth questioning whether Farfalle can be modified to a new construction which is provable and can simultaneously achieve all the benefits of Farfalle. In this work, we confirm the feasibility of the latter question through our proposed construction Farasha. In what follows, we first briefly describe our design approach in moving from Farfalle to Farasha and we then list our contributions.

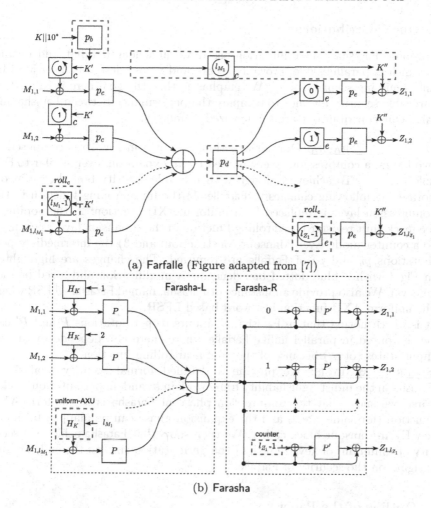

(a) Farfalle (Figure adapted from [7])

(b) Farasha

Fig. 1. A high level overview of Farfalle and Farasha

1.1 Design Rationale of Farasha

In Fig. 1a, a simple but careful observation depicts that Farfalle can alternatively be viewed as a composition of a parallel keyed hash construction (up to the input of p_d) and a parallel PRF construction (from p_d to the PRF output), which is similar to the well-known Hash-then-PRF composition for constructing a PRF. We focus on similar building blocks to construct a permutation-based parallelizable PRF with provable security. Our main idea is to extend the well-known parallelizable keyed hash algorithm [14] to a public permutation and then combine it with the permutation based CTR-mode PRF [3,4].

1.2   Our Contributions

We propose Farasha[1], a permutation-based variable length input and output PRF which is parallelizable, provably secure and whose design is motivated by Farfalle's missing security proof. We emphasize that the goal here is to analyze the provable security and not to compare the performance between Farasha and Farfalle. Our contributions are summarized as follows.

1. DESIGN OF FARASHA: Our construction as shown in Fig. 1b is composed of two layers: a compression layer followed by an expansion layer similar to Farfalle(Fig. 1a). To achieve a design with provable security bounds, we incorporate the following changes to Farfalle: 1) the linear rolling function in the compression layer is replaced by a uniform AXU function; 2) the nonlinear feedback shift register based rolling function in the expansion layer is changed to a counter mode Even-Mansour construction; and 3) the intermediate permutations p_b and p_d of Farfalle are removed. The changes are highlighted in Fig. 1 with a blue dotted box denoting a modification and a red one for removal. We also provide an instance of Farasha, named Farasha-wLFSR where the uniform AXU function is a word based LFSR.

    It is worth noting that in Farasha, all inputs to permutations P and P' can be computed in parallel unlike Farfalle where there is a dependency among input states (of p_e) because of the nonlinear rolling function.

2. SECURITY ANALYSIS: We provide a detailed formal security analysis of Farasha in the indistinguishability framework in a random permutation model. First, we show that the compression phase of Farasha is a ϵ-uniform-AXU function (for some $\epsilon > 0$) and the expansion phase can be mapped to multi-key Even-Mansour block cipher. We then show that Farasha achieves a security of minimum of keysize or half the permutation size. In the end, we give insights on the security of Farfalle.

1.3   Outline of the Paper

The rest of the paper is organized as follows. In Sect. 2, we define our notation and give a brief overview of the security model and keyed hash functions. Section 3 presents the design of Farasha along with its salient features. We provide the security analysis of Farasha in Sect. 4. In Sect. 5, we provide a discussion on improved security of Farasha, the choice of AXU functions and their performance trade-offs, and insights on the security of Farfalle. Finally, we conclude the paper in Sect. 6.

2   Preliminaries

In this section, we describe the notation used throughout the paper, our security model, and some well-known constructions which are relevant to this work.

---

[1] Farasha means butterfly in Arabic.

2.1   Notation and Security Model

Fix $n, m \in \mathbb{N}$. We use $\{0,1\}^n$ and $\{0,1\}^*$ to denote the set of all bit strings of length n and variable length bit strings, respectively. For any $X \in \{0,1\}^*$, $|X|$ denotes the length of X in bits. The size of a set S is also denoted by $|S|$ if the meaning is clear from the context. We use $X_1, \cdots, X_u \xleftarrow{n} X$ to denote the n-bit block partitioning of X where $|X_i| = n$ for $1 \le i \le u-1$ and $1 \le |X_u| \le n$. Also, $pad_n(X)$ denotes the bit string obtained by appending X with 1, followed by 0's, so that its length becomes the nearest multiple of n. For $X, Y \in \{0,1\}^n$, $X \oplus Y$ and $X\|Y$ denote the bitwise XOR and concatenation operators, respectively. By $X \leftarrow\!\$ \{0,1\}^n$, we mean X is picked uniformly at random from the set $\{0,1\}^n$. Further, $\mathsf{Perm}(n)$ denotes the set of all n-bit permutations while $\mathsf{Func}(n, m)$ refers to the set of all n-bit to m-bit functions. For $n = m$, we write $\mathsf{Func}(n, n)$ as $\mathsf{Func}(n)$. We define $\mathsf{msb}_i(X)$ as the leftmost i bits of a string X. Finally, $\Pr[X = x]$ denotes the probability that a random variable X takes value x.

For our security analysis, we consider an adversary $\mathcal{A}$ which is an algorithm that is given access to one or more oracles $\mathcal{O}$. After interacting with $\mathcal{O}$, it outputs a bit $w \in \{0,1\}$. We denote this event by $\mathcal{A}^{\mathcal{O}} \mapsto w$. We always consider computationally unbounded adversaries, i.e., their computational time is always measured in terms of number of oracle queries (say q). For any two oracles $\mathcal{O}$ and $\mathcal{P}$, the advantage of distinguishing $\mathcal{O}$ from $\mathcal{P}$ is then defined as

$$\mathsf{Adv}_{\mathcal{O}}^{\mathcal{P}}(\mathcal{A}, q) := \Big| \Pr[\mathcal{A}^{\mathcal{O}} \mapsto 1] - \Pr[\mathcal{A}^{\mathcal{P}} \mapsto 1] \Big|. \tag{1}$$

2.2   Keyed Hash Functions

Let $k, t \in \mathbb{N}$ and $\epsilon > 0$. A keyed hash function H is a deterministic algorithm from $\{0,1\}^k \times \{0,1\}^* \to \{0,1\}^t$ with $H(K, M) = T$. For a fixed key K, we denote it by H_K. We now state some relevant definitions related to the keyed hash functions (adapted from [16][Section 7.1 and 7.2]).

Definition 1. *[Almost XOR Universal Hash Function (AXU)] Let $\Delta \in \{0,1\}^t$. We say H_K is ϵ-AXU if for any two distinct messages M and M', we have*

$$\Pr[K \leftarrow\!\$ \{0,1\}^k \mid H_K(M) \oplus H_K(M') = \Delta] \le \epsilon \tag{2}$$

Definition 2. *[Uniform Hash Function] Let $\Delta \in \{0,1\}^t$. We say H_K is ϵ-uniform if for any message M, the following holds:*

$$\Pr[K \leftarrow\!\$ \{0,1\}^k \mid H_K(M) = \Delta] \le \epsilon \tag{3}$$

Definition 3. *[Uniform AXU Function] We say H_K is ϵ-uniform-AXU if H_K is both ϵ-uniform and ϵ-AXU.*

Note that in the above definitions, the number of queries is not present. Accordingly, to formulate the security of H_K (which usually relies on the hash output being secret) against adversaries with q queries, we define the distinguishing game setup for each of these definition and give its adversarial advantage.

Adversarial Setup for H_K as an AXU. Here the goal of the adversary is to find the Xor-difference of the hash of two messages. For the security of the secret key, hash values are always kept secret (typically via encryption) and this process is often referred to as a blinding operation on the hash. The blinding operation is modelled with the help of a random oracle: a function that returns an independent random value for every new input.

For a query of the form (M, Δ), the responses of the oracles are as follows.

- Real world $\mathcal{O}$: Here, the key $K \leftarrow\!\!{\scriptstyle\$} \{0,1\}^k$ is sampled along with a secret random oracle $\mathcal{RO}_1$;. The challenger returns $\mathcal{RO}_1(H_K(M) \oplus \Delta)$.
- Ideal world $\mathcal{P}$: $\mathcal{RO}_2(M, \Delta)$ with a secret random oracle $\mathcal{RO}_2$.

For an adversary $\mathcal{A}$ making q queries, the advantage is given by

$$\mathsf{Adv}_H^{\mathrm{axu}}(\mathcal{A}, q) := \left| \Pr\left[\mathcal{A}^{\mathcal{O}} \mapsto 1\right] - \Pr\left[\mathcal{A}^{\mathcal{P}} \mapsto 1\right] \right| \tag{4}$$

Note that Eq. 4 is identical to the *blinded key hash (bhk)* model defined in [29].

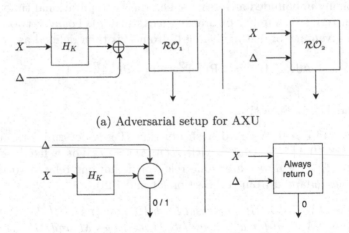

(a) Adversarial setup for AXU

(b) Adversarial setup for uniformity

Fig. 2. Adversarial setups for keyed-hash functions

Adversarial Setup for H_K as Uniform Function. Here the adversary's goal is to find a message along with its hash-value and a query is of the form (X, Δ). The real world oracle returns whether $H_K(X) = \Delta$ is true or false. The ideal world always returns false as shown in Fig. 2b. The advantage is defined as,

$$\mathsf{Adv}_H^{\mathrm{uni}}(\mathcal{A}, q) := \left| \Pr\left[K \leftarrow\!\!{\scriptstyle\$} \{0,1\}^k \mid H_K(M_i) = \Delta\right] \right| \tag{5}$$

Adversarial Setup for H_K as a Uniform-AXU. Here the adversary is given access to both oracles, that of an AXU function and a uniform function, and the goal is to distinguish the real world from the ideal world.

2.3   Even-Mansour Block Cipher

The Even-Mansour (EM) construction [27], builds a b-bit block cipher from a b-bit public permutation P. The original construction (dual key Even-Mansour), based on a pair of b-bit keys K_1 and K_2, is defined as $E^P_{K_1,K_2}(M) = P(M \oplus K_1) \oplus K_2$ where M is a b-bit message. Dunkelman *et al.* [25] showed that the original EM scheme is not minimal in terms of key size and they presented the Single-key Even-Mansour (SEM) block cipher with the same security level. The single key Even-Mansour (SEM) is given by $E^P_K(M) = P(M \oplus K) \oplus K$.

SEM in Multi-key Setting with Independent Keys. The security bounds of SEM in the multi-key setting is given by Theorem 1.

Theorem 1 (Security of Multi-key EM [35]). *In a multi-key setting with μ EM block-cipher instances with μ independent keys, the distinguishing advantage of an adversary is bounded by*

$$\mathsf{Adv}^{\mathrm{prp}}_{EM}(\mathcal{A}, \sigma, \mu) \leq \frac{\sigma^2}{2^b} + \frac{2\sigma q_p}{2^b} \tag{6}$$

where σ is the total number of construction queries (across all μ instances) and q_p is the number of primitive queries to P.

SEM in the Modified Key Setting. In contrast to μ independent keys as in Theorem 1, we consider keys which are the output of an ϵ-uniform-AXU keyed hash function H_K, where $K \twoheadleftarrow\$ \{0,1\}^k$. Figure 3 depicts this setting and we provide a security proof of SEM with these multiple keys in Theorem 2.

Theorem 2 (Security of SEM in the modified key setting). *Let $\epsilon, k > 0$, $K \twoheadleftarrow\$ \{0,1\}^k$ and $H_K : \{0,1\}^k \times \{0,1\}^\star \to \{0,1\}^k$ be a ϵ-uniform-AXU. Consider μ SEM instances with keys $K_i = H_K(M_i)$ for $i = 1, \cdots, \mu$. Then, in a multi-key setting, the distinguishing advantage of an adversary is bounded by*

$$\mathsf{Adv}^{\mathrm{prp}}_{EM}(\mathcal{A}, \sigma, \mu) \leq \sigma^2 \epsilon + 2\sigma q_p \epsilon \tag{7}$$

where σ is the total number of construction queries (across all μ instances) and q_p is the number of primitive queries to P.

Proof. The proof is analogous to the proof of Theorem 1 and details are provided in Appendix A.3 for completeness.

Corollary 1. *Theorem 2 can be trivially extended to the dual-key variant of EM cipher.*

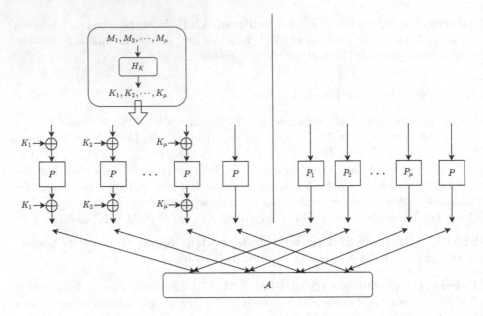

Fig. 3. Multi-key SEM game setup in the modified key setting

2.4   PRP-PRF Switching

To bound the advantage of an multiple EM block cipher as a PRF, we extend the PRP-PRF switching lemma [18] to the multi-key setting as follows.

Lemma 1. *The advantage of switching μ independent PRPs to PRFs is bounded by*

$$\mathsf{Adv}_{prp}^{prf}(\mathcal{A}, \sigma, \mu) \leq \frac{\sigma^2}{2} \frac{1}{2^b} \tag{8}$$

where σ is the total number of queries to μ PRP instances.

3   Farasha Specification and Features

In this section, we formally introduce Farasha - a PRF with provable security bounds. We describe its building blocks and one of the instance. We also highlight the salient features of Farasha by comparing it with Farfalle.

3.1   The Farasha PRF

Farasha is a variable length input and variable length output PRF. As shown in Fig. 1 (dashed boxes), Farasha consists of two layers[2], namely Farasha-L and

---

[2] Farasha means butterfly in Arabic. Here Farasha-L and Farasha-R correspond to the left and right wing of a butterfly, respectively.

Farasha-R. The core components of these layers include (1) public permutations P and P' which operate on a b-bit state; and (2) a fixed input-size keyed hash function H that takes as input a counter and a secret key K of length k satisfying $k \leq b$ and outputs a b-bit message digest. We now explain Farasha-L and Farasha-R in detail.

3.1.1   Description of Farasha-L

In a nutshell, Farasha-L is a compression function similar to the compression layer of Farfalle. We simply abstract the linear rolling function of Farfalle (see Fig. 1a) to a keyed hash function which is a uniform-AXU. Let $M_i \in \{0,1\}^*$ be the i-th input message. Let $\ell_{M_i} \geq 1$ such that $(M_{i,1}, \cdots, M_{i,\ell_{M_i}}) \overset{b}{\leftarrow} pad_b(M_i)$. For a fixed key K, denote the keyed hash function by $H_K(\cdot)$. Then Farasha-L computes a b-bit secret state X_i by first applying the function $P \circ H_K$ to ℓ_{M_i} blocks of message M_i in parallel and then computing the XORed value of outputs. Formally, we have $X_i = \bigoplus_{j=1}^{\ell_{M_i}} P(H_K(j) \oplus M_{i,j})$. An algorithmic description of Farasha-L is provided in Algorithm 1.

Algorithm 1: Farasha-L

Input: k-bit secret key K with $k \leq b$; message M_i with
$\qquad (M_{i,1}, \cdots, M_{i,\ell_{M_i}}) \overset{b}{\leftarrow} pad_b(M_i)$
Output: $X_i \in \{0,1\}^b$
1 $X_i \leftarrow 0^b$
2 **for** $j = 1$ *to* ℓ_{M_i} **do**
3 $\quad \mid \quad X_i \leftarrow X_i \oplus P(H_K(j) \oplus M_{i,j})$
4 **end**
5 **return** X_i

3.1.2   Description of Farasha-R

Farasha-R is a fixed input and variable length output PRF analogous to Farfalle (see Fig. 1a). The output of Farasha-L is used as the key for Farasha-R, such that each Farasha-R invocation has a different key (using a different input message). We modify the expansion layer of Farfalle to the counter-mode based Even-Mansour-like construction as follows. Let X_i be the output of Farasha-L corresponding to the message M_i. Further, let N be the required number of PRF output bits with $\ell_{Z_i} = \lceil \frac{N}{b} \rceil$. For $1 \leq j \leq \ell_{Z_i}$, we compute the j-th output block as $Z_{i,j} \leftarrow X_i \oplus P'(X_i \oplus (j - 1))$. Note that for the last output block, we do the truncation if N is not a multiple of b. The entire procedure is illustrated in Algorithm 2.

3.2   Farasha-wLFSR: An Instance of Farasha

We present an instances of Farasha, where H_K is an LFSR. We call this instance as Farasha-wLFSR. For the concrete LSFR, we consider word-based ones, using

Algorithm 2: Farasha-R

Input: b-bit secret state X_i

Output: N bits of PRF with $\ell_{Z_i} = \lceil \frac{N}{b} \rceil$

1 $Z_i \leftarrow \varepsilon$

2 for $j = 1$ to ℓ_{Z_i} do

3 $Z_{i,j} \leftarrow X_i \oplus P'(X_i \oplus (j-1))$

4 $Z_i \leftarrow Z_i || Z_{i,j}$

5 end

6 return $\mathsf{msb}_N(Z_i)$

---

the method described in [28]. Consider an LSFR with state size of 256 bits arranged into 4 64-bit words, initialised with as $S_0 = K$. If $S_j = (x_0, x_1, x_2, x_3)$ is the state at time j, then the next state S_{j+1} is computed as

$$S_{j+1} = (x_1, x_2, x_3, (x_0 \lll 3) \oplus (x_3 \ggg 5)). \tag{9}$$

Note that this LFSR initialized with $S_0 = K$, is shown to be a uniform AXU [17,28].

3.3   Salient Features of Farasha

Our main goal while designing Farasha is to have a parallel permutation-based PRF construction with provable security. In addition to achieving this goal, Farasha, by design, incorporates the following salient features.

Simple and Versatile Design. Farasha is a simple construction with fewer building blocks compared to Farfalle. The utilized uniform AXUs in Farasha-L could be versatile and platform-specific rather than a specific LFSR based rolling function in Farfalle. The permutation p_d and function $roll_e$ are required in the Farfalle expansion phase to augment the non-linearity provided by a limited rounds permutation p_e (e.g. Xoodoo[6] in Xoofff). With p_e replaced by a random permutation, these two components can be replaced with a simple counter as in a CTR-mode PRF design.

Independent Input States in Farasha-R. An LFSR based compression phases in both Farasha and Farfalle can be mapped to matrix multiplication operations, enabling independent computations for all input blocks to permutation P. The same holds true for inputs to P' in the expansion phase of Farasha, which uses a simple counter addition. On the other hand, Farfalle uses a non-linear function $roll_e$, which introduces a dependency amongst the inputs in the expansion phase. The independence of states in the expansion phase gives an additional advantage for Farasha in terms of implementation (for example, multi-CPU implementation).

Small State Size. Farfalle requires $3b$ bits of state registers in both the compression and expansion phases. For Farasha, the state size required for the two phases is $k + 2b$ and $2b$, respectively. Overall, the state size of Farasha is smaller than Farfalle.

4   Security Analysis of Farasha

In this section, we discuss the security of Farasha in a single-user setting and show that it is birthday-bound secure. We start this section by explaining our adversarial setup. Next, we state our main result in Theorem 3 and provide its security proof. Before proceeding to the proofs, we recall some notations which will be used throughout this section.

Notation. Let $\epsilon > 0$, $t \geq 0$ and $k, b \in \mathbb{N}$ with $k \leq b$. Fix $\mathcal{K} = \{0,1\}^k$ and $\mathcal{Y} = \{0,1\}^b$. Let $H : \mathcal{K} \times \mathbb{N} \to \mathcal{Y}$ be a ϵ-uniform-AXU. Let $K \leftarrow_\$ \mathcal{K}$, $P, P' \leftarrow_\$ \mathsf{Perm}(b)$, and Rand be a function that for each input $M_i \in \{0,1\}^*$ returns a random string $Z_i \in \{0,1\}^*$. Let $M_i = M_{i,1} \| \cdots \| M_{i,\ell_{M_i}}$ consists of $\ell_{M_i} = \lceil \frac{|M_i|}{b} \rceil$ b-bit blocks. We pad the last message block if it is not a multiple of b. Similarly, we have $Z_i = Z_{i,1} \| \cdots \| Z_{i,\ell_{Z_i}}$ for some $\ell_{Z_i} \geq 1$. Note that $Z_{i,\ell_{Z_i}}$ may not be a full block, however, for the simplicity of analysis we take $|Z_{i,\ell_{Z_i}}| = b$. Furthermore, we write Farasha-L and Farasha-R as $\mathsf{F_L}$ and $\mathsf{F_R}$, respectively.

For $M_i = M_{i,1} \| \cdots \| M_{i,\ell_{M_i}}$, let $(j, M_{i,j})$ denote the tuple corresponding to the j-th message block $M_{i,j}$ of M_i. Now, for $M_i \neq M_i'$, we say two tuples are identical if both $j = j'$ and $M_{i,j} = M_{i',j'}$. In our proof, we denote σ as the total number of distinct tuples $(j, M_{i,j})$ within the q messages $M_1, \cdots, M_q$.[3]

4.1   Adversarial Setup

Consider a deterministic and computationally unbounded adversary $\mathcal{A}$ which tries to distinguish $\mathcal{O} := (\mathsf{Farasha}_K^{H,P,P'}, P^\pm, P'^\pm)$ (real world) from $\mathcal{P} := (\mathsf{Rand}, P^\pm, P'^\pm)$ (ideal world). The notation $P^\pm$ denotes that both P and P^{-1} queries can be made. The advantage of adversary $\mathcal{A}$ for the PRF security of Farasha is defined as

$$\mathsf{Adv}_{\mathsf{Farasha}}^{\mathrm{prf}}(\mathcal{A}) := \left| \Pr\left[K \leftarrow_\$ \mathcal{K} : \mathcal{A}^{\mathsf{Farasha}_K, P^\pm, P'^\pm} \mapsto 1\right] - \Pr\left[\mathcal{A}^{\mathsf{Rand}, P^\pm, P'^\pm} \mapsto 1\right]\right|. \tag{10}$$

To compute an upper bound on the adversarial advantage in Eq. 10 (later given in Theorem 3), we first define the data (inputs, outputs) available to an adversary after its interaction with oracle $\mathcal{O}$ or $\mathcal{P}$. The input-output pairs are collected in a transcript τ. We say τ is attainable, if it can be obtained with a non-zero probability in the ideal world.[4]

---

[3] For instance, if $M_1 = a\|a\|a\|a$ and $M_2 = a\|a\|b\|b$, then there are 6 distinct tuples.
[4] This means there exists a random function Rand which on an input $M_i \in \{0,1\}^*$ returns a random string $Z_i \in \{0,1\}^*$.

Transcripts from Construction Queries. Let the adversary $\mathcal{A}$ makes q construction queries to $\mathcal{O}$ or $\mathcal{P}$, in the forward direction only. We summarize the inputs and outputs of these queries in the following transcript.

$$\tau_c = \{(M_i, Z_i) \mid M_i, Z_i \in \{0,1\}^*, \, 1 \leq i \leq q\}. \tag{11}$$

We only consider valid queries here, i.e., $M_i \neq M_{i'}$ for $i \neq i'$ in τ_c.

Transcripts from Primitive Queries. Let the adversary $\mathcal{A}$ makes q_p and $q_{p'}$ primitive queries to P and P', respectively. The transcripts are summarized as follows.

$$\tau_p = \{(u_i, v_i) \mid u_i, v_i \in \{0,1\}^b, \, P(u_i) = v_i, \, 1 \leq i \leq q_p\}$$
$$\tau_{p'} = \{(u_i, v_i) \mid u_i, v_i \in \{0,1\}^b, \, P'(u_i) = v_i, \, 1 \leq i \leq q_{p'}\} \tag{12}$$

Note that each of the sets $\tau_p, \tau_{p'}$ does not contain duplicates.

Transcripts After Releasing Keying Material. After its interaction with oracles $\mathcal{O}$ and $\mathcal{P}$, and before $\mathcal{A}$ outputs its final decision, we release the secret keying material used in the construction. This only improves the adversarial success probability and can be done without loss of generality. We first release the secret key K used in the construction. In the real world, K is the actual key used in the construction, and in the ideal world K is sampled uniformly from $\mathcal{K}$. The release of key-material provides additional inputs of permutation P arising from the key K, which are denoted as $\tau_{c,p}$ and are given by

$$\tau_{c,p} = \{A_{i,j} \mid A_{i,j} = H_K(j) \oplus M_{i,j}, \text{ for } 1 \leq i \leq q, 1 \leq j \leq \ell_{M_i}\} \tag{13}$$

Thus, the entire transcripts can be denoted as $\tau = (\tau_c, \tau_p, \tau_{p'}, K)$ or equivalently as $\tau = (\tau_c, \tau_p, \tau_{p'}, \tau_{c,p})$.

4.2   Main Result on the PRF Security of Farasha

Theorem 3 (PRF security of Farasha). *Let* $\epsilon > 0$ *and* $k, b \in \mathbb{N}$ *with* $k \leq b$ *and* $K \leftarrow_\$ \mathcal{K}$. *Consider* Farasha $:= \mathsf{F_R} \circ \mathsf{F_L}$ *as defined in Sect. 3.1 where* $\mathsf{F_L}$ *is a uniform-AXU based on a* ϵ-*uniform-AXU* H_K *and a random permutation* $P \leftarrow_\$ \mathsf{Perm}(b)$, *and* $\mathsf{F_R}$ *is a fixed input and variable output length PRF based on a random permutation* $P' \leftarrow_\$ \mathsf{Perm}(b)$. *For any adversary* $\mathcal{A}$ *making* q *construction queries (with* σ *being the number of distinct tuples* $(j, M_{i,j})$ *over all* q *queries),* σ' *output blocks (each query consisting of* l_{Z_i} *output blocks and* $\sigma' = \sum_{i=1}^q l_{Z_i}$), q_p *primitive queries to* P *and* $q_{p'}$ *primitive queries to* P',

$$\mathsf{Adv}^{\mathrm{prf}}_{\mathsf{Farasha}}(\mathcal{A}, q, q_p, q_{p'}, \sigma, \sigma') \leq \left(\frac{\sigma^2}{2}\epsilon + \sigma q_p \epsilon + \frac{\sigma^2}{2}\frac{1}{2^b}\right) + \left(\frac{3\sigma'^2}{2}\frac{1}{2^b} + \frac{2\sigma' q_{p'}}{2^b}\right).$$

Proof. The basic idea of proof is as follows. In Step-1, we observe that $\mathsf{F_R}$ can be mapped to a multi-key EM construction where the output of $\mathsf{F_L}$ is the key for every EM instance. In Step-2, we show that $\mathsf{F_L}$ is a uniform-AXU function and analyse $\mathsf{F_R}$ in the modified key-setting (given in Theorem 2). Next, we describe these two steps in details.

Step 1: In Farasha, the component F_R generates the PRF outputs. Thus, from the construction, it follows that

$$\mathsf{Adv}^{\mathrm{prf}}_{\mathsf{Farasha}}(\mathcal{A}, q, q_p, q_{p'}, \sigma, \sigma') := \mathsf{Adv}^{\mathrm{prf}}_{F_R}(\mathcal{A}', q, q_{p'}, \sigma') \tag{14}$$

for an adversary $\mathcal{A}'$. Note that in the following, we introduce the intermediate adversaries (similar to $\mathcal{A}'$) if the meaning is clear from the context.

Now, a closer look at Farasha shows that F_R is a CTR-mode PRF where the counter values are encrypted using the EM block cipher with key X_i. Since the key changes per input message M_i, it is an instance of the multi-key Even Mansour block cipher. Note that F_R is a block-cipher based construction with its output indistinguishable from a random PRP. To compute the advantage of F_R as a PRF, we apply the PRP/PRF switching for the EM block-cipher instances (with a total of σ' queries). The advantage is captured by Lemma 1 and we have the following:

$$\mathsf{Adv}^{\mathrm{prf}}_{F_R}(\mathcal{A}', q, q_{p'}, \sigma') \le \mathsf{Adv}^{\mathrm{prf}}_{EM}(\mathcal{A}'', q, q_{p'}, \sigma')$$
$$\le \mathsf{Adv}^{\mathrm{prp}}_{EM}(\mathcal{A}'', q, q_{p'}, \sigma') + \frac{\sigma'^2}{2}\frac{1}{2^b} \tag{15}$$

Step 2: The EM keys here resemble the SEM in the modified key setting (as discussed in Theorem 2) where they satisfy the ϵ'-uniform-AXU property, for a given $\epsilon' > 0$. As shown in Sect. 4.3, F_L is a ϵ'-AXU, however there is also an additional advantage arising from the number of AXU queries using the hash values ($X_i = F_L(K, M_i)$ for $i = 1, \cdots, q$). We denote this advantage by $\mathsf{Adv}^{\mathrm{u\text{-}axu}}_{F_L}$. Consequently, the first term in Eq. 15 is given by

$$\mathsf{Adv}^{\mathrm{prp}}_{EM}(\mathcal{A}'', q, q_{p'}, \sigma') \le \sigma'^2 \epsilon' + 2\sigma' q_{p'} \epsilon' + \mathsf{Adv}^{\mathrm{u\text{-}axu}}_{F_L}(\mathcal{B}, q, q_p, \sigma) \tag{16}$$

Now, by Lemma 2, we have

$$\mathsf{Adv}^{\mathrm{u\text{-}axu}}_{F_L}(\mathcal{B}, q, q_p, \sigma) \le \frac{\sigma^2}{2}\epsilon + \sigma q_p \epsilon + \frac{\sigma^2}{2}\frac{1}{2^b} \tag{17}$$

Note that $\epsilon' = 2^{-b}$ when there is no collision among X_i's. Thus, substituting $\epsilon' = 2^{-b}$ in Eq. 16, and combining Eqs. 15–17, we have

$$\mathsf{Adv}^{\mathrm{prf}}_{\mathsf{Farasha}}(\mathcal{A}, q, q_p, q_{p'}, \sigma, \sigma') \le \left(\frac{\sigma^2}{2}\epsilon + \sigma q_p \epsilon + \frac{\sigma^2}{2}\frac{1}{2^b}\right) + \left(\frac{3\sigma'^2}{2}\frac{1}{2^b} + \frac{2\sigma' q_{p'}}{2^b}\right). \tag{18}$$

The first two terms in Eq. 16 are given by Theorem 2 and the proof of Eq. 17 is given in Sect. 4.3.

Remark 1. Theorem 3 shows that for $\epsilon = 2^{-k}$, Farasha achieves a birthday-bound security in the key-size k and the permutation-size b, i.e., $\min\{k/2, b/2\}$.

4.3   Uniform AXU Bound of Farasha-L

Recall that for $M_i \in \{0,1\}^*$, we have $\mathsf{F_L}(K, M_i) = \bigoplus_{j=1}^{\ell_{M_i}} P(H_K(j) \oplus M_{i,j})$ where $K \leftarrow_\$ \mathcal{K}$, $P \leftarrow_\$ \mathsf{Perm}(b)$ and H_K is a ϵ-uniform-AXU. In Lemma 2, we give the uniform-AXU bound of Farasha-L, i.e., the adversarial advantage $\mathsf{Adv}_{\mathsf{F_L}}^{\text{u-axu}}$.

Lemma 2 (Uniform AXU bound of $\mathsf{F_L}$). *Let $\epsilon > 0$ and $k, b \in \mathbb{N}$ with $k \leq b$. Let $K \leftarrow_\$ \mathcal{K}$, $P \leftarrow_\$ \mathsf{Perm}(b)$ and H_K be a ϵ-uniform-AXU. Consider $\mathsf{F_L}$ as defined above. For any adversary $\mathcal{A}$ making q construction queries (with σ being the number of distinct tuples $(j, M_{i,j})$ over all q queries) and q_p primitive queries to P,*

$$\mathsf{Adv}_{\mathsf{F_L}}^{\text{u-axu}}(\mathcal{A}, q, q_p, \sigma) \leq \frac{\sigma^2}{2}\epsilon + \sigma q_p \epsilon + \frac{\sigma^2}{2}\frac{1}{2^b}. \tag{19}$$

Proof. From the transcript $\tau = (\tau_c, \tau_p, \tau_{p'}, \tau_{c,p})$, the subset of interest to $\mathcal{A}$ is $(\tau_c, \tau_p, \tau_{c,p})$. To prove the AXU (resp. uniformity) bound for $\mathsf{F_L}$, we look at the XOR difference of the $\mathsf{F_L}$ output of two messages (resp. output of a message) when the number of queries made by the adversary are q. We divide the proof into three steps, with the first two steps capturing the adversary's advantage: (1) replace P by a random function $\rho \leftarrow_\$ \mathsf{Func}(b)$, (2) define bad events and bound their probability and (3) prove the $\frac{1}{2^b}$-uniform-AXU property when P is replaced by a random function ρ and no bad events occur.

Step 1: PRP-PRF switching. For the sake of brevity, let $\mathsf{F_L}'$ be $\mathsf{F_L}$ when P is replaced by a random function. Since there are σ distinct tuples $(j, M_{i,j})$ and $H_K(j) \oplus M_{i,j}$ is input to P, the number of calls to P is bounded by σ. By the PRP-PRF switching lemma [18], we have

$$\mathsf{Adv}_{\mathsf{F_L}}^{\text{u-axu}}(\mathcal{A}, q, q_p, \sigma) \leq \frac{\sigma^2}{2}\frac{1}{2^b} + \mathsf{Adv}_{\mathsf{F_L}'}^{\text{u-axu}}(\mathcal{A}', q, q_p, \sigma). \tag{20}$$

Step 2: Accounting bad events. We define the following two events as bad events.

- $\underline{\mathsf{Bad}_1}$: Collision in the set $\tau_{c,p}$, i.e., $H_K(j) \oplus M_{i,j} = H_K(j') \oplus M_{i',j'}$ for $(j, M_{i,j}) \neq (j', M_{i',j'})$. If $j = j'$, we have $M_{i,j} \neq M_{i',j'}$ and hence there will be no collision. If $j \neq j'$, a collision implies $H_K(j) \oplus H_K(j') = M_{i,j} \oplus M_{i',j'}$, with the probability of this event bounded by ϵ (since H_K is ϵ-AXU). With the number of distinct input-tuples $(j, M_{i,j})$ being σ, the probability of a collision is at most $\binom{\sigma}{2}\epsilon \leq \sigma^2\epsilon/2$.
- $\underline{\mathsf{Bad}_2}$: Collision in the sets $\tau_{c,p}$ and τ_p, i.e., there exists $A_{i,j} \in \tau_{c,p}$ and $(u_r, v_r) \in \tau_p$ such that $A_{i,j} = u_r$. A collision between an element of $\tau_{c,p}$ (computed as $H_K(j) \oplus M_{i,j}$) and $(u_r, v_r) \in \tau_c$ implies $H_K(j) = u_r \oplus M_{i,j}$. Since H is ϵ-uniform, the probability of this event is bounded by ϵ. With $|\tau_{c,p}| \leq \sigma$ and $|\tau_p| = q_p$, the probability of a collision in the two sets is at most $\sigma q_p \epsilon$.

Now, we define $\mathsf{F_L}''$ as $\mathsf{F_L}'$ when neither Bad_1 nor Bad_2 occurs. Then, accounting for the probability of the bad events, we have

$$\mathsf{Adv}_{\mathsf{F_L}}^{\text{u-axu}}(\mathcal{A}, q, q_p, \sigma) \leq \left(\frac{\sigma^2}{2}\epsilon + \sigma q_p \epsilon + \frac{\sigma^2}{2}\frac{1}{2^b}\right) + \mathsf{Adv}_{\mathsf{F_L}''}^{\text{u-axu}}(\mathcal{A}'', q, q_p, \sigma) \tag{21}$$

Step 3: Bounding $\mathsf{Adv}^{\text{u-axu}}_{\mathsf{F_L}''}$. We show that $\mathsf{F_L}''$ is both $1/2^b$-uniform and $1/2^b$-AXU. We highlight that ρ is a random function in $\mathsf{F_L}''$ with no collisions in inputs to ρ.

- $\mathsf{F_L}''$ is $1/2^b$-uniform: $\mathsf{F_L}(K, M_i)$ computed as $\bigoplus_{j=1}^{\ell_{M_i}} \rho(H_K(j) \oplus M_{i,j}))$ is uniformly distributed as each input to ρ is distinct with each output of ρ being uniformly distributed. Thus, $\Pr[\mathsf{F_L}(K, M_i) = Y]$ is $1/2^b$ and $\mathsf{F_L}''$ is $1/2^b$-uniform.

- $\mathsf{F_L}''$ is $1/2^b$-AXU: For any given message pair (M_1, M_2), we show that the XOR difference of $\mathsf{F_L}(K, M_1) \oplus \mathsf{F_L}(K, M_2)$ is uniformly distributed. Let

$$\Delta = \bigoplus_{j=1}^{\ell_{M_1}} \rho(H_K(j) \oplus M_{1,j}) \oplus \bigoplus_{j=1}^{\ell_{M_2}} \rho(H_K(j) \oplus M_{2,j}). \tag{22}$$

Without loss of generality, assume that $\ell_{M_1} \geq \ell_{M_2}$. Since $M_1 \neq M_2$ there always exists an index j^* such that the message blocks M_{1,j^*} and M_{2,j^*} differ. If $\ell_{M_1} > \ell_{M_2}$, then take $j^* = \ell_{M_1}$ and if $\ell_{M_1} = \ell_{M_2}$, choose j^* as a block-index where M_1 and M_2 differ. Accordingly, we rewrite Eq. 22 as

$$\Delta = \rho(H_K(j^*) \oplus M_{1,j^*}) \oplus \Big(\bigoplus_{j=1, j \neq j^*}^{\ell_{M_1}} \rho(H_K(j) \oplus M_{1,j}) \odot \bigoplus_{j=1}^{\ell_{M_2}} \rho(H_K(j) \oplus M_{2,j}) \Big).$$
$$\tag{23}$$

Since the term at index j^* is independent of the rest of the right-hand side of Eq. 23, and ρ is a random function, the term at index j^* is uniformly distributed. Hence, the probability of Δ being equal to $\mathsf{F_L}(K, M_1) \oplus \mathsf{F_L}(K, M_2)$ is $1/2^b$. Thus $\mathsf{F_L}''$ is 2^{-b}-AXU.

Substituting $\mathsf{Adv}^{\text{u-axu}}_{\mathsf{F_L}''} = 1/2^b$ proves the lemma.

Remark 2. It is crucial to note that $\mathsf{F_L}$ is not 2^{-b}-uniform-AXU if the adversary is allowed unbounded number of queries. It satisfies uniform-AXU property with a bounded number of queries with the advantage given in Lemma 2. When no bad event happens, $\mathsf{F_L}$ is 2^{-b}-uniform-AXU (exactly as $\mathsf{F_L}''$ in Step 3 above). Furthermore, it is always possible to construct queries of the form $M_1 = (M_{1,1}, M_{1,2})$, $M_2 = (M_{2,1}, M_{2,2})$, $M_3 = (M_{1,1}, M_{2,2})$ and $M_4 = (M_{2,1}, M_{1,2})$ so that $\bigoplus_{i=1}^{4} X_i = 0$. However, since X_i's are secret, nothing is revealed about $X_i \oplus X_j$.

5   Further Insights on Farasha and Farfalle

5.1   Farasha Based on Regular-Size Keys

In Theorem 3, we have shown that Farasha achieves only $k/2$ bits of security for k-bit key. A natural question is whether this can be improved to full k bits of security. To answer this, we present Farasha#, a variant of Farasha. Farasha# is exactly similar to Farasha, except for the fact that we expand the master key K to another $2k$-bit key K' (satisfying $2k \leq b$) by a single call of the b-bit permutation P''. The key K' and the message M are then used as inputs to Farasha. This extension of Farasha to Farasha$^{\#}$ is shown in Fig. 4 and the security proof is given in Appendix A.2. Note that the permutation P'' is analogous to the permutation p_b in Farfalle.

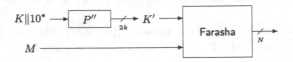

Fig. 4. A generic diagram of Farasha$^{\#}$

5.2   On Performance Trade-Offs in Farasha

Although the goal of this work is to understand the provable security aspects, we now highlight that the design choices in Farasha could provide different performance trade-offs. For instance, given a 8-bit micro controller, we can choose H_K as an LFSR over finite field $\mathbb{F}_{2^8}$. We could further select a primitive feedback polynomial that allows either efficient implementations or require low latency. Similarly, one could choose an LFSR for 32 and 64-bit architectures. In the case where hardware resources are not limited, a designer may choose H_K as a finite field multiplier (similar to AES-GCM). Moreover, since Farasha use public permutations, then for concrete instantiations, we could choose any secure permutation or its round-reduced variant (given that it is also secure) based on the performance requirements. All-in-all, based on the use-case and performance requirements, we could select an appropriate H_K and permutation.

We also believe that the Farasha-L can be abstracted to any generic uniform AXU function. Then it gives many new choices for AXUs. One interesting example is that 4-round AES with uniform and independent keys is an 2^{-113}-AXU [21].

5.3   Discussion on the Security of Farfalle

While the goal of Farfalle is to have an efficient design with security claims, as opposed to provable security, we can analyse Farfalle in the random permutation model under the following assumptions:

- $roll_c$ is a uniform-AXU: The authors of Farfalle mention that $roll_c$ should posses the properties of a uniform-AXU, i.e., "*Informally, an adversary not knowing K shall not be able to predict the mask value $roll_c^i(K)$ for any i in a reasonable range, nor the difference between any pair of mask values $roll_c^i(K)$ and $roll_c^j(K)$ for any $i \neq j$ in that range*" [7, Section 2.3]. In fact for $roll_c$ being an LFSR with primitive feedback polynomial, this property holds.

– p_b, p_c, p_d and p_e are random permutations: While the authors do not make this assumption (and use a 6-round Xoodoo instead), we analyze the overall Farfalle construction where permutations are modelled as a random permutation.

Under these assumptions, we can show that Farfalle is birthday bound secure in the random permutation model. We omit the details of proof due to space limitation and will provide them in the full version of the paper.

6 Conclusion

In this work, we have proposed Farasha, a permutation-based variable length input and output pseudo random function, which is parallelizable and provably secure. The Farasha PRF relies on a uniform almost xor universal hash function and a counter for its provable security. We presented Farasha-wLFSR, where the uniform AXU is an LFSR whose output state is always secret. We then proved that Farasha is birthday-bound secure and also have shown that a slight modification ensures full security in the key-size. Moreover, we discussed different AXUs and the security of Farfalle in the random permutation model. Finally, since our work presents the first formal treatment of Farasha and Farfalle, finding more tight bounds for these constructions is another interesting research direction. We also believe this work will bring new insights to the readers in further understanding the provable security of Farfalle-like constructions.

Acknowledgments. The authors would like to thank the reviewers of SAC 2022 for their insightful comments which improved the quality of the paper.

A   Security Proofs

A.1   Proof of Lemma 1

Proof. Let σ_i be the number of queries to P_i. By the PRP/PRF switching lemma, the advantage after switching P_i by PRF ρ_i is bounded by $\frac{\sigma_i^2}{2 \cdot 2^b}$. Since the permutations as well as the functions are independent of each other, the total advantage of the μ switchings is given by

$$\frac{1}{2}\frac{1}{2^b}\sum_{i=1}^{\mu}\sigma_i^2 \leq \frac{1}{2}\frac{1}{2^b}\left(\sum_{i=1}^{\mu}\sigma_i\right)^2 = \frac{\sigma^2}{2 \cdot 2^b}. \tag{24}$$

A.2   PRF Security of Farasha$^{\#}$

In Farasha$^{\#}$ (see Sect. 5.1), we first expand a k-bit key K to a $2k$-bit key $K' = P''(K)$. The key K' is then used as a key for Farasha. Denote the modified left-side as Farasha-L$^{\#}(K, M) =$ Farasha-L$(P''(K), M)$. Then, the security of Farasha$^{\#}$ follows from Lemma 3.

Lemma 3 (PRF security of Farasha$^{\#}$). *Consider* Farasha *as defined in Theorem 3 and additionally let* $P'' \leftarrow\!\!\$ \, \mathsf{Perm}(b)$ *and* Farasha-L$^{\#}$ *as defined above. Then for adversaries* $\mathcal{A}, \mathcal{A}'$, *we have*

$$\mathsf{Adv}^{\text{u-axu}}_{\mathsf{Farasha\text{-}L}^{\#}}(\mathcal{A}) \leq \frac{q_{p''}}{2^k} + \mathsf{Adv}^{\text{u-axu}}_{\mathsf{Farasha\text{-}L}}$$

$$\implies \mathsf{Adv}^{\text{prf}}_{\mathsf{Farasha}^{\#}}(\mathcal{A}') \leq \frac{q_{p''}}{2^k} + \mathsf{Adv}^{\text{prf}}_{\mathsf{Farasha}}, \qquad (25)$$

where $q_{p''}$ *is the number of primitive queries to* P''.

Proof. With another public permutation P'' for the key expansion, $P''^{\pm}$ is the additional (primitive) oracle available to the adversary $\mathcal{A}$. Let $\mathcal{A}$ make $q_{p''}$ primitive queries to P'' and denote its input-output pairs as $\tau_{p''} = \{(u_i, v_i) \,|\, P''(u_i) = v_i, 1 \leq i \leq q_{p''}\}$. Now, in addition to all cases in proof of Theorem 3, we need to consider an additional bad event, i.e., when one of the queries in $\tau_{p''}$ matches the key K. The probability of this event is at most $q_{p''}/2^k$. Given that the construction after the key expansion is identical to Farasha-L, accounting for this term in Lemma 2 (resp. Theorem 3) gives the adversarial advantage of Farasha-L$^{\#}$ (resp. Farasha$^{\#}$) as given in Eq. 25. This proves the lemma.

A.3   Proof of Theorem 2

Proof Idea. Let (M_{ij}, C_{ij}) denote the j-th plaintext and ciphertext pair corresponding to the EM instance with key K_i, i.e., E_{K_i}. Furthermore, (x_j, y_j) denote the input/output of the j-th public permutation query. The bad events are identical to the independent keys analysis done in [35], and are as follows.

$$\exists\, i, i', j, j' : i \neq i' : M_{ij} \oplus M_{i'j'} = K_i \oplus K_{i'} \quad \vee \quad C_{ij} \oplus C_{i'j'} = K_i \oplus K_{i'} \qquad (26a)$$

$$\exists\, i, j, j' : M_{ij} \oplus x_{j'} = K_i \qquad\qquad \vee \quad C_{ij} \oplus y_{j'} = K_i \qquad (26b)$$

The probabilities that Eq. 26a and Eq. 26b hold is bounded by ϵ due to the ϵ-uniform-AXU property. The rest of the proof is identical to the one in [35], and the $1/2^b$ term can be generalised to ϵ with $\epsilon = 1/2^b$ for independent keys.

Proof. The adversarial model for the modified key setting is depicted in Fig. 3, with an adversary $\mathcal{A}$ having bidirectional access to $\mu+1$ oracles $(\mathcal{O}_1, \cdots, \mathcal{O}_\mu, \mathcal{O})$. In the ideal world, these are $(P_1, \cdots, P_\mu, P) \leftarrow\!\!\$ \, \mathsf{Perm}(n)^{\mu+1}$. In the real world, these are $(E_{K_1}, \cdots, E_{K_\mu}, P)$, where $E_{K_i}(M_{ij}) = P(M_{ij} \oplus K_i) \oplus K_i$ for $i = 1, \cdots, \mu$. Note that, in this setting, the keys K_i are the output of a keyed hash function H_K and satisfy the ϵ-uniform-AXU property. The adversary makes σ_i queries to oracle $\mathcal{O}_i$ (resp. q_p queries to oracle $\mathcal{O}$), which are captured in transcripts τ_i for $1 \leq i \leq \mu$ (resp. τ_p). Thus, the transcripts in the real-world are:

$$\tau_i = \{(M_{ij}, C_{ij}) \,|\, M_{ij}, C_{ij} \in \{0,1\}^b, \; E_{K_i}(M_{ij}) = C_{ij}, \; 1 \leq i \leq \sigma_i\}$$

$$\tau_p = \{(x_i, y_i) \,|\, x_i, y_i \in \{0,1\}^b, \; P(x_i) = y_i, \; 1 \leq i \leq q_p\} \qquad (27)$$

We assume the adversary never makes duplicate queries, so that $M_{ij} \neq M_{ij'}, C_{ij} \neq C_{ij'}, x_j \neq x_{j'}, y_i \neq y_{j'}$ for all i, j, j' where $j \neq j'$. We denote the total number of keyed (or construction) queries by $\sigma = \sum_{i=1}^{\mu} \sigma_i$.

After all the queries by $\mathcal{A}$ are done, but before it outputs its decision, the key K (of the hash function H_K) in the real world and a dummy key in the ideal world is released to the adversary. This enables the adversary to compute the keys $(K_1, \cdots, K_\mu)$. The interaction of $\mathcal{A}$ with the oracles can be summarized by a transcript $\tau = \{K, \tau_1, \cdots, \tau_\mu, \tau_p\}$ or equivalently, $\tau = \{K_1, \cdots, K_\mu, \tau_1, \cdots, \tau_\mu, \tau_p\}$.

Without loss of generality we assume that $\mathcal{A}$ is deterministic. Given the fixed deterministic adversary $\mathcal{A}$, we denote the probability distribution of transcripts in the real world by X, and in the ideal world by Y. We say that a transcript τ is attainable if it can be obtained from interacting with $(P_1, \cdots, P_\mu, P)$, i.e., $\Pr[Y = \tau] > 0$. In our proof, we use the H-coefficient technique, as given by Lemma 4.

Lemma 4. *(H-coefficient Technique [36]). Let us consider a fixed deterministic adversary $\mathcal{A}$, and let $\mathcal{T} = \mathcal{T}_{good} \cup \mathcal{T}_{bad}$ be a partition of the set of attainable transcripts. Let δ be such that for all $\tau \in \mathcal{T}_{good}$*

$$\frac{\Pr[X = \tau]}{\Pr[Y = \tau]} \geq 1 - \delta \tag{28}$$

Then, $\mathsf{Adv}_{EM}^{prp}(\mathcal{A}, \sigma) \leq \delta + \Pr[Y \in \mathcal{T}_{bad}]$.

We say that a transcript $\tau \in \mathcal{T}$ is bad if two different queries result in the same input (or output) to P, were $\mathcal{A}$ interacting with the real world. Stated formally, τ is bad if one of the following conditions is met:

$$\exists\, i, i', j, j' : i \neq i' : M_{ij} \oplus M_{i'j'} = K_i \oplus K_{i'} \quad \vee \quad C_{ij} \oplus C_{i'j'} = K_i \oplus K_i' \tag{29a}$$

$$\exists\, i, j, j' : M_{ij} \oplus x_{j'} = K_i \qquad\qquad \vee \quad C_{ij} \oplus y_{j'} = K_i \tag{29b}$$

A transcript that is not a bad transcript, is referred to as a good transcript.

Upper Bounding $\Pr[Y \in \mathcal{T}_{bad}]$. We want to upper bound the event that a transcript τ in the ideal world satisfies Eq. 29a or 29b. Recall that for $i = 1, \cdots, \mu$, keys K_i satisfy the ϵ-uniform-AXU property. For any fixed $i \neq i'$, there are at most $2\sigma_i \sigma_{i'}$ possible plaintext pairs and ciphertext pairs. With keys satisfying ϵ-AXU property, the probability of satisfying the condition in Eq. 29a is bounded by $2\sigma_i\sigma_{i'}\epsilon$. Analogously, for any fixed i, there are at most $2\sigma_i q_p$ distinct values in Eq. 29b. Since the keys are also ϵ-uniform, the probability of satisfying the condition in Eq. 29b is bounded by $2\sigma_i q_p \epsilon$. Therefore,

$$\Pr[Y \in \mathcal{T}_{bad}] \leq \left(\Sigma_i \Sigma_{i' < i} 2\sigma_i \sigma_{i'} \epsilon\right) + \left(\Sigma_i 2\sigma_i q_p \epsilon\right)$$
$$\leq \sigma^2 \epsilon + 2\sigma q_p \epsilon.$$

Lower Bounding Ratio $\Pr[X = \tau]/\Pr[Y = \tau]$. Let us consider a good and attainable transcript $\tau \in \mathcal{T}_{good}$. Then, denote by $\Omega_X = 2^b \cdot 2^b!$ the set of all possible

oracles in the real world and by $comp_X(\tau) \subseteq \Omega_X$ the set of oracles in Ω_X compatible with transcript τ. Define $\Omega_Y = 2^b \cdot (2^b!)^{\mu+1}$ and $comp_Y(\tau)$ similarly. According to the H-coefficient technique:

$$\Pr[X = \tau] = \frac{|comp_X(\tau)|}{|\Omega_X|} \text{ and } \Pr[Y = \tau] = \frac{|comp_Y(\tau)|}{|\Omega_Y|} \tag{31}$$

First, we calculate $|comp_X(\tau)|$. As $\tau \in \mathcal{T}_{good}$, there are no two queries in τ with the same input or output of the underlying permutation. Any query tuple in τ, therefore, fixes exactly one input-output pair of the underlying oracle. Because τ consists of $\sigma + q_p$ query tuples, the number of possible oracles in the real world equals $(2^b - \sigma - q_p)!$. By a similar reasoning, the number of possible oracles in the ideal world equals $\prod_{i=1}^{\mu}(2^b - \sigma_i)! \cdot (2^b - q_p)!$. Therefore,

$$\Pr[X = \tau] = \frac{(2^b - \sigma - q_p)!}{2^b \cdot 2^b!} \tag{32}$$

$$\Pr[Y = \tau] = \frac{\prod_{i=1}^{\mu}(2^b - \sigma_i)! \cdot (2^b - q_p)!}{2^b \cdot (2^b!)^{\mu+1}}$$

$$\leq \frac{(2^b - \sigma - q_p)! \cdot (2^b!)^{\mu}}{2^b \cdot (2^b!)^{\mu+1}} \tag{33}$$

$$= \frac{(2^b - \sigma - q_p)!}{2^b \cdot 2^b!} = \Pr[X = \tau]$$

It then follows that $\Pr[X = \tau]/\Pr[Y = \tau] \geq 1$. Thus,

$$\mathsf{Adv}_{EM}^{\mathrm{prp}}(\mathcal{A}, \sigma) \leq \Pr[Y \in \mathcal{T}_{bad}] \leq \sigma^2 \epsilon + 2\sigma q_p \epsilon.$$

This proves the theorem.

References

1. Aumasson, J., Henzen, L., Meier, W., Naya-Plasencia, M.: Quark: a lightweight hash. J. Cryptol. **26**(2), 313–339 (2013). https://doi.org/10.1007/s00145-012-9125-6
2. Aumasson, J.-P., Jovanovic, P., Neves, S.: NORX: parallel and scalable AEAD. In: Kutyłowski, M., Vaidya, J. (eds.) ESORICS 2014. LNCS, vol. 8713, pp. 19–36. Springer, Cham (2014). https://doi.org/10.1007/978-3-319-11212-1_2
3. Bernstein, D.J.: Chacha, a variant of Salsa20. In: Workshop Record of SASC (2008). cr.yp.to/papers.html#chacha
4. Bernstein, D.J.: The Salsa20 family of stream ciphers. In: Robshaw, M., Billet, O. (eds.) New Stream Cipher Designs. LNCS, vol. 4986, pp. 84–97. Springer, Heidelberg (2008). https://doi.org/10.1007/978-3-540-68351-3_8
5. Bernstein, D.J., et al.: GIMLI: a cross-platform permutation. In: Fischer, W., Homma, N. (eds.) CHES 2017. LNCS, vol. 10529, pp. 299–320. Springer, Cham (2017). https://doi.org/10.1007/978-3-319-66787-4_15
6. Bertoni, G., Daemen, J., Peeters, M., Assche, G.: CAESAR submission: Ketje v2 (2014). http://ketje.noekeon.org/Ketjev2-doc2.0.pdf

7. Bertoni, G., Daemen, J., Hoffert, S., Peeters, M., Assche, G.V., Keer, R.V.: Farfalle: parallel permutation-based cryptography. IACR Trans. Symmetric Cryptol. **2017**(4), 1–38 (2017). https://tosc.iacr.org/index.php/ToSC/article/view/801
8. Bertoni, G., Daemen, J., Peeters, M., Van Assche, G.: Sponge-based pseudorandom number generators. In: Mangard, S., Standaert, F.-X. (eds.) CHES 2010. LNCS, vol. 6225, pp. 33–47. Springer, Heidelberg (2010). https://doi.org/10.1007/978-3-642-15031-9_3
9. Bertoni, G., Daemen, J., Peeters, M., Van Assche, G.: Duplexing the sponge: single-pass authenticated encryption and other applications. In: Miri, A., Vaudenay, S. (eds.) SAC 2011. LNCS, vol. 7118, pp. 320–337. Springer, Heidelberg (2012). https://doi.org/10.1007/978-3-642-28496-0_19
10. Bertoni, G., Daemen, J., Peeters, M., Van Assche, G.: Sponge functions. In: Hash Functions Workshop (2007). https://keccak.team/files/SpongeFunctions.pdf
11. Bertoni, G., Daemen, J., Peeters, M., Van Assche, G.: Keccak specifications. Submission to NIST (Round 2) (2009)
12. Bertoni, G., Daemen, J., Peeters, M., Van Assche, G.: Permutation-based encryption, authentication and authenticated encryption. DIAC (2012)
13. Beyne, T., Chen, Y.L., Dobraunig, C., Mennink, B.: Dumbo, jumbo, and delirium: parallel authenticated encryption for the lightweight circus. IACR Trans. Symmetric Cryptol. **2020**(S1), 5–30 (2020). https://doi.org/10.13154/tosc.v2020.iS1.5-30
14. Black, J., Rogaway, P.: A block-cipher mode of operation for parallelizable message authentication. In: Knudsen, L.R. (ed.) EUROCRYPT 2002. LNCS, vol. 2332, pp. 384–397. Springer, Heidelberg (2002). https://doi.org/10.1007/3-540-46035-7_25
15. Bogdanov, A., Knežević, M., Leander, G., Toz, D., Varıcı, K., Verbauwhede, I.: SPONGENT: a lightweight hash function. In: Preneel, B., Takagi, T. (eds.) CHES 2011. LNCS, vol. 6917, pp. 312–325. Springer, Heidelberg (2011). https://doi.org/10.1007/978-3-642-23951-9_21
16. Boneh, D., Shoup, V.: A Graduate Course in Applied Cryptography (2020). cryptobook.us
17. Chakraborty, D., Sarkar, P.: A general construction of tweakable block ciphers and different modes of operations. IEEE Trans. Inf. Theory **54**(5), 1991–2006 (2008). https://doi.org/10.1109/TIT.2008.920247
18. Chang, D., Nandi, M.: A short proof of the PRP/PRF switching lemma (2008). http://eprint.iacr.org/2008/078
19. Daemen, J., Hoffert, S., Assche, G.V., Keer, R.V.: The design of Xoodoo and Xoofff. IACR Trans. Symmetric Cryptol. **2018**(4), 1–38 (2018). https://doi.org/10.13154/tosc.v2018.i4.1-38
20. Daemen, J., Hoffert, S., Peeters, M., Assche, G.V., Keer, R.V.: Xoodyak, a lightweight cryptographic scheme. IACR Trans. Symmetric Cryptol. **2020**(S1), 60–87 (2020). https://doi.org/10.13154/tosc.v2020.iS1.60-87
21. Daemen, J., Lamberger, M., Pramstaller, N., Rijmen, V., Vercauteren, F.: Computational aspects of the expected differential probability of 4-round AES and AES-like ciphers. Computing **85**(1-2), 85–104 (2009). https://doi.org/10.1007/s00607-009-0034-y
22. Daemen, J., Massolino, P.M.C., Mehrdad, A., Rotella, Y.: The subterranean 2.0 cipher suite. IACR Trans. Symmetric Cryptol. **2020**(S1), 262–294 (2020). https://doi.org/10.13154/tosc.v2020.iS1.262-294
23. Dobraunig, C., Eichlseder, M., Mendel, F., Schläffer, M.: Ascon v1.2: lightweight authenticated encryption and hashing (2021). https://doi.org/10.1007/s00145-021-09398-9

24. Dobraunig, C., Grassi, L., Guinet, A., Kuijsters, D.: CIMINION: symmetric encryption based on Toffoli-Gates over large finite fields. In: Canteaut, A., Standaert, F.-X. (eds.) EUROCRYPT 2021. LNCS, vol. 12697, pp. 3–34. Springer, Cham (2021). https://doi.org/10.1007/978-3-030-77886-6_1

25. Dunkelman, O., Keller, N., Shamir, A.: Minimalism in cryptography: the even-mansour scheme revisited. In: Pointcheval, D., Johansson, T. (eds.) EUROCRYPT 2012. LNCS, vol. 7237, pp. 336–354. Springer, Heidelberg (2012). https://doi.org/10.1007/978-3-642-29011-4_21

26. Dworkin, M.J.: SP 800-38D: recommendation for block cipher modes of operation: Galois/counter mode (GCM) and GMAC. National Institute of Standards & Technology (2007)

27. Even, S., Mansour, Y.: A construction of a cipher from a single pseudorandom permutation. J. Cryptol. **10**, 151–162 (1997). https://doi.org/10.1007/s001459900025

28. Granger, R., Jovanovic, P., Mennink, B., Neves, S.: Improved masking for tweakable blockciphers with applications to authenticated encryption. In: Fischlin, M., Coron, J.-S. (eds.) EUROCRYPT 2016. LNCS, vol. 9665, pp. 263–293. Springer, Heidelberg (2016). https://doi.org/10.1007/978-3-662-49890-3_11

29. Gunsing, A., Daemen, J., Mennink, B.: Deck-based wide block cipher modes and an exposition of the blinded keyed hashing model. IACR Trans. Symmetric Cryptol. **2019**(4), 1–22 (2019). https://doi.org/10.13154/tosc.v2019.i4.1-22

30. Guo, J., Peyrin, T., Poschmann, A.: The PHOTON family of lightweight hash functions. In: Rogaway, P. (ed.) CRYPTO 2011. LNCS, vol. 6841, pp. 222–239. Springer, Heidelberg (2011). https://doi.org/10.1007/978-3-642-22792-9_13

31. Jean, J., Nikolic, I., Peyrin, T., Seurin, Y.: Deoxys v1. 41. Submitted to CAESAR **124** (2016). https://competitions.cr.yp.to/round3/deoxysv141.pdf

32. Krovetz, T., Rogaway, P.: The software performance of authenticated-encryption modes. In: Joux, A. (ed.) FSE 2011. LNCS, vol. 6733, pp. 306–327. Springer, Heidelberg (2011). https://doi.org/10.1007/978-3-642-21702-9_18

33. McGrew, D., Viega, J.: The Galois/counter mode of operation (GCM). Submission to NIST Modes of Operation Process **20**, 0278–0070 (2004)

34. Minematsu, K.: Parallelizable rate-1 authenticated encryption from pseudorandom functions. In: Nguyen, P.Q., Oswald, E. (eds.) EUROCRYPT 2014. LNCS, vol. 8441, pp. 275–292. Springer, Heidelberg (2014). https://doi.org/10.1007/978-3-642-55220-5_16

35. Mouha, N., Luykx, A.: Multi-key security: the even-mansour construction revisited. In: Gennaro, R., Robshaw, M. (eds.) CRYPTO 2015. LNCS, vol. 9215, pp. 209–223. Springer, Heidelberg (2015). https://doi.org/10.1007/978-3-662-47989-6_10

36. Patarin, J.: The "coefficients H" technique. In: Avanzi, R.M., Keliher, L., Sica, F. (eds.) SAC 2008. LNCS, vol. 5381, pp. 328–345. Springer, Heidelberg (2009). https://doi.org/10.1007/978-3-642-04159-4_21

37. Peyrin, T., Seurin, Y.: Counter-in-tweak: authenticated encryption modes for tweakable block ciphers. In: Robshaw, M., Katz, J. (eds.) CRYPTO 2016. LNCS, vol. 9814, pp. 33–63. Springer, Heidelberg (2016). https://doi.org/10.1007/978-3-662-53018-4_2

38. Rogaway, P., Bellare, M., Black, J.: OCB: a block-cipher mode of operation for efficient authenticated encryption. ACM Trans. Inf. Syst. Secur. **6**(3), 365–403 (2003). https://doi.org/10.1145/937527.937529

39. Rogaway, P., Shrimpton, T.: A provable-security treatment of the key-wrap problem. In: Vaudenay, S. (ed.) EUROCRYPT 2006. LNCS, vol. 4004, pp. 373–390. Springer, Heidelberg (2006). https://doi.org/10.1007/11761679_23

A Sponge-Based PRF with Good Multi-user Security

Arghya Bhattacharjee[1], Ritam Bhaumik[1,2]([✉]), and Mridul Nandi[1]

[1] Indian Statistical Institute, Kolkata, Kolkata, India
bhaumik.ritam@gmail.com
[2] Inria, Paris, France

Abstract. Both multi-user PRFs and sponge-based constructions have generated a lot of research interest lately. Dedicated analyses for multi-user security have improved the bounds a long distance from the early generic bounds obtained through hybrid arguments, yet the bounds generally don't allow the number of users to be more than birthday-bound in key-size. Similarly, known sponge constructions suffer from being only birthday-bound secure in terms of their capacity. We present in this paper Muffler, a multi-user PRF built from a random permutation using a full-state sponge with feed-forward, which uses a combination of the user keys and unique user IDs to solve both the problems mentioned by improving the security bounds for multi-user constructions and sponge constructions. For D construction query blocks and T permutation queries, with key-size $\kappa = n/2$ and tag-size $\tau = n/2$ (where n is the state-size or the size of the underlying permutation), both D and T must touch birthday bound in n in order to distinguish Muffler from a random function.

Keywords: Sponge · Multi-User · PRF · public permutation

1 Introduction

Multi-user Security. The study of provably secure symmetric-key modes has traditionally revolved around the single-user setting, where a single user generates the keys of the various underlying primitives and uses them to respond to all subsequent adversary queries. However, it has long been recognised that often a more practically relevant scenario is the multi-user setting, where several users generate their own keys independently, and the adversary can query any or all of them. The notion of multi-user security was first introduced by Bellare, Boldyreva and Micali [3].

One of the possible reasons why research in this direction did not garner sufficient interest is that it was established quite at the outset that when μ

R. Bhaumik—This project has received funding from the European Research Council (ERC) under the European Union's Horizon 2020 research and innovation programme (grant agreement no. 714294 - acronym QUASYModo).

© The Author(s), under exclusive license to Springer Nature Switzerland AG 2024
B. Smith and H. Wu (Eds.): SAC 2022, LNCS 13742, pp. 459–478, 2024.
https://doi.org/10.1007/978-3-031-58411-4_21

users are involved, the security bound does not degrade by more than a factor of μ. This generic bound looked like a satisfactory conclusion to the problem at that time; however, with the rapidly increasing expected number of users in practice, it has been evident for some time now that this degradation can be quite significant.

This realisation has led to a growing interest in recent times in dedicated security analyses of modes for the multi-user settings, which have been shown to yield bounds much better than the generic one.

Multi-user Degradation. As noted by Biham [14], there exists a faster generic key-recovery attack on any block cipher in the multi-key setting compared to the single-key setting. In this work Biham established the key-recovery trade-off $\mu T = 2^\kappa$ where μ denotes the number of users, κ is the key-size of a symmetric-key algorithm and T is the time (mainly the number of primitive calls used in the target algorithm).

As shown by Hong and Sarkar [26], and by Biryukov et al. [15], the stream cipher time-memory-data tradeoffs can be applied to the block cipher setting as well, assuming that a plaintext is encrypted under multiple keys. Their work generalizes the findings of Biham. The observation that recovering one key out of a large group of keys can often be easier is applicable to any deterministic symmetric-key algorithm, as is done for MACs by Chatterjee, Menezes, and Sarkar [17].

By using standard hybrid argument the above trade-off can be shown to be tight [29]. Whenever the number of users increases rapidly, the multi-user security is no longer κ bits (which is usually a desirable level of security). In this paper, one of the main motivations is to recover κ-bit security even in the multi-user model. Previously there were some attempts based on randomization (e.g., randomized GCM in TLS 1.3 [6]). However, it still suffers from the high key-collision probability among users which adds a term like $\mu^2/2^\kappa$ to the bound. Thus, for a large number of users, this construction is still birthday bound on the key-size.

Sponge-Based Constructions. A popular and useful design paradigm for modes in recent years has been the sponge-based constructions [8], which was used in the SHA3 hash function Keccak. In the sponge mode the internal state of the public permutation is split into an r-bit part to be released to the adversary and a hidden c-bit part; r and c are called the *rate* and *capacity* of the construction respectively. With the rise in popularity of permutation-based designs, the efficiency and security of sponges have increasingly drawn the attention of researchers. Till now all sponge constructions have been limited to the birthday bound in terms of its capacity [1, 10, 11]. This is mainly due to the length-extension of sponge construction. In other words, the security bound of the sponge-based PRF is mostly determined by the term $D^2/2^c$, where D is the data available to the adversary (measured by the number of construction queries).

Our second motivation of the paper is to improve this bound for sponge constructions by introducing a simple variant. Our variant enables to obtain

$\min\{(c+r)/2, c\}$ bit security. When we consider the multi-user model, our bound turns out to be roughly $\min\{(c+r)/2, c, \kappa\}$. With appropriate choice of parameters of c and r, we can achieve almost optimal security.

1.1 Our Contributions

We present in this paper Muffler, a multi-user PRF built from a random permutation using a full-state sponge with feed-forward, which uses a combination of the user keys and unique user IDs to improve the security bounds both for multi-user constructions and sponge constructions. For D construction query blocks and T permutation queries, with key-size $\kappa = n/2$ and tag-size $\tau = n/2$, both D and T must touch birthday bound in n in order to distinguish Muffler from a random function.

Comparison to Full-State Keyed Duplex [20]. Our proposed construction is similar to the full-state Duplex, with an added feed forward of the processed key into the final permutation call. We also replace the IV used in Duplex with a unique ID assigned to each user. The bound we obtain for the multi-user case is better than the bound in [20]. Eqn. 2 in [20] suggests that the dominating terms in their bound is $q_{iv}T/2^{\kappa}$ and $LT/2^{c}$, where κ is the key-length, c is the capacity, q_{iv} is the maximum number of keys which are called on the same IV, T is the offline complexity, and L is the number of *repeated paths*, i.e., repeated message prefix to the same key; unless IV is refreshed for every user (or for every t users for a small t), we can expect q_{iv} to be of the order of u, the number of users, and if IV is used as an ID, L is of the order of D, so their security term always has either a $uT/2^{\kappa}$ term (multi-user degradation of the single-user $T/2^{\kappa}$ term) or a $DT/2^{c}$ term (signifying birthday-bound in capacity). Our design solves both these problems.

1.2 Related Work

Initial works can be traced back to Biham [14] in symmetric cryptanalysis and Bellare et al. [3] in public-key encryption. Biham [14] considered the security of block ciphers in the multi-target setting and later Biryukov et al. [15] refined it as a time-memory-data trade-off to demonstrate how one can take advantage of the fact that recovering a block cipher key out of a large group of keys is much easier than targeting a specific key. The same observation can be applied to any deterministic symmetric-key algorithm, as done for MACs by Chatterjee et al. [17]. Bellare et al. [6] first formalized a multi-user secure authenticated encryption scheme and also analyzed countermeasures against multi-key attacks in the context of TLS 1.3. Andreeva et al. [1] considered the security of the outer and inner keyed sponge in the multi-user setting, a proof which internally featured a security analysis of the Even-Mansour block cipher in the multi-user setting. The direction of multi-user security got subsequently popularized by Mouha et al. [29], leading to various multi-user security results [2,24] with security bounds almost independent of the number of users involved.

Since Chatterjee et al. [17], multi-user security of MACs has been studied by Morgan et al. [28] and Bellare et al. [5]. The security of DbHtS (Double-block Hash-then-Sum) in the multi-user setting has been analysed by Shen et al. [31], Guo et al. [22] and Datta et al. [21]. Multi-user security of XORP[3] (bitwise-xor of 3 outputs of n-bit pseudorandom random permutations with domain separated inputs) has been analysed by Bhattacharya et al. [13]. Various other related works can also be found [7,16,25–27].

The multi-user security of various other modes has been of significant research interest in recent years. One such class of functions is the cascade family [4]; Bellare, Bernstein and Tessaro have studied the multi-user security of AMAC [2], a cascade-based MAC function. Some other constructions of interest in the context of multi-user security have been the key-alternating ciphers [24], Tweakable Even-Mansour [23], and double encryption [25]. Bose, Hoang and Tessaro presented a multi-user security analysis of AES-GCM-SIV [16]. Another direction of research for sponge constructions has been that of indifferentiability [9].

2   Preliminaries

Mathematical Preliminaries and Notation. For integers i, j with $i \leq j$, $[i..j]$ will denote the set $\{k \mid i \leq k \leq j\}$. The notation for $[1..j]$ will be abbreviated to $[j]$. $\{0,1\}^m$ will denote the set of all binary strings of length m, and $\{0,1\}^{\geq m}$ will denote all binary strings of size at least m. For a finite set S, $|S|$ will denote its size. Thus, $|\{0,1\}^m| = 2^m$.

For a binary string x of length m, and i, j such that $i \leq j \leq m$, $x[i..j]$ will denote the contiguous substring of x starting at the i-th bit and ending at the j-th bit. For a finite set S and a random variable X, we say X is *uniformly sampled* from S, denoted $X \xleftarrow{\$} S$, if for each $x \in S$, $\Pr[X = x] = 1/|S|$.

Thus, when a binary string of length m is uniformly sampled, every string is picked with a probability $1/2^m$. A *random function* $f : S \longrightarrow \{0,1\}^m$ samples $f(x)$ uniformly from $\{0,1\}^m$ for each $x \in S$. A function $f : S_1 \longrightarrow S_2$ is called *injective* if for any distinct $x_1, x_2 \in S_1$, $f(x_1) \neq f(x_2)$. An injective function from S to S is called a *permutation* over S. For two binary strings x, y, $x\|y$ will denote their concatenation. For $b \in \{0,1\}$ and $m \geq 0$, b^m will denote the m-bit string with each bit identical and equal to b. We fix n to be the *block-size* for the rest of this paper, and each member of $\{0,1\}^n$ is considered a block. The function $\mathsf{fixl}(\cdot, \cdot)$ fixes the last bit of a block, i.e., for a block x and a bit b,

$$\mathsf{fixl}(x, b) := x[1..n-1]\|b.$$

For $m \in [0..n-1]$ and $x \in \{0,1\}^m$, $x\|10^*$ denotes the block $x\|1\|0^{n-m-1}$. (We will sometimes use the term *incomplete block* to describe an m-bit string with $m \in [0..n-1]$.) $X \longleftarrow x$ denotes the assignment of the value x to the variable X.

Sampling a Random Permutation. We say P is a *partially-determined permutation* if for two subsets $\mathrm{dom}(P)$ and $\mathrm{ran}(P)$ of $\{0,1\}^n$ of equal size P is an injective function from $\mathsf{dom}\,(P)$ to $\mathsf{ran}\,(P)$. We take $|P| = |\mathsf{dom}\,(P)| = |\mathsf{ran}\,(P)|$. For a partially-determined permutation P and a pair (x, y) with

$$x \in \{0,1\}^n \setminus \mathsf{dom}\,(P),\ y \in \{0,1\}^n \setminus \mathsf{ran}\,(P),$$

we can *add* (x, y) to P, by extending the definition of P to include $P(x) := y$.

Note that this adds x to $\mathsf{dom}\,(P)$ and y to $\mathsf{ran}\,(P)$. When sampling a *random permutation* P, queries to P or P^{-1} are answered while keeping track of the partially-determined P. For any *forward query* x (i.e., a query to P), if $x \in \mathsf{dom}\,(P)$, $P(x)$ is returned; else a y is sampled uniformly from $\{0,1\}^n \setminus \mathsf{ran}\,(P)$ and returned, and (x, y) is added to P. Similarly, for any *backward query* y (i.e., a query to P^{-1}), if $y \in \mathsf{ran}\,(P)$, $P^{-1}(y)$ is returned; else an x is sampled uniformly from $\{0,1\}^n \setminus \mathsf{dom}\,(P)$ and returned, and (x, y) is added to P. Thus, for any $x \notin \mathsf{dom}\,(P)$ and $y \notin \mathsf{ran}\,(P)$, the probability that a forward query x will return y or a backward query y will return x is $1/(2^n - |P|)$. As long as $|P| \leq 2^{n-1}$, we can use the simpler bound $1/2^{n-1}$.

Single-User PRF Game in the Public Permutation Model. Let $f_1[P] : S \longrightarrow \{0,1\}^m$ be a function which uses a permutation P as an underlying primitive (we assume all its components other than P and the secret key are publicly computable), and $f_0 : S \longrightarrow \{0,1\}^m$ be a random function. In the Single-User PRF Game in the Public Permutation Model, an adversary $\mathcal{A}$ makes a series of forward and backward queries to P, called the *permutation queries* (or the *offline queries*), and a series of queries to an oracle $\mathcal{O}$, called the *construction queries* (or the *online queries*). $\mathcal{O}$ is either the real oracle $\mathcal{O}_1$, which returns $f_1[P](x)$ when x is queried; or it is the ideal oracle $\mathcal{O}_0$, which returns $f_0(x)$ when x is queried. In the *post-query phase*, i.e., after all the permutation queries and construction queries have been answered, the oracle $\mathcal{O}$ may decide to reveal certain additional information to $\mathcal{A}$. Finally, $\mathcal{A}$ returns a bit b, and wins if $\mathcal{O} = \mathcal{O}_b$. Note that the permutation queries and responses are visible to $\mathcal{O}$, so we can assume that all queries are handled by $\mathcal{O}$ itself. The advantage of $\mathcal{A}$ against $f_1[P]$ when it makes D blocks of construction queries and T blocks of permutation queries is defined as

$$\mathbf{Adv}^{\mathcal{A}}_{f_1[P]}(D, T) := |\mathrm{Pr}_1\,[\mathcal{A}\text{ wins}] - \mathrm{Pr}_0\,[\mathcal{A}\text{ loses}]\,|,$$

where $\mathrm{Pr}_1\,[\cdot]$ denotes probability under the real oracle and $\mathrm{Pr}_0\,[\cdot]$ denotes probability under the ideal oracle. The (D, T)-*PRF-advantage* of $f_1[P]$ is defined as

$$\mathbf{Adv}^{\mathrm{PRF}}_{f_1[P]}(D, T) := \max_{\mathcal{A}} \mathbf{Adv}^{\mathcal{A}}_{f_1[P]}(D, T).$$

The Multi-user Version of the Game. We consider the case where $\mathcal{A}$ can access $f_1[P]$ as μ different users. Each user has an independently sampled secret key, and a unique public ID of variable length. The adversary's construction queries can specify an user index $u \in [\mu]$, specifying which user's key-ID pair to use for evaluating the call. The domain of the random function f_0 (that the ideal oracle uses) is $[\mu] \times S$ in this game. With D and T as before, the advantage of $\mathcal{A}$

against $f_1[P]$ is defined identically as in the single-user version, except with the additional parameter μ in the notation. The (μ, D, T)-*multi-user-PRF-advantage* of $f_1[P]$ is defined as

$$\mathbf{Adv}_{f_1[P]}^{\mathsf{MU\text{-}PRF}}(\mu, D, T) := \max_{\mathcal{A}} \mathbf{Adv}_{f_1[P]}^{\mathcal{A}}(\mu, D, T).$$

We will also call the Multi-User PRF game with the parameters μ, D, T as described above a (μ, D, T)-MU-PRF-game.

Coefficients H Technique. For bounding the MU-PRF-advantage of a function $f_1[P]$, we can use a result called the Coefficients H Technique. It is a proof method by Patarin [30] that was modernized by Chen and Steinberger [18,19] and generalized by Hoang and Tessaro [24] in their expectation method. Suppose the partially-determined P at the end of the query phase is revealed to the adversary by the real oracle. Note that this P contains the history of both the permutation queries and the calls to P or P^{-1} by the oracle itself while evaluating $f_1[P]$ at the construction queries. Since all the other parts of the construction calls are publicly computable, this partially-determined P includes complete information about the game. We will call it a *transcript* of the game and denote it as $\widetilde{P}$. Suppose we can define a simulator for the ideal oracle, which can produce a valid transcript $\widetilde{P}$ which looks like it comes from the real oracle, unless it encounters certain *bad* events. If for some $\epsilon > 0$ for any (μ, D, T)-MU-PRF-game we can show that $\Pr_0$ [a bad event is encountered] $\leq \epsilon$, and that for a valid transcript $\widetilde{P}$, $\Pr_0 \left[\widetilde{P} \right] \leq \Pr_1 \left[\widetilde{P} \right]$, then the Coefficients H Technique tells us that

$$\mathbf{Adv}_{f_1[P]}^{\mathsf{MU\text{-}PRF}}(\mu, D, T) \leq \epsilon.$$

(Note that when we talk of the probability of a transcript $\widetilde{P}$, what we really refer to is the probability that a game ends up with transcript $\widetilde{P}$.) The original result of the Coefficients H Technique is slightly more general, but in this paper we will only be interested in the special case of it described above.

3   A PRF with Multi-user Security

The Muffler[P] *Construction.* Muffler[P] is a multi-user PRF based on a public random permutation P. Each user, in addition to having an independent random key of κ bits, for some $\kappa \in [n]$, also has a unique public ID. A user's ID is first hashed to a single block, which the adversary can compute by querying the public permutation, but cannot control. The key and hashed ID of an user are prefixed to each message queried to her, and the entire sequence of blocks is absorbed into a full-state sponge. The output of the first P call is squeezed out and fed-forward into the input of the last P call, and the top τ bits (for some $\tau \in [n]$) are squeezed out of the sponge at the end and released as the τ-bit output. The working of Muffler[P] is illustrated in Fig. 1, and the algorithm is described in Algorithm 1.

```
Module hashID
input  : t - 1 complete ID blocks id₁, id₂, ..., id_{t-1} and one incomplete
          (possibly empty) ID block id*_t
output: hashed ID H

begin
    V ⟵ 0
    for j ⟵ 1 to t - 1 do
        U ⟵ V ⊕ id_j
        V ⟵ P(U)
    end for
    U ⟵ fixl(V ⊕ pad(id*_t), 1)
    H ⟵ P(U)
end

Module PRF
input  : hashed ID H, κ-bit user key K, ℓ - 1 complete message blocks
          M₁, M₂, ..., M_{ℓ-1} and one incomplete (possibly empty) message
          block M*_ℓ
output: τ-bit tag T

begin
    X ⟵ K ∥ 0^{n-κ}
    Z ⟵ P(X)
    X ⟵ Z ⊕ H
    Y ⟵ P(X)
    for j ⟵ 1 to ℓ - 1 do
        X ⟵ Y ⊕ M_j
        Y ⟵ P(X)
    end for
    X ⟵ Y ⊕ pad(M*_ℓ) ⊕ Z
    Y ⟵ P(X)
    T ⟵ chop(Y)
end
```

Algorithm 1: The algorithm for the Muffler[P] construction. pad(x) denotes $x\|10^*$; chop(x) denotes $x[1..\tau]$.

Notation for Security Game. In this game there are μ users $\mathcal{U}_1, \ldots, \mathcal{U}_\mu$. We denote the key and ID for $\mathcal{U}_u$ as $K^{(u)}$ and $\mathrm{id}^{(u)}$ respectively. We let

$$\mathsf{H}^{(u)} := \mathcal{H}[P]\left(\mathrm{id}^{(u)}\right),$$

where $\mathcal{H}[P]$ is the hash function to be defined shortly. The adversary $\mathcal{A}$ makes T permutation queries. For $i \in [T]$, we say $i \in \mathcal{P}^f$ when the i-th permutation query is made to P, (i.e., it's a *forward* query); then the query is denoted U^i and the response is denoted V^i; we say $i \in \mathcal{P}^b$ when the i-th permutation query is made to P^{-1}, (i.e., it's a *backward* query); then the query is denoted V^i and the response is denoted U^i. Thus for each $i \in [T]$,

$$P(\mathsf{U}^i) = \mathsf{V}^i.$$

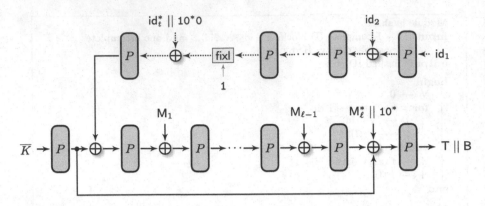

Fig. 1. The Muffler construction. P is a public random permutation; $\overline{K} := K||0^{n-\kappa}$; $\mathrm{id}_1, \ldots, \mathrm{id}_t^*$ is the ID corresponding to key K, where id_t^* may have less than n bits (when id_t^* has n or $n-1$ bits, the final block being added after fixl() in the figure is the padding block); $\mathsf{M}_1, \ldots, \mathsf{M}_\ell^*$ is the message where M_ℓ^* may have less than n bits; tag T is obtained by chopping off the last $n - \tau$ bits of the final output. The dotted lines represent offline computations.

For $u \in [\mu]$, $\mathcal{A}$ further makes q_u construction queries to $\mathcal{U}_u$, with

$$q := \sum_{u \in [\mu]} q_u;$$

for $i \in [q_u]$, the i-th query to $\mathcal{U}_u$ is denoted $\mathsf{M}^{(u,i)}$. There are $\ell^{(u,i)}$ blocks in $\mathsf{M}^{(u,i)}$, with

$$D_u := \sum_{i \in [q_u]} \ell^{(u,i)};$$

for $j \in [\ell^{(u,i)}]$ the j-th block of $\mathsf{M}^{(u,i)}$ is denoted $\mathsf{M}_j^{(u,i)}$, where $\mathsf{M}_{\ell^{(u,i)}}^{(u,i)}$ just denotes the final incomplete (possibly empty) block of $\mathsf{M}^{(u,i)}$ after 10^* padding. Finally, we let

$$D := \sum_{u \in [\mu]} D_u,$$

which denotes the total number of blocks queries to the construction. The total number of query blocks including construction queries and permutation queries is $D + T$. Let

$$\mathcal{Q} := \{(u, i) \mid u \in [\mu], i \in [q_u]\}$$

be the set of all construction query indices, and let

$$\mathcal{I} := \left\{ (u, i, j) \mid (u, i) \in \mathcal{Q}, j \in \left[\ell^{(u,i)} \right] \right\}$$

be the set of all construction query block indices. In addition, we define a slightly different set of construction query block indices, to be useful in the subsequent analysis:

$$\mathcal{I}^{\pm} := \left\{ (u,i,j) \mid (u,i) \in \mathcal{Q}, j \in \left[2..\ell^{(u,i)} + 1 \right] \right\}.$$

Padding the IDs. We use a 10*0 padding on the IDs to bring their length up to a multiple of n bits. This injective padding scheme ensures that the last bit is always 0, and the first bit following the un-padded ID is always 1, with a variable number of 0 bits inserted in between to adjust the length. (Note that when the final ID block is of length n bits or $n-1$ bits, this padding scheme appends an entire padding block to the ID.)

Hashing the IDs. The hashing of the IDs consists of a series of chained calls to the permutation, with one bit tweaked before the final call. We assume that these calls are made as part of the forward permutation queries by the adversary. Let $t^{(u)}$ be the number of blocks in $\mathsf{id}^{(u)}$ after padding, and let the blocks be $\mathsf{id}_1^{(u)}, \ldots, \mathsf{id}_{t^{(u)}}^{(u)}$. Then we assume for each $u \in [\mu]$ there are indices $i_1^{(u)}, \ldots, i_{t^{(u)}}^{(u)} \in \mathcal{P}^f$ such that

$$\mathsf{U}^{i_1^{(u)}} = \mathsf{id}_1^{(u)},$$
$$\mathsf{U}^{i_j^{(u)}} = \mathsf{V}^{i_{j-1}^{(u)}} + \mathsf{id}_j^{(u)} \qquad\qquad \text{when } 2 \leq j \leq t^{(u)} - 1,$$
$$\mathsf{U}^{i_{t^{(u)}}^{(u)}} = \mathsf{fixl}\left(\mathsf{V}^{i_{t^{(u)}-1}^{(u)}} + \mathsf{id}_{t^{(u)}}^{(u)}, 1 \right).$$

4   Main Security Result

We now state the main result of this paper.

Theorem 1 (Security Bound). *Let $\mathcal{A}$ be a PRF adversary, trying to differentiate a $\mathsf{Muffler}[P](\kappa, \tau)$ construction for μ users from an ideal random function $f : [\mu] \times \{0,1\}^{\geq n} \longrightarrow \{0,1\}^{\tau}$. Suppose $\mathcal{A}$ makes q construction queries, consisting of D blocks in all, and T permutation queries, including forward and backward queries. Then, for integer parameters θ_1 and θ_2,*

$$\mathbf{Adv}_{\mathcal{A}}^{PRF} \leq \frac{\theta_1 T}{2^{n-\tau}} + \frac{\theta_2 T}{2^{\kappa}} + \frac{2^{\tau}}{\theta_1!} \cdot \left(\frac{D}{2^{\tau}} \right)^{\theta_1} + \frac{2^n}{\theta_2!} \cdot \left(\frac{D^2}{2^n} \right)^{\theta_2} + \frac{\mu^2}{2^{2\kappa}}$$
$$+ \frac{D^2 + 2DT + 2qD + 2\mu D + \mu^2 + 6\mu T}{2^n} + \frac{\mu^2 T + \mu^3}{2^{n+\kappa}}.$$

Making Sense of the Bound. The bound above is rather complicated for taking in at a glance, so we now simplify it a bit by substituting certain typical parameter values we have in mind. First we assume that μ and q are of the same order as D, which gives the bound.

$$\mathbf{Adv}_{\mathcal{A}}^{\mathrm{PRF}} \leq \frac{\theta_1 T}{2^{n-\tau}} + \frac{\theta_2 T}{2^{\kappa}} + \frac{2^{\tau}}{\theta_1!} \cdot \left(\frac{D}{2^{\tau}}\right)^{\theta_1} + \frac{2^n}{\theta_2!} \cdot \left(\frac{D^2}{2^n}\right)^{\theta_2}$$
$$+ \frac{D^2}{2^{2\kappa}} + \frac{6D^2 + 8DT}{2^n} + \frac{D^2 T + D^3}{2^{n+\kappa}}.$$

Typical values for κ and τ would be about $n/2$ each, so substituting that gives us

$$\mathbf{Adv}_{\mathcal{A}}^{\mathrm{PRF}} \leq \frac{\theta_1 T + \theta_2 T}{2^{n/2}} + \frac{2^{n/2}}{\theta_1!} \cdot \left(\frac{D}{2^{n/2}}\right)^{\theta_1} + \frac{2^n}{\theta_2!} \cdot \left(\frac{D^2}{2^n}\right)^{\theta_2}$$
$$+ \frac{7D^2 + 8DT}{2^n} + \frac{D^2 T + D^3}{2^{3n/2}}.$$

We choose the parameters θ_1 and θ_2 large enough so that the coefficients $2^{n/2}/\theta_1!$ and $2^n/\theta_2!$ are small. For example, when $n = 128$, choosing $\theta_1 \geq 21$ and $\theta_2 \geq 34$ ensures that either coefficient is less than 1. For further simplification, we can choose $\theta_1 \approx 2n/3$ and $\theta_1 \approx n/3$ to get

$$\mathbf{Adv}_{\mathcal{A}}^{\mathrm{PRF}} \leq \frac{nT}{2^{n/2}} + 2\left(\frac{D}{2^{n/2}}\right)^{2n/3} + \frac{7D^2 + 8DT}{2^n} + \frac{D^2 T + D^3}{2^{3n/2}}.$$

This shows that we can allow both D and T to go up to the birthday-bound in n without breaking the security of $\mathsf{Muffler}[P]$. The only degradation is a factor of n in the first term of the simplified bound.

5   Proof of Security

Real Oracle. We begin by describing in detail the specific oracles we choose for this game. In the real oracle, the user key $K^{(u)}$ for each $u \in [\mu]$ is initially sampled uniformly from $\{0,1\}^{\kappa}$. For each $i \in [q_u]$, we first set (Fig. 2)

$$\mathsf{X}_0^{(u,i)} = K^{(u)} \| 0^{n-\kappa},$$
$$\mathsf{Y}_0^{(u,i)} = P\left(\mathsf{X}_0^{(u,i)}\right).$$

Next we incorporate the hashed user ID by setting

$$\mathsf{X}_1^{(u,i)} = \mathsf{Y}_0^{(u,i)} + \mathsf{H}^{(u)},$$
$$\mathsf{Y}_1^{(u,i)} = P\left(\mathsf{X}_1^{(u,i)}\right).$$

Then comes the message blocks: for each $j \in [2..\ell^{(u,i)}]$ we set

$$\mathsf{X}_j^{(u,i)} = \mathsf{Y}_{j-1}^{(u,i)} + \mathsf{M}_{j-1}^{(u,i)},$$
$$\mathsf{Y}_j^{(u,i)} = P\left(\mathsf{X}_j^{(u,i)}\right).$$

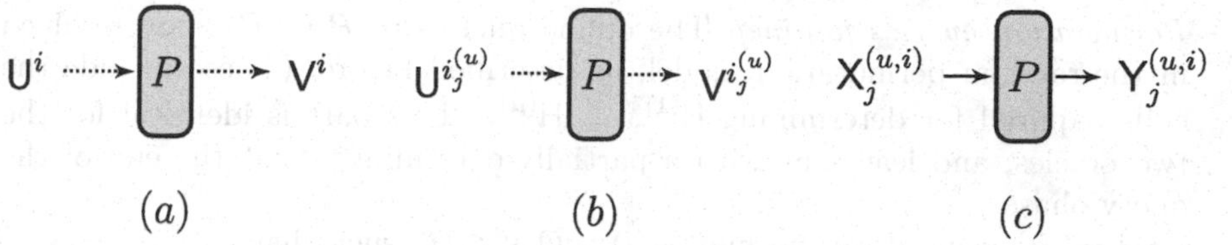

$$\mathsf{U}^i \dashrightarrow \boxed{P} \longrightarrow \mathsf{V}^i \qquad \mathsf{U}^{i^{(u)}_j} \dashrightarrow \boxed{P} \dashrightarrow \mathsf{V}^{i^{(u)}_j} \qquad \mathsf{X}^{(u,i)}_j \longrightarrow \boxed{P} \longrightarrow \mathsf{Y}^{(u,i)}_j$$

$$(a) \qquad\qquad\qquad (b) \qquad\qquad\qquad (c)$$

Fig. 2. Notation for real oracle computations. **(a)** i-th call to public permutation P; **(b)** j-th (offline) call to P while hashing the ID of user u; **(c)** j-th (online) call to P while processing i-th construction query to user u.

For the final call to P, we feed forward the output of the first call by setting

$$\mathsf{X}^{(u,i)}_{\ell(u,i)+1} = \mathsf{Y}^{(u,i)}_{\ell(u,i)} + \mathsf{Y}^{(u,i)}_0 + \mathsf{M}^{(u,i)}_{\ell(u,i)},$$
$$\mathsf{Y}^{(u,i)}_{\ell(u,i)+1} = P\left(\mathsf{X}^{(u,i)}_{\ell(u,i)+1}\right).$$

The output is

$$\mathsf{T}^{(u,i)} := \mathsf{Y}^{(u,i)}_{\ell(u,i)+1}[1..\tau].$$

Additionally we denote

$$\mathsf{B}^{(u,i)} := \mathsf{Y}^{(u,i)}_{\ell(u,i)+1}[\tau+1..n].$$

$\mathsf{T}^{(u,i)}$ is returned immediately to the adversary at the end of the i-th query to $\mathcal{U}_u$. Note that all the P calls above are executed in the random permutation model. The partially determined P is revealed to the adversary at the end of the query phase.

Ideal Oracle. The sampling mechanism of the ideal oracle is described below. Certain bad events can be encountered during the sampling process. Once a bad event is encountered, the subsequent behaviour of the ideal oracle is left undefined. (One can for instance imagine that after encountering a bad event, the ideal oracle only outputs random bits for the rest of the game.)

– *Construction queries [online]:* The queries are resolved in the random oracle model: for each $u \in [\mu], i \in [q_u]$, we sample $\mathsf{Y}^{(u,i)}_{\ell(u,i)+1}$ uniformly from $\{0,1\}^n$, and define

$$\mathsf{T}^{(u,i)} := \mathsf{Y}^{(u,i)}_{\ell(u,i)+1}[1..\tau],$$
$$\mathsf{B}^{(u,i)} := \mathsf{Y}^{(u,i)}_{\ell(u,i)+1}[\tau+1..n].$$

$\mathsf{T}^{(u,i)}$ is returned to the adversary in response to the i-th query to $\mathcal{U}_u$.
 • badCC occurs if we can find θ_1 distinct pairs $(u_1, i_1), \ldots, (u_{\theta_1}, i_{\theta_1}) \in \mathcal{Q}$ such that

$$\mathsf{T}^{(u_1,i_1)} = \ldots = \mathsf{T}^{(u_{\theta_1}, v_{\theta_1})}.$$

- *Permutation queries [offline]:* The offline queries to P or P^{-1} are resolved in the random permutation model, as described before. (These include the calls required for determining $H^{(1)}, \ldots, H^{(\mu)}$.) This part is identical for the two oracles, and leaves us with a partially-determined P at the end of the query phase.
  - badCP occurs if we can find $(u, i) \in \mathcal{Q}, i' \in [T]$ such that

$$Y^{(u,i)}_{\ell^{(u,i)}+1} = V^{i'}.$$

  - badPE occurs if we can find θ_2 distinct pairs $(u_1, i_1), \ldots, (u_{\theta_2}, i_{\theta_2}) \in \mathcal{Q} \in [\mu] \times \mathcal{P}^f$ such that

$$H^{(u_1)} + V^{i_1} = \ldots = H^{(u_{\theta_2})} + V^{i_{\theta_2}}.$$

- *Internal sampling:* A triple $(u, i, j) \in \mathcal{I}$ is called *fresh* if one of the following is true:
  - $i = 1$;
  - $i \geq 2, j = \ell^{(u,i)}$;
  - $i \geq 2, j \in [2..\ell^{(u,i)} - 1]$ and for each $i' \in [i-1]$ with $\ell^{(u,i')} \geq j+1$ we can find $j' \in [j-1]$ such that $M^{(u,i)}_{j'} \neq M^{(u,i')}_{j'}$, i.e., the $(j-1)$-block prefix of the i-th query to user u was not a proper prefix of an earlier query to the same user.

Let $\mathcal{F}$ denote the set of all fresh (u, i, j) triples. For $(u, i, j) \in \mathcal{I}$, the (u, j)-ancestor of i is the smallest i_0 such that for each $j' \in [j-1]$, $M^{(u,i)}_{j'} = M^{(u,i_0)}_{j'}$. Note that this automatically implies that $(u, i_0, j) \in \mathcal{F}$. Now we describe the sampling order of the internal inputs and outputs of P, which is done at the end of the query phase:

Step 1: For each $(u, i, j) \in \mathcal{F}$, sample $Y^{(u,i)}_j$ uniformly from $\{0, 1\}^n$.
  - badYC occurs if we can find $(u, i, j) \in \mathcal{F}, (u', i') \in \mathcal{Q}$ such that

$$Y^{(u,i)}_j = Y^{(u',i')}_{\ell^{(u',i')}};$$

  - badYP occurs if we can find $(u, i, j) \in \mathcal{F}, i' \in [T]$ such that

$$Y^{(u,i)}_j = V^{i'};$$

  - badYY occurs if we can find distinct $(u, i, j), (u', i', j') \in \mathcal{F}$ such that

$$Y^{(u,i)}_j = Y^{(u',i')}_{j'}.$$

Step 2: For each $(u, i, j) \in \mathcal{I} \setminus \mathcal{F}$, set

$$Y^{(u,i)}_j := Y^{(u,i_0)}_j,$$

where i_0 is the (u, j)-ancestor of i.

Step 3: For each $(u, i, j) \in \mathcal{I}^{\pm}$, set

$$\mathsf{X}_j^{(u,i)} := \mathsf{M}_{j-1}^{(u,i)} + \mathsf{Y}_{j-1}^{(u,i)}, \qquad\qquad j \leq \ell^{(u,i)},$$
$$:= \mathsf{M}_{j-1}^{(u,i)} + \mathsf{Y}_{j-1}^{(u,i)} + \mathsf{Y}_1^{(u,i)}, \qquad j = \ell^{(u,i)} + 1.$$

- badXP occurs if we can find $(u, i, j) \in \mathcal{I}^{\pm}, i' \in [T]$ such that

$$\mathsf{X}_j^{(u,i)} = \mathsf{U}^{i'};$$

- badXX occurs if we can find $(u, i, j), (u', i', j') \in \mathcal{I}^{\pm}$ such that

$$\mathsf{X}_j^{(u,i)} = \mathsf{X}_{j'}^{(u',i')}.$$

Step 4: For each $(u, i, j) \in \mathcal{I}^{\pm}$, add $\left(\mathsf{X}_j^{(u,i)}, \mathsf{Y}_j^{(u,i)}\right)$ to P.

Step 5: For each $u \in [\mu]$ sample $K^{(u)}$ uniformly from $\{0,1\}^{\kappa}$ and set $\mathsf{X}_0^{(u,1)} := K^{(u)} \| 0^{n-\kappa}$.

Step 6: For each $u \in [\mu]$, if $\mathsf{X}_0^{(u,1)} \in \mathrm{dom}\,(P)$ set $\mathsf{Y}_0^{(u,1)} := P\left(\mathsf{X}_0^{(u,1)}\right)$, else sample $\mathsf{Y}_0^{(u,1)}$ uniformly from $\{0,1\}^n \setminus \mathrm{ran}\,(P)$ and add $\left(\mathsf{X}_0^{(u,1)}, \mathsf{Y}_0^{(u,1)}\right)$ to P.

Step 7: For each $u \in [\mu]$ set

$$\mathsf{X}_1^{(u,1)} := \mathsf{Y}_0^{(u,1)} + \mathsf{H}^{(u)}.$$

- badHP occurs if we can find $u \in [\mu], i \in [T]$ such that

$$\mathsf{X}_1^{(u,1)} = \mathsf{U}^i;$$

- badHX occurs if we can find $(u', i', j') \in \mathcal{I}^{\pm}$ such that

$$\mathsf{X}_1^{(u,1)} = \mathsf{X}_j^{(u',i)};$$

- badHH occurs if we can find distinct $u, u' \in [\mu]$ such that

$$\mathsf{X}_1^{(u,1)} = \mathsf{X}_1^{(u',1)}.$$

- badHK occurs if we can find $u, u' \in [\mu]$ such that

$$\mathsf{X}_1^{(u,1)} = \mathsf{X}_0^{(u',1)}.$$

Step 8: For each $u \in [\mu]$ add $\left(\mathsf{X}_1^{(u,1)}, \mathsf{Y}_1^{(u,1)}\right)$ to P.

Step 9: For each $(u, i) \in \mathcal{Q}$ with $i > 1$ set

$$\mathsf{X}_0^{(u,i)} := \mathsf{X}_0^{(u,1)}, \quad \mathsf{Y}_0^{(u,i)} := \mathsf{Y}_0^{(u,1)}, \quad \mathsf{X}_1^{(u,i)} := \mathsf{X}_1^{(u,1)}.$$

At the end of the internal sampling phase, the partially-determined P is revealed to the adversary. (Note that the last step of the ideal oracle does not affect the game, and is only included for the convenience of our analysis.)

472   A. Bhattacharjee et al.

Table 1. Classification table of bad events.

Event	Definition	Range of Indices	Bound
badCC	θ_1-collision in $\mathsf{T}^{(u,i)}$	$(u,i) \in \mathcal{Q}$	$(2^\tau/\theta_1!) \cdot (q/2^\tau)^{\theta_1}$
badCP	$\mathsf{Y}^{(u,i)}_{\ell^{(u,i)}+1} = \mathsf{V}^{i'}$	$(u,i) \in \mathcal{Q}, i' \in [T]$	$\theta_1 T/2^{n-\tau}$
badPE	θ_2-collision in $\mathsf{H}^{(u)} + \mathsf{V}^i$	$u \in [\mu], i \in \mathcal{P}^f$	$(2^n/\theta_2!) \cdot (\mu D/2^n)^{\theta_2}$
badYC	$\mathsf{Y}^{(u,i)}_j = \mathsf{Y}^{(u',i')}_{\ell^{(u',i')}}$	$(u,i,j) \in \mathcal{F}, (u',i') \in \mathcal{Q}$	$qD/2^n$
badYP	$\mathsf{Y}^{(u,i)}_j = \mathsf{V}^{i'}$	$(u,i,j) \in \mathcal{F}, i' \in [T]$	$DT/2^n$
badYY	$\mathsf{Y}^{(u,i)}_j = \mathsf{Y}^{(u',i')}_{j'}$	$(u,i,j), (u',i',j') \in \mathcal{F}$	$D^2/2^{n+1}$
badXP	$\mathsf{X}^{(u,i)}_j = \mathsf{U}^{i'}$	$(u,i,j) \in \mathcal{I}^\pm, i' \in [T]$	$DT/2^n$
badXX	$\mathsf{X}^{(u,i)}_j = \mathsf{X}^{(u',i')}_{j'}$	$(u,i,j), (u',i',j') \in \mathcal{I}^\pm$	$D^2/2^{n+1}$
badHP	$\mathsf{X}^{(u,1)}_1 = \mathsf{U}^i$	$u \in [\mu], i \in [T]$	$\mu T/2^{n-1} + \mu D/2^n +$ $\mu^2 T/2^{n+\kappa} + \theta_2 T/2^\kappa$ $+ \mu T/2^{n-1}$
badHX	$\mathsf{X}^{(u,1)}_1 = \mathsf{X}^{(u',i)}_j$	$(u',i',j') \in \mathcal{I}^\pm$	$qD/2^n$
badHH	$\mathsf{X}^{(u,1)}_1 = \mathsf{X}^{(u',1)}_1$	$u, u' \in [\mu]$	$\mu^2/2^{n+1}$
badHK	$\mathsf{X}^{(u,1)}_1 = \mathsf{U}^i$	$u \in [\mu], i \in [T]$	$\mu T/2^n + \mu D/2^n +$ $\mu^3/2^{n+\kappa} + \mu^2/2^{2\kappa}$

Proof of Theorem. Let $\widetilde{P}$ denote the partially-revealed P at the end of the interaction of $\mathcal{A}$ with the chosen oracle. When obtained from the real oracle, $\widetilde{P}$ contains all the probabilistic information of the game; when obtained from the ideal oracle, in the absence of bad events (which could result in unpredictable, inconsistent or incomplete transcripts), it also contains all the probabilistic information of the game. Let σ be the size of $\mathsf{dom}\left(\widetilde{P}\right)$. Since all P-responses are sampled in the random permutation model in the real oracle,

$$\Pr_1\left[\widetilde{P}\right] = \frac{1}{2^n \cdot (2^n - 1) \cdot \ldots \cdot (2^n - \sigma + 1)}.$$

In the ideal oracle, some of the P-responses are sampled in the random permutation model, and some are sampled uniformly. Suppose σ_1 of the P-responses are sampled uniformly. Then (Fig. 3)

$$\Pr_0\left[\widetilde{P}\right] \leq \frac{1}{(2^n - \sigma_1) \cdot (2^n - \sigma_1 - 1) \cdot \ldots \cdot (2^n - \sigma + 1)} \cdot \left(\frac{1}{2^n}\right)^{\sigma_1}.$$

Thus, $\Pr_0\left[\widetilde{P}\right] \leq \Pr_1\left[\widetilde{P}\right]$, given that no bad event occurs. Coefficient H Technique tells us then that

$$\mathbf{Adv}^{\mathrm{PRF}}_{\mathcal{A}} \leq \Pr_0\left[\mathrm{bad}\right],$$

where bad is the event that one of the twelve events badCC, badCP, badPE, badYC, badYP, badYY, badXP, badXX, badHP, badHX, badHH and badHK is

Query-Response Phase

Online

for $(u,i) \in \mathcal{Q}$:

$Y^{(u,i)}_{\ell(u,i)+1} \xleftarrow{\$} \{0,1\}^n$

$T^{(u,i)} \longleftarrow Y^{(u,i)}_{\ell(u,i)+1}[1..\tau]$

$B^{(u,i)} \longleftarrow Y^{(u,i)}_{\ell(u,i)+1}[\tau+1..n]$

$T^{(u,i)} \longrightarrow \mathcal{A}$

check for badCC

Offline

for $i \in E_p$:

$V^i \xleftarrow{\$} \{0,1\}^n \setminus \operatorname{ran}(P)$

$P \longleftarrow P \cup \{(U^i, V^i)\}$

$V^i \longrightarrow \mathcal{A}$

check for badCP, badPE

for $i \in D_p$:

$U^i \xleftarrow{\$} \{0,1\}^n \setminus \operatorname{ran}(P)$

$P \longleftarrow P \cup \{(U^i, V^i)\}$

$U^i \longrightarrow \mathcal{A}$

Internal Sampling Phase

for $(u,i,j) \in \mathcal{F}$:

$Y^{(u,i)}_j \xleftarrow{\$} \{0,1\}^n$

check for badYC, badYP, badYY

for $(u,i,j) \in \mathcal{I} \setminus \mathcal{F}$:

$i_0 \longleftarrow (u,j)$-ancestor of i

$Y^{(u,i)}_j \longleftarrow Y^{(u,i_0)}_j$

for $(u,i,j) \in \mathcal{I}^-$:

$X^{(u,i)}_j \longleftarrow M^{(u,i)}_{j-1} + Y^{(u,i)}_{j-1}$

for $(u,i) \in \mathcal{Q}$:

$X^{(u,i)}_{\ell(u,i)+1} \longleftarrow M^{(u,i)}_{\ell(u,i)} + Y^{(u,i)}_{\ell(u,i)} + Y^{(u,i)}_1$

check for badXP, badXX

for $(u,i,j) \in \mathcal{I}^{\pm}$:

$P \longleftarrow P \cup \{(X^{(u,i)}_j, Y^{(u,i)}_j)\}$

for $u \in [\mu]$:

$K^{(u)} \xleftarrow{\$} \{0,1\}^\kappa$

$X^{(u,1)}_0 \longleftarrow K^{(u)} \| 0^{n-\kappa}$

if $X^{(u,1)}_0 \in \operatorname{dom}(P)$:

$Y^{(u,1)}_0 \longleftarrow P(X^{(u,1)}_0)$

else :

$Y^{(u,1)}_0 \xleftarrow{\$} \{0,1\}^n \setminus \operatorname{ran}(P)$

$P \longleftarrow P \cup \{(X^{(u,1)}_0, Y^{(u,1)}_0)\}$

$X^{(u,1)}_1 \longleftarrow Y^{(u,1)}_0 + H^{(u)}$

check for badHP, badHX, badHH, badHK

$P \longleftarrow P \cup \{(X^{(u,1)}_1, Y^{(u,1)}_1)\}$

$P \longrightarrow \mathcal{A}$

Fig. 3. Behaviour of Ideal Oracle

encountered by the ideal oracle. If we rename them $\mathsf{bad}_1, \ldots, \mathsf{bad}_{12}$, we have by the union-bound

$$\mathbf{Adv}_{\mathcal{A}}^{\mathrm{PRF}} \leq \sum_{i=1}^{12} \mathrm{Pro}\left[\mathsf{bad}_i\right].$$

We shall show that the twelve probability terms on the right-hand side can be bounded as shown in Table 1. The bound in the theorem is obtained simply by adding them up.

6   Bounding the Bad Probabilities

Probability of badHP. Recall from Sect. 4 that badHP occurs if we can find $(u, i) \in \mathcal{Q}$ such that

$$\mathsf{X}_1^{(u,1)} = \mathsf{U}^i.$$

We can rewrite this as

$$\mathsf{Y}_0^{(u,1)} + \mathsf{V}_{\iota(u)}^{i^{(u)}} = \mathsf{U}^i.$$

Now we consider several cases:

Case 1: $\mathsf{X}_0^{(u,1)} \notin \mathrm{dom}\,(P)$. For fixed u, by the randomness of $\mathsf{Y}_0^{(u,1)}$ the collision has a probability $\leq 1/2^{n-1}$. There are at most μ choices for u and at most T choices for i. Thus,

$$\mathrm{Pro}\left[\mathsf{badHP} : \mathrm{Case}\ 1\right] \leq \frac{\mu T}{2^{n-1}}.$$

For each of the other cases, we need two simultaneous collisions, so we bound the joint probability by looking at one or the other or both, as needed.

Case 2: $\mathsf{X}_0^{(u,1)} = \mathsf{X}_{j'}^{(u',i')}$ for some $(u', i', j') \in \mathcal{I}^{\pm}$. We can rewrite this second collision equation as

$$\mathsf{X}_0^{(u,1)} = \mathsf{M}_{j'-1}^{(u',i')} + \mathsf{Y}_{j'-1}^{(u',i')}$$

when $j' \leq \ell^{(u',i')}$, and as

$$\mathsf{X}_0^{(u,1)} = \mathsf{M}_{j'-1}^{(u',i')} + \mathsf{Y}_{j'-1}^{(u',i')} + \mathsf{Y}_0^{(u',i')}$$

when $j' = \ell^{(u',i')} + 1$. Fix u, u', i', j', and let i'_0 be the $(u', j' - 1)$-ancestor of i'. Then we can further rewrite this collision equation as

$$\mathsf{X}_0^{(u,1)} = \mathsf{M}_{j'-1}^{(u',i')} + \mathsf{Y}_{j'-1}^{(u',i'_0)} \quad \text{or}$$
$$\mathsf{X}_0^{(u,1)} = \mathsf{M}_{j'-1}^{(u',i')} + \mathsf{Y}_{j'-1}^{(u',i'_0)} + \mathsf{Y}_0^{(u',i')},$$

depending on whether $j \leq \ell^{(u,i)}$ or $j = \ell^{(u,i)} + 1$. By the randomness of $\mathsf{Y}_{j'-1}^{(u',i'_0)}$ this collision has a probability of $1/2^n$. There are μ choices for u and D choices for (u', i', j'). Thus,

$$\mathrm{Pro}\left[\mathsf{badHP} : \mathrm{Case}\ 2\right] \leq \frac{\mu D}{2^n}.$$

<u>Case 3:</u> $X_0^{(u,1)} = X_0^{(u',1)}$ for some $u' < u$ such that $X_0^{(u',1)}$ was not in $\mathrm{dom}\,(P)$ when it was sampled. Then we can rewrite the first collision equation as

$$Y_0^{(u',1)} + V_{t(u)}^{i(u)} = U^i.$$

For fixed u, u', i, by the randomness of $Y_0^{(u',1)}$ this collision has a probability $\leq 1/2^{n-1}$. We can rewrite the second collision equation as

$$K^{(u)} = K^{(u')}.$$

For fixed u, u', this collision has a probability of $1/2^\kappa$. Thus the joint collision has a probability $\leq 1/2^{n+\kappa-1}$. There are at most $\binom{\mu}{2}$ choices for u, u' and T choices for i. Thus,

$$\mathrm{Pr}_0\left[\mathsf{badHP} : \text{Case } 3\right] \leq \frac{\binom{\mu}{2} \cdot T}{2^{n+\kappa-1}} \leq \frac{\mu^2 T}{2^{n+\kappa}}.$$

<u>Case 4:</u> $X_0^{(u,1)} = U^{i'}$ for some $i' \in \mathcal{P}^f$. Note that i' cannot be $i_{t(u)}^{(u)}$, since $X_0^{(u,1)}$ and $U^{i_{t(u)}^{(u)}}$ differ in the last bit. For fixed u, i', by the randomness of $K^{(u)}$, this second collision has a probability of $1/2^\kappa$ if $U^{i'}[\kappa + 1..n] = 0^{n-\kappa}$, and 0 otherwise. We can rewrite the first collision equation as

$$V^{i'} + V_{t(u)}^{i(u)} = U^i.$$

Since badPE has not occurred, for each choice of i, there are at most θ_2 choices of (u, i'), which makes the total number of choices for (u, i, i') at most $\theta_2 T$. Thus,

$$\mathrm{Pr}_0\left[\mathsf{badHP} : \text{Case } 4\right] \leq \frac{\theta_2 T}{2^\kappa}.$$

<u>Case 5:</u> $X_0^{(u,1)} = U^{i'}$ for some $i' \in \mathcal{P}^b$. For fixed u, i', by the randomness of $U^{i'}$, this second collision has a probability $\leq 1/2^{n-1}$. As in the previous case, we can rewrite the collision equation as

$$V^{i'} + V_{t(u)}^{i(u)} = U^i.$$

Since choosing i and u fixes i', there are at most μT choices for u, i, i'. Thus,

$$\mathrm{Pr}_0\left[\mathsf{badHP} : \text{Case } 5\right] \leq \frac{\mu T}{2^{n-1}}.$$

Taking union-bound over the four cases, we have

$$\mathrm{Pr}_0\left[\mathsf{badHP}\right] \leq \frac{\mu T}{2^{n-1}} + \frac{\mu D}{2^n} + \frac{\mu^2 T}{2^{n+\kappa}} + \frac{\theta_2 T}{2^\kappa} + \frac{\mu T}{2^{n-1}}.$$

Due to space limitation, we omit the proof of bound of the less critical bad events here and refer the interested readers to the full version of the paper [12].

7   Conclusion and Future Works

This paper proposed a simple variant of the full-state absorption sponge PRF. This variant provides higher security than existing constructions which were birthday-bound in the capacity. In addition we consider the multi-user security which is stifled by the $T\mu/2^k$ bound (for all basic constructions). To get something close to k-bit security, nonce-based or randomized constructions have been considered in the past. In this paper we consider a completely different and more realistic approach, based on a user-id (which is assumed to be unique for each user). We use this approach to bypass the need to maintain nonce or generate random salts. Our construction also allows arbitrary lengths of ID. To the best of our knowledge, it is the first deterministic stateless construction to achieve k-bit security in the multi-user security game. There are some natural follow up research questions which could be studied in future:

1. We prove the security in the known ID model in which user-IDs are given to an adversary. Can we consider a stronger adversary in which adversary can choose an ID adaptively (chosen-ID model)?
2. For the sake of simplicity of proof, we keep tag output to be at most $n/2$. Can we consider multiple squeezing phase to generate larger tag output (without degrading the security)?
3. Is it possible to analyse the security of this construction eliminating the multi-collision factor? This would help us to obtain some matching attack. In other words, can we prove that our bound is tight?
4. Can we find another efficient design which can solve all the above problems and may give better security results?

References

1. Andreeva, E., Daemen, J., Mennink, B., Van Assche, G.: Security of keyed sponge constructions using a modular proof approach. In: Leander, G. (ed.) FSE 2015. LNCS, vol. 9054, pp. 364–384. Springer, Heidelberg (2015). https://doi.org/10.1007/978-3-662-48116-5_18
2. Bellare, M., Bernstein, D.J., Tessaro, S.: Hash-function based PRFs: AMAC and its multi-user security. In: Fischlin, M., Coron, J.-S. (eds.) EUROCRYPT 2016. LNCS, vol. 9665, pp. 566–595. Springer, Heidelberg (2016). https://doi.org/10.1007/978-3-662-49890-3_22
3. Bellare, M., Boldyreva, A., Micali, S.: Public-key encryption in a multi-user setting: security proofs and improvements. In: Preneel, B. (ed.) EUROCRYPT 2000. LNCS, vol. 1807, pp. 259–274. Springer, Heidelberg (2000). https://doi.org/10.1007/3-540-45539-6_18
4. Bellare, M., Canetti, R., Krawczyk, H.: Pseudorandom functions revisited: the cascade construction and its concrete security. In: Proceedings of the 37th Annual Symposium on Foundations of Computer Science, pp. 514–523. IEEE (1996)
5. Bellare, M., Krovetz, T., Rogaway, P.: Luby-Rackoff backwards: increasing security by making block ciphers non-invertible. In: Nyberg, K. (ed.) EUROCRYPT 1998. LNCS, vol. 1403, pp. 266–280. Springer, Heidelberg (1998). https://doi.org/10.1007/BFb0054132

6. Bellare, M., Tackmann, B.: The multi-user security of authenticated encryption: AES-GCM in TLS 1.3. In: Robshaw, M., Katz, J. (eds.) CRYPTO 2016. LNCS, vol. 9814, pp. 247–276. Springer, Heidelberg (2016). https://doi.org/10.1007/978-3-662-53018-4_10

7. Bernstein, D.J.: The Poly1305-AES message-authentication code. In: Gilbert, H., Handschuh, H. (eds.) FSE 2005. LNCS, vol. 3557, pp. 32–49. Springer, Heidelberg (2005). https://doi.org/10.1007/11502760_3

8. Bertoni, G., Daemen, J., Peeters, M., Van Assche, G.: Sponge functions. In: ECRYPT Hash Workshop, vol. 2007. Citeseer (2007)

9. Bertoni, G., Daemen, J., Peeters, M., Van Assche, G.: On the indifferentiability of the sponge construction. In: Smart, N. (ed.) EUROCRYPT 2008. LNCS, vol. 4965, pp. 181–197. Springer, Heidelberg (2008). https://doi.org/10.1007/978-3-540-78967-3_11

10. Bertoni, G., Daemen, J., Peeters, M., Van Assche, G.: Duplexing the sponge: single-pass authenticated encryption and other applications. In: Miri, A., Vaudenay, S. (eds.) SAC 2011. LNCS, vol. 7118, pp. 320–337. Springer, Heidelberg (2012). https://doi.org/10.1007/978-3-642-28496-0_19

11. Bertoni, G., Daemen, J., Peeters, M., Van Assche, G.: On the security of the keyed sponge construction. In: Symmetric Key Encryption Workshop, vol. 2011 (2011)

12. Bhattacharjee, A., Bhaumik, R., Nandi, M.: A sponge-based PRF with good multi-user security. Cryptology ePrint Archive, Paper 2022/1146 (2022). https://eprint.iacr.org/2022/1146

13. Bhattacharya, S., Nandi, M.: Luby-Rackoff backwards with more users and more security. In: Tibouchi, M., Wang, H. (eds.) ASIACRYPT 2021. LNCS, vol. 13092, pp. 345–375. Springer, Cham (2021). https://doi.org/10.1007/978-3-030-92078-4_12

14. Biham, E.: How to decrypt or even substitute des-encrypted messages in 228 steps. Inf. Process. Lett. **84**(3), 117–124 (2002)

15. Biryukov, A., Mukhopadhyay, S., Sarkar, P.: Improved time-memory trade-offs with multiple data. In: Preneel, B., Tavares, S. (eds.) SAC 2005. LNCS, vol. 3897, pp. 110–127. Springer, Heidelberg (2006). https://doi.org/10.1007/11693383_8

16. Bose, P., Hoang, V.T., Tessaro, S.: Revisiting AES-GCM-SIV: multi-user security, faster key derivation, and better bounds (2018)

17. Chatterjee, S., Menezes, A., Sarkar, P.: Another look at tightness. In: Miri, A., Vaudenay, S. (eds.) SAC 2011. LNCS, vol. 7118, pp. 293–319. Springer, Heidelberg (2012). https://doi.org/10.1007/978-3-642-28496-0_18

18. Chen, S., Steinberger, J.: Tight security bounds for key-alternating ciphers. Cryptology ePrint Archive, Report 2013/222 (2013). https://ia.cr/2013/222

19. Chen, S., Steinberger, J.: Tight security bounds for key-alternating ciphers. In: Nguyen, P.Q., Oswald, E. (eds.) EUROCRYPT 2014. LNCS, vol. 8441, pp. 327–350. Springer, Heidelberg (2014). https://doi.org/10.1007/978-3-642-55220-5_19

20. Daemen, J., Mennink, B., Van Assche, G.: Full-state keyed duplex with built-in multi-user support. In: Takagi, T., Peyrin, T. (eds.) ASIACRYPT 2017. LNCS, vol. 10625, pp. 606–637. Springer, Cham (2017). https://doi.org/10.1007/978-3-319-70697-9_21

21. Datta, N., Dutta, A., Nandi, M., Talnikar, S.: Tight multi-user security bound of DbHtS. Cryptology ePrint Archive, Paper 2022/689 (2022). https://eprint.iacr.org/2022/689

22. Guo, T., Wang, P.: A note on the security framework of two-key DbHtS MACs. Cryptology ePrint Archive, Paper 2022/375 (2022). https://eprint.iacr.org/2022/375

23. Guo, Z., Wenling, W., Liu, R., Zhang, L.: Multi-key analysis of tweakable even-mansour with applications to minalpher and OPP. IACR Trans. Symmetric Cryptol. **2016**(2), 288–306 (2017)
24. Hoang, V.T., Tessaro, S.: Key-alternating ciphers and key-length extension: exact bounds and multi-user security. In: Robshaw, M., Katz, J. (eds.) CRYPTO 2016. LNCS, vol. 9814, pp. 3–32. Springer, Heidelberg (2016). https://doi.org/10.1007/978-3-662-53018-4_1
25. Hoang, V.T., Tessaro, S.: The multi-user security of double encryption. In: Coron, J.-S., Nielsen, J.B. (eds.) EUROCRYPT 2017. LNCS, vol. 10211, pp. 381–411. Springer, Cham (2017). https://doi.org/10.1007/978-3-319-56614-6_13
26. Hong, J., Sarkar, P.: New applications of time memory data tradeoffs. In: Roy, B. (ed.) ASIACRYPT 2005. LNCS, vol. 3788, pp. 353–372. Springer, Heidelberg (2005). https://doi.org/10.1007/11593447_19
27. Luykx, A., Mennink, B., Paterson, K.G.: Analyzing multi-key security degradation. In: Takagi, T., Peyrin, T. (eds.) ASIACRYPT 2017. LNCS, vol. 10625, pp. 575–605. Springer, Cham (2017). https://doi.org/10.1007/978-3-319-70697-9_20
28. Morgan, A., Pass, R., Shi, E.: On the adaptive security of MACs and PRFs. In: Moriai, S., Wang, H. (eds.) ASIACRYPT 2020. LNCS, vol. 12491, pp. 724–753. Springer, Cham (2020). https://doi.org/10.1007/978-3-030-64837-4_24
29. Mouha, N., Luykx, A.: Multi-key security: the even-mansour construction revisited. In: Gennaro, R., Robshaw, M. (eds.) CRYPTO 2015. LNCS, vol. 9215, pp. 209–223. Springer, Heidelberg (2015). https://doi.org/10.1007/978-3-662-47989-6_10
30. Patarin, J.: The "coefficients H" technique. In: Avanzi, R.M., Keliher, L., Sica, F. (eds.) SAC 2008. LNCS, vol. 5381, pp. 328–345. Springer, Heidelberg (2009). https://doi.org/10.1007/978-3-642-04159-4_21
31. Shen, Y., Wang, L., Gu, D., Weng, J.: Revisiting the security of DbHtS MACs: beyond-birthday-bound in the multi-user setting. In: Malkin, T., Peikert, C. (eds.) CRYPTO 2021. LNCS, vol. 12827, pp. 309–336. Springer, Cham (2021). https://doi.org/10.1007/978-3-030-84252-9_11

Author Index

B. Smith and H. Wu (Eds.): SAC 2022, LNCS 13742, pp. 479–480, 2024.
https://doi.org/10.1007/978-3-031-58411-4

Printed in the United States
by Baker & Taylor Publisher Services

Printed in the United States
by Baker & Taylor Publisher Services